THE BRITISH YEAR BOOK OF INTERNATIONAL LAW

THE BRITISH YEAR BOOK OF INTERNATIONAL LAW 1985

FIFTY-SIXTH YEAR OF ISSUE

OXFORD
AT THE CLARENDON PRESS
1986

Oxford University Press, Walton Street, Oxford OX2 6DP
Oxford New York Toronto
Delhi Bombay Calcutta Madras Karachi
Kuala Lumpur Singapore Hong Kong Tokyo
Nairobi Dar es Salaam Cape Town
Melbourne Auckland
and associated companies in
Beirut Berlin Ibadan Nicosia

OXFORD *is a trade mark of Oxford University Press*

ISBN 0-19-825547-0

ISSN 0068-2691

The British Year Book of International Law is an annual publication, starting with Volume 52 (1981). Subscriptions £65 (U.S. $120 for subscribers in the U.S.A., £55 for those in the U.K.), postage included. Subscriptions should be sent to Journals Subscriptions Department, Oxford University Press, Walton Street, Oxford OX2 6DP, U.K., or placed through a subscription agent or bookseller

Printed in Great Britain
at the University Printing House, Oxford
by David Stanford
Printer to the University

Editorial Communications should be addressed as follows:

Articles and Notes:
PROFESSOR IAN BROWNLIE
All Souls College, Oxford, OX1 4AL.

Books for Review:
PROFESSOR D. W. BOWETT
Queens' College, Cambridge, CB3 9ET.

CONTENTS

THE PERSISTENT OBJECTOR RULE AND THE DEVELOPMENT OF CUSTOMARY INTERNATIONAL LAW*

By JONATHAN I. CHARNEY[1]

I. THE PERSISTENT OBJECTOR RULE IN PUBLIC INTERNATIONAL LAW

THE role of the dissenting State in the development of customary international law is difficult to identify. The positivists clearly held that no rule of international law could be binding on a State without its consent.[2] Most modern theories of international law do not require that express consent be found before a rule of customary international law can be held to be binding on a State. Many authorities argue that a State can be bound by a rule of customary international law even though the State neither expressly nor tacitly consented to the rule.[3] The Socialist States appear

[1] Professor of Law, Vanderbilt University. Appreciation is given to Jeffrey A. Green, JD, Vanderbilt University School of Law 1984, who served as the research assistant for this article. Professor Anthony D'Amato's comments on the treatment, in an early draft, of his writings are also appreciated.

[2] Vattel, *Le Droit des gens* (trans. Chitty, 1857), Preliminaries section 26, at p. 62. See also *The SS 'Lotus' (France* v. *Turkey), PCIJ*, Series A, No. 10, pp. 4, 18 (1927); Hudson, *World Court Reports* (1935), vol. 2, pp. 20, 35. The Court speaks of international law being created by States' 'own free will'. In *The Scotia*, 81 US (14 Wall.) 170 (1872), the Supreme Court stated, '. . . it is recognition of the historical fact that by common consent of mankind, these rules have been acquiesced in as of general obligation': ibid. at p. 188. In *The Antelope*, 23 US 66 (1825), the Court at p. 122 requires that there be the consent of the State before a rule of international law can be applied to it. Chief Justice Cockburn wrote in *The Queen* v. *Keyn*, 2 Ex. Div. 63 (1876), 'To be binding, the law must have received the assent of the nations who are bound by it. This assent may be express, as by treaty or the acknowledged concurrence of governments, or may be implied from established usage . . .': ibid. at p. 202. Hackworth wrote: 'customary . . . international law is based on the common consent of nations extending over a period of time of sufficient duration to cause it to become crystallized into a rule of conduct': *Digest of International Law*, vol. 1 (1940), p. 1. See also *Tinoco* case, *Great Britain* v. *Costa Rica* (1923), *Reports of International Arbitral Awards*, vol. 1, pp. 375, 381. See the discussion of this point in MacGibbon, 'Customary International Law and Acquiescence', this *Year Book*, 33 (1957), p. 115. Jaffe has argued that consent is required for the system only and is not necessary in the case of specific rules: *Judicial Aspects of Foreign Relations* (1933), p. 90.

[3] Most Western writers reject the view that express consent is required for the creation of a new international law because the view does not present an accurate description of the development of international law. See, e.g., Akehurst, 'Custom as a Source of International Law', this *Year Book*, 47 (1974–5), pp. 1, 23; Brierly, *The Law of Nations* (6th edn., 1963), pp. 51–3; and Fitzmaurice, 'The General Principles of International Law Considered from the Standpoint of the Rule of Law', *Recueil des cours*, 92 (1957–II), pp. 1, 36–47. In practice, States are bound by rules to which they have not given their express consent. D'Amato has written, 'The World Court has had numerous occasions to apply customary international law, and yet nowhere has it held as a matter of general customary law that the defendant state must have consented to the rule in question in order to be bound by it': *The Concept of Custom in International Law* (1971), p. 190. See also ibid. at pp. 194, 198 and 246, and D'Amato, 'On

to require the presence of consent but permit a finding of consent based on the most indirect evidence.[4] No authority would permit a State unilaterally to opt out of an existing rule of customary international law,[5] and few would permit new States to choose to exempt themselves from such rules.[6]

Even though most authorities recognize that a State is not required to have expressly consented to be bound by a rule of customary international law, virtually all authorities maintain that a State which objects to an *evolving* rule of general customary international law can be exempted from its obligations. Thus the recent tentative draft of the *Restatement of the*

Consensus', *Canadian Yearbook of International Law*, 8 (1970), pp. 104, 108. H. Lauterpacht identified three types of international law: universal, general and particular:

> 'There is no clear definition of universal international law. On the face of it it seems to mean an international law binding on all or practically all states. . . . Properly understood, it is international law which is binding on all states regardless of their consent; most of them may have consented to it, and this is probably the way in which the bulk of conventional international law has come into existence. However, such consent is not essential. When in *West Rand Central Gold Mining Co.* v. *The King* [[1905] 2 KB 391], Lord Alverston declared as binding upon English courts rules of international law to which the United Kingdom has given its assent or which are so generally accepted that it is inconceivable that a civilized State should refuse its consent to them, he was referring to universal international law'

(*International Law* (ed. E. Lauterpacht), vol. 1 (1970), p. 267). See also Waldock, 'General Course on Public International Law', *Recueil des cours*, 106 (1962–II), pp. 1, 50; Lauterpacht, op. cit. above at p. 64; dissent of Judge Lachs in the *North Sea Continental Shelf* cases (*Federal Republic of Germany/Denmark*; *Federal Republic of Germany/Netherlands*), *ICJ Reports*, 1969, pp. 3, 229; De Visscher, 'Reflections on the Present Prospects of International Adjudication', *American Journal of International Law*, 50 (1956), pp. 467, 472–3; Kelsen, *Principles of International Law* (1952), pp. 307, 311–17; O'Connell, 'Sedentary Fisheries and the Australian Continental Shelf', *American Journal of International Law*, 49 (1955), pp. 185, 194. While Henkin appears to require consent to a new rule he implies that consent includes acquiescence: *How Nations Behave* (2nd edn., 1979), pp. 33–4.

[4] Tunkin writes: 'A rule of conduct, being the result of universal practice, becomes a customary norm of international law only if it has been accepted or recognized by the states as juridically binding as a norm of law': 'Remarks on the Juridical Nature of Customary Norms of International Law', *California Law Review*, 49 (1961), pp. 419, 422, 423; and see Tunkin, 'Co-Existence and International Law', *Recueil des cours*, 95 (1958–III), pp. 1, 12–14. But even Tunkin does not require express consent; he allows it to be implied: '[i]t may be assumed that recognition of one or another rule as a norm of international law by a large number of states can serve as a basis for the assumption that this norm has won general recognition. However, this is an assumption only, and not a final conclusion', *California Law Review*, 49 (1961), at p. 429. See Akehurst, *A Modern Introduction to International Law* (5th edn., 1984), pp. 31–2; Alexidze, 'Legal Nature of *Jus Cogens* in Contemporary International Law', *Recueil des cours*, 172 (1981–III), pp. 219, 246.

[5] *Restatement of the Foreign Relations Law of the United States* (*Revised*) (hereinafter *Restatement*), section 102, Comm. (d) (Tentative Draft No. 6, 12 April 1985); dissenting opinion by Judge Azevedo, *Asylum* case (*Colombia/Peru*), *ICJ Reports*, 1950, pp. 266, 336; Akehurst, op. cit. (previous note), at p. 18; Akehurst, loc. cit. above (p. 1 n. 3), at p. 25; Fitzmaurice, 'The Law and Procedure of the International Court of Justice, 1951–54: General Principles and Sources of Law', this *Year Book*, 30 (1953), pp. 1, 24–6; MacGibbon, loc. cit. above (p. 1 n. 2), at p. 138.

[6] *Restatement*, section 102, Comm. (d); Akehurst, op. cit. above (n. 4), at pp. 19–22; Akehurst, loc. cit. above (p. 1 n. 3), at pp. 27–8; D'Amato, *The Concept of Custom in International Law* (1971), at pp. 191, 192. Tunkin argues that newly emerging States may withhold their consent if they do so at the time they enter the international system: *California Law Review*, 49 (1961), at p. 428, and *Recueil des cours*, 95 (1958–III), at pp. 60–1. It is argued that empirical data demonstrate that new States are not bound by existing international law: Alexandrowicz, 'Empirical and Doctrinal Positivism in International Law', this *Year Book*, 47 (1974–5), pp. 286, 289; Anand, *New States and International Law* (1972).

Foreign Relations Law of the United States (*Revised*) states in Comment (d) to section 102:

Dissenting views and new states . . . [I]n principle a dissenting state which indicates its dissent from a practice while the law is still in the process of development is not bound by that rule of law even after it matures. . . . A state that enters the international system after a practice has ripened into a rule of international law is bound by it.[7]

The tentative draft of the *Restatement* could be interpreted to permit the dissenting State to invoke an exemption merely by indicating its disagreement with a practice in a timely manner. Other authorities draw the rule more narrowly, requiring the State to have actively and persistently maintained an objection to the evolving rule of law.[8] Thus Akehurst wrote that a State which 'opposes the rule in the early days of the rule's existence (or formation) and maintains its opposition consistently thereafter' may prevent a rule of customary international law from becoming binding on it.[9]

[7] *Restatement*, section 102, Comm. (d). See also ibid. at section 131, Comm. (b). This rule is founded upon the position of the *Restatement* that acceptance by individual States of new general international law is not required. Rather, a new rule must only be 'accepted as such by the international community of states . . .': ibid. (Tentative Draft Number 6), section 102 (1). The use of the term 'international community of States' places the focus on the community in general as opposed to individual States. This view is reinforced in the Introductory Note to this draft where it is said 'general law depends on general acceptance': ibid., at p. 19. While the next sentence begins with the statement, '[l]aw cannot be made by the majority for all', it continues with a reference to the persistent objector rule which makes it clear that some type of majority will make law for the community but that individual States may be exempted under certain conditions. Similarly, the statement on the previous page that actions of the UN 'influence the development of international law but only when accepted by states' refers to 'states' in a collective sense: ibid. at p. 18.

The Chief Reporter of this *Restatement*, Professor Henkin, appears to have taken a somewhat different position in his own work: see above, p. 1 n. 3.

[8] Because there exists a difference of opinion as to whether the objection must be persistent, some authorities refer to the rule as the 'persistent objector rule', and others refer to it as the 'objector rule' or 'dissenting State rule'. This article will refer to the rule as the 'persistent objector rule' but the thesis does not necessarily turn on the question of whether or not the objection must be persistent.

[9] Akehurst, loc. cit. above (p. 1 n. 3), at p. 24. See MacGibbon, 'Some Observations on the Part of Protest in International Law', this *Year Book*, 30 (1953), pp. 292, 318–19; Akehurst, loc. cit. above (p. 1 n. 3), at pp. 25, 32; Fitzmaurice, loc. cit. above (p. 2 n. 5), at p. 26; Lauterpacht, op. cit. above (p. 1 n. 3), at pp. 65–6, 443; Thirlway, *International Customary Law and Codification* (1972), p. 110; Verzijl, *International Law in Historical Perspective* (1968), vol. 1, pp. 37–8; Waldock, loc. cit. above (p. 1 n. 3), at p. 50; *Fisheries* case (*United Kingdom* v. *Norway*), *ICJ Reports*, 1951, p. 116 at pp. 131, 138–9; separate opinion of Judge De Castro, *Fisheries Jurisdiction* case (*United Kingdom/Iceland*), ibid., 1974, pp. 3, 91–2. Kelsen appears to have argued that international law is binding even on the dissenting State: op. cit. above (p. 1 n. 3), at pp. 316–17.

MacGibbon argues, 'In the event of repetition of the acts protested against or the continuation of the situation created by them, it is clear that scant regard will be paid to the isolated protest of a State which takes no further action to combat continued infringements of its rights. Failure to supplement the initial expression of disapproval will not unreasonably give rise to the presumption either that its opposition could not be supported by any show of legal right, or that . . . it was for some reason indifferent to the outcome': loc. cit. above, at p. 310. See also ibid., at pp. 311, 314.

Some argue that an objection may never be effective against a rule of international law that is *jus cogens*: Thirlway, op. cit. above, at p. 110; *Anglo-Norwegian Fisheries* case, Reply of the UK (28 November 1950), *ICJ Pleadings, Oral Arguments, Documents*, 1951, vol. 2, pp. 291, 428–9. If, however, a rule of *jus cogens* comes into force through the same process that creates customary international law a dissenting State may be able to invoke the persistent objector rule. It would only be

The International Court decision that writers primarily rely upon to support this rule is the *Anglo-Norwegian Fisheries* case. In that judgment the International Court of Justice made an alternative finding that a coastline delimitation rule put forward by the United Kingdom 'would appear to be inapplicable as against Norway, in as much as she has always opposed any attempt to apply it to the Norwegian coast'.[10]

It is interesting that this rule has been given attention in the new *Restatement* when it was absent from the earlier *Restatement*.[11] This development may reflect the United States' and other Western developed countries' belief that their influence over the evolution of international law is eroding. Accordingly, they must seek a haven from objectionable changes by invoking this rule.[12] Increased attention to the persistent

after the rule of *jus cogens* comes into force that a dissenting State could not then dissent and seek an exemption from the rule of law. See below, p. 19 n. 81. See also Alexidze, loc. cit. above (p. 2 n. 4), at pp. 253–4. See, generally, Robledo, 'Le *jus cogens* international sa genèse, sa nature, ses fonctions', *Recueil des cours*, 172 (1981–III), p. 7; Schwelb, 'Some Aspects of International *Jus Cogens* as Formulated by the International Law Commission', *American Journal of International Law*, 61 (1967), p. 946; and *Restatement*, section 102, Comm. (k).

[10] *Fisheries* case, *ICJ Reports*, 1951, p. 116 at p. 131. Norway raised the rule first in its Counter Memorial (31 July 1950), *Fisheries* case (*United Kingdom* v. *Norway*), *ICJ Pleadings, Oral Arguments, Documents*, 1951, vol. 1 at pp. 381–4. The response of the UK to Norway's argument and supporting citations was to argue that the decline of extreme positivism put the argument in question, particularly in matters involving fundamental principles: Reply of the UK, ibid., vol. 2 at pp. 428–9. Norway's response is found at Duplique soumise par le Gouvernement du Royaume de Norvège, ibid., vol. 3, p. 1, at pp. 291–6. See Fitzmaurice, loc. cit. above (p. 2 n. 5), at pp. 25, 26; Fitzmaurice, loc. cit. above (p. 1 n. 3), at pp. 99–101. The treatment of the rule by the International Court of Justice may not be consistent. In the *Fisheries* case the persistent nature of the Norwegian behaviour was clear: *ICJ Reports*, 1951, p. 116 at p. 131. In the other important case in this area, the *Asylum* case (*Colombia* v. *Peru*), *ICJ Reports*, 1950, p. 266, the operative Peruvian objection was based merely on its refusal to become a party to a single convention. It was maintained in a dissenting opinion that Peru's behaviour had not been consistent. See dissenting opinion by Judge M. Caicedo Costilla, ibid., at pp. 359, 367–8. See also dissenting opinion by Judge Lachs in the *North Sea Continental Shelf* cases, *ICJ Reports*, 1969, p. 3 at pp. 232, 238.

[11] The last *Restatement* only addressed the question of the role of the dissenting State in the context of the dynamics of the development of a new rule of law:

'e. *Objection to practice as means of preventing its acceptance as rule of law.* The growth of practice into a rule of international law depends on the degree of its acceptance by the international community. If a state initiates a practice for which there is no precedent in international law, the fact that other states do not object to it is significant evidence that they do not regard it as illegal. If this practice becomes more general without objections from other states, the practice may give rise to a rule of international law. Because failure to object to practice may amount to recognition of it, the objection by a state to a practice of another is an important means of preventing or controlling in some degree the development of rules of international law':

Restatement of the Law, Second, Foreign Relations Law of the United States (1965), section 1, Comm. (e).

[12] Key examples in which the Western developed States' power may be slipping are found in the law of the sea where the developed maritime States resisted both the expansion of the territorial sea to 12 miles and the development of the 200-mile exclusive economic zone. In the end they have been forced to adjust to the new rule of law that was imposed upon them by the international community. They may now face similar losses in the case of the law for the deep sea-bed. See Charney, 'The Law of the Deep Seabed Post UNCLOS III', *Oregon Law Review*, 63 (1984), pp. 19, 46–52.

The question of the law for the deep sea-bed is addressed in the *Restatement* (Tentative Draft No. 6), at section 523. Comment (e) states that while the deep sea-bed regime in the Convention on the Law of the Sea might emerge as general international law, the US would not be bound by the new rule of law since it had rejected the regime: ibid., at p. 120. See also section 131, Comm. (b).

objector rule may also reflect the emphasis on State sovereignty that the newly emerging States have encouraged.[13] This rule, however, is particularly difficult to reconcile with the view that consent is not required before a rule of customary law can bind the State.

It is the purpose of this article to examine the persistent objector rule in order to ascertain its real contribution to the development of customary international law. The importance of the rule may increase in the future, and its inclusion in the *Restatement* may presage a return to a more consent-oriented analysis of international law.

II. Support for the Persistent Objector Rule

(a) *In General*

While the overwhelming majority of international law writers accept the persistent objector rule, support for the rule in State practice and judicial decisions is limited. The writers appear to have no difficulty reconciling their acceptance of the persistent objector rule with their rejection of the requirement that a State must consent to a rule of international law.

Brierly both accepted the persistent objector rule and rejected consent as a necessary element of customary law formation:

> The truth is that states do not regard their international legal relations as resulting from consent, except when the consent is express, and that the theory of implied consent is a fiction invented by the theorist; only certain plausibility is given to a consensual explanation of the nature of their obligations by the fact, important indeed to any consideration of the methods by which the system develops, that, in the absence of any international machinery for legislation by majority vote, a *new* rule of law cannot be imposed upon states merely by the will of other states.[14]

Brierly proceeded from this passage to criticize further the consensual theory of international law without any explanation of why his arguments mandating a rejection of that theory might not also require rejection of the persistent objector rule. He did not provide any examples of State practice that would support his assertion that new customs cannot be imposed on States 'merely by the will of other states'.

A more recent writer, Brownlie, sought to identify the basis of the persistent objector rule but did not provide a satisfying explanation:

> *The persistent objector*. The way in which, as a matter of practice, custom resolves itself into a question of special relations is illustrated further by the rule that a state may contract out of a custom in the process of formation. Evidence of objection must be clear and there is probably a presumption of acceptance which

[13] Akehurst, op. cit. above (p. 2 n. 4), at pp. 19–22.

[14] Brierly, op. cit. above (p. 1 n. 3), at p. 52.

is to be rebutted. The toleration of the persistent objector is explained by the fact that ultimately custom depends on the consent of states.[15]

Brownlie justified the rule by reference to a dependence of custom on consent. But he cannot mean that custom depends upon the express consent of States since, at the same time, he declares that both passive and subsequent objectors are bound by customary law.[16] Thus, custom must depend on the implied consent of States, but Brownlie does not disclose to us the rules that determine when consent is to be implied and when it is not. Brownlie is of the view that consent is to be implied in the absence of initial active dissent. Without more, however, the passage quoted above does not explain, but merely restates, the persistent objector rule.[17] Many others report the existence of the persistent objector rule but with little explanation and few supporting authorities.[18]

(b) *D'Amato's Special Custom Analysis*

Only D'Amato appears to reject the rule. His argument has two parts. First, he argues that the persistent objector rule is incompatible with the theory that public international law is not founded upon the specific consent of States to rules of law.[19] Secondly, he argues that the authorities cited in support of the persistent objector rule either do not support the rule in fact or are limited to situations in which a special, rather than general, rule of customary international law is relevant.[20] He maintains that the persistent objector rule is appropriate in the case of a special custom since such a custom represents a derogation from generally applicable legal obligations by a limited group of States.[20] To require consent in that limited circumstance would be compatible with the general jurisprudence of public international law.

[15] Brownlie, *Principles of Public International Law* (3rd edn., 1979), pp. 10–11, (2nd edn., 1973), p. 10, (1st edn., 1966), p. 8.

[16] Ibid. (3rd edn.).

[17] As is true in the case of most writers on this subject, limited references are given to support the rule. In only the third edition of his book does Brownlie provide support for the rule, and then only for the first sentence of the above-quoted passage. Reference is to 'the views of Judge Gros in his Separate Opinion in the *Nuclear Tests Case*, (Australia v. France), ICJ Reports (1974), p. 253 at pp. 286–9': op. cit. above (n. 15), 3rd edn., p. 10.

[18] Waldock reports the existence of the rule and relies on passages in the judgments of the International Court of Justice in the *Fisheries* case and the *Asylum* case: loc. cit. above (p. 1 n. 3), at pp. 49–50. He does not endeavour to reconcile this rule with the view that rules of international law are not based on State consent. Fitzmaurice similarly relies on the judgment in the *Fisheries* case for the rule notwithstanding his elaborate rejection of the consent theory: loc. cit. above (p. 2 n. 5), at pp. 24–6; and loc. cit. above (p. 1 n. 3), at pp. 36–47, 99–101. The Soviet jurist Alexidze also reports the existence of the rule: loc. cit. above (p. 2 n. 4), at p. 246. Prosper Weil seems to place this rule near the centre of the classical theories of custom: Weil, 'Towards Relative Normativity in International Law?', *American Journal of International Law*, 77 (1983), pp. 413, 433–4, 437–8. Other writers who report the existence of the rule are identified at p. 3 n. 9, above.

[19] D'Amato, *The Concept of Custom in International Law* (1971), at p. 261. See also ibid. at pp. 187–95.

[20] Ibid. at pp. 233–4, 248–9, 252–4, 261.

D'Amato and Akehurst have engaged in a strenuous debate over whether the case authorities that appear to support the persistent objector rule involve only special customs.[21] They have focused particularly on the passage in the *Fisheries* case quoted above. D'Amato argues that the Court was referring to a theoretical special custom of Norway and the UK forbidding the use of straight baselines.[22] Akehurst argues that the passage addresses the general proposition that Norway's persistent objection to the 10-mile bay rule had immunized it from the obligations under the rule.[23]

D'Amato's analysis is based on the distinction between general and special customs. The classic example of a special custom is found in the *Asylum* case which also serves as an authority for the persistent objector rule.[24] In that case, Colombia alleged that Peru was bound by a Latin-American custom permitting the asylum in question. Colombia had the burden of arguing that the relevant group of States had created a special custom:

> The Party which relies on a custom of this kind must prove that this custom is established in such a manner that it has become binding on the other Party. The Colombian Government must prove that the rule invoked by it is in accordance with a constant and uniform usage practised by the States in question, and that this usage is the expression of a right appertaining to the State granting asylum and a duty incumbent on the territorial State.[25]

Colombia relied on evidence of practice by Latin-American States and certain international agreements in an attempt to establish this regional custom.[26] Nevertheless, the Court concluded that no uniformity of practice had been shown sufficient to find a custom among Latin-American States and continued:

> The Court cannot therefore find that the Colombian Government has proved the existence of such a [regional or local] custom. But even if it could be supposed that such a custom existed *between certain Latin-American States* only, it could not be invoked against Peru which, far from having by its attitude adhered to it, has, on the contrary, repudiated it. . . .[27]

D'Amato uses this case as the prime example of his position that the persistent objector, although bound by general customary law, is not bound

[21] Ibid.; Akehurst, loc. cit. above (p. 1 n. 3), at pp. 24–5.

[22] D'Amato, *The Concept of Custom in International Law* (1971), at pp. 252–4, 261; id., *Canadian Yearbook of International Law*, 8 (1970), at pp. 110–11 n. 27; id., 'The Concept of Special Custom in International Law', *American Journal of International Law*, 63 (1969), pp. 211, 221; id., 'The Concept of Human Rights in International Law', *Columbia Law Review*, 82 (1982), pp. 1110, 1144. The distinction between special and universal rules of international law is also drawn by Fitzmaurice, loc. cit. above (p. 2 n. 5), at pp. 68–9. See also MacGibbon, loc. cit. above (p. 1 n. 2), at pp. 122, 123.

[23] Akehurst, loc. cit. above (p. 1 n. 3), at p. 25. See also Thirlway, op. cit. above (p. 3 n. 9), at p. 110.

[24] *Asylum* case, *ICJ Reports*, 1950, p. 266.

[25] Ibid., at p. 276. See also *Restatement*, at section 102, Comm. (e).

[26] *Asylum* case, *ICJ Reports*, 1950, at pp. 275–7.

[27] Ibid., at pp. 277–8 (emphasis added).

by special, here regional, custom.[28] Unfortunately, his attempt to impose this limitation on the *Anglo-Norwegian Fisheries* case causes him to define the role of a special custom so broadly that the distinction he seeks to draw lacks significance.

In order to make the distinction between special and general custom, D'Amato has had to find the matter under discussion in the *Anglo-Norwegian Fisheries* case to be a special custom. As the reader will recall, Norway argued that it was not bound to use the conservative baseline rules advocated by the UK. It argued that the 10-mile bay closing line rule advocated by the UK did not have the force of law and that it had a right to use its system of straight baselines. The Court held for Norway.

> [The United Kingdom] has not abandoned its contention that the ten-mile rule is to be regarded as a rule of international law.
>
> In these circumstances the Court deems it necessary to point out that although the ten-mile rule has been adopted by certain States both in their national law and in their treaties and conventions, and although certain arbitral decisions have applied it as between these States, other States have adopted a different limit. Consequently, the ten-mile rule has not acquired the authority of a general rule of international law.
>
> In any event the ten-mile rule would appear to be inapplicable as against Norway inasmuch as she has always opposed any attempt to apply it to the Norwegian coast.[29]

D'Amato argues thus:

> . . . the Court considered the ten-mile rule both in general and in special custom. It upheld Norway on the general ground because of the division of state practice throughout the world. And it upheld Norway on the special ground because, as between Norway and Great Britain, Norway had not consented to the practice (indeed she had opposed it). Here the Court was in effect saying that Norway's delimitation of bays was not unreasonable in light of general customary practice, and therefore Great Britain could not *limit* Norway's rights within the ambit of reasonableness unless Norway consented to the establishment of such a special custom.[30]

Thus, according to D'Amato, there were two grounds for the judgment, general and special custom. The first ground states that under general international law Norway was free to draw a system of straight baselines within a range of reasonableness. The second ground is dependent on the first. It provides that initially Norway had the right to draw its straight baselines unless it consented to relinquish that right in a special custom with the UK.[31] But what was this rule that the UK had put forward? It was

[28] D'Amato, *The Concept of Custom in International Law* (1971), at pp. 252–4.

[29] *Fisheries* case, *ICJ Reports*, 1951, at p. 131.

[30] D'Amato, *The Concept of Custom in International Law* (1971), at p. 261.

[31] D'Amato took a similar approach in his more recent analysis of the judgment in the *North Sea Continental Shelf* cases, arguing that the Federal Republic of Germany had rights in its continental shelf to its geological limits and only if it had by special custom consented to the equidistance rule could those rights be dislodged: *Columbia Law Review*, 82 (1982), at pp. 1142–3. To the contrary, the

a general rule of customary international law that limited straight baselines to 10 mile closing lines of bays for all States. The UK did not seek to apply a special custom to Norway but rather a general rule. Thus under D'Amato's analysis any new general rule put forward by a State can be effectively denied applicability to an objecting State without further inquiry.[32] He calls this process the denial of a special custom, but it is hard to distinguish it from the process of developing rules of general customary international law.[33] The result in either event is that a State can resist a new rule by objecting to it at an early date.

(c) *Judicial Opinions*

Even the judicial opinions upon which writers normally rely do not represent the strongest authorities in support of the concept of the persistent objector. In the two International Court of Justice judgments discussed above, the *Anglo-Norwegian Fisheries* case and the *Asylum* case,[34] the passages that arguably support the rule are merely secondary bases for the Court's decisions. In both, the Court had previously found that the substantive rule of law did not exist in the first place. The Court then went on to allow that even if the rule were international law, the objecting States in these cases would not legally be obligated to abide by the rule.[35]

Writers also rely on separate or dissenting opinions to support the existence of the rule. Thus Akehurst relies on Judge Azevedo's dissent in the

Court never placed the geological limit in such a pre-eminent position. At most, one could argue that the Court was engaged in an effort to discover the true boundary law that already existed. See Charney, 'Ocean Boundaries Between Nations: A Theory for Progress', *American Journal of International Law*, 78 (1984), pp. 582, 585–6, 587–93.

[32] The Court's judgment implies that Norway's system of straight baselines is opposable to all States, with the possible theoretical exception of a State that had expressly protested Norway's claim. It is doubtful that a special custom could be binding on States not party to the special custom: Akehurst, loc. cit. above (p. 1 n. 3), at pp. 29, 31; D'Amato, *The Concept of Custom in International Law* (1971), at p. 46; *contra*, Thirlway, op. cit. above (p. 3 n. 9), at pp. 136–9.

[33] D'Amato, in his book *The Concept of Custom in International Law* (1971), directly addressed the question of the definition of special custom: at pp. 241–4, 246–63. While he catalogued a few cases according to whether they concerned a general custom or a special custom (at p. 252), in the end he admitted that he could not define special custom: '. . . the examples are too few to spell out all the elements of special custom in international law. Nor can we be sure that there exist generalizable elements of special custom, for out of the practice of states may emerge many varied rules relating to different types and situations of special custom': ibid., at p. 263.

In his recent article on the subject, D'Amato appeared to tie the concept of a special custom and the requirement of consent closely to States' rights in territory: *Columbia Law Review*, 82 (1982), at p. 1144. His analysis in this article started from the proposition that a State cannot lose rights in territory without its consent. Such consent may be acquired 'through the process of special custom . . .': at pp. 1143–4. While this may be an uncontroversial proposition it does not help to define the role of special custom. The critical question to be answered in the two relevant cases discussed in this article, the *Fisheries* case and the *North Sea Continental Shelf* cases, is not whether a State may be involuntarily forced to relinquish territory, but rather whether the State had rights in the territory in the first place: ibid., at pp. 1140–4.

[34] *Fisheries* case, *ICJ Reports*, 1951, at p. 131; *Asylum* case, ibid., 1950, at pp. 277–8.

[35] *Fisheries* case, ibid., 1951, at p. 131; *Asylum* case, ibid., 1950, at pp. 277–8; D'Amato, *The Concept of Custom in International Law* (1971), at pp. 117–18.

Asylum case[36] and on the separate opinion of Judge van Wyk in the *South West Africa* cases.[37] Support may also be found in Judge Ammoun's separate opinion in the *North Sea Continental Shelf* cases, as well as Judge Gros's separate opinion in the *Nuclear Tests* case.[38] Yet none of these opinions constitutes a holding of the Court itself.

The more recent *Fisheries Jurisdiction* case presented an interesting situation in which the persistent objector rule might have been directly invoked. As the Court reports, Iceland and the UK had engaged in a long-term dispute over Iceland's attempts to enforce a claim of exclusive fishery jurisdiction beyond 3 nautical miles from its coastline.[39] The UK had consistently taken the position in its relations with Iceland and all other coastal States that the limit of the exclusive fisheries jurisdiction of coastal States was 3 nautical miles and that the waters beyond that limit were subject to the high seas freedom to fish held by all States. Only in 1961 did the UK enter into an agreement with Iceland whereby the UK agreed to object no longer to Iceland's 12-mile fishery zone. The exchange of notes left open questions concerning a further extension of Iceland's fisheries jurisdiction. The agreement also contained a consent by both parties to the jurisdiction of the International Court of Justice in relation to such a further extension.[40] The instant litigation was precipitated by Iceland's assertion and attempted implementation of a 50-nautical mile exclusive fishery zone. The UK objected to the further extension and, after negotiations failed, it invoked the consent to jurisdiction of the Court to commence the suit.[41]

Despite the fact that Iceland refused to participate in the litigation, the Court issued a judgment on the merits of the UK's claim. The Court never directly ruled on the question of the legality under international law of the 50-mile fishery zone. It did, however, hold that the Icelandic claim 'is not opposable to the United Kingdom'.[42] One cannot be certain whether this holding is based on the persistent objector rule as a matter of customary international law or on the obligations that emanated from the exchange of notes.[43] Judge Waldock's separate opinion, however, came closer to invoking the rule. He pointed out the UK's prompt and consistent rejections of the claim and found that the claim 'is not opposable to the United Kingdom

[36] Akehurst, loc. cit. above (p. 1 n. 3), at p. 25 n. 5; *Asylum* case, dissenting opinion of Judge Azevedo, *ICJ Reports*, 1950, p. 332 at pp. 336–7.

[37] Akehurst, loc. cit. above (p. 1 n. 3), at p. 25 n. 5; *South West Africa* cases (*Ethiopia* v. *South Africa*) (*Liberia* v. *South Africa*), *Second Phase*, separate opinion of Judge van Wyk, *ICJ Reports*, 1966, pp. 3, 65, at pp. 169–70. In the *South West Africa* cases two of the judges would have applied the anti-*apartheid* rule to South Africa despite its persistent objection to the rule: separate opinion of Judge Tanaka, ibid., at pp. 250, 293–4; separate opinion of Judge Padilla Nervo, ibid., at pp. 443, 470. See D'Amato, *Canadian Yearbook of International Law*, 8 (1970), at pp. 117–20.

[38] *North Sea Continental Shelf* cases, *ICJ Reports*, 1969, p. 3, separate opinion of Judge Ammoun at p. 131; separate opinion of Judge Gros, *Nuclear Tests* case, ibid., 1974, p. 253 at pp. 286–9.

[39] *Fisheries Jurisdiction* case, ibid., at pp. 10–22.

[40] Ibid., at p. 13.

[41] Ibid., at pp. 15–16.

[42] Ibid., at p. 29. See also p. 30.

[43] Ibid., at pp. 29–30.

under *general international law*'.[44] Judge De Castro took the opposite view, and argued that a 12-mile limit to the fisheries zone could not apply to Iceland because it had persistently objected to any such limit.[45]

Despite the UK's continued support of the traditional high seas regime, the Court did hold that the UK and Iceland had an obligation to negotiate their respective fishery interests in the context of a newly developed rule of international law giving the coastal state 'preferential rights' in the living resources adjacent to their coastlines.[46] While the judgment states that the UK had accepted that rule, the basis for this statement appears to stretch the Court's own report of the UK's position.[47] In sum, while the Court did not reject the persistent objector rule, neither did it take advantage of the opportunity to bolster the rule. Its ambiguous treatment of the subject may have even facilitated Iceland's future behaviour. The ruling did not effectively restrain Iceland's continued enforcement of its claim against the UK, and today Iceland's 200-mile exclusive economic zone is securely in place.[48] It would thus appear that the record of this conflict does not resolve questions relating to the vitality of the persistent objector rule.

(d) *State Practice*

One can look in vain through writers' discussions of the persistent objector rule for references to State practice that clearly support the rule. In addition, recent events cast doubts about the viability of the rule. A number of examples arise in the context of the law of the sea. For some time, the UK, the US and Japan led the fight against the expansion of coastal State jurisdiction. As indicated already, the UK had little success in its dispute with Iceland.

Owing to Japan's island status and its substantial reliance on fish products, it has had a major interest in maximizing the freedoms of the seas in order to minimize restrictions on its distant water fisheries and commerce to and from its territory. It has strenuously resisted the movement towards the expansion of coastal State jurisdiction in the oceans. When, in the mid 1960s, Australia, Mexico, New Zealand, the Republic of Korea and the US claimed their 12-mile exclusive fishery zones, Japan made its position clear that the area beyond the 3-mile territorial sea was high seas open to fishing by all nations. It then proceeded with diplomatic efforts to resolve the dispute. While at one point Japan threatened to take New Zealand to the International Court of Justice on the issue, in the end it entered into agreements with each of these countries, which temporarily resolved

44 Ibid., separate opinion of Judge Waldock, at pp. 106, 120 (emphasis added). See dissenting opinion of Judge Gros, ibid., at pp. 126, 148–9. See also judgment of 25 July 1974, ibid., at pp. 23–6, 29–31, and joint separate opinion, ibid., at pp. 45, 46.

45 Ibid., separate opinion of Judge De Castro at pp. 91–2.

46 Ibid., at pp. 32, 34.

47 Ibid., at pp. 14, 29.

48 Anand, 'A New Legal Order for Fisheries', *Ocean Development and International Law*, 11 (1982), pp. 265, 280.

the dispute.[49] In all but the agreement with the Republic of Korea pragmatic solutions were reached whereby Japanese fishermen obtained limited access to specified areas for a determinate period of time without a Japanese acknowledgement of the legality of the coastal State's fishery zone. The agreement with the Republic of Korea contained an express mutual recognition of the right of each State to establish a 12-mile fishery zone.[50] The agreements were intentionally ambiguous on the question of whether international law permitted the coastal State unilaterally to establish a 12-mile exclusive fishery zone. Thus one can interpret the events as demonstrating that Japan had to obtain permission from these coastal States to fish in their fishery zones. Viewed from this perspective, the events implicitly establish the *de facto* effect of these unilateral claims. On the other hand, the record could also be interpreted to establish that Japan's high seas rights in the areas had been vindicated because the coastal States were compelled to permit Japanese fishing in portions of these zones and to obtain the Japanese agreement to relinquish rights to pursue fishing in other parts of these zones.[51] In the end, however, the strong forces favouring the 12-mile fishery zone and then the 200-mile zone overwhelmed the Japanese tenacious efforts to resist these changes. It has accepted the new law of the sea with its 12-mile territorial sea and 200-mile exclusive economic zone.[52] Its status as a persistent objector was of little value in the face of these changes in international law.

[49] The 1967 Agreement between the United States of America and Japan concerning Certain Fisheries off the Coast of the United States of America, signed 9 May 1967, *United Nations Treaty Series*, vol. 685, p. 254, reprinted at Oda, *The International Law of the Ocean Development: Basic Documents*, vol. 2 (1975), p. 136; the 1968 Agreement on Fishing by Japanese Vessels in Waters Contiguous to the Mexican Territorial Sea, signed 7 March 1968, entered into force 10 June 1968, *United Nations Treaty Series*, vol. 683, p. 257, reprinted at Oda, op. cit., at p. 152; the 1967 Agreement on Fisheries between Japan and New Zealand, signed 12 July 1967, entered into force 26 July 1968, *United Nations Treaty Series*, vol. 683, p. 45, reprinted at Oda, op. cit., at p. 160; the 1968 Agreement on Fisheries between Australia and Japan, signed 27 November 1968, entered into force 24 August 1969, *United Nations Treaty Series*, vol. 708, p. 201, reprinted at Oda, op. cit., at p. 162; Agreement on Fisheries between Japan and the Republic of Korea, signed 22 June 1965, entered into force 18 December 1965, *United Nations Treaty Series*, vol. 583, p. 51, reprinted at *International Legal Materials*, 4 (1965), p. 1128.

[50] The diplomatic records of the Japanese efforts on this matter have been collected in Oda and Owada, *The Practice of Japan in International Law 1961–1970* (1982), pp. 149–70. See also Oda, 'International Law of the Resources of the Sea', *Recueil des cours*, 127 (1969–II), pp. 355, 392–6. Even in 1969 Professor Oda seemed to recognize the futility of the Japanese efforts in this regard: ibid.

[51] This ambiguity is made clear in the Japanese diplomatic record. See Oda and Owada, op. cit. (previous note); and Oda, loc. cit. (previous note).

[52] For a recent and comprehensive review of Japan's oceans interests and activities, see Friedheim *et al.*, *Japan and the New Ocean Regime* (1984). While, externally, Japan actively opposed the expansions of coastal State jurisdiction, a study of the internal politics in Japan reveals that there was much conflict: Fukui, 'How Japan Handled UNCLOS Issues: Does Japan Have an Ocean Policy?', ibid., at pp. 21, 36–40, 44–51; Akaha, 'A Cybernetic Analysis of Japan's Fishery Policy Process', ibid., at pp. 173, 198–210. The Japanese change of position in favour of these expansions was critically influenced by its increased international isolation as demonstrated by State practice and the negotiations at the Law of the Sea Conference: Fukui, loc. cit. above, at pp. 39 and 47; Yanai and Asomura, 'Japan and the Emerging Order of the Sea—Two Maritime Laws of Japan', *Japanese Annual of International Law*, 21 (1977), pp. 48, 71, 72.

See, generally, Jones, 'Freedom of Fishing in Decline: The Fishery Conservation and Management

Only reluctantly in 1983 did the US accept the view that States could legally claim territorial seas in excess of 3 nautical miles.[53] Until that announcement, it was also a persistent objector to territorial sea claims beyond 3 nautical miles. Similarly, it objected to the development of extended resource zones in the water column for many years. In both circumstances, its status as an objector was often met by coastal States' enforcement of their broad claims.[54] Ultimately, the US was forced to accept the new zones.[55]

Even today, the US continues to maintain that highly migratory species of tuna are exempt from coastal State jurisdiction beyond the territorial sea.[56] While the international law may not be completely settled, it appears

Act of 1976 and the Implications for Japan', *California Western International Law Journal*, 11 (1981), pp. 52, 91–104; Ouchi, 'A Perspective on Japan's Struggle for Its Traditional Rights in the Oceans', *Ocean Development and International Law*, 5 (1978), p. 107; Ouchi, 'Japanese Perspective on the Law of the Sea', *Proceedings of the American Society of International Law*, 71 (1977), p. 159; Park, 'The Sino-Japanese–Korean Sea Resources Controversy and the Hypothesis of a 200-Mile Economic Zone', *Harvard International Law Journal*, 16 (1975), pp. 27, 35–7; Yanai and Asomura, loc. cit. above. For a review of the effects of the 200-mile zone on Japanese fishing, see Tanaka, 'Japanese Fisheries and Fishery Resources in the Northwest Pacific', *Ocean Development and International Law*, 6 (1979), p. 163.

[53] This acceptance came in the Statement of the President on the Exclusive Economic Zone of 10 March 1983, which accompanied the Exclusive Economic Zone Proclamation of the same date (Proclamation No. 5030, *Federal Register*, 48 (1983), No. 50, at p. 10605). In the statement the President said:

'Today I am announcing three decisions to promote and protect the oceans interests of the United States in a manner consistent with those fair and balanced results in the Convention [on the Law of the Sea] and international law.

'First, the United States is prepared to accept and act in accordance with the balance of interests relating to traditional uses of the oceans—such as navigation and overflight. In this respect, the United States will recognize the rights of other states in the waters off their coasts, as reflected in the Convention, so long as the rights and freedoms of the United States and others under international law are recognized by such coastal states.'

('United States Oceans Policy', Statement by the President, 10 March 1983, *Weekly Compilation of Presidential Documents*, vol. 19, no. 10, p. 383 (14 March 1983))

[54] Some indication of the magnitude of the conflict can be obtained by a review of the expenses incurred by the US to reimburse fishermen for their losses and fines resulting from exercises of coastal State jurisdiction that the US maintains is illegal. In fiscal year 1981 the US paid $8,600,000 in accordance with the Fishermen's Protective Act, 68 Stat. 883, 22 USC section 1971 f., on claims under the programme to protect ships from foreign seizure: *Catalogue of Federal Domestic Assistance*, 1982, pp. 495–6. Payment in fiscal year 1981 out of the Fishermen's Guarantee Fund, section 7 of the Fishery Conservation and Management Act (FCMA), 16 USC sections 1812–13, was $1,777,000: ibid., at p. 111. Payment out of the Fishermen's Guarantee Fund in fiscal year 1982 was $2,314,800: *Update to Catalogue of Federal Domestic Assistance*, 1983, p. E-24. Payment in the same year for the protection of ships from foreign seizure was $1,600,000: ibid., at p. E-82. Payment under the Fishermen's Guarantee Fund for fiscal year 1983 was $1,516,799: *Catalogue of Federal Domestic Assistance*, 1984, p. 111. Payment for the protection of ships from foreign seizure under the FCMA in fiscal year 1983 amounted to $17,000: ibid., at pp. 515–16.

[55] See above, n. 53.

[56] In the President's Statement which accompanied his Exclusive Economic Zone Proclamation (loc. cit. above, n. 53), he said: 'My proclamation does not change existing United States policies concerning the continental shelf, marine mammals, and fisheries, including highly migratory species of tuna which are not subject to United States jurisdiction. The United States will continue efforts to achieve international agreements for the effective management of these species': Statement, loc. cit. above (n. 53). This position is codified in legislation: FCMA, loc. cit. above (n. 54).

that the claims of many interested coastal States and the text of the Law of the Sea Convention would support the view that such species of fish are within the coastal States' jurisdiction in the exclusive economic zone.[57] Despite the fact that the US would have a persistent objector status, it has been subjected to serious enforcement actions by coastal States.[58] Those coastal States appear to be unwilling to treat the US as exempt from the new rule.

The Western developed States have found themselves in a similar persistent objector status in the case of the law regarding compensation for expropriation. While these States have argued that the prompt, adequate and effective compensation standard was, and continues to be, the applicable rule of law, much of the rest of the world utilizes less generous standards even in cases involving nationals of the objecting States.[59] The erosion of the argument for the higher standard has been further emphasized in Tentative Draft Number 6 of the *Restatement of the Foreign Relations Law of the United States* (*Revised*), which uses the standard of just compensation,[60] and in a judgment of the Iranian–US Claims Tribunal

[57] Virtually all coastal States claim jurisdiction over fish within their 200-mile zones. Very few of them make distinctions based on the species of fish for this purpose. See Charney, 'The Exclusive Economic Zone and Public International Law', *Ocean Development and International Law*, 15 (1985), p. 233 at n. 69.

[58] In a recent incident that obtained significant news coverage the Solomon Islands impounded a US tuna boat valued at $3.5 million. As a result, the US imposed trade sanctions on the Islands. A similar incident arose in 1982 in which Papua New Guinea seized another US tuna vessel: 'Tuna Fishing Causes a Row between US and Pacific Islands', *The Christian Science Monitor*, 9 October 1984, p. 16; 'Solomons Ban US Tuna Ships and Say Soviets Might be OK', ibid., 29 August 1984, p. 2; 'Pacific Atolls Show Feisty Independence', *The New York Times* (Late City Final Edition), 24 October 1982, sec. 4, p. 2, col. 3.

Similar actions against United States tuna boats have resulted in the imposition of US trade sanctions against Mexico and Ecuador: 'Billion-Dollar-Tuna Fish Sandwich', *The Christian Science Monitor*, 25 September 1980, p. B1; 'For Reagan and Mexican, A Quick Tour of the Issues', *The New York Times* (Late City Final Edition), 14 August 1983, sec. 4, p. 2, col. 3; 'Why Mexico Threw its U.S. Fishing Accords Overboard', *The Christian Science Monitor*, 30 December 1980, p. 3; 'Mexico Ends Agreements with U.S. on Fishing', *The Washington Post* (Final Edition), 29 December 1980, sec. 1, p. A8; 'U.S. in Reprisal, Bans Imports of Tuna from Ecuador', *The New York Times* (Late City Edition), 7 November 1980, sec. A, p. 7, col. 4; 'The "Tuna War" With Mexico', ibid., 31 July 1980, sec. D, p. 1, col. 3; 'U.S. Seeks Tuna Pact with Mexico', ibid., 17 July 1980, sec. A, p. 8, col. 3.

[59] See UN General Assembly Resolution on Permanent Sovereignty over Natural Resources, GA Res. 1803 (XVII), *General Assembly Official Records*, 17th Session, Supplement 17 (A/5217), at p. 15 (1962); Trade and Development Board of UNCTAD Resolution on Permanent Sovereignty over Natural Resources, Res. 88 (XII), *UN Conference on Trade and Development Official Records*, 12th Session, Supplement 1, at p. 1, UN Doc. TD/B/423 (1973); UN General Assembly Resolution on Permanent Sovereignty over Natural Resources, Res. 3171 (XXVIII), *General Assembly Official Records*, 28th Session, Supplement 30 (A/9030) at p. 52 (1974); UN General Assembly Declaration on the Establishment of a New International Economic Order, GA Res. 3201 (S-VI), *General Assembly Official Records*, Sixth Special Session, Supplement 1 (A/4559), at p. 3 (1974); *Restatement of the Foreign Relations Law of the United States* (Tentative Draft No. 3, 15 March 1982), section 712, Reporters' Notes, p. 1; Lillich, 'The Valuation of Nationalized Property in International Law: Toward a Consensus or More "Rich Chaos"?', in *The Valuation of Nationalized Property in International Law* (ed. Lillich), vol. 3 (1975), pp. 190–204; Schachter, 'Compensation for Expropriation', *American Journal of International Law*, 78 (1984), p. 121.

[60] *Restatement* (Tentative Draft No. 6), at section 712 (1); ibid., at Comm. (c) and (d); ibid., at Reporters' Notes 2 and 3. The approach taken by the Reporters on this matter has produced strong

which held that the standard of compensation due to a US claimant for nationalization of a company is its 'going concern value'.[61] The persistent objector rule does not appear to have substantially protected the objecting States from these developments.

Neither South Africa nor Rhodesia realized advantages from the persistent objector rule in their efforts to maintain *apartheid*. The vast majority of States and commentators are of the view that *apartheid* violates international law.[62] At the same time, South Africa and Rhodesia (prior to the establishment of Zimbabwe) persistently objected to the norm. Nevertheless, this status did not immunize South Africa and Rhodesia from the apparent consensus of the international community that they are obligated not to practise *apartheid*. The persistent objector status did not in any way protect them from the pressure exerted by the international community to force them to conform to the norm.[63] In all respects, the international community has treated them as serious violators of a rule of international law, their status as a persistent objector notwithstanding.

In each of the examples given above, the persistent objector rule does not appear to have significantly helped the State or States that have resisted the new developments. No case, however, is clear cut. In all of the cases that one could identify, it might be argued that the alleged pre-existing law was never law, that the new law is not yet settled, or alternatively, that the persistent objector rule was of assistance in some imperceptible way. Such explanations of the examples, however, do not so much support the viability of the rule as demonstrate the very tenuous nature and limited usefulness of the rule itself.

Equally, situations that might be identified as ones in which the persistent objector rule was of assistance are rarely clear cut. Thus, the Scandinavian States' maintenance of a 4-mile territorial sea in the face of claims that the limit might not exceed 3 miles can be viewed as a persistent objector case. Questions arise, however, as to whether the 3-mile rule was established as the general rule of law and whether the Scandinavian States' rights did not derive from prescription that ultimately depended

negative reactions from some interested sectors. See Claggett, 'Protection of Foreign Investment Under the Revised Restatement', *Virginia Journal of International Law*, 25 (1984), p. 73; Robinson, 'Expropriation in the Restatement (Revised)', *American Journal of International Law*, 78 (1984), p. 176.

[61] American International Group, Inc./American Life Insurance Company and the Islamic Republic of Iran/Central Insurance of Iran, AWD 93-2-3, Iran–US Claims Tribunal, The Hague, 19 December 1983, reprinted at *International Legal Materials*, 23 (1984), p. 1, reported at *American Journal of International Law*, 78 (1984), p. 454.

[62] See *Barcelona Traction* case (*Belgium* v. *Spain*) (*Second Phase*), *ICJ Reports*, 1970, pp. 3, 32; *Restatement*, at section 702 (f); ibid., Comm. (i); ibid., Reporters' Notes, p. 7; and Brownlie, op. cit. above (p. 6 n. 15), (3rd edn.) at pp. 596–8. Brownlie points out that there is an alternative view that the rule against race discrimination is based on specific international agreements: ibid., at p. 597.

[63] For a comprehensive collection of relevant materials up to 1973, see Sohn and Buergenthal, *International Protection of Human Rights* (1973), pp. 373–504, 634–739. See also Note, 'Economic Sanctions Against South Africa: Problems and Prospects for Enforcement of Human Rights Norms', *Virginia Journal of International Law*, 22 (1982), p. 345; Gupta, 'South Africa, Human Rights and the United Nations', *India Quarterly*, 38 (1982), p. 334.

upon the acquiescence of the international community and not the Scandinavian States' status as persistent objectors.

In conclusion, the proponents of the persistent objector rule have not put forward persuasive evidence of State practice or even judicial opinions that would definitively establish the persistent objector rule. At the same time, it must be acknowledged that there is widespread support for the existence of the rule in the publications of writers and individual judicial opinions.

III. Consent and Customary International Law

Most writers forbear from claiming that consent is the basis for obligation under international law even though they support the persistent objector rule[64] which permits a State to be exempt from a rule of international law by dissenting in a timely manner. It is difficult to see how the acceptance of this rule does not reflect an acceptance of the consent theory of international law. If a mere objection to an evolving rule of law can prevent application of that rule to the State, then each State has the unilateral power to decide whether or not to be bound by the rule.

Some authorities seek to avoid this logical difficulty by relying on the doctrine of tacit consent. Thus, if a rule is evolving and a State does not object, it is assumed to have consented to the rule.[65] As others have pointed out, this tacit consent is a mere fictional creation of academicians which has no basis in the realities of the States' behaviour.[66] The tacit consent rule is not easily reconciled with the generally accepted rule that new States are bound by existing rules of international law to which they had never consented.[67] Furthermore, the tacit consent rule does not explain why silent dissenters and dissenters who make their objections known after the rule has become international law are bound.[68]

When the question of consent is directly addressed, most writers argue that States do not have the free will to decide whether or not to be bound by rules of international law. The obligation to conform to rules of international law is not derived from the voluntary decision of a State to accept or reject the binding force of a rule of law. Rather, it is the societal context which motivates States to have an international law and obligates them to conform to its norms.

Brierly, for example, argued that nothing in the nature of consent *per se*

[64] See authorities cited above at p. 3 n. 9. Brierly's statement at p. 5 n. 14, above, is a good example of this apparent inconsistency.

[65] See above, p. 2 n. 4; Lauterpacht, op. cit. above (p. 1 n. 3), at pp. 65–6; MacGibbon, loc. cit. above (p. 1 n. 2), at pp. 139–45.

[66] Kelsen rejected attempts to save the consent theory by assuming tacit consent where no express manifestation of consent exists: op. cit. above (p. 1 n. 3), at pp. 311–17. See Akehurst, op. cit. above (p. 2 n. 4), at pp. 31–2; De Visscher, *Theory and Reality in Public International Law* (translation, rev. edn., 1968), pp. 153–7. See also Fitzmaurice, loc. cit. above (p. 1 n. 3), at p. 40.

[67] See previous note. But see above, p. 2 n. 6.

[68] See above, p. 1 n. 3; Thirlway, op. cit. above (p. 5 n. 9), at pp. 110, 133.

can create an obligation: a more fundamental rule, to the effect that consensual agreements ought to be kept, exists. Thus he stated:

> But a contract or treaty is capable of having . . . juridical effect only because there exists an underlying general rule of law to the effect *pacta sunt servanda*, and we may well speak of a legal obligation as consensual, meaning only that the occasion out of which it arises is a consensus of parties, and not intending to imply that its ultimate basis, the rule of law which gives binding effect to the consensus, is itself consensual in character.[69]

Fitzmaurice also argued that consent is not necessary.

> If a rule is necessary, or if the existence of a system of rules is a necessary condition of a certain state of affairs, the rule or system must also necessarily be binding, or it would not fulfil, or be able to fulfil its function. Practising international lawyers need perhaps look no further than to considerations of this type for the obligatory character of their system. It is something that arises logically and inevitably out of the requirements of international intercourse, relations and transactions. It is an inherent necessity of the case, and no theory of consent need be postulated in order to account for it.[70]

For Kelsen the basis of customary law is not founded on express or implied consent but on 'the general principle that we ought to behave in the way our fellow men usually behave and during a certain period of time used to behave'.[71] Kelsen rejected attempts to save the consent theory by assuming tacit consent where no express manifestation of consent exists.[72] To hold non-consenting States bound by way of 'tacit consent' was, for Kelsen, to rely on a fiction of an equivalent nature to the fictions that must be relied upon by natural law theories.[72] Kelsen argued that the notion that consent is the source of obligation in international law results from the traditional, but discarded, theory of sovereignty and social contract.[73] But the idea that States are truly 'sovereign' is merely a fiction: 'the states, subjected to international law are, by their very nature, no more "sovereign" than the individuals, subjected to the national legal order, are, by their very nature, "free"'.[74] Kelsen rejected the consent theory because he was unable to accept the fictions that must be utilized to make the theory conform to reality and because without these fictions the theory is unacceptable. In his words:

> It is certainly possible to assume that a state is bound by international law only if it recognizes this law as binding upon it, just as it is possible to assume that an individual is bound by national law only if he recognizes this law as binding upon

[69] Brierly, *The Basis of Obligation in International Law* (1958), p. 10; see also Brierly, op. cit. above (p. 1 n. 3), at p. 53.

[70] Fitzmaurice, loc. cit. above (p. 1 n. 3), at pp. 39–40. Corbett wrote that the 'cause of international law is the desire of states to have their necessary mutual relations regulated with the greatest possible rationality and uniformity': 'The Consent of States and the Sources of the Law of Nations', this *Year Book*, 6 (1925), pp. 20, 22. See also Henkin, op. cit. above (p. 1 n. 3), at pp. 29–31, 49–68.

[71] Kelsen, op. cit. above (p. 1 n. 3), at p. 307.

[72] See ibid. at p. 311.

[73] Ibid., at pp. 315–16.

[74] Ibid., at p. 316.

him. In other words, it is possible to proceed from the assumption that the state is sovereign, i.e., the highest legal authority, just as it is possible to start from the assumption that the individual is free and hence can be bound only by his own will. But there is hardly a writer ready to accept all the consequences of such an assumption.[75]

De Visscher criticized the consent theory because it superimposes on customary international law an *ex post facto* contractual analysis when, in reality, new customary law is the result of repeated exercises of power combined with the proper *opinio juris* (which is not equivalent to consent, either actual or implied).[76]

If it is the societal context that is the source of the obligation to conform to specific rules of international law, then consent, either express or tacit, is irrelevant to the obligation. It may also appear to follow that if the societal context is the source, then an objection at any time, persistent or not, is irrelevant to the binding effect of a rule of law. If this is true, there is no place in international law for the persistent objector rule. A similar conclusion that the rule has no place in international law is reached if one maintains that consent is the basis of obligation. In that case, a particular persistent objector rule is redundant.

Only if one actually believes in the reality of the tacit consent theory of international legal obligation might there be any room for the persistent objector rule. In that case, it is difficult to limit its application only to overt dissent commenced at the formative stages of law development. One also has to refute the powerful arguments of Kelsen and others that tacit consent is a fiction.

Akehurst focuses on this issue in his defence of the persistent objector rule. His argument is based on the premiss that no rule of international law would ever emerge from a system that requires the unanimous consent of all States to a new rule. He argues that a State must either be able to opt out of a new rule of customary international law, or the system must accept some form of majority voting. Akehurst is unable to accept that such a majority voting system exists (or is workable), because it is impossible to agree about the size of the majority necessary or the degree to which different States' votes should be weighted. Therefore, he accepts the only alternative: namely, that a State may contract out of a new rule.[77] Given the possibility of contracting out by the persistent objector rule, no system of majority voting is required to create new norms, because '[p]ractice followed even by a small number of States can create new customary rules, provided the practice be consistent'.[78]

Akehurst's rejection of a system of majority voting, however, on which

[75] Kelsen, op. cit. above (p. 1 n. 3), at p. 317.

[76] De Visscher, op. cit. above (p. 16 n. 66), at pp. 153–7. See also Akehurst, op. cit. above (p. 2 n. 4), at pp. 31–2.

[77] Akehurst, loc. cit. above (p. 1 n. 3), at pp. 23–7. See also p. 3 n. 7, above.

[78] Akehurst, loc. cit. above (p. 1 n. 3), at p. 26. See also Akehurst, op. cit. above (p. 2 n. 4), at p. 31.

depends his conclusion that dissenting States must be allowed to opt out of developing law, does not appear to be well founded. First, despite Akehurst's assertions that 'it would be impossible to reach agreement about the size of the majority required',[79] a system of weighted majority decision-making already seems to be the basis upon which customary international law has traditionally developed. In practice, a weighted majority calculation must be undertaken to determine whether an emerging rule of customary law has attained the level of adherence necessary to qualify it as customary international law. In making these calculations the weight accorded to the behaviour of particular States varies according to the power of the State and the significance of its interest in the subject-matter of the rule. It is true that one cannot precisely set out the details of how this weighted system operates, but it is not possible to deny that the system exists.[80] Thus, contrary to the position adopted by Akehurst, the fact that States may disagree on the weight to be given particular 'votes' or the size of the 'majority' required does not make such a system unacceptable. If it were unacceptable, one would have to deny the legitimacy of the modern international legal system.

Secondly, a system of weighted majority decision-making should not be avoided simply because it requires the imposition of the will of the majority on minority States. To hold that States cannot be bound against their will is simply a return to the discarded consensual theory of international law. In fact, States are often bound against their will. Not only are new States, as well as passive and subsequent objectors, bound, but all States are bound by rules of *jus cogens* whether they presently consent to be so bound or not.[81] If the weight and power of the majority of the

[79] Akehurst, loc. cit. above (p. 1 n. 3), at p. 26. See also Verzijl, op. cit. above (p. 3 n. 9), at p. 37.

[80] Akehurst, loc. cit. above (p. 1 n. 3), at pp. 14, 22, 23, 39–40; Akehurst, op. cit. above (p. 2 n. 4), at pp. 31–2; Baxter, 'Treaties and Custom', *Recueil des cours*, 129 (1970–I), pp. 24, 66; Bishop, 'General Course of Public International Law', ibid., 115 (1965–II), pp. 151, 227; D'Amato, *The Concept of Custom in International Law* (1971), at pp. 64–5; De Visscher, op. cit. above (p. 16 n. 66), at p. 154; H. Lauterpacht, *The Development of International Law by the International Court* (1958), at p. 368; Tunkin, *Recueil des cours*, 95 (1958–III), at pp. 17–18, 70; and see above, p. 3 n. 7. A 1964 textbook published by the Soviet Institute of International Relations states: 'The relativity of the element of generality expresses itself in the fact that for the arising of a customary norm, it is non-obligatory that all governments without exception acknowledge and apply it. Its acknowledgement on the part of the majority of governments, having the main role and greatest importance in international relations, appears to be necessary and sufficient practice': Kozhevnikov (ed.), *Mezhdunarodnoye Pravo* (1964), p. 42, translation in D'Amato, *Canadian Yearbook of International Law*, 8 (1970), at p. 109.

[81] It is the author's view that if the persistent objector rule is good law, the rule could apply to the development of all new rules of international law, including rules of *jus cogens*. See above, p. 3 n. 9. Arguments that the persistent objector rule does not apply to the creation of rules of *jus cogens* must be founded on the theory that the international community of States can impose rules of law on States notwithstanding their active and timely dissent. By accepting the view that rules of *jus cogens* are not subject to the persistent objector rule, one must be stating that rules of *jus cogens* are so important that the international legal system can override dissenting States' views. Since the same international legal system must be used to support both rules of *jus cogens* and 'normal' rules, one must conclude that the international legal system is capable of overriding the position of the dissenting State. The distinction, therefore, is not based on legal theory but on the strength of the will of the international community. In the case of *jus cogens* the community will use greater power to impose law on the dissenting State. The

international community can impose duties on States against their will in these situations, there is no reason why the persistent objector should be treated any differently.

Akehurst's defence of the persistent objector rule as a necessary safety valve for States which are unwilling to go along with the majority also raises the question whether international law requires that States be bound by a single uniform rule. International law is clear that a single unvarying rule of behaviour is rarely required. Variations are permitted, but those variations are permissible only with the consent or acquiescence of the interested States. For example, Fitzmaurice addressed this question in his 1957 Hague lecture. He pointed out that situations are often identified as exceptions to a rule of international law. Rather than exceptions to the law itself, he characterized many of these situations as falling within 'the exception created or recognized by the law itself'.[82] Thus the rule of law created by the international community as a whole has built into it provisions for various circumstances. Similarly, in the case of prescriptive rights, the State that maintains rights not included within the rule of law may obtain an exemption from the rule by way of prescription, a process which requires the international community to have acquiesced in the right that is claimed. Prior to the vesting of the prescriptive right the deviating State would be a violator of the law.[83]

It is also well accepted that, with the exception of rules that are *jus cogens*, States may vary rules of international law in their bilateral and multilateral relations *inter se* by agreement.[84] Even fewer than all the parties to an international agreement may enter into a special agreement under certain con-

persistent objector rule would then be seen not as a rule based on the inherent nature of the international legal system, but as a desirable rule that responds to gradations of importance of international rules. See Weil, loc. cit. above (p. 6 n. 18), at pp. 426–7.

Interestingly, a counter-argument to this view that the persistent objector rule is overriden by *jus cogens* might be that it is in just such *jus cogens* cases that the dissenting State has the most interest in preserving its freedom from the new rule. Rules of *jus cogens* could be seen as presenting a greater challenge to State sovereignty than most other rules of international law. Once a rule of *jus cogens* becomes law, the State is forbidden to diverge from it even by agreement with other States of similar preference.

[82] Fitzmaurice, loc. cit. above (p. 1 n. 3), at pp. 108–9.

[83] Ibid., at pp. 111–12.

[84] The legality of such agreements was implicit in the *Asylum* case, *ICJ Reports*, 1950, at pp. 274–8. See also D'Amato, *The Concept of Custom in International Law* (1971), at p. 131; Akehurst, loc. cit. above (p. 1 n. 3), at p. 31; Fitzmaurice, loc. cit. above (p. 1 n. 3), at pp. 96–108; Fitzmaurice, 'The Law and Procedure of the International Court of Justice: General Principles and Substantive Law', this *Year Book*, 27 (1950), pp. 1, 15–16; Jessup, 'Non-Universal International Law', *Columbia Journal of Transnational Law*, 12 (1973), pp. 415, 416; Thirlway, op. cit. above (p. 3 n. 9), at pp. 120–4.

There is no dispute that in their relations *inter se* State parties to an international agreement can bind themselves to rules different from customary international law. See Vienna Convention on the Law of Treaties, Articles 53 and 64, UN Doc. A/Conf. 39/27, reproduced at *American Journal of International Law*, 63 (1969), p. 875, and *International Legal Materials*, 8 (1969), p. 679, which prohibits only treaties that contravene rules of *jus cogens*; and International Law Commission Report, *Yearbook of the International Law Commission*, 1966, vol. 2, pp. 169, 247–9. See also Gaja, '*Jus Cogens* Beyond the Vienna Convention', *Recueil des cours*, 172 (1981–III), p. 271; Rozakis, *The Concept of* Jus Cogens *in the Law of Treaties* (1976); Sztuki, *Jus Cogens and the Vienna Convention on the Law of Treaties* (1974).

ditions establishing rules applicable to their relations *inter se* that vary the terms of the primary agreement.[85]

All of the rules identified above have a common attribute. The State or States that seek to vary their behaviour from a single uniform standard must have the consent or acquiescence of all other States to be affected by the behaviour. The persistent objector rule is different. It would permit the dissenting State by unilateral act to exempt itself from a rule of law in its relations with all other States.

IV. Is there a Role for the Rule?

At this point it might be wise to conclude that regardless of one's theory of international law, the persistent objector rule has no legitimate basis in the international legal system. Not only is the rule hard to reconcile with the current theories of international law, but the evidence which might be produced to support the rule is weak indeed. This conclusion does not explain why so many reputable international law authorities explicitly report the existence of the rule. Perhaps its *raison d'être* can be found in the dynamics of international law development.

While Akehurst's arguments may be wanting, he has focused on the dynamics of law development. Customary international law is not static. It changes as the patterns of State behaviour change and *opinio juris* evolves to reflect current realities of obligation. Extant rules of law are subjected to change. Nations forge new law by breaking existing law, thereby leading the way for other nations to follow. Ultimately, new patterns of behaviour and obligation develop.[86]

In the early stages a number of States may object to the new behaviour, but over time social pressures and modern realities will cause those reluctant States to conform to the new norm. On the other hand, some will seek to retain the traditional rule. The persistent objector rule becomes directly relevant when those resisting States continue to dissent from the new norm after it has replaced the old norm. At this stage the persistent objector rule promotes disharmony and discord in international relations. The international community will exert pressure to force the objector to conform to the new normative standard. As Akehurst and Fitzmaurice have pointed out, this pressure will be extreme, and few, if any, objectors will persevere to maintain their status long after the new norm becomes settled.[87] In fact, the two International Court of Justice cases which appear to support the persistent objector rule both arise in circumstances in which the new rule itself was in substantial doubt.[88] Thus, it was significantly easier for the

[85] Vienna Convention, loc. cit. (previous note), Article 41. See Kearney and Dalton, 'The Treaty on Treaties', *American Journal of International Law*, 64 (1970), pp. 495, 524. See, generally, Sinclair, *The Vienna Convention on the Law of Treaties* (2nd edn., 1984).

[86] Fitzmaurice, loc. cit. above (p. 1 n. 3), at p. 113.

[87] Akehurst, loc. cit. above (p. 1 n. 3), at p. 27; Fitzmaurice, loc. cit. above (p. 1 n. 3), at p. 111.

[88] See text at p. 9 n. 34, above.

objector to maintain its status. No case is cited for a circumstance in which the objector effectively maintained its status after the rule became well accepted in international law. In fact, it is unlikely that such a status could be maintained in light of the realities of the international legal system.[89] This is certainly the plight that befell the US, the UK and Japan in the law of the sea. Their objections to expanded coastal State jurisdiction were ultimately to no avail, and they have been forced to accede to 12-mile territorial seas and 200-mile exclusive economic zones.[90]

It appears, therefore, that the persistent objector rule, if it really exists, focuses more on the process of law development than on the status of a State under stable international law. Its utility, if any, is to provide the State which objects to the evolution of a new rule of law with a tool it may use over the short term in its direct and indirect negotiations with the proponents of a new rule.[91] The objecting State is armed with the theoretical right to opt out of the new rule. The proponents of the new rule are, as a consequence, encouraged to accommodate the objecting State or to utilize greater power to turn the objecting State to their will. At the same time, the persistent objector rule serves to soften the threat that the force of 'law' will impose a new and objectionable rule on the State that is content with the status quo. The persistent objector rule permits the objecting State to feel secure that it is not directly threatened, in an overt legal way, by changes in the law which it opposes. The legal system thereby appears to be fair and to permit an accommodation of views in the evolution of rules of law. It will be the political and social realities of the new status quo that will force the objecting State to conform to the new rule of law or the rest of the international community to accept on the basis of prescription the

[89] The *Fisheries Jurisdiction* case, discussed at pp. 10–11 nn. 42–8, above, would appear to support the proposition that a persistent objector cannot persevere. Despite the British persistent objections to a fishery zone beyond a narrow territorial sea, Iceland continued to enforce its claim against British fishermen. See above, p. 11 n. 48. Ultimately, the 200-mile resource zone became established in international law and the British have ceased to resist. See generally Charney, loc. cit. above (p. 14 n. 57).

Akehurst has written,

> 'Unless dissenting States are numerous, they seldom maintain their dissent for long. Resolutions passed by large majorities at meetings of international organizations will remind them how isolated they are. The views of writers, insofar as they reflect State practice, will be used to reinforce the opinion of the majority of States and to put pressure on the minority to conform.
>
> 'Moreover, the practical difficulties which the dissenting States are likely to experience in enforcing their rights will cause them to change their attitude':

loc. cit. above (p. 1 n. 3), at p. 27. See, generally, Akehurst, op. cit. above (p. 2 n. 4), at pp. 8–11; Baxter, loc. cit. above (p. 19 n. 80), at pp. 73–4, 102–3; Tunkin, *California Law Review*, 49 (1961), at p. 428. *Contra*, Verzijl, op. cit. above (p. 3 n. 9), at pp. 37, 38. It is interesting to note that the example Verzijl uses to support the rule is historical. The objecting State is no longer an objector.

[90] See text at pp. 12–14 nn. 52–8, above.

[91] The idea that a rule of international law could exist to give a State leverage in the development of applicable rules may be found in the International Law Commission's discussion of *rebus sic stantibus*: 'there may remain a residue of cases in which, failing any agreement, one party may be left powerless under the treaty to obtain any legal relief from outmoded and burdensome provisions. It is in these cases that the *rebus sic stantibus* doctrine could serve a purpose as a lever to induce a spirit of compromise in the other party': International Law Commission Report, *Yearbook of the International Law Commission*, 1966, vol. 2, pp. 169, 258.

dissenter's unique status. It will not be a formal rule of uniform obligation that will procure conformity.

Viewed in this light, the persistent objector rule may be seen to be closely linked to the doctrine that in order to determine whether a rule of international law exists, one must examine the views and practices of the States whose interests are particularly affected.[92] If the particularly affected States have not behaved in ways that conform to the purported rule of law, the International Court of Justice will be reluctant to hold in favour of that rule.[93]

If any State will be the persistent objector, it will be the particularly affected State. Such a State will have interests directly at stake in the matter that is the subject of the rule of law under study. If it finds that the new rule is contrary to its interests, it will oppose the rule and will work for its rejection. As a particularly affected State, it will have leverage in determining the evolution of the applicable rule of law and will have the theoretical option of invoking the persistent objector rule.[94] Thus both of these rules have one purpose, to force an accommodation of interests in the international community with respect to the evolution of new rules of law.

It is as such a persistent objector and particularly affected State that the US is seeking to pursue its interest in highly migratory species of tuna.

[92] *North Sea Continental Shelf* cases, *ICJ Reports*, 1969, at pp. 42–5. See also joint separate opinion of Judges Forster, Bengzon, Jiménez De Aréchaga, Nagendra Singh and Ruda, *Fisheries Jurisdiction* case, ibid., 1974, at pp. 50–1; D'Amato, *The Concept of Custom in International Law* (1971), at pp. 41–3; Akehurst, loc. cit. above (p. 1 n. 3), at pp. 1–3.

[93] *North Sea Continental Shelf* cases, *ICJ Reports*, 1969, at pp. 42–5; dissent of Judge Gros, *Fisheries Jurisdiction* case, ibid., 1974, at pp. 135–6; dissent of Judge Petrén, ibid., at p. 161. See also MacGibbon, loc. cit. above (p. 3 n. 9), at p. 319; Thirlway, op. cit. above (p. 3 n. 9), at p. 110.

[94] A situation in which the particularly interested State doctrine makes it unnecessary to consider the persistent objector rule is presented in the case of sovereign immunity. While the Western developed States have favoured the doctrine of restrictive sovereign immunity, the Eastern European socialist States have continued to favour the traditional doctrine of complete sovereign immunity. The Eastern European States have been effective in blocking the development of a universal rule of restrictive sovereign immunity. They have been effective for two reasons: (1) they represent a significant group of States that have resisted the restrictive immunity rule; (2) they are particularly interested States. As a consequence of this conflict, it might be concluded that there is no normative rule.

This situation has led the reporters of the *Restatement of the Foreign Relations Law of the United States* (*Revised*) to conclude:

'there is no general principle of sovereign immunity, not even a general principle of restrictive immunity . . ., from the law of another state. In general, then, unless otherwise provided by special agreement, activities of a foreign state, whether they are "governmental" or "commercial" in character, are subject to local law [jurisdiction to prescribe], even though, as to the former, the foreign state is immune from enforcement of that law by domestic courts, administrative bodies, or police action [jurisdiction to adjudicate and enforce]':

Part IV (2) (A) (Tentative Draft No. 5, 5 April 1984), 'Immunity of Foreign States from Jurisdiction to Prescribe', Introductory Note at p. 6.

The persistent objector rule would become clearly relevant only if there were few or unimportant States resisting the restrictive immunity rule. In that case the rule would be deemed to be binding on all States except the persistent objectors. While these differences may appear to lie on continuum, the difference is significant. In the first instance, a totally disinterested uninvolved State would be bound by the traditional rule of absolute immunity. In the second, that same State would be bound by the new restrictive immunity rule.

While the developing law may be adverse to the US position, it is using its political and economic leverage to forge a more acceptable result. Its legal status may have some marginal value in this effort but, as in the case of the 12-mile territorial sea and the 200-mile exclusive economic zone, the law will settle and the US can be expected to abandon its positions if they do not prevail.

When the rule does settle, there may be a few States that may continue to maintain an objection to a new rule of law. If they are few, they will not be able to block a finding that the new rule represents international law. While in theory or in a court of law they may invoke the persistent objector rule, the realities of the societal pressure will require either that they conform to the new rule or that a new accommodation be reached.[95]

In conclusion, it appears that the persistent objector rule is, at best, only of temporary or strategic value in the evolution of rules of international law. It cannot serve a permanent role, unless, of course, one really does believe that States have the independence freely to grant or withhold their consent to rules of customary international law.

[95] In the face of increased isolation, Japan chose to conform to the expansions of coastal State jurisdiction in the oceans rather than to continue its resistance. See p. 12 n. 52, above, and the accompanying text.

IS THERE AN INTERNATIONAL LAW OF REMEDIES?*

By CHRISTINE GRAY[1]

ONE of the most striking things to anyone starting to read about remedies in international law, whether self-help or judicial remedies, is that they tend to be treated as a distinct subject, often merely as an afterthought. That is, the substantive rules on particular areas are discussed; what States should do is considered. But if the consequences of breaches of these rules are mentioned at all in this context this usually just takes the form of an examination of State protests at the behaviour of other States as evidence of the content and existence of the suggested rule.[2] After the discussion of substantive law there may follow separate sections on State responsibility and international claims, on judicial settlement and on reprisals, often included in the discussion of the use of force. It is clear why this pattern has been commonly adopted for its convenience is obvious, but it does carry with it a danger of distortion. And even though there are signs that slightly more attention is now being paid to remedies in international law,[3] the tendency is still to treat remedies separately from the substantive rules, as a coherent separate subject.

This question is now being considered by the International Law Commission as part of its work on State responsibility. Its long struggles with this project are notorious. The first attempt (with García Amador as Special Rapporteur) to codify the rules on State responsibility for injury to aliens had to be abandoned because of differences over the substantive rules. So when the Commission tried again (with Judge Ago as Special Rapporteur) it adopted a radical change of approach in response to the earlier difficulties. It decided that when dealing with State responsibility it was unrealistic to try to define the rules placing obligations on States, the violations of which would engage State responsibility, for that would mean trying to codify the whole of international law from the point of view of responsibility. Instead the Commission tried to separate general principles of State responsibility from particular rules applicable to wrongful acts.

After ten years' work the Commission has now produced Part I of the

[1] MA, Ph.D., Fellow of St Hilda's College, Oxford. This article is based on a paper given at a meeting of the International Law Association in Oxford in July 1985. The author would like to thank the participants at that meeting for their helpful criticism of the paper. This article deals with some of the main themes in her forthcoming book, *Judicial Remedies in International Law*.

[2] Despite their different terminology, this is also the approach of the McDougal school.

[3] See, e.g., Oliver in Lillich (ed.), *International Law of State Responsibility for Injuries to Aliens* (1983), p. 61; Brownlie, *System of the Law of Nations—State Responsibility Part I* (1983), p. 199.

Draft Articles on State Responsibility. This is not the place for a detailed discussion of the value of this product,[4] but there must be considerable doubt as to whether all the effort has produced a worthwhile result. Probably what has attracted most attention and controversy is the provision on international crimes, that certain behaviour by States is not merely unlawful but criminal.[5] And it may be this rather than any of the more general objections that finally undermines any hope of acceptance for the Commission's work. What is important for the purposes of this article is that on this question of international crimes the International Law Commission has clearly not been able to maintain the distinction between general principles and particular substantive rules.

The difficulties involved in its attempt to evolve general principles of State responsibility and to keep them separate from particular substantive rules are even more apparent in the Commission's discussion (with Riphagen as Special Rapporteur) of Part II of the Draft Articles on 'Content, Forms and Degree of Responsibility'.[6] To follow the general rules on when a State incurs responsibility it is planned that there should be general rules on the consequences of responsibility. The Special Rapporteur seems to be asking himself 'What should happen if there is a breach of international law?'. But to find the answer he has not looked at State practice in any detailed or systematic way, despite pleas from other members of the Commission. He does not appear to have looked to see what happens if there is a breach of treaty or customary law or other rule of international law.

There is an interesting contrast here with the International Law Commission's work on 'International Liability for Injurious Consequences

[4] See Brownlie, op. cit. (previous note).

[5] '*Article 19—International Crimes and International Delicts*

'1. An act of a State which constitutes a breach of an international obligation is an internationally wrongful act, regardless of the subject-matter of the obligation breached.

'2. An internationally wrongful act which results from the breach by a State of an international obligation so essential for the protection of fundamental interests of the international community that its breach is recognized as a crime by that community as a whole, constitutes an international crime.

'3. Subject to paragraph 2, and on the basis of the rules of international law in force, an international crime may result, *inter alia*, from:

(a) a serious breach of an international obligation of essential importance for the maintenance of international peace and security, such as that prohibiting aggression;
(b) a serious breach of an international obligation of essential importance for safeguarding the right of self-determination of peoples, such as that prohibiting the establishment or maintenance by force of colonial domination;
(c) a serious breach on a widespread scale of an international obligation of essential importance for safeguarding the human being, such as those prohibiting slavery, genocide and *apartheid*;
(d) a serious breach of an international obligation of essential importance for the safeguarding and preservation of the human environment, such as those prohibiting massive pollution of the atmosphere or of the seas.

'4. Any internationally wrongful act which is not an international crime in accordance with paragraph 2 constitutes an international delict': *Yearbook of the International Law Commission*, 1976, vol. 2, part 2, p. 117.

[6] *Yearbooks of the ILC* from 1980.

arising out of Acts not prohibited by International Law'.[6] For this latter project the Commission has undertaken a detailed study of State practice.[7] It may yet turn out that this more controversial and rather tentatively undertaken project, attacked by one writer as 'fundamentally misconceived . . . the contagion may produce general confusion in respect of the principles of state responsibility',[8] will be more fruitful than the Commission's work on the more familiar topic of State responsibility.[9]

In their work on State responsibility it seems that the Special Rapporteur and many of his colleagues have assumed that there are general principles on what they call the 'Content, Forms and Degree' of responsibility. This seems misguided. For although it is entirely possible that an examination of State practice would reveal general principles, it is not justifiable to assume this result a priori.

It is true that the Special Rapporteur accepts that there may be some special regimes of responsibility. Draft Article 3 provides:

> The provisions of this part apply to every breach by a State of an international obligation, except to the extent that the legal consequences of such a breach are prescribed by the rule or rules of international law establishing the obligation, or by other applicable rules of international law.[10]

But this type of provision allowing for special regimes of responsibility is yet another indication that it is not possible completely to separate general principles from particular substantive rules, and shows that the idea that Part I or Part II of the Draft can provide general principles is an illusion. And, moreover, the International Law Commission's approach in Part II implicitly excludes the possibility that there are *only* special regimes of responsibility and that there is no general regime.

Where then does the Special Rapporteur turn in his hunt for general principles? Not to the vast and admittedly difficult to handle mass of State practice. Nor—and this comes as a relief—to the *Chorzów Factory* case and its famous pronouncement:

> The essential principle contained in the actual notion of an illegal act—a principle which seems to be established by international practice and in particular by the decisions of arbitral tribunals—is that reparation must, as far as possible, wipe out all the consequences of the illegal act and re-establish the situation which would, in all probability, have existed if that act had not been committed.

[7] See UN Doc. A/CN. 4/384.

[8] See Brownlie, op. cit. above (p. 25 n. 3), at p. 50.

[9] e.g. it is suggested on the basis of State practice that even 'massive pollution of the atmosphere or the seas' is better dealt with as an injurious consequence arising out of acts not prohibited by international law than as an international crime.

[10] *Yearbook of the ILC*, 1982, vol. 1, p. 199. Apart from the strangeness of the last phrase, this article has been criticized as incompatible with Article 17 of Part I which sets out the rule that the source of an obligation does not affect the regime of responsibility (ibid., 1981, vol. 1, p. 138). In fact there is no incompatibility between the two articles: under Article 3 it is not the source of the rule that affects the regime of responsibility but its content. Particular rules may themselves specify the consequences of their breach.

> Restitution in kind or, if this is not possible, payment of a sum corresponding to the value which a restitution in kind would bear; the award, if need be, of damages for loss sustained which would not be covered by restitution in kind or payment in place of it—such are the principles which should serve to determine the amount of compensation due for an act contrary to international law.[11]

For the Special Rapporteur warns that this should not necessarily be accepted as a general rule, but should be treated with caution:[12] we should not turn to the decisions of international tribunals for general rules on the consequences of State responsibility.

He gives various reasons for this, of varying strength:

(i) that the powers of tribunals differ, they may be given wide or restricted powers, and they are involved in a special task rather than in the application of general rules,
(ii) that they are limited by their judicial function and by the fact that they are dealing with States,
(iii) that they may be deciding the case a long time after the alleged breach,
(iv) that in judicial reparation the obligation to stop a breach may be submerged,
(v) that they generally do not pronounce on the most serious wrongs and have been mainly concerned with injury to aliens, and
(vi) that they are not always explicit about the way the amount of damages is assessed,[13]

and concludes that:

> In short for the purposes of drafting articles dealing with the content, forms and degree of international responsibility in general and independent of the existence of a machinery for implementation, they [sc. judicial and arbitral decisions] are of limited value.[14]

This approach stands in marked contrast to that of most writers who, in dealing with the consequences of responsibility, concentrate, often exclusively, on judicial remedies. It leads the Special Rapporteur to play down the importance of the *Chorzów Factory* case and to reject the idea that *restitutio in integrum* is the primary remedy in international law and that its equivalent is invariably required where *restitutio* is impossible.

So the Special Rapporteur in his search for general rules is not looking at State practice nor at the decisions of international tribunals. Rather his arguments on the consequences of State responsibility appear to be based on a priori reasoning or 'legal logic'. If this could be interpreted simply as rather obscure shorthand for 'my long experience of State practice and

[11] *PCIJ*, Series A, No. 17, at p. 47.

[12] *Yearbook of the ILC*, 1981, vol. 1, p. 215; ibid., 1981, vol. 2, part 2.

[13] Ibid., 1981, vol. 2, part 1, pp. 83–4, 92–3; ibid., 1981, vol. 1, p. 126; and see Reuter, ibid., at p. 129; Ushakov, ibid., at p. 134.

[14] Ibid., 1981, vol. 2, part 1, p. 92.

of arbitral and judicial decisions' perhaps it would be acceptable, but that does not seem to be what is meant. And this approach—the reliance on legal logic—is familiar also in other writers when they come to consider remedies. Thus Cheng asserts that the obligation to make reparation for an international wrong is vital to the existence of any legal system. He says:

> The judicial essence of responsibility is that it imposes an obligation upon every subject of law who commits an unlawful act to wipe out all the consequences of that act and to re-establish the situation which would, in all probability, have existed if that act had not been committed. It is a logical consequence flowing from the very nature of law and is an integral part of every legal order.[15]

Similarly Fitzmaurice claims that the notion of international responsibility would be devoid of content if it did not involve the liability to make adequate reparation.[16] Perhaps the best-known judicial statements on this topic are those of Judge Huber in the *Spanish Zone of Morocco* claims[17] that 'Responsibility is the necessary corollary of a right. All rights of an international character involve international responsibility. If the obligation in question is not met, responsibility entails the duty to make reparation', and of the Permanent Court of International Justice in *Chorzów Factory (Jurisdiction)* case[18] that 'it is a principle of international law that the breach of an engagement involves an obligation to make reparation in an adequate form. Reparation therefore is the indispensable complement of a failure to apply a convention, and there is no necessity for this to be stated in the convention itself.'

It does not seem obviously true that the question of remedies for breaches of international law is one of logic rather than an empirical question. But even assuming for the moment that it is a question of legal logic, we are left with an odd contrast between the ideal world of what legal logic requires, what any legal system must have—whether it is restitution, nullity or full reparation—and what goes on in practice. Clearly not every breach of international law is followed by reparation; if the test *ubi remedium ibi ius* is applied, it might seem that there is not much international law. That is not to say that breaches of international law are often or usually cost free, but it may serve as a reminder not to be too influenced by judicial remedies in any general discussion of the consequences of breaches of international law. For international tribunals it may be true enough that responsibility once established involves a duty to make reparation, but generally reparation and responsibility have a limited role in international relations. Even if we reject Kelsen's premiss that a sanction is the only necessary condition for a legal system, we may accept as realistic his argument that reparation

[15] *General Principles of Law as Applied by International Courts and Tribunals* (1953), p. 389.
[16] This *Year Book*, 27 (1950), p. 1.
[17] *Reports of International Arbitral Awards*, vol. 2, p. 615 at p. 641.
[18] *PCIJ*, Series A, No. 9, at p. 21.

is not a necessary condition, that although an obligation to make reparation may be stipulated in the abstract by general international law, it is possible that the obligation will not come into existence in a concrete case:

For an obligation to make reparation exists only if an international delict has been committed, and there is, under general international law, no objective authority, especially no court, competent to ascertain the existence of a delict. This function is left by general international law to the states concerned. Consequently a state may consider itself to be under an obligation to make reparation only if it admits that it has committed a delict, that is to say, if there is an agreement of the states concerned in this respect. However, such agreement might not be reached. Even if it has been reached it does not suffice to establish the concrete obligation to make reparation. The state responsible for a delict is not obliged to comply with any unilateral demand for reparation made by the injured state. They must also come to an agreement concerning the content of reparation to be made. As long as these agreements concerning the existence of the delict and the content of the reparation are not concluded, it is hardly possible to assume the existence of a concrete obligation to make reparation.[19]

He concludes that

In view of the situation which exists under general international law, it is even possible to assume that general international law does not impose upon the delinquent state the obligation to make reparation and upon the injured state the obligation to try to get reparation from the state responsible for the delict before resorting to reprisals or war against the latter. On this assumption, general international law only provides that by an agreement concerning reparation of the material and moral damage caused by the delict, and by the fulfilment of the obligation established by this agreement, the delinquent state can avoid the sanctions provided by international law.[20]

Clearly just because reparation is often not forthcoming for a breach of international law, that does not mean that there is no rule requiring it. But if the suggested rule is widely divorced from normal practice then at least we should be cautious, *first*, with respect to the International Law Commission's approach of seeking general principles on the content, forms and degree of State responsibility without sufficient study of State practice. The problems now facing the International Law Commission in its search for general principles are enormous.[21] The range of international wrongs is wide and the International Law Commission's attempt to divide them into categories is far from simple; should the categorization depend on the importance of the rule broken, or on the importance of the consequences of the breach, or on the type of injury involved? Is it possible to lay down

[19] Kelsen, *Principles of International Law* (2nd edn., by Tucker, 1966), at p. 18. Kelsen's views on the necessity of a sanction are accepted with little discussion by Bissonnette, *La Satisfaction comme mode de réparation en droit international* (1952), and Reitzer, *La Réparation comme conséquence de l'acte illicite en droit international* (1938). The latter also accepts Kelsen's arguments that the duty to make reparation cannot be based on natural law, nor is it a necessary element in every legal system.

[20] Kelsen, op. cit. (previous note), at p. 19.

[21] See discussion in *Yearbook of the ILC*, 1981, vol. 1, pp. 136ff.

rules as to different regimes of responsibility for different types of wrong, whatever the classification adopted? The whole question of international crimes is controversial and the practical difficulties overwhelming; is a centralized enforcement mechanism essential? What is to be the role of the United Nations? Would judicial and arbitral tribunals be able to decide on responsibility for international crimes? The question of the relation between reprisals and reparation is raised by Part I of the Draft Articles.[22] According to Article 30,

> The wrongfulness of an act of a State not in conformity with an obligation of that State towards another State is precluded if the act constitutes a measure legitimate under international law against that other State, in consequence of an internationally wrongful act of that other State.

But the commentary says only that some wrongs justify reparation only and not reprisals, that some justify reprisals provided reparation is sought first, and that for some breaches (for example, of humanitarian law) counter-measures are not acceptable. What breaches of which rules are to be followed by what mixture of reprisals and reparation remains to be worked out in Part II. And the question whether financial compensation is always required for breaches of international law[23] will have to be settled. In its work on Part I the International Law Commission agrees that damage is not necessary for there to be a breach of international law;[24] the implications of this for remedies are still unclear. These problems raised by the work of the Commission show yet again that it is not possible to keep separate 'primary' substantive rules of responsibility and general principles, and consequently that the quest for general rules on the regime, or even regimes, of responsibility may be a hopeless one.

Secondly, it is important to avoid a court-centred view when discussing in general the consequences of breaches of international law. The Special Rapporteur at the beginning of his work said that his aim was not only to describe rules on State responsibility, but also to help international tribunals.[25] But his subsequent emphasis on the special nature of tribunals' decisions on remedies brought him to argue that these decisions should not be used as sources for general rules. And, conversely, it follows that the general rules evolved by the Special Rapporteur and the Commission will not be of much use to tribunals. This is another qualification on the generality of the International Law Commission's draft provisions.

In the work of the Commission it is possible to detect an interesting progression from the first to the second set of draft articles presented by the Special Rapporteur on the 'Content, Forms and Degree of State

[22] Ibid., 1979, vol. 2, part 2, p. 115.

[23] As is argued by Fitzmaurice, this *Year Book*, 17 (1936), p. 82 at p. 109; Brownlie, *International Law and the Use of Force by States* (1963), pp. 379ff.; García Amador, Sohn and Baxter, *Recent Codification of the Law of State Responsibility for Injuries to Aliens* (1974), at p. 143.

[24] *Yearbook of the ILC*, 1973, vol. 2, p. 183; ibid., 1976, vol. 2, part 1, pp. 7ff.

[25] Ibid., 1981, vol. 1, p. 126.

Responsibility'. The first set seemed designed to give guidance to tribunals even though the provisions were very general.[26] Members of the Commission criticized them for their generality and for not adequately reflecting jurisprudence. There was also some doubt as to whether they extended beyond State responsibility for injury to aliens.[27] The second set of proposed draft articles shows a very different approach;[28] they do not seem

[26] *Yearbook of the ILC*, 1981, vol. 1, p. 126:

'*Article 1*

A breach of an international obligation by a State does not, as such and for that State, affect [the force of] that obligation.

'*Article 2*

A rule of international law, whether of customary, conventional or other origin, imposing an obligation on a State, may explicitly or implicitly determine also the legal consequences of the breach of such obligation.

'*Article 3*

A breach of an international obligation by a State does not, in itself, deprive that State of its rights under international law.

'*Article 4*

Without prejudice to the provisions of article 5:

1. A State which has committed an internationally wrongful act shall:

(a) discontinue the act, release and return the persons and objects held through such act, and prevent continuing effects of such act; and
(b) subject to article 22 of Part 1 of the present articles, apply such remedies as are provided for in, or admitted under, its internal law; and
(c) re-establish the situation as it existed before the breach.

2. To the extent that it is materially impossible for the State to act in conformity with the provisions of paragraph 1 of the present article, it shall pay a sum of money to the injured State, corresponding to the value which a fulfilment of those obligations would bear.

3. In the case mentioned in paragraph 2 of the present article, the State shall, in addition, provide satisfaction to the injured State in the form of an apology and of appropriate guarantees against repetition of the breach.

'*Article 5*

1. If the internationally wrongful act is a breach of an international obligation concerning the treatment to be accorded by a State [within its jurisdiction] to aliens, whether natural or juridical persons, the State which has committed the breach has the option either to fulfil the obligation mentioned in article 4, paragraph 1, under (c), or to act in accordance with article 4, paragraph 2.

2. However, if, in the case mentioned in paragraph 1 of the present article,

(a) the wrongful act was committed with the intent to cause direct damage to the injured State, or
(b) the remedies referred to in article 4, paragraph 1, under (b) are not in conformity with an international obligation of the State to provide effective remedies, and the State concerned exercises the option to act in conformity with article 4, paragraph 2, paragraph 3 of that article shall apply.'

[27] Ibid., 1981, vol. 1, pp. 208 ff.

[28] Ibid., 1982, vol. 1, p. 199:

'*Article 1*

An internationally wrongful act of a State entails obligations for that State and rights for other States in conformity with the provisions of the present part 2.

'*Article 2*

The performance of the obligations entailed for a State by its internationally wrongful act and the exercise of the rights for other States entailed by such act should not, in their effects, be manifestly disproportional to the seriousness of the internationally wrongful act.

[*footnote continued opposite*

designed to guide tribunals. Are tribunals in need of such guidance? Is this an area where something could be contributed by the Commission?

The earliest modern arbitral tribunal to make decisions on the award of damages was the tribunal set up under Article 7 of the 1794 Jay Treaty.[29] The tribunal assumed that international law, or, strictly, the law of nations, was the source of the rules to be applied on the assessment of damages. Some of its awards were very brief and not clearly reasoned, but others gave more detailed consideration to the question of damages than many later cases.[30] In many ways not much progress towards the development of a coherent body of law that could be called the international law of remedies has been made since then. The Jay Treaty tribunal and later tribunals apparently assumed that just as the rules governing responsibility for treatment of aliens were rules of international law, so were those on remedies and in particular on the assessment of damages.

But tribunals seem to have worked in isolation; they rarely referred to decisions of other tribunals on this question of remedies. Before the twentieth century this can be explained by the fact that reports of the

'*Article 3*

The provisions of this part apply to every breach by a State of an international obligation, except to the extent that the legal consequences of such a breach are prescribed by the rule or rules of international law establishing the obligation or by other applicable rules of international law.

'*Article 4*

An internationally wrongful act of a State does not entail an obligation for that State or a right for another State to the extent that the performance of that obligation or the exercise of that right would be incompatible with a peremptory norm of general international law unless the same or another peremptory norm of general international law permits such performance or exercise in that case.

'*Article 5*

The performance of the obligations entailed for a State by its internationally wrongful act, and the exercise of the rights for other States entailed by such act, are subject to the provisions and procedures embodied in the Charter of the United Nations.

'*Article 6*

1. An internationally wrongful act of a State, which constitutes an international crime, entails an obligation for every other State:

(a) not to recognize as legal the situation created by such act; and
(b) not to render aid or assistance to the author State in maintaining the situation created by such act; and
(c) to join other States in affording mutual assistance in carrying out the obligations under (a) and (b).

2. Unless otherwise provided for by an applicable rule of international law, the performance of the obligations mentioned in paragraph 1 is subject mutatis mutandis to the procedures embodied in the United Nations Charter with respect to the maintenance of international peace and security.

3. Subject to Article 103 of the United Nations Charter, in the event of a conflict between the obligations of a State under paragraphs 1 and 2 above, and its rights and obligations under any other rule of international law, the obligations under the present article shall prevail.'

And see pp. 203 ff. for discussion of these articles.

[29] Moore, *History and Digest of the International Arbitrations to which the United States has been a Party* (1898), vols. 3 and 4 (hereinafter Moore, *International Arbitrations*), and *International Adjudications* (1929–33), vol. 4.

[30] See, e.g., *The Betsey*, Moore, *International Adjudications*, vol. 4, pp. 194, 240, and *The Neptune*, ibid., p. 372.

decisions of tribunals were not readily available, but, even when they had become available, the twentieth-century cases also show only very occasional references to other tribunals on this point, and those mostly only to 'generally recognized principles'. Nor do the *compromis* contain detailed provisions on remedies in general, or the assessment of damages in particular. And the arbitrators did not, on the whole, discuss general principles or give detailed explanations of their awards of damages. In practice, the decision seems to be left to the discretion of the arbitrator; it is possible to infer from the awards that their aim was generally to give full compensation and in some decisions this aim was made express.[31] But that alone does not provide much guidance.

The result is a remarkable collection of conflicting decisions on the assessment of damages. Awards made on the basis of equity do not seem different from those based on law, neither does the admission of responsibility by the defendant State make any difference. Nor have tribunals developed any coherent theory of the relationship between their remedies and rules on the assessment of damages and those of municipal law. It is true that at first sight their decisions may look similar to those of municipal law, but this is only because of the similarity of subject-matter. There are few references to particular systems of municipal law, and those mostly on questions of interest and lost profits.[32] In fact it seems clear that municipal law could not in the nineteenth century and cannot today provide general principles that would help international tribunals. The *International Encyclopaedia of Comparative Law* shows the wide differences of method and result in the assessment of damages between different States, even within the so-called families of legal systems.[33] The recent debate arising out of the Bhopal disaster in India over whether victims would be able to bring actions in the United States rather than in India is just one graphic reminder of these differences. Hersch Lauterpacht's claim that there are rules on the assessment of damages—on the award of interest and on lost profits—that are common to all legal systems seems over-optimistic.[34]

[31] *Norwegian Shipowners'* claims, *Reports of International Arbitral Awards*, vol. 1, p. 307; *Cheek* claim, Moore, *International Arbitrations*, pp. 1899 and 5068; *Delagoa Bay Railway Company* case, ibid., p. 1865; *Union Bridge Company* case, *Reports of International Arbitral Awards*, vol. 6, p. 138.

[32] On interest, contrast the *Russian Indemnity* case (*Reports of International Arbitral Awards*, vol. 11, p. 421), where reference to municipal systems was made to justify the award of interest, with the *Georges Pinson* case (ibid., vol. 5, p. 327), where it was held that the rules of civil law governing interest on private pecuniary debts had no direct relevance to the question of interest under international law, since the rules regarding the latter had developed independently and in entirely different spheres from those prevailing with reference to moratory interest in private law. Both these cases refer in general terms to 'civil law' and 'private legislation'. However, in some cases specific rules of particular legal systems are referred to in order to fix the rate of interest appropriate. See the *Delagoa Bay Railway Company* case, loc. cit. (previous note), the *Orinoco Steamship Company* case (*Reports of International Arbitral Awards*, vol. 9, p. 181) and the *Religious Properties* case (ibid., vol. 1, p. 7). Tribunals also refer to municipal law to justify the award of lost profits, as in the *Cape Horn Pigeon* case (ibid., vol. 9, p. 51).

[33] See particularly Stoll, vol. 11, chapter 8; Treitel and Eorsi, vol. 7, chapter 16.

[34] *Private Law Sources and Analogies of International Law* (1927), at p. 143.

Here, as so often, the danger is that any general principle that can be derived from municipal legal systems may be so general as to be no guide at all; and taken in isolation from the rules that give it substance it may lack any content. In many legal systems the rule that interest is required as compensation for a delay in the payment of a fixed sum of money is only a starting-point and subject to many modifications. As for the other universal rule proposed by Lauterpacht, that of compensation for lost profits, this is certainly allowed in all major legal systems, but different methods are employed in the assessment and limitation of such damages; the term 'lost profits' has no fixed meaning.

The mass of international arbitral practice on the assessment of damages—of the 435 arbitral tribunals counted by Stuyt between 1794 and 1970 261 were concerned with claims for damages[35]—does not seem to have produced coherent rules on damages.[36] This may be confirmed by the well-known decision at the 1930 Hague Codification Conference by the Subcommittee on Damages that it was best to leave this question for development by the jurisprudence of arbitral tribunals as there had not yet been sufficient crystallization of the principles to warrant codification.[37]

Nor is the position on other judicial remedies for breaches of international law made clear by the arbitral practice. The one thing that is obvious is that their award is not common. Most *compromis* do not make any provision on jurisdiction to award remedies,[38] so what remedies are available depends on the practice of the tribunals and on one's conception of the judicial role in cases involving States, that is, on principle. Here, as in the general discussion of remedies, it is the latter, and its relation with the former, that causes problems, in particular in the continuing debate over the primacy or availability of *restitutio in integrum* as a remedy in international law.

The cases involving restitution, whether legal or material, are few and well known.[39] Their rarity, and the fact that their award is generally made on the basis of a *compromis* that makes express provision for this, count against the primacy of *restitutio in integrum* in international law.[40] The

[35] Stuyt, *A Survey of International Arbitrations* (1972).

[36] For an exhaustive collection of arbitral decisions on the award of damages, see Whiteman, *Damages in International Law* (1937). The most detailed discussions of these decisions are those of Personnaz, *La Réparation du préjudice en droit international public* (1939), and of Reitzer, op. cit. above (p. 30 n. 19).

[37] League of Nations Publication 1930.V.17, p. 134.

[38] This weakens one of the Special Rapporteur's arguments as to why tribunals should not be expected to provide generally applicable rules on reparation. See above at p. 28 n. 13.

[39] *L'Affaire Martini*, *Reports of International Arbitral Awards*, vol. 2, p. 979; *Nicaragua* v. *El Salvador*, ibid., vol. 3, p. 1871; *L'Affaire de la Société Radio-Orient*, ibid., vol. 3, p. 1871; *Spanish Zone of Morocco* claims, ibid., vol. 2, p. 615. There are many arbitral awards that order the return of sums of money unlawfully seized (e.g. the *Orinoco Steamship Company* case, ibid., vol. 9, p. 297). However, this is perhaps a special case in that it is not the actual coins or notes that were seized whose return is demanded but their monetary equivalent.

[40] See Alvarez de Eulate, 'La "Restitutio in Integrum" en la Práctica y en la Jurisprudencia Internacionales', *Revista de Ciencia y Técnica Jurídica*, 29–32 (1971–2), p. 11. In his apparently

opposing arguments are clearly rehearsed in the awards in the *Texaco*[41] and *Liamco*[42] cases (but were not made by the respondent party, Libya, which did not appear) and today the prevailing view among writers seems to be against the primacy of restitution, and for its availability (whilst acknowledging that its award is unlikely to be common).[43] There are no clear examples of the award of injunctions by arbitral tribunals in the absence of express provision for this by the parties. Finally, in international as in municipal law, the declaratory judgment was slow to develop as a remedy for a breach of the law, that is, as a remedy in its own right independent of any claim for damages, restitution or an injunction. There are in international arbitral practice a few awards of nominal damages that may perhaps be included under this heading of declaratory judgment,[44] but the only straightforward example of its use as a remedy for a breach of international law is in the cases of *The Carthage* and *The Manouba*.[45]

Have the decisions of the PCIJ and of the ICJ led to greater certainty on this question of remedies in international law? As far as the assessment of damages is concerned only two awards have been made, although this remedy was requested at some stage in about a third of the cases brought to the Court. Awards were actually made in the *Wimbledon*[46] and *Corfu Channel*[47] cases, and the assessment of damages was discussed in the *Chorzów Factory* case.[48] But there are some unusual features in these cases.[49] Also, on the actual methods of assessment of damages the Court in each case worked in isolation; it did not refer to arbitral practice or even to its own earlier decisions. These factors make it difficult to extract general rules from the decisions. It is important not to exaggerate this difficulty, and some of the writers who have examined the question of damages in

exhaustive study of *restitutio in integrum* in diplomatic and arbitral practice he does not distinguish between those cases where express provision for the award of *restitutio* was made in the *compromis* and those where no such provision was made. The arbitrator in *BP* v. *Libya* (53 ILR 297) drew this distinction, and his survey of those agreements where express provision was made for *restitutio in integrum* led him to conclude that 'Such treaties and compromis are not numerous and consistent enough to be regarded as evidence of a uniform State practice'.

41 53 ILR 389.

42 *International Legal Materials*, 20 (1981), p. 1.

43 See, e.g., Brownlie, op. cit. above (p. 25 n. 3); Greenwood, this *Year Book*, 53 (1982), p. 27.

44 *Brower* case, *Reports of International Arbitral Awards*, vol. 6, p. 109; *Compagnie Générale des Asphaltes* case, Whiteman, op. cit. above (p. 35 n. 36), p. 833.

45 *Reports of International Arbitral Awards*, vol. 11, pp. 449, 463.

46 *PCIJ*, Series A, No. 1. In fact no payment of these damages was ever made: see *PCIJ*, Series E, No. 1, p. 167.

47 *ICJ Reports*, 1949, p. 1.

48 *PCIJ*, Series A, No. 13.

49 e.g. in *The Wimbledon* Germany did not contest the amount claimed for demurrage, deviation and fuel, and no question of lost profits arose. The award of interest from the date of the judgment was made without any reference to international arbitral practice. In the *Chorzów Factory* case the value of the property illegally seized was to be assessed at the time of the indemnification—an extremely unusual decision. In both this and the *Corfu Channel* case a very wide discretion was left to experts appointed by the Court. In the latter the Court adopted the more usual date of the time of injury for the assessment of value, but did so without any mention of the *Chorzów Factory* case.

international law have claimed to be able to extract general rules from the practice of arbitral tribunals and the Court.[50] But as soon as they go beyond general rules on causation, the process by which they extract their suggested rules seems somewhat mysterious. Some concentrate on the few decisions of the World Court; others apparently select certain arbitral decisions as authoritative because they approve of the reasoning and result, perhaps because these are familiar to them from their own legal systems.

Of course there is nothing strange or objectionable about such a process; this approach to a mass of cases is familiar in municipal law textbooks also. But there is a difference between international and municipal law here in that in the latter courts do not operate in isolation but develop consistent approaches over time.

The jurisdiction of the International Court to award restitution, specific performance or an injunction, in the absence of express provision for this, remains controversial. Much depends on how much significance is to be attached to the fact that these remedies have been requested of the Court by States.[51] For the Court has never unequivocally made any of these awards in the absence of express provision.[52] The *Iranian Hostages* case[53] finally raised this question of the Court's jurisdiction to issue an order to the parties rather than merely a declaratory judgment on the interpretation and application of a treaty, in a case where the agreements between the parties made no reference to remedies. But it raised the question only by implication: the Court gave no express consideration to the question. In its application the United States had asked the Court 'to adjudge and declare' that Iran had violated its legal obligations to the US; that Iran 'is under a particular obligation immediately to secure the release of all United States nationals currently being detained within the premises of the United States Embassy in Tehran and to assure that all such persons and all other United States nationals in Tehran are allowed to leave Iran safely'; that Iran shall pay reparation to the US; and 'that the Government of Iran submit to its competent authorities for the purpose of prosecution those persons responsible for the crimes committed against the premises and staff of the United States Embassy and against the premises of its

[50] See, e.g., Personnaz, op. cit. above (p. 35 n. 36); Reitzer, op. cit. above (p. 30 n. 19); Brownlie, op. cit. above (p. 25 n. 3); Mann, this *Year Book*, 48 (1976–7), p. 1; and most textbooks.

[51] *Anglo-Iranian Oil Company* case, *ICJ Reports*, 1952, p. 93; *Nottebohm* case, ibid., 1955, p. 4; *Interhandel* case, ibid., 1959, p. 6; *Chorzów Factory* case, *PCIJ*, Series A, No. 13, p. 57; *Nuclear Test* cases, *ICJ Reports*, 1974, pp. 253, 457; *Right of Passage* case, ibid., 1960, p. 6; *Diversion of Waters from the Meuse* case, *PCIJ*, Series A/B, No. 70.

[52] In the *Free Zones of Upper Savoy and the District of Gex* case, *PCIJ*, Series A, No. 24, the Court made an order to France to withdraw its customs boundary. However, express provision had been made for the Court to do at least this in the Special Agreement from which it derived its jurisdiction. The *Temple of Preah Vihear* case, *ICJ Reports*, 1962, p. 6, is said by Mann (loc. cit. above (n. 50)) to be a case where a mandatory order was issued, but it is quite clear from the Court's discussion of its jurisdiction in this case that this judgment is declaratory rather than a mandatory order.

[53] *ICJ Reports*, 1980, p. 3.

Consulates'. This leaves it unclear whether a declaration or an order (or both) was being requested.

The Court found that Iran had violated its obligations to the US and went on to say that it

> *Decides* that the Government of the Islamic Republic of Iran must immediately take all steps to redress the situation resulting from the events of 4 November 1979 and what followed from these events, and to that end:
>
> (a) must immediately terminate the unlawful detention of the United States Chargé d'affaires and other diplomatic and consular staff and other United States nationals now held hostage in Iran, and must immediately release each and every one and entrust them to the protecting Power (Article 45 of the 1961 Vienna Convention on Diplomatic Relations);
> (b) must ensure that all the said persons have the necessary means of leaving Iranian territory, including means of transport;
> (c) must immediately place in the hands of the protecting Power the premises, property, archives and documents of the United States Embassy in Tehran and of its Consulates in Iran;
>
> *Decides* that no member of the United States diplomatic or consular staff may be kept in Iran to be subjected to any form of judicial proceedings or to participate in them as a witness . . .[54]

But if this is the first case in which the Court has issued an order to a State party, rather than merely declaring that there is an obligation on it to act in a certain way, then the Court made this breakthrough with a remarkable lack of discussion. In the absence of express discussion some uncertainty remains; does the Court regard an order as simply equivalent to a declaratory judgment that there is an obligation to act in a certain way? Does it simply assume that both are equally within its jurisdiction whether under a *Chorzów Factory* type compromissory clause or under the Optional Clause?

For in the jurisprudence of the ICJ perhaps the most notable development is the rise of the declaratory judgment as a remedy in itself for a breach of international law. The PCIJ gave declaratory judgments mostly for the purpose of interpreting a treaty or contract or settling a question of territorial sovereignty.[55] Obviously there can be no absolutely clear-cut distinction between such a judgment and a declaration that there has been a violation of international law,[56] but the form of the judgment is different.

[54] *ICJ Reports*, 1980, at pp. 44–5.

[55] It has been said that the *Mavrommatis* (*Jerusalem*) *Concessions* case (*PCIJ*, Series A, No. 5, at p. 51) is an example of the PCIJ giving a declaratory judgment that there has been a breach of international law: see García Amador in García Amador, Sohn and Baxter, op. cit. above (p. 31 n. 23), at p. 98. But such an interpretation is probably not justified. The Court decided that as there had not been any loss to Mavrommatis the claim for damages must fail. There was no indication that it considered the first part of its judgment to be a declaratory judgment that there had been a breach of international law, in itself a remedy for the claimant State. Rather the Court completely rejected the claim on behalf of Mavrommatis.

[56] This can be seen in the application of Article 177 of the EEC Treaty. See Collins, *European Community Law in the United Kingdom* (3rd edn., 1984), pp. 123ff.

It is in the practice of the ICJ that the declaratory judgment takes on a new importance as itself constituting satisfaction for an injured State,[57] stating an obligation to behave in a certain way[58] and stating that there has been a breach of international law.[59]

If we take the declaratory judgment as the norm in the practice of the ICJ, rather than reparation, let alone restitution,[60] this may serve as a reminder that not every breach of international law should be met by a demand for money. The appealing rhetoric of money should not be over-used. It is interesting in this context to consider the jurisdiction of the European Court of Justice in actions against member States. It is generally accepted that a judgment of the Court under Articles 169 and 170 of the EEC Treaty[61] is purely declaratory, that the Court is restricted to stating that a member State has or has not failed to fulfil its obligations, and that it is left to the member State to decide on the measures necessary for it to perform the obligations incumbent on it as a result of the judgment.[62] Of course in the absence of an express ruling by the European Court some doubt must remain. But rather than advocate a more extensive jurisdiction for the European Court of Justice[63] it might be wiser to recognize the peculiar suitability for international relations of the type of declaratory judgment used by the European Court, especially when accompanied by the wide range of municipal and Community remedies available to individuals and enterprises under Community law.[64]

If there is little guidance to be gained from the jurisprudence of the World Court on the assessment of damages and the availability of other remedies against States, it is perhaps not surprising that the specialized tribunals also have done little to build a coherent body of rules in this area.[65] This is not the place for a detailed study of the work of the European Court of Human Rights under Article 50 of the European Convention on

[57] *Corfu Channel* case, *ICJ Reports*, 1949, p. 3.

[58] *Temple of Preah Vihear* case, ibid., 1962, p. 5.

[59] *Fisheries Jurisdiction* case, ibid., 1974, pp. 3, 175.

[60] See Vallat, *Yearbook of the ILC*, 1981, vol. 1, p. 211.

[61] Articles 140–2 of the Euratom Treaty are essentially similar, but the procedure established under the ECSC Treaty, Article 88, differs from that under the other two treaties. And it is only under the ECSC Treaty that there is provision for sanctions to be employed against member States in the event of their violation of treaty obligations. These are to be imposed by the High Authority, not the Court. In fact, this power has never been used.

[62] Schermers, *Judicial Protection in the European Communities* (3rd edn., 1983), at section 429; Gaudet, in Schwebel (ed.), *The Effectiveness of International Decisions* (1967), p. 309; Amphoux, in Ganshof van der Meersch (ed.), *Le Droit des Communautés Européennes* (1969), section 1042.

[63] As Wyatt does: *European Law Review*, 7 (1982), p. 147.

[64] See below at p. 42 n. 77.

[65] Also, although Lillich and his associates have claimed that the decisions of national claims commissions have contributed to the development of international law (see Lillich, *International Claims: their Adjudication by National Claims Commissions* (1962)), the unilateral nature of the decisions and the lack of uniformity between the decisions of different commissions severely restrict their significance. Cf. the accounts in Lillich, *International Claims: Post-war British Practice* (1967); Weston, *International Claims: Post-war French Practice* (1971); Yates, *Virginia Journal of International Law*, 13 (1971–3), p. 554.

Human Rights,[66] nor of that of the various international administrative tribunals.[67] Under Article 50 the European Court of Human Rights has the power to afford just satisfaction to an individual injured by violation of his human rights. Although the *Ringeisen*[68] and *Neumeister*[69] cases refer to international law as relevant to the decisions of the Court, on this question of just satisfaction the Court has not turned to international practice for guidance and does not refer to international jurisprudence. Indeed it is doubtful whether international jurisprudence could give much assistance, for traditionally satisfaction is a remedy for injury to a State's honour and dignity. Nor can the decisions on the assessment of damages for moral injury to individuals guide the European Court of Human Rights, since the calculation of compensation for moral injury is necessarily an arbitrary process. Apart from its acknowledgement that it does not have the power to order States to adopt certain behaviour, the European Court of Human Rights does not seem to have followed any one coherent policy on satisfaction for moral injury. Sometimes it allows pecuniary compensation, but the amounts vary considerably and without explanation; at other times it says that a declaratory judgment that there has been a breach of the Convention constitutes in itself sufficient satisfaction for the victim. The Court does not explain its choice in each case between a financial award and a declaratory judgment, nor is there any obvious criterion that accounts for the choices.

International administrative tribunals—the UN and International Labour Organization tribunals and the European Court of Justice under Articles 179 and 215 of the EEC Treaty—have produced a substantial body of decisions involving the award of judicial remedies. But although each has developed its own characteristic style of judgment, they have not developed clear rules on the assessment of damages. They do not look to each other's jurisprudence, nor to municipal legal systems,[70] nor to international arbitral practice. Nor have they achieved internal consistency: both on the relatively straightforward assessment of past losses by employees and on the more difficult question of future losses there is wide variation between and within the different tribunals. Specialized tribunals, like the early arbitration tribunals, operate in isolation; for them, too, remedies seem something to be invented anew in each case.

Of course it is often the tendency, sometimes the weakness, of writers to seek uniformity, to look for coherent sets of rules. The harm caused by the present diversity should not be exaggerated. But the differences between modern commercial arbitral awards highlight the continuing uncertainty.

[66] See Gray, *Human Rights Review*, 6 (1981), p. 153.

[67] See Jenks, *The Proper Law of International Organizations* (1962); Akehurst, *The Law Governing Employment in International Organizations* (1967); Schermers, *Judicial Protection in the European Communities* (3rd edn., 1983).

[68] Series A, No. 15.

[69] Series A, No. 8.

[70] Except in *Howrani's* case (UN Administrative Tribunal judgment no. 11) and *Keeney's* case (UN Administrative Tribunal judgment no. 12).

Like cases are not treated alike and results are unpredictable. The differences between the arbitrators in *BP* v. *Libya*,[71] *Texaco*,[72] *Liamco*[73] and *Aminoil*[74] show fundamental uncertainties in the international law of remedies—on whether restitution is the primary remedy in international law, on whether it is a possible remedy and if so when, on methods of assessing compensation, and on the relationship between the assessment of damages for an unlawful act and of compensation for a lawful act.

But these cases do suggest some interesting possibilities; perhaps out of the uncertainty new approaches to the international law of judicial remedies may be found. *First*, these oil arbitrations suggest that even if general principles of municipal law cannot be of much assistance in the working out of methods of assessing compensation, the provisions of the defendant State's municipal law might be used, if reliance on this is permissible in the absence of a choice of law clause. This would amount to a type of modified national standard of treatment of aliens.

The problems involved in this type of approach in a non commercial case may be seen in the recent *Filartiga* case.[75] This case was brought in the US by two Paraguayans who alleged that the defendant, another Paraguayan, had tortured and murdered a member of their family in Paraguay. The case was brought under the 1789 Alien Tort Claims Act. This provides that federal courts shall have 'original jurisdiction of any civil action by an alien for a tort only, committed in violation of the law of nations'. There were two possible interpretations of this: first that the existence of a violation of international law is significant only for providing the courts with jurisdiction and that once this was established the court should then apply conflicts of laws principles which would lead it to the substantive law of Paraguay; or, secondly, that international law is to be applied as the substantive law, to determine the decision on the merits.

In its decision on the appropriate remedy the District Court apparently blurred the distinction between these two interpretations. It found that international law did not ordain detailed remedies for torture but that international instruments on torture referred to the necessity for redress and compensation in accordance with national law and for the States parties to ensure that torture was an offence in criminal law. That is, international law by prohibiting torture had established a standard and referred to national States the task of enforcing it; it was for the court to apply national law to give effect to the norms of international law, and national law included conflicts of laws. Because the case had links with Paraguay, the court should consider the interests of Paraguay to the extent that these did not inhibit the enforcement of the applicable law or conflict with the public policy of the US. Therefore the Court should look first to

71 53 ILR 297. 72 Loc. cit. above (p. 36 n. 41). 73 Loc. cit. above (p. 36 n. 42).

74 *International Legal Materials*, 21 (1982), p. 976.

75 *Filartiga* v. *Pena-Irala*, 577 F Supp. 860 (US District Court, EDNY, 10 January 1984). Strictly, this was not a case against a defendant State.

Paraguayan law to determine the remedy for the violation of international law. The magistrate to whom the question of damages was initially referred for a report found that Paraguayan law did not allow punitive damages and awarded a sum of $375,000 for pain and suffering, loss of companionship, disruption of family life and expenses. But the District Court did not accept the magistrate's recommendation; it held that because Paraguayan law did not allow punitive damages and because Paraguay had not undertaken to prosecute the defendant, Paraguayan law did not provide an adequate remedy. The objective of international law in making torture punishable as a crime could only be met by imposing punitive damages. The Court accepted that these were not commonly awarded by international tribunals and accordingly invoked the *I'm Alone* case[76] but otherwise relied on United States cases to justify its $10 million award.

The District Court's argument that, because torture is an international crime, the objectives of international law can only be met by the imposition of punitive damages does not seem compelling; a combination of criminal action and civil action is envisaged by the relevant international instruments and the absence of the former does not necessarily justify the transformation of the latter into an action for punitive damages. The Court's rejection of Paraguayan law—a rather summary rejection—and its enormous award based on US cases are open to criticism.

The *Filartiga* case shows clearly the extreme disparities between States in their methods of assessing damages. The question must arise whether these disparities rule out any prospect of general acceptance of the assessment of damages on the basis of the law of the defendant State. It is, therefore, significant that States setting up international standards by treaty are turning to municipal law for enforcement mechanisms and as a source of remedies. In customary international law the idea of the international criminal responsibility of individuals for offences such as slavery, piracy, war crimes and crimes against humanity is long-established. More recently treaties have been made to bind contracting States either to prosecute or to extradite those allegedly guilty of offences such as hijacking and attacks on diplomats when caught on their territory.[77] This method of turning to

[76] *Reports of International Arbitral Awards*, vol. 3, p. 1609.

[77] e.g. there are three conventions dealing with the problem of attacks on aircraft: the 1963 Tokyo Convention on Offences and Certain Other Acts Committed on board Aircraft (entered into force 4 December 1969), *International Legal Materials*, 2 (1962–3), p. 1042; the 1970 Hague Convention for the Suppression of the Unlawful Seizure of Aircraft (entered into force 14 October 1971), ibid., 10 (1971), p. 133; and the Montreal Convention for the Suppression of Unlawful Acts against the Safety of Civil Aviation (entered into force 26 January 1971), ibid., 10 (1971), p. 1151. See discussion by McWhinney, *The Illegal Diversion of Aircraft and International Law* (1975); Abramovsky, *Columbia Journal of Transnational Law*, 13 (1974), p. 381, and ibid., 14 (1975), p. 451; Thomas and Kirby, *International and Comparative Law Quarterly*, 22 (1973), p. 163. See also the Convention on the Prevention and Punishment of Crimes against Internationally Protected Persons (entered into force 20 February 1977), *International Legal Materials*, 13 (1974), p. 41, and discussion by Bloomfield and Fitzgerald, *Crimes against Internationally Protected Persons: Prevention and Punishment* (1975), Rozakis, *International and Comparative Law Quarterly*, 23 (1974), p. 32, and Wood, ibid., p. 791; the Convention on the Suppression and Punishment of the Crime of *Apartheid* (entered into force 18 July

municipal law mechanisms and remedies to deal with breaches of international law, of imposing municipal criminal liability on an individual rather than attempting to impose international responsibility on his State or to establish an international criminal tribunal, may be seen also in treaties on polluting and ultrahazardous activities. For example, the 1954 Convention for the Prevention of the Pollution of the Sea by Oil[78] prohibits the discharge of oil within specified areas and requires flag States to make contravention of this prohibition an offence under their own laws. Treaties also provide for the imposition of civil liability under municipal law: several treaties on aviation, nuclear and maritime activities and on the utilization of river basins require that States parties ensure a municipal remedy for damage caused by certain defined activities.[79] That is, municipal law procedures are used to enforce acceptable standards and modes of behaviour. The treaties create a uniform regime, binding on States parties under international law, and it is left to the parties to implement the regime under their own legal systems.

Alternatively, if international tribunals prove unwilling in their decisions on the assessment of damages to look to the municipal law of the defendant State, the oil arbitrations and particularly the *Aminoil* case suggest another, related, way forward. It is true that in this case the tribunal was assessing the compensation due in consequence of a legitimate nationalization by Kuwait, but its approach could have a more general application and be used also for the assessment of damages for unlawful acts. In the *Aminoil* case the tribunal did not search for general rules of international law on the assessment of compensation:

> The tribunal considers that the determination of the amount of an award of 'appropriate' compensation is better carried out by means of an enquiry into all the circumstances relevant to the particular concrete case, than through abstract theoretical discussion.[80]

It invoked the notion of 'the contractual equilibrium' and the 'legitimate expectations of the parties' created by that. Compensation was to be assessed in the light of the particular relationship between the parties and particularly on the basis that Kuwait welcomed foreign investment and that 'over the years, Aminoil had come to accept the principle of a moderate estimate of profits, and it was this that constituted its legitimate expectation'.

1976), *International Legal Materials*, 13 (1974), p. 50; the Convention on Torture as an International Crime (not yet in force), ibid., 19 (1980), p. 647; the Convention on the Physical Protection of Nuclear Material (not yet in force), ibid., 18 (1979), p. 1419.

[78] Entered into force 26 July 1958; ibid., 9 (1970), p. 1.

[79] See, e.g., the Paris Convention on Third Party Liability in the Field of Nuclear Energy, *American Journal of International Law*, 55 (1961), p. 1082; the 1969 International Convention on Civil Liability for Oil Pollution Damage (entered into force 19 June 1975), *International Legal Materials*, 9 (1970), p. 617; and the 1974 Nordic Environment Protection Convention (entered into force 5 October 1976), ibid., 13 (1974), p. 591.

[80] Ibid., 21 (1982), at p. 1033.

This type of approach, of basing the assessment of compensation on the particular relationship between the parties, was adopted also by the Special Rapporteur of the International Law Commission in his work on 'International Liability for Injurious Consequences arising out of Acts not prohibited by International Law'.[81] His scheme envisages the payment of reparation as a last resort arising only when the other provisions have not prevented the occurrence of harm. Sections 4–7 govern the assessment of compensation; these are very flexible guidelines: everything depends on their interpretation and application in a particular situation.[82]

[81] *Yearbook of the ILC*, 1982, vol. 1, p. 224.

[82] '*Section 4*

1. If any activity does give rise to loss or injury, and the rights and obligations of the acting and affected States under the present articles in respect of any such loss or injury have not been specified in an agreement between those States, those rights and obligations shall be determined in accordance with the provisions of this section.

The States concerned shall negotiate in good faith to achieve this purpose.

2. Reparation shall be made by the acting State to the affected State in respect of any such loss or injury, unless it is established that the making of reparation for a loss or injury of that kind or character is not in accordance with the shared expectations of those States.

3. The reparation due to the affected State under the preceding article shall be ascertained in accordance with the shared expectations of the States concerned and the principles set out in section 5; and account shall be taken of the reasonableness of the conduct of the parties, having regard to the record of any exchanges or negotiations between them and to the remedial measures taken by the acting State to safeguard the interests of the affected State. Account may also be taken of any relevant factor including those set out in section 6, and guidance may be obtained by reference to any of the matters set out in section 7.

4. In the two preceding articles, "shared expectations" include shared expectations which:

(a) have been expressed in correspondence or other exchanges between the States concerned or, insofar as there are no such expressions,

(b) can be implied from common legislative or other standards or patterns of conduct normally observed by the States concerned, or in any regional or other grouping to which they both belong, or in the international community.

'*Section 5*

1. The aim and purpose of the present articles is to ensure to acting States as much freedom of choice in relation to activities within their territory or control as is compatible with adequate protection for the interests of affected States.

2. Adequate protection requires measures of prevention that as far as possible avoid a risk of loss or injury and, insofar as that is not possible, measures of reparation; but the standards of adequate protection should be determined with due regard to the importance of the activity and its economic viability.

3. Insofar as may be consistent with the preceding articles, an innocent victim should not be left to bear his loss or injury; the costs of adequate protection should be distributed with due regard to the distribution of the benefits of the activity; and standards of protection should take into account the means at the disposal of the acting State and the standards applied in the affected State and in regional and international practice.

4. To the extent that an acting State has not made available to an affected State information that is more accessible to the acting State concerning the nature and effects of an activity, and the means of verifying and assessing that information, the affected State shall be allowed a liberal recourse to inferences of fact and circumstantial evidence in order to establish whether the activity does or may give rise to loss or injury.

'*Section 6*

Factors which may be relevant to a balancing of interests include:

1. The degree of probability of loss or injury (i.e. how likely is it to happen?);

[*footnote 82 continued on pp. 45 and 46*

2. The seriousness of loss or injury (i.e. an assessment of quantum and degree of severity in terms of the consequences);

3. The probable cumulative effect of losses or injuries of the kind in question—in terms of conditions of life and security of the affected State, and more generally—if reliance is placed upon measures to ensure the provision of reparation rather than prevention (i.e. the acceptable mix between prevention and reparation);

4. The existence of means to prevent loss or injury, having regard to the highest known state of the art of carrying on the activity;

5. The feasibility of carrying on the activity by alternative means or in alternative places;

6. The importance of the activity to the acting State (i.e. how necessary is it to continue or undertake the activity, taking account of economic, social, security or other interests?);

7. The economic viability of the activity considered in relation to the cost of possible means of protection;

8. The availability of alternative activities;

9. The physical and technical capacities of the acting State (considered, for example, in relation to its ability to take measures of prevention or make reparation or to undertake alternative activities);

10. The way in which existing standards of protection compare with:

(a) the standards applied by the affected State; and
(b) the standards applied in regional and international practice;

11. The extent to which the acting State:

(a) has effective control over the activity; and
(b) obtains a real benefit from the activity;

12. The extent to which the affected State shares in the benefits of the activity;

13. The extent to which the adverse effects arise from or affect the use of a shared resource;

14. The extent to which the affected State is prepared to contribute to the cost of preventing or making reparation for loss or injury, or of maximizing its benefits from the activity;

15. The extent to which the interests of:

(a) the affected State; and
(b) the acting State

are compatible with the interests of the general community;

16. The extent to which assistance to the acting State is available from third States or from international organizations;

17. The applicability of relevant principles and rules of international law.

'*Section 7*

Matters which may be relevant in negotiations concerning prevention and reparation include:

I. Fact-finding and prevention
1. The identification of adverse effects and of material and non-material loss or injury to which they may give rise;
2. The establishment of procedural means for managing the activity and monitoring its effects;
3. The establishment of requirements concerning the structure and operation of the activity;
4. The taking of measures to assist the affected State in minimizing loss or injury.

II. Compensation as a means of reparation
1. A decision as to where primary and residual liability should lie, and whether the liability of some actors should be channelled through others;
2. A decision as to whether liability should be unlimited or limited;
3. The choice of a forum in which to determine the existence of liability and the amounts of compensation payable;
4. The establishment of procedures for the presentation of claims;
5. The identification of compensable loss or injury;
6. The test of the measure of compensation for loss or injury;
7. The establishment of forms and modalities for the payment of compensation awarded;
8. Consideration of the circumstances which might increase or diminish liability or provide an exoneration from it.

III. Authorities competent to make decisions concerning fact-finding, prevention and compensation

At different phases of the negotiations the States concerned may find it helpful to place in the hands

Several members of the Commission have expressed reservations over these provisions;[83] one member has doubted whether they would be viable in the absence of specific provision for a dispute settlement mechanism.[84]

These draft provisions are apparently intended to serve as guidelines both for States parties involved in negotiating a settlement and for a third party authorized to make recommendations or decisions on compensation. They certainly represent a marked departure from the traditional approach of arbitral and judicial bodies on the assessment of damages: the reparation 'shall be ascertained in accordance with the shared expectations of the States concerned', 'account shall be taken of the reasonableness of the conduct of the parties', and account may also be taken of listed 'relevant factors'. These provisions have been attacked for not providing objective standards. But this is an area where objective standards and perhaps even general principles seem to be extremely elusive goals. The attempt to balance interests, despite the obvious difficulties involved, is more likely to produce economically efficient and/or socially just results (and—more important—results acceptable to the States involved) than the simple imposition of strict liability with a consequent duty to pay damages assessed according to traditional rules. But the implementation of any new set of guidelines to supplement existing rules on the assessment of damages by more flexible rules on compensation for harm caused by lawful activities is hardly an immediate possibility.

It may be that the approach in the *Aminoil* case is simply an open acknowledgement of what has been the common practice of judicial and arbitral tribunals on remedies: tribunals have not referred to each other's decisions nor have they developed their own coherent systems of rules on remedies. It is not clear that the International Law Commission would be able to do much to assist tribunals, either by way of codification or by progressive development of the law on remedies. It might be possible and desirable for tribunals to adopt a consistent policy on their jurisdiction, in the absence of express provision, to award remedies other than damages. But, given the controversy, this would be a difficult question for the International Law Commission to resolve. On the question of the assessment of damages it may not ever be possible for tribunals to evolve a set of general rules applicable in all cases and specific enough to give guidance. Earlier attempts at codification show the difficulties clearly.[85] Rather than follow this approach it would be better to accept the present lack of uniformity, and either turn to a particular municipal system (rather than

of their national authorities or courts, international organizations or specially constituted commissions, the responsibility for making recommendations or taking decisions as to the matters referred to in I and II.'

[83] See, e.g., *Yearbook of the ILC*, 1982, vol. I, p. 277.

[84] Yankov, ibid., at p. 224.

[85] See García Amador, Sohn and Baxter, *Recent Codification of the Law of State Responsibility for Injuries to Aliens* (1974).

general principles of law) for guidance or accept that the case by case approach to decisions on the basis of the relationship between the parties may be inevitable. At present it is clear that the mass of arbitral and judicial practice has fallen somewhat short of producing an international law of remedies.

THE SHATT-AL-ARAB RIVER BOUNDARY: A LEGAL REAPPRAISAL*

By KAIYAN HOMI KAIKOBAD[1]

I. Introduction

THE history of the boundary regime between Iran and Iraq in the region of the Shatt-al-Arab river is a long and complex one, and, accordingly, there has appeared, over a number of years, a considerable amount of literature on questions relating to the history, politics and law of this sector of the border.[2] However, this body of work suffers from some difficulties. For one thing, although a number of scholarly studies regarding the Iran–Iraq boundary and the war of 1980 have appeared since the commencement of hostilities between the two States, most of them tend not to be exhaustive legal examinations of the Shatt-al-Arab sector. For another, some of the writings on this topic are outdated in so far as they were written in a period prior to the conclusion of the Algiers Protocol of 1975 and the developments preceding and succeeding the hostilities. Moreover, some of this work is either inspired by official sources or is not entirely objective in presentation and analysis. Furthermore, in certain cases, writers and commentators have attempted to address themselves to legal questions without adequate knowledge of either the law or the political history of the case, both of which are, as with every boundary case, essential for an objective appreciation of the status of the boundary regime. In view of this situation, and especially the continuing hostilities between Iran and Iraq,

[1] BA (Punjab), LLB (Karachi), LLM (London), Ph.D. (London); Advocate, Bar Council, Punjab.

[2] Some of the more important published works on this subject in terms of history and analysis are Al-Izzi, *The Shatt-al-Arab River Dispute in Terms of Law* (Baghdad, 1972) and *The Shatt-al-Arab Dispute: A Legal Study* (London, 1981); Ismael, *Iraq and Iran: Roots of Conflict* (Syracuse, 1982); Amin, *International and Legal Problems of the Gulf* (London, 1981) and 'The Iran–Iraq Conflict: Legal Implications', *International and Comparative Law Quarterly*, 31 (1982), p. 167; Tahir-Kheli (ed.), *The Iran–Iraq War: New Weapons, Old Conflicts* (New York, 1983); El-Azhary (ed.), *The Iran–Iraq War* (London, 1984); Dessouki (ed.), *The Iraq–Iran War, Issues of Conflict and Prospects for Settlement* (Princeton, 1981). Some of the older works are: E. Lauterpacht, 'River Boundaries: Legal Aspects of the Shatt-al-Arab Frontier', *International and Comparative Law Quarterly*, 9 (1960), p. 208; Edmond, 'The Iraqi-Persian Frontier, 1639–1938', *Asian Affairs*, 62 (1975), p. 147 and *Kurds, Turks and Arabs* (Oxford, 1957); Melamid, 'The Shatt-al-Arab Boundary Dispute', *Middle East Journal*, 22 (1968), p. 351; Khadduri and Dixon, 'Passage through International Waterways', in Khadduri (ed.), *Major Middle Eastern Problems in International Law* (Washington, DC, 1972); Akhtar, 'The Iraqi–Iranian Dispute over the Shatt-al-Arab', *Pakistan Horizon*, 22 (1969), p. 213; Ryder, 'The Demarcation of the Turco-Persian Boundary in 1913–1914', *Geographical Journal*, 66 (1925), p. 237. For official governmental publications see *A Review of the Imposed War by the Iraqi Regime upon the Islamic Republic of Iran* (Legal Department, Ministry of Foreign Affairs, Iran, 1983); *Comment on the Iranian Claims concerning the Iraqi–Iranian Frontier Treaty of 1937, and the Legal Status of the Frontier between the two Countries in the Shatt-al-Arab* (Ministry of Foreign Affairs, Baghdad, 1969); and *Facts concerning the Iraqi–Iranian Frontier* (Ministry of Foreign Affairs, Baghdad, 1960).

a reappraisal of the legal aspects of the boundary regime in the Shatt-al-Arab region may not necessarily be a superfluous essay.[3] The objective of this work is to analyse the various problems regarding the Shatt-al-Arab (henceforth referred to as the Shatt) frontier in the context of the general and specific principles of international law relating to boundaries. It is recognized that the Shatt region is only a very small sector of an extensive 550-mile frontier; but it is this region which has generated problems and uncertainties and, consequently, the investigation has been confined, in the main, to this sector.

II. Geographical Description of the Region

The Euphrates and Tigris rivers flow through the Mesopotamian plains in Iraq in a general north-west to south-east direction. The two rivers meet at Kornah (Qornah), and, from this point to where they flow into the Persian Gulf, the waters are known as the Shatt-al-Arab river. The areas of land on either side of the Shatt between Kornah and the Gulf are flat and marshy. On the eastern side the lands are surrounded by the Zagros mountains which lie wholly in Iran. Informed sources hold the view that the land lying between the Iranian plateau and the Shatt is geographically part of the Mesopotamian plain, the greater part of which is within Iraq today.[4] To the west of the Shatt is an extensive tract of low-lying alluvial desert drained by the Khor Zubair. The latter flows into the Khor Abdulla, a large tidal creek flowing south-east into the Gulf.[5] The belts of land on either side are ringed with date plantations. Low tides uncover vast tracts of marshy land at the mouth of the Shatt.[6] Further to the west, the terrain rises gently to form the great sand-deserts on the northern edges of the Arabian plateau. Downstream from Kornah on the right, or western,[7] bank of the Shatt lies Basra. Further downstream is Khoramshar, or Mohammara as it was once known.[8] It is situated on the left bank and lies astride the Karun river, or the Haffar Canal, which flows into the Shatt

[3] The political and historical account of this boundary dispute is based almost entirely on unpublished archival material housed in the India Office Records and Library, London, England. A substantial amount of this material originated in the Foreign Office. The India Office was not only kept informed on all matters which affected British interests in India, the Persian Gulf and other adjacent areas, but also participated directly by seconding officials for frontier advice, investigations and expeditions and boundary demarcation. The records referred to belong to the series entitled *Letters, Political and Secret* (L/P & S), Nos. 10, 11 and 12 (Files and Collections).

[4] Eastern Department, Foreign Office, *Memorandum on the Frontier between Persia and Turkey, and Persia and Iraq: 1639–1934* (8 January 1935), Foreign Office, Persia Confidential Print (henceforth PCP), E 171/32/34 at PZ 462 (1935), in L/P & S/12/2869 (henceforth referred to as the *Eastern Department Memorandum*).

[5] Naval Intelligence Division, *Iraq and the Persian Gulf* (1944), p. 61.

[6] This phenomenon caused legal problems regarding the exact position of the line at the mouth of the Shatt.

[7] In keeping with usage, the terms left and right banks will be employed to refer to the east and west of the Shatt.

[8] Although Khoramshar is the current name, Mohammara, for purposes of this study, is deemed to be the more appropriate one inasmuch as the latter name was used throughout the history of the dispute up to 1937. The use of the name Mohammara does not reflect political bias.

from the north-east. The Karun river, which flows in a general south-west direction towards Mohammara, joins the Haffar Canal some miles to the east of Mohammara. The Bamishere river flows generally parallel to the Shatt on its eastern side, and empties its waters into the Gulf. It is believed that at one time the Bamishere constituted the eastern branch of the Shatt; it receives its waters today from the Karun which it leaves at the point where the latter flows into the Haffar Canal. This configuration has led to the creation of the island of Abadan, or Al Khizr, its earlier name, at the north-western head of which is the port of Abadan. Approximately 75 miles to the north of Mohammara is Hawizeh, and south-east of the latter, about 30 miles to the east of Mohammara, is the old town of Fellahiyeh.

III. A General Historical Provenance of the Boundary Problem

(a) *The Location and Description of the Boundary*

The boundary between Iraq and Iran begins in the north near a peak approximately 40 miles north-east of Ruwandiz in Iraq (36° 38′ N, 44° 32′ E), at north latitude 37° 10′ and east longitude 44° 48′, the tri-junction of the Iraqi, Iranian and Turkish boundaries. It extends generally south-south-east along the high watersheds of the Zagros mountains and then along a tributary of the Little Zab. The boundary subsequently follows the Little Zab and the Baneh rivers in a southerly direction leaving the upper basin of the Qala Chulun tributary of the Little Zab and the upper tributaries of the Diyala to Iraq. It then crosses the Diyala near Halabia and runs along a defile east of the river in a general south-westerly direction towards Qasr-e-Shirin and Khanaqin in the Zohab region. These are the so-called 'transferred territories' which were the subject of some controversy in the early part of this century.[9] From this point, the boundary runs south-eastwards along the western edges of the Zagros, or the Pusht-i-Kuh, leaving the plains in Iraq and Luristan in Persia. It runs to Al Miqdadiyah, then south-east to Mandali, Badra and to a point approximately 32 miles west of Dezful. The alignment then descends southwards into the plains and after it reaches the eastern tributary of the Karkheh river, the boundary tends generally south-west and south through featureless marshy tracts. West of Hawizeh the boundary line runs south along a marsh canal to the 31° parallel, whence it turns east along it up to a point east of the 48° meridian, at Khushk-i-Basri. It then turns south in a straight line to the Shatt which it meets about 8 miles west of Mohammara.

The boundary south of this point constitutes the main area of controversy and has over the course of more than a century been modified on several occasions. By virtue of the Baghdad Treaty of 1975, which is

[9] Below, p. 58.

the latest agreement regarding the location of the frontier, the boundary runs along 'the thalweg, i.e. the median line of the main navigable channel at the lowest navigable level, starting from the point at which the land frontier between Iran and Iraq enters the Shatt Al Arab and [continues] to the sea'.[10]

(b) *Early History of the Boundary Question*

The Ottoman Empire began to gain ascendancy in Mesopotamia in the sixteenth century and direct administration began in 1546. After having extended its frontiers, the Ottoman Empire began a series of wars with Persia over questions of territory in Mesopotamia; but the treaties of peace which followed the wars never defined the exact location of the frontier between the Persian and Ottoman Empires. Questions were resolved by vague and general attributions of parcels of territory. Thus the Treaty of Zohab of 17 May 1639[11] between Sultan Murad IV of Turkey and Shah Safi of Persia, which is one of the earliest treaties assigning territories to the two States, failed to delineate a boundary as such. On 4 September 1746 the two States signed the Treaty of Kurdan and reaffirmed the territorial divisions of the Treaty of Zohab.[12] These provisions were subsequently confirmed by the Ottoman and Persian rulers in the first Treaty of Erzeroum, signed on 28 July 1823.[13] However, no precise definition of the demarcation was attempted. The northern end of the Perso-Russian frontier was determined by the Treaty of Turkmanchai of 1828 between the Persian and Russian Empires: it was defined as lying along the Aras (Araxes) range at Mount Ararat.[13]

The second Treaty of Erzeroum of 31 May 1847[14] also attempted to resolve territorial questions by general attribution of territory, but inasmuch as it did so partly by reference to the Shatt, a degree of delineation and certainty entered the treaty. It is discussed in some detail below.

[10] Article 2. Text: Legal Department, Ministry of Foreign Affairs, Iran, *A Review of the Imposed War* (1983), Annex, p. 163.

[11] For text, see PCP 10007, Reg. P1742 (1912), in L/P & S/10/266, and *British Foreign and State Papers*, vol. 105, pp. 763–6. However, it may be noted that altogether five versions of the Treaty were produced at various times at the Conferences at Erzeroum held between 1844 and 1847: see Canning despatch of 18 July 1844 in PCP 12044 of 16 March 1912: *Notes on Treaties between Turkey and Persia relative to the Frontier Question: 1639 to 1822*, Reg. P1326 (1912), in L/P & S/10/266.

[12] FO Research Department, *Memorandum on the Persian Frontier* (31 January 1947), PCP E 10136/4029/34, Ext. 1133 in L/P & S/12/1201 (henceforth referred to as the *Research Department Memorandum*), text: PCP 10007, Reg. P1742. An annexed article says that 'the frontiers and boundaries of Sultan Murad Khan shall be correctly ascertained and the governors of the frontiers shall refrain from actions which are opposed to friendship': PCP 10007, Reg. P1742. See also Enc. 1 in Lowther to Grey (23 April 1912), PCP 17845, Reg. P2869/70 (19 July 1912), in L/P & S 10/291.

[13] *Research Department Memorandum*; text: PCP 10007, Reg. P1742.

[14] For text, see *British and Foreign State Papers*, vol. 45, p. 874; Parry, *Consolidated Treaty Series*, vol. 101, p. 86. Both are French language texts. For the English text see Appendix No. 1, in Iraqi letter to Secretary-General, Council of the League of Nations (29 November 1934), *League of Nations Official Journal*, 16 (1935); and Al-Izzi, *The Shatt-al-Arab River Dispute in Terms of Law* (1972), Annex 1, p. 123.

(c) *The Development of the Frontier Question after 1843*

1. *The Conferences and Treaty of Erzeroum, 31 May 1847*

At the Conferences of Erzeroum, both Persia and Turkey advanced claims to Mohammara and the lands to the north and east of it, including Tamar and Hafar, and submitted evidence in respect thereof.[15] The British representatives, who like their Russian counterparts acted as Mediating Commissioners, concluded that on the balance of probabilities Turkey had valid rights to Mohammara.[15] However, Count Nesselrode, the Russian Vice-Chancellor, recommended that Mohammara and the left bank be ceded to Persia and that she be assured the freedom of navigation in the Shatt.[15] In March 1845 the British and Russian envoys jointly recommended the cession of Mohammara and of all the places dependent upon Persia and that the latter be granted full rights of navigation in the Shatt.[15] Turkey agreed in principle but made it clear that she would have 'rights of property to the river, the course of which was still to belong wholly and exclusively to the Porte, which only granted freedom of passage to Persia . . .'.[16] A draft treaty was drawn up in which Article 2 stipulated that Turkey agreed to cede to Persia the city, port and anchorage of Mohammara and the island of Al Khizr. Thereafter Britain and Russia gave, upon Turkey's insistence, written assurances to her regarding the meaning of some of the articles, including the extent of the cession at Mohammara.[17] The treaty was signed on 31 May 1847. Ratification was at first withheld by the Persian representative who objected to the assurances given by the Mediating Powers. Pressure, however, was brought to bear upon the Persian Plenipotentiary, and eventually he 'acceded . . . to the demands of the Porte in the form of an official note addressed to the Mediating Representatives'.[18] Turkey then requested a formal statement of the assurances from Britain and Russia. The 'explanatory note' was communicated to Turkey by Britain on 26 February 1848 and in the following month she ratified the treaty.[19]

[15] *Memorandum respecting the Frontier between Mohammara and Turkey* (3 April 1912), by A. Parker, PCP 14638, Reg. 1595 (24 March 1912), in L/P & S/10/266, henceforth referred to as the *Parker Memorandum*.

[16] Lord Palmerston to Lord Bloomfield (12 July 1850), *Parker Memorandum*, Appendix H.

[17] Ibid. For the published text of the written assurances, see Appendix 1 to Iraqi Letter to Secretary-General, League of Nations, 29 November 1934, *League of Nations Official Journal*, 16 (1935); Al-Izzi, *The Shatt-al-Arab River Dispute in Terms of Law* (1972), Annex 2, pp. 126–8. Other assurances include statements to the effect that Persia would not be entitled to put forward claims in regard to regions on the right bank and that both parties would abstain from fortifying the banks of the Shatt. For Ottoman reply, see Appendix 1, loc. cit. For Persian delegate's reply, see Appendix 6 to Persian letter to League Council, 8 January 1935, *League of Nations Official Journal*, 16 (1935), p. 216.

[18] *Parker Memorandum*. Cf. Lowther to Grey (5 April 1912), No. 81 M, Reg. P1326 (1912), in L/P & S/10/266.

[19] *Parker Memorandum*. See also Shipley Report: *The Turco-Persian Frontier Commission, 1912*, PCP 12714 (19 March 1913), Reg. 1353 (4 April 1913), in L/P & S/10/267.

Article 2 of the Treaty of Erzeroum stipulated that

> the Ottoman Government formally recognizes the unrestricted sovereignty of the Persian Government over the city and port of Mohammara, the island of Khizr, the Abadan anchorage, and the lands on the eastern bank, that is to say, the left bank—of the Shatt-al-Arab, which are in the possession of tribes recognized as belonging to Persia. Further, Persian vessels shall have the right to navigate freely without let or hindrance on the Shatt-al-Arab from the mouth of the same to the point of contact of the frontiers of the two Parties.

The Persian Government abandoned all her claims to the city and province of Suleimani. Article 2 also recorded an undertaking given by the Persian Government 'to cede to the Ottoman Government all the lowlands—that is to say, the land in the western part of the province of Zohab . . .'. The Ottoman Government undertook to cede the eastern or mountainous part of the said province. Article 3 of the treaty provided for the appointment of commissioners 'for the purpose of determining the frontiers between the two States in conformity with the preceding article'.

2. *Demarcation attempts: 1850–2*

Two Boundary Commissioners from Persia and Ottoman Turkey and two Mediating Commissioners from Britain and Russia assembled at Mohammara in 1850 and at Zohab in 1851 and 1852.[20] Turkey and Persia failed to adopt a mutually acceptable interpretation of Article 2 of the treaty. While the Ottoman Commissioner agreed to cede the town and port of Mohammara, he refused to transfer even 'an inch of the surrounding territory'.[21] It was argued that the cession of Mohammara and Abadan did not imply that the boundaries between them lay in that direction: Abadan was an island and Mohammara an enclave. All that was required of the Commissioners was the determination of the frontier between Turkey's left bank possessions and Persia's Khuzistan dominions.[22] This interpretation was unacceptable to both the Mediating Commissioners and Persia.[23] The former proposed a line, on the basis of Colonel Williams's recommendations, which ran from the mouth of the Shatt along its left bank and lay across the Haffar Canal; it then ran 'up the Shatt al Arab to the mouth of the Abu Djudei Canal, a distance of a geographical league . . . from the Haffar; and thence in as straight a line as circumstances will admit of to the town and district of Hawiza [Hawizeh] . . .'.[24] The Persian Government objected at first to the recommended line[25] but on British insistence agreed on 25 May 1850 to accept it. However, the Turkish

[20] *Parker Memorandum*; *Eastern Department Memorandum*.

[21] *Parker Memorandum*.

[22] Ibid., and *Eastern Department Memorandum*.

[23] Ibid. See also Sir Stratford Canning to Lord Palmerston, Constantinople, 30 May 1850, Appendix G, *Parker Memorandum*; Palmerston to Bloomfield, ibid.

[24] Col. Williams, as quoted in *Parker Memorandum*.

[25] Ibid.; see also letter of Persian Prime Minister to British and Russian Ministers, 25 May 1850, *Eastern Department Memorandum*.

Government rejected the proposed line, 'and it was agreed, but as a purely provisional arrangement, and expressly pending a final adjustment, to accept the status quo . . . but a long wrangle took place as to what was the status quo, and nothing precise was generally accepted'.[26]

3. *The identic map and the agreement of 1869: further attempts at demarcation*

In 1869 the British and Russian ambassadors in Constantinople presented the Turkish Foreign Minister with what subsequently came to be referred to as the 'identic map'.[27] It was prepared on a scale of 1:73500 and covered the entire length of the Turco-Persian borderlands between latitude 30° in the south on the Gulf, to latitude 40° in the north in the Caucasus mountains.[28] The areas covered lay within a 'frontier zone' ranging from 20 to 50 miles, but no line was delineated upon it. The ambassadors urged the Ottoman Government to agree a boundary with Persia by delineating a line within the stipulated zone, and suggested that if there were any difficulties in this respect it could refer to the British and Russian Governments.[29] On 3 August 1869 Turkey and Persia concluded an agreement for the preservation of the status quo regarding the frontier 'such as was defined by the Commissioners of the four Powers'.[30] In 1870 the British and Russian representatives in Tehran communicated a copy of the identic map and their proposals to the Persian Government.[31] Three years later the agreement, or Protocol as it was also called, was renewed,[32] and Persian and Turkish boundary Commissioners met in 1874 in Constantinople to proceed with the demarcation of the frontier on the basis of the detailed identic map.[33] They were joined by British and Russian representatives in 1875 and 1876, whose efforts, none the less, failed to induce the Turkish and Persian Commissioners to delineate, either by delimitation or demarcation, a mutually acceptable frontier.[33]

4. *The Tehran Protocol of 1911 and the Boundary Protocol of 1913*

The unsettled state of affairs at the frontier continued to generate political difficulties. For one thing, Turkey began attempting to assert her influence in Mohammara and adjacent areas in the late nineteenth and early twentieth centuries, a development the British Government viewed

[26] *Parker Memorandum.*

[27] *Eastern Department Memorandum.* A copy of this map, prepared by the Southampton Survey, is in the possession of the India Office Library, London.

[28] Ibid. See also *Research Department Memorandum*, and Wilson to Cox, 26 May 1909, Enc. 2 in Barclay to Grey, 9 September 1909, PCP 35732, Reg. 1356 (1912), L/P & S/10/266.

[29] *Eastern Department Memorandum.*

[30] Ibid. For text, see Parry, *Consolidated Treaty Series*, vol. 139, pp. 425–6 (French language translation). See Articles 2, 4 and 7.

[31] Ibid. See also Wilson to Cox, 26 May 1909, loc. cit. above (n. 28).

[32] Wilson to Cox, 26 May 1909, loc. cit. above (n. 28).

[33] *Eastern Department Memorandum.*

with alarm.[34] For another, the question of a commission for the superintendence and levying of dues on shipping in the Shatt raised issues of rights to the river.[35] Britain wished to secure the most favourable agreement for the Sheikh of Mohammara and Persia[36] and hence her interests dominated the sector of the boundary between the Gulf and 32° north latitude. Russian interests in the borders stretched from the Mount Ararat trijunction to 36° north latitude. Between 32° and 36° north latitude there was an overlap of interests of the two Mediating Powers. Local investigations had established that the locally observed line ran not along the left bank but along the middle of the Shatt from its mouth to a point near Falliyeh and then along the *medium filum aquae* of a narrow canal in the Shatt to Daiji, whence it ran on *terra firma* northwards to Hawizeh.[37] The Foreign Office realized, however, that it could not persuade Turkey to abandon the left bank boundary and therefore favoured adopting a balanced course of action in which the 1850 line was to continue in principle while the locally observed line was to be urged only for specific areas in order to accommodate Persian grievances.[38] Thus on 18 July 1912 the FO communicated a memorandum to the Turkish Ambassador in London in which the former proposed adopting a line which followed the left bank of the Shatt except in the sector between a point south of the Mohammara anchorage and Daiji. In this sector the line ran along the middle of the Shatt.[39] This would enable Persia to continue to control the anchorage of Mohammara and other parts of the river consistent with the genuine requirements of the Sheikh of Mohammara. Turkey was in principle agreeable to this proposition but required a *quid pro quo* in the form of territorial concessions in the Zohab province situated between 32° and 36° north latitude.[40] Following further local investigations, proposals and counter-proposals relative to the Zohab, both Britain and Russia agreed to accommodate the greater part of Turkish demands in the sector.[41] In

[34] See Consul McDouall to Cox, 12 June 1909, Enc. 4 in Barclay to Grey, 9 September 1909, PCP 35732, Reg. 1356 (1912), L/P & S/10/266; Grey to O'Conor, 25 February 1908, PCP 5428, Reg. 2914 (6 March 1908), L/P & S/10/132; and Baxter, 'Relations between Persia and Iraq' (4 June 1928), PCP 2936/29/35, Reg. P3641 (1928), L/P & S/10/1229 (henceforth referred to as the *Baxter Memorandum*).

[35] See Cox to MacMahon, 9 March 1912, Reg. 1356 (12 April 1912), L/P & S/10/266.

[36] Ibid.; and see Parker's remarks to Cox letter of 23 May 1912: enclosure in Foreign Office to India Office, 31 May 1912, PCP 22191, Reg. 1950–1 (1912), in L/P & S/10/266.

[37] Wilson to Cox, 12 March 1910, enclosure in Cox to Grey, 8 May 1910, PCP 18938, Reg. 1356 (12 April 1912). See also Wilson to Cox, 5 May 1912, enclosure in Cox to Hirtzel, 5 May 1912, No. M. 11 in Reg. 2184 (7 June 1912), L/P & S/10/266.

[38] See generally, Foreign Office to India Office, 31 May 1912, PCP 22191, Reg. 1950–1; Grey to Buchanan, 11 April 1912, P1356, Reg. 1350 (10 April 1912); and Minute Note to Reg. 2184 (7 June 1912), in L/P & S/10/266.

[39] Enclosure No. 1, memorandum on Mohammara Frontier communicated to Turkish Ambassador, in Grey to Buchanan, 17 July 1912, PCP 30379, Reg. 2981–2 (25 July 1912), L/P & S/10/291. See also 'declaration' of 29 July 1913: PCP 35336 (29 July 1913), Reg. P3371, in L/P & S/10/430.

[40] Parker Minutes, 4 March 1913, PCP 10716, P1048 (1912), and 7 March 1913, PCP 11389, P1142 (1913), in L/P & S/10/267.

[41] See generally correspondence in L/P & S/10/267, L/P & S/10/291 and L/P & S/10/430.

a similar fashion agreement was also reached in respect of the areas lying between Hawizeh and the Shatt.[42] At this stage Persia took no part in the negotiations. Her major contributions were the conclusion at Tehran of a protocol with the Ottoman Government on 21 December 1911 in respect of the establishment of a basis of negotiations and the procedure to be followed for the delimitation of the boundary, and the resultant negotiations with Turkey in March 1912.[43]

After the Anglo-Russian and Ottoman negotiations had produced informal agreement on all outstanding issues, a conference attended by all four States was convened in Constantinople in November 1913. On 17 November the parties signed the Boundary Protocol.[44] The alignment between Hawizeh and the sea ran along the left bank of the Shatt except in the waters off the Mohammara anchorage, where it ran along the middle of the Shatt, and the narrow strip of water up to Daiji, after which point the line ascended land and ran northwards to Hawizeh. The islands of Mohalla, its two smaller islands, the four islands between Shutait and Moaviyeh and the islands opposite Maukouli were transferred to Persia. Article 5 provided that 'when a section of the frontier has been demarcated that section will be considered as definitely fixed, and will not be open either to a further examination or to a revision'. The Protocol was concluded and the boundary demarcated on the mutual understanding that the alignment in question was a result of the interpretation of the general provisions of the Treaty of Erzeroum.

5. *Boundary demarcation proceedings, 1914*

The map following p. 105 (Fig. 2) is intended to illustrate the demarcation proceedings which were initiated in January 1914. The sector between the mouth of the Shatt and the Khaiyin Canal–Nazaliyeh junction was demarcated at the second meeting on 21 January 1914.[45] The southern terminus was fixed at 2 miles south of the Sheikh's fort, at north latitude 87°.[46] Six boundary pillars were placed at the extreme edge of the lands drained by the Nahr Khayin and the *medium filum aquae* at Tujawait extending northwards was determined accurately and recorded. By 28 October 1914 the entire boundary, except a small section in Kotur

[42] See generally correspondence in L/P & S/10/266 and L/P & S/10/291.

[43] Text: Parry, *Consolidated Treaty Series*, vol. 215, p. 138: French language. For English language texts see Appendix 7 to Persian reply to Secretary-General, League of Nations, loc. cit. above (p. 53 n. 17); Al-Izzi, *The Shatt-al-Arab River Dispute in Terms of Law* (1972), Annex 3, p. 129.

[44] Text: See Appendix 2 to Iraqi letter to Secretary-General, League of Nations, 29 November 1934, loc. cit. above (p. 53 n. 17), and Al-Izzi, op. cit. (previous note), Annex 4, pp. 131–41.

[45] Ryder Report, undated, Reg. 1577 (1 April 1915); and Wratislaw Notes of Turco-Russian Frontier from Mohammara to Vaneh, enclosure in Wratislaw to Grey, 21 December 1914, Persia and Central Asia Print 88900, Reg. P2202/5094 (4 June 1915), in L/P & S/10/522. See also Proceedings of the Boundary Commission (translation) in Reg. 7173 (1920), in L/P & S/10/932.

[46] Proceedings of the Boundary Commission, loc. cit. (previous note). See also description in tabular form: Enclosure in Chief Political Officer, Basra, to Officer in Charge, Arab Bureau, DMI Cairo, 28 May 1917, Reg. P2852 (1917), in L/P & S/10/522.

(which now lies in Turkey) had been marked out on the ground up to Mount Ararat.[47] As such, the entire Iran–Iraq boundary stood demarcated on the basis of the Protocol of 1913. The Boundary Commission recorded its work in eighty-seven subsidiary protocols and a *tableau descriptif* of the frontier.[48] The demarcated line was drawn on ten sets of the identic map and upon ten sets of twenty-five sheets of a supplementary map; each sheet was signed.[49] However, the proceedings were never ratified, a fact which was to cause some difficulties at a later period of time.

6. *The Treaty of 1937*

At the end of the First World War, Turkey concluded the Mudros Armistice and handed over Mesopotamia to British forces. Subsequently the territory was placed under a British mandate which lapsed when Iraq emerged as an independent State on 3 October 1932. In 1921 Raza Shah ascended the Persian throne and brought with him a vigorous nationalist foreign policy.[50] For a variety of reasons, both general and specific questions continued to be raised in respect of the frontier. First, Iran questioned the validity of the 1913 Protocol, which had deprived her of Chia Surkh and other prospective oil-bearing areas in the Zohab, the so-called transferred territories.[51] Secondly, Iran had no rights to the Shatt: ships anchored at Abadan, now a major port with its British oil refinery, were, in contrast to the situation at Mohammara, in Iraqi national waters. Moreover, she was excluded from jointly carrying out the lighting, buoying and dredging of the bar and safe navigation in the river, which was the exclusive responsibility of the Basra Port Authority. Yet an estimated 80 per cent of the shipping, which generated one-third of the revenues for the Authority, was bound for either Abadan or Mohammara.[52] It was clear therefore that the existence of Basra as a first-class port depended on the Abadan trade.

Support for the 'invalidity' of the 1913–14 settlement came from the fact that the Turkish Government had renounced the Protocol of 1913 in so far as it applied to the Turco-Iranian frontier.[53] Further, Iran felt that

[47] Ryder Report, loc. cit. above (p. 57 n. 45). See also Minute Note by Major Marrs, Reg. 7173 (1920), in L/P & S/10/932.

[48] For text, see Appendix 2B of Iraqi letter to Secretary-General, League of Nations, 29 November 1934, loc. cit. above (p. 53 n. 17).

[49] *Eastern Department Memorandum.*

[50] Persia will henceforth be referred to as Iran.

[51] *Baxter Memorandum.* See also letter from British Embassy at Baghdad to FO, 29 March 1933, PZ2502 (1933), in L/P & S/12/2869: Iran wanted the creation of a zone for joint exploitation of all minerals which lay between the 1913 and 1847 lines.

[52] *Baxter Memorandum.* See also Iran Minister, Baghdad, to Iraqi Foreign Minister, 18 August 1936, enclosure in British Embassy, Baghdad, to FO, 22 August 1936, PZ6431 (1936), in L/P & S/12/3803. By 1935 ninety per cent of the dredging dues came from ships calling at Abadan only: see Appendix A, 'Report of Narrative of Events', 28 November 1935, PCP E69949/32/34, PZ170 (1936), in L/P & S/10/2870. All shipping at Abadan was British.

[53] Clive to Chamberlain, 12 January 1928, PCP E587/55/34, Reg. P774 (1928), in L/P & S/10/1229.

'times have changed sufficiently since [the] Treaty of Erzeroum to justify her in wishing for equal rights in the river with Iraq . . .'.[54]

The British Government, who continued to exercise a significant measure of influence in the foreign affairs of Iraq, appreciated Iran's difficulties especially in the matter of the Abadan anchorage and the problems for Basra if Iran developed alternative ports away from the Shatt.[55] In March 1929 Britain assured Iran that she would lend assistance regarding her reasonable demands for frontier rectification.

The uncertainties regarding the boundary prompted frontier incidents in the Shatt[56] and the areas to the north in Amara Liwa, Kut Liwa and Diala.[57] On 20 September 1931 Iran notified Iraq that the 1913 Treaty had not been officially recognized,[58] and on 29 November 1934 Iraq requested the Council of the League of Nations to intervene on the question of the boundary and the 1913–14 settlement.[59] At the same time, however, both parties continued to pursue negotiations between themselves with Britain acting as adviser to the Government of Iraq. The petition at the Council of the League was therefore 'adjourned' in May 1935. In January 1936 the Iraqi Government recommended the conclusion of a new boundary agreement and a separation of conservancy issues in the Shatt, and agreed in principle to cede the Abadan anchorage, as opposed to half of the width of the river. As *quid pro quo* Iran was to acknowledge the alignment of 1913.[60] These proposals were followed by further negotiations relative to the extent of the cession in the Shatt. By January 1937 both sides had agreed that it would be effected by drawing a line 4 miles in length in the middle (or the *thalweg*) of the river between the northern end of Shutait island and Jetty No. 1 of the Abadan anchorage.[61] The remainder of the alignment would follow the course of the 1913 line. Several other matters, including that of 'equality of interests' in the Shatt regarding the navigation of merchant ships and warships of the contracting parties, joint control of dredging, maintenance of the navigable channel and other questions concerning navigation and prevention of smuggling were also keenly

[54] Clive to FO, 4 March 1929, Reg. P1933 (1929), in L/P & S/10/1098.

[55] *Baxter Memorandum.* See also, generally, 'Perso-Iraqi Frontier: Proposals for a New Policy', 30 December 1936, E7925/10/34, next to PZ500 (1937), in L/P & S/12/3803; memorandum by Committee on Imperial Defence, 13 September 1934, E5719/197/34 in PZ6165 (1934), in L/P & S/12/2869; and Clive to FO, 9 January 1929, Reg. P364 (1929), and FO to Clive, 8 February 1929, Reg. P1174 (1929), in L/P & S/10/1098.

[56] See, generally, PZ 7798 (1934); PZ5610 (1934); Minute Note PZ6702 (1934), in L/P & S/12/2869.

[57] Iraqi Minister for Foreign Affairs to Persian Minister, Baghdad, 14 August 1934, PZ5847 (1934); and Iraqi Minister for Foreign Affairs to Secretary-General, League of Nations, November 1934, enclosure in Humphrys to Simon, 22 November 1934, PCP E7220/197/34, PZ7798 (1934), in L/P & S/12/2869.

[58] PZ6689 (1931), in L/P & S/12/45.

[59] See her letter to Secretary-General, League of Nations, 29 November 1934 in *League of Nations Official Journal*, 16 (1935), p. 196. For Iranian reply, 8 January 1935, see ibid., p. 216.

[60] Knatchbull-Hugessen to FO, 6 January 1936, PZ213 (1936); 15 January 1936, PZ399 (1936), in L/P & S/12/3803. It also recommended a treaty of friendship.

[61] Clerk-Kerr to FO, 23 January 1937, PZ667 (1937), in L/P & S/12/3803.

discussed,[62] but they are peripheral to the present study and hence excluded. A treaty was signed at Tehran on 4 July 1937[63] incorporating the terms mentioned above. Ratifications were exchanged by the parties at the Central Bureau, Ministry of Foreign Affairs, in Baghdad on 20 June 1938.[64] On 8 December 1938 the two States concluded a treaty which provided for the constitution of a Boundary Commission with powers to reinstall pillars in accordance with Article 3 of the Treaty of 1937.[65] The Commission met in the same month and (in addition to the existing sixty pillars)[66] installed sixty-eight new boundary pillars, the first of which was located at the confluence of the Shatt with the Khayin, and the last at Khushk-i-Basri.[67] It appears that Iran unilaterally withdrew from the demarcation proceedings in May 1940.[67] Negotiations between Iraq and Britain regarding the conclusion of a convention in respect of conservancy and control of the Shatt were undertaken but no favourable progress was made and the negotiations were subsequently abandoned at the outbreak of the war of 1939–45.[68]

7. *The Algiers Protocol and Baghdad Treaty of 1975*

Notwithstanding the Treaty of 1937, the Shah of Iran, Reza Shah, and his son, who ascended the throne in 1941, continued to raise questions regarding the boundary in the Shatt and refused to accept the left bank as the dividing line.[69] In April 1969 matters came to a head and Iraq threatened not to allow any Iranian ship to navigate in the Shatt.[70] On 27 April 1969 the Ministry of Foreign Affairs, Iran, announced that the Treaty of 1937 had been abrogated.[71] Support for this measure was based on arguments to the effect that the treaty perpetuated a fundamental inequality of the contracting parties; that Iraq had not carried out her obligations accruing under the treaty and it was therefore she who had effectively abrogated the treaty; that the treaty had terminated on grounds of a fundamental change of circumstances; and that the treaty had failed to

[62] See, generally, correspondence in L/P & S/12/3803 and L/P & S/12/3804.

[63] For text, see *League of Nations Treaty Series*, vol. 90, no. 4423, p. 241; *British Foreign and State Papers*, vol. 141, p. 1081.

[64] Peterson to Halifax, 28 June 1938, PCP E4194/127/38, PZ5924 (1938), in L/P & S/12/3804; Consul General for Iraq at Bombay to Government of India, External Affairs Department, 7 July 1938, PZ528 (1938), in L/P & S/12/3804.

[65] Peterson to Halifax, 22 December 1938, PCP E75/75/34, PZ1001 (1939), in L/P & S/12/3804. Text: enclosure in ibid.

[66] Al-Izzi, op. cit. above (p. 57 n. 43), p. 39, quoting Al Rawi, *International Borders* (Cairo, 1970), p. 501.

[67] *Facts concerning the Iraqi-Iranian Frontier* (Ministry of Foreign Affairs, Baghdad, 1960).

[68] Aide-Mémoire, Baghdad Embassy, April 1945, PZ1930 (1945), in L/P & S/12/3804.

[69] Ismael, *Iraq and Iran: Roots of Conflict* (Syracuse, 1982), pp. 18–20; Amin, *International and Legal Problems of the Gulf* (London, 1981), pp. 74–5.

[70] See, generally, *Yearbook of the United Nations*, 23 (1969), pp. 245–6: Letters exchanged between Iran, Iraq and President, Security Council, between April and July 1969. Also see Amin, 'The Iran–Iraq Conflict: Legal Implications', *International and Comparative Law Quarterly*, 31 (1982), p. 167 at p. 173; Ismael, op. cit. (previous note), pp. 18–20.

[71] *Yearbook of the United Nations*, 23 (1969), p. 245.

apply the *thalweg* or median line principle.[72] These arguments will be analysed elsewhere.[73]

Relations between the two States continued to decline and a military clash occurred in April 1971 in the Khanaqin region. Thereafter intermittent border incidents continued to occur between the two States in the period 1971–4.[74] In February 1974 Iraq requested the Security Council to intervene. A resolution calling for bilateral negotiations was passed and a ceasefire was arranged by the Security Council on 7 March 1974.[75] Negotiations were initiated, and at the Summit Conference of the Organization of Petroleum Exporting Countries, convened in Algiers in March 1975, the Shah of Iran and the President of Iraq held two meetings.[76] In the joint communiqué of 6 March 1975, or Algiers Declaration, the two States agreed, *inter alia*, to 'effect a definitive demarcation of their land frontiers on the basis of the Protocol of Constantinople, 1913 and the *procès verbaux* of the Delimitation of Frontier Commission of 1914'; and to 'delimit their fluvial frontiers according to the thalweg line'.[77] Effectively, therefore, Iraq finally yielded to Iran's ancient demand, and abandoned the left bank line. The communiqué went on to declare that both parties would commit themselves to exercising strict control along the frontier 'with a view to putting a definitive end to all acts of infiltration of a subversive character no matter where they originate from'. It appears that this provision constituted a *quid pro quo* for Iraqi abandonment of the left bank frontier and has important implications in the context of the boundary problem.[78] According to Ramazani, however, Iraq decided to agree to a *thalweg* line in the interests of greater domestic power and unity within OPEC.[79] At any rate, a protocol embodying the principles of agreement was signed at Tehran on 17 March 1975 following meetings of the Foreign Ministers of Iran, Iraq and Algeria.[80] In Baghdad on 13 June 1975 the Shah of Iran and the President of Iraq signed the Treaty of International Boundaries and Good Neighbourliness.[81] Appended to this were

[72] See, generally, Iranian letters to President, Security Council, 1 and 9 May 1969: S/9190 and S/9200, and of 2 September 1969: S/9425: *Yearbook of the United Nations*, 23 (1969), p. 246. See also addresses of Iranian Minister for Foreign Affairs to UN General Assembly, October 1969 (24th Session): *UN Monthly Chronicle*, 6 (1969), November, pp. 120–1; and of Iranian Permanent Representative, Mr Vakil, October 1971: ibid. 8 (1971), October, p. 164.

[73] Below, pp. 69–79.

[74] *Yearbook of the United Nations*, 28 (1974), pp. 252–6; Ismael, op. cit. above (p. 60 n. 69), p. 20.

[75] Ismael, op. cit. above (p. 60 n. 69), p. 20.

[76] Ibid.; and Amin, *International and Legal Problems of the Gulf* (1981), p. 81.

[77] Joint Communiqué between Iran and Iraq, 6 March 1975. For text, see Appendix 6 in Ismael, op. cit. above (p. 60 n. 69), pp. 60–2. Generally, see ibid., pp. 21–2; Amin, 'The Iran–Iraq Conflict', loc. cit. above (p. 60 n. 70), pp. 176–8; Pipes, 'A Border Adrift: Origins of the [Iran–Iraq] Conflict', in Tahir-Kheli (ed.), *The Iran–Iraq War, New Weapons, Old Conflicts* (New York, 1983), p. 20.

[78] Below, pp. 86ff.

[79] Ramazani, 'Iran's Search for Regional Cooperation', *Middle East Journal*, 30 (1976), p. 177 at p. 177; Amin, loc. cit. above (p. 60 n. 70), p. 177; Pipes, loc. cit. above (n. 77), pp. 20–1.

[80] Amin, loc. cit. above (p. 60 n. 70), p. 177; see also *A Review of the Imposed War by the Iraqi Regime upon the Islamic Republic of Iran* (Legal Department of the Ministry of Iran, Teheran, 1983), pp. xiii–xiv.

[81] For text, see Annex 1 in *A Review of the Imposed War*, op. cit. (previous note); Appendix 9 and 10,

three protocols.[82] Article 2 of the Baghdad Treaty confirms that the frontier in the Shatt will be that which is delimited on the basis of the protocols and their annexes. Article 4 stipulates that the provisions of the three protocols shall constitute an integral part of the Treaty and will be final and permanent in character. Article 5 provides that in keeping with the inviolability of the frontier, the land and river boundaries shall be inviolable, permanent and final. In the Protocol concerning the Delimitation of the River Frontier, the two States agree in Article 2 that the 'boundary line in the Shatt . . . shall follow the thalweg line, i.e. the median line of the main navigable channel when the water level is at its lowest navigable level, beginning from the point where the territorial borderline is projected at the Shatt . . . through the sea'. Article 3 stipulates that the line has been demarcated (i.e. delimited) in certain joint maps at meetings of the Foreign Ministers in April 1975 which approved, *inter alia*, the minutes of the committee entrusted with the demarcation of the Perso-Iraqi water boundary. In terms, therefore, the left bank boundary was finally and officially abandoned by Iraq in favour of a *thalweg* line division. As a result of this development, the special boundary regimes set up in the Abadan and Mohammara anchorages became redundant. With respect to land boundaries, there appears to be some confusion as to which State benefited. According to Dr Amin, the Baghdad Treaty transferred about 200 square miles to Iran,[83] while Mr Heikal writes that 200 square kilometres were apportioned to Iraq.[84]

The Baghdad Treaty of 1975 was ratified by the parties on 22 June 1976 and 'its implementation went ahead with considerable smoothness'.[85] However, Iraq failed to reconcile herself with the loss of the Shatt, and with the ascent to power of the Ayatollah Khomeini in Iran in February 1979 relations between the two States deteriorated.[86] Iraq, dissatisfied with the frontier, now demanded a revision of the boundary treaty.[87] Hostilities broke out between the States in early September 1980 and have continued ever since. On 17 September 1980 Iraq abrogated the Baghdad Treaty of 1975. The persistence of belligerency has precluded the resolu-

Ismael, op. cit. above (p. 60 n. 69), pp. 62–5. The text appearing at *International Legal Materials*, 14 (1975), p. 1133, which is a reprint from the *Baghdad Observer*, appears to be neither definitive nor official, and therefore those appearing in the former sources are recommended.

[82] The three protocols, the texts of which appear as Annexes in *A Review of the Imposed War*, op. cit. above (p. 61 n. 80), are: Protocol concerning the Delimitation of the River Frontier between Iran and Iraq; Protocol concerning the Re-demarcation of the Land Frontier; and Protocol concerning Security on the Frontier between Iran and Iraq.

[83] Amin, 'The Iran–Iraq Conflict', loc. cit. above (p. 60 n. 70), p. 178; and *International and Legal Problems of the Gulf* (1981), p. 82; see also Pipes, loc. cit. above (p. 61 n. 77), p. 25 n. 34.

[84] Heikal, *Iran: The Untold Story* (New York, 1982), pp. 205–6. See also Pipes, loc. cit. above (p. 61 n. 77).

[85] Amin, 'The Iran–Iraq Conflict', loc. cit. above (p. 60 n. 70), p. 178.

[86] *A Review of the Imposed War*, op. cit. above (p. 61 n. 80), pp. xv–xx.

[87] Amin, 'The Iran–Iraq Conflict', loc. cit. above (p. 60 n. 70), p. 178; *A Review of the Imposed War*, op. cit. above (p. 61 n. 80).

tion of the Shatt boundary question although it appears that the Government of Iraq is inclined to annul the abrogation of the treaty in question and to accept the 1975 line. A formal settlement, however, will have to await a cessation of hostilities.[88]

IV. The Principal Legal Issues

An examination of the principal legal issues relating to the boundary dispute may conveniently be separated into two broad areas of enquiry, i.e. the legal regime of the boundary before and after 1975. The gradual westward expansion by Iran into Iraqi/Arab dominated territories over the course of the nineteenth and twentieth centuries culminated in 1975 when she concluded the Baghdad Treaty and acquired control of the Shatt up to the line of its *thalweg*. The treaty, hence, not only represents—at least before the war broke out—the latest phase, but also the logical conclusion of a process which had been evolving since ancient times, and thus merits consideration as a major watershed in the history of the frontier.

(a) *The Legal Regime of the Boundary before 1975*

1. *General*

An examination of the historical facts of the dispute clearly shows that Ottoman rule existed to a considerable degree on either side of the Shatt and that with the passage of time the Pashas of Baghdad and Basra began to lose control over the territories on the left bank. They managed, however, to retain jurisdiction over the Shatt itself with the result that the left bank of the river became traditionally regarded as the frontier separating the dominions of the Ottoman rulers and the Persian kings.

The Treaty of Erzeroum of 1847 attempted to regularize the situation prevailing along the frontier. To that end the two parties recognized each other's mutually exclusive territorial control on the left and right bank of the Shatt respectively, with the proviso that the left bank of the river up to the sea was to be regarded as the frontier between them. It is to be noted that on the strength of the facts on record the analysis presented above ignores the Turkish interpretation of the 1847 treaty, viz. that the frontier lay well to the east of the lands drained by the Karun, including Gabon. The attitude adopted by the Mediating Powers confirmed, by way of their attempts at demarcation, that the frontier established by the Treaty of Erzeroum in 1847 lay along the left bank and not the middle of the Shatt. While it is true that the line delimited by the Mediating Commissioners was not legally binding on either party inasmuch as Turkey had failed to accept it, the merits of this line lie in the fact that it serves as evidence of the location of the boundary as perceived by the Mediating Commissioners; and it is significant that such perception was based not only on the plain

[88] Below, p. 92.

facts of possession but also of a fair and reasonable interpretation of the terms of the treaty in question.[89] It is also legally significant that Persia, the State which had initially challenged the left bank boundary, agreed to accept the 1850 alignment determined by the Mediating Commissioners. Again, while this acceptance did not result in any legally binding allocation of territory and could not prejudice Iran's position *vis-à-vis* the 1850 line, it serves as evidence that on the balance of probabilities Iran recognized the fact that she had little or no valid claim beyond the left bank. Although the parties could not adopt a mutually acceptable demarcation, they agreed, in the Treaty of 1869, to preserve the status quo regarding the frontier 'such as was defined by the Commissioners of the four Powers'. This treaty, which was renewed in 1873, effectively precluded the development of a situation which would have prejudiced the legal rights of either party, and thus precluded the introduction of claims based on prescription, acquiescence and recognition. The result, of course, was an entrenchment of the territorial status quo.

Notwithstanding the treaties of 1869 and 1873, and the objectives thereof, the evidence is clear that the status quo was indeed upset over a considerable period of time. By the first decade of the twentieth century Persian officials had apparently consolidated their control over the territories on the left bank. Their unopposed activities right up to the middle of the Shatt began to acquire, at least on the local level and on the basis of repute, the colour of rightful authority, with the result that the boundary as observed locally came to be regarded as lying in the middle of the Shatt. Had Persia insisted then on a midline boundary on the basis of acquiescence, it is arguable that she might have made out a good case; she would, nevertheless, have had difficulty in reconciling her claims with the disclaimers contained in the treaties of 1869 and 1873. It may, at any rate, be futile to go into this particular issue in view of the conclusion of the treaty of 1913 and the demarcation proceedings of 1914 wherein the parties agreed, once again, that the left bank of the Shatt was to continue to be the dividing line. Hence, even if Persia had been able to establish the claim that the alignment in the Shatt had shifted westwards to the half-way mark, it would have been largely without legal relevance inasmuch as she, on the assumption that the locally observed line in the river had acquired a degree of validity, ultimately abandoned it in favour of the left bank frontier. In one sense, therefore, the 1913 treaty and the demarcation of 1914 reaffirmed the ancient frontier in the greater part of the Shatt, entrenching further the left bank line, and nullifying all 'on-site' developments contrary to the left bank boundary which had occurred in the period immediately preceding the 1913–14 agreements.

The Treaty of 1937 gave Iran a greater part of and rights to the Shatt; but the essential feature, which was that the greater part of the frontier ran along the eastern edge of the Shatt, remained constant. The median line

[89] Above, pp. 53–4.

opposite the anchorage at Abadan was clearly seen as a derogation from the main lie of the alignment, and a concession to Iran. From the above analysis it is clear that the two States were agreed in principle on the 'true' location of the boundary, and there was accordingly no dispute, at least in law and theory, as to where the boundary was located. On this view of the matter the boundary dispute was essentially political in nature. The difficulties did not lie in differing interpretations regarding the law governing the boundary regime, or where exactly the alignment ran along the bank which, in principle, would have left the matter unsettled to some degree. The difficulties between the States lay in accepting and reconciling themselves to the boundary.

The legal effect of successive recognition of the left bank boundary is not without importance. It implied that each State acknowledged the title of the other State to the territory lying on either side of the frontier line and thus precluded the States from subsequently challenging the legality of the attribution of territory by the boundary. In the *Eastern Greenland* case,[90] the Permanent Court of International Justice took into consideration the fact that Norway had concluded with Denmark a series of bilateral agreements; and that there were various multinational agreements to which both Norway and Denmark were contracting parties, and in which Greenland had been 'described as a Danish colony, or as forming part of Denmark, or in which Denmark had been allowed to exclude Greenland from the operation of the agreement'.[91] 'In accepting', the Court held, 'these bilateral and multilateral agreements as binding upon herself, Norway reaffirmed that she recognized the whole of Greenland as Danish; and thereby she has debarred herself from contesting Danish sovereignty over the whole of Greenland, and in consequence, from proceeding to occupy any part of it'.[92]

In the *Temple* case,[93] one of the questions considered by the International Court was that of Thailand's subsequent recognition and reaffirmation of the boundary depicted in the Annex 1 map. It observed that Thailand had had several opportunities of raising with the French authorities the question of the incorrect depiction on that map. In 1925 and 1937 she concluded with France the Treaties of Friendship, Commerce and Navigation, and although they were not boundary treaties as such, they provided for a general process of revision or replacement of previous agreements. However, these treaties excluded the boundary settlements of 1893, 1904 and 1907 from their scope of operation.[94] 'Thereby', the Court concluded, 'and in certain more positive provisions, the Parties confirmed the existing frontiers whatever they were.'[95] It also held that it was difficult to overlook the fact that in the Treaty of 1937 Thailand (then Siam) had reaffirmed the established frontier.[96]

[90] *PCIJ*, Series A/B, No. 53 (1933). [91] Ibid., p. 68. [92] Ibid., pp. 68–9.
[93] *ICJ Reports*, 1962, p. 6. [94] Ibid., pp. 27–8. [95] Ibid., p. 27.
[96] Ibid. See also the separate opinions of Judge Sir Gerald Fitzmaurice, p. 62, and Judge Alfaro,

Similarly, in the *Rann of Kutch* arbitration[97] the question of successive recognition of a boundary arose in the context of a complex of official documentation, including governmental administrative records, gazettes, maps and the like published over a period spanning almost a century.[98] There was, however, no boundary treaty between the British Indian Province of Sind and the autonomous native State of Kutch. It was argued by India that this documentation constituted recognition of the northern edge of the Rann as the alignment between Kutch and Sind. The Chairman of the Court of Arbitration held in favour of India, and although he acknowledged the fact that there were many difficulties of interpretation and of facts in the documentation, he ruled that these statements and maps 'constitute acts of competent British authorities which—if viewed as being in response to claims by Kutch or other Indian States that the Rann was Indian State territory—may be interpreted as acquiescence in or acceptance of, such claims . . .'.[99] In respect of several series of wide-ranging maps, the Chairman, Judge Lagergren, observed that 'the cumulative effect of the publication of official maps, in conjunction with other acts or omissions by the British authorities, and the interpretation placed on the maps by those concerned at the time, might be such that the maps must be given decisive weight in determining the issues confronting the Tribunal'.[100]

In the *Beagle Channel* arbitration[101] both Argentina and Chile claimed title to the three disputed islands lying in the mouth of the channel on the basis of the line delimited in the Boundary Treaty of 1881. While the Court of Arbitration was requested to interpret the treaty in order to determine the 'true' allocation, Chile also contended that several official Argentine decrees, which dealt with the administrative divisions of Argentine national territory and were issued in the period between 1883 and 1904, tended to confirm and corroborate her claims.[102] It was pointed out that none of the decrees showed the disputed islands as being under Argentine administrative control, notwithstanding the fact that they indicated specific boundaries. The Court ruled in favour of Chile.[103]

pp. 39–43. Cf. oral argument of Soskice, Counsel for Thailand, *ICJ Pleadings*, 1962, *Temple of Preah Vihear* case, vol. 2, pp. 288, 320–3, regarding Thailand's non-recognition.

97 50 ILR 1; *Reports of International Arbitral Awards*, vol. 16, p. 1.

98 50 ILR 1, at pp. 217ff.

99 Ibid., at p. 500. See also the *Minquiers* case (*ICJ Reports*, 1953, p. 47) regarding British reliance on several international instruments and correspondence as evidence of French recognition of Britain's sovereignty over the island groups: *ICJ Pleadings*, 1953, *Minquiers and Ecrehos* case, vol. 1, pp. 49–73 and pp. 113–24.

100 50 ILR 1, at p. 486. See also p. 514.

101 Award of 18 April 1977 (HMSO, 1977).

102 Ibid., p. 102.

103 Ibid., p. 106. See also the *Arbitral Award of the King of Spain* case (*ICJ Reports*, 1960, p. 192), wherein the International Court held that there had been 'repeated acts of recognition by Nicaragua' of the boundary award of 23 December 1906 (p. 214) and that it was 'no longer open to Nicaragua to go back upon that recognition . . .': p. 213. It the *Western Sahara* advisory opinion (*ICJ Reports*, 1975, p. 12), Morocco contended that a series of international acts, including treaties, exchanges of letters

Cognate with the presentation above is the point that successive recognitions by treaty can be seen as confirmation of the view that the States in question were disposed towards achieving a maximum degree of territorial stability and finality. Both Iraq and Iran were determined, it appears from the treaties, not to subject the established boundary to fundamental changes, and to permit modifications only in small sectors of the line, viz. at Mohammara and Abadan with a view to accommodating the legitimate territorial problems of Iran. By and large, these States wished to maintain the location of the boundary and, consequently, to reaffirm the attribution of territory effected by the line in question. This point has particular significance in the context of the legal problem created by the abrogation of the treaties of 1937 and 1975, and will be dealt with in some detail at the appropriate place.[104] It may be sufficient to note here that the doctrine of finality and stability of boundaries, which is one of the more fundamental principles relating to the international law of boundaries, places great emphasis on the conclusive nature of the resolution of all territorial and boundary-related problems.[105] States do not look kindly upon a system either of diplomacy or of law which continually challenges the location and validity of a boundary established on the basis of, and existing in, law. In the *Case Concerning the Continental Shelf* (*Tunisia/Libyan Arab Jamahiriya*)[106] the International Court had the opportunity of referring to the status of the land frontier between the two States in order to determine the starting-point of the boundary on the coast. It observed that the boundary was initially settled by virtue of the Convention of 19 May 1910 between the Bey of Tunis, who had come under the protection of France, and the Ottoman Empire.[107] (The boundary was demarcated in the period 1910–11.)[108] The International Court went on to observe that the 1910 line had been

> expressly confirmed by the Treaty of Friendship and Neighbourly Relations concluded on 10 August 1955 between the French Republic (on behalf of Tunisia) and the United Kingdom of Libya, implicitly confirmed by the Treaty . . . of 7 January 1957, which was amended and completed by the Establishment Convention of 14 June 1961, and expressly confirmed by an exchange of letters at the time of signing that Establishment Convention.[109]

It noted that the boundary had 'remained unchanged throughout the vicissitudes of the two World Wars' and that the principle declared in the 1964 Cairo Resolution according to which 'all Member States pledge

and diplomatic correspondence, constituted recognition of her title to territory extending to the south of the Noun and Dra'a. The Court declined to uphold that view: pp. 49–57, but see the separate opinions of Judges Ammoun, pp. 87–92, and de Castro, pp. 161–4.

[104] Below, p. 79.

[105] Kaikobad, 'Some Observations on the Doctrine of Continuity and Finality of Boundaries', this *Year Book*, 54 (1983), p. 119.

[106] *ICJ Reports*, 1982, p. 18.

[107] Ibid., p. 65.

[108] Brownlie, *African Boundaries: A Legal and Diplomatic Encyclopaedia* (London, 1979), p. 141.

[109] *ICJ Reports*, 1982, p. 65.

themselves to respect the borders existing on their achievement of national independence' was exemplified in the continuity of the boundary regime between the parties.[110] Referring also to the principle of continuity of boundaries in the event of a succession of States predicated in Article 11 of the 1978 Vienna Convention on Succession of States in respect of Treaties, the Court concluded that 'the permanence and stability of the land frontier is one of the points where the Parties are in full agreement'.[111]

The rule in question was a central feature in the judgment of the International Court in the *Temple* case. It was observed therein that in general where two States establish a frontier between themselves, one of the primary objectives is to achieve finality and stability. This would, it was ruled, be impossible if the line so established could at any given moment be called into question and its rectification claimed whenever any inaccuracy by reference to a clause in the parent treaty was discovered.[112]

State practice is consistent with this proposition of law. Reference may be made to the boundary dispute between Afghanistan and Pakistan. To some extent the facts are not altogether dissimilar in that the frontier, established by virtue of the Anglo-Afghan agreement of 12 November 1893 and demarcated in the period 1894–6, was confirmed in the treaties of 1905, 1919 and 1921, and in the exchange of notes of 1930. Afghanistan has since challenged the validity of the boundary on several grounds, including the non-applicability of the principles of continuity in the event of State succession, and *rebus sic stantibus* regarding the frontier agreements. In November 1947, three months after the transfer of power to Pakistan, Mr Gerald Fitzmaurice (as he then was), who was Legal Adviser to the Foreign Office, advised the British Government, in a joint opinion with Miss J. Gutteridge, that the boundary treaties and regime established by the treaties were valid and binding on Afghanistan.[113] In a statement to Parliament on 30 June 1949, Mr Noel-Baker, the British Secretary of State for Commonwealth Relations, said that in the opinion of the British Government, 'Pakistan is in international law the inheritor of the rights and duties of the old Government of India and of His Majesty's Government in the United Kingdom in these territories and that the Durand Line [i.e. the Afghan–Pakistani frontier] is the international frontier'.[114]

110 *ICJ Reports*, 1982, pp. 65–6.

111 Ibid., p. 66.

112 *ICJ Reports*, 1962, p. 6 at p. 34. See also the *Grisbadarna* arbitration, *Scott's Hague Court Reports*, p. 121 at p. 130; *State of South Australia* v. *State of Victoria*, [1914] AC 283, at p. 310; *Costa Rica* v. *Nicaragua*, *Moore's International Arbitrations*, vol. 2, p. 1945; *Costa Rica* v. *Panama*, *Reports of International Arbitral Awards*, vol. 11, p. 528, regarding the existence of a traditional river boundary between the disputing States.

113 Opinion of 5 November 1947, in Ext. 8930/47, L/P & S/12/1822, Collection 3/24.

114 Hansard, *House of Commons Debates*, vol. 466, cols. 1491–3, at col. 1491. See also Prime Minister's statement to the House of Commons, 1 March 1956, ibid., vol. 549, col. 1367; E. Lauterpacht, 'The Contemporary Practice of the United Kingdom in the Field of International Law', *International and Comparative Law Quarterly*, 5 (1956), p. 421; and letter transmitted to UN by UK Permanent Representative, 26 February 1965 in *Materials on Succession of States* (UN Legislative Series, New York, 1967: ST/LEG/SER.B/14), pp. 186–7.

The above statement of the law warrants the conclusion that once States agree to allocate territory on the basis of a treaty, and thereafter implement its provisions by way of demarcation, and subsequently reaffirm the treaty and/or the location of the frontier with or without minor modifications to the alignment, it is reasonable to assume that the matter has, in principle, received its quietus and is not to be reopened. To the extent that a boundary agreement is the source of the territorial and boundary-related obligations of both adjacent States, it may be seen as investing title to territory in favour of either State. The subsequent successive reaffirmation or confirmation of the alignment constitutes recognition of the conclusive nature of the boundary regime, which, in turn, precludes the States from contesting the validity of the boundary at a subsequent period of time. It will be seen that each of those treaties, i.e. the treaties of 1847, 1913–14 and 1937, attributed territory to Iran and Iraq, and they were thus vestive of title. In another sense, the treaties of 1913–14 made only modifications to the left bank boundary and were to that extent reaffirming the prevailing alignment. They may be regarded as evidence of the conclusive nature of the allocation of territory made by the States. This implies, furthermore, that both Iran and Iraq were precluded from subsequently challenging the status of the left bank boundary. The question of preclusion will be examined in the context of the unilateral abrogation of the boundary at a more appropriate section of this work, and it will suffice therefore to state here that the left bank boundary was in principle valid and binding upon the two Parties.

2. *Specific issues*

(i) *Midline or* thalweg *in the Shatt.* The question of the midline and/or the *thalweg* in the Shatt is perhaps central to a proper appreciation of the legal regime of the frontier, and accordingly this matter, although familiar to students and writers of international law, is examined in considerable detail. One of the arguments consistently put forward by Iran in earlier[115] as well as more recent times[116] was that the Shatt should be divided along either the middle of the river or the *thalweg*. In support of her claim Iran has argued that it is a well-received rule of international law that when a river divides the territories of two or more States the boundary runs along either the *thalweg* or the median line, and not along either of the

[115] See generally above, pp. 56, 58–9. See also Melamid, 'The Shatt-al-Arab Boundary Dispute', *Middle East Journal*, 22 (1968), p. 351 at p. 354; Edmonds, 'The Iraqi–Persian Frontier, 1639–1938', *Asian Affairs*, 62 (1975), p. 147 at pp. 150–2.

[116] See Iran's letters to the President, Security Council, 1 and 9 May 1969 (including statements of 27 April and 3 May 1969 by Ministry of Foreign Affairs, Iran): S/9190 and S/9200 and Add. 2; and letter of 2 September 1969: S/9425. See also Iraq's letters to President, Security Council, 29 April 1969: S/9185; 13 May 1969: S/9205; 11 July 1969: S/9323 and Corr. 1: *Yearbook of the United Nations*, 23 (1969), p. 246. See also Statement by Iraqi Minister of Foreign Affairs to General Assembly, 3 October 1980: Annex to *The Iraqi–Iranian Dispute: Facts and Allegations* (Ministry of Foreign Affairs, Iraq, 1981); *Facts Concerning the Iraqi–Iranian Frontier* (id., 1960); *Comment on the Iranian Claims concerning the Iraqi–Iranian Frontier Treaty of 1937* (id., 1969); and Ismael, *Iraq and Iran: Roots of Conflict* (Syracuse, 1982), p. 26.

two banks of the river; and, hence, the left bank alignment cannot be upheld in law. In his reply to the Iraqi representative's address to the Council of the League of Nations in February 1935, the Persian Minister, Mr Kazemi, claimed that the Treaty of Erzeroum '[did] not say a word about giving to the Porte the whole of the Shatt . . . in full sovereignty', and concluded:

> It does not fix in direct, clear and categorical terms the frontier on the bank beyond the waters of the river; yet this should have been made quite explicit in absolute and formal terms, if the intention were to depart from the fundamental principle of the equal sovereignty of the two riparians as far as the middle of the river.[117]

At the outset, it is to be noted that although the concept of the median line is different from that of the *thalweg*, the two terms were apparently often employed interchangeably by officials of the Government of Iran and the Foreign Office in Britain. While it is generally accepted that the term *medium filum aquae* is the line of geographic equidistance in the river, i.e. it divides the river lengthways in equal proportions, there is some difficulty in attributing an equally precise meaning to the term *thalweg*. Both lawyers and geographers have observed that this term is susceptible of varying interpretations. Thus, the term *thalweg* can be understood as being either the median line in the main navigable channel, or the continuous line of deepest soundings, and according to some commentators, even the axis of the safest and most accessible channel for the largest ships.[118] The precise meaning, however, of the term is of little or no consequence to this particular study inasmuch as nothing material turns on the question of the exact location of the *thalweg*, and it will therefore be sufficient to proceed on the understanding that, for purposes of this analysis, the term *thalweg* refers to the median line of the main navigable channel. This, at any rate, is the view that is most widely accepted. A question of greater importance is whether Iran was correct in claiming that there exists a fundamental principle of international law which requires the maintenance of a median line boundary which could only be displaced by express agreement. This question requires some analysis of the law and practice of States relative to boundary lines in navigable rivers.

A discussion of frontier delimitation in respect of rivers may be appropriately prefaced by a brief historical survey. In so far as State practice is concerned, the development of the law has not, according to Professor Verzijl, been uniform: different regions in Europe have had diverse

[117] *League of Nations Official Journal*, 16 (1935), p. 118; see also p. 120.

[118] Bouchez, 'The Fixing of Boundaries in International Boundary Rivers', *International and Comparative Law Quarterly*, 12 (1963), p. 789 at p. 793; E. Lauterpacht, 'River Boundaries: Legal Aspects of the Shatt al Arab Frontier', ibid. 9 (1960), p. 208; McEwen, *International Boundaries of East Africa* (Oxford, 1971), pp. 78–9; Jones, *Boundary Making* (Washington, DC, 1945), pp. 114–17; Verzijl, *International Law in Historical Perspective*, vol. 3 (1971), pp. 563–5; Cukwurah, *The Settlement of Boundary Disputes in International Law* (Manchester, 1967), pp. 51–4; Al-Izzi, *The Shatt al Arab River Dispute in Terms of Law* (1972), pp. 70–3.

experiences.[119] In medieval times, the main rivers of Europe were governed by the legal regime of *stratae regiae* or, literally, the street of the Holy Roman Empire. Riparian 'states' (towns, areas, etc.) could only exercise rights appertaining to jurisdiction, navigation, fishery and the like in broad rivers in so far as such rights had been expressly granted to them by the Empire. In the absence of such grant, the territorial rights of the riparians were limited by the bank of the river, while the Empire exercised exclusive sovereignty over it, up to and including its natural inundation area irrespective of the territorial claims of the riparians.[120]

However, in the Balkans the general trend, as seen in treaty provisions between Russia, Austria and Turkey, was to leave either the entire river to one of the States or to fix their respective boundaries along both banks of the river, thus ascribing to the latter the status of 'no man's land'.[121] Verzijl observed that he 'did not find much indication which could support the conscious acceptance in early times of the idea of a river condominium proper, and the express partition of a river into two strips divided by its median line, let alone divided along its *thalweg*, was still very rare'.[122] For other parts of Europe, he found no evidence of any 'fixed general customary rule' regarding the division of rivers. The view, therefore, that nations adhered at first to 'the principle of co-dominion, which assigned to the opposite riverain proprietors rights of sovereignty over the entire stream'[123] has to be tempered somewhat with the foregoing observations.

There is no doubt, however, that the concept of a median line division did eventually gain greater currency among the States in Europe, and by the time Hugo Grotius wrote *De jure belli ac pacis libri tres* in 1625 he could observe that 'in case of doubt the jurisdiction of two States bordering on the same river extends to the middle of the stream . . .'.[124] This technique, nevertheless, was found not to be free from difficulties in navigable rivers. The *medium filum aquae* did not necessarily correspond with the channel of navigation in the river, and a vessel following the main channel was likely to find itself on either side of the boundary in the course of its passage. Thus by the beginning of the nineteenth century States began to adopt the *thalweg* as their boundary in navigable rivers as opposed to a median line

[119] Verzijl, op. cit. (previous note), pp. 540–1.

[120] Ibid. On a discussion of such medieval grants, see *The Twee Gebroeders*, 3 C Rob. 336, at pp. 344–7.

[121] Verzijl, op. cit. above (p. 70 n. 118), p. 543.

[122] Ibid. In this context, see the *Grisbadarna* case, *Scott's Hague Court Reports*, p. 122 at p. 129; and below.

[123] Hyde, *International Law Chiefly as Interpreted and Applied by the United States* (1945), vol. 1, p. 443; see also *New Jersey* v. *Delaware*, 291 US 361, at p. 381; *Minnesota* v. *Wisconsin*, 252 US 273, at p. 282.

[124] *De jure belli ac pacis libri tres* (translation by F. W. Kelsey, 1925: Carnegie Endowment for International Peace, Washington, 1964), book II, chap. III, no. 18 (p. 218). Also see Vattel, *The Law of Nations* (1773) (translation by J. Chitty, London, 1834), book I, chap. 22, no. 266; Pufendorf, *De jure naturae et gentium libri octo* (1688) (translation by Oldfather, 1934: Carnegie Endowment for International Peace, New York, 1964 (vol. 2)), book IV, chap. VII, p. 594.

division.[125] Gradually, the notion of the *thalweg* delimitation evolved as a principle of law. As Professor Hyde observed,

> The principal boundary treaties concluded [in this period] afford abundant evidence of the fact that States have generally taken great care to express their acceptance of the principle of thalweg and have avoided the use of words the literal meaning of which might encourage the inference that the contracting parties sought to retain the old method of establishing a frontier.[126]

In general terms, the principle is that, in the absence of an agreement or evidence to the contrary, wherever a navigable river divides the territories of two (or more) States, the boundary lies, or is to be drawn, along the *thalweg* of the river.[127]

A notable feature of international jurisprudence is that there is a virtually complete absence of any detailed comment on the law of the *thalweg* and the *medium filum aquae*. This is especially conspicuous in view of the fact that tribunals *have* delimited boundaries along the *thalweg* of rivers in their judgments and arbitral awards. The explanation may be that in almost all the cases regarding river boundaries there have been no controversies regarding the extent of territorial sovereignty widthways in the water-courses: disagreement, more often than not, has been confined to the question of the location of the boundary on *terra firma*. Thus in the *British Guiana–Brazil Boundary* arbitration,[128] the Arbitrator, King Victor Emmanuel of Italy, fixed the boundary in the *thalweg* of the rivers Ireng (Mahu) and Takutu.[129] Similarly in the *Northeastern Boundary* arbitration,[130] between Great Britain and the United States, King William I of the Netherlands drew the 'line of convenience' along the *thalweg* of the St John and St Francis rivers, an alignment which neither of the parties had claimed.[131] In the *British Guiana–Venezuela Boundary* arbitration,[132] the tribunal, in an award delivered in October 1899, fixed the frontier along the mid-stream of a number of rivers.[133] It is noteworthy that Article 4(b) of the *Compromis* of February 1897 provided that 'The Arbitrators

[125] Hyde, op. cit. above (p. 71 n. 123), p. 444; Verzijl, op. cit. above (p. 70 n. 118); Twiss, *The Law of Nations* (Oxford, 1884), pp. 249–50; Westlake, *International Law*, Part I, Peace (Cambridge, 1904), p. 141. An interesting example of this change can be seen in part of the boundaries between the US and Canada. The 1783 Treaty and subsequent demarcation commissions of 1822 established the boundary in the geographical centre of the waters between the eastern terminus and the Neebish Falls situated in the water communication between Lakes Huron and Superior. However, the Webster–Ashburton Treaty of 1842 adopted the *thalweg* for the sector beginning at the Neebish Falls and ending at the Lake of Woods: Verzijl, op. cit. above (p. 70 n. 118), p. 556; *Moore's International Arbitrations*, vol. 1, pp. 162–95.

[126] Hyde, op. cit. above (p. 71 n. 123), p. 445 n. 4.

[127] Brownlie, *African Boundaries: A Legal and Diplomatic Encyclopaedia* (1979), p. 17; Bouchez, loc. cit. above (p. 70 n. 118), p. 799; McEwen, loc. cit. above (p. 70 n. 118), pp. 78–84; E. Lauterpacht, loc. cit. above (p. 70 n. 118), pp. 216–22; Cukwurah, op. cit. above (p. 70 n. 118). For older authorities, see Hyde, op. cit. above (p. 71 n. 123), pp. 444–9; and Hall, *International Law* (8th edn., 1934), p. 147; Wharton, *A Digest of the International Law of the United States* (Washington, DC, 1887), pp. 95–7, and Hackworth, *A Digest of International Law*, vol. 1 (Washington, DC, 1940), pp. 570–4.

[128] *Reports of International Arbitral Awards*, vol. 11, p. 21.

[129] Ibid., p. 23.

[130] *Moore's International Arbitrations*, vol. 1, p. 127.

[131] Ibid., p. 134.

[132] *British Foreign and State Papers*, vol. 92, p. 160.

[133] Ibid., p. 161. However, the boundary was drawn along the northern bank of the River Cuyueni.

may recognize and give effect to rights and claims vesting on any other ground whatever valid according to international law, and on any principles of international law which the Arbitrators may deem to be applicable to the case'.[134]

In the *Alaska Boundary* arbitration,[135] the tribunal was called upon to identify, *inter alia*, the 'true' Portland Channel along which part of the boundary was to run. According to the United States the inlet running south of Wales and Pearse Islands was the Portland Channel because, *inter alia*, 'the Channel contended for [by her] was the deepest, broadest and by far the most important because it is in fact the only really navigable and safe one'.[136] In her written argument, the US relied heavily upon the doctrine of the *thalweg* and controverted the British claim that the channel lay along the northern side of the above-mentioned islands, describing it as a 'narrow rocky and really unnavigable channel'.[136] In his oral address, Sir Robert Finlay, Counsel for Great Britain, argued that the *thalweg* doctrine was irrelevant to the dispute inasmuch as the question was one of identity of the 'true' channel, and not where the boundary lay in the undisputed channel.[137] He admitted, however, that there was some confusion as to whether the US regarded both the inlets as one channel separated by islands or whether there were two distinct channels.[138] The tribunal, which unanimously agreed that the boundary ran along the northern side of the Wales and Pearse Islands, based its decision entirely upon the intentions of the negotiators of the boundary treaty of 1825 and Admiral Vancouver's narratives of his journeys, and abstained from commenting upon the *thalweg* doctrine.[139] However, in his individual opinion, Lord Alverstone remarked that in his view 'there is no foundation for the [US] argument in favour of the thalweg doctrine'.[140]

The question of the *thalweg* was also raised in the *Grisbadarna* arbitration[141] wherein the Permanent Court of Arbitration accepted this method of delimitation as a 'rule' of international law but failed to apply it to the case at hand on the basis of the restrictions imposed by the principles of the intertemporal law. For similar reasons, the Permanent Court rejected the claims for a median line division.[142]

It is the *genus* of decisions of national courts which has played the major part in developing the doctrine of the *thalweg* in boundary rivers. In the earlier part of this century, the Supreme Court of the United States of America was seised from time to time of a number of cases which were

[134] See *British and Foreign State Papers*, vol. 89, p. 57 at p. 60. See also the *Island of Timor* case: *Scott's Hague Court Reports*, p. 355.

[135] *Reports of International Arbitral Awards*, vol. 15, p. 491.

[136] *Argument of the United States Before the Tribunal* . . . (Washington, 1903), pp. 41–2.

[137] *Alaska Boundary* Tribunal, *Minutes of Proceedings*, 17 September 1903, pp. 2–6 at pp. 4–5.

[138] Ibid., p. 5.

[139] Award, *Reports of International Arbitral Awards*, vol. 15, pp. 492–3, 495, 501–2, 512–13, 521–3.

[140] Ibid., p. 495.

[141] *Scott's Hague Court Reports*, p. 122.

[142] Ibid., p. 129. Also see the judgment in *Zurich* v. *Schaffhausen*, below, p. 76.

concerned with disputes regarding boundaries in rivers between the various States of the Union. Its decisions have thus become the chief English language source of judicial opinion on this question.[143] In the cases before it, the Court has consistently ruled in favour of the *thalweg* principle. In *Iowa* v. *Illinois*, one of the earliest cases on this matter, Mr Justice Field ruled:

> When a navigable river constitutes the boundary between two independent States, the line defining the point at which the jurisdiction of the two separates is well established to be the middle of the main channel of the stream. The interest of each State in the navigation of the river admits of no other line. The preservation by each of its equal right in the navigation of the stream is the subject of paramount interest. It is, therefore, laid down in all the recognised treatises on international law of modern times that the middle of the channel of the stream marks the true boundary between the adjoining States up to which each State will on its side exercise jurisdiction.[144]

In *Louisiana* v. *Mississippi*,[145] Chief Justice Fuller went on to hold that on occasion the principle of the *thalweg* was applicable in respect of water boundaries to sounds, bays, straits, gulfs, estuaries and other arms of the sea.[146] In *New Jersey* v. *Delaware*,[147] the Supreme Court observed that the underlying rationale of the doctrine of the *thalweg* was one of equality and justice and gave prominence to the fact that if the dividing line were to be placed in the centre of the stream rather than in the centre of the channel the whole track of navigation might be thrown within the territory of one State to the exclusion of the other.[148]

The point, which is particularly worthy of note, but is frequently overlooked in commentaries relating to these cases, is that in none of the disputes did any of the States of the Union lay claim to the entire width of the river which separated them; and that, therefore, the question to which the Supreme Court was confined was whether or not the *thalweg* boundary, as claimed by one State, was, in principle, to be given precedence over the median line division, as claimed by another. Indeed, in some of these cases, the Federal Enabling Acts, which described, *inter alia*, the territorial extent of the States joining the American Union, stipulated that the boundaries of the States in question lay along the middle of certain rivers.[149] Furthermore, in several cases, the delimitation of boundaries along the middle of certain rivers was expressly provided for in treaties concluded between the

[143] See *Iowa* v. *Illinois*, 147 US 1; *Louisiana* v. *Mississippi*, 202 US 1; *Arkansas* v. *Tennessee*, 246 US 158; *Arkansas* v. *Mississippi*, 250 US 39; *Minnesota* v. *Wisconsin*, 252 US 273; *New Jersey* v. *Delaware*, 291 US 361; *Washington* v. *Oregon*, 211 US 127; *Handly's Lessee* v. *Anthony et al.*, 5 Wheat. 374; *Buttenuth et al.* v. *St Louis Bridge Co.*, *Scott's Cases on International Law* (Washington, DC, 1922), p. 206 (123 Ill. 535; 17 NE Rep. 439).

[144] 147 US 1, at p. 7.

[145] 202 US 1.

[146] Ibid., p. 50.

[147] 291 US 361.

[148] Ibid., p. 380.

[149] See *Iowa* v. *Illinois*, 147 US 1, at pp. 10–11, 13–14; *Arkansas* v. *Tennessee*, 246 US 160, at pp. 160ff.; *Arkansas* v. *Mississippi*, 250 US 39, at pp. 41–6; *Nebraska* v. *Iowa*, 143 US 359, at pp. 359–60; *Missouri* v. *Nebraska*, 196 US 23, at pp. 23–35; *Buttenuth* v. *St Louis Bridge Co.*, loc. cit. above (n. 143).

British, French, Spanish and US Governments in the eighteenth and nineteenth centuries in respect of their North American territories.[150] Accordingly, it is important to be reminded of the context in which the Supreme Court made its decisions in favour of the *thalweg* principle and to note that it was not faced with claims of title to the entire width of the river. It can, therefore, hardly be contended that the Supreme Court accepted the proposition that the rule of the *thalweg* had to be applied without qualification to all boundary rivers. On the contrary, it is manifest that the Court did not approve of this interpretation of the law in question. In *Washington* v. *Oregon* the matter before the Court was whether the boundary in the Columbia River, which separated the two States, lay along the 'middle of the north ship channel of the Columbia River'. The territorial extent of Oregon was described in the Act of 14 February 1859 which admitted the State into the Union and provided that part of the boundary lay in the middle of the said north ship channel. It was contended by counsel on behalf of Washington that the 'true boundary line is the varying centre or middle of that channel of the river which is best suited and ordinarily used for the purposes of navigation',[151] and thus the boundary ran along the centre of the southern, or main, channel of navigation. In response to the arguments advanced by Washington, the Court referred, *inter alia*, to some of the earlier decisions passed by it in favour of the *thalweg* principle, and in distinguishing them, observed:

> But in these cases the boundary named was 'the middle of the main channel of the river' or 'the middle of the river' and it was upon such a description that it was held that in the absence of avulsion the boundary was the varying centre of the channel. But there is no fixed rule making [the *thalweg*] the boundary between States bordering on a river . . . Now, if Congress in establishing the boundary between Washington and Oregon had simply named the middle of the river, or the centre of the channel, doubtless it would be ruled that the centre of the main channel, varying as it might from year to year through the process of accretion, was the boundary between the two States . . . However . . . when Congress came to provide for the admission of Oregon . . . it provided that the boundary should be the middle of the north channel. The Courts have no power to change the boundary thus prescribed and establish it at the middle of some other channel.[152]

The Supreme Court, moreover, had recognized, in certain *obiter* passages, that the *thalweg* rule cannot be applied in every case. In *Iowa* v. *Illinois*, it remarked that the reason for and necessity of the *thalweg* rule may not be as cogent in inter-State disputes in the US as it is among European States where there is no central government, 'yet the same rule will be held to obtain unless changed by statute or usage of so great a length of time as to have acquired the force of law'.[153] The same precept was

[150] See *Louisiana* v. *Mississippi*, 202 US 1; *Arkansas* v. *Tennessee*, 246 US 158; *Iowa* v. *Illinois*, 147 US 1; *Vermont* v. *New Hampshire*, 289 US 593.

[151] *Washington* v. *Oregon*, 211 US 127, at p. 129.

[152] Ibid., pp. 134–5.

[153] 147 US 1, at p. 10. See also *Vermont* v. *New Hampshire*, 289 US 593.

adopted in *New Jersey* v. *Delaware* when the Court held that unless prescription or convention had entrenched another rule, the Court was to utilize the formula that would make equality prevail.[154]

Reference may also be made to the decision of the Swiss Federal Court rendered on 9 November 1897 regarding the boundaries of the Cantons of Zurich and Schaffhausen along the Rhine.[155] In this case the Federal Court was seised of claims and facts not entirely dissimilar to the ones obtaining in the Shatt boundary dispute. Schaffhausen claimed that the boundary ran along the left bank of the Rhine leaving the entire width of the river under her jurisdiction. She based her claim on the Confederate award of 1555 which resolved the dispute between the two Cantons by attributing territorial sovereignty over the entire width of the relevant sector of the Rhine to Schaffhausen. Zurich contested this by arguing that the modern concepts of international law were in favour of a median line division and therefore the alignment between the parties lay not along the left bank but in the middle of the Rhine. The Federal Court was not convinced by the arguments of Zurich and in a passage which has particular relevance to the present study observed:

> The circumstances that now, in accordance with the development of objective law, more importance is attached to the doctrine of international law, according to which the boundary of two States divided by a river is usually found in the middle of the said river, and less importance is attached to the actual possession and events of feudal law, cannot now effect any change in the juridical condition determined in such an authentic way any more than it could have done so previously. For the principal question to be decided today is whether the present dispute has not already been decided, at least to a certain extent, in a legally binding manner, and whether thereby a condition has been created which must be guarded according to the principles of acquired rights, regardless of how the dispute would be decided according to the now prevalent norms and conceptions.[156]

[154] 291 US 361, at p. 383. See also *Handly's Lessee* v. *Anthony*, 5 Wheat. 374, at pp. 378–84; *Regina* v. *Mat Erat* (1872), 2 Ky. (Cr.) 86 (Straits Settlements), *Commonwealth International Law Cases*, vol. 8, p. 379; *In re Village of Fort Erie and Buffalo and Fort Erie Public Bridge Co.* (1927), 61 OLR 502, *Commonwealth International Law Cases*, vol. 8, p. 433; *Buttenuth et al.* v. *St. Louis Bridge Co.*, *Scott's Cases on International Law* (1922), p. 212.

[155] See Schindler, 'The Administration of Justice in the Swiss Federal Court in International Disputes', *American Journal of International Law*, 15 (1921), p. 149 at pp. 167–8.

[156] Ibid., pp. 167–8. Translation by Schindler. In another case in respect of a different sector of the boundary, the claims were reversed. Zurich argued that by virtue, *inter alia*, of prescription and *usucapio*, her sovereignty extended up to the northern (or right) bank of the Rhine, while Schaffhausen claimed a median line. The Federal Court held that Zurich had failed to establish her claims in law, and declared that the line lay in the middle of the Rhine: Decision of 28 May 1907, cited in Schindler, ibid., pp. 168–9. See also, in passing, Venezuela's arguments in the *British Guiana–Venezuela* arbitration in respect of the middle distance and natural boundaries. Referring generally to watersheds, she argued: 'Before the rule of the middle distance can be used, it must be found that there is no line of right; that neither party has a superior right to the whole or any determinate part of the disputed territory': *Printed Argument on Behalf of the United States of Venezuela* (New York, 1898), vol. 1, p. 757. In the *Barotse Kingdom Boundary* arbitration, part of the boundary between (Portuguese) Angola and (British Northern Rhodesia) Zambia was located along the left bank of the Kwando river: Brownlie, *African Boundaries: A Legal and Diplomatic Encyclopaedia* (1979), pp. 1067–70.

The point that emerges clearly from the above discussion is that the *thalweg* rule in boundary rivers is not an absolute principle, that is, a 'rule' to be followed whenever a navigable river separates two or more States. The *thalweg* doctrine is applicable only in certain circumstances, and one of these circumstances, apart, of course, from incidents of express agreement between the parties, is a situation in which neither of the parties can adduce evidence in the form either of a treaty, municipal instruments, acquiescence or otherwise, regarding the location of the line in a navigable river. In other words, in such situations, the boundary will, in all the appropriate circumstances, be located in the *thalweg* of the river and neither in the middle of nor along one of the banks of the navigable river. It amounts to this, therefore, as Professor Brownlie observed, that the principles of the *thalweg*, and of the *medium filum aquae* in non-navigable rivers, are essentially presumptions,[157] which may be rebutted by either party upon submission of evidence to the contrary. There is considerable support for this view among the earlier and more contemporary writers on international law.[158] Equally, and this is a concomitant of the foregoing, there is no presumption in favour of exclusive title to both sides of the boundary rivers. Thus in *The Twee Gebroeders*,[159] the Judge, Sir William Scott, observed, in the context of the status of the Groningen Watt, a river running along the Groningen (Dutch) coast, that there was, in principle, a presumption in favour of a communal use of the rivers flowing through the territories of States. He added that while it may be that a State may have, by way of prior settlement, secured possession of the bank of a river, 'the general presumption certainly bears strongly against such exclusive rights, and the title is a matter to be established, on the part of those claiming under it, in the same manner as all other legal demands are to be substantiated, by clear and competent evidence'.[160]

State practice affords corroboration of the view that delimitation by *thalweg* in navigable boundary rivers is not an absolute principle. Although it is true that the greater number of treaties stipulate for either a median line or *thalweg* delimitation, the attribution of the entire width of the river to one of the parties is by no means unknown. Thus, examples of international boundaries which run along the banks of navigable rivers are

[157] Brownlie, op. cit. (previous note), p. 17. In respect of river estuaries and bays, see Verzijl, op. cit. above (p. 70 n. 118), pp. 593–4.

[158] Adami, *National Frontiers in Relation to International Law* (Oxford, 1927), pp. 15, 17, 20–1; G. F. Martens, *The Law of Nations* (Cobbett translation, 4th edn., 1829), pp. 159–60; Twiss, op. cit. above (p. 72 n. 125), pp. 249–51, especially p. 250 n. 33; Wheaton, *Elements of International Law* (6th edn., by Keith, 1929), pp. 384–5; Westlake, op. cit. above (p. 72 n. 125), vol. 1, p. 142; Hall, op. cit. above (p. 72 n. 127), p. 147; Moore, *A Digest of International Law* (Washington, DC, 1906), vol. 1, pp. 616–17; Lindley, *The Acquisition and Government of Backward Territory in International Law* (London, 1926), pp. 272, 276–7; Cukwurah, op. cit. above (p. 70 n. 118), pp. 47–9; Verzijl, op. cit. above (p. 70 n. 118), p. 561; Al-Izzi, op. cit. above (p. 70 n. 118), pp. 72–3.

[159] 3 C Rob. 336; 165 ER 485.

[160] 3 C Rob. 336, at pp. 339 and 346–7; Lindley, op. cit. above (n. 158), p. 276.

to be found in Europe, America and Africa.[161] By virtue of the Franco-Liberian Treaty of 18 September 1907, the boundary between Liberia and the Ivory Coast was drawn along the right, or western, bank of the river Cavally, thereby placing the entire course of the river south of its confluence with the river Noun under French/Ivory Coast sovereignty.[162] The 1907 line, it may be added, was a modification of the *thalweg* regime established by an earlier agreement of 1892. No dispute regarding this sector exists between the States today.[163] In Europe, the Chiers, a tributary of the Meuse, was ceded by Austria in its entirety to France pursuant to Article 21 of the Treaty of 16 May 1769.[164] Certain sectors of the French–Swiss boundary between Mont Delont and Lake Geneva were, by virtue of the agreement signed on 10 June 1891, delimited along the left bank of the L'Eau Noire and the right banks of La Barberine and La Morge, attributing the entire width of the streams to France.[165] In South America the frontier line between Surinam and (French) Guyana runs, on the basis of an agreement signed by the Dutch and French Governors on 9 November 1836, along the right bank of the Maroni river, although, for purposes of navigation in the estuary, the limits, according to the Treaty of 30 September 1915, lie along the median line.[166]

In view of the above discussion of the law and practice on the question, two conclusions may now be drawn. First, it was not unlawful for either Iraq or Iran to have concluded an agreement (or agreements) which adopted the left bank of the Shatt, as opposed to the *thalweg* or median line, as the boundary between them. There is clearly no prohibition in international law against the conclusion of a frontier agreement which attributes the

[161] See, generally, Bouchez, loc. cit. above (p. 70 n. 118), p. 791; and 'The Netherlands and the Law of International Rivers', in Panhuys (ed.), *International Law in the Netherlands* (The Hague, 1978), vol. 1, pp. 215 ff.; Brownlie, op. cit. above (p. 76 n. 156), *passim*; Menon, 'International Boundaries—A Case Study of the Guyana–Surinam Boundary', *International and Comparative Law Quarterly*, 27 (1978), p. 738, at pp. 753–4; Adami, op. cit. above (p. 77 n. 158), pp. 21–2; Verzijl, op. cit. above (p. 70 n. 118), pp. 545–7; Cukwurah, op. cit. above (p. 70 n. 118), p. 47; McEwen, op. cit. above (p. 70 n. 118), pp. 84–6.

[162] Brownlie, op. cit. above (p. 76 n. 156), pp. 358–70; McEwen, op. cit. above (p. 70 n. 118), pp. 85–6.

[163] Brownlie, op. cit. above (p. 76 n. 156), p. 369. See also the boundary along the eastern bank of Ngobwe Creek between Kenya and Tanzania by virtue of the Anglo-German Protocol of 1900: McEwen, op. cit. above (p. 70 n. 118), pp. 84–5. For disputed river boundaries see the Mali–Mauritania frontier along the Senegal river: Brownlie, op. cit., pp. 407–15; and the sector of the river Faleme between Mali and Senegal, ibid., pp. 423–6.

[164] Verzijl, op. cit. above (p. 70 n. 118), p. 545; see, generally, pp. 545–7, 590–610.

[165] Adami, op. cit. above (p. 77 n. 158), p. 22. For disputed river boundaries, see the Ems–Dollard estuary problem between West Germany and the Netherlands. The former claims the entire breadth of the Ems estuary on the ground of historic title, while the Dutch Government argues in favour of the *thalweg* boundary: Bouchez, 'The Netherlands and the Law of International Rivers', loc. cit. above (n. 161), p. 282.

[166] Day (ed.), *Borders and Territorial Disputes* (London, 1982), pp. 376–7. The Dutch Governors' agreement of 1799 in respect of the boundaries of Berbice (now in Guyana) and Surinam settled the frontier along the west, or left, bank of the Corentyne river: see Menon, loc. cit. above (n. 161), pp. 748–55. The Franco-Portuguese frontier agreement of 10 August 1797 delimited the line along the right bank of the Oyapec: see Bouchez, loc. cit. above (p. 70 n. 118), p. 791.

entire width of a river to one of the contracting States, and consequently the objections raised by Iran and other commentators were misconceived. Secondly, no presumption in favour of a *thalweg* or median line boundary can arise in the Shatt. Iran had agreed in three separate agreements concluded in 1847, 1913–14 and 1937 to an alignment which ran, save in the Abadan and Mohammara sectors, along the left bank of the river. Even if a presumption existed at any point in favour of a *thalweg* division, it could easily be rebutted by reference to the treaties mentioned above and the demarcation proceedings of 1914. In the final analysis, therefore, Iran's objections and representations made prior to the conclusion of the Baghdad Treaty of 1975, which challenged the validity of the left bank boundary on the ground that international law recognized only the *thalweg*/median line in navigable rivers, were based on a misunderstanding of the position in law.

(ii) *The abrogation of the Treaty of 1937*. Iran unilaterally abrogated the Treaty of 1937 in April 1969. Several arguments were raised in support of abrogation, one of which was that the boundary stipulated in the treaty ran along the left bank and was therefore invalid. The question of the validity of the left bank alignment has been examined above. The doctrine of *rebus sic stantibus* was also relied upon by Iran which claimed that, inasmuch as there had occurred a fundamental change of circumstances between the parties, the Treaty of 1937 had terminated. Accordingly, the line established by it had ceased to exist. In order to appreciate the validity of this action and arguments submitted in support of it, a survey of the law is essential.

Before examining the role of the *rebus sic stantibus* doctrine, a brief statement regarding the general theory of executed boundary provisions and related matters will be in order. Generally speaking, alignments between States are to be viewed with a maximum degree of continuity on account, *inter alia*, of the fact that boundary treaties have 'dispositive' characteristics, that is to say, they have the effect of creating permanent rights which run and remain with the territory acquired by either State under the terms of the frontier treaty.[167] The logical basis for this proposition is that the delineation of the boundary by treaty constitutes a kind of conveyance of territory between States who thereafter acquire valid title to territory in accordance with the terms of the boundary settlement. Once the treaty is concluded and ratified, the respective rights relating to territory and boundaries are considered transferred and the treaty stands executed. It

[167] O'Connell, *International Law* (2nd edn., 1970), vol. 1, pp. 373–4; and *State Succession in Municipal Law and International Law* (1967), vol. 2, p. 273; McNair, *The Law of Treaties* (1961), pp. 655–64; Haraszti, 'Treaties and the Fundamental Change of Circumstances', *Recueil des cours*, 146 (1975–III), pp. 65–72; Vallat, *Yearbook of the International Law Commission*, 1974, vol. 2, part 1, p. 83; Lester, 'State Succession to Treaties in the Commonwealth', *International and Comparative Law Quarterly*, 12 (1963), p. 475, at pp. 492–5; Udokang, *Succession of New States to International Treaties* (New York, 1972), pp. 377–402; Tyranowski, 'State Succession: Boundaries and Boundary Treaties', *Polish Yearbook of International Law*, 10 (1979–80), p. 115; Fischer Williams, 'The Permanence of Treaties', *American Journal of International Law*, 22 (1928), p. 89.

continues, nevertheless, to serve as evidence of the transfer of territory and location of the alignment. To some extent, the treaty functions not unlike a title deed to land transferred under municipal law. In the words of the late Sir Humphrey Waldock, 'it may be argued that a boundary treaty has constitutive effects and establishes a legal and factual situation which thereafter has its own separate existence . . .'.[168] An attempt to state the law on the matter was made by the International Law Association at its biennial conference in Buenos Aires in 1968. At that conference the Committee on the Succession of New States to Treaties passed a series of resolutions, one of which, No. 8, stated that when a treaty which provided for the delimitation of a national boundary had been executed in the sense that the boundary had been delimited and no further action needed to be taken, the treaty had spent its force and what was succeeded to was not the treaty but the extent of national territory so defined.[169]

It is in this context that the law relating to the doctrine of *rebus sic stantibus* and international boundaries needs to be examined. It is generally accepted that the doctrine of *rebus sic stantibus* is not applicable to those treaties which by definition create situations intended to be permanent in character and duration, such as, *inter alia*, agreements in respect of the delimitation and demarcation of frontiers. Thus the exclusion of frontier treaties from the operation of the doctrine in question constitutes a proviso to the general rule. Some of the rationale behind the existence of this proviso was elicited in the preparatory work conducted by the International Law Commission on the Law of Treaties. In his Second Report on the Law of Treaties, the Special Rapporteur, Sir Humphrey Waldock, introduced a proviso to the fundamental circumstances rule in favour of boundary treaties.[170] By and large there was general agreement among members of the Commission regarding the inclusion of such a proviso.[171] 'Clearly', stated Jiménez de Aréchaga, the Chairman of the Commission at its fifteenth session, 'territorial rights established by a treaty would not be affected by the doctrine of a change in circumstances, because the parties would have no further interest in securing the termination of a treaty already executed'.[172] At the session in January 1966 the member from Austria, Verdross, pointed out that the proviso to the *rebus sic stantibus* doctrine 'was not a special rule, but simply the application of a more general rule to the effect that the *clausula rebus sic stantibus* was not applic-

[168] *Yearbook of the International Law Commission*, 1972, vol. 2, p. 54. See below in the context of the doctrine of *rebus sic stantibus*.

[169] *Report of the Fifty-third Conference (1968)* (London, 1969), p. 589, at p. 598; Commentary, p. 603. But cf. below, p. 81. See also ILA Handbook, *The Effect of Independence on Treaties* (London, 1965), pp. 352–5.

[170] *Yearbook of the International Law Commission*, 1963, vol. 2, pp. 79–85.

[171] See, generally, ibid., vol. 1, pp. 136–63. For views of State governments, see ibid. 1966, vol. 2, pp. 39–42.

[172] Ibid. 1963, vol. 1, p. 150. See also his remarks, ibid. 1966, vol. 1, pp. 83–4. For commentary on this provision, see Lissitzyn, 'Treaties and Changed Circumstances', *American Journal of International Law*, 61 (1967), p. 895.

able to a treaty which had already been fully executed, for reliance on that clause always presupposed the continued existence of obligations flowing from the treaty'.[173] Where a treaty, he added, had been fully executed it ceased to produce any obligation and the clause was inoperative.[173] However, Waldock reminded members of the Commission that the reason for the exclusion of boundary treaties from the *rebus sic stantibus* rule was not that the provisions of those treaties were executed provisions but that treaties of that type were intended to create a stable position.[174] 'It would', he said, 'be inconsistent with the very nature of those treaties to make them subject to the *rebus sic stantibus* rule'.[175] In its definitive form as Article 62, paragraph 2(a), of the Vienna Convention on the Law of Treaties[176] the rule reads:

> A fundamental change of circumstances may not be invoked as a ground for terminating or withdrawing from a treaty:
> (a) If the treaty establishes a boundary. . . .

Furthermore, the question of *rebus sic stantibus* and boundary treaties can be seen in the light of the general rule against the unilateral abrogation of boundary treaties. The views expressed in the preceding paragraphs in respect of the proviso to the *rebus sic stantibus* principle are cognate with and constitute part of the rationale for the general rule against the unilateral abrogation of boundary treaties. Inasmuch as a boundary agreement invests permanent rights in favour of either Party regarding the territorial limits of two (or more) States, it no longer remains within the province of any one State to attempt to deprive the other of the rights vested lawfully in that State. It is the case that States view matters of territory and frontiers with considerable care and caution, and hence if the law were to support a State in attempts at unilateral denunciation of a valid frontier, on whatever grounds, it would create uncertainty and instability in the international community. It is not inconceivable that States dissatisfied with the allocation of territory would be tempted to initiate new contestations over territory or to challenge existing frontier regimes. Clearly the law cannot, and does not, give countenance to such claims and supports the position that a valid boundary treaty is conclusive of all relevant questions and the alignment established cannot be modified or denounced without agreement, express or otherwise, with the coterminous State. Emphasis here is on the word 'valid', and thus a boundary

[173] *Yearbook of the International Law Commission*, 1966, vol. 1, part 1, p. 76.

[174] Ibid., p. 86. See below, in reference to war, boundary treaties and the views of Sir Cecil Hurst, p. 92.

[175] Ibid. See also the observations of Mr De Luna, Member, Sixth Committee, General Assembly, in *General Assembly Official Records*, 18th Session, 792nd meeting, p. 56, paragraph 10 (1963).

[176] UN Document A/CONF.39/27. References to the Convention are made strictly on the basis of the fact that it constitutes evidence of the accepted law on treaties in the international community. Apart from the fact that Article 4 of the Convention precludes retroactive application, Iraq has neither signed nor ratified and Iran, who has signed, has failed to ratify the Convention.

treaty which has never been accepted as valid does not fall within the ambit of this rule.

Considerations of this nature were predicated in draft Article 17, paragraph 4, in the Second Report on the Law of Treaties by Sir Humphrey Waldock, the Special Rapporteur.[177] Draft Article 17 dealt with the question of the denunciation and termination of treaties which contained no provisions regarding their duration or termination. While it enumerated four kinds of treaties which could in certain specified circumstances be denounced, it provided in paragraph 4:

A treaty shall continue in force indefinitely with respect to each party where the treaty:

(a) is one establishing a boundary between two States, or effecting a cession of territory or a grant of rights in or over territory.

In his commentary Waldock explained that paragraph 4, which listed five types of treaty,[178] was based on the premiss that 'the intention of the parties must be presumed to be to establish a permanent treaty regime, in the sense of a regime which will continue indefinitely until revised or terminated by subsequent agreement'.[179] The draft article was presented as Article 53 to the Committee of the Whole at the Vienna Conference in 1968, by which time the reference to frontier agreements had been deleted and the article had undergone substantial changes.[180] In the preparatory meetings of the Committee of the Whole, several amendments to Article

[177] *Yearbook of the International Law Commission*, 1963, vol. 2, p. 64. Cf. draft Article 4, Fitzmaurice, 2nd Report (1957), ibid. 1957, vol. 2, pp. 22–3, 38–9, which was predicated on the rule that 'silence means, in principle, no termination except by general consent': p. 38; and Harvard draft Article 34 which is based on similar premisses, *American Journal of International Law*, 29 (1935), Supplement, pp. 1173–83. For a general review of unilateral denunciation of treaties see McNair, *The Law of Treaties* (1961), pp. 493–505, 539–71, especially pp. 494, 531–3 (on executed territorial treaties); Brierly, *The Law of Nations* (6th edn., 1963), pp. 327–40; Nahlik, 'The Grounds of Invalidity and Termination of Treaties', *American Journal of International Law*, 65 (1971), p. 736 at pp. 746–51; Sinha, *Unilateral Denunciation of Treaty Because of Prior Violations of Obligations by Other Party* (The Hague, 1966); Widdows, 'The Unilateral Denunciation of Treaties containing no Denunciation Clause', this *Year Book*, 53 (1982), p. 83, especially p. 109. Also see Indian Memorial, *ICJ Pleadings*, 1973, *Appeal Relating to the Jurisdiction of the ICAO Council*, pp. 38–44.

[178] Those establishing a special international regime for a particular area, territory, river, waterway or airspace; a treaty of peace, disarmament or maintenance of peace; one effecting a final settlement of an international dispute; a general multilateral treaty providing for the codification or development of international law. Cf. the dictum of the Swiss Federal Court in *Luzerne* v. *Aargau* (1882), wherein the Court observed that a State servitude may be annulled unilaterally under certain circumstances, including *rebus sic stantibus*: Schindler, loc. cit. above (p. 76 n. 155), pp. 164–5; but see below, p. 84 n. 186 for views on the general principle.

[179] *Yearbook of the International Law Commission*, 1963, vol. 2, p. 69. See also draft Article 28: unless the treaty provides otherwise the unilateral termination of a treaty shall not affect the validity of any act performed or of any right acquired under the provisions of the treaty prior to termination. See Minutes of the ILC, ibid., vol. 1, pp. 234–6, especially Mr Lachs who emphasized the importance of permanent rights: p. 235.

[180] Draft Article 17 was criticized by members on the basis, *inter alia*, that it was more liberal in terms of the right to denounce or withdraw from treaties than was generally admitted under customary law, particularly the *pacta sunt servanda* rule: see Minutes of the ILC, ibid., vol. 1, pp. 99–107 and pp. 239–41. See also Commentary to draft Article 39 in the Report of the Commission to the General Assembly, 1963, in ibid., vol. 2, pp. 200–2.

53 were tabled.[181] The main thrust of these amendments was to incorporate reference to the nature and character of the treaty in the provision, a reference which the International Law Commission had decided to exclude from its draft, as one of two grounds on the basis of which alone a State could denounce or withdraw from the treaty. From the records of the meetings of the Committee it is clear that certain members were particularly inclined in favour of the stability of boundary treaties.[182] Accordingly, Article 53 was redrafted and the text adopted by the Committee of the Whole and the Plenary Meeting emerged as the definitive Article 56 of the Vienna Convention.[183] It provided:

> 1. A treaty which contains no provision regarding its termination and which does not provide for denunciation or withdrawal is not subject to denunciation or withdrawal unless:
>
> . . . (b) a right of denunciation or withdrawal may be implied by the nature of the treaty . . .

The problem of unilateral abrogation of boundary treaties was also raised and commented upon by the Commission in its preparatory work on the law of State succession to treaties. In his first report as Special Rapporteur, Sir Francis Vallat observed that there was a 'practical need' to make an exception to the clean-slate principle to deal with boundary and territorial regimes. Otherwise, he said, in every case of succession, States would have a unilateral right to repudiate existing boundaries and territorial rights and obligations created by treaty. He wrote:

> The disturbance to international relations that might follow from such a right of unilateral repudiation is not one that could be lightly contemplated . . . Indeed, the disturbance of existing boundaries is much more likely to create chaos than their maintenance.[184]

In *Costa Rica* v. *Nicaragua*[185] the Central American Court of Justice was seised of the rights of Costa Rica regarding navigation and other facilities over the San Juan River which she alleged had been prejudiced owing to

[181] See Reports of the Committee of the Whole: (A/CONF.39/14) in *United Nations Conference on the Law of Treaties, Official Records, 1st and 2nd sessions*, pp. 177–8.

[182] See observations of Messrs Alvarado (Peru); Martinez Caro (Spain); Kovalev (USSR); Makarewicz (Poland); Myslil (Czechoslovakia); and cf. Alvarez Tabio (Cuba): 59th Meeting, May 1968, ibid., 1st session (A/CONF.39/11), pp. 336–43.

[183] See also draft Article 39 of 1963 which referred, *inter alia*, to the 'character of the treaty': ibid., p. 200. For comments by Governments on draft Article 39, see *Yearbook of the International Law Commission*, 1966, vol. 2, pp. 25–7. Although draft Article 53 of 1966 did not refer to either the nature or character of the treaty in question, the commentary observed: 'Treaties of peace and treaties fixing a territorial boundary are examples of such treaties': ibid. 1966, vol. 2, p. 250. Cf. Briggs, who refers to the 'nature' and 'character' of perpetual treaties as 'a pseudo-scientific notion which refers not to the juridical nature of treaties but to their content and political purpose': 'Unilateral Denunciation of Treaties: The Vienna Convention and the International Court of Justice', *American Journal of International Law*, 68 (1974), p. 51 at p. 64. See Widdows, loc. cit. above (p. 82 n. 177), p. 93.

[184] *Yearbook of the International Law Commission*, 1974, vol. 2, part 1, p. 1 at p. 83. See also pp. 73–83; and Waldock Report, ibid. 1968, vol. 2, pp. 92–3, and ibid. 1972, vol. 2, pp. 44–59.

[185] *American Journal of International Law*, 11 (1917), p. 181.

the conclusion of the US–Nicaraguan Treaty of August 1914. In a passage *obiter*, the Court observed that

> the Cañas–Jerez Treaty (the Treaty of Limits) has preserved its full obligatory force and effect down to the present day, as well by virtue of the categorical holdings in the Cleveland Award [of March 1888] . . . as by virtue of the permanent character of its stipulations. Wherefore, in the absence of mutual consent by the contracting Parties, the treaty cannot be lawfully denounced or held to be dead, nor can the agreements therein stipulated be avoided . . .[186]

The question of the alleged 'lapse' or 'cancellation' of the Treaty of 1859 between Britain and Guatemala has some bearing on the matter. In Article 1 of the Treaty, Guatemala effectively acknowledged British sovereignty over, and ceded large tracts of land to, the British settlement and possessions in the Bay of Honduras, the areas of which were also defined in the said article. In Article 7 both parties 'conjointly' agreed to use their 'best efforts' to establish a line of communication between the capital of Guatemala and 'the fittest place on the Atlantic'. An agreement was concluded in August 1863 with a view to clarifying the obligations of the parties relative to Article 7; but owing to the failure of ratification of the treaty Britain declared herself released from the obligations imposed by Article 7 of the 1859 Treaty. After over fifty years of fruitless negotiations, Guatemala indicated in September 1939 that the 1859 treaty had lapsed in view of Britain's failure to build the line of communication; that therefore the 'cession' of territory to Great Britain was invalid and that the title to the territory had accordingly reverted to Guatemala.[187] Mr L. Anderson, writing on behalf of the Government of Guatemala, recognized the problem of declaring the treaty lapsed or terminated, for he wrote that the treaty had already been executed by way of demarcation of the ceded territory which was in the possession of Great Britain.[188]

The Government of the US had occasion to comment upon the question under consideration in the context of the frontier dispute between Peru and Ecuador.[189] In 1960, the latter unilaterally denounced the frontier agreement of 1942, also known as the Rio Protocol, on grounds of invalidity.

[186] *American Journal of International Law*, 11 (1917), p. 194. In *Luzerne* v. *Aargau*, the Swiss Federal Council observed that treaties which created 'concrete juridical relations' could not be unilaterally denounced: 'such treaties remain binding for both parties as long as no special juridical reason for their annulment has arisen': as cited in Schindler, loc. cit. above (p. 76 n. 155), p. 164.

[187] For a review of the dispute see Anderson, *The Belize Question: Continuation of White Book: Controversy between Guatemala and Great Britain relative to the Convention of 1859 on Territorial Matters* (Ministry for Foreign Affairs, Guatemala, 1940); Mendoza, *Britain and her Treaties on Belize . . .* (Ministry for Foreign Affairs, Guatemala, 1946); Bloomfield, *The British Honduras–Guatemala Dispute* (Toronto, 1953).

[188] Anderson, op. cit. (previous note), pp. 57–8. For views similar to these, see Bloomfield, op. cit. (previous note), pp. 116–19. Of course, Britain does not concede that the treaty was one of cession, but regards it as an acknowledgement by Guatemala of the validity of Britain's existing title.

[189] Whiteman, *Digest of International Law*, vol. 3 (1964), pp. 676–80.

The US, one of the four guarantor States, advised Ecuador against such a course of action and in a telegram to her Government observed:

It is a basic principle of international law that the unilateral will of one of the Parties is not sufficient to invalidate a boundary treaty nor to liberate it from the obligations imposed therein. Only mutual agreement by both Parties can modify its provisions or attribute competence to an international tribunal to judge questions which may arise regarding such an instrument.[190]

On 8 December 1941 China declared war on Japan and announced the (unilateral) abrogation of the Treaty of Shimonoseki of 1895 which had ceded Formosa (Taiwan) and the Pescadores to Japan. In a debate on the status of Formosa in the House of Lords of the British Parliament, it was queried whether the islands had, in view of the abrogation, reverted in principle to China. The Joint Parliamentary Under-Secretary of State for Foreign Affairs, the Marquis of Lansdowne, replied:

According to international law, a State cannot merely by unilateral declaration regain rights of sovereignty which it has formally ceded by treaty. China, therefore, could not and did not regain sovereignty over those territories by the unilateral denunciation of this treaty in 1941.[191]

The conclusions that may be drawn are clear. The unilateral abrogation of the Treaty of 1937 was not a valid course of action on the part of the Government of Iran and the arguments advanced in support of the abrogation of the boundary treaty are legally not persuasive. Consequently, the abrogation did not affect the boundary regime: the alignment in the Shatt continued to run along the left bank save at the ports of Mohammara and Abadan where it ran in the middle of the river. The territorial and boundary-related rights and obligations of both Iran and Iraq continued to exist in law and to bind the States.

3. *General conclusions*

The conclusions which may be drawn regarding the specific issues of the boundary dispute are that before 1975, the boundary line in the Shatt sector was formed by the left bank boundary, except for the sections opposite Mohammara and Abadan which were divided along the median

[190] Ibid., p. 679. See also, in reference to the Afghan abrogation of the 1893 boundary treaty, p. 68 above; and the statement of the British Government to the Secretary-General of the UN, 26 February 1965: *Materials on Succession of States* (UN Legislative Series, ST/LEG/SER.B/14), pp. 186–7. See Wright in reference to the continuity of the ceasefire lines (acting as international boundaries) upon the termination of the relevant treaty: 'The Termination and Suspension of Treaties', *American Journal of International Law*, 61 (1967), p. 1000 at p. 1002.

[191] Hansard, *House of Lords Debates*, vol. 212, cols. 497–9, at col. 497 (13 November 1958); E. Lauterpacht, 'The Contemporary Practice of the United Kingdom in the Field of International Law: Survey and Comment, VII' (1958), in *International and Comparative Law Quarterly*, 8 (1959), p. 193. See also the British statement of 13 November 1962 in the seventeenth session of the Fourth Committee of the General Assembly protesting against Venezuela's unilateral decision to regard the boundary arbitral award of 1899 (between the latter and British Guiana) as null and void: E. Lauterpacht, *The Contemporary Practice of the United Kingdom in the Field of International Law—1962 II*, pp. 161–75 at p. 163, especially p. 173.

line and *thalweg* respectively. Both parties were bound to observe this frontier which existed on the basis of a series of treaties and protocols, beginning with the Treaty of 1847, and ending with the Treaty of 1937. There was in principle and in strict legal terms no question or dispute regarding a median or *thalweg* boundary: Iran had claimed a midline/*thalweg* alignment but had over the years settled for a left bank boundary. Her representations in favour of a median line division were motivated by political considerations and had little, if any, support in law.[192] Similarly, the abrogation of the Treaty of 1937 was an act carried out primarily for political purposes, and had no legal consequences.

Nevertheless, it remains a prerogative of a sovereign State to *request* (as opposed to demand) coterminous States to consider the revision of an alignment which may appear to be less than satisfactory to herself, or to all or any one of them. Boundaries may not be altered *unilaterally*: but there is no sanction against mutual revision. It follows therefore that it was perfectly lawful for Iran to have approached Iraq for a revision of the boundary in the Shatt sector, not on the basis of legal obligation, but on political expediency, goodwill and/or reciprocity.[192] At the same time, it was open to Iraq to accept or reject the overtures made by Iran; Iraq's insistence on the left bank boundary was, under the circumstances, not invalid. In the event, however, Iraq accepted a modification in the frontier and thereby changed the status of the waters of the Shatt. The following section attempts to analyse the post-1975 status of the boundary regime.

(b) *The Legal Regime of the Boundary after 1975*

The location of the boundary in the Shatt region changed radically after the conclusion of the Algiers Protocol and Baghdad Treaty of 1975. Article 2 stated clearly that the boundary ran along the *thalweg*, 'or the median line of the main navigable channel at the lowest navigable level', and accordingly there were no legal, as opposed to technical, problems in appreciating either the location or status of the alignment between the two States thereafter. Legal problems, however, were created in September 1980 when the Government of Iraq abrogated the treaty on the basis of arguments which constituted a mix of legal and political considerations. One of these arguments was that the Shatt and the adjacent province of Ahwaz in Iran were in fact Iraqi territories, and that the Ottoman Empire had relinquished its sovereignty over them and ceded them to Iran.[193] It was also contended that the majority of the inhabitants of Ahwaz were Arabs who had dominated the area ever since Islam had spread in the Mesopotamian region.[194]

[192] Cf. the observations made in the concluding section of this work, below, pp. 102 ff.

[193] Ismael, op. cit. above (p. 60 n. 69), p. 26; Amin, loc. cit. above (p. 60 n. 70), p. 168.

[194] Ismael, op. cit. above (p. 60 n. 69), p. 26. See also *A Review of the Imposed War*, op. cit. above (p. 61 n. 80), pp. xvii–xviii, xx, 5, 77, 92–120; Akhtar, 'The Iraqi–Iranian Dispute over the Shatt-al-Arab', *Pakistan Horizon*, 22 (1969), p. 213 at pp. 216, 217–18.

Another argument put forward by Iraq in support of her abrogation was that Iran had herself 'terminated' the agreement 'by word and deed' prior to Iraq's more formal abrogation. The line of reasoning here was that Iran had secured the *thalweg* boundary in the Shatt, a cession of considerable importance to her, by agreeing to desist from fomenting, provoking or aiding the Kurdish rebellion in Iraq. It was contended that Iran's guarantee regarding the Kurdish insurgency was in the nature of a *quid pro quo* in respect of the cession of the *thalweg* line extended by Iraq. The latter argued that Iran had transgressed this obligation and provided Kurdish rebels with the facility of employing parts of Iranian territory as bases for operations against the national integrity and internal security of Iraq.[195] It was alleged that Iran's leaders were trying to export the Iranian revolution to Iraq. Article 3 of the Baghdad Treaty, it may be noted, provides that the parties 'undertake to exercise strict and effective permanent control over the frontier in order to put an end to any infiltration of a subversive nature from any source on the basis of and in accordance with the provision of the Protocol [and annex] concerning frontier security . . .'. Iraq concluded that 'The elements of the 1975 agreement constituted an indivisible whole, a violation of one aspect rendered the entire treaty null and void'.[196]

These representations may be analysed on two levels. First, it is true that the inhabitants of the region are Arabs, and there is evidence to support the claim that the Shatt and adjacent territories had, at a certain epoch in history, been under the control of the Ottoman Empire. None the less, as the Government of Iraq has itself admitted, the lands were ceded to Persia, and a latter-day examination of the validity or otherwise of a transfer of title to territory which (a) took place over a century ago and (b) was accepted as a valid transfer by the contracting parties at that time, is precluded in principle. The point, which has been explained and emphasized in a preceding section of this work,[197] is that the law does not in principle look favourably upon a re-examination of well-settled incidents of territorial attribution and boundary allocation; and it will not hence be necessary here to analyse the legal implications of the Iraqi representations in greater detail. It may, at any rate, be added that the question of ethnicity of the disputed regions is largely irrelevant to the status of both the territorial and boundary regimes in view of the clear provisions of the Treaties of 1847, 1913–14 and 1937 which attributed the territories on

[195] See Iraqi Letters to President, Security Council, 21 May 1980: A/35/268; 20 June 1980: S/14020; 22 and 24 September 1980: S/14191, S/1492; 25 November 1980 (with Annexes): S/14272; *The Iraqi–Iranian Dispute: Facts and Allegations* (Ministry of Foreign Affairs, Iraq, 1981), p. 4; Iraqi Ministry of Foreign Affairs to Iranian Embassy, 17 September 1980 (Annex): S/14272 and letter of 25 November 1980: S/14272. Cf. Iranian claims of Iraqi subversion: Letters to President, Security Council: 23 July 1980, S/14070; 1 October 1980: S/14206 and 10 November 1980 (with Annex: Iranian Ministry of Foreign Affairs to Government of Iraq): S/14249: *Yearbook of the United Nations*, 34 (1980), pp. 318–19. See generally, Al-Mukhtar, 'The Iraqi Position', in Dessouki (ed.), *The Iraq–Iran War: Issues of Conflict and Prospects for Settlement* (Princeton, 1981), p. 16.

[196] Ismael, op. cit. above (p. 60 n. 69), p. 26.

[197] Above, pp. 67, 79–86.

the left bank of the Shatt to exclusive Persian control and jurisdiction. Similarly, although Iraq's argument to the effect that the Shatt has historically been Iraqi territory is, in principle, correct, her claim has to be seen in light of the fact that over a period of more than half a century, Iraq and her predecessors had ceded progressively greater parts of, and control over, the river to Iran. In 1913–14 she ceded half the breadth of the river opposite Mohammara, and a cession of a similar nature was made in respect of Abadan in 1937. Ultimately, the river was divided along the *thalweg* in 1975. The Baghdad Treaty of 1975, which constitutes, in fact, the latest development in a history of receding Iraqi control over the Shatt, cannot be adjudged as invalid merely on the ground that it establishes the *thalweg* and not the left bank as boundary. Iraq, as the lawful sovereign of the river, had, in principle, the legal right to dispose of any degree of territorial or jurisdictional control over the river to Iran, the party who was ready and willing to accept such transfer of control and title. The previous status of the river, not unlike the earlier status of the adjacent Arab-inhabited regions, cannot by itself invalidate or vitiate the Baghdad Treaty; it became, in fact, an irrelevance to the general question of the status and location of the boundary once the Baghdad Treaty of 1975 had been concluded.[198]

The question which has to be surveyed next is whether Iraq was legally justified in abrogating the treaty, the provisions of which had not been observed and respected by Iran. The burden of Iraq's grievance is that the abrogation of the treaty had only the appearance of being unilateral, and that the treaty was effectively a dead letter at the time of its abrogation by the Government of Iraq in September 1980. Iran was obliged not to aid the Kurdish insurgency in Iraq, a matter of central importance to her, and having transgressed Article 3 had forfeited the right to expect Iraq to continue to observe those provisions which placed obligations upon her. The Baghdad Treaty of 1975 had, as it were, ceased to be the basis on which the boundary regime between the two States rested.

On the face of it, there appears to be some truth in Iraq's general representations. For one thing, it is true that Article 3 did have the character of *quid pro quo*, in the absence of which it is doubtful whether Iraq would have agreed to a *thalweg* boundary. The Kurdish revolt had proved to be a source of considerable disquiet in Iraq and the costs of mounting counter-insurgency operations, in terms of men and *matériel*, were high.[199] She had hoped to gain peace by destroying the insurgents' sources of supply and succour, and with a view to securing this objective, had agreed to meet one of Iran's most valued claims: a *thalweg* boundary in the Shatt. The latter agreed to cease aiding the insurgency and the outcome was seen in Article 2, which provided for a *thalweg* boundary, and Article 3, which contained

198 See below, regarding recognition, pp. 90 ff.

199 Al-Mukhtar, loc. cit. above (p. 87 n. 195), p. 16; Pipes, loc. cit. above (p. 61 n. 77), p. 20; Hunseler, 'The Historical Antecedents of the Shatt al Arab Dispute', in El-Azhary (ed.), *The Iran–Iraq War* (1984), pp. 18–19.

a general obligation on both parties to desist from subversive activities against each other.[200]

In any case, the importance which the two parties ascribed to these articles is reflected in Article 4 of the treaty, which stated:

> The High Contracting Parties confirm that the provisions of the three Protocols and the Annexes thereto,[201] referred to in Articles 1, 2 and 3 above and attached to this Treaty as an integral part thereof shall be final and permanent. They shall not be infringed under any circumstances and shall constitute the indivisible elements of an overall settlement. Accordingly, a breach of any of the components of this overall settlement shall clearly be incompatible with the spirit of the Algiers agreement.

The Algiers Declaration, or Joint Communiqué, of 6 March 1975, provides similar clues. Paragraph 3 of the Communiqué provides that the two contracting parties have decided to delimit their fluvial frontiers according to the *thalweg* line, and accordingly the parties will, *inter alia*, commit themselves to exercising a strict and effective control over their common boundaries with a view to putting a definitive end to all acts of infiltration of a subversive character no matter from where they originate. The two parties also agreed in the same paragraph to consider the arrangements referred to as integral elements of a comprehensive solution. 'Hence', the Communiqué stated, 'any infringement of any of their components shall naturally be contrary to the spirit of the Algiers agreement'.

It is clear, therefore, that there is a strong link between Articles 2 and 3 and that they together constitute the core of the arrangements embodied in the Baghdad Treaty of 1975. It may be argued, therefore, that infringement of the obligation 'to put an end to any infiltration of a subversive nature from any source' destroyed the basis of the understanding on which Iraq had agreed to a *thalweg* line in the Shatt. On this view of the matter, one aspect of the problem can be studied by reference to a question of fact, viz. whether Iran did in fact give aid to the Kurdish insurgents or carry out any other acts which constituted infiltration of a subversive nature. If, on the one hand, evidence cannot be adduced to support the claim that Iran gave aid to the Kurdish insurgency, it would be clear that Iraq's accusations were unfounded and her principal argument in the case for abrogation would fail. If, on the other hand, it can be established that Iran had indeed infringed Article 3, it will have to be seen whether such infringement had any legal effects upon the boundary regime and, if so, what these legal effects are.

To begin with, the law as it stands is that a material breach of a bilateral treaty invests the other State with a right either to terminate or to suspend

[200] Clearly, the obligation to desist from subversive activity had to be a mutual one.

[201] The three protocols attached to the Baghdad Treaty were: the Protocol concerning the Delimitation of the River Frontier between Iran and Iraq; the Protocol concerning the Re-demarcation of the Land Frontier between Iran and Iraq; and the Protocol concerning Security on the Frontier between Iran and Iraq.

the agreement in whole or in part.[202] Article 60 of the Vienna Convention, which may be perceived as being declaratory of the law on the matter, defines, in paragraph 3, a material breach as consisting, *inter alia*, of 'the violation of a provision essential to the accomplishment of the object or purpose of the treaty'. There can be little doubt that Articles 1, 2 and 3 of the Baghdad Treaty fell within this class. The proposition, however, that Iraq therefore has the right to terminate the treaty has, on this view of the matter, to be seen in the light of the following considerations.

First, reference may be made to the text of Article 4. It provides, *inter alia*, that 'a breach of any of the components of this overall settlement shall clearly be incompatible with the spirit of the Algiers Agreement'. However, neither Article 4 nor the Algiers Agreement defines precisely the meaning of the 'spirit' of this agreement. While it is clear that it is an indirect reference to the *quid pro quo* character of the treaty, it is equally clear that the phrase is inconclusive and vague in substance. The important point is that it fails to state the precise legal position of the parties in the event of a breach of any of the 'components' of the Baghdad Treaty, i.e. whether the Baghdad Treaty will be regarded as terminated *ipso facto*, or whether the innocent party will thereafter have, at its option, the right either to terminate or to suspend the treaty in whole or in part. Moreover, it is clear that the parties contemplated the possibility of infringement of the said articles but were content to leave the situation unclarified. In view of the importance of these legal alternatives to both States, their omission suggests that at the time of the negotiations both Iraq and Iran had agreed not to adopt them in Article 4. In other words, the failure, on the one hand, to state the precise legal position of the parties and the boundary regime in the event of infringement, and the inclusion, on the other, of a reference to the 'spirit of the Algiers Agreement' indicates that the parties did not admit the right of unilateral abrogation of the Baghdad Treaty: *expressio unius est exclusio alterius*.

This view, secondly, is supported by the fact that Article 5 provides:

> In keeping with the inviolability of the frontiers of the two States and strict respect for their territorial integrity, the High Contracting Parties confirm that the course of their land and river frontiers shall be inviolable, permanent and final.

This Article, importantly, appears immediately after Article 4 which, it is submitted, has the effect of entrenching Articles 1, 2 and 3 in the Baghdad Treaty. The clear reference to permanence and finality of the land and river

[202] McNair, *The Law of Treaties* (1961), pp. 539–71; Sinha, *Unilateral Denunciation of Treaty Because of Prior Violations of Obligations by Other Party* (The Hague, 1966); Nahlik, 'The Grounds of Invalidity and Termination of Treaties', *American Journal of International Law*, 65 (1971), p. 736; draft Article 20, 2nd Waldock Report, 1963, *Yearbook of the International Law Commission*, 1963, vol. 2, pp. 72–7; Harvard draft Article 27 on the Law of Treaties, *American Journal of International Law*, 29 (1935), Supplement, pp. 1077–96; Garner and Jobst, 'The Unilateral Denunciation of Treaties by one Party because of Alleged Non-Performance by Another Party or Parties', ibid., 29 (1935), p. 569, in reference mainly to the German attempts to terminate her obligations under Part V of the Treaty of Versailles. Cf. Brierly, *The Law of Nations* (6th edn., 1963), pp. 327–8.

frontiers can in one sense be regarded as clarification of the stipulations contained in Article 4, viz. that nothing in Article 4 should be interpreted as having the effect of rendering the boundary void or voidable for any reason whatever.

Third, Article 6 (1) provides that in 'the event of a dispute regarding the interpretation or implementation of this Treaty, the three Protocols or the annexes thereto, any solution to such a dispute shall strictly respect the *course* of the Iranian–Iraqi frontier . . . and shall take into account the need to maintain security on the Iranian–Iraqi frontier in accordance with article 3 . . .'.[203] Hence, it is clear that the parties can, in an issue involving the interpretation or implementation of the Baghdad agreements, dispute or question only the *location* of the frontier, viz. the exact or technical determination of the median line in the *thalweg*, and cannot question the legal status of the regime. In other words, they are precluded from raising any issue which involves questions of the fundamental validity of the general boundary regime. Clearly, Iraq's abrogation has provoked a series of legal problems which relate essentially to the latter position. Furthermore, Article 6 goes on to set out the procedure which the parties are required to adopt in the event of a failure of bilateral negotiations, that is, the processes of mediation (Article 6 (3)) and of arbitration (Article 6 (4), (5) and (6)). Evidently, the parties attached great importance to the resolution of the more technical problems regarding the location of the line in the *thalweg* and were antipathetic to leaving these issues unresolved. Accordingly, it appears inconceivable that the parties would agree to contemplate the possibility of unilateral abrogation of the treaty, an abrogation which would serve to heighten rather than reduce the legal and political complications and uncertainty following infringements of Articles 1, 2 or 3.

Finally, and this point is of some significance, reference may be made to that section of this analysis which examined the matter of the unilateral abrogation of boundaries, and to the conclusions drawn therefrom.[204] The function of a boundary treaty is to define with relative precision the territorial limits within which the contracting Parties may exercise their sovereign powers of control and jurisdiction, and once this has been done, the States acquire real and permanent territorial rights independent, to some extent and in certain circumstances, of the treaty in question. Thus Article 70 of the Vienna Convention provides that in the absence of an agreement to the contrary, the termination of a treaty 'does not affect any right, obligation or legal situation of the parties created through the execution of the treaty prior to its termination'.[205] Furthermore, the International Law Commission, in its Commentary to draft Article 57, which subsequently appeared as the definitive Article 60 of the Vienna Convention, cautioned against the termination or suspension of a treaty

[203] Emphasis added.

[204] Above, pp. 79–85.

[205] Also see Introductory Note to Chapter 5 in *Restatement of the Law, Foreign Relations Law of the United States* (2nd edition, American Law Institute, St Paul, 1965), p. 476.

on the basis of mere allegations of a material breach of the provisions thereof.[206] This, in conjunction with Article 65, would require a State to exercise extreme restraint before deciding to abrogate a treaty.

The conclusion, therefore, is that notwithstanding Iran's alleged actions in promoting the Kurdish insurgency in Iraq, the latter had, in view of all the circumstances of the case, no right to abrogate the Baghdad Treaty. It follows that the boundary in the Shatt continued in law to run along the *thalweg*.

(c) *War and the Baghdad Treaty of 1975*

The hostilities which broke out between Iran and Iraq in September 1980 are still continuing and have succeeded in adding a new dimension to the boundary problem. While the factual political situation is easy to describe, the legal position is, relatively speaking, more complex and the material question here is whether the war has in law affected the status of the territory in the borderlands or the location of the 1975 line. This question can be approached in two forms: first, whether the Iran–Iraq war has had in principle any effect or effects on the Baghdad Treaty; and secondly, whether the war has invested either of the belligerents with the right to make changes in and modifications to the frontier. Both levels of investigation, however, are interrelated and the division is primarily one of convenience.

The first issue can be understood in light of the question whether the outbreak of hostilities between States abrogates bilateral treaties existing between them. The earlier view, held by jurists and States alike, was that all treaties were *ipso facto* abrogated upon the occurrence of war between States.[207] The consensus of opinion today is more sophisticated. It is generally agreed that the universal abrogation of treaties between belligerents has no place either in the law or in the practice of States. The con-

[206] *Yearbook of the International Law Commission*, 1966, vol. 2, pp. 254–5. Articles 65 and 66 of the Convention provide 'procedural safeguards against the possibility that the nullity, termination or suspension of the operation of a treaty may be arbitrarily asserted as a mere pretext for getting rid of an inconvenient obligation': Commentary to draft Article 62 in ibid., p. 262. See also draft Articles 18–20 of the Second Report by Fitzmaurice wherein he leaned heavily in favour of a cautious approach to the question of termination of treaties on the grounds of a fundamental breach: ibid., 1957, vol. 2, pp. 52–6; and Harvard draft Article 27, and commentary, loc. cit. (p. 90 n. 202), pp. 1077, 1089, 1091–2.

[207] For commentaries on the law see McNair, *The Law of Treaties* (1961), pp. 695–728; and 'The Functions and Differing Legal Character of Treaties', this *Year Book*, 11 (1930), pp. 100, 102–5; Rank, 'Modern War and the Validity of Treaties', *Cornell Law Quarterly*, 38 (1952–3), pp. 321–55; O'Connell, *International Law* (2nd edn., 1970), vol. 1, pp. 268–71; La Pradelle, 'The Effect of War on Private Treaties', *International Law Quarterly*, 2 (1948), p. 555; Hurst, 'The Effect of War on Treaties', this *Year Book*, 2 (1921–2), pp. 37–47; Harvard draft Article 35, *American Journal of International Law*, 29 (1935), Supplement, pp. 1183–1204; Verzijl, *International Law in Historical Perspective*, vol. 6 (1973), pp. 371–91; Hackworth, *Digest of International Law*, vol. 5 (1943), pp. 377–90; Whiteman, *A Digest of International Law*, vol. 14 (1970), pp. 490–510; Delbruck, 'Effect of War on Treaties', in Bernhardt (ed.), *Encyclopaedia of Public International Law*, vol. 4 (1982), pp. 310–15; Fitzmaurice, 'The Contribution of the Institute of International Law to the Development of International Law', *Recueil des cours*, 138 (1973–I), pp. 235–6.

tinuation or abrogation of treaties depends not only upon the intention of the contracting States, but upon the nature and content of the treaties as well. The point here is that boundary agreements are recognized as belonging to that category of treaties which are not annulled upon the occurrence of war between two or more States.[208] Although a frontier agreement is deemed to be 'suspended' in certain respects for the duration of the war,[209] it remains valid, and the frontier continues to mark the limits of true sovereignty until changed by a peace or other treaty. While the importance of the continuation in law of boundaries and boundary treaties during hostilities has been acknowledged by many writers including Phillimore and Vattel,[210] there is a singular lack of substantial international jurisprudence relating to the question of the effect of war on boundary or territorial treaties. However, in the *Jaworzina* advisory opinion,[211] the Permanent Court remarked *obiter* that when, as a result of the First World War and the dissolution of the Austro-Hungarian Empire, Poland and Czechoslovakia were re-established as independent States, their frontiers were, generally speaking, indicated by historical and ethnological factors which 'pointed naturally' to the former frontier between Galacia and Hungary. 'With the exception', it said, 'of certain disputed sectors . . . this frontier seems, indeed, to have been adopted by the two States from the very outset as being the natural outcome of these circumstances'.[212]

Similarly, in the *North Atlantic Coast Fisheries* arbitration,[213] Britain argued that whatever rights and liberties the United States enjoyed by virtue of the Treaty of 1783 in respect of fisheries had been abrogated by the occurrence of the war of 1812.[214] The Court failed to give any detailed comments on the matter but noted that:

> International law in its modern development recognises that a great number of Treaty obligations are not annulled by war, but at most suspended by it.[215]

The Supreme Court of the United States has had occasion to review the question of the effect of war on treaties. In *Society for the Propagation of the Gospel* v. *New Haven*[216] the issue was whether the Anglo-American Treaty of November 1794 had been abrogated by the war of 1812. The Court

[208] McNair, op. cit. (previous note), p. 705; Verzijl, op. cit. (previous note), vol. 6, pp. 371–2; Wheaton, *Elements of International Law* (6th edn., by Keith, 1929), pp. 504–6; Moore, *A Digest of International Law* (Washington, 1906), vol. 5, pp. 377–86; Hall, op. cit. above (p. 72 n. 127), pp. 453, 456–7; Westlake, *International Law*, Part II: *War* (Cambridge, 1907), p. 30; Oppenheim, *International Law*, vol. 2 (7th edn., by Lauterpacht, 1952), pp. 302–6; Coleman Phillipson, *Termination of War and Treaties of Peace* (New York, 1916), pp. 250–4, 261–7.

[209] For criticism of this view, see below, pp. 94–5.

[210] *Commentaries Upon International Law* (2nd edn., London, 1873), vol. 3, p. 796. See also Vattel, op. cit. above (p. 71 n. 124), book II, chapter 12, p. 208, no. 192.

[211] *PCIJ*, Series B, No. 8 (1923).

[212] Ibid., p. 20.

[213] *Reports of International Arbitral Awards*, vol. 11, p. 173.

[214] Case of Great Britain, *Proceedings in the North Atlantic Coast Fisheries Arbitration* (Washington, 1912), vol. 4, pp. 43–4; and Case of the United States, ibid., vol. 1, pp. 14–31. See also Oral Arguments by Sir William Robson, ibid., vol. 11, pp. 1655–721.

[215] *Reports of International Arbitral Awards*, vol. 11, p. 181.

[216] 8 Wheaton 464.

observed that where treaties contemplate a permanent arrangement of territorial and other national rights, it would be against every principle of just interpretation to hold them extinguished by the event of war. 'If such', the Court continued, 'were the law, even the Treaty of 1783 so far as it fixed our limits and acknowledged our independence would be gone . . .'.[217] In *State* v. *Reardon*[218] the Supreme Court observed in an *obiter* passage:

> A treaty which establishes a permanent status—such for instance as one fixing a boundary—plainly is not intended to be affected, and is not affected by war.[219]

The theory behind this rule is that the conclusion of a boundary treaty results in the mutual conveyance and acquisition of territorial and boundary-related rights. Inasmuch as a boundary treaty allocates territory to either side in a permanent and conclusive manner, neither State can be allowed to suffer a diminution of territory on account merely of the occurrence of war between the parties. Effectively, therefore, as the Supreme Court of Canada said in *Francis* v. *The Queen*,[220] treaties dealing, *inter alia* with the recognition of independence and the establishment of boundaries are deemed executed and the treaty becomes a muniment or evidence of the political or proprietary title.[221] The nub of the matter is that territorial and boundary-related rights stand transferred to either of the States and exist *independently but on the basis of the treaty*. Issue may be taken with the term 'suspension of boundary treaties' which, it is submitted, is neither adequate nor comprehensive. The first point is that a boundary treaty is but one medium out of several on the basis of which States mutually convey and acquire territorial and boundary-related rights and obligations, and that it is this body of rights and obligations which is paramount. It is not essential for a frontier to exist exclusively on the basis of a treaty or protocol: a valid alignment may be founded on a set of municipal instruments, or a complex of official documentation including maps and governmental records; or upon the evidence of State activity, acquiescence and recognition; and/or a combination of any two or more of these factors. It would, accordingly, be more appropriate to speak of territorial and boundary-related rights rather than boundary treaties as such. However, it appears

[217] 8 Wheaton 464, p. 494.

[218] 120 Kansas 614; 245 *Pacific Reporter* 158.

[219] 245 *Pacific Reporter* 158, at p. 159. In *Techt* v. *Hughes* (229 NY 222; 128 *North Eastern Reporter* 185) Judge Cordozo said: 'Treaties of alliance fall [in war]. Treaties of boundaries and cession, "dispositive" or "transitory" conventions survive': 128 *North Eastern Reporter* 185, at p. 191. In *Karnuth* v. *US* (279 US 231), Mr Justice Sutherland held: '. . . there seems to be fairly common agreement that, at least, the following treaty obligations remain in force [in war] . . . treaties of "cession", boundary and the like . . .': at p. 236. In *Sutton* v. *Sutton* (1830), (1 R & M 663; *British International Law Cases*, vol. 4, p. 362) the British Court of Chancery was concerned with the continuance of proprietary rights of American and British citizens in Britain and the US, as protected under Art. 9 of the Jay Treaty and implemented in 37 Geo. 3, c. 97. Counsel arguing in favour of title queried: 'Were the boundaries so fixed to cease to be the boundaries, the moment that hostilities broke out?': at pp. 672–3. See also the *Trademark Registration* case, Federal Patent Court, Federal Republic of Germany, 27 September 1967: 59 ILR 490, at p. 492.

[220] [1956] 3 DLR (2d) 641.

[221] Ibid., at p. 647.

illogical to describe the legal situation as one of 'suspension' of boundary and territorial rights, one of which is the inviolability of an alignment, the very moment they are transgressed. There would, effectively, be no legal protection if the suspension of the right to secure frontiers could be effected by the violation of that very frontier.[222] It would, on this view of the matter, be more accurate, therefore, to describe the legal situation as one of violation, whether mutual or otherwise, of territorial and boundary rights and obligations. To the extent, however, that the term 'suspension' is employed in juxtaposition to 'abrogation' of treaties during war, it is recognized that the term is not without merit.

Finally, the rule against abrogation of boundaries and boundary treaties is one of several different manifestations of the doctrine of finality and continuity of boundaries. Reference to this doctrine has been made in an earlier part of this study[223] and need not be repeated here. Suffice it to say that several incidents in the history of war and diplomacy give support to the principle in question. The western frontiers of Germany with France, Belgium, Luxembourg and the Netherlands, which were settled on the basis of agreements concluded in the nineteenth century,[224] survived the war of 1939–45. There was a similar restoration of boundaries after the termination of the 1971 Indo-Pakistani war. Article 4 (1) of the Simla Agreement of 3 July 1972 provided that the 'Indian and Pakistani forces shall be withdrawn to their side of the international border'.[225] Similarly, the 'liberation' war of 1979 between Uganda and Tanzania[226] did not affect the territorial delimitation between the belligerents.

However, on a great many occasions in history, the more successful and powerful belligerents have been known to take the opportunity provided by the outcome of the war to effect major or minor changes in the status of the territories of the defeated State by way of annexation, transfer to third State or simple boundary modification. It is this aspect of the matter, i.e. whether or not the war has invested, or is capable of investing either of the belligerent States with the right to effect changes, either unilateral or bilateral, in the boundary, which constitutes the second level of investigation. To an extent the issue can be resolved by reference to the rule stated above, i.e. that a boundary line is not abrogated *in toto* at the outbreak of hostilities and it continues in law to govern the territorial limits of the parties. Accordingly, any unilateral act which, by way of annexation, transfer to third State or boundary modification, deprives

222 On annexation of territory during or after war, see below.

223 Above, pp. 67–9.

224 Treviranus, 'Boundary Settlements between Germany and her Western Neighbours after the Second World War', in Bernhardt (ed.), *Encyclopaedia of Public International Law*, vol. 3 (1982), pp. 71–4 at p. 71.

225 For text, see *International Legal Materials*, 11 (1972), pp. 954–7. See also Joint Statement of Indo-Pakistani Officials on Implementation of the Simla Agreement (30 August 1972), paragraph 3 (ii), ibid., pp. 958–62.

226 Chatterjee, 'Some Legal Problems of Support Role in International Law: Tanzania and Uganda', *International and Comparative Law Quarterly*, 30 (1981), p. 755 at pp. 756–77.

the defeated belligerent State of territory to which she had legal title, is invalid.

Approaching the issue on a more general plane, the threat or use of force by States as an instrument of national policy, or as a medium for the settlement of international disputes, is prohibited in international law,[227] and consequently unilateral changes made by a belligerent State in the status of territory during[228] or after the war by way of annexation or otherwise are unlawful.[229] The outlawry of war is based on various considerations, one of which is *ex iniuria jus non oritur*. Latterly, several multilateral treaties and other instruments have not only condemned the use of force but have reiterated the importance of territorial integrity and the inviolability of frontiers. Article 2 (4) of the Charter of the United Nations, which obliges member States to refrain from the threat or use of force against the territorial integrity or political independence of States, is clearly of the first importance.[230] Reference may also be made to Article 17 of the Charter of the Organization of American States signed in Bogota in April 1948;[231] to Principle 5, Section IV, of the Declaration adopted by the Conference of the Heads of State and Governments of the Non-Aligned Countries at Cairo in 1964;[232] to paragraphs 4 and 10 of Article 1 of the UN General

[227] On the general outlawry of the use of force see Brownlie, *International Law and the Use of Force by States* (Oxford, 1963), pp. 66–122; Lauterpacht, Special Rapporteur, Report on the Law of Treaties, *Yearbook of the International Law Commission*, 1953, vol. 2, pp. 147–9; Waldock, ibid., 1963, vol. 2, pp. 51–2; Schwarzenberger, *International Law as Applied by International Courts and Tribunals*, vol. 2: *The Law of Armed Conflict* (1968), pp. 37–58, especially pp. 50–8; de Aréchaga, 'General Course in International Law', *Recueil des cours*, 159 (1978–I), pp. 86–92; Falk, 'The New States and International Legal Order', *Recueil des cours*, 118 (1966–II), pp. 44–6; Jennings, *The Acquisition of Territory in International Law* (Manchester, 1963), pp. 52–67; Oppenheim, *International Law*, vol. 2 (7th edn., by Lauterpacht, 1952), pp. 151–9, 177–97. See also Article 9 of the draft Declaration on the Rights and Duties of States, *Yearbook of the International Law Commission*, 1949, vol. 2, pp. 287–8. Cf. Castrén, *The Present Law of War and Neutrality* (Helsinki, 1954), pp. 40–7, 50–6, especially 56–7.

[228] Jennings, op. cit. (previous note), p. 52; Schwarzenberger, op. cit. (previous note), pp. 166–73.

[229] Brownlie, op. cit. above (n. 227), pp. 410–23; Jennings, op. cit. above (n. 227), pp. 52–68; Greig, *International Law* (2nd edn., London, 1976), pp. 160–1; Bowett, *Self Defence in International Law* (Manchester, 1958), pp. 29–38; Garner, 'Non-Recognition of Illegal Territorial Annexation and Claims to Sovereignty', *American Journal of International Law*, 30 (1936), pp. 679–88; Lauterpacht, loc. cit. above (n. 227), p. 148; Kelsen, 'The Draft Declaration on Rights and Duties of States', *American Journal of International Law*, 44 (1950), p. 259, at pp. 272–4; Shihata, 'Destination Embargo of Arab Oil: Its Legality Under International Law', ibid., 68 (1974), pp. 591, at pp. 598–608. Cf. Fitzmaurice, 'The Juridical Clauses of the Peace Treaties', *Recueil des cours*, 73 (1948–II), p. 279; Briggs, 'Non-Recognition of Title by Conquest and Limitations on the Doctrine', *Proceedings of the American Society of International Law*, 34 (1940), pp. 80–2; O'Connell, op. cit. above (p. 92 n. 207), p. 432.

[230] For commentary, see Brownlie, 'The Use of Force in Self-Defence', this *Year Book*, 37 (1961), pp. 232–7. See also Article 1 of the General Treaty for the Renunciation of War, *United Kingdom Treaty Series*, No. 29 (1929), Cmd. 3410; and Article 10 of the Covenant of the League of Nations, *American Journal of International Law*, 15 (1921), Supplement, p. 4.

[231] Text in *American Journal of International Law*, 46 (1952), Supplement, p. 43. For other multilateral American agreements, see the Anti-War Treaty of Non-Aggression and Conciliation, 1933; Article 11 of the Convention on Rights and Duties of States, 1933; the Buenos Aires Declaration of 1936; the Lima Declaration, 1938; Second Meeting of the Ministers of Foreign Affairs of the American Republics, Havana, 1940: see Brownlie, op. cit. above (n. 227), pp. 95–107; Whiteman, op. cit. above (p. 92 n. 207), vol. 5 (1965), pp. 874–86.

[232] For text, see *Indian Journal of International Law*, 4 (1964), p. 599 at p. 609. See also Charter of

Assembly Declaration on Principles of International Law Concerning Friendly Relations and Co-operation among States adopted in 1970;[233] and sections 2 and 3 of Article 5 of the General Assembly Resolution on the Definition of Aggression, adopted on 14 December 1974.[234] Article 1 of the Declaration and Article 5 of the Resolution stipulate in terms that the territory of a State cannot be the object of acquisition by another State resulting from the threat or use of force or from aggression.[235] Both articles, furthermore, stipulate that acquisition of territory in such circumstances will not be recognized as lawful.

It is clear that the weight of the opinions of writers and the legal materials is against any unilateral alteration of the status of a territory *durante bello* or following the termination of the war. Fine questions of lawful or unlawful use of force are of no legal consequence to the general principle.[236] However, in the opinion of Professor Julius Stone there is no rule of law 'requiring [the] automatic withdrawal by a military occupant who lawfully entered in [the] course of self defence'.[237] He has also challenged the existence of a rule which precludes the acquisition of title to territory irrespective of the nature of the measures of force used by the acquiring State. 'Such an unqualified rule', he writes, 'would obviously involve the drastic, and in policy incomprehensible, departure from existing international law . . .'.[238] It is submitted, with respect, that this view of the law is difficult to justify.

On this view of the matter, notwithstanding the fact that the war may well be the outcome of a legitimate use of force, as for example self-defence, *unilateral* changes in the status of a territory are to be regarded as unlawful. Certain anomalies in the law would present themselves if there were no provision in favour of universal disqualification. For one thing, the condition of mutual agreement, given *expressis verbis* or otherwise, has always been regarded in contemporary international law as an essential feature in territorial arrangements and allocation between States. The mere fact that a State has exercised force in support of law cannot, on this

the Organization of African Unity, sections 3 and 5 of Article 3; and the Cairo Declaration: Brownlie, *Basic Documents on African Affairs* (Oxford, 1971), pp. 2–9 and 360–1 respectively.

233 Annex to Resolution 2625 (XXV) in *International Legal Materials*, 9 (1970), p. 1292; Brownlie, *Basic Documents in International Law* (3rd edn., 1983), p. 35.

234 General Assembly Resolution 3314 (XXIX), *General Assembly Official Records*, 29th Session, Supplement 31; *International Legal Materials*, 13 (1974), p. 710.

235 While the former does not distinguish between the nature of the force employed, Article 5 of the latter resolution is confined to the acquisition of territory by aggression. (On the significance of the question of lawful use of force and acquisition of territory, see below (main text).) The Six-Power draft of 1970 on the question of defining aggression proposed, *inter alia*, in draft Article 4, that the diminishing of territory or altering of boundaries of a State by the use of illegal force constituted aggression: see UN Doc. A/AC.134/L.17, Annex to Report of the Special Committee, 25th Session, Supplement no. 19, A/8019 (July–August 1970). See also 1971 Draft (A/AC.134/L.32), Annex II to Report, ibid., 26th Session, Supplement no. 19, A/8419 (February–March 1970).

236 Jennings, op. cit. above (p. 96 n. 227), pp. 54–6. In respect of treaties and lawful use of force see below, pp. 99–102. See also Greig, *International Law* (2nd edn., London, 1976), pp. 895–6.

237 Stone, *Conflict Through Consensus* (Baltimore, 1977), p. 59.

238 Ibid., p. 62.

view of the matter, be regarded as a licence to effect unilateral changes in the admitted status of the territory concerned. In his memorandum on the matter of Israel's right to develop new oil fields in Sinai and the Gulf of Suez, the Legal Adviser to the US Department of State, Mr M. Leigh, observed:

> It is difficult to justify a rule that the use of force in self-defence may, during any resulting occupation, give the occupant rights against the enemy sovereign not related to the original self-defence requirement or not required as concomitants of the occupation itself and the occupant's duties. A rule holding out the prospect of acquiring unrestricted access to and use of resources and raw materials would constitute an incentive to territorial occupation by a country needing raw materials, and a disincentive to withdrawal.[239]

The Legal Adviser's comments are equally valid in respect of changes in title. There appears, therefore, to be no reason in general to grant greater legal importance to the fact of the legality of the use of force, used or threatened, as opposed to the fundamental requirement of mutuality in matters of territorial allocation. Moreover, although the concept of self-defence is in principle a question capable of legal determination,[240] it is not entirely free from controversy in terms of interpretation and application.[241]

[239] *Digest of United States Practice in International Law*, 1976, pp. 700–6. See also Report of the Special Committee (on the definition of aggression), 26th Session, loc. cit. above (p. 97 n. 235): 'No one could deny that territorial acquisition resulting from the unlawful use of force was illegal; a State could not annex the territory or part of the territory of another State in the exercise of its right of self-defence, a principle which had long been recognized': at p. 10. Also see statement of Pakistan's representative, Mr M. Mahmud, in this respect: A/C.6/SR.1477, p. 2; Stone, op. cit. above (p. 97 n. 237), p. 64. Cf. Schwebel, 'What Weight to Conquest?', *American Journal of International Law*, 64 (1970), pp. 346–7; and Jennings, op. cit. above (p. 96 n. 227), who gives importance to the role of recognition by the international community exercising its will in a legislative or quasi-legislative capacity in respect of territorial changes effected by a State at the end of a war of self-defence: at p. 56.

[240] Lauterpacht, *The Function of Law in the International Community* (Oxford, 1933), pp. 179–82; Brownlie, 'The Use of Force in Self-Defence', this *Year Book*, 37 (1960), p. 183 at pp. 195, 207–9; Bowett, op. cit. above (p. 96 n. 229), *passim*; Greig, *International Law* (2nd edn., 1976), pp. 876–900, especially pp. 877, 883–7, 892–7.

[241] The main differences of opinion relate to the questions of anticipatory self-defence and armed attack. For the varying interpretations on this see Waldock, 'The Regulation of the Use of Force by Individual States', *Recueil des cours*, 81 (1952–II), pp. 497–8; Brownlie, loc. cit. (previous note), pp. 242–4 and *International Law and the Use of Force* (1963), pp. 257–61, 269–75, 275–80; Bowett, op. cit. above (p. 96 n. 229), pp. 184–93; and 'Reprisals Involving Recourse to Armed Force', *American Journal of International Law*, 66 (1972), p. 4; Higgins, *The Development of International Law through the Political Organs of the United Nations* (London, 1963), pp. 197–210; Kelsen, *Principles of International Law* (2nd edn., New York, 1966), pp. 62–3, 70–2; Stone, *Conflict through Consensus* (1977), pp. 47–50; Greig, op. cit. above (previous note), p. 893; O'Connell, op. cit. above (p. 92 n. 207), pp. 316–18; Farer, 'Law and War', in Black and Falk (eds.), *The Future of International Legal Order* (Princeton, 1971), vol. 3, pp. 30–6 (in reference to nuclear warfare). See also the Questionnaire and Replies on Some Aspects of the Principle of Self-Defence and the Legality of the Use of Force, Part III, *International Law Association Proceedings on the UN Charter, Report of the 48th Session* (New York, 1958), pp. 593–621. On whether self-defence includes rights of intervention, self-help, reprisals etc., see Brownlie, op. cit. above (p. 96 n. 227), pp. 265–8, 272–5, 430, 433–6; Bowett, op. cit. above (p. 96 n. 229), pp. 29ff.; Kelsen, op. cit., pp. 73–80; Greig, op. cit. above (previous note), pp. 878–83; Dugard, 'The OAU and Colonialism: An Inquiry into the Plea of Self-Defence as a Justification for the Use of Force in the Eradication of Colonialism', *International and Comparative Law Quarterly*, 16 (1967), p. 157; Fontenyne, 'Forcible Self Help by States to Protect

Apart from that, it is vulnerable to abuse and, as Professor De Visscher said, 'its exercise in concrete cases always runs into contradictions, owing either to opposing political views or to the uncertainties surrounding the conditions of fact that justify its use'.[242] It is not uncommon today for both belligerents genuinely to claim self-defence and adduce evidence in support of a lawful use of force. Indeed, both Iran and Iraq claim to be acting out of self-defence.[243] Where territorial claims are the basis of the hostilities, questions of self-defence may be intricately tied up with those of title to territory, with the result that a judicial decision regarding self-defence will ultimately turn upon questions of title to territory. In other words, at times a tribunal may have to decide the central issue of title before it can rule on an issue of self-defence.[244] At any rate, the question of title to

Human Rights' in Lillich (ed.), *Humanitarian Intervention and the United Nations* (Charlottesville, 1973), pp. 209–16 (in reference to views expressed in debates of the Special Committee on Principles of International Law Concerning Friendly Relations . . .). Generally, see British Prime Minister's Statement to the House of Commons regarding British intervention in the Suez and subsequent debate: Hansard, *House of Commons Debates*, vol. 558, cols. 1446–1572 (30 October 1956); E. Lauterpacht, 'The Contemporary Practice of the United Kingdom in the Field of International Law, III', *International and Comparative Law Quarterly*, 6 (1957), pp. 325–7; Israeli Representative Herzog, Statement in the Security Council following Entebbe Raid, 9 July 1976: UN Document S/PV.1939 (9 July 1976), *International Legal Materials*, 15 (1976), pp. 1228–31; and Statement of Acting Secretary of State Rush to Professor Rostow, 29 May 1974, in reference to difference between self-defence and reprisals: *Digest of United States Practice in International Law*, 1974, p. 700.

242 *Theory and Reality in Public International Law* (revised edition, translated by P. E. Cobbett, Princeton, 1968), p. 121; Jennings, op. cit. above (p. 96 n. 227), pp. 55–6, 64–5, 66–7, 69–87; Falk, 'The Legal Control of Force in the International Community', in Falk and Mendlovitz (eds.), *The Strategy of World Order*, vol. 2: *International Law* (New York, 1966), p. 306; Kelsen, op. cit. above (previous note), pp. 73–5; Stone, *Legal Controls of International Conflict* (New York, 1954), pp. 243–4. Examples of some of the major abuses of the plea of self-defence are: the German invasion of Norway and of the USSR: see Judgment and Sentences of the International Military Tribunal, Nuremberg, 1 October 1946, in *American Journal of International Law*, 41 (1947), p. 172 at pp. 203–7 and 211–13; the Italian invasion of Ethiopia: see Report of the Committee of the Council of the League of Nations, 5 October 1935, ibid., 30 (1936), Supplement, p. 1: 'The Italian Government informed the Council that the warlike and aggressive spirit in Ethiopia had succeeded in imposing war against Italy . . .': p. 15; and the American War in Vietnam: see Legal Memorandum of the Legal Adviser to the US Department of State, L. C. Meeker, 4 March 1960: 'The Legality of US Participation in the Defence of Vietnam', ibid., 60 (1966), pp. 565–85; and cf. Wright, 'Legal Aspects of the Vietnam Situation', ibid., 60 (1966), pp. 750–69. One aspect of the difficulties in self-defence is reflected in the controversy regarding the 'priority principle' versus the universal approach in matters of State aggression. It featured prominently in the proceedings of the 6th Committee of the General Assembly and the Special Committee commissioned to define aggression: see the Reports of the 25th to 28th Sessions (1970–3) of the Special Committee: No. 19, A/8019 (July–August 1970); No. 19, A/8419 (February–March 1971), No. 19, A/8719 (January–March 1972), No. 19, A/9019 (April–May 1973). The Western Powers initially stood against the priority principle inasmuch as 'it was often impossible to determine who acted first . . . [A] minor first use of armed force might have been provoked or falsified as a pretext for massive retaliation . . .': Ferencz, *Defining International Aggression, The Search for World Peace: A Documentary History and Analysis* (New York, 1975), vol. 2, p. 31; Stone, *Conflict through Consensus* (1977), pp. 44–7. See also 1970 Report of the 6th Committee to the General Assembly, *General Assembly Official Records*, 25th Session, A/8171, p. 4 (19 November 1970).

243 See Iraqi letters of 21 and 24 September 1980 to the President of Security Council: S/14191, S/14192, and Iranian President's letter to Security Council, 1 October 1980: S/14206: loc. cit. above (p. 87 n. 195).

244 O'Connell writes that, where the frontier violated is itself the object of dispute, measures taken by either side cannot be regarded as measures of self-defence within the meaning of Article 51: op. cit. above (p. 92 n. 207), p. 319. See also Bowett, op. cit. above (p. 96 n. 229), pp. 34–8. Writing of the

territory cannot, speaking in broad terms, be seen to be dependent upon a decision pertaining to whether or not a State has exercised force consistent with the principles of the Charter, but upon the substantive issues of law and facts of the dispute in question.

Furthermore, unilateral acquisition of title to territory in such circumstances would leave a way open for States to disguise acts of aggression as those of self-defence with a view to the legitimization of their status in occupied territory. Finally, it is the case that unilateral changes in boundaries and territories tend to exacerbate rather than resolve the fundamental problems between States, and consequently generate greater instability in the region and in the system as a whole. A rule conducive to instability is to be deprecated.

However, having won the war, the dominant State is in a position to seek to extract consent for any agreement from the defeated State with the result that changes effected by a post-war frontier treaty may arguably constitute unilateral measures. The legal issue here is whether a boundary treaty, concluded at the end of hostilities which leave one of the States in a position to extract territorial concessions from the other, may be regarded as a valid agreement capable of creating legal title.

A preliminary answer to this question lies in Article 52 of the Vienna Convention, which is declaratory of customary international law,[245] and provides that a treaty is void if consent thereto has been procured by the threat or use of force in violation of the principles of international law embodied in the Charter of the United Nations.[246] This formulation effectively furnishes a limitation in favour of a legitimate use of force, and this, in conjunction with Article 75, may be seen as representing a logical outcome of the general outlawry of force employed as an instrument of national policy; it reflects a departure from the earlier position of writers on this aspect of the law who sought, *inter alia*, to protect peace treaties in general from being challenged on the ground of coercion but failed to distinguish between treaties concluded by a successful defending State and those dic-

invasion of Goa by India, Wright observes: '[I]f a State were free to occupy territory in the *de facto* possession of another State to which territory it believes it has legal title, attacks would be permissible in every boundary dispute, and the barriers by which the Charter seeks to protect territorial sovereignty would be broken down': 'The Goa Incident', *American Journal of International Law*, 56 (1962), p. 623.

[245] See, generally, Commentary to the final draft Article 49, *Yearbook of the International Law Commission*, 1966, vol. 2, pp. 246–7; Lauterpacht, Special Rapporteur, Report on the Law of Treaties, ibid., 1953, vol. 2, p. 147; Waldock, Special Rapporteur, Second Report, ibid., 1963, vol. 2, pp. 51–2; McNair, *The Law of Treaties* (1961), pp. 206–11; Brownlie, op. cit. above (p. 96 n. 227), pp. 404–5, 408–9 (but he recommends the supervision of the Security Council, p. 408); Schwarzenberger, op. cit. above (p. 96 n. 227), pp. 736–40.

[246] Where the force used is lawful, the treaty cannot be challenged on grounds of coercion. See Lauterpacht, loc. cit. (previous note), p. 150; Waldock, loc. cit. (previous note), p. 52; Brownlie, op. cit. above (p. 96 n. 227), pp. 408–9; De Visscher, op. cit. above (p. 99 n. 242), p. 254. Cf. Stone, *Legal Controls of International Conflict* (1954), pp. xxxi–xxxiii; Grewe, 'Peace Treaties', in Bernhardt (ed.), *Encyclopaedia of Public International Law*, vol. 4 (1982), p. 106: 'Whether the international legal order will be more disturbed than improved by the provision [of Article 52] is also in doubt'.

tated by a successful aggressor.[247] It is submitted that a simplistic recourse to Article 52 is unsatisfactory, not least because where self-defence is claimed by either belligerent, Article 51 of the Charter will become relevant and will accordingly attract all the problems mentioned earlier in respect of lawful use of force, unilateral allocation of, and title to, territory.

Moreover, although the proviso in favour of the lawful use of force is based essentially on the thesis that '[a] State which tramples underfoot the fundamental norm of the present international legal order is fully responsible for its actions',[248] there is, on this view, an underlying and unexpressed assumption that the State employing legitimate force will elect to treat the defeated State in a just and fair manner. That this is not necessarily true in every case is borne out by political history and by the fact that the attitude of the dominant State is dependent upon a host of political factors, only one of which is the fact that the force in question was lawfully employed.

The difficulties attendant upon this approach emphasize the complexity of the question. In principle neither an aggressor nor a State which has taken action in self-defence has the *right* to obtain title as a consequence of the use of force. Hence, a defeated aggressor State, as authoritatively determined by the General Assembly, may nevertheless challenge a treaty which purports to acquire territory on the exclusive justification that the defending State used force consistently with international law. Clearly, the plea of self-defence is not a licence to exact territorial concessions by treaty. The essential criterion in such cases is the requirement of some form of general recognition, such recognition historically normally involving a multilateral peace settlement not confined to the actual parties gaining or losing territory. An *imprimatur* of the General Assembly or an *ad hoc* regional or international convention will constitute evidence of the reasonableness of the terms of the treaty and the conclusive nature of the settlement. Professor (as he then was) Jennings gives great importance to recognition by the international community exerting its will in a legislative or quasi-legislative capacity in respect of territorial changes effected at the end of a war of self-defence.[249]

[247] See Hall, op. cit. above (p. 72 n. 127): '. . . Unless a considerable degree of intimidation is allowed to be consistent with the validity of contracts, few treaties made at the end of a war or to avert one would be binding, and the conflicts of States would end only with the subjugation of one of the combatants or the utter exhaustion of both': at p. 382; also see Wheaton, op. cit. above (p. 93 n. 208), p. 503; Keeton, 'Extraterritoriality', *Recueil des cours*, 72 (1948–I), pp. 350–2; Fitzmaurice, Special Rapporteur, Third Report on the Law of Treaties, *Yearbook of the International Law Commission*, 1958, vol. 2, p. 38: '. . . if peace is a paramount consideration, it must follow logically that peace may, in certain circumstances, have to take precedence for the time being over abstract justice . . .'; Castrén, op. cit. above (p. 96 n. 227), p. 135; Coleman Phillipson, op. cit. above (p. 93 n. 208), pp. 162–3; cf. Brierly, *The Law of Nations* (6th edn., by Waldock, 1963), pp. 318–19; and Van der Molen in *Symbolae Verzijl* (The Hague, 1958): illegal war cannot be legalized by a peace treaty to retain advantages accruing from such a war (pp. 247–8). Generally, see Detter, 'The Problem of Unequal Treaties', *International and Comparative Law Quarterly*, 15 (1966), p. 1069.

[248] Haraszti, 'Reflections on the Invalidity of Treaties', in Haraszti (ed.), *Questions of International Law* (Budapest, 1977), p. 59 at p. 67.

[249] Jennings, op. cit. above (p. 96 n. 227), p. 56.

In the light of these observations, it is clear that the rights created in favour of Iran and Iraq by virtue of the Baghdad Treaty of 1975 are being mutually transgressed on account of the war; but this has not affected title to territory on either side of the alignment, i.e. the *thalweg* in the Shatt. Unilateral measures adopted by either Iraq or Iran incorporating territory on either side of the *thalweg* boundary will not affect the territory allocated by the Baghdad Treaty. At the end of the war, and in the absence of an agreement to the contrary, the *thalweg* line will once again become operational as the international boundary between the parties. Both States will be free to conclude an agreement which either modifies the Baghdad Treaty in terms of relocation of the frontier, or reiterates the continuing validity of the said agreement, or to conclude no agreement regarding boundaries at all. Recognition of the peace treaty by the United Nations will no doubt contribute towards the continued acceptance of the treaty by the parties as a conclusive and final settlement of the boundary questions and all outstanding issues.

V. Statement of Conclusions

A brief commentary on some of the general and specific principles of law elicited in the study will be in order. First, in reference to the question of the *thalweg*, the law as it stands is that there is no absolute rule in favour of the *thalweg* line wherever a navigable river separates two (or more) States. States are free in principle to adopt any alignment which is mutually acceptable to all the coterminous States. In the absence, however, of evidence to the contrary, the *thalweg* in a navigable river will be the dividing line. The rule, thus, is essentially a rebuttable presumption in favour of the *thalweg* and cannot be put any higher than that. Evidence of a line different from that of the *thalweg* may include boundary provisions in a treaty and acts signifying acquiescence and recognition. A rule of law which compels the delimitation of frontiers along the *thalweg* of navigable rivers would be quite impracticable. It would be capable of coming into conflict with situations sanctioned in boundary agreements, rules relative to acquiescence and the historical evolution of frontiers. Moreover, while it would inhibit the freedom of States to seek to adopt alignments of their own choosing, a rule of this kind has no merits in terms of either securing any higher ideals or alleviating more imperative problems between States.

Secondly, there is no principle of international law which justifies the unilateral abrogation of valid frontier agreements. Boundary treaties create real territorial rights which stand permanently transferred in favour of either State, and cannot be terminated either by unilateral abrogation or on the ground of *rebus sic stantibus*. Although allegations of violations of the terms of a boundary treaty cannot in principle serve as grounds for its unilateral abrogation by one of the parties, the interpretation of the terms of the treaty will be relevant to a proper appreciation of the problem.

Thirdly, war may affect, but cannot abrogate, either a boundary regime or a frontier agreement. It is preferable, on this view of the matter, not to speak of a 'suspension' of boundary treaties, but to refer simply to a transgression of boundary and territorial rights, whether mutual or otherwise. It follows that no title can in principle pass in favour of either party through occupation, annexation or otherwise, either *durante bello* or subsequent to the termination of hostilities. The rationale behind this proposition of law is twofold. First, there are considerations relative to permanent territorial rights vested in either State by virtue of the 'dispositive' character of boundary agreements. This constitutes the more classical or traditional approach to the continuity of frontiers. The second and relatively more recent consideration is that the use of force either as a method of settlement of international disputes or as an instrument of national policy is categorically prohibited by international law. Thus, treaties which attempt to modify the status of territories after the conclusion of a war of aggression are invalid, and incapable of creating or transferring valid title. However, if such a treaty were concluded at the end of a legitimate use of force, and were recognized by an international body, for example, the UN General Assembly, as representing fair and reasonable terms for the conclusive settlement of all issues, it would not be considered invalid.

The politico-historical provenance of a frontier question is perceived as assuming considerable legal significance. It is important not only because it provides perspective to the dispute, but also because details of the political history tend to reveal the incidents and distribution of power between the parties and the role played by it in the development of the frontier. Both set of facts, viz. the questions of power and of the historical sources of difficulties, tend to create problems for legal analysis.

As regards the former, although it is in principle external to the legal system, power tends to exercise a degree of influence by determining, *inter alia*, the nature and performance of certain rights and obligations between States. The history of the Shatt question has shown that the distribution of power between Iran and Iraq has frustrated a final and conclusive settlement of *all* the issues, and has on every occasion prompted an agreement which the weaker State was less inclined to accept. Yet in legal terms there were no outstanding problems: the alignment had, in every case, been 'conclusively' settled.

Secondly, the facts have shown that despite the impracticable nature of the left bank boundary Iran had, up to 1975, been unable to secure a line which would have resolved her genuine difficulties in the Shatt. From her perspective, it could be argued that laws which do not take into consideration the equitable needs of a State, rooted not in territorial aggrandizement but in genuine sources of difficulties, inhibit change and are not in touch with political reality. *A fortiori*, a rule of law which accommodates such claims would contribute towards the easing of tension between adjacent States.

Inasmuch as law is a creature of custom and State practice it cannot ignore the evolution of political facts and ideals and must respond to the needs and interests of States. Wherever the law diverges from these needs and interests, its efficacy may be either lost or reduced. Hence, the application of the law in different situations must be tempered with flexibility in order to strike a balance between the rules of law and the exigencies of States.

Although generally correct, these observations merit qualification. First, it is not the rigidity of the law, but the rigidity in the attitude adopted by States, which is ultimately a bar to the accommodation of genuine grievances. Secondly, not only may it be at times impossible to define the term 'genuine', but the resolution of such grievances may well depend upon an infinite range of political criteria far too extensive to be provided for or enumerated in law.

Thirdly, a provision for change will inevitably lead to a periodic review of boundary agreements which in turn will generate, rather than resolve, problems of territorial instability. Indeed the Iran–Iraq war is an apt illustration of the difficulties to which States would be vulnerable if a periodic review of alignments were sanctioned by law.

Finally, the law is not totally oblivious to the imperatives of change. The reconciliation between law and fact is facilitated at times by the doctrine of finality of boundaries. One of the objectives of the principles of acquiescence, estoppel and recognition is to give due weight to situations which, while they may not be totally coincidental with certain treaty provisions, are predominant on the ground. Nor does the law ignore the fact that in certain circumstances the relevance of the principle of equity may be compelling, alleviating as it does the rigours imposed by a strict application of the law. Yet it is in principle reasonable to deny a continuously available process under which calls for revision of boundary regimes in the light of difficulties or changed circumstances may be made. There is, at any rate, no legal bar to the resolution of the problem by way of diplomacy.

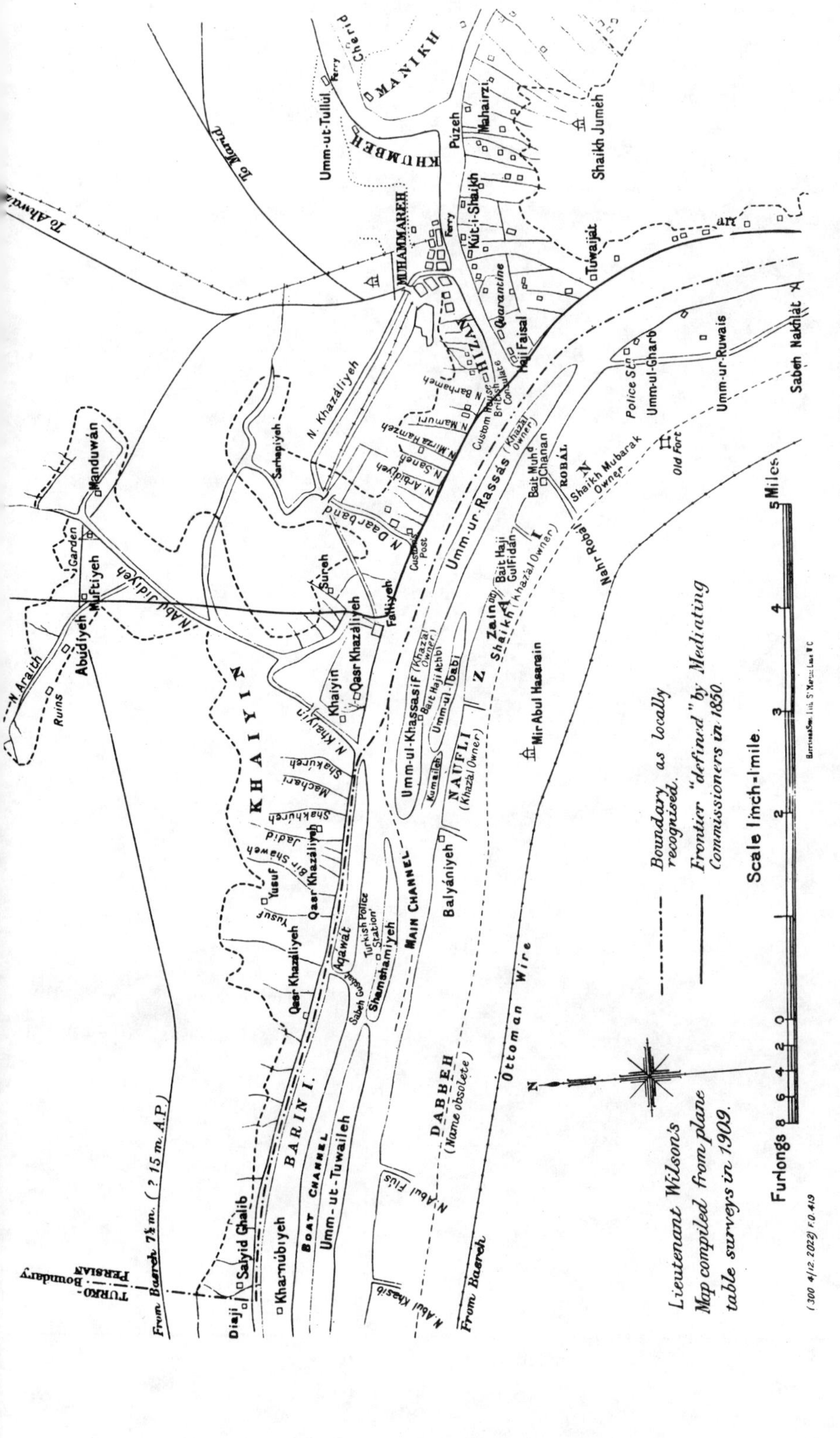

FIG. 1. Map shows part of boundary in the northern sector of the Shatt, as existing in 1909, namely the dotted line in the Shatt. The 1913–14 line conformed to this part of the existing alignment.

(Map reproduced from file L/P & S/10/266, p. 265, India Office Library, London. Unpublished Crown-copyright material reproduced by permission of the Controller of Her Majesty's Stationery Office)

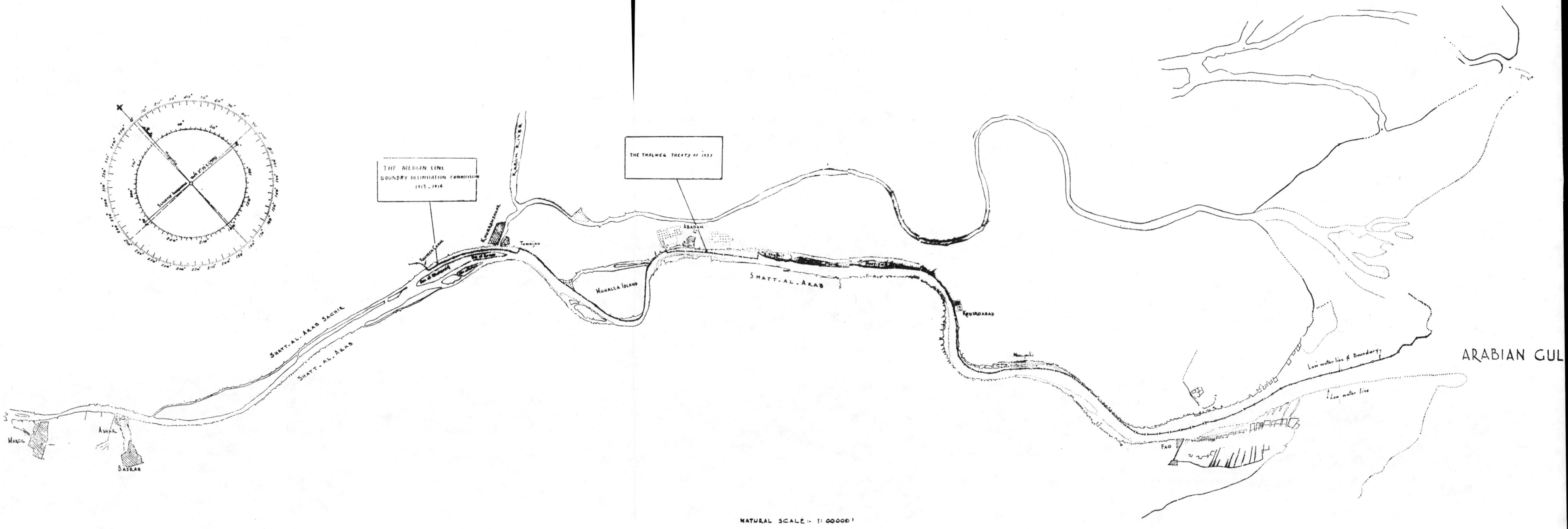

Fig. 2. Map shows the alignment and modifications effected by the 1913–14 and 1937 agreements.

(Reproduced from *Comments on the Iranian Claims concerning the Iraqi–Iranian Frontier Treaty of 1937 and the Legal Status of the Frontier between the two Countries in the Shatt-al-Arab*, Ministry for Foreign Affairs, Baghdad, 1969)

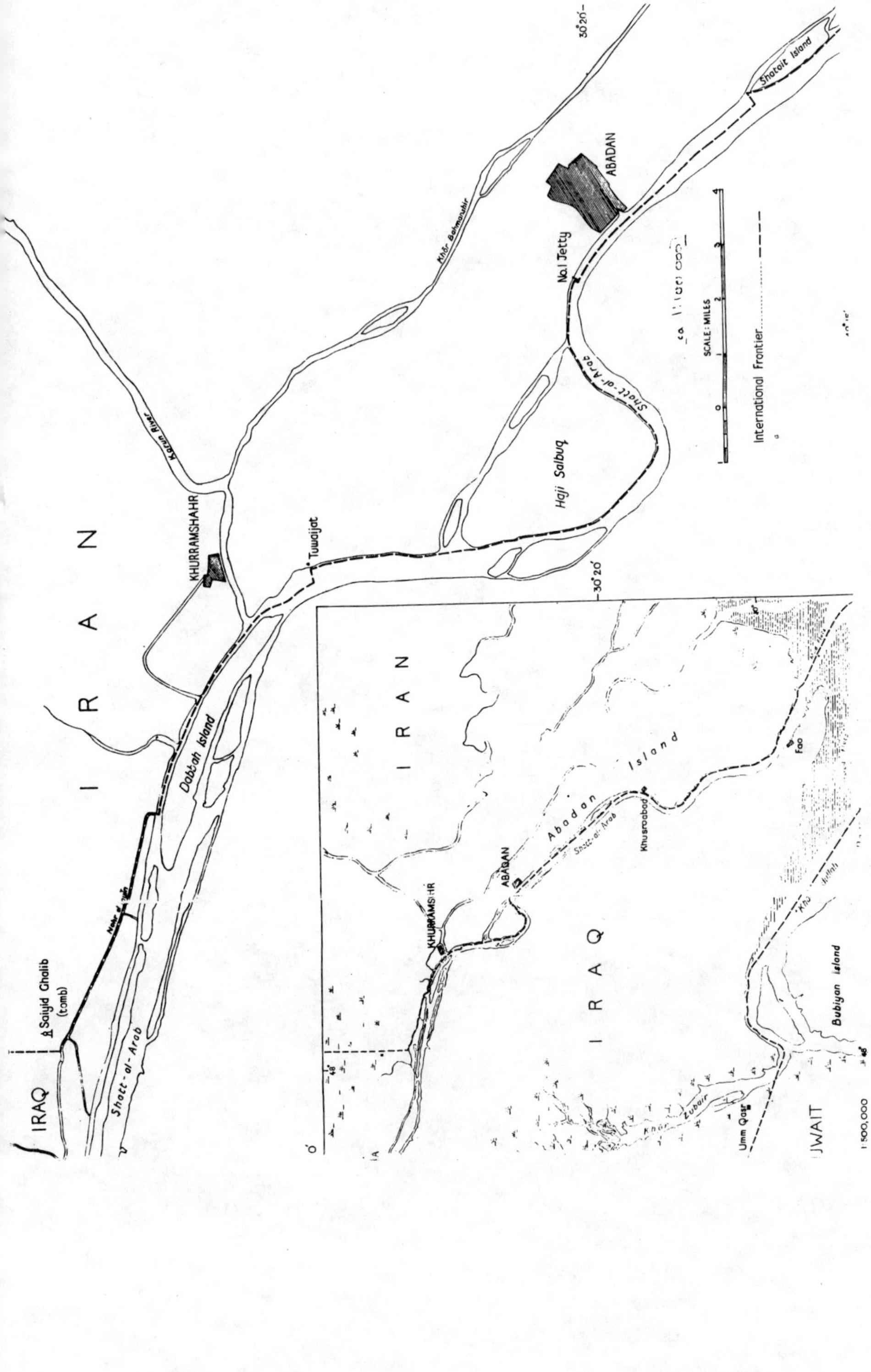

FIG. 3. Map shows the modifications effected by the treaty of 1937.

(Compiled and drawn by J. I. B. January, 1960)

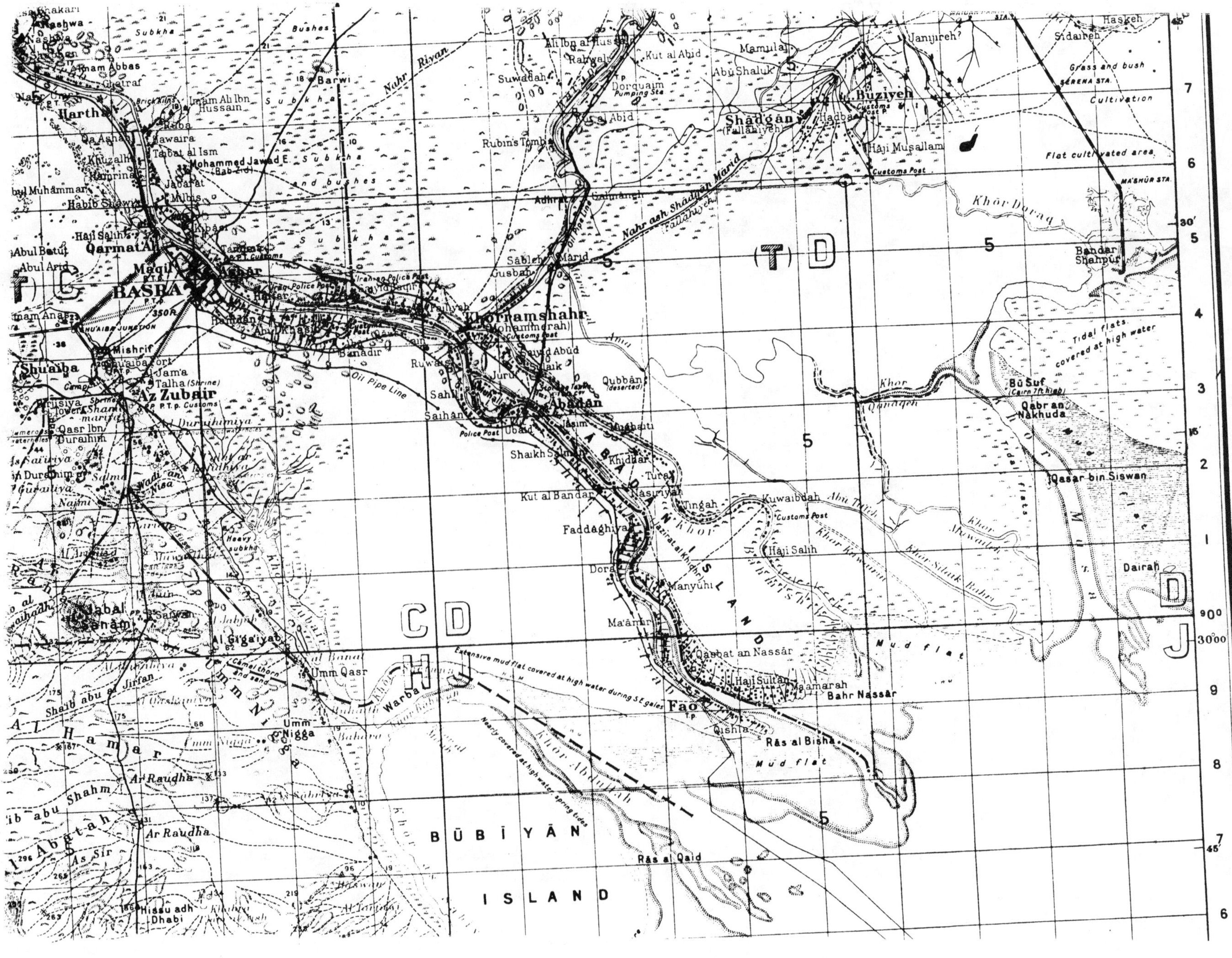

FIG. 4. Map shows the relevant sector of the boundary in detail.

(Geographical Section, General Staff No. 3954, published by War Office, 1955, edition 2—British Crown Copyright, GSGS 1955. Sheet No. GSGS 3956 Basra–Kuwait. 1:500,00)

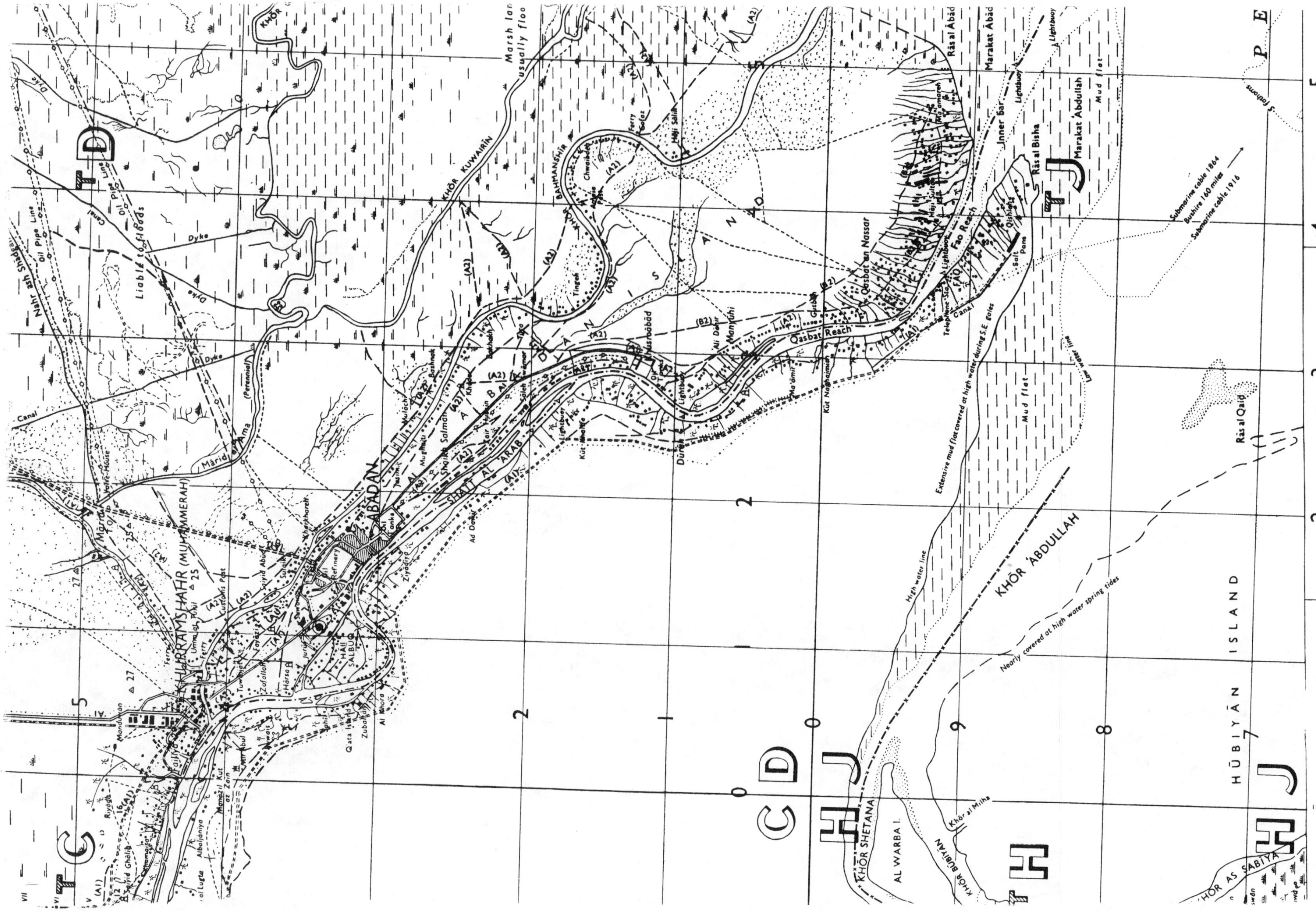

Fig. 5. Map shows relevant sector of the boundary in detail.

(Geographical Section, General Staff No. 3919 (MDR 9002), published by War Office, 1941, 2nd edn. 1948. Series K 501 (GSGS 3919), sheet H-39 (G+M), edition 2—British Crown Copyright, GSGS 1948. 1″ = 4 miles or 1:253,440. Reprinted from second edition. Printed for D. Survey (WO and AM) by Ordnance Survey 7,000/9/58/5812/05)

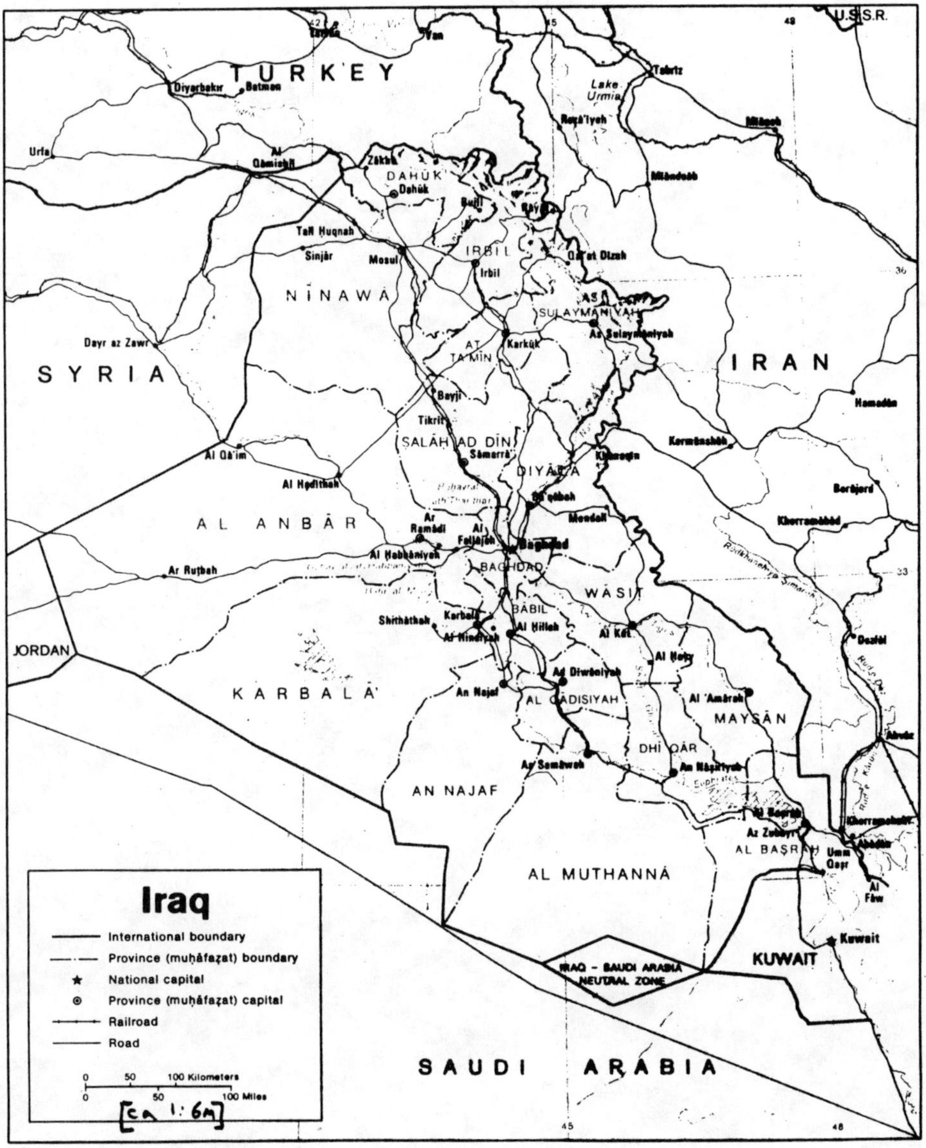

FIG. 6. Map shows the borderland provinces of Iraq and Iran through which the international frontier runs.

THE SEAWARD LIMIT TO CONTINENTAL SHELF JURISDICTION IN CUSTOMARY INTERNATIONAL LAW*

By D. N. HUTCHINSON[1]

I. Introduction

For at least a quarter of a century,[2] States have possessed sovereign rights for the purpose of exploring the sea-bed off their coasts and exploiting its natural resources.[3] Yet, throughout this period, the question of how far seaward these sovereign rights extend has remained the subject of intense controversy. The Convention on the Continental Shelf of 1958[4] and the United Nations Convention on the Law of the Sea of 1982[5] have sought to provide a solution. However, the former is currently operative in the mutual relations of but fifty-four States;[6] whilst the latter is not yet in force, and does not seem likely to be in the near future.[7] The current state of customary international law on the question of the outer limit is therefore of great legal significance: it governs both the mutual relations of States not parties to the Geneva Convention, and the relations between States not parties and those States which are parties to that Convention. It is also a matter of increasing practical importance as, with technological and economic developments, the search for offshore oil and gas moves into ever deeper waters.

II. The Rationale of Continental Shelf Rights

It is customary to distinguish rules which confer exclusive jurisdictional competencies on coastal States from the rules which determine the precise

[1] BA, BCL, Lecturer in Law at University College London.

[2] It is difficult to determine exactly when continental shelf rights became a part of general customary international law. Thirteen years after the Truman Proclamation of 1945, and after much international debate, adverse opinions can still be found at the Geneva Conference of 1958: Sweden, *UNCLOS I Official Records*, vol. 6, p. 3; Greece, ibid., p. 6; Chile, ibid., p. 16; Monaco, ibid., p. 32; and perhaps Cuba, ibid., p. 40. However, the adoption of the Convention on the Continental Shelf must have dispelled these doubts: cf. Spain, ibid., p. 7.

[3] This formulation of the nature of continental shelf rights in customary law is made by the International Court of Justice in the *North Sea Continental Shelf Cases* (*Federal Republic of Germany/Denmark; Federal Republic of Germany/Netherlands*), *ICJ Reports*, 1969, p. 3 at para. 19.

[4] Convention on the Continental Shelf, Geneva, 1958, Article 1.

[5] UN Convention on the Law of the Sea, Montego Bay, 1982, Articles 76 and 84, and Annex II.

[6] *Multilateral Treaties in respect of which the Secretary-General performs depositary functions: Status as of 31st December 1982*, at p. 625. This does not include Senegal, which denounced the Convention in 1976; but it does include Taiwan, since the Government of the Republic of China purported to ratify the Convention on behalf of China in 1970.

[7] According to Article 308, the Convention will come into force twelve months after the deposit of the 60th instrument of ratification or accession. By March 1986, there were twenty-five ratifications.

extent of the spatial area over which those rights exist.[8] This dichotomy is justified by the fact that different sets of reasons may lie behind the two types of rule. For instance, economic interests or security considerations may lie behind entitlement as such, whilst simplicity, ease of ascertainment and so on may lie behind the relevant rule on limits. However, it would seem justified to expect that the rule relating to limits should not seriously conflict with or negate the reasons for which the rule conferring title was recognized. Although it is always open to States to decide otherwise, it would seem reasonable to assume that the limits of any given maritime zone will be based, at least partly, on respect for the reasons behind the rule which confers title. This intimate connection between title and limits was recently confirmed by the International Court in the *Libya–Malta* case. The Court there treated the two issues as one and the same,[9] and talked of the rules relating to the outer limits of continental shelf rights as bases of title;[10] for, as Judge Mbaye noted in his separate opinion, limits 'define the factors which determine rights'.[11] The Court proceeded to oppose the issues of title and limits to the separate domain of the rules on the delimitation of boundaries between overlapping claims; but, even then, it recognized that '[t]he legal basis of that which is to be delimited . . . cannot be other than pertinent':[12] delimitation must be effected 'in a manner consistent with the concepts underlying the attribution of legal title',[13] since, '[o]therwise, the legal concept of continental shelf could itself be fundamentally changed by the introduction of considerations strange to its nature'.[14] If the basis of continental shelf rights is relevant to the distinct issue of delimitation, then how much more is it relevant to the closely related question of limits.

It is therefore in point to review those reasons of policy which appear to have moved the generality of States to invest States with sovereign rights over the sea-bed off their coasts for the purpose of exploring it and exploiting its natural resources.

Advances in technology in the years preceding the Second World War made possible, practically everywhere in the world, the commercial exploitation of the resources of the sea-bed and the subsoil of the shallow coastal seas—primarily, deposits of hydrocarbons. There was thus presented the prospect of a considerable supply of vital raw materials for a very long time to come. They would inure directly to the benefit of whoever harvested them and whichever government administered and taxed this enterprise. However, States were faced with the question of what regime should govern this activity. It was immediately apparent that

[8] *Case Concerning the Continental Shelf* (*Tunisia/Libyan Arab Jamahiriya*), *ICJ Reports*, 1982, p. 17 at para. 44.

[9] *Case Concerning the Continental Shelf* (*Libyan Arab Jamahiriya/Malta*), *ICJ Reports*, 1985, p. 13 at para. 27.

[10] Paras. 34, 39, 43 and 61.

[11] p. 95. In his oral argument for Malta, Weil remarked that legal title relates essentially to the establishment of the outer seaward limits: CR 84/25, pp. 28–9.

[12] Para. 27.

[13] Para. 61.

[14] Para. 48.

regulation by an international organization was not a practical proposition.[15] Broadly speaking, three possibilities remained: a system of free exploitation, akin to freedom of fishing on the high seas; a regime whereby the sea-bed was treated as *res nullius*, open to the exclusive user of that State which might first occupy and exploit it; and some system of exclusive coastal State rights over contiguous sea-bed areas.[16] Opinion rapidly formed in favour of a rule conferring on each State exclusive jurisdiction *ipso facto* and *ab initio* over resource-related activities in the areas of sea-bed off its coasts.[17]

First, and most elementary, it was thought that this was the best way to avoid international conflict. Exclusive and inherent coastal State jurisdiction would preclude the prospect of a dangerous and chaotic 'rush and grab'[18] for valuable submarine resources, which might well occur under a system of unregulated freedom of exploitation or a system of occupation.[19] Otherwise, there was a great potential for conflict through conflicting claims, dual exploitation, squatting and so on.[20] Secondly, exclusive jurisdiction was seen as necessary in order to protect the coastal State against unregulated and unsupervised activities and foreign installations off its coasts, constituting potential threats to its security.[21] This concern was forcefully expressed by several States at the Geneva Conference of 1958.[22] Thirdly, the coastal State was seen to have a special interest in regulating the exploitation of the sea-bed off its coasts, since it would thus be able to control the consequent threat of pollution to its coasts and its fisheries.[23] Fourthly, it was foreseen that deposits underlying the land

[15] Report of the International Law Commission to the General Assembly on the Work of its Second Session, *Yearbook of the International Law Commission*, 1950, vol. 2, p. 384 (hereafter cited as *ILC 2nd Report*).

[16] Cf. Hudson, *Yearbook of the ILC*, 1950, vol. 1, p. 228.

[17] *North Sea* cases, para. 19; Convention on the Continental Shelf, Article 2.

[18] Report of the Special Rapporteur François on the Regime of the High Seas, *Yearbook of the ILC*, 1950, vol. 2, p. 51.

[19] This opinion can be found expressed in divers places: Report of the International Law Commission to the General Assembly on the Work of its Third Session, ibid., 1951, vol. 2, p. 142: para. 4 of the Commentary on draft Article 2 (hereafter cited as *ILC 3rd Report*); Comment by the Government of Sweden on the International Law Commission's Draft Articles of 1951, in Report of the International Law Commission to the General Assembly on the Work of its Fifth Session, ibid., 1953, vol. 2, p. 261 (hereafter cited as *ILC 5th Report*); Venezuela, *UNCLOS I Official Records*, vol. 6, p. 21; Judge Padilla Nervo in the *North Sea* cases at p. 92.

[20] *Petroleum Development* (*Trucial Coast*) *Ltd.* v. *Sheikh of Abu Dhabi*, 18 ILR 144 at p. 156; Brownlie, *Principles of Public International Law* (3rd edn., 1979), p. 226.

[21] The Truman Proclamation on the Continental Shelf (1945), para. 4; Report of the Special Rapporteur François on the Regime of the High Seas, *Yearbook of the ILC*, 1950, vol. 2, p. 51; Vallat, quoted in Report of the Special Rapporteur François on the Continental Shelf, ibid., 1953, vol. 2, p. 5; Turkey, A/C. 6/SR.392, p. 156; Judge *ad hoc* Jiménez de Aréchaga in the *Tunisia–Libya* case at paras. 71–2; *Libya-Malta* case at para. 51; and the oral argument of Lauterpacht in that case at CR 84/23, pp. 60–2.

[22] India, *UNCLOS I Official Records*, vol. 6, p. 12: Uruguay, ibid., p. 34; Colombia, ibid., p. 41; Argentina, ibid., p. 43; USSR, ibid., p. 20; Vietnam, ibid., p. 24.

[23] Loc. cit. above (n. 18). Cf. Res. 2 of the Latin American Meeting on Aspects of the Law of the Sea at Lima, 4–8 August 1970, wherein this thinking was subsequently put to a much wider use: Lay, Churchill and Nordquist, *New Directions in the Law of the Sea*, vol. 1 (1973), p. 237 at p. 240. See also the oral argument of Lauterpacht in the *Libya–Malta* case at CR 84/23, p. 62.

territory of the coastal State might extend seawards. Exclusive coastal State control over these unified deposits was thought necessary to facilitate their rational exploitation, and to preclude the conflict which might arise from dual exploitation.[24] Fifthly, a solution based upon coastal State jurisdiction offered most coastal States political and economic advantages—as the speed with which the Latin American and Gulf States followed the United States' lead by claiming continental shelf zones indicates.[25] For in this way all coastal States were assured of a fair amount of sea-bed and the prospect of considerable natural wealth: the less developed States were protected against the danger that the technologically advanced States would reap all the immediate financial benefits from any shelf deposits off their coasts, as would in all probability have occurred under a regime of free exploitation or occupation.[26] Several Latin American States also found in the continental shelf a useful prop for their claims to extensive fisheries zones.[27]

However, the consideration which seems to have weighed most strongly in favour of exclusive coastal State jurisdiction was that this was the best way in which the law might facilitate the profitable exploitation of the hydrocarbon resources of the coastal sea-bed.[28] It was recognized that the legal regime which would regulate the recovery of these valuable riches should be such as to ensure their 'effective exploitation'.[29] Indeed, there was a clear conviction that, besides facilitating exploitation, the law should promote its economic efficiency, in order that all States consumers of the extracted oil and gas might benefit from lower prices.[30] These policies were necessarily assessed in the light of the current state of exploitation technology and its foreseeable development. At that time, exploitation of the oil and gas reserves of the coastal sea-bed was only possible by means of fixed installations which were heavily dependent on technical support from the adjacent coastal State; and there was no reason to believe that this would change in the foreseeable future. Exclusive coastal State

[24] Truman Proclamation, paras. 2 and 4; Turkey, loc. cit. above (p. 113 n. 21); USSR, *UNCLOS I Official Records*, vol. 6, p. 20.

[25] Hollick, *US Foreign Policy and the Law of the Sea* (1981), p. 372.

[26] Salamanca, *Yearbook of the ILC*, 1956, vol. 1, p. 138; India *UNCLOS I Official Records*, vol. 6, p. 12; Colombia, ibid., pp. 41 and 43; Argentina, ibid., p. 43; Judge Ammoun in the *North Sea* cases at p. 106; Judge *ad hoc* Jiménez de Aréchaga in the *Tunisia–Libya* case at para. 70; Hollick, op. cit. (previous note), at p. 35.

[27] Hollick, op. cit. above (n. 25), at pp. 67–80 and 117–18.

[28] Brownlie, oral argument in the *Libya–Malta* case at CR 84/27, p. 14.

[29] Truman Proclamation, para. 4; Kerno, *Yearbook of the ILC*, 1951, vol. 1, p. 272; *ILC 3rd Report*, p. 142: para. 4 of the Commentary on draft Article 2; Scelle, *Yearbook of the ILC*, 1953, vol. 1, p. 73; *ILC 5th Report*, at p. 215; Report of the International Law Commission to the General Assembly on the Work of its Eighth Session, *Yearbook of the ILC*, 1956, vol. 2, p. 296 (hereafter cited as *ILC 8th Report*); El Salvador, *UNCLOS I Official Records*, vol. 6, pp. 33–4.

[30] Second Report of the Special Rapporteur François on the Regime of the High Seas, *Yearbook of the ILC*, 1951, vol. 2, p. 100, quoting the Rapporteur of the International Law Association; Report of the Special Rapporteur François on the Continental Shelf, ibid., 1953, vol. 2, p. 19, quoting Gidel; *ILC 3rd Report*, p. 142: para. 2 of the Commentary on draft Article 2; 'preserving and prudently utilizing' in para. 2 of the Truman Proclamation.

jurisdiction was therefore the natural regime to regulate these activities. For, even if the coastal State received no such jurisdiction, it would still exercise a highly significant *de facto* control over exploitation off its coasts because of the practical necessity for coastal State support. If foreign enterprises were free in law to exploit the sea-bed off its coasts, the coastal State might use this control to prevent such activities from going ahead against its will, or to subject them to onerous conditions impairing their economic viability. To confer exclusive jurisdiction on the coastal State would avoid such impasses. Even if the coastal State were to act in the best of faith, it would still use its practical control over offshore activities to regulate them in some manner. Coastal State regulation would then exist simultaneously with flag State jurisdiction over the installation in question. Conflicting regulations, legal uncertainties and so on might then render exploitation impracticable or uneconomic; and, even if such a drastic result were not to occur, its economic efficiency might well be impaired. In view of the inevitability of coastal State regulation, unity of control under exclusive coastal State jurisdiction was the most rational choice;[31] and would provide the most 'stable' basis for the exploitation of the coastal sea-bed.[32]

III. The Customary Law as of 1970

Article 1 of the Convention on the Continental Shelf of 1958 provides:

> For the purpose of these articles, the term 'continental shelf' is used as referring (a) to the seabed and subsoil of the submarine areas adjacent to the coast but outside the area of the territorial sea, to a depth of 200 metres or beyond that limit, to where the depth of the superjacent waters admits of the exploitation of the natural resources of the said areas; (b) to the seabed and subsoil of similar submarine areas adjacent to the coasts of islands.

The ensuing articles lay down the legal regime of the continental shelf which is to apply to the area thus defined. This legal regime and these limits, *qua* treaty provisions, are applicable solely to the mutual relations of parties to the Convention. It is possible that the legal regime of the continental shelf in customary law differs from that of the Convention; and, similarly, it is possible that the area to which the customary law regime applies differs from that area defined in Article 1. Whatever is the position with regard to the legal regime of the continental shelf, there is good reason to believe that, by the late 1960s, if not before, the customary law on limits came to be governed by a rule in substance identical to that enshrined in Article 1 of the Geneva Convention.

[31] Gidel, loc. cit. (previous note); François, *Yearbook of the ILC*, 1951, vol. 1, p. 407; Judge Jessup in the *North Sea* cases at pp. 67–8, quoting the memorial of the Federal Republic of Germany; Judge *ad hoc* Jiménez de Aréchaga in the *Tunisia–Libya* case at para. 75; McDougal and Burke, *Public Order of the Oceans* (1962), p. 633.

[32] Brownlie, op. cit. above (p. 113 n. 20), at pp. 224 and 226.

(a) *The Rule in Article 1 as Customary Law*

A survey of State practice in the years up to the end of the 1950s suggests that, if the rule in Article 1 had not come to reflect customary law by the end of that decade, it definitely constituted an emerging rule of general international law. First, between 1945 and 1960, thirty-three States (excluding protectorates) laid claim to exclusive coastal State rights over the sea-bed beyond a narrow territorial sea. Of these, sixteen did not specify any seaward limit to the rights claimed;[33] whilst seven employed the exploitability concept of Article 1, with or without the addition of the 200-metres depth criterion.[34] As will be shown below, those claims which failed to specify a limit can legitimately be counted alongside those which reproduced the formula of Article 1, since the underlying purposes of these two types of claim were identical. Therefore, after allowance has been made for those States which were land-locked and thus had no practical interest in the matter,[35] it can be seen that a significant body of the States then in existence espoused a rule on limits akin to that in Article 1. Moreover, a rule similar to that in Article 1 was adopted in a Resolution of the Inter-American Specialized Conference on 'Conservation of Natural Resources: the Continental Shelf and Marine Waters' at Ciudad Trujillo in 1956.[36] The work of the International Law Commission must also be considered in this respect: not as part of State practice, of course, but as a reflection of it. Whilst it considered the draft articles it produced to be a progressive development in the law,[37] the Commission recognized that the starting-point in its deliberations had to be the existing State practice and the currents of opinion behind it.[38] This process, whereby emerging law was crystallized, was enhanced by the fact that the resulting draft articles and commentaries produced by the Commission were the subject of comment by States, which the Commission in turn took into account in

[33] Argentina, Australia, Brazil, Ceylon, Costa Rica, Greece, Iran, Iraq, Korea (South), Libya, Mexico, Nigeria, Philippines, Saudi Arabia, Spain and the US (despite an accompanying press release, no limit was included in the Truman Proclamation itself). Similar claims were also made by, or on behalf of, five protectorates—Bahrein, Brunei, Kuwait, Qatar and five of the sheikhdoms now constituting the United Arab Emirates—and four claims were made in respect to territories then constituting colonies—Bahamas, British Honduras, British Guiana and Jamaica. Norway, Trinidad and USSR had negotiated treaties delimiting their continental shelf boundaries, although they did not make formal claims to continental shelf zones in this period.

[34] Egypt, Haiti, Honduras, India, Israel, Morocco, Venezuela.

[35] *North Sea* cases, para. 73; see also Judge Lachs, ibid., p. 227.

[36] *Background Material on the Activities in the OAS relating to the Law of the Sea Prepared for Submission to the UN Conference, Geneva, Switzerland, 1958*, p. 30: res. 1.

[37] *Yearbook of the ILC*, 1951, vol. 1, p. 401; *ILC 5th Report*, p. 215.

[38] François, *Yearbook of the ILC*, 1950, vol. 1, p. 215; Yepes and Sandström, ibid.; Hudson, ibid., p. 216. Yepes referred to the contemporaneous State practice on limits as containing the germ of a rule of customary law, which it was the Commission's task to recognize and capture: ibid., 1953, vol. 1, p. 338. At several particular instances, members of the Commission referred to precedents in State practice to vindicate their arguments: e.g. Hudson, ibid., 1950, vol. 1, p. 226; François, ibid., 1951, vol. 1, p. 270; Amado, ibid., pp. 272 and 273.

formulating its subsequent drafts.[39] Thus, although his judgment was sanguine,[40] there was an element of truth in Salamanca's affirmation that the Commission, in adopting the future Article 1, was interpreting a current of opinion among States which had already fixed the outer limit of the continental shelf regime.[41] That the Commission succeeded in capturing the essence of contemporary thinking on limits was confirmed by the widespread acceptability of its draft article at the 1958 Geneva Conference.

This conclusion is bolstered by a consideration of the jurisprudence of the International Court. It was in the *North Sea Continental Shelf* cases of 1969 that the Court first examined Article 1. These cases did not relate directly to the question of the seaward limit of continental shelf rights. The majority judgment accordingly remarked that, in considering the relationship between the Geneva Convention and customary law, 'it has in view solely the delimitation provisions (Article 6) of the Convention, not other parts of it, nor the Convention as such'.[42] However, the Court did find it necessary to consider in some detail the relationship between the various provisions of the Convention and customary law while examining the scope of the power to make reservations under Article 12;[43] and, in so doing, the majority judgment was clearly sympathetic to the proposition that the rules in Articles 1 to 3 of the Geneva Convention represented emergent customary law in 1958 when the Convention was adopted by the Geneva Conference. This proposition is not made *expressis verbis*: it is said that the members of the International Law Commission and the representatives of States at the Geneva Conference considered these articles to represent 'received, or at least emergent, rules of customary international law relative to the continental shelf, amongst them the question of the seaward extent of the shelf'.[44] However, the Court intimates no disagreement with this supposed assessment. Indeed, it seems to sympathize; for the Court itself treats Article 2 as 'enshrining' the fundamental idea of the continental shelf regime in customary law.[45] Judge

[39] Judge *ad hoc* Jiménez de Aréchaga drew attention to this 'important element' in the *Tunisia–Libya* case at para. 41 of his separate opinion.

[40] Statements are prevalent in the Commission and at the Geneva Conference that the rule in Article 1 was not yet a rule of customary law. See, especially, the reactions to the ILC's draft articles of 1956 in the Sixth Committee of the General Assembly: Greece, A/C. 6/SR. 487, p. 32; USSR, A/C. 6/SR. 488, p. 36; Iran, A/C. 6/SR. 490, p. 48; and Australia, A/C. 6/SR. 499, p. 106.

[41] *Yearbook of the ILC*, 1956, vol. 1, p. 138. In his oral argument for Malta in the *Libya–Malta* case, the Maltese Agent, Mizzi, made a similar claim: CR 84/22, p. 63.

[42] Para. 60.

[43] Paras. 63–9. This issue was relevant because the rules in Article 6 were alleged to constitute customary law at the time of the adoption of the Convention, despite the fact that reservations might be made thereto under Article 12. The Court thus considered the relationship between the power to make reservations and customary rules incorporated in a treaty.

[44] Para. 63; see also para. 66. This proposition is reiterated by the Court in the *Tunisia–Libya* case at para. 42.

[45] Para. 19.

Padilla Nervo seems to be of a similar opinion;[46] and Judge Tanaka remarks:

> There is no doubt that Articles 1–3, which constitute the fundamental concept of the continental shelf, are mainly formulated on the basis of the State practice established since President Truman's Proclamation of September 1945, and that, accordingly, they have the character of customary law.[47]

Thus, in the *Tunisia–Libya* case, Judge *ad hoc* Jiménez de Aréchaga had no doubts of where the Court's sympathies lay; for, recalling the treatment of Article 1 in the majority judgment,[48] he stated that the *North Sea* cases 'proclaimed that Article 1 represented a rule of customary international law'.[49]

The International Court considered the rule in Article 1 once more in the *Tunisia–Libya* case of 1982. On this occasion, however, the rule was more germane to the issues before the Court, since the arguments of both parties made it essential to analyse the concept of the continental shelf as it had developed in international law. The Court there used the rule as an essential part of its argument that continental shelf rights might extend beyond the confines of the physical continental shelf.[50] In so doing, the Court was clearly presupposing its customary status. Since neither Tunisia nor Libya was a party to the Geneva Convention, it was solely the concept of the continental shelf in customary international law that was in point. Indeed, the Court made reference to its previous opinion that the rule was regarded in 1958 as reflecting or crystallizing a received, or at least emergent, rule of customary law.[51] Far from disagreeing with this supposed assessment, the Court affirmed that it was 'at a *very early* stage in the development of the continental shelf as a concept of law' that the divorce of the legal shelf from the physical phenomenon was established by the exploitability criterion.[52]

If the rule in Article 1 constituted emergent law at the time of its adoption in 1958, there would seem to be little reason to doubt that it became a positive rule of general customary law by the end of the 1960s. First, the adoption of Article 1 at the Geneva Conference had a certain impact on customary law. The very concept of continental shelf jurisdiction was a recent development, and there were still some doubts, even in 1958, as to whether it had passed into the corpus of general customary law.[53] The Geneva Conference was thus much more than an attempt to produce a multilateral treaty: it represented a source of legal ideas to which State practice, in search of order and uniformity, would inevitably turn.

[46] pp. 95–6. [47] p. 179. [48] Para. 40.

[49] Paras. 46 and 53.

[50] Paras. 41–2. See text at pp. 139–40 nn. 189–95 below.

[51] Para. 42.

[52] Para. 41 (emphasis added).

[53] See p. 111 n. 2 above. Even in 1984, Bowett described the law of the continental shelf regime as 'a world of comparatively young, developing jurisprudence': CR 84/34, p. 28.

This is not to say that all of the provisions of the Geneva Convention were adopted as customary law. As the *North Sea* cases show, they clearly were not. However, in view of its status as an emergent rule of customary law, the adoption of Article 1 clearly constituted a further step in its consolidation.

Secondly, a survey of claims made in the period up to the end of 1971 reveals that the rule in Article 1 did indeed have a significant impact on State practice. By the end of that year, fifty States maintained claims to continental shelf rights which employed the exploitability criterion (with or without the addition of the 200-metres depth criterion), either expressly, or by incorporating it by reference to the Geneva Convention. Twenty-eight of those States were parties to the Convention by that date;[54] twenty-two were not.[55] Furthermore, twenty-four States—eight States parties and sixteen States not parties to the Convention—had made claims which failed to specify any seaward limit.[56] As has already been noted, these claims may legitimately be counted alongside those claims which employed the rule in Article 1. It is therefore evident that a considerable majority of the coastal States then in existence supported the rule in Article 1 in their actual practice, whether they were parties to the Geneva Convention or not. This body of support appears to have been sufficiently representative of the international community, both geographically and politically, for the formation of a rule of general customary law, consisting of States from all continents, both major political systems, and all stages of development.[57] The rule also attracted the support of those States most interested in the question of the seaward limits of continental shelf rights—namely, those States most active in the offshore

[54] Australia, Canada, Denmark, Dominican Republic, Fiji, Finland, France, Haiti, Kampuchea, Israel, Malaysia, Malta, Mauritius, Netherlands, New Zealand, Nigeria, Norway, Portugal, Roumania, South Africa, Spain, Sweden, Thailand, Trinidad and Tobago, USSR, Venezuela and Yugoslavia. The Ukraine should be added, since it is governed on this point by Union legislation. Israel, Norway and Venezuela made claims utilizing the rule long before they became parties to the Convention.

[55] Argentina, Brazil, Costa Rica, Egypt, Federal Republic of Germany, German Democratic Republic, Ghana, Greece, Honduras, Iceland, India, Indonesia, Italy, Liberia, Mauritania, Morocco, Philippines, Sudan, Syria, Uruguay, Vietnam (South) and Yemen (Aden). A similar claim was also maintained in respect of the Bahamas, then still not independent. It might also be added that one of the United Arab Emirates—Fujairah—also employed the rule in Article 1, thus differing from the other sheikhdoms, which did not define the seaward limits of their claims.

[56] The eight States parties were: Albania, Bulgaria, Guatemala, Jamaica, Mexico, Tonga, UK and USA. The sixteen States not parties were: Bahrein, Belgium, Cameroon, Gambia, Guyana, Iran, Iraq, Ireland, Korea (South), Kuwait, Libya, Panama, Qatar, Saudi Arabia, Sri Lanka and the United Arab Emirates (though see previous note). Similar claims were also maintained in respect of Brunei, a British Protected State, and British Honduras, a colony.

[57] On the requirement that support must be geographically and politically representative of the community of States in order that a rule become part of *general* customary law, see: the *North Sea* cases, at para. 73; the separate opinion of Judge Lachs in those cases, at p. 227; *Texaco Overseas Petroleum* v. *Libya*, *International Legal Materials*, 17 (1978), p. 1 at para. 84; the separate opinion of Judge Dillard in the *Fisheries Jurisdiction* case (*United Kingdom of Great Britain and Northern Ireland* v. *Iceland*), *ICJ Reports*, 1974, p. 3 at p. 57. See also the oral argument of Quéneudec in the *Libya–Malta* case, CR 85/10, p. 52.

oil and gas industry, and those States with extensive areas of shallow sea-bed off their coasts.[58]

Thirdly, a considerable number of States on the United Nations Sea-Bed Committee and at the Third UN Conference on the Law of the Sea treated the rule in Article 1 as general customary law, whether they were parties to the Geneva Convention or not. The delegates of several States directly addressed the question of the relationship of the conventional rule on limits to the customary law, and, of these, all but the Japanese and Nepalese[59] affirmed the belief that the rule in Article 1 represented the contemporaneous state of customary law.[60] The celebrated 'Pardo statement' itself made this very proposition.[61] Moreover, many delegations apparently assumed that Article 1 represented customary law; for they concentrated on the proper interpretation of that article when expounding their arguments on the present limits of national jurisdiction.[62] A similar supposition was accepted by all the parties to the *North Sea* cases, including the Federal Republic of Germany, which was not, of course, a party to the Convention.[63] Furthermore, two of the three great declarations on the law of the sea of the early 1970s affirmed the belief that the rule in Article 1, and in particular the exploitability criterion, constituted general customary law. Thus the Montevideo Declaration on the Law of the Sea of 1970 declares it to be a 'basic principle' of the law of the sea that the coastal State possesses exclusive rights over the contiguous sea-bed 'to

[58] On the requirement that a considerable number, or even a majority, of 'interested' States must subscribe to a rule in order that it become general customary law, see: the *North Sea* cases, at paras. 73 and 74; Judge Lachs, loc. cit. (previous note); the *Texaco* case at paras. 84 and 85; Judge Dillard, loc. cit. (previous note).

[59] Japan: A/AC. 135/1/Add. 3; A/AC. 135/SR. 5, p. 4; A/AC. 135/WG. 1/SR. 6, p. 35; and A/AC. 138/SC. 1/SR. 20, pp. 119–20. Nepal: *UNCLOS III Official Records*, vol. 2, pp. 151–2.

[60] Argentina (not a party to the Geneva Convention), A/AC. 138/SC. 1/SR. 11, p. 127; Australia (a party), A/AC. 135/WG. 1/SR. 8, p. 64; Canada (later became a party), A/AC. 138/SC. 1/SR. 8, p. 90, A/AC. 138/SR. 24, p. 82; Honduras (not a party), *UNCLOS III Official Records*, vol. 2, p. 145; Indonesia (not a party), A/AC. 138/SR. 55, p. 126, ibid., vol. 2, p. 169; Malta (a party), A/AC. 138/SC. 1/SR. 7, p. 61; Mexico (a party), A/AC. 138/SR. 58, p. 186, ibid., vol. 2, p. 173; Norway (a party), ibid., vol. 2, p. 164, and ibid., vol. 1, p. 85.

[61] A/C. 1/PV. 1515, p. 38.

[62] There are many instances of this. The most notable examples are Kenya (a party), *UNCLOS III Official Records*, vol. 2, p. 161; Singapore (not a party), ibid., p. 151; Switzerland (a party), ibid., p. 157. The judgment of the International Court in the *Fisheries Jurisdiction* case discounts the relevance of statements made by States at the Third Conference to a consideration of *lex lata*, since even purported assessments of the state of the existing law may be but 'vehicles of their aspirations' on what the law should be: para. 53. Nevertheless, it is submitted that Judges Forster, Bengzon, Jiménez de Aréchaga, Nagendra Singh and Ruda—half of the majority—were right when, in their joint separate opinion, they remarked that it is not possible to 'brush aside entirely those pronouncements of States and consider them devoid of all legal significance': para. 12. For these pronouncements do constitute judgments on the state of the existing law, and are thus some evidence of what that law then was. Moreover, as the five judges stated (para. 13), they are of significance in determining the *opinio juris* of the States in question on a subject regulated by customary law. Since it is the will of States which is creative of rules of law binding upon them, it is of the utmost relevance to find expressions of this will: *SS Lotus* (*France* v. *Turkey*), *Hudson's World Court Reports*, 2 (1927), p. 20 at p. 35; *PCIJ*, Series A, No. 10, at p. 18. In the *Libya–Malta* case, Judge Oda remarked that 'in seeking to ascertain the principles and rules of the law of the sea today, it is unthinkable to overlook all the efforts deployed in the great workshop of UNCLOS III': para. 31.

[63] *ICJ Pleadings*, vol. 1, pp. 61, 393 and 402; vol. 2, pp. 92 and 242.

where the depth of the superjacent waters admits the exploitation of such resources';[64] and the Declaration of Santo Domingo of 1972 states it to be a proposition of *lex lata* that the coastal State has sovereign rights over 'the submarine areas adjacent to the coast, but outside the area of the territorial sea, to a depth of 200 metres or beyond that limit, to where the depth of the super-jacent waters admits the exploitation of the natural resources of the said areas'.[65]

In conclusion, the rule in Article 1 of the Geneva Convention probably represented emergent customary law at the time of its adoption by the Geneva Conference in 1958. In the ensuing decade, by virtue of its widespread acceptance in State practice and in the juridical consciousness of the international community, this rule passed into the corpus of general customary international law.[66]

(b) *The Meaning of the Rule in Article 1*

1. *The relevance of the* travaux préparatoires

It is clearly legitimate to make use of the deliberations of the International Law Commission and the Geneva Conference to interpret the rule in Article 1 *qua* treaty obligation.[67] These *travaux préparatoires* disclose the precise import which the negotiating States intended that rule to have in the relations of those States which were subsequently to become parties to the Convention. However, it is not immediately obvious that these records are relevant to the meaning of that rule *qua* rule of customary law; for the will which was constitutive of this rule *qua* customary law was the will of States that it should constitute a norm of customary law—a will entirely distinct from that of the formulators of Article 1 as a treaty-norm. Nevertheless, it is submitted that the *travaux préparatoires* are, indeed, of immediate relevance to such an assessment.

First, much support for the customary status of the rule in Article 1 is derived from the practice and the attitudes of States parties to the Geneva Convention. It is highly improbable that these States consider the rule in Article 1 binding in one sense *qua* treaty obligation, whilst at the same time treating the same rule as binding in another, different sense *qua* rule of customary law. Indeed, the evidence is that they do not.[68]

[64] Lay, Churchill and Nordquist, *New Directions in the Law of the Sea*, vol. 1 (1973), at pp. 235–6. The adherents to this Declaration were Argentina, Brazil, Chile, Ecuador, El Salvador, Nicaragua, Panama, Peru and Uruguay.

[65] Ibid., pp. 247–9. The adherents to this Declaration were Colombia, Dominican Republic, Guatemala, Haiti, Honduras, Mexico, Nicaragua, Trinidad and Tobago and Venezuela.

[66] See Judge Ammoun in the *North Sea* cases at p. 106; also Judge *ad hoc* Sørensen at p. 247.

[67] Convention on the Law of Treaties, Vienna, 1969, Article 32. It is beyond doubt that the conditions for the admission of preparatory work to supplement the 'primary' means of interpretation are fulfilled in the case of Article 1. Indeed, all commentators have proceeded on this basis.

[68] See, for instance, the arguments made by several States parties to the Geneva Convention which treat the rule in Article 1 as customary law and refer to the true interpretation of the treaty rule in order to divine the meaning of the customary rule: p. 120 n. 62, above; and statements by Sweden, A/C. 1/PV. 1515, p. 55; and USSR, A/AC. 138/SC. 1/SR. 8, p. 80.

Secondly, it would appear that the will of the generality of States, which subsequently made the rule in Article 1 part of customary law, was influenced by the negotiations which preceded the adoption of that rule *qua* treaty obligation. The process of norm-creation was thus identical to that envisaged by the International Court of Justice in the *Fisheries Jurisdiction* case. In that case the Court addressed, *inter alia*, the concept of preferential fishing rights in the adjacent high seas in favour of States which are especially dependent on coastal fisheries for their economic development or whose populations are overwhelmingly dependent thereon for their livelihood. This concept had been introduced by Iceland at the Geneva Conference of 1958, and had been the subject of discussion both there and at the ensuing Conference in 1960. The Court held that such a concept had passed into customary law by the early 1970s.[69] In so doing, the Court held that, subsequently to the 1960 Conference, 'the law evolved through the practice of States *on the basis of the debates* and near agreements at the Conference'.[70] The Court accordingly referred to various proposals, resolutions and, most interestingly, the express reasoning in favour of the proposals at the Conferences in order to elucidate the precise nature of the alleged right and how to give effect to it.[71] A very similar process seems to have occurred with regard to the rule in Article 1. Several States which approved of that rule and participated in drafting it did not become parties to the Geneva Convention, yet proceeded to make continental shelf claims in accordance with that rule. Their understanding of the rule was presumably influenced by the preparatory work.[72] Indeed, as has already been seen, several States which later maintained the status of the rule as customary law referred to its formulation in the Convention and the preparatory work to elucidate its import *qua* customary law.[73]

This should not be surprising. The Convention did not introduce an entirely novel idea in Article 1: it formulated an idea which was already crystallizing in State practice. The preparatory work should thus be directly relevant in ascertaining the meaning of the nascent customary rule. Moreover, the work of the International Law Commission and the Geneva Conference, and the Convention itself, had a great influence on the customary law of the continental shelf, which was then in its infancy.[74] The records of these debates and the Convention text were a readily available point of reference in a highly important field where there was as yet little doctrine and relatively little State practice. It is therefore very

[69] This proposition has been the subject of much criticism on the grounds that the evidence cited by the Court was insufficient to support its conclusion: see, especially, Churchill, *International and Comparative Law Quarterly*, 24 (1975), p. 82 at pp. 94–7. However, the *process* of reasoning used by the Court has not been criticized.

[70] Para. 52 (emphasis added).

[71] Paras. 55–7.

[72] Especially Argentina, Brazil, Egypt, Ghana, Honduras, Iceland, India, Indonesia, Liberia, Morocco, the Philippines, Syria and Uruguay.

[73] p. 120 n. 62 above, and accompanying text.

[74] See p. 111 n. 2 above, and text at p. 118 n. 53.

much in point to make a careful examination of the *travaux préparatoires* of Article 1 in order to ascertain the precise import of the customary rule. Indeed, the International Court did precisely this in the *Tunisia–Libya* case.[75]

2. *The meaning of 'exploitability'*

(i) *Future exploitation and the limits problem.* Once the International Law Commission had accepted the idea of continental shelf rights, it was recognized that a decision on their seaward limit had to be taken.[76] In accordance with the highly practical approach taken by the Commission,[77] one of the main factors necessitating such a decision was the removal of legal uncertainty. As François pointed out, without a decision on limits, petroleum operators would not know which legal regime was applicable to their activities—the continental shelf or the high seas—and investment would be impaired by uncertainty.[78] The optimum solution was therefore a clear and definite fixed limit. At the same time, in view of the intimate relationship between the justification of continental shelf rights and the possibility of exploiting the coastal sea-bed, the Commission had to provide for the possibility that exploitation would occur at greater depths and at greater distances from the coast in the immediate future.[79]

Given the difficulties that existed in the 1950s of foreseeing precisely how the nascent hydrocarbons industry was going to develop, there was an obvious tension between these two basic requirements, which made it difficult to impose a fixed and definite limit. It was evident that advances in technology would make possible the exploitation of the sea-bed at ever greater depths and distances from the coast; and it was recognized that, in accordance with the rationale of the continental shelf regime, coastal State jurisdiction should at least extend to those less deep and distant areas of sea-bed which would become exploitable in the more clearly foreseeable future. The security interests of the coastal State, and its interests in controlling pollution, justified its exclusive control of any exploitation activities that might occur in such areas. It would also be of little point that the continental shelf regime prevented conflicts, and so maintained international order, in areas currently exploitable if dangerous competition were to be countenanced in the areas just beyond.[80] Moreover, the distributive rationale of the regime would be negated if the technologically advanced States were left free to exploit off the coasts of the developing States outside a continental shelf zone fixed according to contemporary requirements only.[81] Lastly, and perhaps most importantly,

[75] Para. 41. Judge *ad hoc* Jiménez de Aréchaga did likewise: paras. 40–5.

[76] *ILC 2nd Report*, p. 384.

[77] See text at p. 124 n. 85 below.

[78] *Yearbook of the ILC*, 1951, vol. 1, p. 270.

[79] Hudson, ibid., 1951, vol. 1, p. 270; François, ibid.; Kerno, ibid., pp. 272 and 273.

[80] See, especially, the comment of the Venezuelan delegate, *UNCLOS I Official Records*, vol. 6, p. 21.

[81] Statement of the Indian delegate, ibid., p. 12.

it was believed that, at least in the foreseeable future, technology would not succeed in breaking the dependence of offshore drilling operations on coastal support. Consequently, if coastal State jurisdiction were not to extend to new areas of sea-bed as they became exploitable, then their exploitation might well be effectively prevented or its profitability impaired.

However, when the International Law Commission and the Geneva Conference turned their attention to the more distant future, it became increasingly difficult to make reliable predictions. It could not then be known whether the more deep and distant areas of the coastal sea-bed would prove to contain any resources worth exploiting;[82] and, if they did, whether their exploitation would ever be practicable. If they could be recovered, it was nevertheless impossible to foresee how this would be done, and whether the regime of the continental shelf would be appropriate to the technology involved:[83] several States raised the possibility of dredging the sea-bed from installations neither fixed to the sea-floor nor dependent on coastal support, and they clearly felt that the continental shelf regime should not regulate such activities.[84] Conversely, if the working of the sea-bed did in fact continue to be conducted from fixed installations and to rely on coastal support, then the considerations advanced above might well justify the extension of the continental shelf regime to the areas of sea-bed in question; but even then it was impossible to be sure, since changes in global politics and economics—and international law itself—might prove to favour another solution.

This uncertainty made it impossible to set a fixed and definite limit which States could be confident would remain permanently valid. However, the Commission saw its task as being essentially a practical one: to agree upon a treaty-text that would be acceptable to States and facilitate the profitable exploitation of the sea-bed for the immediate future.[85] A permanent solution to the limits problem was not vital, therefore. What was important was that at least a temporary solution should be found that would work satisfactorily for some time to come. It was generally recognized that the continental shelf regime would most appropriately regulate those areas of sea-bed which would become exploitable in the more clearly foreseeable future. Consequently, attempts were made to predict just how deep down and how far out exploitation would prove possible, and to fix a specific and definite outer limit accordingly.

[82] A point well made by Eckert in *The Enclosure of Ocean Resources* (1979), at p. 32.

[83] Cf. Report of the Special Rapporteur François on the Regime of the High Seas and Regime of the Territorial Sea, *Yearbook of the ILC*, 1956, vol. 2, p. 9.

[84] Comment by the Government of the Netherlands on the draft Articles concerning the Law of the Sea adopted by the International Law Commission at its Eighth Session, *UNCLOS I Official Records*, vol. 1, p. 110; cf. also the statement of the Israeli delegate that the continental shelf regime regulated drilling only, and not dredging: ibid., vol. 6, p. 17.

[85] Hudson, *Yearbook of the ILC*, 1950, vol. 1, p. 219, and ibid., 1951, vol. 1, p. 270; Spiropoulos, ibid., 1953, vol. 1, p. 75; Lauterpacht, ibid.; François, ibid., p. 79. See also the statement of the Norwegian delegate, *UNCLOS I Official Records*, vol. 6, p. 47.

(ii) *The limits proposed as reflections of exploitability*. Thus, at the second session of the International Law Commission, in 1950, the outer edge of the physical continental shelf was mooted as a limit to coastal State rights. This was not because of any 'inherent validity' which this feature might have possessed, but because the shelf edge was believed to be the practical limit of exploitation for the foreseeable future.[86] Nowhere is this clearer than in the approach of Hudson. Emphasizing the practical approach the Commission had to take, he proposed that the outer limit should follow the possibilities of exploitation[87]—a clear formulation of the exploitability criterion later enshrined in Article 1. Hudson then put forward a parallel proposal that the outer limit be the edge of the physical shelf,[88] having remarked that this was the limit to practical exploitation for the foreseeable future.[89] That he did not regard the shelf edge as possessing any inherent justification as a limit is clear from two further facts. First, he affirmed that, under his second proposal, sea-bed which was not, scientifically speaking, continental shelf would be assimilated thereto if it constituted 'shallow areas',[90] since, if sea-bed was sufficiently shallow to permit exploitation, the continental shelf regime should embrace it. It was to deal with such situations that he introduced his first proposal in favour of the exploitability criterion.[91] Secondly, Hudson affirmed that, if exploitation should actually occur beyond the shelf edge, then rights beyond that limit would be justifiable.[92] In a similar vein, Canada suggested the edge of the physical shelf as an appropriate limit at the Geneva Conference, on the basis that it reflected 'foreseeable practical requirements'.[93]

Just as the shelf edge was proposed as an outer limit because it was thought to reflect the practical limit of exploitation in the foreseeable future, so with the 200-metre isobath and various other isobaths. Indeed, there seems to have been a much more widespread belief that the 200-metre isobath, and not the edge of the physical shelf, was the maximum depth at which exploitation would prove possible in the foreseeable future.[94] The prevalence of this belief would seem to explain the especial influence which this isobath had in the deliberations of the International

[86] Amado, *Yearbook of the ILC*, 1950, vol. 1, p. 220; Hudson, ibid., pp. 218, 219, 229 and 305. In 1953, Zourek opposed a 200-metre depth limit, because it would impede exploitation which might become possible in the foreseeable future, whilst supporting Kozhevnikov's proposal of the shelf edge: ibid., 1953, vol. 1, p. 77.

[87] Ibid., 1950, vol. 1, p. 218.

[88] Ibid., p. 220.

[89] n. 86 above.

[90] *Yearbook of the ILC*, 1950, vol. 1, p. 221.

[91] Ibid., p. 218.

[92] Ibid., p. 219.

[93] *UNCLOS I Official Records*, vol. 6, p. 30; and see the comments of the Canadian Government on the International Law Commission's draft articles of 1956, ibid., vol. 1, p. 76; cf. the attitude of Argentina, ibid., vol. 6, p. 33.

[94] See, especially: Hudson, *Yearbook of the ILC*, 1950, vol. 1, p. 219; François, ibid., 1953, vol. 1, p. 79; Report of the Special Rapporteur François on the Regime of the High Seas, ibid., 1950, vol. 2, p. 51; and Second Report of the Special Rapporteur François on the High Seas, ibid., 1951, vol. 2, p. 101. See also citations at p. 126 n. 98, below.

Law Commission, epitomized in François's Report of 1951: not wishing to confer shelf rights where there was no practical justification,[95] whilst, at the same time, wanting to enable coastal State jurisdiction to extend to wherever exploitation might prove practicable,[96] he suggested the 200-metre isobath as the natural outer limit.[96] Consequently, François and certain other members of the Commission argued for a 200-metre depth limit, contending that such a limit corresponded with the probable limits of exploitation for the foreseeable future;[97] and this reasoning temporarily prevailed in the International Law Commission in 1953.[98]

There would thus seem to be little substance in the suggestions of Goralczyk[99] and Denorme[100] that the 200-metre isobath figured so prominently because it provided a simple conventional line which roughly corresponds to the edge of the physical shelf. What truth there is in this view[101] is explicable on the basis that this isobath was thought to correspond to the edge of the shelf, which, in turn, was thought to be the practical limit to exploitation for the foreseeable future.[102] Indeed, both supporters and critics affirmed that this was the only reason in its favour.[103] Thus, for instance, there can be found the following exchange:

Mr Hudson said that the point at issue was the working limit in the foreseeable future.

Mr François claimed that he had said that himself. Naturally, if technical progress made it possible to exploit the sea-bed beyond the 200 metre limit, it would have to be reviewed. It could be said that the continental shelf extended up to the limit set by the technical possibilities of working the sea-bed and subsoil. He had considered such a definition, but had believed that it was to everyone's interest to determine, at least provisionally, for the guidance of all concerned with the working of any such waters, how far the rights of States extended. That was

[95] *Yearbook of the ILC*, 1951, vol. 2, p. 101. See also Sandström for an identical line of argument, ibid., 1951, vol. 1, p. 298.

[96] Ibid., p. 102; cf. p. 128 n. 118 below.

[97] Ibid., 1953, vol. 1, p. 79.

[98] Sandström, ibid., 1956, vol. 1, pp. 135 and 138; François, ibid., pp. 137–8; *ILC 5th Report*, p. 213; *ILC 8th Report*, p. 296 at para. 3, explaining its decision of 1953 in favour of the 200-metre isobath. It is of interest to note the adherence of Hudson to this view. He repeatedly stressed that shelf rights must run wherever exploitation might prove possible (*Yearbook of the ILC*, 1950, vol. 1, pp. 214 and 219), and, as has been seen, in 1950 he accordingly proposed a version of the exploitability criterion. In 1951, he continued to espouse the same underlying idea (ibid., 1951, vol. 1, pp. 269 and 270), concretizing it this time in a proposal for a 200-metre depth limit (ibid., p. 271).

[99] *Revue iranienne des relations internationales*, 11/12 (1978), p. 121 at p. 129.

[100] *Proceedings of the Fourth Annual Conference of the Law of the Sea Institute: 1969, The Law of the Sea: National Policy Recommendations*, p. 263 at p. 268.

[101] The Court in the *Tunisia–Libya* case more cautiously remarks that the 200-metre depth criterion was incorporated into Article 1 '*partly* as corresponding approximately to the normal outer limit of the shelf in the physical sense': para. 42 (emphasis added).

[102] Hudson, *Yearbook of the ILC*, 1950, vol. 1, p. 226, and ibid., 1951, vol. 1, p. 269; cf. the Report of the Special Rapporteur François on the High Seas, ibid., 1951, vol. 2, p. 101, referring to the deliberations of the 1950 conferences of the International Bar Association and the International Law Association.

[103] Sandström, ibid., 1951, vol. 1, p. 298; Spiropoulos, ibid., 1956, vol. 1, p. 135.

the only reason why he had adopted the limit of 200 metres which was, moreover, to be found in a number of proclamations.[104]

Concomitantly, it was clearly recognized that, if it had been possible to foresee exploitation beyond 200 metres, then another limit would have had to be adopted.[105] Thus François remarked that it was not objectionable in itself to extend exclusive rights beyond 200 metres, but the contingency of exploitation there was so remote that he doubted the necessity of providing for it.[106]

Several States seem to have followed this line of reasoning. Commenting on the draft articles produced by the International Law Commission in 1951, the United Kingdom and the Union of South Africa both suggested the 600-feet isobath as a limit, since they felt that it would be sufficient for all practical purposes for a considerable time to come.[107] On the same grounds, France suggested the 300-metre isobath,[108] whilst Egypt preferred a depth limit, without specifying any particular figure.[109] Subsequently, at the Geneva Conference, the Lebanon proposed the deletion of the exploitability criterion from the Law Commission's draft Article 67, subject to the retention of the 200-metre limit, on the basis that it would never be profitable to exploit beyond such a depth.[110] The UK and the Netherlands used a similar argument to support a 550-metre depth limit,[111] and India to support the 1000-metre isobath.[112]

It may be noted that several suggestions were made in the 1950s that a limit to coastal State rights should be set at a specific distance from the baseline (or the outer limit) of the territorial sea. Significantly, it was argued in support of these limits that the distance chosen, or to be chosen, was, or would be, a reflection of the practical limits of exploitation for the foreseeable future.[113]

(iii) *Exploitability and the failure of proposals for fixed limits*. However, all these proposals were rejected, both by the International Law Commission and by the Geneva Conference. Although they made provision for the immediate future, all the proposed limits might eventually prove to be unsatisfactory. Even in the 1950s, it was possible to foresee that technology would in time open up the sea-bed beyond any fixed limit that

[104] Ibid., 1951, vol. 1, p. 270. François affirms the same proposition earlier on in this same discussion: ibid. Also, François did not believe the substitution of the 200-metre limit for the exploitability criterion in the Commission's draft articles of 1953 to be a change of basic principle; for, as this quotation shows, in his eyes the 200-metre isobath was just an application of the exploitability concept: ibid., 1953, vol. 1, p. 336.

[105] Fitzmaurice, ibid., 1956, vol. 1, pp. 134 and 135; François, ibid., 1953, vol. 1, p. 338.

[106] Ibid., 1956, vol. 1, p. 132.

[107] *ILC 5th Report*, pp. 266 and 265, respectively.

[108] Ibid., pp. 249–50.

[109] Ibid., p. 249.

[110] *UNCLOS I Official Records*, vol. 6, p. 21; similarly, Italy, ibid., p. 17.

[111] Ibid., pp. 36 and 46, respectively.

[112] Ibid., p. 42; and subsequently 550 metres: ibid., p. 46.

[113] Spiropoulos, *Yearbook of the ILC*, 1953, vol. 1, p. 81; El Khoury, ibid., p. 82; and Norway, *UNCLOS I Official Records*, vol. 6, p. 47.

might be chosen. In all probability, the rationale of the continental shelf regime would justify the extension of coastal State rights to the newly exploitable areas immediately beyond; and, although it was increasingly difficult to make forecasts as the sea-bed under consideration became more remote and its exploitation a more distant prospect, nevertheless, continental shelf rights might turn out to be justifiable even there. Fixed limits were thus a less eligible option, since they might well prevent continental shelf rights extending to where they proved to be justified. Moreover, if exploitation continued to be dependent on coastal State support, as would quite probably be the case, then the failure of coastal State rights to extend to the sea-bed beyond a fixed limit would, as a practical matter, prevent its exploitation or render its working inefficient and uneconomic.

Thus, early on in its discussions, the International Law Commission, with the approval of almost every State,[114] rejected the idea that the presence of a physical shelf should be a necessary condition of the existence of continental shelf rights, or that the physical shelf should limit the legal shelf[115]—a decision not disproved by the choice of the term 'continental shelf' to describe the area of sea-bed delineated in Article 1.[116] Its reasoning was that legal concepts should not impede exploitation:[117] if certain areas of sea-bed might become exploitable in the future, then their exploitation should not be prevented by insisting on the presence of a physical shelf as a precondition of legal rights.[118] Moreover, like the edge of the physical shelf, specific isobaths were rejected as limits: exploitation might outstrip any isobath that might be chosen, yet commercial operations might be unjustifiably prevented or hindered by the failure of coastal State rights to extend beyond that limit to embrace the sea-bed in question.[119] To have countenanced such a situation would have been to fly in the face of the idea of the continental shelf as it had been developed in State practice, it was said.[120] The International Law Commission explained its decision of 1956 to supplement the 200-metre depth limit with the exploitability criterion in precisely these terms.[121] The States of the Americas seem to have rejected a simple 200-metre limit on these

[114] e.g. the Report of the Special Rapporteur François on the Continental Shelf, *Yearbook of the ILC*, 1953, vol. 2, p. 37.

[115] *ILC 2nd Report*, p. 384.

[116] See text at p. 133 nn. 147–8 and p. 138 nn. 181–2 below.

[117] Cf. Hudson, *Yearbook of the ILC*, 1950, vol. 1, p. 214.

[118] Loc. cit. above (n. 115). See also *ILC 3rd Report*, p. 141, para. 2 of the Commentary on draft Article 1; and *ILC 8th Report*, p. 253, paras. 6–7 of the Commentary on draft Article 67. Many statements by individual members of the Commission can be found to similar effect, most notably Fitzmaurice, *Yearbook of the ILC*, 1956, vol. 1, p. 74. At the Geneva Conference, India noted that the physical shelf was the practical limit to exploitation for the present, but that there was no reason why this should remain the case; India accordingly favoured the present Article 1: *UNCLOS I Official Records*, vol. 6, p. 12.

[119] Amado, *Yearbook of the ILC*, 1956, vol. 1, pp. 135 and 138; Fitzmaurice, ibid., p. 134.

[120] Salamanca, ibid., p. 133. See the similar remarks of El Salvador at Geneva: *UNCLOS I Official Records*, vol. 6, pp. 24 and 33–4.

[121] *ILC 8th Report*, p. 296, para. 4 of the Commentary on draft Article 67.

grounds at the Ciudad Trujillo Conference of 1956, opting to supplement it with the exploitability criterion;[122] and, at the Geneva Conference, the same argument was used to reject various specific depth limits which were proposed[123] and to support 'exploitability'.[124] Maximum distance limits were rejected for identical reasons.[125]

The International Law Commission and the Geneva Conference therefore fully appreciated the problems posed by the many uncertainties that existed at that time with regard to the future of offshore drilling. It proved more difficult to design a solution that could accommodate them. The most obvious solution was to select a fixed limit capable of providing for the more immediate future and to leave this limit to be revised subsequently if and when the extension of shelf rights to the sea-bed beyond proved justified. However, to require fresh decisions to be taken each time coastal State rights needed extending would not only be cumbersome, but might also effectively prevent exploitation for considerable periods of time in the same way as a permanent fixed limit.[126]

At the same time, a whole body of reasons opposed meeting this uncertainty by means of extensive limits capable of meeting all eventualities—reasons which also led to the rejection of proposals, made several times in the 1950s, that all States should be entitled to shelf rights out to a minimum distance from the coast, irrespective of the depth of the sea-bed, its physical nature and its prospective exploitability.[127] As Amado stressed in 1951, the continental shelf regime applies to areas which previously had been subject to the freedoms of the high seas: any limitation of these freedoms was liable to prejudice the world community, and therefore required full justification.[128] The justification of coastal State title to continental shelf rights was intimately linked to the practicability of the exploitation of the sea-bed from fixed installations, as has already been seen. The necessary corollary was that, where the sea-bed was not open to

[122] *Inter-American Specialized Conference on Conservation of Natural Resources: the Continental Shelf and Marine Waters, Ciudad Trujillo*, 15–28 March 1956, Report of the Rapporteur of Committee One: Continental Shelf, p. 34.

[123] Notably, Canadian and German opposition to a 550-metre depth limit: *UNCLOS I Official Records*, vol. 6, pp. 42 and 37; and US and Colombian doubts about the wisdom of any specific depth limit: ibid., pp. 40 and 41.

[124] See, especially: Colombia, ibid., p. 10; Korea, ibid., p. 32; and El Salvador, ibid., pp. 24 and 33–4.

[125] e.g. Zourek's opposition to El Khoury's proposal, *Yearbook of the ILC*, 1953, vol. 1, p. 82 (which was rejected at ibid., p. 83); François's explanation of the Commission's opposition to distance limits given to the Sixth Committee of the General Assembly in 1956, A/C. 6/SR. 485, p. 26; and Dutch opposition to the Yugoslav proposal at Geneva, *UNCLOS I Official Records*, vol. 2, p. 12.

[126] Cf. p. 131 n. 137, below.

[127] *Yearbook of the ILC*, 1950, vol. 1, p. 224; ibid., 1951, vol. 1, pp. 271–2 and 296; *UNCLOS I Official Records*, vol. 6, p. 32. It is noteworthy that Amado, speaking in favour of a minimum distance limit, argued that the sea-bed in question, however deep, would eventually prove exploitable: *Yearbook of the ILC*, 1950, vol. 1, p. 224, and ibid., 1951, vol. 1, p. 297. Cf. text at p. 127 n. 113 above.

[128] Ibid., 1951, vol. 1, p. 273.

exploitation, coastal jurisdiction could not be justified.[129] Thus François stressed that to recognize continental shelf rights over areas where there was no prospect of exploitation would be utterly inimical to the Commission's thinking[130]—a sentiment echoed at the Geneva Conference.[131] If an expansive limit were adopted, it might turn out that there were no resources worth exploiting in the deeper and more distant areas of sea-bed embraced by such a limit, or their exploitation might prove to be either technically impossible or uneconomic. Exclusive rights would then have been needlessly conferred on the coastal State, and this at a cost: interference with scientific research relating to the sea-bed;[132] conflicts as to whether bottom fisheries are continental shelf resources or not;[133] potential obstruction of military uses of the sea-bed;[134] and so on. Furthermore, even should such areas of sea-bed eventually prove exploitable, the continental shelf regime might turn out not to be appropriate in view of the technology involved or changing economic and political conditions.[135]

(iv) *The exploitability criterion: a final decision postponed.* Therefore, in the 1950s, uncertainty with regard to a whole series of factors made it impossible to take a *final* decision on the outer limit of the continental shelf regime. Indeed, this uncertainty positively favoured postponement until the information which would facilitate an informed and reliable decision became available. Nevertheless, even in this state of uncertainty, certain intelligent decisions could be taken. As has already been seen, there was a generally held belief in the 1950s that exploitation would prove practicable out to the 200-metre isobath in the more immediate future, and that the continental shelf regime would most appropriately regulate the areas of sea-bed involved. A confident decision could therefore be taken, even then, to recognize coastal State rights out to the 200-metre isobath. This would provide all the benefits of a clear and certain limit for a considerable time to come. Hand in hand with this more immediate solution went recognition that if exploitation of the sea-bed, conducted by means similar to those then in existence, should become practicable beyond that isobath, then coastal State jurisdiction should be *capable* of extending to embrace the areas of sea-bed in question: the 200-metre depth criterion was thus not a final limit but was supplemented by the exploitability criterion. If it were perceived that the extension of continental shelf rights to newly

[129] Kerno, *Yearbook of the ILC*, 1951, vol. 1, pp. 272 and 273. See the Second Report of the Special Rapporteur François on the High Seas, ibid., 1951, vol. 2, p. 101; François, ibid., 1951, vol. 1, p. 297; Brierly, ibid.; Hsu, ibid.; Hudson, ibid., pp. 270 and 296–7; Sandström, ibid., p. 298.

[130] Ibid., p. 272; see also *ILC 3rd Report*, p. 141, paras. 7–8 of the Commentary on draft Article 1.

[131] Dominican Republic, *UNCLOS I Official Records*, vol. 6, p. 9; Colombia, ibid., p. 10; and Norway, ibid., p. 47.

[132] Convention on the Continental Shelf, Article 5 (8).

[133] Ibid., Article 2 (4). Several disputes of this nature have indeed arisen, notably the USA–Japan dispute relating to king crab and the Franco-Brazilian lobster dispute.

[134] Brown, *Current Legal Problems*, 22 (1969), p. 181 at pp. 186–7.

[135] See text at p. 124 nn. 83–4 above.

exploitable areas beyond 200 metres was justified, then it should be possible to make coastal State rights extend to the sea-bed in question. If, on the other hand, it were recognized—perhaps after several such extensions—that coastal rights should not extend any further, to newly exploitable areas beyond, then it should be possible to stop the expansion of the continental shelf regime. Since it would be both cumbersome and disadvantageous to require that a fresh decision be taken each time coastal rights required an extension, a *presumption* was created that jurisdiction should extend to wherever exploitation might prove practicable. However, it was merely a presumption; and, should it at some future time be thought illegitimate that coastal rights extend to a certain point, then the presumption would be rebutted and the expansion of continental shelf jurisdiction halted. Thus Oxman writes:

> what the coastal State desiring to extend its jurisdiction under the exploitability criterion was given is a legal argument of varying validity depending on the nature and location of the area, not an unimpeachable right. The process will be the same as that regarding the territorial sea question and other questions of custom and practice. Rights claimed under the exploitability criterion will become universally valid until some State says 'thus far and no further', at which point various international means for settling the question will be brought into play.[136]

The exploitability criterion might thus be seen simultaneously as a means of postponing a final decision on the outer limit and as the institution of a decision-making procedure as to where this final limit should lie. The subsequent decision might be taken in several ways. A conference might amend the rule in Article 1, fixing a definite limit to the expansion of coastal State rights.[137] Alternatively, a general consensus might develop supplementing the rule in Article 1.[138] If no *general* international decision proved possible, then decisions might be taken bilaterally between interested States, either by means of specific treaties and agreements,[139] or through the normal process of claim, protest and acquiescence.[140] This kind of scenario was envisaged by Spiropoulos and

[136] *Journal of Maritime Law and Commerce*, 3 (1972), pp. 245, 445, and 683 at p. 720.

[137] Cf. François, *Yearbook of the ILC*, 1951, vol. 1, p. 270, ibid., 1953, vol. 2, p. 7, and ibid., 1956, vol. 1, p. 137; Kerno, ibid., 1951, vol. 1, p. 272. Here, a subsequent amendment *permitting* expansion beyond the 200-metre isobath is envisaged, but the current of opinion favouring a subsequent review of any limit that might be chosen is thus evident.

[138] Cf. Tunkin, *Theory of International Law* (translated by Butler, 1974), pp. 142–6. Also Vienna Convention on the Law of Treaties, Article 31 (3) (a) (b).

[139] Cf. the solution of parallel declarations recommended by the American Bar Association: Joint Report of Sections of Natural Resources Law, International and Comparative Law, and the Standing Committee on Peace and Law through the United Nations, reproduced in Stone, *Natural Resources Lawyer*, 1970, p. 155 at p. 192.

[140] This process must be distinguished from the normal process of claim and acquiescence. First, the coastal State need undertake no activity at all with regard to its continental shelf, yet, when the sea-bed becomes *capable* of being exploited, then rights presumptively vest. Secondly, the relevant fact which vests rights in the coastal State is the possibility of *exploitation*: other forms of activity, such as the issue of exploration leases, or the possibility of prospecting, cannot vest presumptive rights under the rule in Article 1. Thirdly, under the normal process of claim and acquiescence, if a State makes a

Scelle, who both doubted that any definite limit could be found which would be acceptable to the generality of States.[141] Indeed, Scelle noted that there was at that time no universally valid limit for the territorial sea, yet most States managed to find *modi vivendi*;[141] whilst Hsu, espousing exploitability, remarked that States would adjust their claims if disagreements arose.[142] By whatever particular means this decision-making process might operate, the exploitability criterion, by tying decisions on the extension of coastal State rights to the practical possibilities of exploitation, ensured that they would be taken in the light of all the relevant facts, such as the resource potential of the sea-bed, the technology of new exploitation operations, and contemporary political, economic and legal conditions.

This basic purpose explains the failure of a large number of claims in the 1940s, 1950s and 1960s to specify any outer limit. These claims can thus be counted alongside those using the exploitability formula when determining whether that criterion reflected the customary law on limits, for their purposes are identical. In view of the large number of those claims which existed in the 1950s, this might well explain why the International Court of Justice in the *North Sea* cases could say that the International Law Commission and the Geneva Conference believed Article 1 to encapsulate an existing, or at least an emergent, rule of customary law.[143]

It was therefore the purpose of the exploitability criterion to leave the decision on the final limits of the continental shelf regime until the future. It did this by conferring exclusive rights on the coastal State wherever the sea-bed became exploitable, but with presumptive force only: they would become definitive if no opposition were raised to their extension, but would cease to exist if a decision was taken that they should not be so extended. However, it might be thought that, by adopting the exploitability criterion, a final decision was in fact taken on the outer limit, since it appears on the face of Article 1 that coastal State rights extend with definitive and irrebuttable force to wherever the sea-bed becomes exploitable—even to the abyssal plains and the middle of the world's oceans. The seas might thus be turned into vast 'national lakes', divided between certain coastal States. The exploitability formula was criticized in the International Law Commission,[144] and at the Geneva Conference,[145] on the grounds that it was open to this very interpretation. This feeling persisted in the debates of the UN Sea-Bed Committee—indeed, the

claim to certain rights over the high seas, its action is prima facie a breach of the law, and its claim only becomes valid once other States give their consent to that claim, explicitly or implicitly. In contrast, once the sea-bed becomes exploitable, continental shelf rights are presumptively *valid*, and it is only if States decide against the extension of coastal State rights and protest that these rights *divest*.

141 *Yearbook of the ILC*, 1950, vol. 1, p. 224.

142 Ibid., 1953, vol. 1, p. 82.

143 See text at p. 116 n. 34 and p. 119 n. 56 above.

144 Report of the Special Rapporteur François on the Continental Shelf, ibid., 1953, vol. 2, p. 38.

145 e.g. Lebanon, *UNCLOS I Official Records*, vol. 6, p. 38; Ceylon, ibid., p. 43; France, ibid.

Japanese delegate, Oda, felt this to be the only logical interpretation of Article 1.[146]

Nevertheless, it is impossible to maintain that this decision was in fact taken. The International Law Commission always recognized that, whatever provision on limits was adopted, it was sea-bed areas off the coasts which were in issue, and there would be an area of sea-bed beyond which could not be subject to continental shelf rights. The Commission several times rejected the substitution of the term 'submarine areas' for 'continental shelf' in Article 1, since the former might be read to embrace any sea-bed, even in mid-ocean, whilst 'continental shelf', although not tying the legal regime to the physical phenomenon, at least served to indicate the 'coastal' nature of the sea-bed areas which the Commission had in mind.[147] The word 'adjacent'—and, before it, 'contiguous'—was seen to have much the same purpose.[148] François clearly believed that there was an area of sea-bed beyond the legal continental shelf which would retain its high seas status, even when exploitable by means of fixed installations;[149] and, as Brownlie observes,[150] a similar opinion existed at the Geneva Conference.[151] Indeed, the potential partition of the whole of the world's sea-bed would have been an immense political problem, whereas the approach taken in the 1950s was essentially a practical one—to provide a straightforward, uncontroversial solution, facilitating the profitable exploitation of the coastal sea-bed for the immediate future.[152] Moreover, almost all the States on the UN Sea-Bed Committee immediately agreed that the 'national lakes' interpretation was totally unacceptable. There was a clear consensus that there was, and would remain, an area of sea-bed beyond national jurisdiction,[153] which found expression in a series of General Assembly resolutions passed by massive majorities.[154]

[146] *Recueil des cours*, 127 (1969–II), p. 355 at p. 442; see also A/AC. 138/SC. 1/SR. 6, p. 53. Similarly, Denorme, the Belgian delegate, A/AC. 135/SR. 5, p. 5—a marked contrast with his academic writings!

[147] Kozhevnikov, *Yearbook of the ILC*, 1953, vol. 1, p. 76; François, ibid., p. 77; *ILC 8th Report*, p. 297, para. 9 of the Commentary on draft Article 67; Pal, *Yearbook of the ILC*, 1956, vol. 1, p. 139; Amado, ibid., pp. 134–5. And see text at p. 138, nn. 181–2, below.

[148] Amado, ibid., 1951, vol. 1, p. 271, and ibid., 1953, vol. 1, p. 80.

[149] Report of the Special Rapporteur François on the Regime of the High Seas and the Regime of the Continental Shelf, ibid., 1956, vol. 2, p. 9. However, this statement was made at a time when the 200-metre depth criterion was the only limit favoured by the International Law Commission.

[150] *Proceedings of the Fourth Annual Conference of the Law of the Sea Institute: 1969, The Law of the Sea: National Policy Recommendations*, p. 133 at p. 140.

[151] As has been observed above (text at p. 124 nn. 83–4), several States conceived of the possibility of exploitation of the deep sea-bed by means of dredging, and thought that this would be subject to the high seas regime rather than that of the continental shelf.

[152] See text at p. 124 n. 85 above.

[153] Report of the Ad Hoc Committee to Study the Peaceful Uses of the Sea-Bed and Ocean Floor Beyond the Limits of National Jurisdiction (1968), A/7230, para. 70; also Annex II (Report of the First Session of the Legal Working Group to the Ad Hoc Committee), para. 40. Also, the statement of Darwin, the representative of the UK, A/AC. 138/SC. I/SR. 6, p. 46.

[154] See, especially, the preamble of General Assembly Resolution 2574A (XXIV), and Resolution 2574D (XXIV).

The whole work of the Sea-Bed Committee and the Third UN Conference on the Law of the Sea proceeded on this basis.

(v) *Exploitability: some objections dismissed.* Several commentators have rejected the notion that the exploitability criterion was adopted in order to facilitate the expansion of the continental shelf regime, claiming that its purpose lies essentially elsewhere. Thus Denorme maintains that, as incorporated in Article 1, 'exploitability' was merely a verbal formula, designed to achieve a compromise.[155] Indeed, the Danish Government argued in its favour that the exploitability criterion accommodated the existing and potential claims of States, whilst avoiding the problem that they would probably be unable to agree on a single fixed limit applicable throughout the world.[156] Reference is also made to the rejection of the Korean proposal at the Geneva Conference—that exploitability be the sole criterion of Article 1 and the 200-metre depth criterion be dropped—as indicating that the exploitability criterion was not desired for its own sake, but was merely one part of the 'fall-back' solution represented by the draft articles of the International Law Commission, which was adopted *faute de mieux*.[157]

There is, perhaps, some truth in Denorme's view. Nevertheless, it would be wrong to insist that the exploitability criterion of Article 1 can be explained purely, or even mainly, as an attempt to obscure failure to achieve a more precise solution to the limits issue. On the contrary, it was the natural expression of the thinking on limits current in the 1950s. Moreover, there were good reasons to reject the Korean proposal and to retain the combination of the exploitability criterion with a 200-metre depth limit, as has been shown above.[158]

Some writers have claimed to see another, distinct aspect to the compromise nature of 'exploitability'. Thus Oxman writes: 'it is unlikely that the exploitability criterion would have been adopted had it not been for the vastly unequal distribution of shelf lands'.[159] On this view, which was shared by Judge *ad hoc* Jiménez de Aréchaga in the *Tunisia–Libya* case,[160] exploitability found its way into Article 1 in order to satisfy those States—most notably, of the west coast of Latin America—which are endowed with very narrow physical shelves, and which would thus find little or no benefit in a continental shelf zone the limits of which were fixed at a specific depth or according to the physical nature of the sea-bed.

155 Loc. cit. above (p. 126 n. 100), at p. 265; cf. Brownlie, loc. cit. above (p. 133 n. 150), at p. 140, though Brownlie did not reiterate this claim in his textbook: op. cit. above (p. 113 n. 20).

156 *ILC 5th Report*, p. 245.

157 Brownlie, loc. cit. above (p. 133 n. 150), at p. 140. Norway explained that it had voted in favour of Article 1 in the Fourth Committee at Geneva, unsatisfactory though it was, since it was preferable to no agreement at all: *UNCLOS I Official Records*, vol. 6, p. 47.

158 See text in paragraph following n. 135 at p. 130 above.

159 Loc. cit. above (p. 131 n. 136), at p. 714.

160 Paras. 41–4; see also para. 52, where he describes the open-endedness of the exploitability criterion as if it were an unintended side-effect.

Rather than being unequivocally deprived of any rights over their adjacent sea-bed, they retained a potential claim thereto.

As with Denorme's interpretation, there is some truth in Oxman's view. Throughout the debates of the 1950s, there can be found expressions of concern lest the criterion chosen to govern the limits of the new regime cause 'unjustifiable inequality' and 'discriminate' between States. Thus the International Law Commission recognized the injustice that would be committed to certain States if a physical shelf were made a precondition of continental shelf rights.[161] It also expressed a desire to avoid the unfair effects which might be caused by certain natural features of the sea-bed, such as submarine troughs close to the coast, which, were a depth limit chosen, would cut off the coastal State from extensive shallow areas further seaward.[162] The proposals for a minimum distance limit were clearly prompted by a desire to compensate those States which had little shallow or exploitable sea-bed off their coasts.[163] This same concern to compensate for natural inequalities lay behind the exploitability criterion, at least in the eyes of some of its proponents. García-Amador justified the reintroduction of exploitability into the draft articles of 1956 on the grounds that it preserved the equality of States.[164] Years later, certain delegates at the Third UN Conference on the Law of the Sea were to argue that the insertion of the criterion into Article 1 demonstrated that the continental shelf regime had as one of its integral elements the idea of compensating those States disadvantaged by submarine geography.[165]

Just as Denorme's interpretation of Article 1 must not be overstressed, so with Oxman's. 'Exploitability' did perform a compensatory role in the mouths of lawyers and statesmen, which ensured the acceptability of Article 1 to Chile, Peru and others. Nevertheless, it is pellucid that exploitability did not in truth compensate the geographically disadvantaged. Deep areas beyond narrow continental shelves would remain unexploitable, and therefore beyond coastal State jurisdiction, for a long time to come. Attempts to confer rights over the sea-bed irrespective of its prospective exploitability met with crushing defeats in the International Law Commission and at the Geneva Conference, as has already been seen.

In conclusion, the fact that the rule in Article 1 came to reflect general

[161] *ILC 2nd Report*, p. 384; François, *Yearbook of the ILC*, 1953, vol. 1, p. 74; Chile, *UNCLOS I Official Records*, vol. 6, p. 16; Colombia, ibid., p. 41.

[162] *ILC 5th Report*, p. 214 at para. 66. See also the Report of the Special Rapporteur François on the Continental Shelf, *Yearbook of the ILC*, 1953, vol. 2, p. 38; and Lauterpacht, ibid., 1953, vol. 1, p. 74.

[163] Yepes, ibid., 1951, vol. 1, pp. 270, 271, 296 and 298; Amado, ibid., p. 270; el Khoury, ibid., p. 271. Also Ecuador, A/C. 6/SR. 489, p. 45; Norway, *UNCLOS I Official Records*, vol. 6, p. 5; and the United Arab Republic, ibid., p. 27.

[164] *Yearbook of the ILC*, 1956, vol. 1, pp. 131 and 136. Also Yepes, ibid., 1951, vol. 1, p. 346, and ibid., 1953, vol. 1, pp. 73 and 338; comments of the Cuban Government on the ILC's draft Articles of 1956, *UNCLOS I Official Records*, vol. 1, p. 80; Chile, ibid., vol. 6, p. 16; Korea, ibid., pp. 23 and 32; and Netherlands, ibid., p. 44.

[165] Argentina, *UNCLOS III Official Records*, vol. 2, p. 150; Trinidad and Tobago, ibid., p. 154; Kenya, ibid., p. 161; Mali, ibid., p. 167; Costa Rica, ibid., vol. 1, p. 60.

customary law, at least by the end of the 1960s, did not mean that the seaward limit of the continental shelf regime was settled. Certainly, coastal State rights extended to the 200-metre isobath. Furthermore, it was presumed that, when exploitation became practicable immediately beyond that depth, the regime would probably extend to the sea-bed in question. But exactly how far this extension should continue was undetermined, although it was universally recognized that at some point it should cease. This was left for future determination. Therefore the Government of Iceland could truly say that in 1968 the law on limits was 'in a stage of evolution' and was 'likely to be transformed' by the deliberations of the UN Sea-Bed Committee.[166]

3. *Was a decision in fact taken?*

Many writers and many States have argued that a deliberate decision was in fact taken in the International Law Commission and at the Geneva Conference on how far continental shelf rights should extend. Although the rule in Article 1 might appear open-ended, an ultimate limit was placed on any future extension of the continental shelf regime under the aegis of the exploitability criterion. Thus, in 1969, Brownlie remarked that those who emphasized the exploitability criterion were saying that the law on limits was more open-ended than it in fact was.[167]

(i) *The 'continental shelf' and* maxima pars pro toto. The most popular argument of this type is that a decision was taken to restrict the extension of continental shelf rights to the physical shelf and its immediate environs on the upper part of the continental slope. Thus Brownlie writes that the correct interpretation of the rule in Article 1 is that '[t]he 200 metre depth criterion is subject to the exploitability criterion, but the latter is controlled by the overall general conception of the shelf as a geological feature'.[168] First, it has been pointed out, both by writers[169] and by States themselves,[170] that the International Law Commission chose to retain the term 'continental shelf' in preference to the vague 'submarine areas' to describe the sea-bed delineated in Article 1. Similarly, Article 6 provides for the delimitation of boundaries between overlapping claims where 'the

[166] A/AC. 135/1/Add. 8. See Rembe, *Eastern Africa Law Review*, 7 (1974), p. 65 at p. 90.

[167] Loc. cit. above (p. 133 n. 150), at p. 136.

[168] Op. cit. above (p. 113 n. 20), at p. 227. However, on p. 228 Brownlie seems to indicate that, by the geological concept of the shelf, he in fact means the continental *margin*, since he there contemplates the exploitability criterion carrying the rights of the coastal State down the slope and on to the continental rise. Yet, on p. 227, he uses several of the arguments that he employed in a paper delivered to the Law of the Sea Institute in 1969 (loc. cit above, p. 133 n 150) in order to maintain that the exploitability criterion is limited by the concept of the physical shelf *stricto sensu*, and not the continental margin. For the latter argument, see section 3 (iii) below.

[169] Denorme, loc. cit. above (p. 126 n. 100), at pp. 268–9; Brownlie, loc. cit. above (p. 133 n. 150), at pp. 137 and 186; Henkin, ibid., at p. 172, and *American Journal of International Law*, 63 (1969), p. 504 at p. 507, and ibid., 64 (1970), p. 62 at p. 66; and Oxman, loc. cit. above (p. 131 n. 136), at p. 715.

[170] Cyprus, A/C. I/PV. 1530, pp. 23–5; Sweden, A/C. I/PV. 1527, pp. 48–50; Roumania, A/AC. 135/WG. 1/SR. 6, p. 70.

same area of continental shelf' is adjacent to the coasts of two States; whilst the very title of the treaty is the 'Convention on the Continental Shelf'. National proclamations have likewise claimed rights over the 'continental shelf'. Admittedly, the 200-metre isobath was at the time known to embrace areas beyond the physical shelf proper,[171] and the exploitability criterion would probably carry continental shelf rights some way further down the continental slope. However, according to the principle that 'the name of the major part stands for the whole', the use of the term 'continental shelf', with its definite geological connotations, served to restrict coastal State jurisdiction to the immediate environs of the homonymous physical feature.[172] Secondly, just as the term 'continental shelf' is thought to have a gravitational effect on the exploitability criterion, so with the 200-metre depth criterion. Denorme remarks that the latter was retained because the exploitability formula was not intended to be of major significance.[173] Given the belief, which was widespread in the 1950s, that this isobath roughly coincides with the edge of the physical shelf, these first two arguments are very similar in effect. Thirdly, several writers have pointed out that the International Law Commission, on adopting the present formulation of Article 1 in 1956, explained in its Report to the General Assembly that it was departing from the *strict* geological concept of the continental shelf, since it considered that 'some' departure therefrom was justified.[174] The Commission, it is said, basically adopted the physical shelf as its model for the legal institution, recognizing the legitimacy of some departure, but treating that as exceptional:[175] exploitability was intended to facilitate merely a *limited* extension of legal rights beyond the physical phenomenon.[176]

Nevertheless, it is submitted that this argument cannot succeed. First, it is extremely doubtful that the use of the term 'continental shelf' has much significance with regard to the issue of limits. This appears on the very face of Article 1, which serves to define the usage of that term throughout the Convention; for there it is made clear that 'continental shelf' is a term of art, the precise meaning of which is governed by the ensuing criteria.[177] The term was apt because, in the 1950s, it was clear that the physical phenomenon would be the chief object of practical interest for a

[171] e.g. François, *Yearbook of the ILC*, 1956, vol. 1, p. 138.

[172] Krylov, ibid., 1956, vol. 1, p. 140; and Sandström, ibid., 1951, vol. 1, p. 275. Also Brownlie, loc. cit. above (p. 133 n. 150), at p. 186, in discussion.

[173] Loc. cit. above (p. 126 n. 100), at p. 268. Also Brownlie, loc. cit. above (p. 133 n. 150), at p. 139.

[174] *ILC 8th Report*, p. 297, para. 9 of the Commentary on draft Article 67.

[175] Henkin, *American Journal of International Law*, 64 (1970), p. 62 at p. 69; Denorme, loc. cit. above (p. 126 n. 100), at pp. 268 and 271; Brownlie, op. cit. above (p. 113 n. 20), at pp. 227–8.

[176] Brownlie, loc. cit. above (p. 133 n. 150), at pp. 137 and 140, and see p. 143, where the fundamental position of the physical shelf in the legal institution is clearly expressed. Fourthly, several writers, rather than curbing the expansive effect of the exploitability criterion, have contended that expansion was not its true purpose: see text at pp. 134–5, nn. 155–65 above.

[177] Spiropoulos, *Yearbook of the ILC*, 1953, vol. 1, p. 76.

considerable time to come.[178] However, as it was decided to include areas of sea-bed which were not, scientifically speaking, continental shelf within the scope of the legal regime, so 'continental shelf' came to incorporate shallow areas not technically shelf,[179] the slope within the 200-metre isobath, and then, potentially, exploitable areas beyond. Nowhere is this better exemplified than in the International Law Commission debates of 1956. Fitzmaurice and García-Amador argued that, since the supplementation of the 200-metre depth criterion by the exploitability formula unequivocally indicated that coastal State jurisdiction might extend on to and down the continental slope, the use of the term 'continental shelf' was infelicitous. Nevertheless, a proposal to drop the term was rejected. As François remarked, the Commission, in accepting that term in 1953, had recognized that departure would be made from its strict geological sense. The proposed amendment was thus of 'no consequence' and the argument misplaced.[180] The term 'continental shelf' was preferred, in spite of this departure from the geological sense of the term, first, because it was already current amongst States;[181] and, secondly, because it served to indicate that the rights of the coastal State lay over a restricted area of sea-bed off its coast, and could not cover remote isolated areas, nor the sea-bed in the middle of the oceans.[182] To argue from this term to a proposition on limits is thus to be under the same misapprehension as were Pal and Zourek when they joined the International Law Commission in 1953—a notion of which they were quickly disabused by their colleagues.[183]

The 200-metre depth criterion likewise has little relevance to the proper interpretation of the exploitability criterion. As has been shown above, the combination of these two criteria in Article 1 is explicable without recourse to the idea that the former implies a gravitational effect on the latter.[184]

Furthermore, it is extremely difficult to construe the debates in the International Law Commission as indicating any intention to limit the range of the exploitability criterion. Paucity of reference to the continental slope is little indication of any such intention. The physical shelf and its analogues, such as the Persian Gulf, were the most important areas from a

[178] Fitzmaurice, *Yearbook of the ILC*, 1956, vol. 1, p. 134; in Hudson's words, it was the 'crux' of the problem: ibid., 1950, vol. 1, p. 229.

[179] Brownlie, op. cit. above (p. 113 n. 20), at pp. 227–8.

[180] *Yearbook of the ILC*, 1956, vol. 1, p. 140. Zourek observed that, once it was agreed that there was a lack of congruency between the legal definition and the geological connotation, the fact that the legal term was to include at least some of the slope was a mere technicality, which could be satisfactorily explained in the Commentary: ibid. Amado wished to retain the term (ibid., p. 135), whilst recognizing that exploitability had the potential to carry the coastal State's rights on to the terrace proper (ibid., p. 138).

[181] Sandström, ibid., 1953, vol. 1, p. 76; François, ibid.; Amado, ibid.; *ILC 5th Report*, p. 214, para. 65 of the Commentary; also *ILC 8th Report*, p. 297, para. 9 of the Commentary on draft Article 67.

[182] Text at p. 133 nn. 147–8, above.

[183] *Yearbook of the ILC*, 1953, vol. 1, p. 76; cf. Pal, ibid., 1956, vol. 1, p. 133, where his realization that 'continental shelf' was a term of art is evident.

[184] See text following n. 135 at p. 130 above.

practical perspective at that time, whilst the slope was then of little moment, since it would not be economically exploitable for a long time to come.[185] There are, nevertheless, several observations that the exploitability criterion would take continental shelf rights down the continental slope. However, the issue of 'how far down the slope?' was not addressed, because no intelligent answer could then be given.[186] Although certain isolated statements in the Commission's Report of 1956 do seem to indicate an intention to limit the legal regime to the environs of the shelf edge, the Report also remarked that it had adopted the physical shelf as the basis of its juridical definition only 'to a certain extent'.[187]

This conclusion is corroborated by a consideration of the jurisprudence. As the International Court notes in the *North Sea* cases, it was the discovery that the physical continental shelf was rich in energy resources, which could be exploited commercially, that was at the root of the development of the legal institution.[188] However, as the Court observes in the *Tunisia–Libya* case, the legal concept of the continental shelf, 'while it derived from the natural phenomenon, pursued its own development', so that there arose a 'lack of identity between the legal concept of the continental shelf and the physical phenomenon known to geographers by that name'.[189] It is indeed true that the legal and the physical conceptions do not coincide.[190] For, under the rule in Article 1, the legal shelf does not embrace certain parts of the physical shelf: namely, the sea-bed of the territorial sea, and the deeper areas of the physical shelf, which, in some parts of the world, lie well beyond the 200-metre isobath and the reach of modern exploitation techniques. At the same time, the legal shelf does include sea-bed which is not, scientifically speaking, continental shelf, such as the shelves of islands, and shallow basins such as the North Sea and the Persian Gulf. However, the International Court seems to have in mind more than these technical divergences from the strict physical conception; for it is to the exploitability criterion that it points as the prime cause of the divorce between the legal and the physical shelves. This criterion, it is said, made the outer limit of the legal institution 'clearly open-ended'.[191] Consequently, the legal concept of the continental shelf has undergone a 'widening', and has acquired 'a more extensive connotation' than the physical concept.[192] In his separate opinion, Judge *ad hoc* Jiménez de Aréchaga comes to a similar conclusion.[193] Affirming that the very purpose of the exploitability criterion was to extend coastal State rights to areas beyond the physical shelf,[194] he states that 'the facts of geomorphology, as

[185] François, ibid., 1956, vol. 1, p. 138. [186] See text at pp. 143–4 nn. 222–7 below.

[187] *ILC 8th Report*, p. 297, para. 7 of the Commentary on draft Article 67.

[188] Para. 95.

[189] Para. 42; and see para. 41. Judge *ad hoc* Evensen expressed his agreement with these passages: para. 10. [190] Brownlie, op. cit. above (p. 113 n. 20), at pp. 227–8.

[191] Para. 42.

[192] Para. 41. See also the argument of Weil for Malta in the *Libya–Malta* case: CR 84/25, p. 47.

[193] Para. 40. [194] Paras. 41–4.

well as those of geology, did not constitute a controlling factor in the legal definition of the continental shelf or in the recognition of sovereign rights for its exploration and exploitation'.[195]

Once more, in the *Libya–Malta* case, the attention of the International Court was drawn to the history of the relationship between the legal shelf and its physical homonym. Counsel for Malta made extensive citation of the foregoing passages from the *Tunisia–Libya* case,[196] and the Maltese Agent concluded that '[e]ven in 1958 . . . the constraint on the extent of the shelf was placed by the Convention of that year not on the morphology of the seabed, much less on its geology, but on the progress achieved by technology . . . with the result that there were in fact no definable limits to the extent of the continental shelf'.[197] Consonant with its previous judgment, the Court, whilst noting the physical origins of the legal regime, stated that 'throughout its history' it has become 'more and more a complex and juridical concept'.[198]

(ii) *'Adjacency' as a distance limit*. Henkin has maintained that the use of the term 'adjacency' in Article 1 was intended to imply a maximum limit to the exploitability criterion based on distance from the coast.[199] This opinion is shared by Denorme,[200] and also, it seems, by Goralczyk;[201] and, in the UN debates after 1967, several States used the same argument.[202]

This is by no means a necessary meaning of 'adjacency'. It could equally well mean 'that which lies next to', referring to location, rather than to dimension.[203] If anything, this is its more natural meaning, and the debates of the 1950s provide no ground for reading it otherwise. A few isolated statements can be found suggesting that some notion of closeness was in the minds of at least certain members of the International Law Commission;[204] and, in 1956, both García-Amador and Fitzmaurice explicitly suggested that a maximum distance limit was implicit in the use of the term 'adjacent'.[205] However, as François pointed out at the time, the proposition that this word implied a horizontal limit on the extension of coastal State rights was 'an entirely new idea, foreign to the ones previously adopted by the International Law Commission'.[206] Indeed, the

[195] Para. 44; also para. 46.

[196] CR 84/22, pp. 50 and 51; CR 84/25, pp. 52–3 and 66.

[197] CR 84/22, p. 50.

[198] Para. 34. See also the separate opinion of Judge Mbaye at p. 94.

[199] Loc. cit. above (p. 137 n. 175), at p. 64. The geology of the area within that distance might well be totally irrelevant: ibid.

[200] Loc. cit. above (p. 126 n. 100), at pp. 264 and 273.

[201] Loc. cit. above (p. 126 n. 99), at p. 132.

[202] Malta, A/C. I/PV. 1515, p. 42, A/AC. 138/SC. 1/SR. 7, pp. 61, 62 and 65–6; Belgium, A/AC. 138/SR. 36, p. 92 (Denorme); Singapore, *UNCLOS III Official Records*, vol. 2, p. 151; Switzerland, ibid., pp. 167–8. Sweden, A/C. I/PV. 1527, pp. 48–50, seems to have regarded adjacency as making proximity at least a part of the law on limits.

[203] Brown, *The Legal Regime of Hydrospace* (1971), p. 5.

[204] Second Report of the Special Rapporteur François on the High Seas, *Yearbook of the ILC*, 1951, vol. 2, p. 101; Report of the Special Rapporteur François on the Continental Shelf, ibid., 1953, vol. 2, p. 38; Liang, ibid., 1953, vol. 1, p. 76.

[205] Fitzmaurice, ibid., 1956, vol. 1, p. 134 and 135; García-Amador, ibid., p. 135.

[206] Ibid., p. 137.

notion of a maximum distance limit was decisively rejected several times in the Commission, and subsequently at the Geneva Conference. Such limits were felt to fly in the face of the underlying purpose that was being pursued in the limits debate. Moreover, as Brown has observed, the 200-metre isobath may lie over 200 miles from the coast, as it does off the northern coast of the Soviet Union; yet such areas were definitely considered to be subject to coastal State jurisdiction, despite their distance from the coast.[207]

In fact there is positive evidence that 'adjacent' was intended to be used in its more normal sense of '[an object] lying next to'. The International Law Commission was faced with the problem of an area of shallow sea-bed cut off from another area of shallow sea-bed landward thereof by a deep trough. Though the latter might be 'adjacent' to the coast,[208] the former could not be said so to be, being divorced therefrom by the trough and the other block of sea-bed. Coastal State rights would therefore not extend to that area on a strict interpretation of Article 1. It was felt necessary to make a special 'exception' for certain of the cases where such 'inequitable' results would otherwise follow; so confirming that the Commission used 'adjacency' in its basic sense.[209] If the term were used in the sense of closeness, the presence of a trough would have been irrelevant, as long as the shallow area beyond was close to the coast.[210]

Those who argue that 'adjacency' implies that the juridical shelf must be close to the coast have found support in the judgment of the International Court in the *North Sea* cases. In its majority judgment, the Court at one point addresses the notion of 'adjacency', remarking:

> it is evident that by no stretch of imagination can a point on the continental shelf situated say a hundred miles, or even much less, from a given coast, be regarded as 'adjacent' to it, or to any coast at all, in the normal sense of adjacency, even if the point concerned is nearer to some one coast than to any other. . . . Equally, a point inshore situated near the meeting place of the coasts of two States can often properly be said to be adjacent to both coasts, even though it may be fractionally closer to the one than the other.[211]

It has been contended that, on this basis, the continental shelf regime may not cover areas of sea-bed too far from the coast.[212] However, this is to ignore the context in which this statement occurs. The Court is here

[207] Op. cit. above (p. 140 n. 203), at p. 6. François explicitly noted this fact: *Yearbook of the ILC*, 1953, vol. 1, p. 81.

[208] The analogous term 'contiguous' was used when this debate arose: ibid., 1953, vol. 2, pp. 212 and 214.

[209] Ibid., 1956, vol. 2, p. 297, para. 8 of the Commentary on draft Article 67. See Brown, op. cit. above (p. 140 n. 203), at p. 6.

[210] Cf. Henkin, loc. cit. above (p. 137 n. 175), at p. 64, where he indicates that the nature of the sea-bed contained within the 'adjacent' but exploitable area might well be irrelevant if 'adjacent' means close.

[211] Para. 41.

[212] Henkin, loc. cit. above (p. 126 n. 100), at p. 173, in discussion. Henkin and other reciters of this passage do not address the problem that the 200-metre isobath may lie over 200 miles from the coast: text preceding n. 207, above.

addressing the contention of the Netherlands and Denmark that the basic rationale of continental shelf rights is that the sea-bed in question is close to the coast, and that, in consequence, when drawing boundary lines between overlapping claims, it is only natural that an equidistance line be used, awarding each State those areas of sea-bed closer to it.[213] Finding that State proclamations and treaties use a variety of terms to describe the relationship of the juridical shelf to the coast, and that 'adjacent' is the term most commonly employed, the Court proceeds to see if 'adjacent' is used in the sense of closeness. It takes, in isolation, an area of sea-bed only a hundred miles out—an area clearly within the juridical shelf, since areas less than 200 metres deep can clearly lie further than that from the coast. If 'adjacent' is truly used in the sense of 'close', then this area must be capable of being described as 'adjacent' to the coast. It cannot be so described; thus 'adjacent' is used in its natural sense of 'lying next to', and not as referring to the dimensions of the object described: since if the area considered is taken *in isolation*, it is not 'adjacent' to the coast. (However, if the area is to be treated as *part* of a larger whole, and not in isolation, then that whole can truly be said to be 'adjacent' to the coast.) That proximity is not the basis of shelf rights is thus made clear;[214] and the Court accordingly proceeds to reject the argument that delimitation according to the equidistance method is juristically inevitable. This passage from the Court's judgment therefore disproves, rather than proves, the argument in favour of a distance limit.

(iii) *The base of the slope*. The previous two contentions bear an underlying similarity. Both of them, if true, would not establish a *precise* limit to the expansion of coastal State rights according to the exploitability criterion; rather they would merely establish the *type* of limit and its approximate location. The precise outer limit would thus remain open,[215] and a decision on a specific limit would remain to be taken.[216] The third argument differs in an important respect. It presupposes that a decision was taken in fairly precise terms on how far shelf rights might extend. Technical deliberation on how to convert this limit into a line on the map would be all that was subsequently required.

Thus Finlay has argued that a decision was in fact taken in the 1950s that, should technology develop to permit its exploitation, coastal State rights might extend to the base of the continental slope,[217] but no

[213] Paras. 37–9.

[214] Brown, op. cit. above (p. 140 n. 203), at p. 35.

[215] Denorme, loc. cit. above (p. 126 n. 100), at p. 265.

[216] Cf. ibid., p. 273, where recommendations are made for a specific outer limit.

[217] The landward part of the rise is often mentioned too. However, in so far as Finlay's argument is founded on the taking of a deliberate decision in the 1950s, this cannot be the case. The rise is not mentioned once in any of the debates or in the available scientific evidence: see the Terminology and Definitions Approved by the International Committee on the Nomenclature of Ocean Bottom Features, adopted by the International Committee of Scientific Experts at Monaco in 1952, reproduced at *Yearbook of the ILC*, 1956, vol. 1, p. 131; and the Panamanian delegate remarked that the declivity of the slope ends on contact with the horizontal plane of the ocean floor: *UNCLOS I Official Records*, vol. 6, p. 33.

further.[218] This contention is founded on two pieces of evidence: first, the resolution adopted by the States of the Americas at the Ciudad Trujillo Conference of 1956, which was the main impetus behind the decision of the International Law Commission to supplement the 200-metre depth criterion with the exploitability formula in its draft articles of 1956. This resolution seems to have contemplated that coastal State rights might extend to the base of the slope as such areas became exploitable; for it states:

the seabed and subsoil of the continental shelf, the continental and insular terrace, or other submarine areas, adjacent to the coastal State, but outside the area of the territorial sea, and to a depth of 200 metres or, beyond that limit, to where the depth of the superjacent waters admits of the exploitation of the natural resources of the seabed and subsoil, appertain exclusively to that State and are subject to its jurisdiction and control.[219]

It is assumed that the intention behind this resolution was imported wholesale into the Commission's draft articles when they were amended to include the exploitability criterion. Secondly, it is observed that García-Amador affirmed that the effect of the incorporation of that criterion would be to legitimize (potential) coastal State rights to the base of the slope, despite the fact that the Commission rejected the reference made by the Ciudad Trujillo resolution to the continental terrace.[220]

This argument cannot succeed. Although the American resolution was an important factor in persuading the International Law Commission to add the exploitability criterion, the Commission did not simply adopt the reasoning of the American States. The term was debated, and the Commission adopted it for its own reasons. Moreover, exploitability was not a new idea: the Commission had used it in 1950 and 1951,[221] and, as has been shown, the principle behind it underlay the whole of the Commission's thinking on limits from 1950 to 1956. This argument also ignores the fact that a Panamanian proposal in favour of the very proposition suggested by Finlay was decisively rejected at the Geneva Conference by an overwhelming vote.[222] Although reference was made to the slope—

[218] *American Journal of International Law*, 64 (1970), p. 42 at p. 45; although there is room for rights over the deep ocean floor where equity demands compensation of States with narrow continental terraces: ibid., p. 46. In his textbook, Brownlie seems to subscribe to a similar view: op. cit. above (p. 113 n. 20), at p. 228, and see p. 136 n. 168 above. In so far as Brownlie argues that such a decision was taken in the 1950s, the comments made below on Finlay's argument are equally relevant; but, in so far as his argument is dependent on developments subsequent to the 1950s, see sections 3. (iv) and IV. (b) below.

[219] Loc. cit. above (p. 129 n. 122). The clause 'or other submarine areas' seems to be a true alternative, designed to compensate States lacking an extensive shelf or terrace: Finlay, loc. cit. (previous note), at pp. 44–5 and 46.

[220] *Yearbook of the ILC*, 1956, vol. 1, p. 136.

[221] Cf. Goldie, loc. cit. above (p. 126 n. 100), at p. 282, in discussion.

[222] Thirty-eight votes against, four in favour, with twenty-six abstentions: *UNCLOS I Official Records*, vol. 6, p. 47. Argentina remarked that the Panamanian proposal was a completely novel idea: ibid., p. 39.

often indirectly—in the debates of 1956, there is no indication given of just how far down the slope coastal jurisdiction might extend. Thus the Report of the Commission for 1956 admits extension of coastal State rights beyond the physical shelf, but does not examine the question of how far.[223] Amado and Salamanca remarked that, in accordance with the Commission's purpose on the limits issue, the terrace should not be excluded from coastal control; but they did not say if all of it might be made juridical shelf, or all of it and no more, or clarify the matter at all.[224] Indeed, that no such decision could be intelligently taken is clear from the fact that the Commission did not seem to understand the dimensions of the continental slope. François and Fitzmaurice thought it had no clear meaning;[225] for several, it was an esoteric scientific term which they could not understand;[226] whilst others completely misunderstood its true extent.[227]

(iv) *Leasing practice and the continental slope*. The argument has occasionally been heard that, even though no decision was taken in the 1950s on how far down the continental slope coastal State rights might extend, nevertheless, by the 1970s, certain States had acquired continental shelf rights over much of the adjacent continental slope—and even parts of the continental rise—by issuing licences to private companies for prospecting, test-drilling and exploration, or by making legislative provision for the licensing of these areas.[228] Obviously, such rights cannot have been acquired under the rule in Article 1. That rule can only create rights beyond 200 metres when and where the sea-bed becomes exploitable; whereas the leasing activity in question related solely to prospecting and exploration.[229] Rather, the argument seems to be that the issuing of licences, permits and leases was in the nature of an implicit claim by the coastal State to the right to regulate exploration, and, *a fortiori*, exploitation, of the sea-bed in question. These claims, though well known, encountered no protests, and from this silence on the part of other States can be inferred their consent to the validity of the rights claimed, which consequently became opposable to the rest of the international community. The argument is thus similar to that which was used by the International Court in the *Fisheries* case when it held that, as a result of the failure of the

[223] *ILC 8th Report*, pp. 296–7.

[224] *Yearbook of the ILC*, 1956, vol. 1, pp. 138 and 133, respectively.

[225] Ibid., pp. 132 and 134, respectively; cf. statements about translation difficulties: el Khoury, ibid., p. 134; Krylov, ibid.

[226] Spiropoulos, ibid., p. 135; Salamanca, ibid., pp. 133 and 140.

[227] Thus García-Amador talked of the foot of the terrace as being 500 metres deep: ibid., p. 136; likewise Panama at the Ciudad Trujillo Conference: see Oxman, loc. cit. above (p. 131 n. 136), at pp. 453–4. In fact the average depth of the foot of the slope is 1,830 metres—and it can be up to 5,000 metres deep: Brown, *Sea-Bed Energy and Mineral Resources and the Law of the Sea:* Vol. 1, *The Areas Within National Jurisdiction* (1984), at 1.4 30.

[228] Auburn, *Canadian Bar Review*, 50 (1972), p. 87 at p. 97. Stone is more cautious: loc. cit. above (p. 131 n. 139), at p. 170. See also Brownlie, op. cit. above (p. 113 n. 20), at pp. 226–7. For a review of this leasing practice, see Auburn, loc. cit., at pp. 96–104; and for a detailed table of Canadian leases, see Buzan and Middlemiss, in Johnson and Zacher (eds.), *Canadian Foreign Policy and the Law of the Sea* (1977), p. 5.

[229] Malta, A/AC. 138/SC. I/SR. 7, p. 62.

UK to protest against the Norwegian decrees of 1869 and 1889, of which it had long been apprised, Norway had become entitled to use straight baselines as against the UK.[230]

Considerations of space preclude examination of this argument here. However, even if this argument were valid, it would merely establish that particular States had, by 1970, acquired continental shelf rights over the slope and rise: it would not follow that such a limit was part of *general* customary law. Furthermore, it may be pointed out here that this argument faces several problems, even if it is to serve as a basis for the special claims of particular States. First, as Brownlie points out, it is not always clear that the States which issue these leases and permits intend them to be valid as against, and exclusive of, foreign nationals, rather than merely constituting regulation of the conduct of their own nationals.[231] It is therefore not necessarily the case that leasing practice implies a claim of exclusive continental shelf rights. Secondly, there may be difficulties in fixing other States with the knowledge that leases have been issued.[232] Thirdly, some doubts may exist even then as to whether the issue of leases for prospecting and exploration, as distinct from exploitation, can truly be treated as a claim to continental shelf rights. The argument that sovereign rights could be acquired by means of such leases has been made only once in the whole course of the UN debates since 1967.[233] It met with the immediate reply that rights beyond 200 metres could only be acquired when the sea-bed became exploitable;[234] otherwise, the argument was simply ignored. Fourthly, in the *Tunisia–Libya* case, the International Court gave a cold reception to the argument made by Libya that it had acquired rights, opposable to Tunisia, over the sea-bed depicted in a map which purported to show the area over which Libya's power to issue exploration and exploitation licences existed. The Court accepted that the Petroleum Law of 1955 and Petroleum Regulation No. 1 (to which the map in question was annexed) constituted a claim by Libya to a continental shelf zone; but, as to the *limits* of that zone, the Law, Regulation and map were said to be 'purely internal' and 'domestic' acts, 'not sufficient even for the mere purpose of defining a formal claim at the level of international relations to a maritime or continental shelf boundary'.[235] Although that case related to the delimitation of lateral boundaries between overlapping claims rather than the outer limit, the Court's scepticism with regard to claims founded on leasing practice is revealing.[236]

230 *Fisheries* case (*United Kingdom* v. *Norway*), *ICJ Reports*, 1951, p. 116 at pp. 138–9.

231 Op. cit. above (p. 113 n. 20), at p. 227; see also loc. cit. above (p. 133 n. 150), at pp. 142–3.

232 Cf. *Case Concerning Sovereignty over Certain Frontier Land* (*Belgium/Netherlands*), *ICJ Reports*, 1959, p. 208 at pp. 227–9. This case even involved neighbouring States!

233 Canada, A/C. I/PV. 1529, p. 71, and A/AC. 135/SR. 4, p. 4.

234 p. 144 n. 229 above.

235 Para. 92.

236 In the *Gulf of Maine* case, Canada presented an argument somewhat similar to Libya's. However, the leases issued for the exploitation of the sea-bed were well-known to the US, which

4. *Limits based on the rationale of continental shelf rights*

Many commentators and a considerable number of States have maintained that, in spite of all appearances, there always has been a limit to the seaward extension of coastal State rights implicit in the very rationale of the continental shelf regime. This line of argument is thus distinct from the various contentions discussed above. The latter shared the common feature that the question of limits was said to have been the subject of conscious and deliberate decision during the debates of the 1950s. In contrast, the present line of thought does not search for evidence of a deliberate decision on limits. Rather, it is maintained that, once certain considerations were recognized as justifying coastal State jurisdiction over the adjacent sea-bed, the limits to this jurisdiction were simultaneously fixed in accordance with the well-known maxim '*cessat ratio, cessat lex*'.

(i) *Natural prolongation.* The most well-known argument of this type is the so-called 'natural prolongation' argument, which seems to have its origin in the judgment of the International Court of Justice in the *North Sea Continental Shelf* cases. In a celebrated passage, the Court remarked:

> What confers the *ipso jure* title which international law attributes to the coastal State in respect of its continental shelf, is the fact that the submarine areas concerned may be deemed to be actually part of the territory over which the coastal State already has dominion,—in the sense that although covered with water, they are a prolongation or continuation of that territory, an extension of it under the sea.[237]

This passage has been interpreted as meaning that, in customary law, what justifies the exclusive rights which the coastal State has over the sea-bed off its coasts is the fact that, *physically speaking*, these areas of sea-bed constitute an extension of the coastal State's land territory under the sea—that is, they are its natural prolongation. Taking this as the major premiss, it is then observed that, underlying the surface sediments, the crust of the earth is of two basic types: continental-granitic and oceanic-basaltic.[238] It is the continental-granitic crust which underlies the world's continental landmasses. However, it does not stop at the shore-line: typically, it extends below the sea-bed off the world's coasts to the bottom of the continental slope, and then continues under at least part of the continental rise (where the rise is present). The continental shelf, the continental slope and at least the landward part of the continental rise can thus be said, in

learned about them in detail in the course of inter-governmental correspondence; the US also knew that Canada considered the leases to constitute a claim of shelf rights because of this correspondence. The case thus bears little similarity to the situation under discussion. See *Case concerning the Delimitation of the Maritime Boundary in the Gulf of Maine Area* (*Canada/United States of America*), *ICJ Reports*, 1984, p. 245 at paras. 126–48.

[237] Para. 43; see also para. 19.

[238] See, e.g., Brown, op. cit. above (p. 144 n. 227), at 1.4 29. As Lauterpacht observed in his oral argument for Malta in the *Libya–Malta* case, 'to most readers "natural prolongation" refers to inherent content and structure rather than surface shape': CR 84/23, pp. 66–7.

physical terms, to constitute a continuation below the sea of the continental landmass. Moreover, whilst the continental rise is partly based on oceanic-basaltic crust, the rise itself consists of detritus washed down or slumped from the shelf and slope, and can thus be said to be a geological prolongation of the continents *in toto*.[239] These natural facts serve as the minor premiss of the argument. By means of a syllogism, it is concluded that the coastal State possesses exclusive rights over the whole of the adjacent continental margin, irrespective of its current exploitability.[240] Indeed, coastal States have possessed these rights from the time that the continental shelf regime became part of general customary law.

This argument was first developed by Jennings.[241] It has attracted considerable support: many commentators on the law of the continental shelf, such as Anand[242] and Gardiner,[243] have espoused it; and, at the Caracas session of the Third UN Conference on the Law of the Sea, a considerable number of States deployed it in support of their claim that any future convention must make the outer edge of the continental margin the limit of continental shelf rights in recognition of the position at customary law.[244]

This argument must be distinguished from the other major argument in favour of a margin limit, considered below.[245] The present argument contends that, right from the inception of the continental shelf regime, what has justified the rights which the coastal State exercises over the sea-bed off its shores is that this sea-bed physically prolongs its land territory: consequently, the toe of the continental margin has *always* represented the limit to coastal State rights. This argument might be mistaken. Nevertheless, a second argument might be made that, even if the outer edge of the margin was not the limit in the 1950s and 1960s, it became so by the end of the 1970s, as the result of a conscious decision taken at the Third UN Conference.

[239] Feulner, *Virginia Journal of International Law*, 17 (1976), p. 77 at p. 85; Jennings, *International and Comparative Law Quarterly*, 18 (1969), p. 819 at p. 830.

[240] If it is accepted that all of the rise is continental in nature, 'continental margin' will be understood in its geomorphological sense; if not, and only the landward part of the rise is considered continental, it will be understood in its geological sense: see Brown, op. cit. above (p. 144 n. 227), at 1.4 29.

[241] Loc. cit. above (n. 239), at pp. 821–4 and 829–30.

[242] Anand (ed.), *Law of the Sea: Caracas and Beyond* (1980), p. 145 at pp. 160–3 and 179.

[243] *Revue iranienne des relations internationales*, 11/12 (1978), p. 145 at pp. 151 and 154.

[244] In the Second Committee (for the significance of asterisks, see p. 159 n. 321 below): Argentina*, *UNCLOS III Official Records*, vol. 2, p. 150; Australia, ibid., p. 147; Bangladesh*, ibid., p. 144; Chile, ibid., p. 166; Ecuador, ibid., p. 158; El Salvador*, ibid., p. 149; Honduras, ibid., p. 145; Iceland, ibid., p. 159; Korea (North), ibid., p. 162; Korea (South), ibid., pp. 148 and 196; Mauritius*, ibid., p. 163; Mexico*, ibid., p. 166; New Zealand*, ibid., p. 170; Portugal, ibid., pp. 145–6; Trinidad and Tobago, ibid., pp. 154–5; Turkey*, ibid., p. 158; UK, ibid., p. 200; US, ibid., p. 291; Uruguay*, ibid., p. 153; and Venezuela, ibid., p. 152. In Plenary: Bahamas, ibid., vol. 1, p. 132; Canada*, ibid., p. 97; and Senegal, ibid., p. 164. Several other States supported a margin limit, but without relying on the natural prolongation argument. Burma, ibid., vol. 2, p. 155, and Thailand*, ibid., p. 160, supported a margin limit by reference to the concept of natural prolongation; but they appear to have regarded natural prolongation as justifying jurisdiction solely over the shelf as a matter of *lex lata*, and its use to justify a margin limit as a proposal *de lege ferenda*: see text at p. 149 n. 251 below.

[245] Section IV (b).

It is submitted that the natural prolongation argument propounded by Jennings and his followers is mistaken. To accept the concept of natural prolongation as the basis of coastal State rights and to interpret it in a physical sense—in short, to accept the major premiss outlined above—does not necessarily yield the conclusion that the outer limit to coastal State rights is the edge of the continental margin. For, in so far as the judgment of the International Court can be read as using natural prolongation in a physical sense, there is no evidence to the effect that the Court is employing that term to refer to crustal geology in the way the minor premiss supposes. It may equally well be using the concept in a geomorphological sense, to refer to the prolongation of the land under the sea in the form of a horizontal plateau. The physical continental shelf is just such a feature; and its outer edge would then be an appropriate outer limit. Indeed, there are some indications that, if the Court is using 'natural prolongation' physically, it is using it in the latter sense, rather than the former. For, having observed that the legal institution of the continental shelf arose 'out of recognition of a physical fact', and that 'the link between this fact and the law' remains important, the Court states that '[t]he continental shelf is, by definition, an area physically extending the territory of most coastal States into a species of *platform*':[246] that is, a 'raised level surface'.[247]

Denorme has accordingly interpreted the judgment to support his argument that the legal shelf is limited to the immediate environs of the physical phenomenon.[248] Emery is likewise in disagreement with Jennings's interpretation of the judgment. Referring to Article 76 (1) of the UN Convention on the Law of the Sea of 1982, wherein it is provided that a coastal State's rights extend throughout the natural prolongation of its land territory to the outer edge of the continental margin, he remarks that this constitutes an 'expansion' of the opinion of the Court in the *North Sea* cases, where the concept of natural prolongation was but 'vaguely stated'.[249]

In this connection, it may be noted that, in the debates of the late 1960s and early 1970s, several States recognized the concept of natural prolongation, physically defined, as the basis of coastal State title, and yet they did not think the edge of the margin was the outer limit of continental shelf rights—rather, the edge of the physical shelf and its immediate

[246] Para. 95 (emphasis added).

[247] *Oxford English Dictionary*. Brown, op. cit. above (p. 140 n. 203), at p. 33, further notes that the Court refers exclusively to the continental shelf as the prolongation of the coastal State's land territory, and not to the slope, rise, terrace or margin, although it was well aware of the slope, as it shows at para. 41.

[248] Loc. cit. above (p. 126 n. 100), at pp. 267–8.

[249] *Ocean Development and International Law*, 10 (1981–2), p. 1 at p. 4. See also the judgment of the Chamber in the *Gulf of Maine* case at para. 160; and the dissenting opinion of Judge Oda in the *Libya–Malta* case at paras. 55, 58 and 59. In his oral argument for Malta in the latter case, Weil pungently remarked that '[t]he natural prolongation of 1982 is no longer the one referred to by the Court in 1969': CR85/7, p. 45 (English translation).

environs.[250] Indeed, Burma and Thailand argued that any future convention should take the outer edge of the margin as the seaward limit, relying on the natural prolongation concept; yet they both recognized this would be a 'new' development, an 'extension' of the existing law.[251]

Nevertheless, it is not necessarily the case that, when the International Court talks of natural prolongation in the *North Sea* cases, it is signifying that it is the physical nature of the sea-bed which justifies the coastal State's title. This is, indeed, patent from the Court's judgment. For the Court talks of the continental shelf and the contiguous zone as analogous, in the sense that they are both 'territorial extensions to seaward' of the land territory of the coastal State.[252] The language of 'territorial extension' is clearly another rendition of 'natural prolongation',[253] and yet it is used in a context—the contiguous zone—where it cannot refer to submarine geography at all. The Court itself draws attention to the fact that the contiguous zone relates solely to the water column. What the Court has in mind when it says that these maritime zones are 'territorial extensions to seaward' is that the rights which the coastal State exercises there are extensions seaward of certain aspects of its territorial sovereignty. Thus the Chamber of the International Court in the *Gulf of Maine* case stresses that the concept of natural prolongation merely expresses the 'link' between a State's sovereignty and its sovereign rights to adjacent submerged land, and that this link is just as well, if not better, expressed by the concept of 'adjacency'.[254] However, the seaward extent of the territorial extension of a State's sovereignty clearly varies according to the maritime zone under consideration: the contiguous zone has dimensions different from the continental shelf. Thus the notions of territorial extension and natural prolongation are, by themselves, of no assistance in determining the limits of maritime jurisdiction, for their precise meanings depend on how they are defined.

'Natural prolongation' is employed not only to describe the fact that the coastal State possesses continental shelf rights over the sea-bed off its coasts: it is also used to justify their existence. However, the existence of legal rights cannot be explained and justified merely by referring back to the fact of their existence. The International Court recognizes this in the *North Sea* cases. For it states that the prolongations constituted by the continental shelf regime and by the contiguous zone are both justified on the basis that 'the land dominates the sea':[255] the coastal State has certain interests relating to its land territory which are generally recognized to

[250] Ireland, A/C. I/PV. 1525, p. 6; Israel, *UNCLOS III Official Records*, vol. 2, p. 144; USSR, ibid., p. 161.

[251] Ibid., pp. 155 and 159–60, respectively. Libya opposed a margin limit on these very same grounds: A/AC. 138/SR. 52, p. 93.

[252] Para. 95.

[253] Indeed, at para. 43, where the concept of natural prolongation is articulated, the Court talks of 'a prolongation or continuation of that territory, an extension of it under the sea'.

[254] Para. 103.

[255] Para. 95; and see the argument of Weil for Malta in the *Libya–Malta* case at CR 85/7, pp. 6–7.

merit certain jurisdictional competencies over adjacent marine areas to secure their protection. The area over which these legitimate interests are recognized to justify jurisdiction is the coastal State's 'territorial extension to seaward'—its 'natural prolongation'. What these reasons are, and what is the area over which they justify the extension of coastal State rights, clearly varies between maritime zones. If the Court uses 'natural prolongation' to describe the basis of the coastal State's entitlement to continental shelf rights, then it is employing the term as a form of legal shorthand—a concise way of stating these reasons and the area of sea-bed over which they justify continental shelf rights. Thus, in the *Libya-Malta* case, Weil argued on behalf of Malta that, 'in a true sense', natural prolongation is not the basis of title; rather, it is a 'verbal formula' that serves to express this basis in a concise fashion,[256] 'a linguistic convenience'.[257] Like adjacency, its synonym, it is a relative concept and its content is imprecise. One needs to look further to ascertain what the reasons are which justify the continental shelf regime, and over what area of sea-bed: that is, one needs to see how it is defined.[258]

The recent judgment of the International Court in the *Libya-Malta* case affords compelling evidence that the concept of natural prolongation is indeed a term of art. The Court there held that, by the 1980s, a new rule of customary law had developed, entitling coastal States to claim continental shelf rights out to 200 miles from the coast, irrespective of the depth and the current exploitability of the sea-bed, and even if there is no physical prolongation in the form of a continental margin as understood by Jennings. Nevertheless, the Court continued to maintain that natural prolongation is an 'essential element' in the juridical concept of the continental shelf, constituting the basis of the coastal State's title.[259] It is therefore clear that natural prolongation is an entirely legal idea, as the Court itself states,[260] and does not necessarily possess a physical meaning. The meaning of the term—and, specifically, whether it is used to connote physical prolongation—is entirely dependent on how it is defined. Thus the International Court affirms that, in the 1980s, with the advent of the new 200-mile rule, 'natural prolongation . . . is in part defined by distance from the shore, irrespective of the physical nature of the intervening sea-bed and subsoil'.[261] Judge Mbaye emphasizes this important point in his separate opinion. As he remarks, 'the basis of title . . . in spite of its name (natural prolongation) is entirely legal',[262] and the area of sea-bed to which it justifies title is dependent on how it is 'measured' and 'applied',[263] 'implemented' and 'defined'.[264]

256 CR 85/7, p. 8. See also CR 84/26, p. 5.
257 CR 85/7, p. 32.
258 Ibid., p. 33.
259 Para. 34. On the 200-mile rule, see section IV (a) 1., below.
260 Para. 77.
261 Para. 34.
262 pp. 98; also p. 99.
263 p. 97.
264 p. 95.

Therefore, when the International Court in the *North Sea* cases maintains that natural prolongation is the basis of coastal State title, it cannot be assumed that the Court is professing that it is because of the physical nature of the sea-bed that the coastal State receives jurisdiction—be it in the sense contended by Jennings or that espoused by Denorme. This may or may not be the case, depending on how 'natural prolongation' is defined and implemented.

Before proceeding to an analysis of the judgment of the Court and an examination of the subsequent jurisprudence, it is important to note that the debates of the 1950s afford no support to the argument that coastal State title is based on submarine geology or geomorphology.

First, several States at the Geneva Conference directly addressed the relationship between submarine geography and title, and unequivocally rejected the proposition that the coastal State is entitled to the adjacent sea-bed on the grounds that it physically prolongs its land territory.[265] Moreover, there is a veritable welter of evidence to the effect that the International Law Commission and the States at the Geneva Conference justified the continental shelf regime by reference to considerations of policy quite different in nature from the details of sea-bed geography alluded to by Jennings.[266]

Secondly, if physical fact did found coastal State title, and if this premiss had the significance for limits which the natural prolongation argument suggests, then it would be only natural to expect that the International Law Commission and the Geneva Conference would have been led ineluctably to the choice of some physical phenomenon as the seaward limit of coastal jurisdiction, or to some isobath or distance limit as a convenient substitute. If the coastal State has title because the sea-bed extends its land territory laterally in the form of a plateau, then the edge of the physical shelf would seem the natural limit to the legal shelf; if title is based on the fact that the sea-bed extends the coastal State's land territory geologically, then the foot of the slope would have been the natural choice.[267] However, as has already been seen,[268] the former limit consistently failed to find favour, and the jurisprudence of the International Court has rejected the notion that the legal institution of the continental shelf is tied to the physical phenomenon,[269] whilst a Panamanian proposal at the Geneva Conference in favour of the latter was resoundingly defeated.[270] The rejection of the latter proposal is of especial interest because Jennings's natural prolongation argument was deployed to support it. 'The main claim of the coastal State to the continental shelf is

[265] Chile, *UNCLOS I Official Records*, vol. 6, p. 16; Colombia, ibid., p. 41; Cuba, ibid., p. 25; El Salvador, ibid., p. 24; Peru, ibid., p. 11.

[266] Text at pp. 113–15 nn. 16–32 above.

[267] The rise was then unknown, even, it seems, to experts: p. 142 n. 217 above.

[268] See text at p. 128 nn. 114–18 above.

[269] See text at pp. 139–40 nn. 188–98 above.

[270] p. 143 n. 222 above, and accompanying text. Furthermore, Panama merely proposed the foot of the slope as an outer limit on the operation of the exploitability criterion.

based on the fact that it is the prolongation of its land territory', argued the Panamanian delegate, and, since the continental slope does not differ structurally from the shelf, both features are a 'submerged prolongation of *terra firma*', and therefore should be subject to coastal jurisdiction.[271] The natural prolongation argument could not have been more clearly put; and it could hardly have met with a more unequivocal rejection.

Thirdly, whilst the concept of natural prolongation did find occasional expression in the debates of the 1950s, it appears that, with the exceptions of Panama and Spain, its proponents understood it in a non-physical sense. At the Geneva Conference, the Argentinian delegation remarked that the claims of Chile and Peru to the sea-bed off their coasts were justified since the submarine areas in question were 'extensions of the continent under the sea';[272] and yet the areas of sea-bed claimed by those two States can, in no sense of the word, be said to be physical extensions of their respective land territories, embracing, as they do, large areas of abyssal plain. The delegate of the Dominican Republic stated that the principle underlying limits was that the continental shelf is the 'prolongation' of the coastal State's land territory, and that consequently the decisive criterion was proximity to the coast.[273] At the Third Conference itself, despite the relatively widespread advocacy of natural prolongation in its geological denotation, examples can still be found of States using the concept in a non-physical sense. For example, Kenya accepted the concept as the basis of coastal State title,[274] but, at the same time, rejected the contention that the edge of the margin was the outer limit of continental shelf rights in contemporary law, advocating instead an outer limit of 200 miles.[275] The Roumanian delegate proposed the same limit, declaring that it would render more specific the principle of natural prolongation, which was the basis of coastal State title.[276]

Therefore the debates of the 1950s provide no support for the argument that coastal State title rests on physical prolongation. The judgment of the International Court in the *North Sea* cases is in no way at variance with this historical analysis. In paragraph 43 of its judgment, in a passage already quoted above, the Court affirms that 'natural prolongation' is the basis of coastal State rights over adjacent sea-bed areas: certain reasons justify coastal State title to a certain area off its coast, which is termed the natural prolongation of that State. The Court realizes that the 'natural prolongations' of two States may well overlap, since the reasons founding title suggest that they both have legitimate interests which merit protection in the same area of sea-bed. In such a case, the Court says, it follows that the process of delimiting a boundary line between the areas

[271] *UNCLOS I Official Records*, vol. 6, pp. 32–3; also ibid., p. 5. Spain supported the proposal on similar grounds: ibid., p. 7.

[272] Ibid., p. 2.

[273] Ibid., p. 9.

[274] *UNCLOS III Official Records*, vol. 1, p. 83.

[275] Ibid., vol. 2, pp. 161–2.

[276] Ibid., p. 156.

pertaining to the respective jurisdictions of the two States must be directed towards ascertaining the 'most natural' prolongations of each State, and not allocating to one State areas more naturally appurtenant to the other. The law which governs delimitation should ensure that each State receives those areas of sea-bed where its interests which are protected by the continental shelf regime are the stronger when compared with the interests of the other delimiting State. An intimate connection is thus established between the rationale of title and the norms which govern delimitation: delimitatory norms are directed to ensure respect for the reasons which justify coastal State rights over the shelf. The same connection is made in other significant passages of the Court's judgment,[277] and has recently been reaffirmed in the *Libya–Malta* case.[278]

In view of this close connection between the rationale of coastal State title and the law of delimitation, if it were true that title derives from the physical fact that the sea-bed prolongs the coastal State's land territory, it would be natural to expect delimitatory law to give pride of place to considerations of submarine geology and geomorphology. This, however, the Court does not do. Rather, in detailing the 'equitable principles' which regulate delimitation, it stresses the importance of reflecting coastal geography.[279] The prime concern given to considerations of coastal geography is a direct consequence of the rationale of continental shelf jurisdiction. For, having articulated the principle that 'the land dominates the sea', which is the justification of all coastal State rights over adjacent maritime areas, the Court remarks that 'it is consequently necessary to examine closely the geographical configuration of the coastlines of the countries whose continental shelves are to be delimited'.[280] In contrast, the physical nature of the sea-bed is relegated to a position of little normative value: 'it *can* be *useful* to consider the geology of the shelf'.[281] Furthermore, in the one instance in which the Court adverts to a physical feature of the sea-bed—the Norwegian Trough—no suggestion whatsoever is made that the delimitation between Norway and the UK would have been dictated by that feature, had it not been for the agreement of those States to ignore it.[282]

The Court provides yet another indication of the fact that it does not use

[277] Paras. 85 (c) and 101 (C) (1).

[278] See text at p. 112 nn. 12–14 above.

[279] Para. 96.

[280] Ibid. See also the opinion of Judge *ad hoc* Jiménez de Aréchaga in the *Tunisia–Libya* case at paras. 57–8; and the oral argument of Brownlie for Malta in the *Libya–Malta* case at CR 84/27, pp. 21–2. For an examination of the delimitatory law expounded in the jurisprudence and its connection to the rationale of the continental shelf regime, see Hutchinson, this *Year Book*, 55 (1984), p. 133.

[281] Para. 95 (emphasis added). See also Judge *ad hoc* Jiménez de Aréchaga in the *Tunisia–Libya* case at paras. 60–3.

[282] Para. 45. Feulner claims that this passage supports the proposition that, but for the agreement of the UK and Norway, the axis of the Trough would have governed the delimitation: loc. cit. above (p. 147 n. 239), at pp. 94–5; but it would seem correct, with Bowett, to characterize this passage as 'delphic' and 'obscure': this *Year Book*, 49 (1978), p. 1 at pp. 16 and 17.

natural prolongation in a physical sense in paragraph 43 itself. For it may be noted that the International Court says that the submarine areas attributed to the coastal State 'may be deemed' to be a 'prolongation' of the land territory of the coastal State: not 'are', as would be expected if the Court is adverting to the physical facts of submarine geography as the reason for coastal State jurisdiction. The idea of physical extension is, therefore, of little legal relevance. There must be reasons for an assertion of title, and of a type fit to justify the rights coastal States have over the sea-bed off their coasts. It is submitted that the policy factors outlined at the beginning of this article fulfil this function. 'Natural prolongation' is but a concise way of stating these reasons and the area over which they suggest the extension of certain facets of the coastal State's sovereignty—namely, the sea-bed described by the rule in Article 1. This conclusion, it may be noted, is similar to that of the African writer, Rembe, who observes that the Court stresses 'adjacency' as the basis of coastal State title, in the sense of the existence of a 'rational nexus with relevant coastal State interests'.[283]

In truth, it would have been odd had the International Court employed the concept of natural prolongation in the physical sense contended by Jennings. It would have followed that the coastal State was already vested with exclusive jurisdiction out to the limits of the continental margin. Yet, as Judge *ad hoc* Jiménez de Aréchaga pointed out in his separate opinion in the *Tunisia–Libya* case,[284] this would have been in conflict with the opinion, which the Court clearly held, that the limit of coastal State rights in both conventional and customary law was governed by the rule in Article 1:[285] that rule would have been *functus officio* if the coastal State possessed exclusive rights *ipso facto* and *ab initio* over the whole of the continental margin irrespective of its exploitability, as Brown has pointed out.[286] Jennings has sought to avoid this problem by asserting that, in customary law, the coastal State has sovereign rights over the sea-bed to the edge of the margin, whilst the exploitability criterion regulates the application of the conventional regime between the parties to the Geneva Convention.[287] This argument clearly cannot hold if the rule in Article 1 in fact represented the customary law rule on limits. Moreover, the argument misrepresents the history of the rule in Article 1, which was clearly the result of a protracted attempt to find a generally acceptable limit to the seaward extent of coastal rights.

The subsequent examination of the concept of natural prolongation in the jurisprudence provides few reasons to revise this conclusion. Neither the Court of Arbitration in the *Anglo-French* case nor the Chamber of the International Court in the *Gulf of Maine* case found it necessary to scrutinize the basis of coastal State title. However, both tribunals sound a

[283] Loc. cit. above (p. 136 n. 166), at p. 91.

[284] Para. 46.

[285] See text at pp. 117–18 nn. 44–9 above.

[286] Op. cit. above (p. 140 n. 203), at p. 33.

[287] Loc. cit. above (p. 147 n. 239), at p. 831. See also Stone, loc. cit. above (p. 147 n. 139), at p. 178.

strong note of caution with regard to the type of argument expounded by Jennings and his followers. As the Chamber notes in the *Gulf of Maine* case, the coastal State's entitlement does not arise merely because the adjacent sea-bed can be said physically to prolong its land territory; for '"legal title" to . . . maritime or submarine areas is always and exclusively the effect of a legal operation'. Title arises from the recognition of a rule of law which establishes a link between territorial sovereignty and continental shelf rights, and 'not from any intrinsic merit in the purely physical fact'.[288] The Court of Arbitration in the *Anglo-French* case is likewise at pains to stress that, in international law, the continental shelf is a legal concept and its scope and meaning is determined by rules of law and not by simple physical facts.[289] A rule might arise which justifies the coastal State's title by reference to physical facts: but it is to the law that one must turn to draw the relevant conclusions *vis-à-vis* limits, and not just to the scientific details of sea-bed geography. Indeed, the Chamber in the *Gulf of Maine* case is positively sceptical about Jennings's argument, remarking that the judgment of the Court in the *North Sea* cases 'is well known to have attributed more marked importance to the link between the legal institution of the continental shelf and the physical fact of the natural prolongation than has subsequently been given to it'.[290]

It is also worthy of note that both cases have maintained the 'low key' approach to the place of submarine geography in delimitation law initiated by the *North Sea* cases. There are certain passages in the award in the *Anglo-French* case which seem to indicate that the Court of Arbitration was of the opinion that if the sea-bed to be delimited was not physically continuous, but was disrupted by the presence of a feature so significant as to create one area of sea-bed prolonging the land territory of one State, and another prolonging that of the other, then the delimitation should follow this disruption.[291] Nevertheless, other passages in the award negative this impression. The Court emphasizes that State practice in making delimitation agreements runs counter to giving any 'critical significance' to the physical features of the sea-bed.[292] Such features are placed where they are 'simply as a fact of nature', and 'there is no intrinsic reason' why they should be important in the delimitation process.[293] The Court accordingly ignored the presence of the Hurd Deep and the related Fault Zone in delimiting the continental shelf boundary between the UK and France,

[288] Para. 103. See also the joint separate opinion of Judges Ruda and Bedjaoui and Judge *ad hoc* Jiménez de Aréchaga in the *Libya–Malta* case at para. 21.

[289] *Arbitration between the United Kingdom of Great Britain and Northern Ireland and the French Republic on the Delimitation of the Continental Shelf*, Cmnd. 7438 (HMSO, 1979), paras. 91 and 191.

[290] Para. 91 (though see the dissenting opinion of Judge Gros at para. 11). See also the dissenting opinion of Judge Oda in the *Libya–Malta* case at para. 54.

[291] Paras. 79, 191 and 194. There was no such disruption in the area of sea-bed to be delimited in that case: paras. 2 and 107.

[292] Para. 105. See also the opinion of Judge *ad hoc* Jiménez de Aréchaga in the *Tunisia–Libya* case at para. 44; and the oral argument of Brownlie in the *Libya–Malta* case at CR 85/5, pp. 78–80.

[293] Para. 108.

although it was clearly quite a 'substantial' feature.[294] Commenting on the award, Brown remarks that the moving idea behind the reasoning of the Court is that the geology of the sea-bed is not relevant to delimiting continental shelf boundaries between States;[295] and, more cautiously, Bowett concludes that it is 'highly questionable' whether sea-bed geology has any relevance to the delimitation process.[296] Likewise, the Chamber in the *Gulf of Maine* case plays down the importance of submarine geography in delimitation law, emphasizing that delimitation is a 'legal-political operation' and that it is consequently 'not the case that where a natural boundary is discernible, the political delimitation necessarily has to follow the same line'.[297] Even if substantial sea-bed features are present, dividing the area to be delimited into separate morphological units, they do not dictate the boundary, but constitute 'factors to be used' along with the other 'criteria' of delimitatory law.[298]

The judgment of the International Court in the *Tunisia–Libya* case of 1982 may appear at first sight to be at variance with the interpretation of the concept of natural prolongation suggested here. In a context which seems to indicate that it is using the term in a physical sense,[299] the Court affirms 'the principle that natural prolongation is the sole basis of . . . title'.[300]

However, the Court in fact makes it clear that title is not based on physical prolongation. Several times it states that there is a 'lack of identity between the legal concept of the continental shelf and the physical phenomenon known to geographers by that name'. This divorce of the legal and the physical shelves is attributed to the rule in Article 1, and, particularly, to the expoloitability criterion, which, by creating an 'open-ended' outer limit, is said to have widened the legal institution and given it a more extensive connotation.[301] Indeed, the Court remarks that such thinking is 'implicit in the whole discussion' in the *North Sea* cases of the 'legal rules and principles' applicable to the continental shelf.[302] Therefore, title is not tied to the presence of a physical shelf, as would surely be the case if it derived from the physical prolongation of the coastal State's land territory, and it is definitely not linked to the presence of a continental margin. The Court does proceed to accord a role to the concept of physical prolongation; but, far from being normative, conferring title on the coastal

[294] *Tunisia–Libya* case, para. 66.

[295] *San Diego Law Review*, 16 (1979), p. 461 at pp. 480–1.

[296] Loc. cit. above (p. 153 n. 282), at pp. 15 and 16.

[297] Para. 56. See also the separate opinion of Vice-President Sette-Camara in the *Libya–Malta* case at p. 62.

[298] Para. 46. In these passages, the Chamber is considering the law of continental shelf delimitation only, and has not yet proceeded to determine what elements of that law are relevant in delimiting a single maritime boundary for the sea-bed and the water column: see paras. 192–4.

[299] It is replying to the Libyan argument that to ascertain the geological prolongations of the delimiting States is decisive of the delimitation.

[300] Para. 48.

[301] See text at pp. 139–40 nn. 189–95 above.

[302] Para. 42. See also the separate opinion of Judge *ad hoc* Jiménez de Aréchaga at paras. 45–6 and 58.

State, the Court uses the term descriptively to provide a rough representation of that area of sea-bed to which the continental shelf regime typically applies. Under the rule in Article 1, the physical shelf is the primary, but not the exclusive, domain in which the coastal State exercises its continental shelf rights: the 200-metre isobath corresponds approximately to the edge of the physical shelf and it is only recently that commercial exploitation has outstripped such depths. Consequently the Court, echoing its judgment in the *North Sea* cases,[303] states that, while the legal shelf 'is not to be identified' with the physical feature, the two remain in some way 'linked';[304] and, for the same reason, the Court states that physical natural prolongation, understood as the extension of land territory by way of a 'species of platform',[305] 'define[s], in general terms, the physical object or location of the rights of the coastal State'.[306] Indeed, since it produces the shallow conditions necessary for the application of the rule in Article 1, the physical shelf can, in a sense, be said to constitute 'the justification of continental shelf rights *in some cases*', as the Court notes.[307]

The Court's treatment of delimitation gives little reason to doubt this interpretation of its judgment. The Court notes that considerations of sea-bed geography are relevant in the delimitation process.[308] Certain passages of its judgment seem to go further and attribute crucial significance to any major discontinuities that might exist in the delimitation area.[309] However, these passages must be treated with caution; for, elsewhere, the Court makes it clear that the physical facts of submarine geography only play an important role in delimitation when they do not conflict with the solution suggested by the other principles of delimitatory law. Thus the Court remarks that such features 'would not necessarily be sufficient, or even appropriate' in themselves to determine continental shelf boundaries,[310] stating that it is only 'where the geographical circumstances are appropriate' that they 'may' have 'a role to play'.[311] The Court proceeded to reject the relevance of various submarine features relied on by the parties. One of these features—the Tripolitanian Furrow—was quite substantial, and the refusal of the Court to delimit the continental-shelf boundary along it prompted Decaux to write that 'la Cour semble . . . avoir étayé avec des arguments de fait une position de principe', rejecting the relevance of submarine geography in delimitatory law,[312] and springing from its

[303] Para. 95.
[304] Para. 41.
[305] Para. 47.
[306] Para. 43. The French translation reads '*l'assise*'.
[307] Para. 44 (emphasis added). See also para. 48, where the Court states that 'the natural prolongation of the coastal State is *a* basis of its legal title' (emphasis added).
[308] Para. 44.
[309] Paras. 66–8 and 70. See Hutchinson, loc. cit. above (p. 153 n. 280), at pp. 150–1 and 152–4.
[310] Para. 43.
[311] Para. 44.
[312] *Annuaire français de droit international*, 28 (1982), p. 357 at p. 368.

affirmation that the legal and physical shelves are distinct.[313] Indeed, Vice-President Sette-Camara notes in the *Libya–Malta* case that tribunals have generally been 'very careful' in their treatment of 'natural boundaries' preented by submarine features.[314]

The International Court considered the basis of the continental shelf regime once more in the recent case between Libya and Malta. The Court's attention was directed chiefly to the new 200-mile limit alleged by Malta. However, it did observe that, 'in spite of its physical origins', the legal idea of the continental shelf as the coastal State's natural prolongation under the sea 'has *throughout* its history become more and more a complex and judicial concept'[315]—an opinion shared by several judges in their separate opinions.[316] This clearly echoes the Court's judgment in the *Tunisia–Libya* case, and reaffirms the divorce of the legal and physical shelves.

It may be thought that, despite these passages, the Court in the *Libya–Malta* case did accept the proposition that legal title is derived from physical prolongation. For, having reviewed its previous decisions, discussed above, the Court states that, in so far as 'such jurisprudence appears to ascribe a role to geophysical or geological factors in delimitation, it finds warrant for doing so in a régime of the title itself which used to allot those factors a place'.[317] (It is noteworthy that the Court does not say that its prior decisions ascribe such factors a *decisive* role in delimitation.) However, as has already been seen, the Court in the *Libya–Malta* case throughout its judgment talks of the rules relating to the limits of continental shelf jurisdiction as bases of title[318]—a State has no title to the sea-bed beyond the outer limit. Moreover, the rule on limits—the rule in Article 1—clearly gave the physical nature of the sea-bed an important 'place' in the regime of the continental shelf: under that rule, the outer limit of jurisdiction, and therefore title, is determined directly (the 200-metre depth criterion) or indirectly (the exploitability criterion) by the depth of the sea-bed, and hence its physical nature. Since the features of submarine geography could consequently affect the area of the sea-bed embraced by coastal State jurisdiction,[319] it is only natural that they were treated as relevant to the delimitation of lateral boundaries between overlapping claims.[320] Thus the limited role ascribed to the geology and

[313] *Annuaire français de droit international*, 28 (1982), p. 357, at pp. 368–70. Cf. Zoller, *Revue générale de droit international public*, 86 (1982), p. 645 at pp. 654–5, 656 and 674.

[314] p. 60. This caution is not surprising in view of the great uncertainties which can exist, even between scientists, as to the significance of such features (*Libya–Malta* case, para. 41), and the injustice that boundaries drawn by reference to them might cause (separate opinion of Judge *ad hoc* Valticos, para. 3).

[315] Para. 34 (emphasis added); see also para. 77.

[316] Vice-President Sette-Camara at pp. 65 and 70; and Judge Mbaye at p. 94.

[317] Para. 40.

[318] See text at p. 112 nn. 9–10 above.

[319] Thus, special 'exceptions' had to be made for certain of these features lest they cause blatantly unfair results: see text at p. 141 nn. 209–10 above.

[320] The Court proceeded to accord such features no relevance in the delimitation of continental shelf boundaries out to 200 miles, since, in view of new developments in the law, jurisdiction can exist out to

geomorphology of the sea-bed in the law on delimitation is explicable without recourse to the notion that the physical nature of the sea-bed founds title.

It is to the judgment of the Court in the *North Sea* cases that commentators and States have turned in support of the argument that the rationale of the continental shelf regime justifies its extension to the outer edge of the continental margin. Of the States which deployed the natural prolongation argument at the Caracas Session of the Third UN Conference, approximately half cited the *North Sea* cases in support, whilst the others provided no juridical basis for their assertions.[321] However, one must conclude, with Goralczyk,[322] that, despite a quite widely held view to the contrary, those cases do not provide a sufficient basis for that argument. Indeed, they indicate that it is mistaken; and, in this, they are more than adequately corroborated by the debates of the 1950s and by the subsequent jurisprudence of the International Court. Accordingly, several States at the Third Conference expressly rejected the proposition that the natural prolongation argument represented the contemporary state of the law on limits.[323]

(ii) *Adjacency: a maximum distance limit.* It would seem, therefore, that when the concept of natural prolongation is used in the sense of the basis of the coastal State's title to the sea-bed off its coasts, it refers to the policy reasons which the generality of States have recognized as justifying the extension seawards of certain aspects of coastal State sovereignty, and to the area of sea-bed over which these reasons suggest that the coastal State should receive the rights in question. However, even with the failure of Jennings's natural prolongation argument, it has been suggested that an outer limit has always been inherent in the rationale of the continental shelf regime. This argument has often been presented as a question of the correct interpretation of the term 'adjacency' in the rule in Article 1. Thus Rembe writes that there are three criteria regulating the outer limit under that rule—the 200-metres depth criterion, the exploitability criterion, and adjacency—and it is 'adjacency' which is the most important, restraining the operation of the other two. Consequently, any area claimed under the 200-metres depth criterion or the exploitability formula must also be so related to the coast that it meets the adjacency test, which is said to have the role of maintaining a rational nexus between the area of sea-bed subject to

that distance, whatever the depth and the physical nature of the sea-bed, even if it is deepest abyssal plain: because submarine geography has no bearing on limits, at least out to 200 miles, it is irrelevant to the delimitation of such areas: paras. 39–40 and 48; and Judge *ad hoc* Jiménez de Aréchaga in the *Tunisia–Libya* case at paras. 49, 61 and 62.

321 Of the States listed in n. 244 at p. 147 above, those marked by asterisks referred to the judgment of the Court. All the commentators referred to at p. 147 nn. 241–3 rely on the judgment.

322 Loc. cit. above (p. 126 n. 99), at p. 141.

323 Afghanistan, *UNCLOS III Official Records*, vol. 2, p. 216; Federal Republic of Germany, ibid., p. 165; Iraq, ibid., p. 159; Jamaica, ibid., p. 167; Kenya, ibid., pp. 161–2; Switzerland, ibid., pp. 157–8. This group included Norway, which supported a margin limit, but on other grounds: ibid., p. 164.

the continental shelf regime and coastal State interests.[324] McDougal and Burke[325] and Brown[326] have written to similar effect. However, the argument under consideration is logically distinct from the question of the correct interpretation of 'adjacent' in the rule in Article 1. It is not dependent on finding a conscious and deliberate decision on limits, which was reflected by the insertion of 'adjacent' and its synonyms into Article 1 of the Geneva Convention and into State claims.[327] Rather, it is said that, once certain policies were adopted to justify the continental shelf regime, then an outer limit necessarily came into existence according to the maxim '*cessat ratio, cessat lex*'. The argument can thus be made without reference to the use of the term 'adjacency' in Article 1; but it will be termed the 'adjacency' argument here to distinguish it from the natural prolongation argument discussed above.

Several writers have used an adjacency argument to suggest that an inherent outer limit based on distance from the coast restricted the expansion of continental shelf rights under the exploitability criterion. Rembe makes such an argument, and Brown, writing in 1971, tentatively suggested that a distance of 200 miles might serve as a reasonable starting-point for negotiations.[328] Several States made similar propositions in the 1950s. The Dominican Republic remarked that proximity is the basis of continental shelf rights and that a distance limit accordingly restrained the exploitability criterion.[329] Norway thought that a distance limit should consequently be chosen rather than the rule in Article 1.[330] If reference is made to the policies behind the shelf regime, it is argued that at least several of them point to a distance limitation on the exploitability criterion. Coastal States only have a special interest in controlling pollution up to a certain distance from their coasts. Beyond a certain distance, the coastal State's security is not threatened by the presence of unsupervised foreign installations.[331] There is also likely to be little prospect of land-based deposits stretching seawards beyond a certain distance. Lastly, it is stressed that the element of distributive justice that lies behind the continental shelf regime is opposed to its extension too far seaward. To permit coastal State rights to extend great distances from the coast would benefit only coastal States, and, of them, only those fronting on to broad expanses of ocean. Moreover, of those States, only those with broad continental margins would reap benefits in the form of potential oil and gas reserves. A distance limit would prevent this select group from

324 Loc. cit. above (p. 136 n. 166), at pp. 91–2.

325 Op. cit. above (p. 115 n. 31), at pp. 687–8.

326 Op. cit. above (p. 140 n. 203), at pp. 36 and 38–9.

327 On the use of 'adjacent' and various synonyms in State claims, see the *North Sea* cases at para. 41.

328 Op. cit. above (p. 140 n. 203), at p. 39.

329 *UNCLOS I Official Records*, vol. 6, p. 9; and see text at p. 152 n. 273 above.

330 Ibid., vol. 1, p. 96.

331 The Court in the *Libya–Malta* case recognized that the threat to a State's security decreases with distance: para. 51. It thus felt fewer qualms in shifting the boundary it suggested closer to Malta, since it would still remain at a safe distance from its shores: para. 73.

benefiting too much and preserve a larger area of sea-bed beyond the limits of national jurisdiction for the benefit of all States, including the geographically disadvantaged and the land-locked.

As McDougal and Burke note,[332] it is impossible to point to any specific distance as the appropriate and legally correct limit. This is especially so as the potency of all these policy factors, especially distributive justice, is affected by the nature and the adequacy of the legal regime applicable to the sea-bed beyond national jurisdiction—which, of course, has been the subject of intense debate since the late 1960s. Nevertheless, it is argued, the rationale of the continental shelf regime does indicate the type of limit to which the exploitability criterion is subject. Yet it must be doubted that the policy arguments which were accepted in the 1950s afford a legitimate basis for cutting off coastal State rights at a particular distance from the coast, irrespective of the physical nature of the sea-bed beyond. Whilst it is true that the coastal State's interest in pollution control and security lessen as the distance from land increases, the fundamental purpose of the continental-shelf regime—to facilitate the exploitation of sea-bed resources—appears to militate against a distance limit. If the sea-bed beyond the distance selected were continental shelf, continental slope or continental rise—or, at least, the landward part of the continental rise[333]—then economic interest would still be directed to hydrocarbons; and, since it is probable that exploitation of such deposits will continue to be dependent on coastal support, coastal State rights should be able to extend down the slope and over the rise, should their exploitation prove practicable.[334]

It is, therefore, clear that the rationale of the continental shelf regime did not even suggest that a distance limit was an appropriate type of limit to place upon the expansion of coastal State rights under the exploitability criterion. Whether this was so or not could only be determined in the light of certain facts which are still today unknown: the nature of the technology which will be developed to exploit the hydrocarbon resources of the deeper and more distant areas of sea-bed, and the nature of the legal regime which will govern the exploitation of the sea-bed beyond national jurisdiction. The latter involves highly political calculations. This is, of course, just the reason why States recognized the rule in Article 1—to leave the final decision on limits for subsequent resolution when the salient technological and scientific facts became known and the issue of the legal regime of the area beyond the legal shelf had been dealt with.

(iii) *A minimum distance limit*. Nevertheless, several States at the Third UN Conference argued that a distance limit already formed part of the law

[332] Op. cit. above (p. 115 n. 31), at p. 688.

[333] It is in the landward part of the rise, where the sediments are generally thickest, that the conditions for oil and gas deposits are satisfied: Gardiner, loc. cit. above (p. 147 n. 243), at p. 159.

[334] Also, coastal States would obviously be reluctant to exclude themselves from possible riches to seaward: Eckert, op. cit. above (p. 124 n. 82), at p. 32.

of the continental shelf.[335] The exploitability criterion was said to have proved acceptable to the generality of States because of the unequal distribution of shelf lands. Many States were endowed with narrow physical shelves and would have derived little benefit from the continental shelf regime if the limits of coastal jurisdiction had been set at a specified depth or by reference to the physical nature of the sea-bed. Rather than 'discriminating' against those States, the exploitability criterion was accepted in order to 'compensate' them.[336] The proper way to give expression to this purpose was to extend coastal rights up to a certain distance from the coast, irrespective of the physical nature of the sea-bed. Thus a minimum distance limit was said to be part of the existing law of the continental shelf: all that remained was to select a specific figure.[337]

This argument was clearly erroneous. Whilst the exploitability criterion did have a role to play in the rhetoric of compensation and equal treatment, it is far from compensatory in its effects. Deep areas of sea-bed would clearly remain unexploitable for a very long time to come, and States with little shallow sea-bed off their coasts would thus receive narrow continental shelf zones, whilst States with extensive physical shelves would fare much better. Moreover, in so far as it was alleged that shelf rights existed beyond the 200-metre isobath up to an unspecified distance from the coast, this predicated that shelf rights might exist over the sea-bed regardless of its current exploitability; yet the rule in Article 1 is clearly dependent upon the practicability of exploitation. Attempts to confer shelf rights up to a minimum distance from the coast, irrespective of the prospective exploitability of the sea-bed, were repeatedly and decisively defeated in the International Law Commission and at the Geneva Conference, as has already been observed.[338] Thus, when certain States at the Third Conference argued for compensation and equal treatment by means of a minimum distance limit, they were attempting to introduce a new element into continental shelf law.[339]

IV. Limits Based on New Developments in State Practice since the 1960s

Therefore, by the end of the 1960s, and as the second series of international debates on the legal regime of the sea-bed were getting under way, the question of the outer limit of continental shelf jurisdiction remained unresolved. The rule in Article 1 of the Convention on the Continental Shelf seems to have established itself as a rule of general

[335] See p. 135 n. 165 above and accompanying text. See also Weil's oral argument for Malta in the *Libya–Malta* case at CR 84/25, pp. 46–7; and the separate opinion of Judge Mbaye in that case at p. 95.

[336] See text at pp. 134–5 nn. 159–165 above, for a more detailed exposition of this argument.

[337] Security considerations might also be cited in support: cf. the oral argument of Lauterpacht in the *Libya–Malta* case at CR 84/25, pp. 62–5.

[338] See text at pp. 129–30 nn. 127–35 above.

[339] As Judge Oda notes in the *Libya–Malta* case at para. 52.

customary law by the end of that decade. However, this did not close the issue. Far from it; it was the very purpose of the rule in Article 1 to leave the question of limits for subsequent resolution. Thus several States in the First Committee of the General Assembly and on the UN Sea-Bed Committee observed that the law on limits was 'unresolved', 'open', 'remained to be settled', was 'in a stage of evolution', was 'yet to be defined'.[340] Several remarked that there was no generally accepted norm of international law on limits, in the sense of a final limit which would restrict the extension of national jurisdiction;[341] and the preamble to General Assembly Resolution 2574A (XXIV) of 1969 affirmed that the customary law on the limits of national jurisdiction was 'inconclusive'. Several States explicitly acknowledged that the subsequent establishment of a generally recognized outer limit was thus a political, rather than a legal, question—there was no rule of law which was awaiting discovery or correct interpretation.[342] Accordingly, as the Government of Iceland observed, the law on limits was, in all likelihood, going to be transformed by the deliberations of the UN Sea-Bed Committee and the Third UN Conference on the Law of the Sea.[343] The negotiation and general acceptance of a treaty obligation was what Iceland had in mind. However, in the context of a conference wherein the whole of the international community was to participate, it was probable that the customary law on limits would also be transformed by the treaty-negotiation process. This might be either through the development of a general consensus on what the position was at customary law, regardless of the existence of a treaty, or through the effect which the negotiations might have on State practice in the form of actual claims. Indeed, two major arguments have been made to the effect that an *opinio generalis juris generalis* has developed to supplement or revise the former customary law.

(a) *A 200-Mile Rule*

It is possible to argue that a general consensus has emerged that a distance limit of 200 nautical miles is now a rule of general customary law. However, it is of the greatest importance to note that such a limit can assume two forms. Comparison with the *Fisheries Jurisdiction* case is instructive in this regard. As Judges Forster, Bengzon, Jiménez de Aréchaga, Nagendra Singh and Ruda there made clear in their joint separate opinion, a distinction must be made between a rule that renders

[340] Brazil, A/AC. 138/SR. 19, p. 17; Bulgaria, A/AC. 135/WG. 1/SR. 10, p. 88, and A/AC. 138/SC. 1/SR. 37, p. 17; Honduras, *UNCLOS III Official Records*, vol. 1, p. 82; Iceland, A/AC. 135/1/Add. 8; Kuwait, A/AC. 138/SR. 23, p. 61; UAR, A/C. I/PV. 1528, pp. 48–50.

[341] Belgium, A/C. I/PV. 1529, p. 13; Chile, A/C. I/PV. 1526, pp. 23–5; El Salvador, A/AC. 138/SR. 23, p. 55; France, A/AC. 135/WG. 1/SR. 7, p. 56; Honduras, A/C. I/PV. 1527, p. 31; Iceland, A/AC. 135/SR. 3, p. 6; Malta, A/AC. 135/WG. 1/SR. 7, p. 49 and A/AC. 138/SC. 1/SR. 7, p. 62.

[342] Kuwait, A/AC. 138/SR. 23, p. 61; Libya, A/AC. 135/SR. 17, p. 13, and A/AC. 138/SC. 1/SR. 8, p. 83; Malta, A/AC. 138/SC. 1/SR. 7, p. 65; USA, A/AC. 138/SC. 1/SR. 10, p. 114; Yugoslavia, ibid., p. 116.

[343] A/AC. 135/1/Add. 8.

valid *erga omnes* the extension of jurisdiction up to a certain distance from the coast, and a rule which establishes an obligatory maximum limit and makes claims beyond that distance automatically invalid *erga omnes*.[344] Thus those five judges,[345] in common with the rest of the majority,[346] found that a rule of general customary law had evolved making claims of exclusive fisheries jurisdiction out to 12 nautical miles valid *erga omnes*. However, in marked contrast with the majority judgment, the five judges were willing to proceed and deal with the submission of the UK that a second rule had also developed prohibiting the extension of fisheries jurisdiction beyond 12 miles—an argument which they rejected, finding that there was so much State practice in contravention of the alleged rule that no such norm could be said to exist.[347] States thus remained free to make claims beyond 12 miles: such claims were not automatically validated as against the whole international community, nor were they automatically invalidated and rendered breaches of the law. Rather, the legal validity of such claims would depend on the reactions of other States, being opposable to those States which, when informed, acquiesced, but not to those States which maintained an effective protest.[348]

1. *200-mile claims valid* erga omnes

Although certain commentators have concluded otherwise,[349] there appears to be sufficient evidence to merit the conclusion that by the 1980s, if not before, a 200-mile rule had emerged in the first sense outlined above. Thus, rejecting the argument of Libya to the contrary,[350] the International Court in the *Libya–Malta* case held that 'the development of the law enables a State to claim that the continental shelf appertaining to it extends up to as far as 200 miles from its coast, whatever the geological characteristics of the corresponding seabed and subsoil', its depth, or its current exploitability.[351] The validity of such a rule in no way presupposes that claims beyond that distance are invalid, or that the rule in Article 1 is no longer operative. Indeed, the two rules can coexist quite happily. For, whilst the rule in Article 1 legitimizes claims made according to the criteria of depth and current exploitability, the rule under consideration validates claims made according to another, third, and separate, criterion: that of distance from the coast. The distinction between the two types of limits drawn in the *Fisheries Jurisdiction* case could not be made more clear—if

[344] p. 47, especially paras. 6 and 8.

[345] Para. 7.

[346] Para. 52.

[347] Paras. 20–1.

[348] This point is made clearly in the separate opinion of Judge Dillard at pp. 56 and 60. On the question of effective claim and effective protest, see O'Connell, *The Law of the Sea*, vol. 1 (1982), at pp. 38–44.

[349] e.g. O'Connell, op. cit. (previous note), p. 497.

[350] See, especially, CR 84/31, pp. 47–63, and CR 85/10, pp. 45–7. It is of interest that Libya accepted the 200-mile limit as customary law at one stage in the *Tunisia–Libya* case (LCM para. 3.17), though see later TL 81/75 Ann. 2.

[351] Para. 39; and see the opinion of Judge *ad hoc* Jiménez de Aréchaga three years previously in the *Tunisia–Libya* case at para. 53.

the 200-mile rule was of the second type outlined above, rather than the first, it would invalidate all claims beyond 200 miles and render them breaches of the law.

Two lines of argument have been adduced to justify this conclusion, although they are by no means mutually exclusive. The first argument relies primarily on the debates on the limits of the continental shelf regime which took place at the Third UN Conference on the Law of the Sea and which culminated in the incorporation of the 200-mile rule in Article 76 (1) of the UN Convention. It also relies on the somewhat limited State practice that has occurred in this period by way of claims to continental shelf rights. At the Third Conference, several States made the argument, grounded in notions of distributive justice, that a distance limit of the type under consideration should form at least part of the solution to the limits problem. They argued that the current rule on limits discriminated against those States off whose coasts the sea-bed rapidly falls away, beyond the 200-metre isobath, to depths at which exploitation would long remain impracticable. All coastal States, it was said, whether favoured by submarine geography or not, should be able to claim continental shelf rights out to a distance of 200 nautical miles, irrespective of the depth of the sea-bed and its physical nature, and without having to prove its current exploitability.[352] This argument was a powerful one, and somewhere between seventy and eighty States declared their belief that it should form part of the future treaty settlement at the Caracas Session. This body of support came from two groups of States: one, consisting of between thirty-five and thirty-nine States, supported such a provision, but wished to superimpose a 200-mile rule of the second type discussed above, prohibiting the extension of national jurisdiction beyond that distance;[353] whilst a second group, with between thirty-six and forty declared adherents, argued that the treaty to be produced by the Conference should recognize continental shelf rights beyond 200 miles if certain physical features—specifically, a continental margin—were present.[354] This

[352] See the dissenting opinion of Judge Oda in the *Libya–Malta* case at para. 52.

[353] Afghanistan, Austria, possibly Bhutan, Bolivia, Congo, Denmark, Egypt, France, Gambia, Ghana, Haiti, Israel, Italy, Jamaica, Japan, Kampuchea, Kenya, Lebanon, Lesotho, Liberia, Libya, possibly Saudi Arabia, Singapore, Switzerland, Tanzania, Togo, possibly Tonga, Tunisia, Uganda, Upper Volta and Zaire. The Federal Republic of Germany supported a 200-mile maximum, but subject to the exception that rights validly acquired beyond that distance under the existing law by means of exploitation should be retained. Denmark, Ghana, Jamaica and Pakistan expressed their readiness to drop the 200-mile maximum and accept the possibility of rights beyond that distance. Buzan claims that sixty-three States had adhered to this position by the end of 1974: *Seabed Politics* (1976), p. 221.

[354] Albania, Argentina, Australia, Bahrein, Bangladesh, possibly Burma, Canada, Chile, Costa Rica, Cuba, Ecuador, El Salvador, Honduras, Iceland, India, possibly Indonesia, Ireland, Korea (North), Korea (South), Malawi, Mauritius, Mexico, possibly New Zealand, Nicaragua, Norway, Panama, Peru, Senegal, Spain, Trinidad and Tobago, Turkey, UK, USA, Uruguay, Venezuela and Vietnam. To these States may be added the following, which indicated a certain preparedness to accept the proposition in question: Denmark, Ghana, Jamaica and Pakistan (see previous note). USSR favoured a 200-mile rule of the first type, but not of the second, yet did not support a margin limit at Caracas: see text at p. 174 nn. 417–18 below.

general consensus, which embraced States from all regions of the world and all stages of development, persisted and hardened throughout the Conference, the debate shifting to the question of whether continental shelf rights might extend beyond 200 miles.

A consensus supporting the incorporation of a norm into a treaty text does not suffice to establish the status of that norm as a rule of customary international law.[355] A different kind of consensus is required to achieve this—a consensus that the norm in question is a rule of customary law in force. Even at the Caracas Session of the Conference, certain States did display this attitude with regard to the 200-mile rule: for some, a distance limit of the type under consideration was already part of customary law;[356] for a sizeable group of Latin American States, steadily joined by certain African States, the consensus was just belated recognition of rights over the sea-bed which they had long been claiming. For a great many States, however, it would appear that initially the 200-mile rule was but a proposal for a new treaty obligation. Nevertheless, the widely shared consensus which emerged in 1974 made it immediately clear to all that the great generality of States was willing to accept this proposal without any conditions or any quid pro quo attached. The 200-mile rule thus became a basic assumption in the ensuing negotiations and there was never any doubt that it would be adopted in the future convention.[357] Indeed, the 200-mile rule had attained such widespread and unreserved acceptance by the end of the Geneva Session in 1975 that it was felt that unilateral claims up to that distance did not threaten the negotiating process.[358] If the rule had been merely one element in a larger 'package deal', dependent for its acceptability on the existence of a treaty containing elements of reciprocal consideration, then this could never have been the case. At the date of writing, nineteen States had made claims to a continental shelf of 200 miles,[359] and one State had made a claim of 150 miles.[360]

It is therefore possible to conclude that, by virtue of a generally held *opinio juris*, which formed in the context of the negotiations at the Third Conference and is further evidenced in State practice, the 200-mile rule expressed in Article 76 (1) of the UN Convention is now a part of customary law. Indeed, Judge *ad hoc* Jiménez de Aréchaga in the

[355] Cheng, in Macdonald and Johnston (eds.), *The Structure and Process of International Law* (1983), p. 513 at pp. 528–30.

[356] See text at p. 135 n. 165 and p. 162 n. 335 above.

[357] Op. cit above (p. 165 n. 353), at pp. 221–2. See also Weil's oral argument for Malta in the *Libya–Malta* case at CR 85/7, pp. 42 and 45–6.

[358] Op. cit. above (p. 165 n. 353), at pp. 266–7.

[359] The following States made claims to the outer edges of their continental margins and to 200 miles where the margin does not extend that far: Burma, Dominican Republic, Guyana, Iceland, India, Kampuchea, Mauritania, Mauritius, New Zealand, Pakistan, Senegal, Seychelles, Sri Lanka, Vanuatu, Vietnam and Yemen (Aden). The following States made claims to continental shelf zones of 200 miles: Chile, Costa Rica and Peru. On Kampuchea's claim, see p. 186 n. 492 below.

[360] Madagascar.

Tunisia–Libya case[361] and Judge Mbaye in the *Libya–Malta* case[362] reasoned along these lines.[363] However, the cogency of this first line of argument is open to doubt. For, whilst it is true that the 200-mile limit proved widely acceptable as part of the solution to the limits problem,[364] this has so far been solely in the context of the negotiations for a treaty settlement at the Third Conference. There is little positive evidence in the course of the debates that 200-mile claims were generally acceptable outside a treaty framework. The State practice by way of 200-mile continental shelf claims is still limited, both numerically and to certain regions of the world,[365] and cannot as yet be said to prove conclusively that claims of continental shelf rights out to 200 miles on the basis of distance are generally accepted as a matter of customary law. All that can be said to date, as Zoller remarks, is that, *vis-à-vis* the continental shelf, the 200-mile limit is but 'law in the process of formation'[366]—if recourse is had to the first line of argument only. Indeed, it is noteworthy that the International Court in the *Libya–Malta* case concluded that the 200-mile limit is part of the modern law of the continental shelf 'quite apart from the provision as to distance in paragraph 1 of Article 76'.[367]

However, a second line of argument is available to prove the customary status of the 200-mile rule. As the International Court remarked in the *Libya-Malta* case,[368] confirming the observation it had made in the *Tunisia–Libya* case of 1982,[369] the concept of a 200-mile exclusive economic zone is shown 'by the practice of States' to have become a part of customary law.[370] Throughout the Third UN Conference, at which the idea of the economic zone was developed and elaborated, it was generally understood[371] that, within the zone, the coastal State should possess sovereign rights for the purpose of exploring and exploiting the natural

361 This conclusion is reached on the basis of Article 76 (1) of the UN Convention at para. 52; and the advent of the economic zone as part of customary law (see below) is said to 'confirm' this conclusion: para. 54.

362 Again, the economic zone 'reinforces' the conclusion reached on the basis of Article 76 (1) at p. 94: p. 98.

363 Possibly also Judge *ad hoc* Valticos at para. 9. Sometimes, in his oral argument for Malta, Weil relied solely on the negotiating history of Article 76 to establish the status of the 200-mile rule as customary law: CR 85/7, pp. 47–8; but see ibid., p. 55 and CR 84/24, p. 54, where he relies also on the reception of the economic zone in customary law.

364 Judge Oda in the *Tunisia–Libya* case at para. 129.

365 Quéneudec in oral argument in the *Libya–Malta* case: CR 85/10, p. 51.

366 Loc. cit. above (p. 158 n. 313), at p. 654. Quéneudec described it as *jus emergens* (CR 84/31, p. 50); and Vice-President Sette-Camara described it as a 'trend that cannot yet be considered as a rule of customary international law' in his separate opinion in the *Libya–Malta* case at p. 65.

367 Para. 34.

368 Para. 34; also the opinion of Judge Mbaye at p. 98.

369 Para. 100. See also the separate opinion of Judge *ad hoc* Jiménez de Aréchaga at para. 54; the dissenting opinion of Judge Oda at paras. 120 and 125; and the dissenting opinion of Judge *ad hoc* Evensen at para. 9.

370 Emphasis added. See also the International Law Association, *Report of the 60th Conference, Montreal, 1982*, p. 303 at pp. 305 and 306.

371 With the notable exception of the so-called 'territorialists'—those States favouring a 200-mile territorial sea.

resources of the sea-bed and subsoil, and this understanding was enshrined in Article 56 (1) of the UN Convention. It is by virtue of State practice that the economic zone has passed into the corpus of customary law, as the International Court has observed, and it is not yet clear whether the regime of the zone as developed in State claims is the same in all respects as that in the Convention. However, States have adhered to the formula in Article 56 (1) when claiming economic zones, and the International Law Association's Committee on the Exclusive Economic Zone concluded in its First (Preliminary) Report of 1982 that coastal States enjoy the rights described in that article over the sea-bed and subsoil of the zone in customary law.[372] Continental shelf rights are precisely the same in nature.[373] Consequently, since a State may claim an economic zone out to 200 miles, irrespective of the depth, physical nature and exploitability of the sea-bed, the recognition given to the economic zone concept indicates the general acceptability of claims to continental shelf rights out to 200 miles made solely on the basis of distance. (There is no evidence that the recognition which has been accorded to claims to continental shelf rights in the context of economic zone claims has been given solely on the condition that these rights are claimed as part of a wider economic zone relating also to the superjacent water column.[374] Thus, to claim a 200-mile continental shelf in customary law, a State does not have to claim a full exclusive economic zone.)

Certain commentators, however, have maintained that this second line of argument cannot be employed. This is not merely on the grounds that the economic zone is a juridical concept separate and distinct from that of the continental shelf; for that is beyond contention.[375] Rather, it is said that, although possessing a basically similar judicial nature—involving, as they do, claims to sovereign rights for economic purposes—the rights which a State wields over the sea-bed under the regime of the economic zone differ from continental shelf rights. The general tolerance afforded to claims to 200-mile economic zones therefore does not prove the acceptability of claims to continental-shelf rights out to that distance. Thus Vice-President Sette-Camara treated the discussion of the economic zone in the *Libya–Malta* case as 'unnecessary', since he believed that 'the rights and jurisdiction of the States over the continental shelf and the exclusive economic zone overlap to a considerable degree; but they differ

[372] Loc. cit. above (p. 167 n. 370).

[373] Convention on the Conventional Shelf, Article 2. This article was held to enshrine the fundamental concept of the continental shelf in customary law by the Court in the *North Sea* cases at para. 19.

[374] It may be noted that the ILA's Committee on the Exclusive Economic Zone believed that claims to 200-mile territorial seas, even if they were invalid *qua* territorial sea claims, were valid *qua* economic zones, since the invalidity related solely to those rights claimed in addition to those which might be legitimately claimed under the regime of the economic zone, and there was no reason to suppose that the latter rights might not be severed from the former and the valid part of the claim saved: op. cit. above (p. 167 n. 370), at p. 306.

[375] Para. 34.

in many ways'.[376] Similarly, in his oral argument on behalf of Libya in the *Libya–Malta* case, Quéneudec argued that 'the continental shelf remains subject to its own legal regime, not only when it extends beyond 200 miles, but also within that limit':[377] unlike economic zone rights, which exist solely as from the moment when, and to the extent that, a State decides to institute them by proclamation, continental shelf rights exist *ab initio*, independently of any claim or proclamation.[378] Consequently, he said, the advent of the economic zone does not prove the 200-mile rule *vis-à-vis* the continental shelf.[379]

This objection lacks cogency. According to the UN Convention on the Law of the Sea, the rights which the coastal State exercises over the sea-bed and subsoil of its economic zone are the same in every detail as those which it exercises over its continental shelf. Article 56 (3) provides:

> The rights set out in this article with respect to the sea-bed and subsoil shall be exercised in accordance with Part VI.

Part VI of the Convention defines the regime of the continental shelf. As Judge Oda writes in his judgment in the *Tunisia–Libya* case, it was 'the intention of the authors of the . . . convention that Article 56, paragraph 3, should be interpreted to mean that the régime of the exclusive economic zone will incorporate, in principle, the whole régime of the continental shelf.'[380] Putting it the other way around, Dupuy[381] and Pulvenis[382] write: 'le plateau absorbe le fond de la zone [économique]'. Thus, under the UN Convention, a claim to an economic zone incorporates *ipso jure* a claim of continental shelf rights. Nor would this proposition seem to be confined to the economic zone *qua* treaty law. As Judge Oda notes, from the time of its inception, the concept of the economic zone was chiefly directed at the question of fisheries resources;[383] and, although its extension to the subjacent sea-bed was never in doubt, there was no discussion at all of the nature of the rights which would there be exercised and their relationship to the existing regime of the continental shelf.[384] This is reflected in Part V of the UN Convention.[385] Likewise, in so far as the claims made by States have attempted to detail the jurisdiction exercised in the zone, attention has been directed to fisheries rather than the sea-bed.[386] The underlying assumption, expressed in Article 56 (3), appears to be that the rights over the sea-bed exercised as part of the economic zone pose few problems for legal resolution, since the question has already been adequately dealt with by the law of the continental shelf. Several States have accordingly announced that the sea-bed of their economic zones is regulated by their

[376] p. 71. [377] CR 84/31, p. 57 (English translation). [378] Ibid., p. 56.
[379] Ibid., pp. 55 and 63.
[380] Para. 130. [381] *L'Océan partagé* (1979), p. 109.
[382] *Revue iranienne des relations internationales*, 11/12 (1978), p. 103 at p. 113.
[383] Para. 126.
[384] Para. 113. [385] As Judge Oda notes at para. 119.
[386] As Quéneudec notes in his oral argument in the *Libya–Malta* case: CR 84/31, pp. 60 and 61.

existing legislation relating to the continental shelf.[387] Indeed, as the Chamber of the International Court notes in the *Gulf of Maine* case,[388] the provisions of the UN Convention on the nature and purpose of the economic zone, which clearly include so basic a provision as Article 56 (3), reflect the present state of customary law.[389] Accordingly, in the *Libya–Malta* case, the International Court held:

> Although the institutions of the continental shelf and the exclusive economic zone are different and distinct, the rights which the exclusive economic zone entails over the sea-bed of the zone are defined by reference to the régime laid down for the continental shelf . . . [T]here cannot be an exclusive economic zone without a corresponding continental shelf.[390]

It would seem that the rule of customary law reflected in Article 56 (3) transposes the rules of the continental shelf regime so completely that the continental shelf rights which the coastal State exercises over the sea-bed of its economic zone exist *ab initio* and independently of any proclamation; for the International Court held that the distance criterion was the basis of the titles of both Libya and Malta to the sea-bed in dispute in that case,[391] even though neither of those States had yet claimed an economic zone.[392]

Therefore, since the regimes of the economic zone and the continental shelf with respect to the sea-bed are in fact identical, '[i]t follows that, for judicial and practical reasons, the distance criterion must now apply to the continental shelf as well as to the exclusive economic zone'.[393]

2. *200 miles as a maximum limit*

There is a second sense in which the 200-mile rule may be understood: that is, as a prohibitory limit invalidating all claims to continental shelf rights beyond that distance. Nawaz believed that such a rule was emerging in the UN Sea-Bed Committee;[394] and, at the Caracas Session

[387] Fiji: Marine Spaces Act 1977, section 7; France: Law No. 76–655 relating to the Economic Zone off the Coasts of the Territory of the Republic, Article 2; Ivory Coast: Law No. 77–926 of 17 November 1977 Delimiting the Maritime Zones Placed under the National Jurisdiction of the Republic of the Ivory Coast, Article 4; Mexico: Law Regulating the 8th Paragraph of Article 27 of the Constitution Relating to the Exclusive Economic Zone, Transitional Provision 1; Venezuela: Law Establishing an Exclusive Economic Zone off the Continental and Insular Coasts of the Republic of Venezuela, Article 3 (2). Other States have created identical rules to govern their continental shelf claims and the rights they exercise over the sea-bed of their economic zones—Guyana: Maritime Boundaries Act, No. 10 of 1977, sections 10–14 and 17–20; India: The Territorial Waters, Continental Shelf, Exclusive Economic Zone and Other Maritime Zones Act, No. 80 of 1976, sections 6 (3)–(7) and 7 (4)–(8); Mauritius: Maritime Zones Act 1977, sections 7 and 9; Seychelles: Maritime Zones Act, No. 15 of 1977, section 7; Sri Lanka: Maritime Zones Law, No. 22 of 1976, sections 5 (3) and 6 (3).

[388] Para. 94.

[389] Judge *ad hoc* Jiménez de Aréchaga went even further in his opinion in the *Tunisia–Libya* case, maintaining that the provisions of Part V in general have served as 'the focal point for and authoritative guide to' State practice: para. 54; and, for him, Article 56 (3) therefore definitely reflects modern customary law: para. 55. See also Weil's argument in the *Libya–Malta* case: CR 84/24, p. 53.

[390] Para. 34; also the opinion of Judge Mbaye at p. 98.

[391] Para. 62. [392] Para. 17. [393] *Libya–Malta* case, para. 34.

[394] *Indian Journal of International Law*, 13 (1973), p. 25 at pp. 34 and 37.

of the Third UN Conference, some thirty-nine States argued that coastal State rights should not extend further than 200 miles from the coast.[395] This position remained a widely held one throughout the Conference, though discussion subsequently centred on continental shelf rights beyond that distance; and although the provision finally adopted by the Conference permits the extension of continental shelf rights beyond 200 miles, that was acceptable to this group of States solely as a matter of treaty law.[396]

Nevertheless, it is impossible to maintain that a rule fixing 200 miles as an absolute outer limit, applicable to all continental shelf claims, has become part of customary international law. First, the establishment of a 200-mile maximum limit would have involved certain States being divested of rights which they had validly acquired under the existing law. Under the rule in Article 1, all States received jurisdiction over the sea-bed up to the 200-metre isobath, no matter how far out from the coast that might be. In certain parts of the world, such as Argentina, Australia and the northern Soviet Union, the sea-bed does not reach the 200-metre isobath until well beyond 200 nautical miles from the coast.[397] These States were obviously not prepared to relinquish their claims;[398] and, to that extent at least, a 200-mile limit was not established. The same goes for those States which had undertaken 'exploitation' beyond that distance. Certain States—most notably, Canada—maintained that 'exploitation' had occurred at great depths and distances off their coasts, without protest from other States, and these States were unwilling to renounce rights which they believed they had validly acquired.[399] The Federal Republic of Germany, although it supported the 200-mile limit at the Caracas Session, remarked that this was subject to an exception for those States which had validly acquired rights beyond that distance under the existing law through exploitation.[400]

However, opposition to a 200-mile limit came from many more States than the select group vested with rights beyond that distance under the rule in Article 1—States whose position might otherwise have been more accurately characterized as that of persistent dissenters.[401] A large number of States at the Third Conference maintained that, where the continental margin extends beyond 200 miles, a 200-mile outer limit was totally unacceptable, and that, in such circumstances, it must be recognized that the coastal State's shelf rights extend to the outer edge of the margin.[402]

395 These States are enumerated at p. 165 n. 353 above.
396 See text at pp. 177–81 nn. 431–66 below.
397 p. 141 n. 207 above.
398 See Weil's argument in the *Libya–Malta* case: CR 84/25, pp. 44–5.
399 p. 145 n. 233 above.
400 *UNCLOS III Official Records*, vol. 2, p. 165.
401 *Fisheries* case, p. 131.
402 Albania, Argentina, Australia, Bahamas, Bahrein, Bangladesh, possibly Burma, Canada, Chile, Costa Rica, Cuba, Ecuador, El Salvador, Honduras, Iceland, India, possibly Indonesia, Ireland, Korea (North), Korea (South), Malawi, Mauritius, Mexico, possibly New Zealand, Nicaragua, Norway, Panama, Peru, Portugal, Senegal, Spain, Thailand, Trinidad and Tobago, Turkey, UK,

Indeed, for nearly every one of these States a 200-mile limit was in direct conflict with *lex lata*, which, they maintained, already recognized continental shelf rights over the whole of the continental margin.[403] This group of States maintained its position throughout the Conference. Article 76 (1) of the UN Convention accordingly permits the coastal State to extend its shelf rights beyond 200 miles where the margin extends that far.

In view of this extensive opposition, it is impossible to maintain that a 200-mile limit, applicable to all continental shelf claims, has become a part of customary law. Nevertheless, it would be wrong to say that the support for such a limit has been totally devoid of legal effect. It is now possible to lay claim to the sea-bed up to 200 miles from the coast on the basis of distance, without regard to its depth, exploitability or physical nature. In this context, the 200-mile maximum met with no opposition at the Conference, and remained a basic assumption throughout the negotiations. No claims to continental shelf rights have been made beyond 200 miles purely on the basis of distance. It is firmly established in customary law that exclusive economic rights cannot be claimed beyond 200 miles from the coast;[404] and, in so far as the customary law status of the rule validating claims of continental shelf rights out to 200 miles on the basis of distance is dependent on the reception of the economic zone as a part of customary law,[405] the same limit applies to the continental shelf. Thus, where a claim to continental shelf rights is made solely on the basis of distance, a rule of customary law applies prohibiting such claims beyond 200 miles from the baselines of the territorial sea; but claims founded on bases of entitlement other than distance are not so restricted.

(b) *Natural Prolongation: the Outer Edge of the Continental Margin*

Many writers and States have argued that, in virtue of the concept of natural prolongation, which constitutes the rationale of the continental shelf regime, coastal States were already vested with jurisdiction to the outer edge of the continental margin before the commencement of the Third UN Conference. As has been shown, this argument is mistaken. Nevertheless, as the International Court notes in the *Tunisia–Libya* case, '[t]he concept of natural prolongation . . . was and remains a concept to be examined within the context of customary law and State practice';[406] and the judgment in the *Libya–Malta* case has recently underlined the

USA, Uruguay, Venezuela and Vietnam. The OAS also supported such a limit. Denmark, Ghana, Jamaica and Pakistan indicated a certain preparedness to support such a limit, rather than a 200-mile maximum: p. 165 n. 353 above.

[403] See text at p. 147 n. 244 above.

[404] UN Convention on the Law of the Sea, Article 57; Judge Oda in the *Tunisia–Libya* case at paras. 117, 120, 129 and 130; ILA Committee on the Exclusive Economic Zone: First (Preliminary) Report, loc. cit. above (p. 167 n. 370), at p. 305.

[405] See text at pp. 167–70 nn. 368–93, above.

[406] Para. 43; also para. 73 in fine.

evolutionary nature of continental shelf law, since 'natural prolongation' is now, 'in part', defined by distance from the coast. Accordingly, a second, and distinct, argument can be made for a margin limit. It is conceded that Jennings's interpretation of the *North Sea* cases might indeed be mistaken and that continental shelf rights therefore did not extend to the edge of the margin in the 1960s. Nevertheless, it is said, a new rule of customary law developed in the 1970s conferring jurisdiction over the whole of the continental margin, irrespective of its depth and its current exploitability, and regardless of whether it lies beyond 200 miles from the coast.

At the Caracas Session of the Third UN Conference, thirty-nine States, as well as the Organization of American States, declared their support for such a limit.[407] Nearly all these States maintained this to be the present state of general customary law. There was, therefore, a solid core around which a general consensus might subsequently develop, and its attitude was of the requisite type for the formation of a rule of customary law. It is argued that such a consensus did develop at the Conference, evidenced by the incorporation of the margin rule in all the various negotiating texts, the Draft Convention and, finally, in Article 76 (1) of the Convention itself. Thus, Gardiner writes: 'it was recognised from the start [of the Conference] that the legal definition of the continental shelf ought to take into account the natural prolongation of the land-mass'.[408] Likewise, Anand writes:

> [I]n the *North Sea Continental Shelf* cases, the International Court of Justice ... referred to the continental shelf as the 'natural prolongation' of the land territory of the coastal State. This may be reasonably interpreted to include the whole of the continental margin because it is there that the 'natural prolongation' of the continent ends and the real ocean starts. This principle has now come to be endorsed by the Third U.N. Conference on the Law of the Sea and a consensus has emerged in its favour.[409]

(No matter that this might be an erroneous interpretation of that judgment; for if States will something to be the law, it becomes the law.[410]) And O'Connell wrote that, '[e]xcept for the technicalities of delineation, and the granting of seabed rights to States with continental shelves narrower than 200 nautical miles', the provisions of Article 76 'may be taken to represent the present position in customary international law'.[411] Moreover, in the recent *Libya–Malta* case, both Judge Mbaye[412] and

[407] p. 171 n. 402 above. It may be noted that Buzan writes that forty-nine States had adhered to this position by the end of 1974: op. cit. above (p. 165 n. 353), at p. 220.

[408] Loc. cit. above (p. 147 n. 243), at p. 152; also p. 151.

[409] Loc. cit. above (p. 147 n. 242), at p. 179; also p. 174.

[410] *SS Lotus*, loc. cit. above (p. 120 n. 62).

[411] Op. cit. above (p. 164 n. 348), at p. 497.

[412] pp. 94 and 95.

Vice-President Sette-Camara[413] are clearly of the opinion that Article 76, in so far as it expresses the margin rule, represents customary law.[414] It must be noted that, if the margin rule were part of modern customary law as alleged, the rule in Article 1 would clearly be superseded. For, according to the margin rule, coastal States possess sovereign rights over the whole of their continental margins, irrespective of depth and current exploitability. Furthermore, under that rule, jurisdiction beyond the edge of the continental rise would be prohibited on any grounds other than under the 200-mile rule discussed above.

However, in so far as this argument is based on the negotiations at the Third Conference, it cannot succeed; for it is impossible to maintain that the conditions necessary for the creation of a rule of general customary law have been met. First, several of those States which supported a margin limit recognized that this would constitute a change in the law, and was therefore a proposal about what the law ought to be, rather than an affirmation of what the law already was. Burma and Thailand adopted this position at the Caracas Session,[415] as did Norway.[416] The Soviet Union, by the Seventh Session of the Conference, came to accept the idea of coastal State rights beyond 200 miles where the margin extends that far;[417] but, prior to that, the Soviet delegation had maintained that, according to the principle of natural prolongation, the edge of the physical shelf was the seaward limit of continental shelf rights in customary law.[418]

Secondly, it would be totally wrong to say that a general and settled consensus was immediately established in support of the margin limit. At the Caracas Session, thirty-nine States registered their opinion that coastal State rights should not extend beyond a distance of 200 miles from the coast, even if a continental margin is present;[419] and it is clear that many other States sympathized.[420] It may also be noted that, while not supporting a 200-mile outer limit, the Soviet Union declared its opposi-

[413] pp. 68 and 69.

[414] Indeed, in contrast with O'Connell and Vice-President Sette-Camara, Judge Mbaye treats certain of the detailed provisions of Article 76 on the delineation of the margin limit as customary law—namely, the 350-miles rule in Article 76 (5): p. 94. In his oral argument in the *Libya–Malta* case, Lauterpacht even talked of Article 76 (4) (a) (i) as if it were customary law: CR 84/24, p. 6.

[415] See p. 147 n. 244 and text at p. 149 n. 251 above.

[416] Norway wanted a more precise limit to replace the exploitability criterion; but it was impossible to maintain (and still is) that the edge of the margin represented the current limit of practicable exploitation from fixed installations: *UNCLOS III Official Records*, vol. 1, p. 85, and ibid., vol. 2, p. 164.

[417] Ibid., vol. 9, p. 63; however, even then there was to be a maximum limit of 300 miles.

[418] Ibid., vol. 2, p. 161: a 500-metre depth limit was accordingly proposed, since this isobath embraces the shelf edge in all parts of the world.

[419] These States are enumerated at p. 165 n. 353 above; and eight of these States (Afghanistan, Austria, Gambia, Japan, Kenya, Singapore, Switzerland and Zaire) declared what was implicit in the proposal for a 200-mile maximum limit—that the margin limit was unacceptable.

[420] Buzan puts at sixty-three the number of States which had adopted this position by the end of 1974: op. cit. above (p. 165 n. 353); and Weil stated that this was the majority view in his argument for Malta in the *Libya–Malta* case: CR 85/7, p. 42.

tion to the demands of 'the margineers', as they were called.[421] A large, but indeterminate, number of States persisted in this stance until the end of the decade. Thus the Chairman of the Second Committee, reporting on its work during the Fifth Session, disclosed that, whilst discussion had centred on the definition of the limit to shelf rights beyond 200 miles, some delegations had explained that they had participated in these deliberations in a constructive spirit, in order to negotiate an acceptable treaty provision, but they still adhered to their original position that shelf rights, even as part of a treaty arrangement, should not extend beyond 200 miles from the coast.[422] At the Sixth Session, the Nepalese delegate remarked that over ninety States—land-locked and geographically disadvantaged—had declared themselves in favour of limiting coastal State jurisdiction to 200 miles from the coast;[423] and the Soviet delegation reported that this group had maintained its position during the Seventh Session[424]—indeed, fifteen States can be found to have declared support for a 200-mile outer limit in the brief records of the Plenary debates.[425] The Arab States remained firmly in support of this limit throughout 1978 and 1979;[426] and it was only in 1980 that they finally displayed any readiness to accept a provision recognizing coastal State rights beyond 200 miles, even then maintaining that any such extension must in turn be subject to a distance limit.[427]

There was, therefore, no real consensus in favour of a margin limit, even as part of a treaty settlement, until the final years of the Conference.[428] However, despite such widespread opposition, negotiations immediately centred on finding a way to translate coastal State entitlement to the whole of the continental margin into a precise limit which would prove acceptable to all the States at the Conference, because those States blessed with extensive margins made it clear from the start that recognition of such a limit was a precondition of their adherence to any future treaty.[429] The negotiating texts accordingly incorporated a margin limit, since it was the only formula which offered any realistic chance of achieving a consensus. The opponents of a margin limit must have been all too aware of the fact

421 Loc. cit. above (p. 174 n. 418).

422 A/Conf. 62/L. 17: *UNCLOS III Official Records*, vol. 6, p. 138. See also ibid., p. 43.

423 Ibid., vol. 7, p. 38.

424 Ibid., vol. 9, p. 63.

425 Algeria, Bulgaria, Cameroon, Egypt, German Democratic Republic, Ghana, Hungary, Iraq, Jamaica, Japan, Libya, Nigeria, Poland, Syria and Tunisia.

426 The Arab States placed a proposal for such a limit before Negotiating Group 6 in 1978: NG 6/2. In maintaining this position they acted in accordance with the Recommendations of the Experts on the Law of the Sea of the Member States of the Islamic Conference to the 10th Conference of Foreign Ministers, adopted at Istanbul, 6–9 March 1979: *UNCLOS III Official Records*, vol. 12, p. 68.

427 Report of the Chairman of the Second Committee, A/Conf. 62/L. 51: ibid., vol. 13, p. 83, reporting the statement of the Iraqi delegate on behalf of the group of Arab States to Negotiating Group 6. See also the statement by the delegate of the United Arab Emirates, ibid., p. 21.

428 Even then, some States held out against the margin rule: Judge *ad hoc* Jiménez de Aréchaga in the *Tunisia–Libya* case at para. 52.

429 Loc. cit. above (n. 422). See also the Memorandum of the President of the Conference accompanying the Informal Composite Negotiating Text, A/Conf. 62/WP. 10/Add. 1: *UNCLOS III Official Records*, vol. 8, p. 68.

that the participation of many States was at stake, including States such as Argentina, Canada, Norway, the UK, and the US, whose adherence to any future treaty on the law of the sea was essential.[430] Agreement was finally achieved that the UN Convention should recognize coastal State rights over the continental margin largely because some such agreement had to be reached.

It is, of course, no objection to the formation of a rule of customary law that it is the product of political necessity. However, the third, and major, reason that a rule of general customary law on the lines of Article 76 (1) has not arisen is that the consensus which did finally emerge was of the wrong kind to found a rule of customary law. There is absolutely no indication that the generality of States was prepared to recognize the margin limit irrespective of their adherence to the UN Convention: Article 76 (1) was only acceptable to the generality of States as a treaty rule. It is notorious that the UN Convention on the Law of the Sea is a complex 'package deal'. Various norms were recognized solely in consideration for the acceptance of other normative demands. Such bargains, trade-offs and compromises underpin the whole delicate structure of the Convention. Most of the articles of the Convention thus come with strings attached, linking them to yet other provisions of the treaty. Article 76 (1) is no exception. Mr Castañeda of Mexico, speaking on behalf of the members of the coastal States' co-ordinating group at the Seventh Session, declared that all the issues before Negotiating Groups 4, 5 and 6 constituted a 'package'—the right of access for land-locked and geographically disadvantaged States to the living resources of neighbouring exclusive economic zones, the peaceful settlement of disputes, the definition of the outer limit of the continental shelf and the sharing of revenue derived from the exploitation of the continental shelf. Consequently, all of these topics needed to be dealt with together.[431] The Chairman's report on the work of the Second Committee during the Seventh Session reflects the same understanding.[432]

First, in accordance with the outlines of this 'package deal', many States were not willing to accord coastal States the right to extend their jurisdiction over the continental margin beyond 200 miles unless land-locked and geographically disadvantaged States were accorded in return a satisfactory right of access to the living resources in the economic zones of neighbouring coastal States. The Jamaican delegate remarked that his government believed coastal State rights ought not to extend beyond 200 miles, but that it would accept extension if an equitable solution could be found to the access problem (*inter alia*).[433] Correlatively, as the Mexican delegation affirmed, the 'margineers' were ready to offer such a 'trade-off' in order to secure recognition of the margin limit. Several wide-margin

[430] As Weil noted in his oral argument in the *Libya–Malta* case: CR 85/7, p. 42.

[431] *UNCLOS III Official Records*, vol. 9, p. 57. See also the remarks of the Canadian delegation: ibid., p. 62.

[432] Ibid., p. 49.

[433] Ibid., p. 60; also, ibid., p. 64. Likewise, Uganda, ibid., p. 62.

States took the opportunity to reiterate their readiness to strike such a bargain at the Seventh Session.[434] Thus the Canadian delegation remarked that the limits and access questions were two parts of a whole whose elements could not be considered in isolation.[435]

Secondly, a very large number of States, including coastal States, were only willing to accept claims to the margin beyond 200 miles, and an accompanying diminution of the international area, if there was an obligation to share the revenue derived from the exploitation of the margin beyond that distance.[436] The idea of revenue-sharing seems to have originated in the proposals put to the UN Sea-Bed Committee by the UN in 1970.[437] These proposals recognized that a significant number of States were demanding a margin limit, and that these claims were resisted by much of the international community. As two of the key elements in a suggested compromise,[438] the US proposed that the coastal State should basically have control of the exploitation of the continental margin, but should have to share the benefits it derived with the rest of the international community. At the Caracas Session of the Third Conference, the US discarded the other elements in this proposal, but continued to advocate the same basic trade-off of rights in return for revenue-sharing.[439] Several States which advocated a margin limit expressed agreement with this compromise,[440] whilst several States which opposed the extension of coastal rights beyond 200 miles expressed a readiness to change their minds in return for revenue-sharing.[441] Evidence is littered throughout the records of the Conference that this trade-off played a vital role in securing agreement on the margin limit in Article 76 (1). Despite the continuing confrontation between the '200-milers' and the 'margineers', Njenga, reporting on the work of the Second Committee at the Fifth Session, stated that there was a 'broad consensus' in favour of a margin limit 'on the understanding' that a 'realistic' form of revenue-sharing should be adopted in relation to the margin beyond 200 miles.[442]

[434] Argentina, ibid., p. 59; Brazil, ibid., p. 70; Ecuador, ibid., p. 59; France, ibid., p. 79; Mauritius, ibid., pp. 64–5; New Zealand, ibid., p. 69; Nicaragua, ibid., p. 68; Norway, ibid., p. 60; Pakistan, ibid., p. 68; UK, ibid., p. 66; Uruguay, ibid., p. 76.

[435] Ibid., p. 62.

[436] This 'bargain' has been widely noted: Judge *ad hoc* Jiménez de Aréchaga in the *Tunisia–Libya* case at para. 52; Judge Oda in that case at para. 100 and in the *Libya–Malta* case at para. 57; and Weil in oral argument for Malta in the latter case at CR 85/7, pp. 42–3.

[437] A/AC. 138/25, introduced at A/AC. 138/SR. 29, pp. 9 ff. Pulvenis, loc. cit. above (p. 169 n. 382), at p. 115 n. 21, places its origin in the joint proposal of Afghanistan, Austria, Belgium, Bolivia, Nepal and Singapore: A/AC. 138/SC. II/L. 39, Article 3.

[438] On the compromise nature of the Trusteeship Area, and its place in the wider compromise diplomacy of the US in that period, see Stevenson's statement at A/AC. 138/SR. 65, pp. 61–2.

[439] *UNCLOS III Official Records*, vol. 2, p. 291, introducing A/Conf. 62/C. 2/L. 47. In contrast with subsequent proposals, the duty to share revenue attached to the sea-bed beyond the 200-metre isobath under this proposal, rather than to the sea-bed beyond 200 miles.

[440] Iceland, India, possibly Indonesia, Mauritius and Trinidad and Tobago. Burma, however, rejected such a compromise.

[441] Denmark, Ghana, Jamaica, and possibly Switzerland.

[442] Ibid., vol. 6, p. 43. But see the Report of the Chairman of the Second Committee at ibid., p. 138, which takes a less sanguine view.

At the Seventh Session, Jamaica expressed its readiness to drop its opposition to a margin limit on certain conditions, including a satisfactory system of revenue-sharing with regard to the margin beyond 200 miles;[443] and Switzerland seems to have been of a similar disposition.[444] At the same time, Canada, Ireland, New Zealand and the US expressed their belief that a system of revenue-sharing formed a central part of the emerging package deal on limits.[445] At the Eighth Session, the chairman of the Second Committee reported that, although some States were by then willing to accept coastal State rights beyond 200 miles under the complex formula in the first revision of the Informal Composite Negotiating Text, this was conditional upon a satisfactory outcome to the negotiations on certain related issues, including revenue-sharing.[446] Furthermore, when the Arab States finally dropped their opposition to a continental shelf of more than 200 miles, this was said to be on the understanding that a satisfactory (more generous) system of revenue-sharing was negotiated.[447]

The third element of consideration essential to the adoption of Article 76 (1) was the very definition of the outer limit itself. The 'margineers' claimed that, according to the present state of customary law, coastal States possessed jurisdiction right out to the very edge of the continental rise. Paragraphs 1 and 3 of Article 76 recognize this claim in principle. However, paragraph 2 gives notice that full effect is not accorded to this principle: for coastal rights may not extend beyond the limits prescribed in paragraphs 4, 5 and 6. It was only when the recognition of claims to the continental margin was coupled with these detailed provisions on the delineation of the outer limit that the deadlock between the 'margineers' and the '200-milers' looked like shifting. As the President of the Conference explained on the occasion of the first revision of the Informal Composite Negotiating Text, the series of rules now contained in the various paragraphs of Article 76 represented 'a clear movement away' from the simple margin limit which had figured in the earlier negotiating texts, and constituted a 'compromise' which was 'manifestly [more] acceptable' to most States.[448] Of these paragraphs, it is paragraph 4—the so-called 'Irish amendment'—which is the most celebrated.[449] It contains

443 p. 176 n. 433 above.

444 *UNCLOS III Official Records*, vol. 9, p. 80; see also Yugoslavia, ibid., pp. 69–70.

445 Ibid., pp. 62, 63, 69 and 78, respectively.

446 Ibid., vol. 11, p. 28.

447 Loc. cit. above (p. 175 n. 427).

448 A/Conf. 62/WP. 10/Rev. 1, pp. 18–19.

449 The 'Irish amendment' was introduced in August 1976, but did not receive sufficient acceptance to be introduced into the Informal Composite Negotiating Text. However, it constituted a central element in the revised Soviet paper, NG 6/8, which at last broke the deadlock on the limits issue at the Eighth Session. This paper was adopted by the Chairman of the Second Committee in a compromise text submitted to Plenary: A/Conf. 62/L. 37, at *UNCLOS III Official Records*, vol. 11, at pp. 100–1. This proposal did not attract a consensus, but was incorporated into the first revision of the ICNT, since it seemed to offer a substantially improved prospect of attaining consensus, thus satisfying the criteria laid down for revisions of the ICNT in the Conference decision of April 1978: A/Conf. 62/62, paras. 10–11, at ibid., vol. 5, p. 6.

two alternative methods for the determination of the outer limit where the margin extends beyond 200 miles—the 'Irish Formula' in section (a) (i), and a modified 'Hedberg Formula' in section (a) (ii). Under either of these two formulae, wide-margin States will generally not be able to claim jurisdiction over the entirety of their continental margins. Substantial parts of the continental rise—the exact extent is not clear[450]—are thus subject to the regime developed for the international sea-bed area. The wide-margin States, therefore, were able to present their espousal of the 'Irish amendment' as a major concession on their part to those States which vehemently opposed the extension of shelf rights beyond 200 miles.[451] Thus the New Zealand delegate remarked that the 'Irish amendment' offered the only widely acceptable compromise between recognition of coastal State entitlement over the whole of the continental margin, which was unacceptable to many States, and various 'unacceptable' proposals to cut off the coastal State from the natural prolongation of its landmass by depth or distance criteria.[452] At least some of the '200-milers' welcomed this spirit of compromise.[453] As it was, still more restrictions on margin claims proved necessary before agreement could finally be reached: a combined depth and distance limit on top of the 'Irish amendment';[454] a special provision preventing excessive claims based on submarine ridges;[455] and a Commission on the Limits of the Continental Shelf to police the limits delineated by coastal States according to the rules in Article 76.[456] And this was in addition to the other 'trade-offs' detailed above!

It is, therefore, quite clear that if, as a result of the efforts of a 'campaigning and determined minority',[457] a consensus did finally develop at the Conference in favour of the recognition of coastal State rights over the margin beyond 200 miles, then, nevertheless, that consensus was not of the right type to found a rule of general customary law. Rather, it was intimately related to the existence of a treaty, which not only contained several elements of consideration in return for recognition of a margin

[450] Gardiner states that only 6 per cent of the sea-bed beyond 200 miles out is continental margin, and para. 4 would place only one-half to two-thirds of this area under the continental shelf regime: loc. cit. above (p. 147 n. 243), at p. 166. A Preliminary Study prepared by the UN Secretariat indicated that coastal State jurisdiction would extend to approximately one-third of the margin beyond 200 miles: A/Conf. 62/C. 2/L. 98/Add. 2, *UNCLOS III Official Records*, vol. 4, p. 190.

[451] Gardiner, loc. cit. above (p. 147, n. 243), at pp. 162 and 165; Brown, op. cit. above (p. 144 n. 227), at 1.4 9. See also Argentina, *UNCLOS III Official Records*, vol. 9, p. 59; Canada, ibid., p. 62; Ireland, ibid., vol. 7, p. 36, and vol. 9, p. 63; Norway, ibid., vol. 7, p. 38, and vol. 9, p. 60; UK, ibid., vol. 9, p. 66; USA, ibid., p. 78; and Uruguay, ibid., p. 76. Note the attitude of Argentina, ibid., vol. 13, p. 17. Australia voiced its opposition to the proposal since it did not afford recognition to the Australian claims to the whole of the continental margin: ibid., vol. 9, p. 70.

[452] Ibid., vol. 9, p. 69.

[453] Japan, ibid., vol. 7, p. 37; Nepal, ibid., pp. 36–7.

[454] Article 76 (5).

[455] Article 76 (6).

[456] Article 76 (8) and Annex II. For comment on these various paragraphs and the Annex, see Brown, op. cit., above (p. 144 n. 227), at 1.4 7–18.

[457] Caflisch, *Annuaire suisse de droit international*, 39 (1983), p. 39 at p. 84.

limit, but which also incorporated a series of provisions restraining claims to the margin to the landward part of the continental rise, culminating in an elaborate international machinery to police the delineation of the outer limit. This conclusion is in all respects identical to that reached by Judge Oda in the *Tunisia–Libya* case of 1982. Having reviewed the matter at some length, he concludes:

> It should be crystal clear that Article 76 of the . . . convention is essentially a product of compromise—not consensus—between the conflicting positions of various groups which have different, and sometimes opposite, interests in the use of sea-bed areas. Well may the . . . convention be expected eventually to become binding upon many nations, once it has become widely accepted and received a sufficient number of ratifications. Until that time, there is no doubt that Article 76 is not a provision of any worldwide multilateral convention, and can hardly be considered as enshrining established rules of international law.[458]

Judge *ad hoc* Jiménez de Aréchaga was likewise of the opinion that the margin limit in Article 76 (1) could not be considered to represent customary law.[459] Again, in the *Libya–Malta* case, Judge Oda referred to the 'political compromise' which underlay the recognition of the margin in Article 76;[460] and, in so far as he mentioned the continental margin, he referred to it as a 'new concept . . . in the 1982 Convention'.[461] Moreover, these judicial opinions are in accord with the stance taken by the President of the Third Conference. In his closing speech of 10 December 1982, he stated:

> . . . in the case of article 76, on the continental shelf, the article contains new law in that it has expanded the concept of the continental shelf to include the continental slope and the continental rise. This concession to the broad-margin States was in return for their agreement to revenue-sharing on the continental shelf beyond 200 miles. It is therefore my view that a State which is not party to this Convention cannot invoke the benefits of Article 76.[462]

Furthermore, it is of the greatest interest that certain States are registering their doubts that the margin limit in Article 76 (1) has passed into the corpus of general customary law. In the recent *Libya–Malta* case, both parties, in the course of their oral arguments, cast doubt on the customary status of the first limb of that paragraph. Thus Weil, counsel for Malta, pointed out 'the complex compromise expressed in the various paragraphs of Article 76, supplemented by the establishment of a Commission on the Limits of the Continental Shelf, and, under Article 82 of the Convention, the requirement to make payments or contributions in

[458] Para. 104.
[459] Para. 52. Judge *ad hoc* Evensen referred to it as 'a new accepted trend' at the Conference, but not as law: para. 11.
[460] Para. 58.
[461] Para 62.
[462] *UNCLOS III Official Records*, vol. 17, pp. 136–7.

respect of the exploitation of the continental shelf beyond 200 nautical miles'.[463] He concluded:

> From the foregoing observations it will be apparent that the dividing line between the elements of Article 76 which constitute customary law, and those which do not, . . . runs between the extension of continental shelf rights beyond the 200-mile limit and the fixing of the minimum outer limit of 200 miles. If there is any doubt as to the validity as customary law of certain elements of Article 76, it is only in regard to the extension of continental shelf rights up to the outer edge of the continental margin, and in regard to the complex provisions setting limits to this extension and those providing for payments and contributions.[464]

Quéneudec, counsel for Libya, declared that, of Article 76, only the reference to 'natural prolongation' could be considered part of customary law, and that 'it is difficult to consider' the other elements in that article, 'especially those relating to the determination of the outer limits of the continental shelf', as in accordance with present-day general international law.[465] This is of especial interest, since, three years previously, in the *Tunisia–Libya* case, Libya had argued that the margin limit was then customary law.[466]

It is, of course, possible that a consensus might have developed outside the framework of the UN debates sanctioning claims to the edge of the margin beyond 200 miles. Indeed, it is to the practice of States, and not to the debates of the Third Conference, that the International Court has turned to establish the customary status of the economic zone and the 200-mile rule in the law of the continental shelf. However, to date, there is insufficient State practice to justify the conclusion that claims of continental shelf rights to the outer edge of the margin are valid outside the framework of the new Convention. So far, sixteen—perhaps seventeen—States have explicitly laid claim to the continental margin.[467] To these there must be added a substantial group of States, led by Australia and Canada, which have not as yet made formal claims to the entirety of their margins, but which have consistently maintained that customary law sanctions them. However, as has been seen, this coexists with much known opposition to the validity of these claims. It is thus impossible to maintain that a rule of general customary law has yet emerged making claims to the continental margin beyond 200 miles valid *erga omnes* (although there is

[463] CR 85/7, p. 43 (English translation). He also termed it a 'package deal': ibid.

[464] Ibid., pp. 46–7 (English translation); also ibid., pp. 34, 49, 52–3 and 70.

[465] CR 84/31, pp. 51–2 (English translation); also ibid., p. 41. See also Vallat, CR 84/29, p. 26.

[466] TL 81/75 Ann. 2, quoted by Judge Oda in his dissenting opinion in that case at para. 105. Moreover, Libya claimed parts of the Ionian Abyss as its continental shelf, though over 200 miles from its coasts, under the margin rule in Article 76: see the oral argument of Mizzi in the *Libya–Malta* case at CR 84/22, p. 67, and Lauterpacht at CR 84/24, p. 6.

[467] Bangladesh, Burma, Dominican Republic, Guyana, Iceland, India, Mauritania, Mauritius, New Zealand, Pakistan, Senegal, Seychelles, Sri Lanka, Vanuatu, Vietnam and Yemen (Aden). Kampuchea is a possible addition to this list: see p. 186 n. 492, below. By section 2 (a) of the Continental Shelf Amendment Act of 1977, the Cook Islands (an Associated State of New Zealand) has also lodged such a claim.

clearly agreement that continental shelf rights may never extend beyond the continental rise, other than by means of the new 200-mile rule).

The jurisprudence of the International Court affords no reason to doubt this conclusion. Whilst considering the 'new accepted trends' at the Third UN Conference, the International Court in the *Tunisia–Libya* case remarked that, in so far as Article 76 (1) of the Convention repeats the principle that natural prolongation is a basis of the coastal State's legal title, it introduces no new element.[468] The concept of natural prolongation has formed part of the law of the continental shelf since the judgment of the Court in the *North Sea* cases; but, as has been seen, it has been constantly evolving and the way in which it is defined has changed, culminating in the advent of the 200-mile rule upheld in the *Libya–Malta* case. Thus, as Quéneudec observed, the idea of natural prolongation in Article 76 (1) reflects existing customary law, but the way of defining it by reference to the continental margin is a new idea that cannot yet be considered law.[469]

The Chamber in the *Gulf of Maine* case, whilst examining the 'continental margin' in the delimination area, repeatedly refers to that area of sea-bed by the legal term 'continental shelf',[470] thus indicating that it treats the margin as part of the legal institution. Indeed, it affirms that there have been 'rapid changes' in the law, and delimitations now have 'to share out the potential mineral wealth of continental shelves extending to the continental margin'.[471] However, the Chamber in that case was dealing with a delimitation between two States both of which have long been supporters of the entitlement of the coastal State to the whole of its adjacent margin and have treated this as a proposition of existing customary law. Consequently, by virtue of a 'special' customary rule existing between Canada and the US,[472] the margin limit was indeed applicable.[473] For the purposes of that case, therefore, the margin was indeed continental shelf; but not necessarily according to general customary law.

In the recent *Libya–Malta* case, the International Court several times referred to the fact that, although the new distance rule makes the physical nature of the sea-bed irrelevant up to 200 miles from the coast, it continues to play a part in defining the limits to coastal State rights beyond that distance.[474] However, it would be wrong to consider this as implicit support for the margin limit. Counsel for Malta, Weil, expressed an opinion similar to the Court in this respect,[475] and yet, as has been seen, he rejected the idea that the margin rule in Article 76 (1) represented

[468] Para. 48.
[469] Loc. cit. above (p. 181 n. 465).
[470] Paras. 45, 46, 47 and 50.
[471] Para. 160.
[472] Cf. *Right of Passage over Indian Territory* (*Portugal* v. *India*), *ICJ Reports*, 1960, p. 6.
[473] And see section V, conclusion 9, below. Note that the Special Agreement between the two parties in that case presupposed that the margin was part of the legal shelf: para. 21.
[474] Para. 40; also para. 34.
[475] CR 84/25, p. 68.

customary law.[476] For certain States have already acquired rights beyond 200 miles under the rule in Article 1 where the sea-bed is sufficiently shallow to fall within the 200-metre isobath or the current range of exploitation operations; and, if the rule in Article 1 continues to be a part of customary law, then, where the continental margin extends beyond 200 miles and presents sufficiently shallow conditions, coastal State rights might continue to extend under the aegis of the exploitability criterion. Although the Court at one point seems to envisage the delimitation of the continental margin,[477] it is important to remember that, as Judge Oda points out, [478] it did not even purport to embark on an analysis of the customary status of the first limb of Article 76 (1).

V. Conclusion

The following conclusions may be drawn:

1. By the beginning of the 1970s, if not before, a rule on limits on the lines of that contained in Article 1 of the Convention on the Continental Shelf became part of general customary law.

2. The effect of this rule was automatically to validate claims to continental shelf jurisdiction over the adjacent sea-bed out to the 200-metre isobath. Furthermore, should exploitation of the hydrocarbon resources of the sea-bed immediately beyond that isobath ever prove practicable by means of fixed installations, then coastal State jurisdiction should probably extend to those areas. If exploitation should prove possible well beyond the 200-metre isobath, then no definite answer was given. It was recognized at the time the rule developed that, whilst there was some point at which coastal jurisdiction would cease to be justified, what that point was it was then impossible to tell. A decision on this matter could only be taken in the future, when certain facts relevant to the taking of an informed decision became known. In the meantime, coastal jurisdiction should be able to expand to wherever it proved necessary and desirable. Since a rule which required fresh decisions to be taken each time coastal rights required expansion would be cumbersome and might well prevent exploitation, the rule created a presumption that jurisdiction should extend to wherever exploitation might prove practicable. A deliberate decision that such an extension should not take place would rebut this presumption, and so halt the expansion of coastal State jurisdiction.

3. Arguments that a decision had in fact been taken on how far seawards coastal State rights might extend under the exploitability criterion must fail, since they ignore the fact that it was the very purpose of the rule in Article 1 to defer such a decision.

4. Arguments that a specific rule on limits was inherent in the very rationale of the continental shelf regime must also fail for a similar reason. This includes Jennings's celebrated natural prolongation argument.

[476] Text at p. 181 nn. 463–4 above. [477] Para. 77. [478] Para. 6.

5. In general customary law, the outer limit to the seaward extension of coastal State rights thus remained undetermined at the beginning of the 1970s.

6. By the 1980s, a new rule of general customary law had developed, entitling all coastal States to claim continental shelf rights, valid *erga omnes*, over the sea-bed up to a distance of 200 nautical miles from the baselines of the territorial sea, whatever the depth of the sea-bed at such distances, whether it is currently exploitable or not, and irrespective of its physical nature.

7. Claims beyond 200 miles which are founded solely on the legal basis of distance from the coast or proximity are prohibited. However, claims based on other grounds of entitlement are not prohibited beyond that distance.

8. A rule of general customary law has not yet developed validating *erga omnes* claims over the continental margin beyond 200 miles out to the furthest edge of the continental rise.

9. To these eight conclusions, a ninth might be added. As has been seen, a significant number of States maintain that a rule of general customary law exists validating claims over the whole of the continental margin; but the refusal of many States to accept this proposition has precluded the alleged rule from passing into general customary law and thus binding all States. However, since the former group has continued to affirm this proposition, the rule has become a valid norm of customary law in the relations of those States *inter se*,[479] constituting a 'special', or 'regional', customary law of the type envisioned by the International Court in the *Asylum* case.[480] Therefore, as amongst those States, the former rule of general customary law, as reflected by Article 1 of the Convention on the Continental Shelf, has been superseded by a new rule of 'special' customary law.

10. It is doubtful whether a parallel conclusion can be drawn in the case of those States which resisted the margin limit at the Third Conference, and wished coastal State jurisdiction to be limited to within 200 miles of the coast. In order for a rule of customary law to emerge—be it general or 'special' customary law—there must be a common will that it is a rule in force, and that it binds as customary law, independently of the existence of any valid bonds of treaty obligation. Although a common will existed amongst the supporters of a 200-mile maximum limit, it was not of the requisite kind. The States upholding such a limit at the Third Conference recognized that this was a proposal to effect a change in the law. Moreover, this alteration was not to be achieved by a change in the customary law, but by the creation of a treaty obligation, adjusting the legal position as between parties to the future UN Convention. This

[479] Cheng, loc. cit. above (p. 166 n. 355), at p. 540: conclusion (3); also ibid., p. 549: conclusion (22).
[480] *Asylum* case (*Columbia* v. *Peru*), *ICJ Reports*, 1950, p. 266.

attempt failed; and the 200-mile outer limit remains merely an abortive proposal to create a new treaty obligation.

11. The question therefore remains as to what rule of customary law governs the relations *inter se* of those States which have opposed the margin limit. This can be conveniently discussed in combination with the question of what rules of customary law govern the relations between the adherents and opponents of the margin limit *qua* customary law; for the legal relations between the generality of States and those States which are mutually bound by a 'special' custom are governed by rules of general customary law.[481] As has been seen, certain new rules of general customary law have been established in the 1970s. However, they fail to provide a complete answer to the limits question. Claims may be validly made merely on the basis of distance from the coast; but such claims are prohibited beyond 200 miles. To claim rights over the sea-bed beyond that distance, the coastal State must be able to point to some other generally valid basis of title; as has just been seen, one such basis, in the mutual legal relations of a sizeable group of States, is that the continental margin extends beyond that distance. In the early 1970s the rule in Article 1 provided another such basis, but great doubt may now be felt as to whether this rule still represents general customary law.

Today, forty-two States maintain claims which utilize the rule in Article 1, three of them using the exploitability criterion without reference to the 200-metre isobath limit.[482] Of these States, twenty-seven are parties to the Convention on the Continental Shelf,[483] while fifteen are not.[484] To these forty-two, there may be added twenty-eight claims which do not specify any limit, nine of which have been made by parties to the Convention.[485] Fifty-four States are currently parties to the Convention.[486] However, this level of support for the rule in Article 1 is insufficient to justify the conclusion that it is still a rule of general customary law.

First, a substantial part of the support for the rule in Article 1 is more apparent than real. Several of the States which still employ that rule—such as Argentina, Australia, Indonesia, Norway, Portugal, Spain and Uruguay—have publicly maintained that they are entitled to sovereign rights over the whole of their continental margins, regardless of depth,

[481] Akehurst, this *Year Book*, 47 (1974–5), p. 1 at p. 29.

[482] Indonesia, Norway and the Philippines.

[483] Australia, Canada, Cyprus, Denmark, Fiji, Finland, France, German Democratic Republic, Greece, Haiti, Israel, Malaysia, Malta, Netherlands, Nigeria, Norway, Portugal, Roumania, South Africa, Spain, Sweden, Thailand, Trinidad and Tobago, USSR, Venezuela, Yugoslavia and the Ukraine (which is governed by Union law on such matters).

[484] Argentina, Bahamas, Brazil, Egypt, Federal Republic of Germany, Ghana, Honduras, Indonesia, Italy, Liberia, Morocco, Papua New Guinea, Philippines, Sudan, Syria and Uruguay.

[485] Albania, Bulgaria, Colombia, Jamaica, Mexico, Poland, Tonga, UK and USA. The other nineteen are: Bahrein, Belgium, Belize, Brunei, Cameroon, China, Gambia, Iran, Iraq, Ireland, Korea (South), Kuwait, Libya, Nicaragua, Oman, Panama, Qatar, Saudi Arabia and United Arab Emirates (except Fujairah, which employs the rule in Article 1).

[486] p. 111 n. 6 above.

and irrespective of the fact that the sea-bed in question is currently unexploitable. The same position has been taken by several of those States whose claims specify no outer limit, such as Albania, Ireland, Mexico, the UK and the US.

Secondly, the debates at the Third Conference must have affected the stability of the consensus behind the rule in Article 1. Formally, this might not appear to be so: the rule in Article 1 represented general customary law when the Conference began; various proposals were made to create new treaty rules; and these failed, leaving Article 1 still in force (albeit supplemented by the two new rules described in conclusions 6 and 7). However, support for the rule in Article 1 had never been universal; and almost a decade of proposals for change must have had an unsettling effect.[487] This is especially so, given that all the proposals at the Conference sought to replace the exploitability criterion rather than limit it, and, furthermore, given that one proposal which received strong support—the margin limit—was preferred as *lex lata*.

Thirdly, whereas the tide of State practice was clearly running in favour of the rule in Article 1 at the turn of the 1970s,[488] this tide has definitely turned, and is running in another direction. In the last decade, just one State has signified its consent to be bound by the Convention on the Continental Shelf,[489] whilst, at the same time, one State has denounced it.[490] In the same period, just one State has made a claim employing the formula in Article 1.[491] Meanwhile, eight States which formerly employed that rule announced that they were claiming continental shelf rights over the whole of their continental margins.[492] Three other States replaced the rule in Article 1 with different limits provisions.[493]

Fourthly, and most significantly, the rule in Article 1 no longer has the support of the States most interested in the question of the seaward limits of continental shelf rights. It is undeniable that the support of those States which are blessed with extensive continental margins is vital to the continued existence of a general rule on limits. It is they which are most

[487] Cf. the joint separate opinion of Judges Forster, Bengzon, Jiménez de Aréchaga, Nagendra Singh and Ruda, in the *Fisheries Jurisdiction* case, at paras. 12–13.

[488] Between 1968 and 1972, thirteen States became parties to the Convention on the Continental Shelf, and twenty States made claims employing the rule in Article 1.

[489] The Solomon Islands succeeded in 1981. The previous State to become a party to the Convention was Cyprus in 1974.

[490] Senegal in 1976.

[491] Papua New Guinea, Petroleum Act, No. 46 of 1977, section 2 (c). The previous State to do so was Cyprus in 1974. Ghana and Haiti passed fresh legislation reiterating their adherence to that rule in 1973 and 1977 respectively.

[492] Dominican Republic, Iceland, India, Mauritania, Mauritius, New Zealand, Vietnam and Yemen (Aden). Kampuchea might well be added to this list: the Spokesman on Foreign Affairs stated Kampuchea's claim throughout its natural prolongation (ST/LEG/SER. B/19, 1980, pp. 20–1), but it is unclear whether this claim is superseded or supplemented by the 200-mile continental shelf claim of 1982, which does not mention the continental margin.

[493] Costa Rica dropped it in favour of a 200-mile claim. Oman dropped it in favour of an unspecified limit—a much less momentous change, of course. Kampuchea also replaced its former claim employing the rule: see previous note.

likely to lose valuable hydrocarbon resources should the outer limit be set close in to the coast, and which therefore have a natural motive to disregard any rule on limits that the rest of the international community might recognize. However, the wide-margin States no longer support the rule in Article 1. Rather, they have made formal claims to the whole of their continental margins, or have affirmed that such claims are valid in customary law. Moreover, those States most directly interested in the offshore oil-exploitation industry—Norway, the UK and the US—maintain the same position.

Therefore the rule in Article 1 has probably ceased to be a valid rule of general customary law. The rule still seems to possess some relevance; for a significant number of States still employ that rule to limit their claims to continental shelf rights. The rule in Article 1 would seem to retain its validity as a rule of 'special' customary law in the mutual relations of at least some of these States. It is doubtful, however, whether the rule applies as a 'special' custom in the relations of those States, such as Argentina, Australia, Canada and Norway, which, although they still retain domestic legislation employing the exploitability criterion, have publicly taken the position that States are entitled to lay claim to their continental margins, whether they are currently exploitable or not.

Consequently, the position at customary law is confused. One group of States maintains that the margin limit represents general customary law. These States are bound *inter se* by such a rule, and claims made by other States to the continental margin are opposable to these States.[494] Another group of States appears to maintain that the rule in Article 1 still represents general law, a group to which belong at least some of those States whose claims fail to specify a limit. These States are in their turn bound *inter se* by such a rule, and claims made by other States on the basis of that rule are opposable to them. In addition, all States are bound by the general rules of law stated in conclusions 6 and 7 above. Otherwise, as between these two major groups of States, there are no general rules of law applicable: claims to the foot of the margin are not automatically opposable to the latter group of States; conversely, with the decline of the rule in Article 1, claims to the continental margin beyond 200 miles are not invalid merely because the sea-bed in question remains unexploitable. However, as Judge Dillard points out in the *Fisheries Jurisdiction* case, it does not follow that there is a juridical *lacuna* in the relations between these States, and that no rules of law exist to regulate the seaward extent of shelf claims.[495] Rather, the lawyer must descend from the level of general propositions of law and, instead, undertake an analysis of the bilateral relations between specific pairs of States, examining what claims have been made and whether they have met with recognition, acquiescence or protest.

[494] Cheng, loc. cit. above (p. 166 n. 355), at p. 537.

[495] pp. 58–61.

The law on the limits of continental shelf jurisdiction is therefore in the same position as was formerly the law on the limits of the territorial sea. In this confused state, it is quite likely that Article 76 of the UN Convention, although not yet wholly reflecting the position at customary law, will act as a clear and authoritative guide for future State practice.[496] Moreover, recent history shows that the advantage lies with those States which can act unilaterally to make their claims effective; and, in the case of the continental shelf, this would seem to mean the broad-margin States. If these States persist in the espousal of their claims to the continental margin, it is doubtful whether they can long be effectively opposed.

[496] Brown, op. cit. above (p. 144 n. 227), at 1.4 2.

THE LEGAL VALIDITY OF MILITARY INTERVENTION BY INVITATION OF THE GOVERNMENT*

By LOUISE DOSWALD-BECK[1]

I. Introduction

Since the Second World War, there have been numerous instances of troops being sent to another State allegedly upon invitation of its government. Many texts would support a principle unequivocally in favour of the legality of such intervention, and there is certainly no doubt that a State can legally send troops to another State upon invitation for certain limited operations. The validity of this is recognized, albeit negatively, in General Assembly Resolution 3314 (XXIX) where one instance of aggression is stated to be:

> The use of armed forces which are within the territory of another State with the agreement of the receiving State, in contravention of the conditions provided for in the agreement.[2]

Examples of such limited operations would include the use of peace-keeping forces which do not become involved with internal affairs, certain rescue operations[3] and help with minor disturbances not aimed at the political organization of the country.[4] However, certain recent texts express doubts as to the validity of intervention by invitation where foreign troops are to be used to quell an insurrection. The reasons given for such doubts are variously stated to be the inability of a shaky regime to represent the State as its government, a conflict with the principle of self-determination or a violation of the duty of non-intervention in the internal affairs of another State.

The purpose of this paper is to assess the position of modern international customary law in this respect by studying the meaning and interrelationship of basic theoretical principles of international law, together with an empirical study of relevant interventions undertaken in the last thirty years and State reaction to them. Attention will focus on those

[1] LLB (Bristol), LLM (London), Lecturer in Law at University College London.

[2] 1974 Resolution on the Definition of Aggression No. 3314 (XXIX), Article 3 (e). See also GA Res. 36/103 (1981).

[3] e.g. German help given to the Somalian Government in connection with the highjacked airliner at Mogadishu Airport on 18 October 1977: *Keesing's Contemporary Archives* (henceforth *Keesing's*), p. 28919.

[4] e.g. British help to the Tanganyikan, Ugandan and Kenyan Governments in January 1964 to quell disturbances and disorder in the armed forces who were demanding better conditions and pay: *Keesing's*, pp. 19963–5.

situations where outside help was given to a government which was either in danger of losing its control over the country or had lost such control, and will include instances where peace-keeping forces influenced events in a country.

II. State Representation

The basic principle of State representation in international law is that the government speaks for the State and acts on its behalf.[5] As the Permanent Court of International Justice stated in 1923, 'States can act only by and through their agents and representatives'.[6] This principle is manifest in normal State practice: governments conclude agreements on behalf of the State, the government represents the State in international fora and any representation on behalf of a State is done by its government.

Revolutionaries, on the other hand, have traditionally been treated as enemies[7] of the State in both internal and international law, with the result that any military aid given to rebels in another State has been unequivocally declared illegal.[8] With the possible exception of aid to groups exercising their right of self-determination,[9] the meaning of which will be examined later,[10] there has been no dissent from this view either in case law[11] or in literature.[12] The principle has further been vigorously reaffirmed by the General Assembly on several occasions, including in particular Resolution 2131 (XX) which states that:

> . . . No State shall organize, assist, foment, finance, incite or tolerate subver-

[5] See generally Cheng, *General Principles of Law as applied by International Courts and Tribunals* (1953), pp. 180 ff.

[6] *German Settlers in Poland* advisory opinion, *PCIJ*, Series B, No. 6, p. 22 (1923).

[7] Although recognition of insurgency gives a limited status for certain purposes. See Oppenheim, *International Law*, vol. 1 (8th edn., 1955), pp. 140–1, para. 75 (a). For the effect of recognition of belligerency, see below, p. 196.

[8] On a discussion as to the meaning of Article 7 of Res. 3314 (XXIX) (above, p. 189 n. 2), see Stone, 'Hopes and Loopholes in the 1974 Definition of Aggression', *American Journal of International Law*, 71 (1977), p. 224 at pp. 233–7.

[9] GA Res. 3314 (XXIX) (1974), 2625 (XXV) (1970) and 2621 (XXV) (1970) state that peoples exercising their right to self-determination have the right to receive support. There is basic disagreement as to whether this means military support: see previous note. Res. 2621 (XXV), which states that member States shall render 'moral and material assistance', was adopted with a high negative and abstention vote.

[10] Below, pp. 200–7.

[11] e.g. *Great Venezualan Railroad* case (German–Venezuelan Mixed Claims Commission, 1903), Ralston (ed.), *Venezuelan Arbitrations of 1903*, p. 632 at pp. 635–6, and by implication the ICJ order with regard to the request for the indication of provisional measures in the *Case Concerning Military and Paramilitary Activities in and against Nicaragua* (*Nicaragua* v. *United States*), *ICJ Reports*, 1984, p. 4. at p. 22.

[12] Brownlie, *International Law and the Use of Force by States* (1963), pp. 193, 279 and 370–1; Cheng, op. cit. above (n. 5); Garner, 'Questions of International Law in the Spanish Civil War', *American Journal of International Law*, 31 (1937), p. 66; Borchard, 'Neutrality and Civil Wars', ibid., pp. 305–6; Oppenheim, *International Law*, vol. 2 (7th edn., 1952), para. 298; Higgins, 'International Law and Civil Conflict', in Luard (ed.), *The International Regulation of Civil Wars* (1972), p. 170.

sive, terrorist or armed activities directed at the violent overthrow of the regime of another State . . .[13]

There are in addition numerous statements to this effect by State representatives, including those of delegates during the recent General Assembly and Security Council debates concerning the interventions of the Soviet Union in Afghanistan (1979)[14] and the United States in Grenada (1983).[15]

The apparent exclusiveness of government representation of a State would logically lead to the conclusion that a State could not violate Article 2 (4) of the United Nations Charter (or previously the Kellogg–Briand Pact 1928) if the government invited such intervention, for the interests and affairs of that State would be synonymous with those of the government. The traditional law was thus clearly stated by Garner in his editorial comment on the Spanish Civil War as follows:

The outbreak of insurrection in a state has no effect on its juridical status as a member of the international community. It does not alter the duty of non-intervention in its affairs which other states are under . . . .[16]

[There is a] sound distinction between the rights and duties of a state *vis-à-vis* the recognized legitimate government of another state and rebel forces engaged in the effort to overthrow it. There is no rule of international law which forbids the government of one state from rendering assistance to the established legitimate government of another state with a view of enabling it to suppress an insurrection against its authority. . . . If assistance is rendered to the legitimate government it is not a case of unlawful intervention as is the giving of assistance to rebels who are arrayed against its authority.[17]

Oppenheim states that intervention which is in principle forbidden 'is always *dictatorial* interference, not interference pure and simple'.[18] He then illustrates the latter type of interference, by implication not forbidden, by quoting two instances of military help given to a foreign government to quell an insurrection.[19]

If we were to assume, at this juncture, that these statements still represent the law, then the essential test to establish the legality of an intervention would be the valid consent of a legitimate government. The

[13] Declaration on the Inadmissibility of Intervention in the Domestic Affairs of States and the Protection of their Independence and Sovereignty (1965), para. 2. See also GA Res. 380 (v) (1950), 2625 (xxv) (1970) and 36/103 (1981).

[14] Security Council debates, 5 January 1980, UN Doc. S/PV.2185, S/PV.2186; 6 January 1980, S/PV.2187, S/PV.2188, S/PV.2190; General Assembly 6th Emergency Special Session, 10–14 January 1980.

[15] Security Council debates, 25 October 1983, UN Doc. S/PV.2487; 26 October 1983, S/PV. 2489; 27 October 1983, S/PV.2491; General Assembly debate, 2 November 1983, UN Doc. A/38/PV.43.

[16] *American Journal of International Law*, 31 (1937), at p. 67.

[17] Ibid., p. 68.

[18] Oppenheim, *International Law*, vol. 1 (8th edn., 1955), p. 305 (emphasis added).

[19] Several other authors assume this to be the law, e.g. Borchard, *American Journal of International Law*, 31 (1937), pp. 305 and 306; Woolsey, *Introduction to the Study of International Law* (5th edn., 1877), para. 42. Higgins, quoting Hyde, states this to be the traditional law, in Luard (ed.), *The International Regulation of Civil Wars* (1972), chapter 9, p. 170. See also Ronzitti, *Italian Yearbook of International Law*, 1 (1975), p. 192.

identification of the 'government' of a State as that State's valid representative in international law would thus be the primary task. There is, unfortunately, a lack of modern judicial authority in this respect. However, there are a number of old arbitral decisions which are pertinent and it is necessary to examine recent and present-day practice.

(a) *Early Arbitral Decisions*

The case law of past international arbitrations has consistently attested that the group which is in fact the master of the nation is the legitimate government of the State. In the *Dreyfus* case of 1901 the arbitrator stated that:

> According to a principle of international law . . . today universally admitted, the capacity of a government to represent the State in its international relations does not depend in any degree upon the legitimacy of its origin, so that . . . the usurper who in fact holds power with the consent express or tacit of the nation acts . . . validly in the name of the State . . .[20]

Further, in the *Garrison* case of 1885 the tribunal stated that '. . . every government, properly so called, is a government de facto'. With regard to what constituted a 'de facto' government, the tribunal stated that it was 'a government which . . . commands the habitual respect and obedience of the bulk of the people'.[21] The Commission in the *Hopkins* case of 1926, which considered the validity of certain postal orders issued under the revolutionary government of Huerta, stated as follows:

> The binding force of such acts of the Huerta administration as partook of [a] personal character . . . will depend upon its real control and paramountcy . . . over a major portion of the territory and a majority of the people . . . Once it had lost this control, it would not be more than one among two or more factions wrestling for power as between themselves.[22]

Recognition, on the other hand, is treated in these cases as relatively unimportant. The *Cuculla* case of 1868 concerned a military insurrection in Mexico led by Mr Zuloaga, who took over the capital from which the constitutional President fled. Major European governments recognized the Zuloagan government and it appeared that the American Minister had also done so. Some time afterwards, the previous President, who had not lost control of the rest of the country, retook the capital. The tribunal, in finding that the Zuloagan regime was not a government in international law, stated:

> Where then is the evidence of a de facto government? The possession of the capital will not be sufficient, nor recognition by the American Minister . . . Recognition is based on the pre-existing fact; it does not create the fact.

[20] Quoted in Cheng, op. cit. above (p. 190 n. 5), p. 188.

[21] Moore, *International Arbitrations*, vol. 4, p. 3548 at p. 3553.

[22] US–Mexico General Claims Commission (1926), *American Journal of International Law*, 21 (1927), p. 160 at pp. 164–5.

Habitual obedience of the members of a political society (of the 'bulk' of them) must, in fact, exist to constitute a government.[23]

A widely quoted judgment is that of the *Tinoco Concessions* arbitration of 1923 where the arbitrator assessed the relative value of recognition and *de facto* control:

The non-recognition by other nations of a government . . . is usually appropriate evidence that it has not attained the independence and control entitling it by international law to be classed as such. But when recognition *vel non* of a government is by such nations determined by inquiry, not into its *de facto* sovereignty and complete governmental control, but into its illegitimacy or irregularity of origin, their non-recognition loses something of evidential weight on the issue with which those applying the rules of international law are alone concerned. . . . Such non-recognition for any reason, however, cannot outweigh the evidence disclosed by this record before me as to the *de facto* character of Tinoco's government, according to the standard set by international law.[24]

It is clear from these cases that *de facto* control over the nation was the principal criterion in assessing the existence of a government. In addition to this, however, some cases speak of evidence that the government reflects the will of the people as being important. In the above mentioned *Cuculla* case, in particular, much stress was placed on the fact that the Zuloagan government represented 'the spasm of a dying power',[25] and that the ousted President embodied the true popular choice:

It will be seen how absurd it is to claim that on the 27th day of January 1858 'the habitual obedience' of the 'bulk' of the people of the United Mexican States had been shown to the . . . armed pretension of the Zuloaga brigade. Sufficient time had not elapsed to acertain the sentiments of the people of the numerous and widely extended Mexican states. As soon as they *could* act they came with arms in their hands to suppress the revolutionary attempt (odious to them) . . . no man can doubt that the vast majority of the Mexican people refused obedience to Zuloaga and adhered to the constitutional government making good their rights by force of arms.[26]

In the *Bolivar Railway* case of 1903, the tribunal saw changes in government as 'expressions of a change of national will'.[27]

Might one infer from such statements that a regime with *de facto* control could not be a government in international law if it did not have the approval of the majority of the people? It is submitted that such a postulate, however worthy, is untenable. These cases were decided at a time when notions of democracy were at best embryonic and certainly not widespread. It is significant that the *Cuculla* case referred to the 'sentiments of the people' being realized by force of arms. The national will would thus be more accurately expressed as the strongest group in a

[23] Moore, *International Arbitrations*, vol. 3, p. 2873 at pp. 2876–7.
[24] Ibid., vol. 1, p. 369.
[25] Loc. cit. above (n. 23), at p. 2876.
[26] Ibid., at p. 2877.
[27] Quoted in Cheng, op. cit. above, (p. 190 n. 5), at p. 190.

country. Nevertheless, it would appear from the *Jansen* case of 1868 that a regime would only be considered a valid government if it had control of the country without the aid of a foreign power, and thus truly represented the strongest and most influential body of nationals of that State. This case concerned the validity of the acts of the Emperor Maximilian, an Austrian archduke, who had been installed by the French after their invasion of Mexico in 1863. The tribunal stated that a change in government must be done either through a secure and permanent conquest, or through a revolution within the State. In the words of the decision:

> the latter . . . must be supported by the mass of the people and rest upon their consent. . . . Should foreign intervention aid this change we can never regard the fact as accomplished or as resulting upon the favour of the people unless the new government is strong enough to maintain itself after the foreign aid shall be withdrawn.[28]

The acts of Maximilian's regime were thus found not to be the acts of a government and were consequently void.

(b) *State Practice*

As there are no recent international cases dealing with the validity of governments, it is proposed to assess the law on the subject in the light of present State practice with regard to recognition and quasi-recognition of governments. Although it is appreciated that political motives rather than legal criteria influence some decisions on the recognition of any particular regime, a general State practice with regard to which group is taken to represent the State must be prima facie very strong evidence of the customary law as to the existence of a 'government'.

A review of modern practice reveals that State practice conforms to a significant degree to the criteria enunciated in the arbitrations summarized above. In particular, the existence of *de facto* control is generally the most important criterion in dealing with a regime as representing the state.[29] The recent move towards dispensing with formal recognition in favour of a policy of dealing with regimes according to whether they have control of the country further strengthens the criterion of *de facto* control. Thus in 1980 the British Foreign Secretary stated the following policy:

> We shall continue to decide the nature of our dealings with regimes which come to power unconstitutionally in the light of our assessment of whether they are able . . . to exercise effective control of the territory of the State concerned, and seem likely to continue to do so.[30]

[28] Moore, *International Arbitrations*, vol. 3, p. 2902 at p. 2927.

[29] See in particular Bundu, 'Recognition of Revolutionary Authorities: Law and Practice of States', *International and Comparative Law Quarterly*, 27 (1978), p. 18. Also, note Dr Mendelson's letter in *The Times*, 10 November 1983, in connection with the US intervention in Grenada, in which he stressed the criterion of effective control in identifying the incumbent government.

[30] Hansard, *House of Lords Debates*, vol. 408, cols. 1121–2 (28 April 1980).

This policy which originated as the so-called 'Estrada' doctrine of Mexico, has now been followed by several other States including France, Spain and the US. This pragmatic approach avoids the problems of a State officially recognizing an unpopular regime and being perceived by some as thereby denoting approval of that regime.[31]

With regard to regimes imposed by a foreign power, there is some evidence that the line taken in the *Jansen* case has been followed to some extent this century, strengthened by the Stimson doctrine of non-recognition following the illegality of the acquisition of territory by conquest. The latter was the natural consequence of the principle *ex injuria jus non oritur* following the Kellogg–Briand Pact 1928, although the legal basis of the decision taken in the *Jansen* case itself is less certain. Although the principle of non-recognition of a situation, including a government, arising out of the illegal use of force was frequently applied by States in the 1930s and 1940s,[32] the last thirty years have seen a considerable diminution of instances where governments imposed by a foreign power have been left unrecognized. Thus the governments of Eastern Europe, although at first unrecognized after the Second World War, were all eventually accorded recognition. The same is true of the government led by Mr Kadar in Hungary which was unrepresented in the UN between 1957 and 1963 but was subsequently recognized. Although there have been quite a few instances of governments installed as a result of foreign intervention,[33] the non-recognition of the Heng Samrin regime in Kampuchea,[34] and in particular the non-recognition of this regime in the UN, stands out as the sole recent example of a general policy by States of withholding recognition from a government as such. Other instances of widespread non-recognition, in particular with regard to the governments of Rhodesia after 1965, South West Africa, the Bantustans and, more recently, Northern Cyprus, have turned on the status of those territories and thus concern State recognition rather than government recognition only. The apparent trend in the last two decades towards acceptance of governments in power as the representatives of a State despite foreign control may well be further reinforced by the adoption of the Estrada doctrine and the dropping of the formal act of recognition. Time will tell whether this trend will be reversed by further instances of non-recognition of the type following Vietnam's invasion of Kampuchea.

The analysis of law undertaken thus far would support the proposition that a regime may only be legally entitled to invite outside military help if it is a 'government' within the meaning of international law, and must

[31] The US, e.g., has frequently in the past withheld recognition in order to voice disapproval of a regime.

[32] See Brownlie, *International Law and the Use of Force by States* (1963), pp. 410–18.

[33] Recent examples being the Soviet invasion of Afghanistan in 1979 and the US invasion of Grenada in 1983, both of which were condemned as illegal by the vast majority of States.

[34] Vietnamese troops invaded Kampuchea on 25 December 1978, overthrowing the government of Pol Pot and installing on 7 January 1979 the leader of the Popular Liberation Front, Heng Samrin.

therefore be in *de facto* control. If, on the other hand, it needs to request assistance to quell an insurrection, i.e. a rebellion of some magnitude, it is by definition not in *de facto* control and thus cannot speak for the State. This conclusion has been articulated by several writers. Hall stated that

> . . . the fact that it has been necessary to call in foreign help is enough to show that the issue of the conflict would without it be uncertain, and consequently that there is a doubt as to which side would ultimately establish itself as the legal representative of the state.[35]

Thomas and Thomas in their book on intervention and civil war have adopted the same view:

> A consent by a government in time of civil conflict to an intervention on the part of another state to establish and maintain that government could hardly be called the consent of the state, for the very fact of civil war would show that the identity of the legal representative of the state was in doubt.[36]

A more detailed consideration of the problem has been undertaken by Quincy Wright in his editorial comment on the US intervention in Lebanon in 1958,[37] and it is interesting to see that this argument follows exactly the type of reasoning articulated above in analysing the role and capability of a government:

> The state is an abstract entity and cannot speak except through its government. . . . It is presumed that a government in firm possession of the territory of a state, even if not generally recognized can speak for the state. . . . There is a presumption, on the other hand, that a government, even if generally recognized, cannot speak for the state if it is not in firm possession of the state's territory. In international law, the *de facto* situation is presumed to overrule the *de jure* situation . . .[38]

In support of this statement, Quincy Wright quotes several authors of the same opinion, including Hall, and concludes that this is the predominant opinion. It is doubtful, however, whether this last assertion is correct, at least as far as traditional international law writers are concerned, for, as has already been seen,[39] there is a widespread view that the traditional law favours intervention by invitation of the government but not by invitation of the rebels. The only situation where traditional texts require neutrality[40] on the part of third States is on recognition of belligerency, which can in theory be done if the civil war fulfils four conditions:

(i) Existence of civil war and general hostilities;

[35] *A Treatise on International Law* (8th edn., 1924), p. 347.

[36] *Non-Intervention: the Law and its Impact in the Americas* (1956), p. 94.

[37] 'United States Intervention in the Lebanon', *American Journal of International Law*, 53 (1959), p. 112.

[38] Ibid., p. 120.

[39] See above, p. 191 nn. 16–19.

[40] Note, however, that there is also a view that recognition of belligerency turns a civil war into a real war and thus a third State can join either side or choose to remain neutral: Oppenheim, *International Law*, vol. 2 (7th edn., 1952), para. 298.

(ii) Occupation and a measure of orderly administration of a substantial part of national territory by the insurgents;
(iii) Observance of the rules of warfare on the part of insurgent forces acting under a responsible authority;
(iv) A practical necessity for third states to define their attitude.[41]

Recognition of belligerency has not, however, been given since the American Civil War and there must thus be serious doubts whether the notion has not fallen into desuetude. Textbooks regularly repeat this doctrine as part of the law, but the real test is whether States seriously view it as a legal reality in modern times, and its total non-use, although not conclusive evidence, must nevertheless be carefully assessed. It is certainly true that a large number of civil wars will not comply with the criteria mentioned above; in particular, the third is regularly sadly neglected. The second criterion will also frequently pose problems as a large number of internal conflicts are characterized by a number of insurgent forces fighting separately against the central government and often simultaneously against each other as, for example, Lebanon since 1975, the Congo 1960–4, Afghanistan from 1978 and Chad since 1965. There have, however, been situations which have generally conformed to the four criteria, notably the Nigerian–Biafran War. It may be that given the general disapproval of secession,[42] belligerency has not been recognized in that situation and other similar ones, particularly in Africa. On the other hand, it is submitted that a more likely explanation is the replacement of the doctrine of belligerency in modern international law by the doctrine of non-intervention in the internal affairs of States, the meaning of which will be examined later.

However, whatever the status of the doctrine of belligerency, the situations to be considered will in practice be ones where belligerency is not officially recognized, and thus the question remains whether a State beset by civil war is capable of inviting outside help even though its 'government' is not in *de facto* control of the State. It is submitted that although the case law reviewed above would at first sight support Quincy Wright's assertion that 'a government, even if generally recognized, cannot speak for the state if it is not in firm possession of the state's territory', State practice does not bear this out. It is certainly the case that, generally speaking, a new regime will rarely receive recognition or be treated as a government unless it is in *de facto* control of the country. The few exceptions to this practice, such as the UN Council on Namibia or the instant recognition of the UN-inspired government of Adoula in the Congo in 1961, are based on obvious policy considerations. However, it is also the general practice that governments which were once in control of the country continue to be recognized and *do* act on behalf of the State well beyond the moment they lost control and up until the time that

[41] Ibid., para. 76. [42] Below, p. 201.

another identifiable group has gained control of the country. Thus in Lebanon, for example, UNIFIL was installed in 1978 on the basis of the consent of the government,[43] and it was also assumed that the Lebanese Government could validly request the assistance of the Multinational Forces in 1982.[44] During this period, however, the Lebanese Army only had precarious control of a part of the capital city and some other small pieces of territory in conjunction with the Phalange militia. Furthermore, to speak in terms of a beleaguered government fighting rebel forces would be a fiction in the case of Lebanon as the warring militias were in the main the private armies of the old families whose members make up successive Lebanese cabinets. Similarly in the Congo, ONUC was dispatched to that country in 1960 on the basis of the invitation of the Congolese leaders Kasavubu and Lumumba, who were unable to keep the army or country under control. Not only were there several changes of government during ONUC's operation, but also the identity of the government was frequently difficult to ascertain, and even in the relatively quiet periods large areas of the country were not under the government's control. Unless the Security Council prescribes enforcement measures under Chapter VII, the practice has been that the dispatching of UN peace-keeping forces requires the consent of the State, and for this purpose the ineffective regimes in the Congo and Lebanon in 1960 and 1978 were considered to have validly given that consent. Further, the Multinational Forces were installed in Beirut in accordance with bilateral agreements between the Government of Lebanon and each of the four States. If one wishes to argue that peace-keeping forces are different from a force invited by a government to quell an insurrection because they are not supporting one side or another, then one is invoking a different rule of law, i.e. the principle of non-interference, not the non-existence of government because of lack of *de facto* control.

There are other examples of regimes accepted as the government of the country although they have little control over the country. In Afghanistan, the People's Democratic Party of Afghanistan which took over government by a *coup d'état* in April 1978, led by Mr Taraki and his successor Mr Amin, was accepted by other States as Afghanistan's government. Yet according to a survey made by *Le Monde* in August 1978, the internal conflict had made about 80 per cent of the territory insecure and the government at that time controlled only about half of

[43] UNIFIL was installed following Israel's invasion of southern Lebanon on 15 March and its withdrawal after Security Council Resolution 425.

[44] The Multinational Forces consisting of French, US and Italian troops were first deployed in Beirut in August 1982 in order to supervise the evacuation of PLO and Syrian troops from Beirut, following the bombardment of Beirut by Israeli forces after the latter's invasion into Lebanon on 6 June 1982. After the evacuation, the Multinational Forces withdrew, but were recalled in September 1982 at the request of the Lebanese Cabinet after the massacre in the Palestinian refugee camps of Sabra and Chatila. In February 1983 British troops joined the Multinational Forces, which remained in Lebanon until March 1984.

the country's people concentrated in populated areas.[45] In the Security Council debates following the Soviet invasion in December 1979, most delegates discounted the explanation of President Amin's invitation as untenable as he was subsequently assassinated, but it was assumed that he could have spoken for the State as the leader of the government. Similarly in other States involved in civil war where rebels hold large areas, such as Chad, Angola, El Salvador and Ethiopia, the government is accepted as representing the State in all the usual ways.

It would appear, therefore, that recognition is in practice extremely important. A crucial difference between modern times and the period when the arbitrations earlier referred to were decided is that with the present, near universal, membership of the UN, the representation of a regime on behalf of a State in that body gives a legitimacy to that regime which mere individual State recognition would not. Practice shows that although *de facto* control is generally required of a new regime, recognition will rarely be withdrawn from an established regime, even once it has lost control, if there is no new single regime in control to take its place.[46] Indeed, it has been stated by Oppenheim[47] that premature recognition of a new government is an international wrong against the old government, and this opinion is shared by other jurists.[48] On the other hand, mere withdrawal of recognition without recognition of a new regime would leave a country without representation, and although the United Kingdom decided to recognize no government in Kampuchea after the invasion of the Vietnamese, the general practice, as indicated above, is to continue to treat the beleaguered regime as the valid representative. This approach also has the advantage of practicality in a situation where most of the country is controlled by many separate rebel groups, often hostile to each other. Thus, for example, at least eight separate groups were fighting against the Taraki regime in Afghanistan in 1978–9, no less than eleven rival groups were fighting President Malloum in Chad in 1979 and a similar number of different factions were involved in the Lebanese civil wars. There is, however, one exception in recent times, where no regime was recognized as the government during a civil war, and that was the particularly unusual circumstance which prevailed in the Dominican Republic in 1965. A three-man civilian junta, which had overthrown the democratically elected President Juan Bosch, had ruled the Dominican Republic since 1963. On 25 to 26 April 1965 the junta was overthrown by a military revolt headed by supporters of Señor Bosch, but then almost immediately civil war broke out between

[45] *Keesing's*, p. 29878.

[46] An exception was Hungary between 1956 and 1963, but the new regime was unrecognized for a time as it was installed by a foreign power.

[47] *International Law*, vol. 1 (8th edn., 1955), para. 74.

[48] e.g. Warbrick, 'The New British Policy on Recognition of Governments', *International and Comparative Law Quarterly*, 30 (1981), p. 568 at p. 569, and in same volume Nedjati, 'Acts of Unrecognised Governments', p. 388 at p. 389.

supporters of Bosch on the one hand and supporters of the civilian junta on the other.[49] The OAS, which subsequently sent a peacekeeping force, mediated between the two factions treating neither as a government,[50] and in the Security Council debates, which were called following the US intervention in the country, neither faction was entitled to speak as the representative of that country as such, but they were at one point permitted to put forward their views *qua* factions.[51] This situation was unusual because civil war broke out shortly after the *coup d'état*, before the new government was able firmly to establish itself but at the same time after the old government had been ousted. However, as the normal practice is to continue the recognition of an old regime until a new recognizable regime is *de facto* in control of the country, it is submitted that one cannot argue a duty of non-intervention on the basis of non-existence of government alone. If one argues that a government which is losing control cannot ask for help, the ground for prohibiting such help must be found in another norm.

III. Self-Determination

Self-determination may be defined as the right of a people to choose its own economic, social and political system. A number of eminent authorities have based their theory of the inability of a third State to aid the existing government in a civil war on this principle: Professors Brownlie[52] and Bowett[53] have both stated that apart from policy considerations making such intervention undesirable, it would conflict with the principle of self-determination. Friedmann has stated that such an intervention 'becomes an instrument to prevent social change which is a vital aspect of national self-determination'.[54] Quincy Wright has based his theory on the invalidity of such intervention not only on the basis of the non-existence of government, but also on the basis of self-determination:

> Armed intervention . . . is not permissible by invitation of either the recognized or the rebelling faction in the case of civil strife. If it were, the 'right of revolution' implicit in the concepts of state sovereignty and self-determination would be denied. In a situation of civil strife, the *state* is temporarily inhibited from acting. A government beset by civil strife is not in a position to invite assistance in the name of the state.[55]

It is not intended, in this paper, to review the evidence relating to the existence of the norm of self-determination. As Professor Higgins wrote

[49] *Keesing's*, p. 20813.

[50] *Keesing's*, p. 20813–17.

[51] *Security Council Official Records*, 20th Year, 1212th meeting (19 May 1965).

[52] Op. cit. above (p. 195 n. 32), at p. 327. Brownlie also based his argument on the principle of non-intervention in internal affairs: see below, p. 208 n. 90.

[53] 'The Interrelation of Theories of Intervention and Self-Defence' in Moore (ed.), *Law and Civil War in the Modern World* (1974), chapter 2.

[54] 'United States Policy and the Crisis of International Law', *American Journal of International Law*, 59 (1965), p. 857 at p. 866.

[55] *The Role of International Law in the Elimination of War* (1961), p. 61.

in 1972, 'Self-determination . . . [is] by now established as a legal right. What is far from clear is the "self" to whom this applies.'[56] Although it might be argued that such uncertainty as to the recipient of a right may well cast doubt as to its existence, the overwhelming authority[57] affirming the norm of self-determination does not allow for such doubt. One must instead concentrate on attempting to identify the groups to which the norm applies and to define the content of the rule in practice.

It can be stated with some certainty that the right of self-determination applies to existing states and to non-self-governing territories of the type perceived as colonial. With regard to other groups it is submitted that the principle of self-determination is not at present interpreted so as to include them, with the probable exceptions of the Palestinians and the majority in South Africa. Particular support for these last-mentioned groups is in effect responsible for what would at first appear to be a wide definition of groups entitled to self-determination. Thus, for example, in Geneva Protocol I 1977[57] international conflicts for the purpose of the Protocol are stated to include:

> Armed conflicts in which peoples are fighting against colonial domination and alien occupation and racist regimes in the exercise of their right of self-determination . . .

Although the principle is widely defined, treaty provisions are to be interpreted in their context, in accordance with the object and purpose of the treaty, and in the light of subsequent practice indicating the meaning of a provision.[58] It is submitted that an accurate interpretation of UN resolutions may be achieved using the same method by analogy. It is significant that paragraph 6 of the General Assembly's landmark Resolution 1514 (xv) of 1960 stressed the undesirability of splitting a territorial unit:

> Any attempt at the partial or total disruption of the national unity and the territorial integrity of a country is incompatible with the purposes and principles of the Charter of the United Nations.

Further, despite the fact that the false units created by the colonial powers, especially in Africa and Lebanon, are particularly susceptible to unrest, the Organization of African Unity has decided as a matter of policy not to permit alteration of the colonial boundaries,[59] and the general policy of the UN is to maintain present territorial groupings.[60] This

[56] 'International Law and Civil Conflict', in Luard (ed.), *The International Regulation of Civil Wars* (1972), p. 186.

[57] In particular, Article I of both UN Human Rights Covenants 1966; Article 1 (4) of Geneva Protocol I 1977 Additional to the Geneva Conventions of 1949; ICJ advisory opinion on the *Western Sahara, ICJ Reports*, 1975, p. 12 at pp. 31–3.

[58] Vienna Convention on the Law of Treaties 1969, Article 31.

[59] OAU Resolution on Border Disputes 1964: text in Brownlie, *African Boundaries* (1979), p. 10.

[60] 'Secessionist groups have in the main received little or no support, for example, Biafra was only recognized by five States, and no international recognition is or was given to such groups as the

author would agree with Pomerance's assessment of self-determination as defined by UN policy:

> Today potential claimants (Biafrans, Katangans . . . and a host of other secessionists) are told . . . 'You are not really under "colonial" or "alien" rule at all; you are part of a non-colonial "self" entitled to its territorial integrity'.[61]

The UN operation in the Congo particularly illustrates the wish to prevent secession. Although the original mandates of ONUC stressed that internal affairs should not be interfered with, a later resolution of the Security Council called for 'All appropriate measures to prevent the occurrence of civil war in the Congo including . . . the use of force, if necessary, in the last resort'.[62] The Secretary-General's report of 29 June 1964 with regard to the withdrawal of ONUC stated that the difficulties in the Congo were of an unusual nature, the main origins being found in the absence of a genuine and sufficiently widespread sense of national identity. The report went on as follows:

> The United Nations cannot permanently protect the Congo or any other country from internal tensions and disturbances created by its own organic growth towards unity and nationhood.[63]

The stress is thus on the unity and independence of the State, rather than on the free aspirations of the people.[64] It would logically follow that if a government were to ask for external aid to suppress a secessionist movement, such aid would not necessarily offend against the principle of self-determination, unless that particular unit has been recognized by the international community as entitled to self-determination. The fact that the Palestinians in particular have been named by the UN as a group entitled to self-determination indicates that the principle of self-determination could theoretically apply to other groups, although there is little evidence to that effect at present.[65] It is, however, not inconceiv-

Kurds, Armenians, Eritreans, the people of the Ogaden, Southern Sudanese, Nagas, Tamils, East Timorese, etc.

[61] Pomerance, *Self-Determination in Law and Practice* (1982), p. 15.

[62] Security Council Resolution 161 of 21 February 1961: UN Doc. S/4741.

[63] Report of the Secretary-General on the withdrawal of the UN Force in the Congo and on other aspects of the UN operation, UN Doc. S/5784 (29 June 1964): *Security Council Official Records*, 19th Year, Supplement for Jan.–June 1964, p. 259 at p. 293, para. 145 of the report. See also a statement by U Thant in the context of the Biafran secession: 'The United Nations has never accepted and I do not believe it will ever accept the principle of secession of a part of its Member State': *UN Monthly Chronicle*, February 1970, p. 36.

[64] Although the principle of self-determination might sound dynamic and conducive to change in accordance with the wishes of peoples, it is in fact presently interpreted to be of such limited application, i.e. limited almost exclusively to decolonization, that the picture envisaged by present international law is one of great rigidity; once decolonization is complete, the rule against secession, coupled with the rule against the acquisition of territory by conquest, would in effect freeze the political map in perpetuity! In practice, of course, changes occur, generally through the legally dubious use of force which is subsequently recognized as, for example, in the case of Bangladesh in 1971.

[65] Apart from the majority in South Africa, instances of other groups being singled out by the UN as entitled to self-determination outside the colonial context are rare. The election held in West

able for perceptions to change with regard to which groups are entitled to self-determination, and other non-colonial entities might at some future time be recognized.[66]

The right of a people to self-determination is, generally speaking, becoming increasingly the right belonging to people within a unitary State, and therefore the content of the norm for people of independent States must now be considered. Article 1 (1) of both UN Human Rights Covenants describes self-determination as follows:

> All peoples have the right of self-determination. By virtue of that right they freely determine their political status and freely pursue their economic, social and cultural development.

This norm would appear to have been interpreted as the right of a State's people to choose its own form of government without outside interference. It is submitted, however, that given the reality of modern State representation and the attitude of the majority of State representatives, this does not necessarily mean a government chosen by free regular multi-party elections. Although it is true that the UN has on a number of occasions recommended such elections for certain territories,[67] and has organized plebiscites for territories gaining independence,[68] the people of a State is not generally considered to be deprived of its right to self-determination by virtue of a government imposed by a *coup d'état* or single-party rule, provided that the government consists of persons belonging to the people perceived as being entitled to self-determination. Particularly illustrative in this respect are the Security Council debates following the US invasion of Grenada and the Soviet Union's invasion of Afghanistan,[69] because although the discussion was obviously highly coloured by the overriding question of the use of force, the statements made by the delegates nevertheless highlight the different attitudes towards the meaning of self-determination. The US delegate in her

Irian in 1969 which was supervised to some extent by the UN might be cited as one such example, but it has been stated by some commentators that it was a spurious exercise and in effect legitimized the Indonesian annexation: Pomerance, op. cit. above (p. 202 n. 61), pp. 32–3. For examples of UN inactivity in the face of annexation of the territories of certain groups by contiguous countries after decolonization, see Pomerance, ibid., p. 20.

[66] See in particular Professor Nanda's view that culturally different groups which are suffering grave human rights abuses should be entitled to self-determination: Nanda, 'Self-Determination in International Law', *American Journal of International Law*, 66 (1972), p. 321, and 'Self-Determination under International Law—Validity of Claims to Secede', *Case Western Reserve Journal of International Law*, 13 (1981), p. 257 at pp. 275–80.

[67] Note, for example, the recent General Assembly resolution calling for UN supervised elections in Kampuchea (GA Res. 35/6 of 1980), following GA Res. 34/22 (1979) which in para. 10 'Resolves that the people of Kampuchea should be enabled to choose democratically their own government . . .'.

[68] Togoland 1957; Western Samoa 1961; Cameroons 1961. These plebiscites determined whether the population favoured independence or integration with another State and thus related to the status of the territory rather than the type of government as such.

[69] 25 October 1983 and 25 to 26 December 1979 respectively.

address on 27 October 1983[70] asserted that the US intervened to restore self-determination to the people of Grenada and that proof of that would be a free press, free trade unions and free elections. It will be remembered that the regime which was ousted by the US intervention appeared to be a repressive and arbitrary one which was alleged to be responsible for the murder of the former prime minister, Mr Bishop, various ex-cabinet ministers and members of the population during a demonstration. However, only four[71] States which spoke in the Security Council debates equated the right to self-determination with voting for a free democratic government. The delegates of those States which participated in the intervention[72] spoke of the restoration of democracy in Grenada and might possibly be considered by implication to be referring to self-determination. The majority of delegates, on the other hand, when referring to self-determination assumed that the Grenadian people were exercising their right of self-determination before the intervention. It is, in this author's view, most significant that States represented by dictatorships, in particular, spoke most enthusiastically about the right of the people of a country to choose their own form of government. This view was most clearly expressed by the delegate of the Lao People's Democratic Republic:

> if the American people prefer its form of democracy, that is its business . . . if the Grenadian people has decided to choose a social system that seems appropriate to it, that is its business . . . This emanates from the right of people to self-determination.[73]

Other States[74] which criticized the intervention on the grounds of self-determination stressed outside interference as being the factor which led to a denial of self-determination. The following statements serve as an illustration of this approach:

Mexico

> It is a manifest denial of the right of peoples to self-determination . . . The people of Grenada alone is allowed freely to decide its own government, without foreign interference.[75]

Zimbabwe

> The choosing of a government and of leadership is the sovereign prerogative of the people of each country and must be exercised without external interference and influence.[76]

[70] UN Doc. S/PV.2451.

[71] The UK, Ecuador, Guatemala, and also Venezuela by implication.

[72] The decision to invade was taken by the States members of the Organization of East Caribbean States, i.e. Antigua and Barbuda, Dominica, St Kitts, Nevis, St Lucia, St Vincent and the Grenadines and Monserrat; and participation was invited and accepted by the US, Barbados and Jamaica.

[73] Security Council debate, 26 October 1983: UN Doc. S/PV.2489.

[74] See also speeches by the delegations of Poland, Bolivia, Algeria, Cuba, Benin, Egypt, Peru, Yugoslavia, Colombia, Mozambique, Dominican Republic.

[75] Security Council debate, 25 October 1983: UN Doc. S/PV.2487.

[76] Security Council debate, 27 October 1983: UN Doc. S/PV.2491.

India

[The movement of the non-aligned countries] has always re-affirmed the right of all countries to preserve their independence . . . and the right of their peoples to choose their own political, economic and social systems and to pursue their own development free from any external interference or pressures.[76]

The Netherlands, after stating its concern that the US action was incompatible with the principles of the Charter, then stated

The people of Grenada must be able to exercise their fundamental right to self-determination, free from outside interference.[76]

France deplored the intervention, stressed the right of the self-determination of peoples and then stated that

Everything must be done to allow [the people of Grenada] . . . to regain the right to decide their fate independently and in full sovereignty.[77]

A particularly scathing attack was delivered by Syria which stated that the US action was 'a flagrant violation of the inalienable right of the people of Grenada to self-determination and the structuring of its society free from any outside intervention', and then went on as follows

. . . the major problem facing the world today is that the United States is trying to impose its values on the whole world. It is therefore depriving the peoples of that world of the right to rebuild their countries in accordance with their local circumstances based on their cultural values and national priorities.[77]

During the General Assembly Debate, Syria openly opposed a Belgian draft amendment calling for free elections in Grenada[78] to be added to the resolution condemning the intervention,[79] on the grounds that it would interfere with Grenada's internal affairs. The draft amendment was in fact adopted by a narrow majority.[80]

Basically similar attitudes were expressed in the debate following the Soviet Union's invasion of Afghanistan although, as expected, Eastern bloc States and their allies supported the Soviet Union's version of events. As with the Grenada debate, the main criticism of the invasion was centred around its being a violation of the principle of non-intervention in internal affairs. However, those States which additionally referred to the principle of self-determination again stressed the non-intervention aspect as paramount, the UK being the sole State which referred to the right of the Afghan people *democratically* to determine their own future.[81] Afghanistan had been governed by single party rule since the overthrow of the monarchy in 1973, first under President Daud, who founded the sole 'National Revolutionary Party', and subsequently by Presidents Taraki and Amin in 1978 and 1979 respectively, who led the 'People's

[77] Loc. cit. above, p. 204 n. 73.

[78] General Assembly, 38th Session, agenda item 145: A/38/L.9 (2 November 1983).

[79] GA Res. 38/7.

[80] 71–23–41.

[81] Security Council debate, 5 January 1980: UN Doc. S/PV.2186.

Democratic Party'. Not only was the government in power at the time of the invasion a dictatorship, but there is also no indication whatever that the various groups fighting against the government had any democratic leanings. In this context it is noteworthy that the policies of the Taraki regime which provoked the greatest resistance were the land distribution programme, opposed by large landowners, and measures to improve the condition of women, in particular the literacy campaign and the abolition of bride price.[82] According to a recent report, there are at least thirty-seven active rebel groups in Afghanistan, ranging from royalists to Maoists and all types of Muslim sects.[83]

This total lack of democratic institutions did not deter delegates from characterizing the invasion as the event which denied the people of Afghanistan their right to self-determination. Thus, in contrast to later statements by the US in the Grenada debate, the US delegate to the Security Council debate on Afghanistan spoke as follows:

> A member State of this world organization had been invaded by massive contingents of troops from another state. Its government has been overthrown. Its leaders have been killed, its people have been silenced. . . .

The delegate then urged the Soviet Union to withdraw 'and to allow the people of Afghanistan to conduct their own affairs, to choose their own leaders without outside pressure and interference'.[84]

Many other delegates spoke in a similar vein:

Liberia

> Foreign armed intervention cannot be justified when used to crush the free political expression of the people.[84]

Venezuela

> General information shows that a struggle began between various institutions and political and social currents, which is obviously part of an internal process to determine the political, economic and social future of the country in response to the aspirations of Afghan society.[85]

Australia

> The people of Afghanistan are entitled to work out their future for themselves without fear of interference from outside.[86]

Nigeria

> The people of Afghanistan . . . must contrive to exercise the right to choose their own form of government, as in the past, and not by coercion through the presence of foreign troops.[87]

[82] *Keesing's*, p. 29878.
[83] *International Herald Tribune*, 28 May 1985, p. 5.
[84] Security Council debate, 6 January 1980: UN Doc. S/PV.2187.
[85] Security Council debate, 6 January 1980: UN Doc. S/PV.2188.
[86] Loc. cit. above, n. 84.
[87] General Assembly 6th Emergency Special Session, 10 to 14 January 1980.

Egypt

[The intervention in Afghanistan] constitutes disregard of the right of each people to choose its political, economic and social regime freely and without any external interference.[88]

It is clear from the speeches[89] that the content of the right to self-determination, that is the right of a people to choose its own government, means in effect the absence of outside interference. It does not appear to mean, in the minds of the majority of States, the right to democratic representation or even that the government should reflect the will of the majority of the people. Rather it requires that the government be drawn from a group of people perceived as entitled to self-determination, even if that government actually represents a minority interest within that group and rules by force. Thus the community of States identifies those entities entitled to independence, which at present are, in practice, existing States, previously colonized territories within colonial boundaries, people subjected to racist regimes, i.e. the majority in South Africa, and the Palestinian people. The substance of the right for these entities is that the individuals comprising the government should be a group of their number, which in practice frequently takes power by strength rather than ballot.

The right to self-determination of peoples, so interpreted, does not therefore create a norm in any way different from that stated already in the *Jansen* case, for the stress is on the absence of outside interference rather than the quality of internal government. To speak of the rule of non-intervention as being based on the right of self-determination might give the impression that the individuals within a State have a genuine right to choose their government, which unfortunately they do not have in customary international law. Although the norms of non-intervention in internal affairs and self-determination are closely interlinked, the former being to a large degree based on the latter, it is submitted that a rule of non-intervention is more realistically based on a norm of non-interference in the affairs of another *state* rather than on the largely illusory notion of self-determination of *peoples*. In the UN debates following the invasions of Afghanistan and Grenada, all the delegates referred to the norm of non-interference in the internal affairs of States, whereas only some of them expressly spoke of self-determination.

IV. The Inadmissibility of Interference in the Internal Affairs of States

An immediate logical problem arises when considering the principle of non-interference in the internal affairs of States. There is certainly

[88] Security Council debate, 5 January 1980: UN Doc. S/PV.2185.

[89] Similar statements were made in the Security Council debate by the representatives of Pakistan, Japan, Spain, Somalia, Italy, West Germany, France, Saudi Arabia, New Zealand and Norway. See further in the General Assembly debate statements by the representatives of Bangladesh, Austria, Ivory Coast, Bahrain, Oman and Morocco.

sufficient evidence that such a principle exists as a rule of international customary law,[90] but if the State is said to be exclusively represented by the government, then an invitation by the government to quell an insurrection would not interfere with the affairs of that State. It is submitted that the principle of self-determination does not really vest the legal right of the representation of a State in the people as that principle protects the State from external interference rather than vesting any right in the people as such. It is proposed therefore to study the factual content of the principle of non-intervention in the internal affairs of a State by analysing State practice and then extracting from that material a theoretical conclusion.

Certain General Assembly resolutions deal directly with the principle of non-intervention, the most relevant of which is the Declaration on the Inadmissibility of Intervention in the Domestic Affairs of States and the Protection of their Independence and Sovereignty of 1965.[91] The pertinent part of this Declaration reads as follows:

> No State has the right to intervene, directly or indirectly, for any reason whatever, in the internal and external affairs of any State. Consequently, armed intervention and all other forms of interference or attempted threats against the personality of the State or against its political, economic and cultural elements, are condemned.
>
> . . . no State shall organize, assist, foment, finance, incite or tolerate subversive, terrorist or armed activities directed towards the violent overthrow of the regime of another State, or interfere in civil strife in another State.

This prescription was repeated in the General Assembly Declaration on Principles of International Law concerning Friendly Relations and Co-operation among States of 1970:[92]

> Every State has the duty to refrain from organizing, instigating, assisting or participating in acts of civil strife or terrorist acts in another State or acquiescing in organized activities within its territory directed towards the commission of such acts, when the acts referred to in the present paragraph involve a threat or use of force.

The phrases 'interfere in civil strife in another State' and 'assisting or participating in acts of civil strife' would appear to be general and wide enough to cover a prohibition on the furnishing of assistance to a government to suppress an internal rebellion. The *travaux préparatoires*[93] to Resolution 2131 of 1965 are unfortunately not conclusive in that

[90] Evidence is almost exclusively to be found in State practice rather than in writings. However, Brownlie wrote in 1963 that there are objections to aid being given to a government, *inter alia* because it conflicts with the principle of non-interference in internal affairs: op. cit. above (p. 195 n. 32), at p. 327.

[91] GA Res. 2131 (xx), adopted on 21 December 1965 by 109–0–1 (UK abstaining).

[92] GA Res. 2625 (xxv), adopted on 24 October 1970 without a vote.

[93] General Assembly, 20th Session, General Committee meetings 160, 161; First Committee meetings 1395–1406, 1420, 1422, 1423; Plenary meetings 1340, 1408; Report of the First Committee: UN Doc.A/6220.

the issue was not directly debated. The original draft resolution was introduced by the Soviet Union, whose delegate in the First Committee attacked the US policies in Vietnam, the Dominican Republic and the Congo. The whole debate took place at a time of general decolonization when the sympathy of the Third World was with colonized peoples trying to achieve independence and to maintain it without interference whilst these newly-established States were still weak and finding their feet. There was much discussion, therefore, about forms of subversion other than direct military force, and this is reflected in the final text. Several of the speeches during the debates of the First Committee could be read as a prohibition against supporting an incumbent regime, although whether the speakers would then accept such a prohibition as applying to their own regime, when its time came, is debatable. Thus, when Cuba criticized US policy, its delegate spoke as follows:

> . . . the real reason for the presence of the US troops in the Dominican Republic was to prevent certain institutional and social changes which the US opposed—though there was no principle or rule of international law which entitled any State to pass judgment on political or social developments in another State.
>
> . . . Cuba, like many other Latin American countries, had in the past been governed by dictators who had ruthlessly oppressed the Cuban people. All those dictatorial regimes had been supported by the US government, they had been maintained in power by US military and economic assistance. . . . The present Cuban government, however, had the full support of the Cuban people . . .[94]

The only two delegates who appeared to speak directly on the problem were those of Argentina and Italy. Argentina, in considering the right to call for outside help, stated as follows:

> While it was strongly opposed to any form of interference, Argentina did not go so far as to deny the right of weak countries to conclude agreements to ensure their security and defence, and in exceptional cases to call on foreign military assistance. Such agreements, however, should only be concluded when the government concerned was in full possession of its governmental prerogatives and was supported by the people and its representatives. On the other hand, their value would be extremely debatable if they were concluded in a highly revolutionary situation on the basis of a personal decision taken in desperation.[95]

The delegate did not appear to distinguish between those agreements concluded at a time of government stability but invoked during a revolutionary crisis, and those actually concluded in the latter situation. The Italian delegate, after supporting efforts to abolish colonization and racial segregation, then stated:

> . . . no war was lawful and no one had the right to intervene in any way, either for or against movements or governments, according to how he judged them; such was the essence of non-intervention and of the protection that ought to be granted to the independence and freedom of States. Italy would, therefore, have

[94] Ibid., First Committee meeting no. 1396.

[95] Ibid., First Committee meeting no. 1398.

preferred to consider how best to make possible and even encourage peaceful changes for enlisting the progress of mankind in any sphere. . . .[96]

Other statements by delegates during the First Committee meetings stressed the need for decolonization and the need to prevent neo-colonial domination in newly-independent States.

Several speeches by East European delegates criticized the US for using force which prevented certain revolutions, particularly in Vietnam. Thus:

Yugoslavia

There were some [Powers] who were arrogating to themselves the right forcibly to prevent other peoples from choosing their own social and political systems and to obstruct their struggle for liberation.[97]

Bulgaria

The chief cause of tension in the modern world was the brutal use of force by the Imperialist Powers to hold up economic, social and political change and to preserve their own domination over entire countries and peoples . . .

. . . the uprising of the South Vietnamese was their own internal affair which would be settled equitably without loss of life. Like every other people, the South Vietnamese had the right to decide their own destiny and institutions. Their true representatives were the National Liberation Front, which enjoyed the support of the overwhelming majority of the population and of world opinion.[98]

One can certainly extract from the overall tenor of the speeches the idea that the principle of non-intervention was aimed at allowing certain changes of government and would thus entail the illegality of aiding either side in a revolution. However, a proviso to such a statement is the fact that several speeches expressly endorsed help given to groups fighting against colonial rule,[99] and aid given to a government at its request for its self-defence against outside intervention.[100]

As already indicated, the whole debate was largely motivated by the desire to eliminate colonial power and by East–West rivalry. Such political considerations would not matter if the rule of customary law emerged

[96] General Assembly, 20th Session, First Committee meeting no. 1402.

[97] Ibid., First Committee meeting no. 1401.

[98] Ibid., First Committee meeting no. 1405.

[99] e.g. speeches by the delegates of Kenya and Tunisia at the 1402nd meeting and the United Arab Republic at the 1403rd meeting.

[100] e.g. speeches by the delegate of the US at the 1423rd meeting. Also note the Report of the Special Committee on Principles of International Law concerning Friendly Relations and Co-operation among States 1965: General Assembly 20th Session, Annex 3, agenda items 90–4 at p. 116. The proposal by the UK on the meaning of non-intervention included the following statement in the commentary: '(5) In the event that a State becomes a victim of unlawful intervention practised or supported by the Government of another State, it has the right to request aid and assistance from third States, which are correspondingly entitled to grant the aid and assistance required. Such aid and assistance may, if the unlawful intervention has taken the form of subversive activities leading to civil strife in which the dissident elements are receiving external support and encouragement, include armed assistance for the purpose of restoring normal conditions.'

as a stable norm to be applied in any situation. However, it is not clear merely from studying the *travaux* that such a stable norm was intended to continue to apply with regard to all States once decolonization was complete and indigenous governments were entrenched in the new States. The speech by the delegate of Kenya, for example, might be seen in this respect with some apprehension, for although the majority of the speech would endorse a general norm of non-intervention, the permanent validity of the present government was also implied, which does not bode well for a positive approach towards any future revolution:

> In certain circumstances it might be justifiable for a people of a given country to seek a change in government. But when a liberation movement had as its objective the overthrow of a popularly elected government, it became a threat to the life of a nation and its citizens. It was that kind of revolution that must be condemned because it was merely a movement of terror and subversion inspired or engineered from outside to serve the interests of a foreign power or foreign powers.
>
> The people of Kenya had carried out their own revolution in the years 1952–1956 in the face of overwhelming British military opposition, and there was no room for another.[101]

A pessimistic impression of the longevity of a general norm of non-intervention applying to aid to either side might well be received if one studies the recent Declaration on the Inadmissibility of Intervention and Interference in the Internal Affairs of States of 1981.[102] This does not refer specifically to a prohibition on interference in civil strife, but instead stresses the prohibition of encouraging or tolerating activities aimed at the overthrow of another government. The operative provisions of this resolution are to be found in the Annex, which

> Solemnly declares that:
>
> 1. No State or group of States has the right to intervene or interfere in any form or for any reason whatsoever in the internal and external affairs of other States.
>
> 2. The principle of non-intervention and non-interference in the internal and external affairs of States comprehends the following rights and duties:
>
> . . .
>
> II (a) The duty of States to refrain in their international relations from the threat or use of force in any form . . . to disrupt the political, social or economic order of other States, to overthrow or change the political system of another State or its Government . . .
>
> . . .
>
> (f) The duty of a state to refrain from the promotion, encouragment or support, direct or indirect, of rebellious or secessionist activities within other States, under any pretext whatsoever, or any action which seems to disrupt the unity or to undermine or subvert the political order of other States.
>
> . . .

[101] Loc. cit. above, p. 210 n. 96.

[102] GA Res. 36/103, adopted on 9 December 1981 by 120–22–6.

(n) The duty of a State to refrain from organizing, training, financing and arming political and ethnic groups on their territories or the territories of other States for the purpose of creating subversion, disorder or unrest in other countries.

(o) The duty of a State to refrain from any economic, political or military activity in the territory of another State without its consent.

These provisions are not helpful in assessing whether a government may be supported in an internal conflict, as the stress is on the duty not to support the rebels and paragraph (o) begs the very question. One of the preambular paragraphs could be interpreted more generally, viz:

Conscious also of the imperative need to put a complete end to any threat of aggression, any recruitment, any use of armed bands, in particular mercenaries, against Sovereign States, so as to enable the peoples of all States to determine their own political, economic and social systems without external interference or control.

However, this paragraph is situated after two previous preambular paragraphs, the first of which expresses concern at the 'frequent recourse to the threat or use of force . . . and all other forms of intervention or interference' against States 'with the aim of overthrowing their Governments'. The second refers to the need to withdraw all foreign forces engaged in military occupation,

so that peoples under colonial domination, foreign occupation or racist regimes may freely and fully exercise their right to self-determination, in order to enable peoples of all States to administer their own affairs, and determine their own political, economic and social systems without external interference and control.

Could this Declaration be interpretated as narrowing the scope of the duty of non-interference so that it only encompasses the traditional rule not to aid rebels against the government? The Declaration was unfortunately not discussed either in committee or in the plenary meeting of the General Assembly, and was adopted with twenty-two developed nations voting against it. Its normative value as a resolution is therefore minimal, but there is no indication that the nations which voted negatively either agreed or disagreed with the above-quoted paragraphs or with their one-sided treatment of non-intervention. These countries' objection almost certainly related to those paragraphs in the Annex which dealt with developed States' economic and military defence activities.

It is submitted that a review of the General Assembly resolutions and their *travaux préparatoires* does not lead to a conclusive result, and although the earlier resolutions would allow one to postulate a principle of absolute non-intervention in internal strife, actual State practice must now be studied to see how the norm has been interpreted.

(a) *Cases of Intervention since 1956*

If State practice were to be assessed on the basis of what States have actually done, one would find a good number of interventions undertaken either to prop up existing regimes or to reinstate those just fallen on the basis of either real or alleged invitations from those governments. Examples of interventions where the existence of an invitation was undisputed are those in Lebanon and Jordan in 1958, Stanleyville in 1964 and Chad since 1968. In June 1985 the Governments of Zimbabwe, Tanzania and Mozambique met in Harare to consider military intervention to help Mozambique end an armed rebellion.[103] However, the US involvement in Vietnam cannot be seen as a case of an undisputed invitation, as there was disagreement as to the right of the South Vietnamese Government to speak for an independent State and the majority of the General Assembly perceived Vietnam as one country.[104] Another special case is that of the Lebanon from 1982 to 1984 when the Multinational Forces were sent, *inter alia*, to help the Lebanese Army regain authority in Beirut. The actions of the US contingent effectively supported the Christian Phalange faction as the Lebanese Army at the time fought together with the Phalange against the Syrian-based Druse and Shi'ite Muslim militias.[105] Instances of intervention where there is serious doubt as to both the existence of an invitation and the legal capacity of the allegedly inviting regime to request military aid are those in Hungary 1956, the Dominican Republic 1965, Afghanistan 1979 and Grenada 1983.

However, if one uses Government statements as the yardstick for the assessment of State practice indicating international customary law, a surprisingly consistent practice has emerged since 1956. The justifications given by the intervening or supported governments as well as State reaction to such interventions tend consistently to indicate the need to show significant outside support for the rebels so that the intervention is characterized as a collective defence action rather than an involvement in internal strife. Debate in the UN is of course characterized by a great deal of bias as States frequently speak and vote for those States with which they have political ties. However, although facts are often twisted, exaggerated or simply altered, statements as to the law are fairly consistent even if not expressed as carefully or unequivocally as one would like. It is significant that in those situations where there was no doubt as to the existence of an invitation from the recognized government, the intervention was nevertheless justified as undertaken because of outside help to the rebels.

103 *International Herald Tribune*, 14 June 1985, p. 2.

104 This is evidenced by GA Res. 32/3, adopted on 14 October 1977, requesting economic aid to the newly admitted Socialist Republic of Vietnam which contained the following statement: 'Expressing profound admiration to the courageous Vietnamese people in their struggle for independence and national reunification and their constant efforts devoted to national reconstruction . . .'.

105 See *Keesing's*, pp. 32533–4 and 32890–1; *The Times*, 8, 9, 14, 19 and 22 September 1983.

1. *Intervention based on an undisputed invitation*

(i) *Jordan 1958*. On 14 February 1958 the merger of the Kingdoms of Jordan and Iraq (the 'Arab Federation') was proclaimed. King Faisal of Iraq was appointed Head of State and King Hussein of Jordan Deputy Head of State, with each retaining constitutional authority in his own kingdom. In the week of 14 July King Faisal and other leading figures were assassinated in a *coup d'état* and the new regime, which achieved success in a few hours and met no opposition, declared an Iraqi Republic. On 17 July an Iraqi radio station directed several broadcasts to Jordan calling on the Jordanian people to 'rise in a great revolution and break their chains just as they were broken in Iraq and wipe out the rotten monarchy just as it was wiped out in Iraq'.[106] King Hussein, who had in the meantime assumed the powers of Head of the Arab Federation, requested on the same day military aid 'as a temporary measure to protect our borders from surrounding enemies', and emphasized that the decision was taken in accordance with Article 51 of the UN Charter.[107] The UK sent about 2,000 men. In a statement to the House of Commons this was justified as an action under Article 51 of the Charter as King Hussein had stated that Jordan's territorial integrity was threatened by the movement of Syrian forces across her northern frontier and by the infiltration of arms, and thus British action was intended to help Jordan maintain her independence.[108] During the last few days in July, it was reported[109] that some fifteen persons, alleged to be infiltrators from Syria with a number of weapons and ammunition, had been arrested on the Jordanian–Syrian border. The Union of Jordan and Iraq was ended by King Hussein on 2 August by decree.

(ii) *Lebanon 1958*. Lebanon in 1958 was in a state of tension. Her stability depended on a delicate balance of sectarian interests, the structure of which was affirmed in the National Pact of July 1943.[110] This was an oral agreement between two prominent politicians by which the Lebanese Christians would accept Lebanon's 'Arab face' and refrain from any allegiance with a Western power, and the Muslims would agree to accept Lebanese sovereignty and refrain from seeking to merge Lebanon with any part of the Arab world. Representation in Parliament was agreed to be that of six Christians to five Muslims, which was based on a population census of 1932. It was also essential that major interests were represented in the Cabinet. In 1958 President Chamoun, who feared the popularity of President Nasser in Lebanon and the idea of a united

[106] *Keesing's*, p. 16305. See also the speech of the British delegate in the Security Council debate on Jordan, 831st meeting of 17 July 1958: *Security Council Meetings*, vol. 55.

[107] Ibid., speech of the Jordanian Minister.

[108] Ibid., speech of the British delegate.

[109] *Keesing's*, p. 16305.

[110] For general historical background to Lebanon, see Gordon, *The Republic of Lebanon* (1983); Gilmour, *Lebanon: the Fractured Country* (1983).

Arab State, much talked of at that time, decided to join the Baghdad Pact by which the US would help any government threatened with communist subversion. Lebanon was the only Arab State to do this and it seemed to many to be a repudiation of the National Pact. Chamoun had in fact already made himself unpopular by ensuring the defeat of eminent Muslim opponents in the 1957 elections through various electoral devices and by having as his Prime Minister (traditionally a Sunni Muslim) a pro-Western politician with little real following. Thus he denied the Muslim community adequate representation and, worse still, was believed to covet a second term as President, forbidden under the Constitution.[111] On 8 May 1958, after the assassination of an anti-Chamoun journalist, clashes occurred, but the civil war did not become extensive as the army refused to become involved and some major Maronite figures remained in opposition to Chamoun. However, after the overthrow of the pro-Western monarchy in Iraq, Chamoun and his supporters decided to ask for US military help.

The Lebanese Government had previously, on 22 May 1958, asked the Security Council of the UN to consider the situation in Lebanon which, it said, was caused by infiltration of arms and men from Syria and by a radio and press campaign against the Lebanese authorities in the United Arab Republic.[112] As a result, the Security Council adopted a resolution[113] on 11 June whereby an Observation Group was dispatched to Lebanon. On 14 July President Chamoun asked for outside help, and the next day the US troops began to arrive. In the Security Council Meetings of 15 July, the US argued that help was sent to combat the outside threat:

> The territorial integrity of Lebanon is increasingly threatened by insurrection stimulated and assisted from the outside . . . [the presence of the US forces] is designed for the sole purpose of helping the government of Lebanon at its request in its efforts to stabilize the situation brought on by threats from outside . . .[114]

The US was generally supported by her Western allies[115] in the Security Council, the delegate of France, in particular, stating:

[111] It was believed that Chamoun had intended to submit a constitutional amendment to enable him to seek another term. In May and June of 1958, opposition leaders called for the immediate resignation of Chamoun. On 8 July, however, Chamoun gave an assurance in an interview that he intended to relinquish the Presidency at the end of his present term in office. In the event, Chamoun did not formally seek a second term and elections were held on 31 July by which General Chehab was elected President. Despite the fact that opposition leaders had stated on 29 July that a condition of their support for Chehab was the immediate resignation of Chamoun, he continued in office until 23 September 1958 when his constitutional term ended: *Keesing's*, pp. 16293 and 16439.

[112] *United Nations Yearbook*, 1958, p. 36.

[113] S/4023 adopted at Security Council meeting 825 by 10–0–1 (Soviet Union abstaining). The draft Resolution was submitted by Sweden.

[114] Speech of the US delegate before the 827th meeting of the Security Council on 15 July 1958: *Security Council Meetings*, vol. 54.

[115] United Kingdom at the 827th meeting, loc. cit. (previous note); Canada and China at the 828th meeting, 15 July 1958, ibid.

. . . for two months now Lebanon . . . has been struggling against a revolt which would certainly have ended by now, if it had not been supported from outside.

The delegate then went on to say that the US action was 'justified under the provisions of Article 51 of the Charter'.[116]

It is to be noted, however, that Japan[117] and Sweden[118] had reservations, as the findings of the UN Observation Group did not establish outside infiltration but stated that there was little doubt that the vast majority of the armed men were Lebanese.[119] The Observation Group's findings were doubted by Lebanon and the US, which maintained their version of facts. Not surprisingly, the Soviet delegate attacked the intervention and stated that the events in Lebanon were a popular movement against the 'reactionary government of Chamoun' and that the US was intervening in the internal affairs of the country.[120] However, on the subject of President Chamoun's invitation, he went on to say that:

It is no secret . . . that these rulers are political puppets of the United States and that their requests are inspired by the United States State Department.[120]

A statement by the Swedish delegate could also indicate that a request by the government might be a justification in itself:

. . . to the extent that we are confronted with a decision of a State to request assistance from another State in order to stabilize the internal situation in the State, this is not a question falling directly within the jurisdiction of the United Nations.[121]

The Swedish delegate justified this statement by reference to Article 2 (7) of the Charter and then went on to say that, as no armed attack had occurred within the meaning of Article 51 of the Charter, the Observation Group in Lebanon should be suspended.

These statements of the Soviet and Swedish delegates might indicate that the norm of non-intervention in internal affairs was not well developed at that stage and that the justification of the invitation by the government may have still had some validity. However, the disapproval of the Soviet Union received more support in the General Assembly[122]

116 828th meeting of the Security Council, 15 July 1958, ibid.

117 829th meeting of the Security Council, 16 July 1958, ibid.

118 830th meeting of the Security Council, 16 July 1958, ibid.

119 First Report of UNGIL of 3 July 1958: UN Doc. S/4040. In the Second Report of UNGIL submitted on 30 July 1958, it was stated that the infiltration of arms which might be taking place could not be on anything more than a limited scale and was largely confined to small arms and ammunition. The Group stated that this could be expected with an open and largely unguarded frontier, but that although they patrolled the border areas, they could not detect the infiltration of any men crossing the border for the purpose of fighting: UN Doc. S/4069.

120 827th meeting of the Security Council, 15 July 1958.

121 Loc. cit. above, n. 118.

122 General Assembly Plenary meetings nos. 732–46 held from 8 to 21 August 1958, 3rd Emergency Special Session: *United Nations Yearbook*, 1958, p. 46. Unfortunately the debates themselves are not published: see *General Assembly Official Records*, 1958–9, vol. 13 A (8), index to the 3rd Emergency Special Session.

which, on considering the interventions in Jordan and Lebanon, unanimously adopted Resolution 1237[123] by which States pledged themselves to 'abstain from any action calculated to change established systems of government' and which called on States to observe 'strict non-interference in each other's internal affairs'. It is also of relevance that Jordan, Lebanon and the intervening States justified their actions on the basis of Article 51 even though the invitations were undoubtedly given.

(iii) *Stanleyville 1964*. Shortly after the UN peacekeeping force left the Congo,[124] Mr Tshombe was sworn in as leader of a government of reconciliation[125] although there was still a great deal of rebel activity.[126] In Stanleyville Mr Gbenye, who called himself the President of the Congolese People's Republic, announced on 29 October that since the Belgians were aiding the government forces, his regime would no longer guarantee the safety of Belgian subjects and their property, and he ordered all whites in the area to be placed under house arrest. On 21 November Mr Tshombe authorized the Belgian Government to send a rescue force to evacuate civilians in the area, and this was done on 24 November.[127]

At the Security Council meetings[128] which considered this operation, a number of views were put forward. The representatives of a large number of African countries[129] contended that the mission was undertaken to enable the Tshombe government to take over Stanleyville without endangering the foreigners. It is to be noted that Mr Tshombe was unpopular with some governments as he was perceived as being a neo-colonial leader.[130] As the representative of Mali put it:

> The real purpose of the aggression had been to seize Stanleyville, and then to consolidate their imperialistic hegemony over the Congo under cover of their puppets.[131]

These governments thus characterized the operation as an illegal intervention because it was perceived as an attempt to deny genuine African rule.[132] The representative of Tanzania directly disputed the legality of the Tshombe government:

> . . . the very unrest and civil war in the Congo was proof enough that many Congolese questioned the legality of Mr Tshombe's government.

[123] Adopted on 21 August 1958. [124] 30 June 1964. [125] 10 July 1964.

[126] In late 1964, it was estimated that insurgents controlled more than 150,000 square miles of territory consisting of large parts of eight provinces: *Keesing's*, p. 20561.

[127] *Keesing's*, p. 20561.

[128] Security Council meetings nos. 1170–8 (9 to 17 December 1964) and 1181, 1183–9 (21–30 December 1964): *General Assembly Official Records*, 20th Session, Supplement (A/6002) (1964–5).

[129] The Republic of the Congo (Brazzaville), Ghana, Guinea, Mali, Algeria, Kenya, Burundi, Uganda, Tanzania and Morocco. The representative of the Soviet Union made the same allegation.

[130] See, e.g., the speech of the representative of Guinea, 1171st meeting, para. 491: loc. cit. above (n. 128). [131] Ibid., para. 499.

[132] See in particular, the speeches of the representatives of the United Arab Republic at the 1174th meeting, loc. cit. above (n. 128), and Kenya, ibid.

The Stanleyville operation had constituted an intervention because it had been a conspiracy to impose upon the people of the Congo the disputed authority of the Tshombe government. . . .[133]

To be compared with these statements are those of the delegates of Nigeria[134] and the Ivory Coast.[135] They both stated that Mr Tshombe's government, which was the country's legitimate government, had the right to ask for military aid in the face of subversive help to the rebels which was being given by other African countries. The intervening States themselves vigorously denied undertaking the operation to support the government against the rebels but maintained that it was purely a humanitarian rescue mission carried out with the authority of the legitimate government:

Belgium

The Stanleyville operation had not been a military operation; it had not been intended as assistance to the Congolese army . . .[136]

United States

[The operation] had constituted no intervention in Congolese or African affairs . . . the only purpose of the mission had been to save innocent people . . .

Such statements are not, of course, positive indications that military help to the Congolese Army would not have been acceptable, but it certainly reflects a desire not to be perceived as providing such aid. The tenor of the speeches in general can be seen as indicating a duty of non-intervention unless the assistance is requested by the legitimate government to offset outside interference.

(iv) *Chad.* Chad became an independent nation in August 1960, but since 1965 has been beset by almost continuous civil strife.[137] French forces were involved between 1968 and 1980 and 1983–4 at the request of successive governments, and in 1981 Libyan forces were stationed in Chad at the request of the Oueddei government, which took power with the help of Libyan support. In August 1968, President Tombalbaye, who had imposed one-party rule in Chad since 1961, appealed for and was granted French military assistance in north-eastern Chad where government forces were in conflict with rebel elements. In the early years of French support, perceptions as to the role of the French troops differed: President Tombalbaye claimed several times that the rebellion was encouraged and supported from abroad and that this justified the appeal

[133] Security Council, 1178th meeting.

[134] Ibid., 1176th meeting.

[135] Ibid., 1177th meeting.

[136] Ibid., 1173rd meeting.

[137] For a detailed history of the civil war in Chad, see Thompson and Adloff, *Conflict in Chad* (1981).

for French troops.[138] The French authorities, on the one hand, explicitly stated that they did not believe that there was foreign intervention.[139] On the other hand, the help provided was said to be of a limited nature and directed at providing administrative and advisory assistance as well as some equipment.[140] It is to be noted, however, that the French military involvement was criticized by the opposition party headed by M Mitterand,[141] and the government in its reply stated that although there was no evidence of help to the rebels from Libya, the frontier between Chad on the one hand, and Libya and Sudan on the other, was difficult to control.[142]

In April 1975, President Tombalbaye was overthrown and replaced by General Malloum. A new military agreement was drawn up in 1976 with the French Government by which the number of military instructors to train the army of Chad was increased, but it is noteworthy that the French Prime Minister, M Chirac, stated that the French military personnel would 'not intervene directly against the rebellion'.[143] During 1976, however, increasing Libyan involvement in Chad became apparent. Libya occupied the Aozou strip[144] in Northern Chad consisting of some 27,000 square miles and had been supporting a rebel group led by Mr Habre.[145] A dispute between Mr Habre and the Libyan Government that year resulted in the replacement[146] of Mr Habre by Mr Oueddei as leader of the 'Frolinat'[147] forces. Throughout 1978, heavy fighting took place between the government and the various rebel forces, Mr Oueddei's group receiving Libyan aid. During that year, France sent troops[148] and aircraft to Chad, but a French communiqué stressed that the troops would not be employed in military engagements, but were there to train the Chad army and provide 'technical assistance'.[149] Although a government of

[138] Vernhes and Bloch, *Guerre coloniale au Tchad* (1972), p. 23; statement in Government White Paper, 5 November 1969: *Keesing's*, p. 24035; broadcast by President Tombalbaye, 18 October 1970: ibid., p. 24672; statement by President Tombalbaye on the occasion of the visit to Chad of President Pompidou, January 1972: ibid., p. 25120.

[139] Statement by French military delegate in Chad, March 1969; similar comment by French Government in reply to opposition criticism, 1970: ibid., p. 24035.

[140] Statement of French Government spokesman, 28 August 1968: ibid., p. 23073; announcement by French Government, 2 September 1969: ibid., p. 23548; statement of French meeting of ministers, January 1970: ibid., p. 24035.

[141] Vernhes and Bloch, op. cit. above (n. 138), at p. 62.

[142] *Keesing's*, p. 24035.

[143] 6 March 1976: *Keesing's*, p. 27744.

[144] Thompson and Adloff, op. cit. above (p. 218 n. 137), pp. 61, 67; also Lanne, *Tchad–Libye: la querelle des frontières* (1982), pp. 228, 230, 234.

[145] *Keesing's*, p. 28136.

[146] 18 October 1976, in an announcement on 3 January 1977: ibid., p. 28307.

[147] Front de Liberation Nationale du Tchad. Until 1977, the rebel group called 'Frolinat' had been led by a Dr Sidick, based in Algiers, and had been at odds with Mr Habre's group. It was reported in July 1976 that this original Frolinat was superseded by a group of the same name led by Mr Habre: ibid., p. 28136.

[148] Reports differ as to the number of troops and advisers: France stated that it had sent 150 troops, but a report in the *Guardian* on 22 April estimated a figure of about 650: ibid., p. 29397.

[149] 26 April 1978: ibid., p. 29395. See also a statement by the French Minister for Co-operation that the French troops were engaged on a defensive basis only and were not participating in any offensives against Frolinat.

national unity was negotiated in August 1978, with Mr Habre as Prime Minister and General Malloum remaining President,[150] fighting continued and large areas of territory were captured from the government forces[151] supported by the French.[152] In March 1979 a conference on national reconciliation was held resulting in a government of national unity with Mr Oueddei as provisional Head of State.[153] The mainstream rebels, now involved in government, turned against Libya, which reacted by launching offensives into northern Chad and by supporting discontented rebel groups which were unrepresented in the government.[154] Eventually, in August of that year, an accord of national reconciliation was signed in Lagos in which eleven factions were represented, the new government being formed under the Presidency of Mr Oueddei. At this stage, the French began a withdrawal of their troops, but delayed its completion because of a request by Mr Oueddei that they stay until the arrival of an African peace-keeping force.[154] In 1980, however, the government broke down, owing principally to a power struggle between Mr Oueddei and Mr Habre, and Mr Habre's forces[155] were defeated in December 1980 by forces loyal to Mr Oueddei with the aid of massive Libyan support.[156] On 6 January 1981 the governments of Chad and Libya announced a proposed union between the two countries and the sending by Libya, at the request of Chad, of military personnel to help preserve security and peace. State reaction to this event is indicative of international hostility to major foreign involvement. An extraordinary meeting of the OAU[157] resulted in a communiqué condemning the action and reaffirming the Lagos agreement of August 1979.[158] On 8 January 1981 the French Foreign Ministry issued a statement condemning the proposed union and included the assertion that '. . . in response to requests from the Chad government, France had often given that country aid and protection but had never interfered in its internal affairs and had withdrawn its own troops in line with the Lagos accord'.[159] The following day, the French Government announced that it intended to send troop reinforcements to Africa at the request of any country which was linked to France by a defence and co-operation agreement and which feared that its security was in danger.[160]

[150] *Keesing's*, p. 29397.

[151] 'Forces armées tchadiennes' (FAT).

[152] On the role and official stance of the French troops, see Thompson and Adloff, op. cit. above (p. 218 n. 137), at p. 85.

[153] *Keesing's*, p. 30064.

[154] Ibid., pp. 30065–7.

[155] 'Forces armées du nord' (FAN).

[156] *Keesing's*, p. 31159.

[157] Held 10 to 14 January 1981 in Lomé, Togo.

[158] Full text in *Keesing's*, p. 31159.

[159] Ibid., p. 31160.

[160] On the basis of this, France reinforced its military presence in the Central African Republic to support the government of Mr Dacko which France had helped install after overthrowing Mr Bokassa in September 1979. Requests for help by the Governments of the Ivory Coast, Senegal and Gabon were approved. It was also reported that France was seeking to station other troops in countries considered to be sensitive to Libyan-inspired 'subversion' such as Cameroon and Niger: *Keesing's*, p. 31160.

It would appear that by the end of 1981, Mr Oueddei became resentful of Libyan influence, and Libyan troops left in November of that year. The civil war reintensified and by June 1982 Mr Habre had outmanœuvred the other factions, took the capital, and became official Head of State on 19 June.[161] However, renewed fighting broke out in mid-1983 between government troops and Libyan-based rebels loyal to Mr Oueddei. French troops again became involved at Mr Habre's request. On 28 June 1983 President Mitterand accused Libya of directly supporting the rebel forces and stated that France would supply aid to Chad under the terms of the 1976 Co-operation Agreement.[162] Until January 1984, the troops were officially[163] not taking part in combat operations and Chad radio criticized France for leaving the Chad troops to stand alone against 'Libyan tanks and aircraft'.[164] However, in January 1984, the French ministry stated that there was evidence of the presence of Libyan personnel in Chad, and consequently French troops were ordered to engage hostile forces.[165] French troops withdrew late in 1984[166] after a suggestion by Libya that both countries withdraw their forces.

The various interventions in Chad have not been the subject of any substantial debate at the United Nations[167] and one is therefore left with little evidence on which to assess the opinions of the governments involved and the outcome of the OAU meeting referred to. It is submitted that the persistent reliance placed on the existence of outside intervention by the Chad Government when requesting help, and the insistence by the French Government that it was not taking part in hostile operations against Chad rebels, are consistent with a norm forbidding the giving of aid to a government when the effect of such aid is to interfere with internal affairs. It is particularly interesting that the aid given by France was described as being in effect proportionate to the outside help and that France denied openly engaging in the conflict until the presence of Libyan personnel was ascertained. This would indicate an action of collective self-defence in conformity with Article 51 of the Charter and with the principle of proportionality of response in self-defence actions. The supply of arms and training to a national army even during a civil war was, on the other hand, considered to be not inconsistent with a duty of non-interference. With regard to Libyan involvement in 1981, the OAU response made it quite plain that African countries would not tolerate a situation where a government was kept in power with active outside involvement and which jeopardized the independence of the State.

[161] Ibid., p. 31677.

[162] Ibid., p. 32591.

[163] Statement by French defence minister, Mr Hernu, on 9 August 1983.

[164] 9 September 1983: *Keesing's*, p. 32593.

[165] Ibid., p. 33007.

[166] The withdrawal took place between 25 September and 10 November 1984.

[167] On 16 March 1983 the Chad Government had complained to the UN of Libyan aggression, and the Security Council on 6 April called on the two sides to reconcile their differences: decision of the Security Council, UN Doc. S/15688, *Security Council Official Records*, 38th Year, 2430th meeting.

(v) *Mozambique 1985*. It was reported[168] in June 1985 that the leaders of Mozambique, Zimbabwe and Tanzania had met in Harare to discuss possible military intervention by Zimbabwe and Tanzania to help Mozambique end an armed rebellion. Mr Machel's government had been involved for the previous five years in a struggle with guerillas of the Mozambican National Resistance Movement, which had forces operating in all of the country's provinces and in the suburbs of the capital. Until 1984 the rebels had been aided by South Africa and it was hoped that the non-aggression treaty concluded with South Africa in 1984 would end their support. It was stressed by the three governments that the help was necessary because of South African support to the rebels, although South Africa denied official involvement. It remains to be seen whether the military intervention will take place and whether outside involvement will continue to be stressed as a justification.

2. *Interventions where the existence or validity of the invitation is disputed*

(i) *Hungary 1956*. During the autumn of 1956, mass demonstrations took place in Hungary involving students, workers and soldiers demanding political reform. On 14 October Mr Nagy, who had been Prime Minister between 1953 and 1955 but was expelled as a traitor and Titoist, was readmitted to the Hungarian Workers' Party.[169] On 23 to 24 October fighting broke out[170] and martial law was declared, and on 24 October it was announced that Mr Nagy had taken over the Premiership and that the Government had appealed to the Soviet Union to restore order. Mr Gerö, First Secretary, had made the appeal,[171] but Mr Nagy promised broad democratization.[172] On the next day the insurrection spread and it was becoming clear that the bulk of the Hungarian armed forces were on the side of the insurgents.[173] Between 29 and 31 October Mr Nagy announced the end of single-party rule, the formation of an all-party government, free elections and a decision to leave the Warsaw Pact,[174] and appealed to the UN to guarantee Hungary's neutrality.[175] In the meantime, Mr Kadar, also readmitted to the Communist Party, had

[168] *International Herald Tribune*, 14 June 1985, p. 2. This newspaper account has been verbally confirmed as accurate by a diplomatic official of the Zimbabwe Embassy, London, although at the time of writing an official statement had not yet been released.

[169] *Keesing's*, p. 15189. For greater detail on the Hungarian revolution and its background, see Vali, *Rift and Revolt in Hungary* (1961); Lomax, *Hungary 1956* (1976); Pryce-Jones, *The Hungarian Revolution* (1969). Although the recitations of facts coincide, historians appear to differ in their opinions as to the character and motivations of the principal characters involved, in particular those of Nagy, Gerö and Kadar.

[170] Vali, op. cit. (previous note), at pp. 268–77; Lomax, op. cit. (previous note), at pp. 109–20.

[171] *Keesing's*, p. 15189; Vali, op. cit. above (n. 169), p. 276.

[172] *Keesing's*, p. 15190; Vali, op. cit. above (n. 169), p. 284.

[173] On the failure of the first Soviet intervention, see Vali, op. cit. above (n. 169), p. 277; Lomax, op. cit. above (n. 169), p. 120.

[174] *Keesing's*, p. 15191; Vali, op. cit. above (n. 169), pp. 297–301; Pryce-Jones, op. cit. above (n. 169), pp. 89 and 96.

[175] *Keesing's*, p. 15192, and *United Nations Yearbook*, 1956, p. 67.

replaced Mr Gerö as First Secretary. In the first days of November Soviet forces built up in Hungary and despite Mr Nagy's protest to the UN, Soviet forces overthrew the government on 4 November.[176]

The Security Council had already begun considering the matter in late October 1956. On 27 October France, the UK and the US requested a meeting to consider an item entitled 'The Situation in Hungary' pursuant to Article 34 of the Charter. They stated that foreign military forces in Hungary were violently repressing the rights of the Hungarian people secured by the 1947 Treaty of Peace.[177] In the debate, which was held the next day, the Soviet delegate objected to the inclusion of the item on the agenda, stating that discussions by the Council would amount to an interference in internal affairs as it was the right of the Hungarian Government to ask for aid to suppress the counter-revolutionary uprising. He added that the US was financing subversive activities against the Government of Hungary.[178] This debate took place before Mr Nagy officially appealed to the UN, and it is interesting that the other members of the Security Council concentrated on the nature of the uprising and did not consider whether Mr Gerö had the capacity to issue a request to Soviet forces or indeed whether the request had taken place. Only the delegate of France at this meeting expressly doubted the existence of a request, but he then went on to say that in any case there was no justification in the Warsaw Pact for the use of force to suppress Hungarians as that treaty only provided for such force in the event of foreign aggression.[178] The other delegates devoted themselves to an examination of the nature of the uprising and found it to be a genuine case of Hungarians rebelling against Soviet repression. As the delegate of the UK expressed it

> . . . it is evident that what is really happening in Hungary is a popular nation-wide movement for the recovery of liberty and independence.[178]

At both this meeting and further meetings of the Security Council held between 2 and 4 November 1956, all delegations other than the Soviet Union concentrated on the fact that this was a genuine uprising of the people and made statements of principle reaffirming the norms of non-intervention in internal affairs and self-determination of peoples. The situation in Hungary was, of course, a particularly blatant example of one country totally repressing virtually the entire population of another, rather than one where one faction with some following is using foreign help to quell rebels. However, certain statements were made which appeared to give the principle of non-intervention in internal affairs a wide interpretation. Thus the Peruvian delegate stated that the Warsaw Pact only permitted the use of troops in the event of external aggression, but

[176] *Keesing's*, p. 15192; Vali, op. cit. above (p. 222 n. 169), pp. 360, 371–7. For eye-witness accounts and documents, see Lasky (ed.), *The Hungarian Revolution* (1957).

[177] *United Nations Yearbook*, 1956, p. 67.

[178] 746th meeting of the Security Council, 28 October 1956, *Security Council Official Records*, 11th Year, vol. 47.

that even if their actual use were legitimate under the agreement, it would be contrary to Article 2 (4) of the Charter and the general principle of non-intervention.[179] The delegate of Iran made an unequivocal statement:

> . . . we always regard with profound distrust the presence of foreign troops on the territory of another State and, although we are sometimes obliged to tolerate their presence because the country whose territory is occupied has consented to the occupation, we can never agree to the use of such troops to stifle popular movements, even if the government whose territory is occupied has consented to their use or asked for it.[180]

In the meeting of the Security Council of 4 November, the Soviet delegate stressed his allegation that subversive activities in Hungary had been financed by the US, helped by Austria, and then went on to say that

> The events in Hungary have shown quite clearly that a counter-revolutionary underground movement has been organized in that country with help from abroad . . . Everything points to the fact that the rebels have operated on the basis of a pre-arranged plan . . .[181]

A US draft resolution[182] condemning the intervention was vetoed by the Soviet Union and the matter was then transferred to the General Assembly to be considered pursuant to General Assembly Resolution 377 (v)[183] for the consideration of appropriate steps.

Before the General Assembly that same day[184] the Soviet delegate reiterated his assertion that foreign subversion[185] was partly responsible for the rebellion by 'reactionary forces' and that it was these forces which had caused all the destruction and chaos. He then stated that the Nagy government fell on 4 November as a result of a 'number of democratic statesmen [who] demanded the removal of the Nagy cabinet and took the government of the country into their own hands.' This new government, he said, appealed to the Soviet troops for assistance. A number of countries then spoke condemning the intervention,[186] and all placed the main stress of their argument on the fact that the Soviet Union was repressing a popular movement and that this was a gross interference in Hungary's internal affairs and a denial of the right of the people of Hungary to self-determination.

[179] 746th meeting of the Security Council, 28 October 1956, and 752nd meeting, 2 November 1956, loc. cit. above (p. 223 n. 178).

[180] 746th meeting of the Security Council, 28 October 1956, loc. cit. above (p. 223 n. 178).

[181] 754th meeting of the Security Council, 4 November 1956, loc. cit. above (p. 223 n. 178).

[182] UN Doc. S/3730/Rev. I, voted on 4 November 1956, 9–1–1 (Yugoslavia abstaining).

[183] 'Uniting for Peace Resolution', 3 November 1950.

[184] 564th meeting, 4 November 1956, *General Assembly Official Records*, 2nd Emergency Special Session, vol. 11.

[185] The countries named were the US, which was said to be providing financial support, and Austria and West Germany, which allegedly allowed the rebels to operate in their territory.

[186] Spain, Canada, Italy, Dominican Republic, Greece, UK, Belgium, New Zealand, Turkey, France.

A draft Resolution submitted by the US condemning the intervention, and calling on the governments of Hungary and the Soviet Union to permit observers to report to the UN, was adopted by a large majority.[187] The relevant parts of the resolution read as follows:

. . . Convinced that recent events in Hungary manifest clearly the desire of the Hungarian people to exercise and to enjoy fully their fundamental rights, freedom and independence,

Condemning the use of Soviet military forces to suppress the efforts of the Hungarian people to reassert their rights,

Noting moreover the declaration of 30 October 1956 by the Government of the Union of Soviet Socialist Republics of its avowed policy of non-intervention in the internal affairs of other States,

Noting the communication of 1 November 1956 of the Government of Hungary to the Secretary-General regarding demands made by that Government to the Government of the Union of Soviet Socialist Republics for the instant and immediate withdrawal of Soviet forces,

Noting that the intervention of Soviet military forces in Hungary has resulted in grave loss of life and widespread bloodshed among the Hungarian people,

Taking note of the radio appeal of Prime Minister Imre Nagy of 4 November 1956,

1. Calls upon the Government of the Union of Soviet Socialist Republics to desist forthwith from all armed attack on the people of Hungary and from any form of intervention, in particular armed intervention, in the internal affairs of Hungary;
2. Calls upon the Union of Soviet Socialist Republics to cease the introduction of additional armed forces into Hungary and to withdraw all of its forces without delay from Hungarian territory;
3. Affirms the right of the Hungarian people to a government responsive to its national aspirations and dedicated to its independence and well-being;
4. Requests the Secretary-General to investigate the situation caused by foreign intervention in Hungary, to observe the situation directly through representatives named by him, and to report thereon to the General Assembly at the earliest moment, and as soon as possible to suggest methods to bring an end to the foreign intervention in Hungary in accordance with the principles of the Charter of the United Nations;
5. Calls upon the Government of Hungary and the Government of the Union of Soviet Socialist Republics to permit observers designated by the Secretary-General to enter the territory of Hungary, to travel freely therein, and to report their findings to the Secretary-General.

It is to be noted that although the resolution specifically refers to the appeal of Mr Nagy, there are also statements of principle of a general

[187] General Assembly Resolution 1004, adopted 4 November 1956 by 50–8–15; four of the countries which abstained (Indonesia, Ceylon, Nepal and Burma) said that they did so because of lack of instructions at such short notice, but subsequently supported the resolution. Three countries, India, Yugoslavia and Lebanon, stated that they supported the principle of non-intervention but thought that some of the strong language was unhelpful. The countries that voted against consisted solely of East European satellite nations and Albania.

character. Statements by delegates at further meetings of the General Assembly again stressed the fact that the rebellion was a popular movement, and very little, if any, attention was paid to the technical competence of any particular governmental figure to request assistance. There are also several speeches which looked at the nature of the principle of non-intervention and do certainly seem to indicate the inadmissibility of repressing a revolution, viz:

Brazil

> The employment of foreign troops to fight an internal revolt when the Hungarian people was trying to decide its destiny was indefensible.[188]

Ceylon

> We certainly do not welcome foreign forces in a country under any pretext whatsoever, whether it be for the restoration of order or whether it be to uphold the law of the land.[188]

Costa Rica

> The very fact of one country trying to justify the dispatch of its army to interfere in the affairs of another country on the grounds that there are in that country elements of this or that type . . . is a palpable admission of intervention . . .[188]

Nepal

> My government is opposed to the practice of stationing foreign troops in another country, under any pretext whatsoever. The armed intervention of a big country in the affairs of a small country, even on the plea that a request came from the latter, is apt to interfere with the free expression of the will of the people, and to that extent it is apt to hinder the process of democracy.[189]

As the General Assembly had met under the auspices of the Uniting for Peace Resolution, a number of further meetings were held, resulting in further resolutions,[190] in which the UN tried to secure the amelioration of conditions in Hungary. There was a great deal of distress articulated at reports of massacres, deportations and other brutalities, but as the governments of the Soviet Union and Hungary refused to co-operate with the General Assembly's requests, the matter was eventually dropped.

(ii) *The Dominican Republic 1965*. In 1963, a three-man civilian junta overthrew Mr Bosch who had been the first freely elected President in thirty-eight years. On 25 to 26 April 1965 this junta was in turn overthrown by a military revolt headed by Mr Caemaño which consisted of supporters of Mr Bosch. Almost immediately, civil war broke out

188 569th meeting of the General Assembly, 8 November 1956, loc. cit. above (p. 224 n. 184).

189 585th meeting of the General Assembly, 20 November 1956, *General Assembly Official Records*, 11th Session, vol. 11 A (1).

190 GA Res. 1005, 1006, 1007, 9 November 1956; 1008, 10 November 1956; 1127, 1128, 1129, 21 November 1956; 1130, 4 December 1956; 1131, 12 December 1956; 1132, 10 January 1957.

between Mr Caemaño's units and those led by Mr Wessin, an extreme right-wing officer who was one of the leaders of the coup which overthrew Mr Bosch. Central authority collapsed as fighting took place between the two factions. It appeared that Mr Caemaño was supported by most of the Army, but was opposed by the Air Force, by an armoured unit at the San Isidro air base and by the small Navy. After two days of fighting, Mr Caemaño held the central part of Santo Domingo and some of the suburbs, and Mr Wessin held the rest of the capital and the San Isidro base where the three-man junta installed itself. On 28 April US marines landed in the Dominican Republic and by 30 April had evacuated some 2,500 civilians, but continued to send in more forces.[191]

During the Security Council debates, the US delegate justified the incursion as follows:

> . . . while the PRD planned and during its first hours led the revolutionary movement against the government of Reid Cabral, a small group of well-known communists, consistent with their usual tactics, quickly attempted to seize control of the revolution and of the armed bands in the streets. Quite clearly this group was acting in conformity with directives issued by a communist conference that met in Havana in late 1964 and printed in Pravda on 18th January 1965 . . . This deliberate effort to promote subversion and overthrow governments in flagrant violation of all norms of international conduct is responsible for much of the unrest in the Caribbean area. In the face of uncontrollable violence, the government which had replaced the Reid Cabral government also quickly crumbled in a few days . . . In the absence of any governmental authority, Dominican law enforcement and military officials informed our Embassy that the situation was completely out of control, that the police and the government could no longer give any guarantee concerning the safety of Americans or of any foreign nationals and that only an immediate landing of United States forces would safeguard and protect the lives of thousands of Americans and thousands of citizens of some thirty other countries . . . Faced with that emergency, the threat to the lives of its citizens, and a request for assistance from those Dominican authorities still struggling to maintain order, the United States on the 28th April dispatched the first of the security forces that we have sent to the island.[192]

The delegate then went on to stress that they were not interfering in the internal affairs of the country, but on the contrary, were preventing outside interference:

> . . . the United States government has no intention of seeking to dictate the political future of the Dominican Republic. We believe that the Dominican people, under the established principle of self-determination, should select their own government through free elections . . . Our interest lies in the re-establishment of constitutional government and, to that end, to assist in maintaining the stability essential to the expression of the free choice of the Dominican people . . .
> . . . as President Johnson has emphasised, the United States will never depart from its commitment to the preservation of the right of all of the free people of this

[191] *Keesing's*, p. 20813.

hemisphere to choose their own course without falling prey to international conspiracy from any quarter. . . . the people of that country must be permitted to choose the path of political democracy, social justice and economic progress.[192]

With regard to the 'request for assistance' to which the delegate referred, it is not clear from which authorities it emanated, or the content and purpose of the request. Official source material does not give evidence of such a request. The only direct reference to a communication is to be found in a television broadcast to the nation by President Johnson given on 2 May 1965,[193] in which he refers to a cable sent by the US Ambassador stationed in Santo Domingo:

. . . the cable reported that Dominican law enforcement and military officials had informed our Embassy that the situation was completely out of control, and that the police and the government could no longer give any guarantee concerning the safety of Americans or of any foreign nationals.

The President went on to state that this Ambassador then reported that an immediate landing of troops was necessary to save the civilians.[194] The official White House press release issued on 28 April does not give an exact source or evidence of a request. It simply states that:

The United States government has been informed by military authorities in the Dominican Republic that American lives are in danger. These authorities are no longer able to guarantee their safety and they have reported that the assistance of military personnel is now needed for that purpose.[195]

There is thus considerable doubt not only as to the existence of a direct request, but also as to whether the request could have any validity since, as the delegate himself stated, there was no governmental authority. It would also appear that the alleged request related solely to the evacuation of foreign nationals rather than an intervention in the civil war as such. Diplomatic reaction to the intervention was generally unfavourable, but there was some support for the US action in the Security Council. The UK delegate stated that the only Dominican forces which had any recognizable claim to be in a position to maintain order had declared their inability to do so, and requested the US to take steps to protect foreign nationals. The delegate then expressed gratitude for the evacuation of British subjects.[196] The delegate of the Netherlands also expressed gratitude for the evacuation of its citizens, but purposely refrained from making a statement on the legality of the intervention as such.[197]

With regard to the central issue, i.e. the suppression of communist rebels, only Nationalist China openly supported the arguments of the US.

[192] 1196th meeting of the Security Council, 3 May 1965, *Security Council Official Records*, 20th Year, vol. 72.

[193] *United States Department of State Bulletin*, 52 (1965), pp. 744–8.

[194] The Ambassador's cable was stated to have arrived on 28 April 1965.

[195] Loc. cit. above (n. 193), p. 738.

[196] 1198th meeting of the Security Council, 4 May 1965, loc. cit. above (n. 192).

[197] 1203rd meeting of the Security Council, 7 May 1965, loc. cit. above (n. 192).

It stated that the principle of self-determination can only be exercised in unfettered freedom, and that communism is invariably imposed on a country by a small minority acting under the instigation and in the interests of another foreign power.[198] Statements by other delegates were coloured by the fact that the Organization of American States had in the meantime sent a team to mediate in the crisis and had on 8 May negotiated a cease-fire. Much emphasis was therefore placed on the encouragement of OAS efforts. Nevertheless, statements of principle were made which either expressly or impliedly disapproved of the intervention. Thus France, after supporting the principle of non-intervention in internal affairs, stated that this intervention was exercised against a group which claimed to have constitutional legality. The French delegate went on to say that the actual US operation went beyond what was necessary to evacuate foreign citizens.[199] The delegate of Uruguay disputed the US view that revolutions are no longer the internal affairs of countries when their object is to establish a communist dictatorship, for in his opinion this doctrine would be inconsistent with the principle of self-determination.[199] Malaysia, whilst supporting the efforts of the OAS, emphasized that there should be no intervention in the affairs of another State,[200] whilst Jordan wondered whether events in the Dominican Republic would have reached such a crisis if they had been left to take their natural course.[201] The delegate of the Ivory Coast elaborated the principle of non-intervention in the internal affairs of States and said that it includes the duty not to send armed elements into another State unless requested to do so by the 'legally constituted government'. He then said, however, that in civil wars, where either side is backed by a foreign element, this principle is flouted, and added that in the Dominican Republic, those who were defending constitutional legality 'have paid the price'.[202] The Soviet delegate, not surprisingly, characterized the intervention as an interference in internal affairs, and an act of 'imperialism'.[203] He also quoted from various newspapers, including the *New York Times*, *The Times* and *Le Monde*, to the effect that very few communists were involved in the revolution and that there was no proof of support by Cuban communists.[204]

[198] 1202nd meeting of the Security Council, 6 May 1965, loc. cit. above (p. 228 n. 192).
[199] 1198th meeting of the Security Council, 4 May 1965, loc. cit. above (p. 228 n. 192).
[200] 1202nd meeting of the Security Council, 6 May 1965, loc. cit. above (p. 228 n. 192).
[201] 1200th meeting of the Security Council, 5 May 1965, loc. cit. above (p. 228 n. 192).
[202] 1203rd meeting of the Security Council, 7 May 1965, loc. cit. above (p. 228 n. 192).
[203] 1196th meeting of the Security Council, 3 May 1965, loc. cit. above (p. 228 n. 192).
[204] 1203rd meeting of the Security Council, 7 May 1965, loc. cit. above (p. 228 n. 192). Further condemnation outside UN debates was reported as follows: Latin American delegates at the OAS meeting: *Keesing's*, p. 20813; Senator Fulbright, Chairman of the Senate Foreign Relations Committee stated that the US action was an intervention against a social revolution and temporarily in favour of a corrupt military oligarchy: ibid., p. 20985. In the debates of the UK House of Commons, Mr Noel-Baker of the Labour party said that the dispatch of US troops at the invitation of a 'fascist' military junta was a violation of the OAS Charter and of the UN Charter. Mr Bosch himself, in a radio interview to the US on 3 May 1965, expressed surprise at President Johnson's assertion that

The subsequent action by the OAS reflected the desire not to favour one side or the other, and prolonged negotiations led to agreement in August 1965 for the inauguration of a provisional President pending elections.[205] These were held the following year, and after Mr Balaguer was sworn in as President in July 1966, the Inter-American peace-keeping force withdrew.[206] There can be no doubt that the reaction of other States to the US action indicated serious doubt as to its legitimacy. Apart from certain references, discussion did not turn on the legitimacy of the requesting body or on whether such a request took place, but instead concentrated on the issue of non-intervention in internal affairs. It is, in this respect, significant that the US stressed outside support given to a small number of communists which purportedly created the danger and which needed to be suppressed. The existence of significant communist subversion was evidently disbelieved and thus States viewed the matter as an internal affair of the Dominican Republic.

(iii) *Afghanistan 1979*. On 27 April 1978 the government of President Daud[207] was overthrown and replaced by a government largely composed of the People's Democratic Party (PDP)[208] and led by Mr Taraki.[209] This party declared that it would rid the country of its aristocracy and would start land reform, nationalization and other socialist reforms.[210] Almost immediately, however, there were reports of clashes between Army units and tribesmen which became progressively more intense during that year. By October 1978 heavy fighting in eastern Afghanistan led to a large flow of refugees into neighbouring Pakistan,[211] and, on 12 March 1979, a rebellion broke out in the western city of Herat which was crushed by government forces.[211] During 1979, the rebellion, led by a large number of different Moslem groups, spread and there were also several incidents of mutiny and desertion by the regular army.[212] In the meantime, both the Afghan Government and the Soviet Union accused outside

communists had taken over control. He stated that the uprising was entirely democratic and not under communist control, and asserted that the forces of the right could have been crushed but for the arrival of the US marines which 'smashed the democratic' revolution: *Keesing's*, p. 20813.

[205] Ibid., p. 20986.

[206] Ibid., p. 21481.

[207] Mr Daud had himself taken power in a *coup d'état* which overthrew the monarchy on 17 July 1973 and which created single party rule.

[208] The PDP was launched in 1965 but was banned until 1978 as being too pro-Communist.

[209] The *coup d'état* on 28 April 1978 was executed by the 'Armed Forces Revolutionary Council', under Col. Abdul Qadir, which proclaimed the annulment of President Daud's constitution. The AFRC then proclaimed the establishment of the Democratic Republic of Afghanistan and became part of a new thirty-five-member council, containing leading members of the PDP, which elected Mr Taraki as Chairman.

[210] *Keesing's*, p. 29037.

[211] Ibid., p. 29641.

[212] On 22 April 1979 a mutiny took place at Jalalabad; on 2 May 1979 a mutiny of two battalions was crushed by a commando unit from Kabul; on 17 May 1979 a mechanized brigade deserted and joined the Panthan rebel forces; on 27 May 1979 some 700 Afghan soldiers joined the rebel forces; on 5 August 1979 heavy fighting in Kabul was said to be a mutiny of regular troops at the Bale Hissar Fort in Kabul: *Keesing's*, p. 29878.

powers of helping the revolutionaries. On 3 April 1979 Mr Amin, the Prime Minister, said that his government had proof of 'armed imperialist involvement in the conspiracy against our revolution' but did not mention countries by name.[213] With regard to the rebellion in Herat, the Afghan Government alleged that the rebellion was helped by Iran, which denied the accusation. In *Pravda* it was alleged that 'one of the principal leaders of the counter-revolutionary forces' had on the eve of the Herat rebellion been 'received at the highest level' in Washington.[213] A further report in *Pravda* alleged that the rebels in Afghanistan were getting help from reactionary elements, in particular Pakistan, China, the US, Egypt and West Germany. The US and Pakistan denied allegations of involvement.[214]

In September 1979 Mr Taraki died in mysterious circumstances and Mr Amin was elected President. Mr Amin dismissed many ministers and officials, and replaced them with his own followers, and then took steps to strengthen the position of the PDP by, *inter alia*, rewriting the constitution.[215] The armed rebellion in Afghanistan continued unabated, and there were reports that on 21 September 1979[216] the Soviet Union moved ten companies of combat troops into Afghanistan, and that the Afghan Government received more Soviet equipment on 9 October.[217] In mid-December a build-up of Soviet troops began to take place in Afghanistan and on 25 to 26 December 1979 an estimated 4–5,000 Soviet combat troops and equipment were airlifted into Kabul. A coup took place on 27 December and Mr Amin was killed. There were conflicting suggestions as to how his death occurred, some suggesting that he was executed, and others indicating that he was killed during fighting at the Palace, but not at Soviet hands.[218] There are also reports that the groundwork for the intervention was laid between August and October 1979, during which time a Soviet official made a pessimistic assessment of the military position of the regime in Afghanistan. Certain assessments in the Western press were to the effect that Mr Amin was unpopular with the Soviet Government and that he had rejected Soviet proposals for the introduction of combat forces to assist the Afghan Army.[218] Although the precise facts are not known, the Soviet Union chose to interpret the event as the overthrowing by Mr Karmal of Mr Amin, who was described by Moscow radio as 'tyrannical, murderous' and 'an agent of US Imperialism'.[219] A statement by the Government of Afghanistan was reported in *Tass* to have been broadcast on 28 December to the effect that the Government

[213] Ibid., p. 29641.
[214] Ibid. It was also reported that on 21 March 1979 Mr Majadded, a rebel leader, had said that all Western countries had refused to supply his movement with arms and other help.
[215] *Keesing's*, p. 30031.
[216] Six days after Mr Amin assumed the Presidency.
[217] *Keesing's*, p. 30031.
[218] Ibid., pp. 30229–30.
[219] Broadcast on 27 December 1979.

of Afghanistan had repeatedly asked for help from the Soviet Union to offset the interference from the external enemies of Afghanistan. Another broadcast on 31 December stated that as soon as 'armed incursions and provocations from outside' ceased, there would be no more need for the aid which was given.[220] Mr Karmal, who headed the new regime, had been Deputy Prime Minister under the first Taraki government, but was then later dismissed following differences with Mr Amin and had remained exiled in Czechoslovakia. The composition of Mr Karmal's cabinet included many who had been supporters of Mr Taraki.

Immediate diplomatic reaction to the incursion was hostile[221] and this was reflected in the debates that took place before the UN. On 3 to 4 January 1980, more than fifty nations, including ten Islamic countries, signed a motion calling for a meeting of the Security Council which met on 5 January. After two days of debate, a draft Resolution condemning the intervention was vetoed by the Soviet Union,[222] but the General Assembly, which met on 10 January, overwhelmingly passed a Resolution deploring the intervention.[223] The principal operative paragraphs of this Resolution read as follows:

> [the General Assembly]
>
> (i) Reaffirms that respect for the sovereignty, territorial integrity and political independence of every State is a fundamental principle of the Charter of the United Nations, any violation of which on any pretext whatsoever is contrary to its aims and purposes;
>
> (ii) Strongly deplores the recent armed intervention in Afghanistan, which is inconsistent with that principle;
>
> (iii) Appeals to all States to respect the sovereignty, territorial integrity, political independence and non-aligned character of Afghanistan and to refrain from any interference in the internal affairs of that country;
>
> (iv) Calls for the immediate, unconditional and total withdrawal of the foreign troops from Afghanistan in order to enable its people to determine their own form of government and choose their economic, political and social systems free from outside intervention, subversion, coercion or constraint of any kind whatsoever . . .

Before the Security Council the Soviet Union argued that the Government of Afghanistan had over the previous two years repeatedly appealed to the Soviet Union for military assistance in order to repel armed intervention from the outside.[224] The military contingent was sent, he said, exclusively for this purpose and was based on the appropriate provisions

[220] *Keesing's*, p. 30229.

[221] The reactions of various States are summarized in *Keesing's*, p. 30233.

[222] The Resolution received thirteen affirmative votes, and the Soviet Union and East Germany voted against: UN Doc. S/13729, *Security Council Official Records*, 35th Year, Supplement (1980).

[223] GA Res. ES-6/2, adopted by 104–18–18. Subsequent General Assembly Resolutions have been passed deploring the intervention and the continuing presence of Soviet troops: 35/37 (1981); 37/37 (1982); 38/29 (1984).

[224] Security Council debate, 5 January 1980: UN Doc. S/PV.2185.

of a treaty between the two countries of 1978.[225] In a speech later that same day,[226] the Soviet delegate outlined the nature of the outside intervention: the placing of agents to foment internal counter-revolution, the training and arming of subversive groups and the use of Pakistan's territory to set up centres for this purpose. He then quoted from several western newspapers to support his assertions. The State of Afghanistan, represented by Mr Dost of the Karmal regime,[227] stated that Mr Amin, 'playing into the hands of US Imperialism' had engineered a plot resulting in the assassination of Mr Taraki, and that Mr Amin's regime had brought suffering to the people of Afghanistan. The threat that this posed to the April revolution, together with attacks from abroad, resulted in the rising of the 'Afghan national liberation army' on 27 December. He went on to say that the Soviet Union sent contingents to Afghanistan in response to a request by that country, initially made by Mr Taraki and repeated by Mr Amin. The main purpose, he said, was to remove the threats posed from abroad and to repel foreign armed attacks.[228]

With the exception of a few close allies of the Soviet Union who accepted the latter's version of events, the delegates of those countries who spoke before the Security Council and the General Assembly rejected these assertions. It is significant that the speeches did not focus upon the existence of a request or the authority of a particular person to make such a request to any great extent, but instead concentrated on an assessment of whether the rebellion in Afghanistan was in fact of an internal nature. It is true that several countries[229] discounted the possibility of a request having existed before the intervention because of the subsequent death of Mr Amin. One would not, they said, ask for aid in order to be oneself overthrown. However, these countries, as well as those who did not mention the alleged request, stressed the principle of non-intervention in the affairs of States, the right of a people to choose a government without outside interference, and in effect looked at the real purpose of intervening as the yardstick for assessment. They found that the rebellion was an expression of discontent by the Afghan people themselves and was thus an internal affair of Afghanistan. As the delegate of the UK stated, the Soviet troops were there in reality 'to quell a rebellious people'.[230] Saudi Arabia stated that the Soviet Union invaded Afghanistan 'to subdue opposition to an existing government and to install another authority subservient to the Soviet Union' and that this was

[225] Treaty of Friendship, 5 December 1978. The treaty states, *inter alia*, that the parties 'will consult together and with the consent of both parties, take appropriate measures in order to ensure the security, independence and territorial integrity of both countries'.

[226] UN Doc. S/PV.2186.

[227] Several countries, including the UK, stressed that the representation of the Karmal government before the Security Council did not imply recognition of that government.

[228] Security Council debate, 6 January 1980: UN Doc. S/PV.2187.

[229] Pakistan, China, UK, US, Singapore, Spain, Malaysia, Costa Rica, Liberia, Portugal, Panama, Zaïre and France.

[230] UN Doc. S/PV.2186.

an interference with the internal affairs of a State. The delegate of Italy, among others,[231] stated that the facts did not point to the existence of acts of subversion by third countries. He went on to say that the intervention 'represents open interference in a situation characterized by an internal conflict but not by foreign aggression', and that the people of a country must be able to decide their own destiny. Venezuela[232] stated that information on Afghanistan showed 'a struggle between various institutions and political and social currents'. This is, the delegate stated, 'part of an internal process to determine the political future of the country and should not be interfered with by external actions of the type denounced here'. These speeches specifically indicate the inadmissibility of the use of force to quell a popular rebellion and many other speeches refer to the right of a people to choose a government without outside interference and state that an interference of this type would be a breach of the principle of non-interference in internal affairs.[233] The delegate of Liberia further elaborated on why this was clearly an act of interference. He said that if there had been infiltrators from abroad, this could have been dealt with by a limited contigent on the southern border to prevent their continued entry. The mass use of troops thus indicated another purpose. Foreign armed intervention, he went on to say, cannot be used 'to crush the free political expression of the people'.[234]

The reliance of the Soviet Union on alleged outside interference and the arguments used by States in condemning the intervention do clearly further indicate a general norm of non-intervention prohibiting the repression of a rebellion genuinely stemming from popular discontent within the country.

(iv) *Grenada 1983*. Grenada became an independent State in 1974. By its written constitution, the Queen of the United Kingdom became nominal Head of State and was represented by a Governor-General[235] whose functions were largely ceremonial.[236] At the time of independence, the Prime Minister of Grenada was Sir Eric Gairy who continued in that office after the elections in 1976. It has been reported that although constitutionally elected, Gairy was corrupt and that he used a gang of armed retainers to intimidate critics.[237] On 13 March 1979 the New

[231] e.g. Liberia, the Netherlands, US, New Zealand, Senegal.

[232] Security Council debate, 6 January 1980: UN Doc. S/PV.2188.

[233] e.g. Pakistan, Japan, Egypt, Singapore, Norway, Spain, Liberia, Portugal, Netherlands, Jamaica, Zambia, Yugoslavia, Panama, Tunisia, Australia, France, West Germany. Also, before the General Assembly: Senegal, Sweden, Nigeria, Bangladesh, Austria, Ivory Coast, Bahrain, Oman, Morocco and others.

[234] Security Council debate, 6 January 1980: UN Doc. S/PV.2187.

[235] Constitution of Grenada, 7 February 1974, sections 19 and 57.

[236] See, e.g., sections 57–68 of the Constitution.

[237] A description is to be found in the Fifth Report of the Foreign Affairs Committee, *Parliamentary Papers*, 1981–2, House of Commons, Paper 47, in Annex B of the House of Commons Second Report of the Foreign Affairs Committee on Grenada, ibid., 1983–4, House of Commons, Paper

Jewel Movement led by Mr Bishop carried out a *coup d'état* and the new 'People's Revolutionary Government' suspended the constitution and carried out a series of reforms. Although he was personally popular in Grenada, Mr Bishop's left-wing politics and friendship with Fidel Castro of Cuba incurred increasing concern on the part of the US Government which then applied economic and diplomatic pressure on Grenada.[238] During the summer of 1983, increasing disagreement within the NJM Central Committee resulted in a decision, resisted by Mr Bishop, that power should be shared between Mr Bishop and Mr Coard. The crisis reached a head on 12 October 1983 when the committee voted to keep Mr Bishop under house arrest.[239] On 19 October 1983 a crowd of several thousand, led by the former Foreign Minister,[240] freed Mr Bishop from his house and then stormed the army garrison. When the army sent reinforcements, a number of people were killed, and Mr Bishop and several former Ministers were summarily executed. The same day the formation of a Revolutionary Military Council was announced, headed by Mr Austin, and this body imposed a shoot-on-sight curfew.

On 21 October 1983 the Organization of East Caribbean States[241] met in Barbados and informed representatives of Jamaica, Barbados, Trinidad, the UK and the US that military intervention was contemplated and that their countries were invited to participate. On Sunday, 23 October a formal written invitation was sent to the US Government by the OECS.[242] There are conflicting reports and a great deal of speculation as to when the US decided to intervene. It appears that a US task force bound for the Mediterranean was directed to the Caribbean on either 20[243] or 21 October,[244] and there appears to be evidence that the decision in the White House was made some time on Saturday, 22[245] or Sunday, 23 October.[246] The relevance of this speculation is that the

226, at p. xiv. See also *Grenada: A Parliamentary Report*, released by the Department of State and the Department of Defence, Washington DC (reprinted by the US Information Agency, December 1983).

238 Report of the Foreign Affairs Committee, loc. cit. (previous note), at pp. vi, xiv and xliv.

239 Ibid., p. ix, and Department of State Report, loc. cit. above (n. 237), pp. 9–21.

240 Mr Whiteman. The previous day, 18 October, five Ministers loyal to Mr Bishop resigned, and according to one unsubstantiated report Mr Bishop had been expelled from the party on 17 October and Mr Coard announced as Prime Minister: Department of State Report, loc. cit. above (n. 237), p. 21, and Report of the Foreign Affairs Committee, loc. cit. above (p. 234 n. 237), p. ix.

241 Member States are Antigua and Barbuda, Dominica, St Kitts, Nevis, St Lucia, St Vincent, the Grenadines with Montserrat.

242 The meetings of the OECS and other countries and surrounding events are described in the text of a speech delivered by Mr Adams, Prime Minister of Barbados, on television, Wednesday, 26 October. The text of the speech was kindly provided by the Barbados High Commission, London.

243 *The Economist*, 10 to 16 March 1984, p. 21.

244 Speech of the Prime Minister of Barbados (see above, n. 242).

245 *The Economist*, 10 to 16 March 1984, p. 32.

246 According to a report in the *Sunday Times*, 30 October 1983, the National Security Council had authorized the Pentagon to draw up a contingency plan on Thursday, 20 October, but the actual decision to go ahead took place on Sunday, 23 October, largely as a result of the frustration felt after the bombing of the US headquarters in Beirut that day.

Governor-General of Grenada was alleged to have invited the intervention of the US in conjunction with the OECS. However, according to his own account, he decided to agree to the intervention late on Sunday evening, 23 October, although he had told an official earlier that day that he was against military intervention.[247] The only written evidence of an invitation is one dated 24 October to the Prime Minister of Barbados which was apparently received after the intervention took place.[248] There is thus serious doubt as to whether the intervention, which took place on Tuesday, 25 October 1983, was as a result of an invitation by any authority in Grenada.[249] There is also the further legal problem of whether such an invitation, i.e. one given by a ceremonial Head of State directly against the interests and wishes of the *de facto* seat of power, could have any validity. It is not intended, in this article,[250] to delve into this particular question, but instead to study the justifications given for the intervention and diplomatic reaction to them.

At the Security Council Meeting held on 25 October 1983[251] the representative of the US justified the intervention essentially on two grounds, first, to protect US citizens on the island and, secondly, as a response to a request by the OECS. The following day the Prime Minister of Dominica and chairman of the OECS stated[252] that the Governor-General of Grenada had requested the intervention pursuant to Article 8 of the OECS Treaty providing for collective self-defence.[253] She said that the member States of OECS had been concerned over the extensive military build-up in Grenada over the last few years, and that such disproportionate military might in the hands of an unstable and brutal regime posed a serious threat to the security of the OECS countries. She went on to say that it was the intention of the OECS countries, once the threat was removed, to invite the Governor-General to assume executive authority pending elections. The other participating States spoke in a similar vein, for example:

Antigua and Barbuda

Backed by Cuban and communist troops, a few mad men seized power and foisted on the backs of our black brothers and sisters a revolutionary junta with Cubans and Russians as advisers. When the people gathered in large numbers

[247] Interview given by the Governor-General, Sir Paul Scoon, for BBC Television's *Panorama*, on Monday, 31 October: BBC transcript recorded from transmission.

[248] Report of the Foreign Affairs Committee, loc. cit. above (p. 234 n. 237), p. xvi.

[249] For further details as to events before and surrounding the intervention in Grenada, see Doswald-Beck, 'The Legality of the United States' Intervention in Grenada', *Netherlands International Law Review*, 31 (1984), p. 355, and *Indian Journal of International Law*, 24 (1984), p. 200.

[250] Cf. loc. cit. (previous note), at pp. 371–3 and 216–19 respectively, in which this particular question is considered. The issue was considered on the assumption that the traditional law permitting aid to suppress a rebellion as a result of an invitation by a government was still valid.

[251] Security Council debate, 25 October 1983: UN Doc. S/PV.2487.

[252] Security Council debate, 26 October 1983: UN Doc. S/PV.2489.

[253] For the relevant part of the letter requesting intervention, see text to n. 248, above, and loc. cit. above (n. 249), at pp. 370 and 216 respectively.

and removed Mr Bishop from house detention, the crowd was dispersed with shells and bullets. . . . This state of affairs constituted a serious threat to the security and peace of the region.[254]

St Lucia

It was the Governor-General of Grenada in whom executive authority in Grenada rests . . . who made a formal request to the Organization of Eastern Caribbean States (OECS), of which Grenada is a member, for assistance to remove what he saw as a threat to his people and what at that stage had also become a threat to our subregion.[255]

St Vincent and the Grenadines

The severity of the curfew imposed on Grenada convinced the member States of the OECS that the existing regime was unstable and its conduct unpredictable. We feared not only later reprisals that would have been imposed *en masse* against defenceless citizens of Grenada, but its ability to act aggressively against our own national interest.[256]

The Caribbean States thus stressed the need to use force by way of self-defence and that the request came from the constitutional authority who was, in effect, attempting to save the people from a repressive regime helped by other communist States. The United States subsequently further justified the intervention as being, in effect, necessary for its own defence. In an Address to the Nation on 27 October 1983 President Reagan stated that the amount of military equipment found on Grenada proved that a Cuban occupation of the island was planned, and that Grenada was thus about to become a Soviet–Cuban colony, being prepared as a 'major military bastion to export terror . . .'. He then stated that US security could be threatened in faraway places.[257]

With regard to State reaction to the intervention and justifications given, the vast majority of States, including the traditional allies of the US, characterized the intervention as illegal. It is particularly illuminating that, in the debates which followed, both in the Security Council and the General Assembly, the justification that the Governor-General requested the intervention is barely mentioned at all, and certainly no one, excepting the intervening States, made any effort to consider whether he had authority to request an intervention. Instead the delegates considered the justifications separately, and decided that not only were the US students in Grenada in no danger, but also that there was no need for any action in self-defence. Virtually every delegate who spoke

[254] Security Council debate, 26 October 1983: UN Doc. S/PV.2489.

[255] Security Council debate, 27 October 1983: UN Doc. S/PV.2491. See also an interview with Mr Compton, Prime Minister of St Lucia, in which he gives details as to how he feared the situation in Grenada would pose a threat to the other countries, including his own: *International Herald Tribune*, 21 November 1983.

[256] Security Council debate, 27 October 1983, UN Doc. S/PV.2491. See also similar statements by the delegate of Barbados at the same debate.

[257] *Weekly Compilation of Presidential Documents*, 21 October 1983, p. 1502.

stated that the intervention was a violation of the principle of non-intervention in internal affairs. Although some delegates showed sympathy from a moral viewpoint with the plight of the people of Grenada and the concerns of neighbouring countries, they none the less found the intervention to be an illegal interference in internal affairs.[258] With regard to direct statements on the nature of the norm of non-intervention, there are numerous statements to the effect that no country has the right to dictate the form of government of another country. Two statements, one by the Seychelles and the other by France,[259] speak of the need to show, *inter alia*, a request by the legitimate authorities of the country. Whether this would legitimate an intervention with no outside threat was not made clear. France preceded that statement, however, with the following assertion:

> France is devoted to respect for the principles of non-use of force in international relations and of non-intervention in the internal affairs of States and deeply deplores this armed intervention.[259]

These statements by France could be rationalized by her approach in Africa, i.e. the sending of help on request which does not involve direct military action against rebels unless there is an outside involvement. Other statements, however, are more consistent with a duty not to intervene and influence internal events in any circumstance. Thus, Thailand stated before the General Assembly that events in Grenada before the US action reflected unhealthy trends, but 'Whether we like it or not, and whether that course was one democratically chosen by the people or not, it was an internal matter for Grenada'.[260] There are also numerous general statements to the effect that the people of a country must be left to decide their own affairs, some of which have been already quoted above when considering the principle of self-determination.[261] When considering the principle of non-intervention in internal affairs, much stress was placed on the duty to settle disputes peacefully, the rule of non-use of force except in self-defence and the assertion that peoples cannot choose their own government in the presence of foreign armies:

Trinidad and Tobago

> We believe that the people of Grenada must be given a chance to resolve their problems in a context, not of fear and trepidation, but one in which they themselves will be able to see to their own affairs. They will not be able to do so if there are foreign armies on their soil.[262]

[258] See, e.g., speeches by the delegates of the UK, Netherlands and Chile, 27 October 1983: loc. cit. above (p. 237 n. 256).

[259] Both in Security Council debate, 26 October 1983, loc. cit. above (p. 237 n. 254).

[260] General Assembly debate on Grenada, Wednesday, 2 November 1983, 43rd meeting: UN Doc. A/38/PV.43.

[261] See text to pp. 204–5 nn. 73–7, and pp. 206–7 nn. 84–9, above.

[262] Loc. cit. above (n. 260).

Finland

The government of Finland has followed with concern the developments in Grenada which have led to the use of force and to outside interference in the internal affairs of that country. International disputes should be settled by peaceful means through negotiations without resorting to force which is prohibited in the Charter of the United Nations.[262]

Ethiopia

In the conspicuous absence of external aggression, the action taken by the US . . . cannot but constitute clear and direct intervention in the internal affairs of Grenada.[263]

China

The Chinese government consistently maintains that the affairs of a country should be handled exclusively by the people of that country, free from all outside interference . . . [the USA has] wantonly trampled underfoot the independence and territorial integrity of a sovereign State and intervened in its internal affairs.[264]

Although these statements are not necessarily conclusive evidence that aid to a government constitutes intervention in internal affairs, the general tenor of the debate, and those statements relating to self-determination, with their stress on lack of outside interference, would support a norm of total non-interference in civil strife. Additionally, it is to be noted that participating States continued the general pattern evident since 1956 of stressing outside involvement as a basis for intervening. The fact that third States reacted to the justification with these general statements, and in effect ignored the Governor-General's alleged invitation, must again indicate that a technical plea of invitation is not considered to be the crucial point, but rather whether there has, in fact, been an interference in the affairs of another State and with its people's total independence.[265]

3. *Peace-keeping forces in the Congo 1960–4 and in the Lebanon 1982–4*

It is not intended to study these peace-keeping forces at length as the issue of the type of force used by such troops is complicated by considerations peculiar to peace-keeping as such. Thus with regard to UN forces, institutional law becomes relevant, and questions relating to

[263] Loc. cit. above (p. 236 n. 251).

[264] Loc. cit. above (p. 236 n. 252). See also in particular statements by the delegates of the Congo, Sweden, Australia, Belgium and Canada in the General Assembly debates (loc. cit. above, p. 238 n. 260), and Security Council debates: on 25 October, Mexico, Guyana; 26 October, Algeria, Pakistan; 27 October, Ecuador, Malta, Venezuela, India, Yugoslavia, Colombia, Tanzania and Brazil.

[265] The General Assembly adopted a resolution condemning the intervention: Res. 38/7, adopted 2 November 1983 by 108–9–27. Those States which abstained explained their vote by stating that although they considered the action to be illegal, they wished that the Resolution had given some indication of the difficult situation on the island, and that the delegates had been able to debate the matter before voting.

the powers of the Secretary-General, and of the Security Council outside Chapter VII, as well as the meaning of Article 2 (7) of the Charter, fall outside the scope of this paper. With regard to the Multinational Forces deployed in Lebanon, the fact that they were designated as peace-keeping forces, and that four nations were involved, means that perceptions as to their function were bound to be affected. Thus statements relating to their competence will not be such strong evidence with respect to non-intervention as with the case of the more traditional example of a State intervening to help a beleaguered government against rebels. However, as these two particular peace-keeping operations became involved in internal fighting, a study of the principle of non-intervention would not be complete without some reference to their activities.

(i) *The Congo*. After the Congo became independent on 30 June 1960, a mutiny took place among the soldiers of the Congolese army and, amid general chaos, Belgium flew in paratroops in an attempt to restore order and supervise the evacuation of European nationals. On 12 July the Congolese leaders, Mr Kasavubu and Mr Lumumba, appealed to the UN for assistance to meet 'the external aggression' of the Belgian Government.[266] On 13 July a further telegram to the UN stressed that 'the purpose of the aid requested is not to restore the internal situation in the Congo, but rather to protect the national territory against acts of aggression committed by Belgian metropolitan troops'.[266] The Secretary-General of the UN, during and after the setting up of ONUC, consistently stressed the duty not to become involved in internal affairs. Thus in his First Report the Secretary-General stated that:

> The United Nations Units must not become parties in internal conflicts [and] . . . they cannot be used to enforce any specific political solution of pending problems or . . . influence the political balance decisive to such a solution.[267]

The same report reiterated the basic rule against the use of force except in self-defence, although, as has already been seen,[268] ONUC was later authorized to use force as a last resort to prevent civil war. Although ONUC did in practice become involved to some degree, the position was maintained throughout that the force would not become involved with controversy as to governmental representation, but would instead concentrate on maintaining international peace. This was expressly stated in a Security Council Resolution of 9 August 1960:

> The United Nations force in the Congo will not be a party to, or in any way intervene in or be used to influence the outcome of any internal conflict, constitutional or otherwise.[269]

266 UN Doc. S/4382.

267 First Report of the Secretary-General: UN Doc. S/4389.

268 See text p. 202 n. 62, above.

269 UN Doc. S/4426.

At the withdrawal of ONUC, the Secretary-General's report reaffirmed this position:

> The United Nations operation in the Congo at all times has scrupulously avoided intervention in the internal affairs of that country; it has not taken sides in political or constitutional differences . . .[270]

(ii) *Lebanon*. After the massacre in the Palestinian refugee camps of Sabra and Chatila in Beirut, the Multinational Forces (consisting of US, Italian and French troops, and later joined by a British contingent) were invited back to Beirut[271] to assist the Lebanese Government to restore law and order in the Beirut area and assure the safety of the civilian population there.[272] Lebanon at the time was a mosaic of military factions giving only token recognition to a central government. In most of the north and east, Syrian forces were in control, interspersed with detachments of Palestinians and National Movement militias. To the south were the Israelis who had invaded a few months previously and various Lebanese factions. From October 1982, the Lebanese Army attempted to take control of Beirut and its environs, but found itself increasingly fighting together with the Phalange militia against the combined forces of the Shiʿite Amal Movement and the Druse which were backed by the Syrians. The Multinational Forces found themselves fired upon several times but the US contingent, and to a lesser extent the French, became involved in the fighting in a way that exceeded normal expectations of action in self-defence. The problem was not only that the Phalange militia was led by the President's family, but also that the Army was commanded by a Maronite Christian. The impartiality of the Army was thus seriously questioned and indeed, later in the conflict, large-scale desertions took place by Muslim soldiers to the rebel factions.[273] From September 1983, the US began bombarding muslim positions, particularly in the Chouf mountains, and in that month, the French staged air strikes against Druse and Syrian targets. Throughout the operation, however, the US and French based their actions on self-defence.[274] In particular, a White House statement of 13 September asserted that the US would do what was necessary to defend itself but that they would not support operations by the Lebanese Army.[275] In the meantime, both the US and the Lebanese Governments blamed foreign forces for the fighting in

[270] Loc. cit. above (p. 202 n. 63), at p. 290, para. 139.

[271] September 1982.

[272] Exchange of Notes between the Government of the UK and the Government of the Lebanese Republic concerning the deployment of a British contingent to the Multinational Force in Lebanon, Beirut, 31 January 1983: Cmnd. 8823.

[273] *The Times*, 22 September 1983, and *Keesing's*, p. 32980.

[274] Statement of French Defence Minister of 22 September 1983 (*The Times*, 23 September 1983); US statements of 13 September (*The Times*, 14 September 1983), 19 September (*The Times*, 20 September 1983), 21 September (*The Times*, 22 September 1983).

[275] *The Times*, 14 September 1983.

Lebanon.[276] Indeed, the Lebanese Government and pro-Phalangist Christian newspapers asserted that the Lebanese Army was fighting foreigners and that there was no civil war![277] There was, however, serious criticism of the extent of US involvement which was not considered to be in keeping with the proper task of a peace-keeping force.[278] The Multinational Forces finally withdrew in March 1984, after the Lebanese Army and Phalange militia had in effect been defeated.

Statements relating to both these peace-keeping operations would support the notion that third parties should not become involved with internal political problems, and although the mandate of the Multinational Forces included the task of helping the Lebanese Army in Beirut, it was not generally accepted that it extended to active involvement with army action against the rebels. It is also interesting that 'foreign' involvement was stressed by both the Lebanese and the Congolese Governments in respect of their civil wars.

(b) *Theoretical Assessment*

The essential theoretical problem facing the acceptance of a norm forbidding aid to a government is caused by the basic principle that the government acts for the State. However, it is submitted that there is sufficient evidence that such a prohibitory norm does in fact exist and this must therefore be rationalized with other basic assumptions of international law. It is, in this author's opinion, not helpful to base such a norm on a 'right' of revolutionaries to rebel[279] as there is overwhelming evidence that such rebels, other than recognized national liberation movements, have no personality in international law.[280] It is not possible, therefore, for a State to owe a duty in law to such rebels not to intervene against them. The absolute prohibition against aid to such rebels is further evidence in this respect.[281]

With regard to self-determination it is conceded that *recognized* groups[282] do have a certain personality in international law and there is a

[276] White House statements of 12 September 1983 (*The Times*, 13 September 1983); statements by President Gemayel of 18 September 1983 (*The Times*, 19 September 1983).

[277] *The Times*, 20 September 1983.

[278] See the initiative for a cease-fire by UK, France and Italy, and concern expressed in this context, *The Times*, 24 September 1983. Also criticism by Mr Healey (Labour opposition party), who charged that the US was aiming to make Lebanon a protectorate run by the Christian minority and that a settlement ought to include a shift of power to the Muslims: *The Times*, 19 September 1983. The US Government was further criticized by many in Congress following a particularly heavy bombardment on 8 to 9 February 1984: *Keesing's*, pp. 32890–1.

[279] See, e.g., text to p. 200 n. 55, above.

[280] The *travaux préparatoires* to Geneva Protocol II additional to the Red Cross Conventions 1949 and relating to internal armed conflicts illustrate the fact that States in no way wanted there to be any appearance of personality being accorded to rebel movements and thus insisted that the term 'party' should not be included in the text.

[281] See text to pp. 190–1 nn. 11–15, above.

[282] These include principally the people within a State as one group, but also those peoples expressly indicated as entitled to self-government. 'Recognition' of the latter is usually effected by

duty not to jeopardize their independence. As explained earlier, however, the norm of self-determination is essentially negative in its effect, i.e. it involves the duty not to impose a foreign government on recognized groups. As decolonization is completed, the norm becomes increasingly synonymous with a duty not to impose a foreign government on the people of another State. However, despite the fact that the norm is largely negative in its effect, it can be seen as forming a basis for non-intervention with the recognized group as the recipient of the legal duty not to intervene. In particular it strengthens and complements the principle of non-intervention in the internal affairs of States, which, in this author's opinion, has a sounder theoretical basis, particularly as the identification of the recipient of the duty does not pose the same problem as with self-determination.

The duty not to intervene in the civil strife of another State can only be rationalized by perceiving the recipient of the duty as the State *in abstracto*. The personality of the State as such thus holds the right and for the purpose of this norm the government does not exclusively represent the State. As the representative of Peru stated in the Security Council following the Soviet invasion of Hungary:

> . . . the United Nations admitted Hungary as a nation; it regarded Hungary as a moral and international entity and in admitting Hungary, it was thinking not of some particular government or regime representing a government but of the international personality of Hungary.[283]

The personality of the State, having as its components territory and people, could thus be represented by a body other than the regime in power, if that body is perceived as more truly representing the State, as is the case now with Kampuchea. Such a body would be in a position to complain of the breach of the duty of non-intervention against the State. It is probably because of the lack of an identifiable body to represent the State that this is not being done in respect of Afghanistan.[284] A successor government would also be able to bring a claim in law against another State on the basis that it had violated international law by keeping in power a previous regime in the face of a popular insurrection.

Third States might arguably be seen as beneficiaries of a duty not to interfere in civil strife, although whether they would have sufficient *locus standi* to bring a legal claim against an intervening State is debatable. The famous *obiter dictum* of the International Court of Justice relating to 'obligations *erga omnes*'[285] has yet to be applied in practice. The Court

UN Resolutions which have been approved by a large majority and which are repeated until the said group achieves self-government or association with a neighbouring country. An organization may be accepted as representing the 'people', e.g. the PLO for the Palestinians, and SWAPO for the Namibians.

[283] 752nd meeting of the Security Council, 2 November 1956.

[284] See, e.g., *International Herald Tribune*, 28 May 1985.

[285] *Barcelona Traction, Light and Power Co.* case (*Belgium* v. *Spain*). *ICJ Reports*, 1970, p. 3, at paras. 33–4.

specifically mentioned the outlawing of acts of aggression as such an obligation and one would need to assess whether intervention in civil strife amounts to aggression in this sense. The subject is not directly dealt with in the General Assembly Resolution on the definition of aggression, or in Resolutions 2131 (xx) and 2625 (xxv). There is a fairly widespread view that the duty of non-intervention is implicit in Article 2 (4) as 'political independence' implies free and unhampered development for States,[286] and intervention might thus be said to amount to aggression. The subject has not, however, received extensive examination, and given the persistent disagreements as to the exact meaning of aggression, particularly with regard to the relevance of motive,[287] it is not intended to explore the issue further here.

As to whether the norm of non-intervention is a part of Article 2 (4), regardless of whether it also amounts to an act of aggression, it would seem unlikely that an action to aid a government against rebels was perceived as contrary to Article 2 (4) when it was drafted, given the fact that generally accepted customary law at that time did not forbid it. Such a prohibition has therefore arisen as a newly developed and separate customary norm and tends to be referred to as such, although it is, of course, possible for the interpretation of Article 2 (4) to evolve so as to include a wide prohibition against intervention. One would have to rely on the words 'political independence' to encompass such a rule as a government is, of course, perfectly entitled to invite lawful military assistance which does not violate the norms of self-determination and non-intervention in internal affairs. The final issue which must be considered is whether a State can intervene to help a government against rebels on the basis of a treaty concluded between the States authorizing such action.

(c) *Treaties Authorizing Intervention for the Purpose of Maintaining a Form of Government*

There is very scant consideration of this issue among writers, most discussion being centred around the existence or otherwise of the doctrine of *jus cogens* when considering the legality of treaties authorizing the use of force. There would appear to be agreement that, on the assumption that *jus cogens* is a valid category, treaties authorizing an act of aggression would be invalid. This would beg the question of whether a breach of the rule of non-intervention in internal affairs amounts to aggression, or is a breach of some other peremptory norm generally recognized as one from which no derogation is permitted.

Writers seem to be divided in their opinions as to the status of such treaties or of provisions to that effect in treaties: certain writers have

[286] See, in particular, the Report of the Special Committee on Principles of International Law concerning Friendly Relations and Co-operation among States, loc. cit. above (p. 210 n. 100), at para. 216.

[287] See p. 190 n. 8, above.

expressed the view that such interventions are legitimate,[288] whilst Brownlie would appear to express serious doubt in this respect by linking the question to intervention in civil war in general.[289] Oppenheim, whilst admitting that there was opinion to the contrary, supports the validity of such treaties:

> A State that has guaranteed by treaty the form of government of another State, or the reign of a certain dynasty over the same, has a right to intervene in case of a change in the form of government or of the dynasty, provided that the treaty of guarantee was concluded between the respective States and not between their monarchs personally.[290]

Other writers who would appear to support the validity of such a treaty are Thomas and Thomas, and Winfield. They argue that a treaty of this type would not be valid if concluded during a civil war, because it would be done without the acquiescence of a considerable number of citizens.[291] On the other hand, they appear to support the validity of such a treaty if it was concluded when the government was stable. Winfield stated that such treaties, although politically unwise, were sufficiently common in the past (albeit often evaded), and that an individual State can waive the right of non-intervention. His reasoning and assertion, however, can now be seriously questioned in the light of a statement he made immediately prior to his consideration of treaties authorizing intervention. He expressed the view that certain treaties are illegal, such as those sanctioning slave trading, because they would amount to an 'international crime' and a 'breach of an absolute duty' the right of which is resident in the members of the international circle.[292] Keeping in mind the fact that his article was published in 1924, it is more than possible that developments in the law relating to armed conflict since that date would have led him to conclude that treaties sanctioning intervention are similarly illegal.

The reasoning given by Thomas and Thomas also needs careful scrutiny. They begin by outlining the views of Hodges[293] and Hall[293] who maintain that such treaties would be illegitimate, as their object is to violate a principle of international law. The principle referred to is the independence and sovereignty of States which would be compromised by such a treaty. Thomas and Thomas, on the other hand, challenge this reasoning by pointing out that a State is free to give up part of its independence, or extinguish it altogether by, for example, a voluntary merger into another State. It would be a strange conclusion, they go on to say, if a State could not consent to a less drastic curtailment of its

[288] e.g. Hall, *A Treatise on International Law* (6th edn., 1909), pp. 285–6; Hodges, *The Doctrine of Intervention* (1915), pp. 37–8; Stowell, *Intervention in International Law* (1921), p. 439.

[289] Op. cit. above (p. 195 n. 32), pp. 321 and 327.

[290] Op. cit. above (p. 191 n. 18), at p. 309.

[291] Winfield, 'The Grounds of Intervention in International Law', this *Year Book*, 5 (1924), p. 149 at pp. 157–8; Thomas and Thomas, op. cit. above (p. 196 n. 36).

[292] Loc. cit. (previous note), at p. 155.

[293] Op. cit. above (n. 288).

sovereignty. Although at first sight, this would seem a powerful argument, it is submitted that it is specious. There is no norm of international law prohibiting a voluntary merger of a State with another, but there is a norm prohibiting actions contrary to Article 2 (4) of the UN Charter and prohibiting intervention in the internal affairs of States. This is because States have an interest in preventing the illegal use of force between States, whereas they have no such interest relating to mergers, unless they are created by the use of force, as was the case with Libya and Chad in 1981. Thomas and Thomas then conclude that the illegality of consent to such a treaty 'is not in accord with usage or with law'.[294] It is submitted that such a conclusion is to be questioned, not only because of the fallacy of their argument, but also because practice is at best equivocal with regard to such treaties. There are indeed many treaties providing for intervention, but they tend to specify third party involvement as a basis for such intervention.[295] Further, some States have questioned the legality of such a treaty provision on the grounds that it would contravene Article 2 (4) of the Charter and that the Charter must prevail over other inconsistent treaties by virtue of Article 103. It has also been argued that it would be void following the doctrine of *jus cogens*, and that it would contravene the principles of non-intervention in the internal affairs of States and self-determination.[296]

An example of a recent intervention, allegedly on the basis of a treaty guaranteeing a type of government, was that by Turkey in Cyprus in 1974. On its independence, a Treaty of Guarantee was signed between Cyprus, on the one hand, and Greece, Turkey and the UK, on the other, to ensure the independence of Cyprus and to guarantee its Constitution. Article I of the Treaty stipulates the prohibition of activity on the part of Cyprus leading either to union with any State or to partition of the island. It also states that Cyprus undertakes to ensure 'respect for its Constitution'. The rights and obligations of the guarantors are set out in Article IV of the Treaty which reads as follows:

> In the event of a breach of the provisions of the present Treaty, Greece, Turkey and the United Kingdom undertake to consult together with respect to the representations or measures necessary to ensure observance of those provisions. In so far as common concerted action may not prove possible, each of the three guaranteeing Powers reserves the right to take action with the sole aim of re-establishing the state of affairs created by the present Treaty.

Cyprus has on several occasions argued before the UN that this treaty is a violation of its right to self-determination as it was forced upon it as

[294] Op. cit. above (p. 196 n. 36).

[295] See, for example, Brownlie, op. cit. above (p. 195 n. 32), at pp. 319–20, and also the treaties referred to by the Soviet Union in relation to her intervention in Afghanistan, the US in relation to her invasion of Grenada, and France's treaties with African countries: above, p. 220.

[296] Panama, Security Council debate on Afghanistan, 7 January 1980: UN Doc. S/PV.2190; Senegal, General Assembly 6th Emergency Special Session, 10 to 14 January 1980; Cyprus, below, pp. 247–8.

a condition of independence. It has further argued that is also amounts to an interference in its internal affairs and that Article IV, in particular, is invalid as it might be interpreted so as to authorize unilateral intervention by any of the guaranteeing powers. Cyprus argued this in particular before the Security Council in 1963 after the outbreak of communal violence, but the Security Council abstained from expressing an opinion on the validity of the Treaty.[297]

The events in 1974 began with the seizure of power on 15 July 1974 by Mr Sampson from Archbishop Makarios, who called for a meeting of the Security Council to consider the crisis. There was a great deal of evidence that the Greek military Government was behind the coup, and the Sampson government consisted mostly of people who favoured union with Greece (Enosis).[298] On 20 July Turkey invaded the country and after a few days captured a triangle of territory amounting to about 40 per cent of the island. The Security Council met in emergency session that day[299] and Turkey defended the intervention on the basis of the Treaty of Guarantee, as being necessary following Greece's interference in Cyprus which amounted to a violation of the treaty. The representative of Cyprus condemned the intervention as an act of aggression and argued that it could not be defended by reference to the treaty:

> With regard to . . . the words in the Treaty of Guarantee: 'In so far as common or concerted action may not prove possible', of course I do not for a moment think that common and concerted action by the three guarantors to protect independence or territorial integrity carries the meaning that these three would act together by using their aircraft and battleships to invade Cyprus and bomb it . . . Those words 'concerted action' mean lawful action, peaceful action, through measures of representation, through the Security Council and through other means, not through aggression, which under the Charter of the United Nations is forbidden. There should be no use of force except in self-defence . . . Therefore the words 'concerted action' mean lawful action. In consequence, when the Treaty says, 'When concerted action may not prove possible, each of the guarantors reserves its right to take action', it means lawful action. It does not mean that each of them has the right to invade Cyprus . . .[299]

Cyprus' arguments were developed in greater detail before the General Assembly Special Political Committee:[300]

> Turkey, in an attempt to mollify international public opinion and to cover up its crime against peace, has invoked the legal fiction of having purportedly acted under the so-called Treaty of Guarantee of 1960. The said Treaty, however, does not and would not give such a right of military intervention by force as it

[297] See in particular Schwelb, 'Some Aspects of International *Jus Cogens* as formulated by the International Law Commission', *American Journal of International Law*, 61 (1967), at pp. 952–3.

[298] *Keesing's*, pp. 26662 and 26664.

[299] Security Council debate, 20 July 1974: UN Doc. S/PV.1781.

[300] *General Assembly Official Records*, 29th Session, Special Political Committee, 922nd and 923rd meetings (29 October 1974).

would then, by coming into conflict with the basic provisions of the Charter of the United Nations, be invalidated under Article 103 of the Charter.[301]

He then went on to state that in any case Turkey did not intervene to re-establish the constitutional order, but to partition the island, and that this was obvious from the way in which it drove out the Greek Cypriot inhabitants from the captured territory and its administration of the said territory.

The reaction of third States to the Turkish intervention was confined to a general condemnation of any interference in internal affairs, and the validity of the Treaty of Guarantee was not assessed by the delegates. There was generally a recognition that Greece was partly responsible for the crisis, but already in the Security Council debate of 20 July, when Turkish motives could have been perceived in a favourable light, the general reaction was to disapprove of the military action. For example, the delegate of the UK spoke as follows:

> My government deplores the pressures and interventions which contributed to the Turkish action on Cyprus, and for which Greece must bear a heavy share of the responsibility. However, this invasion in no way serves the hopes for peace of the Turkish community on Cyprus, or indeed the cause of peace in the world. Neither can we be convinced that foreign military intervention in Cyprus, from whatever quarter and by whatever means, has at any time been justifiable. We oppose any intervention in the internal affairs of a member State of the United Nations.[302]

France, the only third party to mention the treaty, expressed the opinion that the intervention was contrary to its provisions:

> We cannot but deplore the delays which took place and which prevented concerted action on the part of the Council, and which incited one of the parties to violate one of the provisions of the Treaty of Guarantee and to resort to force in order to preserve interests which should have been preserved by peaceful means.[302]

The Soviet Union's initial statement appeared to condone Turkish action in that the delegate stressed Greek military interference as the cause of the situation and the necessity of restoring the constitutional arrangements in Cyprus and the Government headed by Archbishop Makarios.[302] However, the Soviet Union supported the Security Council Resolution[303] calling for the withdrawal of all foreign troops, and at a later meeting of the Security Council, condemned the continuing presence of foreign troops:

> . . . Resolution 353 (1974) must be implemented in all its parts and all its provisions. That is the only way to put an end to foreign intervention in the internal affairs of the Republic of Cyprus and to give the Cypriots, both Turkish

[301] Special Political Committee, 923rd meeting.
[302] Security Council debate, 20 July 1974: UN Doc. S/PV.1781.
[303] Security Council Res. 353: see below, p. 249 n. 307.

and Greek, the opportunity freely to decide their own destiny and their own affairs.[304]

Other States who spoke at the Security Council meeting of 20 July generally condemned both the Greek intervention against the constitutional Government of Cyprus and the Turkish intervention. The delegate of Costa Rica, in particular, lamented the lack of Security Council action before 20 July and said:

> Perhaps such action . . . might have sufficed so as not to have to deplore at this stage the Turkish intervention on the island, which my delegation in no way accepts nor can justify, because whatever the reasons for which it was carried out they in no way attenuate the character of an unjustified violation of the territorial integrity of another State.[305]

With regard to the status of the Cyprus Constitution, the statements of delegates do not give a consistent picture. Some, such as Iraq and Mauritius,[305] expressly approved the need to restore the constitutional order of Cyprus but without condoning the Turkish action. Others, such as Indonesia and Kenya,[305] stressed the fact that the problems of Cyprus must be solved by the Cypriot people without the military involvement of foreign elements influencing the outcome. India appeared by implication to disapprove of the Treaty of Guarantee as a concept:

> It is a dangerous concept to sanction external intervention in an independent State on the grounds of ethnic or religious affinities. The future of Cyprus, its constitutional arrangements and so forth are, in our opinion, for the people of Cyprus themselves to determine, in conditions of peace, freedom and democracy.[306]

On 20 July the Security Council passed Resolution 353, calling on 'all States to respect the sovereignty, independence and territorial integrity of Cyprus' and demanding 'an immediate end to foreign military intervention in the Republic of Cyprus that is in contravention of [those] provisions . . .'.[307] A later resolution adopted on 16 August 1974[308] recorded its 'formal disapproval of the unilateral military actions undertaken against the Republic of Cyprus', thereby in effect condemning the Turkish intervention.

The Cyprus affair is an interesting event to consider because the Treaty of Guarantee was aimed at preserving a democratic constitutional structure which gave appropriate representation to the two populations on the island. It was thus not in the same category as a treaty to preserve a 'dynasty', the very word being somewhat old-fashioned in connotation,

[304] Security Council debate, 27 July 1974: UN Doc. S/PV.1785.

[305] Security Council debate, 20 July 1974: UN Doc. S/PV.1781.

[306] Security Council debate, 27 July 1974: UN Doc. S/PV.1785.

[307] Adopted unanimously on 20 July 1974.

[308] Res. 360 adopted by 11–0–3 (abstaining Soviet Union, Byelorussian Soviet Socialist Republic, Iraq; China did not participate in voting).

or a 'government', which could include the most unrepresentative of regimes. Further, the Turkish intervention took place after an undisputed breach of the treaty involving interference in Cyprus by Greece. Despite these political and legal points in favour of the Turkish action, it is interesting that the general reaction was one of disapproval even before Turkey began to partition the island, and the Soviet Union based its initial stand on the prior Greek intervention.

There is thus a strong presumption against military action in another country which may be seen as an intervention in internal affairs, and in the light of this, a treaty authorizing intervention to support any regime is of dubious worth. Whether such a treaty is void by reason of *jus cogens* is a more difficult question, and the doctrine has yet to be applied in judicial practice. It is not intended, in this article, to consider in detail the doctrinal merits, or otherwise, of Article 103 of the Charter, or of the theory of *jus cogens*, which has been debated fully in other works. It would seem to this author, however, that an appropriate test is an assessment of whether a judicial body, in particular the International Court of Justice, would sanction a treaty authorizing military intervention in another State. If, by way of conjecture, States A and B conclude a treaty to invade State C, and after a change of heart State B no longer wishes to abide by the treaty, this author would consider it very unlikely that the Court would find State B in breach of the treaty and order appropriate reparation for State A. A treaty between States A and B to maintain a form of government in B is different from the above in that B is a party to the treaty. However, as the norm of non-intervention in internal affairs is directed at the protection of the State in the abstract, and excludes for this purpose the government of any moment from representing the State, it is arguable that the State as such cannot be seen as agreeing to such intervention. The principle of non-intervention is also closely linked with the principle of self-determination, which would also be violated if such an intervention were directed against a major rebellion so as, in effect, to keep a government in place at the will of the intervening State. Such a treaty is not so different, in effect, from Winfield's example of a treaty sanctioning slave-trading.[309] It is to be seriously doubted that the International Court of Justice would order reparation for State A if State B reneged on a treaty obligation between the two countries to supply slaves from State B to State A. Although necessarily conjecture, it is submitted that the likelihood of such a treaty being declared void is quite high. A treaty authorizing military intervention to maintain a form of government could be viewed with equal disfavour, in particular if its effect is to create a domination by the intervening State against the other, or if all constitutional change in a State is rendered impossible.

[309] Text to p. 245 n. 292, above.

V. Conclusion

It is submitted that there is, at the least, a very serious doubt whether a State may validly aid another government to suppress a rebellion, particularly if the rebellion is widespread and seriously aimed at the overthrow of the incumbent regime. The combination of Resolutions 2131 (xx) and 2625 (xxv), taking into account the motivation behind these resolutions, of the fact that States justify such interventions on the basis of prior outside intervention, and of the number of statements stressing true independence, self-determination and non-intervention in internal affairs, provides substantial evidence to support a theory that intervention to prop up a beleaguered government is illegal. Although it is true that occasions have occurred in which States have given such aid, the reaction to such interventions indicates the need to show effective involvement by a third State. In the case of Afghanistan in particular, States were unconvinced that substantial subversion was proved, mere propaganda or the obtaining of arms in third countries not being, it seems, enough. This is supported by the example of US action in the Lebanon in 1958 when the members of the Security Council were interested in establishing whether men and arms were being infiltrated from Syria into Lebanon. The same would be true of the other fact situations reviewed. An alternative defence to intervention would be the assertion by the intervening State that aid is limited to arms and/or advice and that it does not involve direct action against the rebels. This was stated to be the case by France when giving military aid to the Government of Chad. In this context, it is to be noted that there appears to be no prohibition against States providing governments with weapons and other military supplies during a civil war, and thus the norm of non-intervention does not put governments and rebels on exactly the same footing.

It might be argued that States justify their interventions on the basis of self-defence in order to provide an extra excuse and thus be more acceptable politically. It is submitted, however, that the consistency of this practice has by now hardened into a legal requirement and the view that self-defence is the only justification for the individual use of force in the Charter is strengthened by the new customary norm of non-intervention in internal affairs. Another possible objection could be the view that statements by States are a less secure basis for international customary law than their actions. This assertion must be viewed in the light of the fact that events are very differently perceived by different observers. As international law is principally auto-interpretative, each State will act according to its own perception of the facts, which may be very different from that of another State. Statements as to the law, however, provide a more secure basis for an identifiable norm, provided that such statements are made as assertions of *lex lata* rather than *lex ferenda*. The latter category would include standards which are vaguely agreed to be striven for, such as certain human rights and especially those pertaining to economic development. So-called 'soft law' and 'lip-service' can be distinguished from *opinio juris* in that the latter relates to rights and duties immediately applicable and having concrete legal effects. Further, some violations of the law are not going to eliminate the existence of that law, whereas consistent opposite behaviour will render the alleged norm 'lip-service' rather than customary law. Much human rights 'law' is unfortunately in the former category, whereas it is submitted that States are not in practice supporting tottering governments as a pattern of normal behaviour and the weight of normative statements against such behaviour would indicate the existence of a customary law to that effect.[310]

With regard to the origin of the norm of non-intervention in internal affairs, this can best be seen, in this author's opinion, in the *travaux préparatoires* to Resolution 2131. The ideological differences between the East and West blocs and the support by the former of rebel movements attempting to reject the yoke of colonialism[311] gave rise to an interest in the 1950s and 1960s in seeing the success of certain rebellions against established governments. The principle of non-intervention in internal affairs is, in effect, an attempt to limit outside neo-colonial attempts to influence events in other countries for the interests of the intervening country. The policy behind the norm is a recognition that countries intervene in practice for their own benefit and major powers have an interest in not allowing the influence of an adversary power to be strengthened in this way. The policy interest of weaker countries is self-evident as well as the general wish to avoid the escalation of violence. It is to be expected, however, that these norms will be broken when a State considers it imperative to do so in certain circumstances, or when it considers that it can be got away with, but this is quite normal with any legal system and does not in itself derogate from the norm when that norm is clearly expressed and not in doubt. It is submitted that this is the case with the law of non-intervention in internal affairs.

The effect of this new customary law is to revolutionize the traditional law, which held that a State can intervene to help a government suppress a rebellion unless belligerency is declared. It has already been argued that the doctrine of belligerency may well have fallen into desuetude and in this author's opinion, the old formulation has been totally replaced by the new law of non-intervention in internal affairs. It is this that now regulates intervention in civil war and represents the modern law.

[310] There have been the occasional statements to the contrary and these have been indicated in the text. However, they are remarkably few considering the fact that traditional textbooks affirm a right to help a government to suppress a rebellion. Total consistency cannot be expected but the great bulk of statements are in favour of total non-interference by military means.

[311] The Soviet Union having an interest in reducing the power and influence of the Western States.

NON-GOVERNMENTAL INTERFERENCES WITH HUMAN RIGHTS*

By M. FORDE[1]

I. INTRODUCTION

Human rights are values to which human beings are entitled and include respect for their individual humanity, freedom of choice as to how they should spend their lives, equality of treatment and of opportunity, and access to the means by which they can enjoy health, knowledge, affection, wealth and power. While governments are the most flagrant violators of these rights, individuals and non-governmental entities can cause extensive deprivations of them too. Individuals, either acting alone or in concert with others, kill, maim, enslave, incarcerate, humiliate and economically damage fellow human beings. There are Churches that bar women from access to the higher religious offices, and private clubs that exclude women from membership. Ethnic, religious and political discrimination by employers, professional associations and educational institutions is not unknown today. And the press, radio, television, private police forces and detective agencies persistently infringe on privacy. Like most rules of customary and conventional international law, those contained in international human rights conventions are aimed primarily at governmental violations of guaranteed freedoms. This article considers the status of non-governmental, or private, interferences with such freedoms.[2]

II. NATIONAL CONSTITUTIONAL LAW

States with human rights provisions in their constitutions have been confronted with a similar question, viz. whether private individuals and organizations, as well as the State and other public bodies, must respect those guarantees. In some countries, such as the United States of America, the entrenched rights as a rule may be invoked only against governmental acts. In others, such as the Federal Republic of Germany, private actors can also be obliged to respect those rights. In still other countries, for example the Eastern European communist States and, until very recently, France, human rights guarantees may be invoked against administrative and private action but they do not constrain the supreme form of

[1] Lecturer in Law, University College, Dublin.

[2] Little has been written so far on this important question. See Eissen, *Nordisk Tidsskrift for International Ret*, 32 (1962), p. 230; Drzemczewski, *European Human Rights Convention in Domestic Law* (1983), chap. 8; Eissen in *René Cassin Amicorum Discipulorumque Liber* (1971), vol. 3, pp. 151–62; and Sohn, *American University Law Review*, 32 (1982), at pp. 31–2.

governmental action, viz. legislation. Accordingly, it is instructive to consider briefly the general position under national Bills of Rights before examining the international conventions.[3]

(a) *The United States of America*

The US Bill of Rights, which takes the form of amendments to the US Constitution,[4] has had an enormous influence on the contents and functions of national Bills of Rights—and not merely in countries where the US wields considerable political influence. The most striking feature of the US Bill of Rights, and one which the English Bill of Rights of 1688[5] and the French Declaration of the Rights of Man and of the Citizen of 1789[6] did not share, is that it empowers a bench of judges to strike down as void legislation that contravenes the entrenched guarantees.[7] Another notable feature is that its provisions have been perceived as affording protection against governmental interferences with the enumerated freedoms but not against private prima facie interferences.[8] For example, prior to the enactment of the US Civil Rights Act of 1964[9] there were some US trade unions which, though representing black workers, refused to admit them into membership. When this practice was challenged, a Federal Court of Appeals ruled that the Constitution's 'due process' clause, which *inter alia* proscribes racial discrimination, could have no application to the practices of essentially private organizations, such as trade unions.[10]

There is some support for outcomes such as this both in the history and in the very terms of the US Bill of Rights. The first nine Amendments were adopted in response to widespread demands at the ratification debates on the 1787 constitutional instrument for entrenched protections for the individual. Whereas the 1787 document safeguarded the prerogatives of the several States of the federation, it was felt that individual freedom too should be guaranteed against a potentially over-mighty federal government. Thus in 1833 when a form of expropriation without compensation by a State Government was challenged as a violation of the Fifth Amendment's guarantee of private property, the Supreme Court ruled that this Amendment 'must be understood as restraining the power of the

[3] See Horan, *International and Comparative Law Quarterly*, 25 (1976), p. 848.

[4] But some human rights provisions are contained in the original body of the Constitution: Articles I (9) (ii) and (iii) and (10) (i), and III (2) (iii) and 3 (ii).

[5] 1 Wm. & Mary, Session 2, chap. 2.

[6] Incorporated originally into the French Constitution of 3 September 1791. For text, see Debbasch and Pontier, *Les Constitutions de la France* (1983), pp. 8–10.

[7] *Marbury* v. *Madison* (1803), 5 US (1 Cranch) 137.

[8] See Tribe, *American Constitutional Law* (1978), chap. 18, and Gunther, *Cases and Materials on Constitutional Law* (10th edn., 1980), chap. 11.

[9] Now 42 US Code 5 section 2000e–2 (c).

[10] *Oliphant* v. *Brotherhood of Locomotive Firemen and Enginemen* (1956), 156 F Supplement 89, aff'd. (1958), 262 F 2d 359, cert. denied (1959), 359 US 935. See Wellington, *Yale Law Journal*, 70 (1961), p. 345, and *United Brotherhood of Carpenters and Joiners* v. *Scott*, 77 L Ed. 2d 1049 (1983).

general [i.e. federal] government, [but] not as applicable to the States'.[11] The very terms of some of the early Amendments underline the fact that they were principally if not exclusively directed against federal action; the First Amendment stipulates that 'Congress shall make no law' against free speech, etc.,[12] and the Seventh Amendment's guarantee of a right to jury trial in civil actions is addressed only to the federal courts.[13]

The post-Civil War Amendments, on the other hand, were addressed to State and, more recently, to both State and federal action.[14] Ever since the *Civil Rights* cases,[15] these provisions have been construed as having no application to mere private prima facie interferences with the protected interests. Mr Justice Bradley said there, with regard to the Fourteenth Amendment:

> It is State action of a particular character that is prohibited. Individual invasion of individual rights is not the subject-matter of the amendment . . . It nullifies and makes void all State legislation, and State action of every kind, which impairs the privileges and immunities of citizens of the United States, or which injures them in life, liberty or property without due process of law, or which denies to any of them the equal protection of the laws . . . Positive rights and privileges are undoubtedly secured by the Fourteenth Amendment; but they are secured by way of prohibition against State laws and State proceedings affecting those rights and privileges . . .[16]

The courts, however, have grafted a number of qualifications on to this 'State action' doctrine, which can only be very imperfectly summarized here.

The constitutional guarantees apply to an ostensibly private actor who performs what in fact is essentially a public function. For instance, in *Marsh* v. *Alabama*,[17] Jehovah's Witnesses who were distributing religious literature refused to leave the sidewalk of a privately owned company town, for which they were prosecuted for criminal trespass. The US Supreme Court upheld the contention that their constitutional right to religious freedom had thereby been denied. The Court took the view that private property used as a town not unlike 'ordinary' towns becomes public or State property for the purpose of the constitutional guarantee. In the words of Mr Justice Black:

> the circumstance that the property rights . . . here involved . . . were held by others than the public, is not sufficient to justify the State's permitting a [private]

[11] *Barron* v. *Baltimore* (1833), 32 US (7 Pet.) 243.

[12] But cf. Crosskey, *Politics and the Constitution in the History of the United States* (1953), pp. 1056–82.

[13] This right has not been extended via the Fourteenth Amendment to actions in State courts.

[14] The Thirteenth Amendment, which forbids slavery and involuntary servitude, might be regarded as an exception to this pattern.

[15] (1883), 109 US 3.

[16] Ibid. at p. 11. For an account of the repercussions of this decision on the federal legislative power, see Frantz, *Yale Law Journal*, 73 (1964), p. 1353, and Gunther, op. cit. above (p. 254 n. 8), chap. 11, section 3.

[17] (1946), 326 US 501.

corporation to govern a community of citizens so as to restrict their fundamental liberties and the enforcement of such restraint by the application of a State statute.[18]

Secondly, private conduct in which the State involves itself extensively is subject to the constitutional constraints. In *Burton* v. *Wilmington Parking Authority*,[19] for example, the defendant public authority owned and managed a car-park which included spaces for letting to business enterprises in order to make the park fully self-supporting. One space was let to a restaurateur, who installed most of the equipment necessary to convert it into a restaurant. He refused to serve blacks, who then claimed that their constitutional right to the 'equal protection of the laws' had been violated. Overruling the State court, the Supreme Court held that the racial discrimination here was backed by sufficient State action to trigger the constitutional guarantee. According to Mr Justice Clark

> By its inaction, the Authority, and through it the State, has not only made itself a party to the refusal of service [to blacks], but has elected to place its power, property and prestige behind the admitted discrimination. The State has so far insinuated itself into a position of interdependence with [the restaurant] that it must be recognized as a joint participant in the challenged activity, which, on that account cannot be considered to have been so 'purely private' as to fall within the scope of [the equal protection guarantee].[20]

(b) *France and Eastern Europe*

The French Constitution of 1958[21] states in its preamble that '[t]he French people solemly proclaim their attachment to the Rights of Man . . . as they are defined by the Declaration of 1789 and completed by the Preamble to the Constitution of 1946 . . .' . Therefore, apart from the references in the 1958 instrument to equality before the law and the right to vote, the guarantee that political parties and groups shall have freedom of action, and the Article 66 proscription on arbitrary detention, the substance of the French 'Bill of Rights' is contained in the 1789 Declaration of the Rights of Man and of the Citizen[22] and in the preamble to the 1946 Constitution.[23] In at least two respects the French Bill of Rights differs fundamentally from the American model, and indeed has more in common with the human rights guarantees in the constitutions of the Eastern European communist States.

The rights enumerated are not confined to what may be called the traditional civil liberties (such as equality, freedom of expression and of association, etc.), which are capable of being given a relatively precise

[18] *Marsh* v. *Alabama* (1946), 326 US 501 at p. 509. Cf., e.g., *Hudgens* v. *NLRB* (1976), 424 US 507.
[19] (1961), 365 US 715.
[20] Ibid. at p. 725. Cf., e.g., *Moose Lodge No. 107* v. *Irvis* (1972), 407 US 163.
[21] Of 4 October 1958. For text, see Debbasch and Pontier, op. cit. above (p. 254 n. 6), pp. 277–97.
[22] See above, p. 254 n. 6.
[23] Of 27 October 1946. For text, see Debbasch and Pontier, op. cit. above (p. 254 n. 6), pp. 243–4.

content and, consequently, can be enforced in courts in somewhat the same way as private law rights. For the 1946 preamble also guarantees what are called economic, social and cultural rights, such as the rights to work and to the 'conditions necessary to [the] development . . . [of] the individual and the family', to 'health protection, material security, rest, and leisure' and to 'equal access . . . to education, professional training, and culture'. These latter rights often cannot be given a specific content. Moreover, they are not appropriate for court enforcement in the same way as the traditional rights are. There are weighty objections against courts ruling on many types of claims relating to, for example, social security and work, in that on account of their composition and procedures, courts are not equipped to determine what proportion of the national budget should be allocated to social benefits, employment subsidies and the like. And there is always the possibility of legislators being unwilling to raise, or indeed incapable of raising, the taxes that are needed to fund some ambitious spending programme decreed by the court in the name of human rights. The courts' task would be more difficult still if the Constitution itself contained a balanced budget requirement.[24]

Since the Revolution of 1789 the dominant French politico-legal tradition has been hostile to any judicial review of legislation on the American model. That a bench of judges should be given the power to abrogate measures adopted by a representative legislature was perceived as inconsistent with the principle of democratic government, even where the issues concern the traditional civil liberties as opposed to the broader social, economic and cultural rights.[25] Similarly, in Eastern Europe judicial review is regarded as a contradiction of the principle of democratic centralism.[26] More recently in France, the *Conseil Constitutionnel*, a largely non-judicial body, has been given power to determine whether legislation adopted by Parliament and awaiting promulgation is 'in conformity with the Constitution';[27] but there are great differences between the *Conseil*'s composition and procedures and the US Supreme Court.[28]

On the other hand, the courts in France and Eastern Europe do not hesitate to apply their national Bill of Rights standards to private relations. For example, whereas the German Democratic Republic's constitutional guarantees of a socialist education for all[29] will never be invoked by courts there to strike down aspects of the government's educational programme, those guarantees are relied on by the courts to favour people who pursue

[24] Cf. US Senate Joint Res. 58, 97th Congress, 2nd Session, 4 August 1982; see *Harvard Law Review*, 96 (1983), p. 1600.

[25] See Beardsley, *Supreme Court Review* (1975), p. 189.

[26] See Roussillon, *Revue du droit publique et de la science politique en France et à l'étranger*, 93 (1977), p. 55.

[27] Article 61 of the 1958 Constitution.

[28] See Luchaire, *Le Conseil Constitutionnel* (1980).

[29] Constitution of 27 September 1974, Articles 25 and 26.

that education and to disfavour those who do not. Thus in a child custody dispute it was held that the fact that a three-year old child was raised predominantly by his father should not prejudice the mother's claim to custody when she had spent most of the child's life at a university in a different town exercising her right to education.[30] Similarly, the family courts indirectly enforce the constitutional duty to work by denying alimony to divorced women who do not work, even in situations where there are small children to raise.[31] In France the 1946 preamble's guarantee of the right to strike applies to private as well as to public sector employment,[32] while celibacy clauses in private sector employment contracts are unenforceable because they are inconsistent with that preamble's guarantees of the right to marry and to work.[33] In 1982 Professor F. Luchaire, one of France's leading constitutional lawyers, published a major paper entitled *Les fondements constitutionnels du droit civil*.[34]

(c) *The Federal Republic of Germany*

The 'Basic Rights' provisions of the Constitution of the Federal Republic of Germany[35] have more in common with the US than with the (at least, pre-*Conseil Constitutionnel*) French model, in that the substantive guarantees are confined to the traditional civil liberties type of rights, and the Federal Constitutional Court is empowered to invalidate any law that contravenes those guarantees.[36] However, whereas it is accepted as axiomatic that the US Bill of Rights does not lay down standards for private conduct, and in France it has never been seriously questioned that the 1789 Declaration's and the 1948 preamble's norms may be taken into account in adjudicating controversies involving private relations, this very issue has been the source of considerable dispute in the Federal Republic, and has spawned an enormous literature under what has become known as the *Drittwirkung* (absolute, or third party, effect) debate.[37]

Certain of the Basic Rights provisions suggest that the enumerated guarantees may be invoked only against governmental action of one form

[30] Judgment of 2 February 1971, *Neue Justiz*, 25 (1971), pp. 405–6.

[31] e.g. judgments of 8 September 1958, *Neue Justiz*, 13 (1959), pp. 248–9, and of 2 December 1975, *Neue Justiz*, 30 (1976), pp. 113–14.

[32] e.g. judgment of Cour de Cassation (sociale) of 14 January 1960, *Droit Social*, 1960, p. 491.

[33] e.g. judgment of Cour de Cassation (sociale) of 7 February 1968, in Capitant *et al.*, *Les Grands Arrêts de la jurisprudence civile* (7th edn., 1976), no. 18.

[34] *Revue trimestrielle du droit civil*, 81 (1982), p. 245. Cf. Temple Lang, *Irish Jurist*, 6 (1971), p. 237, and Bognetti, Italian Report in *Proceedings of XIth International Congress of Comparative Law* (1982), pp. 429–48.

[35] Of 23 May 1949. For text, see Finer (ed.), *Five Constitutions* (1979), pp. 198–205.

[36] See Béguin, *Le Contrôle de la constitutionnalité des lois en République Fédérale d'Allemagne* (1982), and Kauper, *Michigan Law Review*, 58 (1960), p. 1091.

[37] See Lewan, *International and Comparative Law Quarterly*, 17 (1968), p. 571, and Scheuner in *René Cassin Amicorum Discipulorumque Liber* (1971), vol. 3, pp. 253–68.

or another; thus, for example, Article 1 (3) states that '[t]he following basic rights shall be binding as directly valid law on legislation, administration and the judiciary', and the concluding provision, Article 19 (4), that '[s]hould any person's rights be infringed by public authority, he may appeal to the courts'. On the other hand, the way some of the specific rights are formulated suggests that they apply *vis-à-vis* private conduct too, most notably the trade union freedom guarantee, Article 8 (3):

> The right to form associations to safeguard and improve working and economic conditions shall be guaranteed to everyone and to all professions. Agreements which seek to restrict or hinder this right shall be null and void; measures directed to this end shall be illegal.

The formulation of certain other guarantees is capable of being construed as applying or as not applying to private conduct, for instance Article 3 (2) that '[m]en and women shall have equal rights'. This could be read as proscribing private discrimination; but against this, the term rights may connote legal entitlements conferred on persons by the State. It is possible, however, to find a compromise position in the Basic Law's very first clause, that '[t]he dignity of man shall be inviolable. To respect and protect it shall be the duty of all State authority.' Assuming that the enumerated rights are all aspects of the 'dignity of man', this provision could be interpreted as meaning that where private interferences with these rights happen without an adequate legal remedy being available to the victims, then the State is in breach of its constitutional obligations. Indeed, this argument could be extended further by saying that where such a situation is allowed to continue, the private actors may be regarded as agents of the State, which is aware of and tolerating their activities.

The influential academic writings on the *Drittwirkung* question are divided into two major camps. There are those who contend that the guarantees such as to sexual equality, freedom of expression, etc., apply directly to private conduct, i.e. that private interference with these freedoms is a direct violation of the Basic Law's provisions.[38] The opposing view, which is supported by the majority of writers, is that these provisions do not place obligations directly on individuals, but do so indirectly by filling out the general clauses of the Civil Code, and notably Article 826, which states that '[a] person who wilfully causes damage to another in a manner contrary to good morals (*güte Sitten*) is obliged to compensate the other for the damage', and Article 138 which provides that '[a] juristic act that is contrary to good morals is void'. Thus, to take the person excluded from a private association on account of his or her race or sex: once damage (which need not be financial) is established, this could be regarded as a wrong contrary to *güte Sitten*, the anti-discrimination provision of the Basic Law giving content to the good morals standard. Similarly, expelling someone from an organization because of his

[38] e.g. Nipperdey, *Grundrechte und Privatrecht* (1961).

religious or political opinions could, if authorized by that body's rules, be regarded as enforcing contract provisions which are against good morals. The Federal Constitutional Court and the Administrative Court have come down on the side of 'indirect' application in this way. At one time the Labour Court preferred the 'direct' approach, but more recently it has adopted the 'indirect' approach; while the Federal Supreme Court in some instances has 'indirectly' applied the Basic Law, but in other cases has taken an ambiguous stance.[39]

III. International Conventions and State Responsibility

There are some international conventions that deal with human rights matters and that provide for penalties on individuals who contravene the standards contained in them. For instance, the Convention on the Prevention and Punishment of the Crime of Genocide[40] stipulates that 'Persons committing genocide . . . shall be punished, whether they are constitutionally responsible rulers, public officials or private individuals'.[41]

Some provisions in international human rights instruments make it clear that States Parties to them either incur or do not incur responsibility for private or non-governmental interferences with various rights that are guaranteed. Where the very nature or terms of a particular guarantee or its *travaux préparatoires*, or the convention in question's general clauses or preamble, do not throw light on the matter, one must fall back on the general principles governing State responsibility.

(a) *The Specific Guarantees*

Sometimes the very terms of the guarantee in question will indicate that States Parties will not be held responsible for private interferences with the protected interest. Thus, Article 7 of the European Convention on Human Rights, which forbids *ex post facto* criminal legislation and heavier penalties, by definition can apply only to State action. Articles 10 and 8 of that Convention suggest that they proscribe only governmental interferences. The former's right of freedom of expression 'include[s] freedom to . . . impart information and ideas without interference by *public authority*';[42] and the latter's guarantee of privacy adds that '[t]here shall be no interference by a *public authority* with [its] exercise . . .' .[43] The second

[39] For a summary of the cases, see Lewan, loc. cit. above (p. 258 n. 37), pp. 579–91.

[40] Of 9 December 1948. For text, see Brownlie, *Basic Documents on Human Rights* (2nd edn., 1981), pp. 31–4.

[41] Article IV.

[42] Article 10 (1) (emphasis added). Cf. *The Sunday Times* case, judgment of European Court of Human Rights, 26 April 1979, Series A, No. 30, 2 EHRR 245 (1979–80).

[43] Article 8 (2) (emphasis added). Cf. *Paton* v. *United Kingdom*, European Commission of Human Rights, 13 May 1980, 3 EHRR 408 (1981), and de Meyer in Robertson (ed.), *Privacy and Human Rights* (1973), pp. 255–75.

sentence of that Convention's right to education is formulated like the post-Civil War Amendments to the US Constitution; it requires that '*the State shall* respect the right of parents to ensure such education and teaching in conformity with their own . . . convictions.[44]

The *travaux préparatoires* of several other Articles suggest that certain undertakings were not intended to trigger State responsibility in respect of private prima facie infringements. For instance, an earlier draft of what was to become Article 26 of the International Covenant on Civil and Political Rights (the general non-discrimination clause)[45] was rejected at the instigation of the United Kingdom and Greece on the grounds that the law does not prohibit all types of discrimination in private relations.[46] A similar draft of what is now the Fourth Protocol to the European Convention on Human Rights was rejected by the Council of Europe's Legal Committee, in the words of the Chairman Rapporteur, because

> A general non-discrimination clause is liable to cause insoluble problems, for instance, in regard to the treatment of foreigners it might also cover private or social relations which are not within the province of the law. Such a provision might put all member countries under the obligation to write into their legislation effective guarantees against discrimination in every field of activity, including such private matters as the employment of workers in private enterprises, the lease of dwellings, the limitation by private associations or trade unions of their membership to certain categories of people, and so on.[47]

There can also be found provisions that unquestionably envisage State responsibility arising out of private interferences with certain protected interests. These come in two different forms. One is the straightforward declaration that States Parties will be held responsible for private action, as is the case, for example, with the freedom of expression guarantee in the American Convention on Human Rights, where it is provided that '[t]he right of expression may not be restricted by indirect methods or means, such as the abuse of . . . *private controls* over newsprint, radio broadcasting frequencies, or in the equipment used in the dissemination of information'.[48] Perhaps the best known example of the other form is Article 2 (d) of the International Convention on the Elimination of All Forms of Racial Discrimination,[49] which stipulates that '[e]ach State Party shall prohibit and bring to an end, by all appropriate means, including legislation as

[44] First Protocol, Article 2 (emphasis added). Cf. *Kjeldsen et al.* v. *Denmark*, European Court of Human Rights, 7 December 1976, Series A, No. 23, 1 EHRR 711 (1979–80).

[45] 'All persons are equal before the law. The law shall prohibit *any discrimination* and guarantee to all persons equal and effective protection against discrimination on [the enumerated] grounds' (emphasis added): Article 124 of the draft as submitted by the Commission on Human Rights, Report of the 10th Session (1954), *Economic and Social Council Official Records*, 18th Session, Supplement no. 7, E/2573, Annex 1 B.

[46] (1961), General Assembly, 3rd Committee, 16th Session.

[47] (1959), Consultative Committee of the Council of Europe, *Report on the Second Protocol to the Convention on Human Rights*, Doc. 1057, p. 12, 17 November 1959.

[48] Article 13 (3) (emphasis added).

[49] Of 21 December 1965. For text, see Brownlie, op. cit. above (p. 260 n. 40), pp. 150–63.

required by the circumstances, racial discrimination by *any person*, group or organization'.[50] Yet even though it is clear from the *travaux préparatoires* that a major objective of this latter Convention was to stamp out private racialism, it is arguable that the Convention's very terms do not in fact require States Parties to adopt measures against each and every form of private discrimination on the grounds of race. For racial discrimination is defined in Article 1 (1) as unequal treatment in the public domain: 'any distinction [etc.] which . . . impair[s] the . . . exercise, on an equal footing, of human rights and fundamental freedoms in the political, economic, social, cultural or any other field of *public life*'.[51] As for the specific content of the basic non-discrimination obligation, Article 5 enumerates entitlements the vast majority of which by definition can be interfered with only by public authorities, for instance, the guarantees of equal treatment in the organs administering justice (Article 5 (a)), in the political process and the public service (5 (c)) and in relation to nationality, internal migration, emigration and returning to one's own country (5 (d) (i)–(iii)). That other rights—such as to choice of spouse, to own property and to inherit—are classified as 'civil rights' (5(d)), suggests that they are perceived as traditional civil liberties, i.e. to be protected against 'direct' governmental infringements. And the fact that certain of the rights—such as to protection against violence and bodily harm, and to access to various facilities which are used by the general public (5 (b) and (f))—are expressly stated as applying to private action, lends support to the argument that the other entitlements were not intended to be protected against non-governmental infringements outside the public domain.[52]

It is instructive to consider a situation not unlike that which confronted the English Courts in two recent cases.[53] A white man leaves property in trust for his child, but subject to a provision that the interest in it shall be forfeited if the child shall marry any person not of the Caucasian race. If the courts in a State Party to the Racial Discrimination Convention uphold such a clause, is this not a violation of the guarantees against discrimination in the rights to choice of spouse and to inherit therein enshrined?[54] If the Convention's provisions are applied literally, the answer must be yes.[55]

There are, moreover, certain rights which by their very nature must envisage governmental responsibility for failure to ensure that they are respected by private individuals and organizations. This clearly is the case

[50] Emphasis added. See too Article 2 (e) of the Convention on the Elimination of All Forms of Discrimination Against Women.

[51] Emphasis added. On this question, see Schwelb, *International and Comparative Law Quarterly*, 15 (1966), pp. 996 and 1017–31, and Elkind, *University of Pittsburg Law Review*, 32 (1971), pp. 307 and 310–19.

[52] Cf. *Dockers' Labour Club and Institute* v. *Race Relations Board*, [1976] AC 285.

[53] *Blathwayt* v. *Baron Cawley*, [1976] AC 397, and *In re Tuck's Settlement Trusts*, [1978] 1 Ch. 49 (CA).

[54] Article 5 (d) (iv) and (vi).

[55] Cf. Cruz, *Racial Discrimination* (1977), pp. 117–18 and 227–8.

for such guarantees as those against slavery or servitude, and against forced or compulsory labour, in that the principal forms of servitude cannot exist without the active support of the State.[56] When the law does not make human beings chattels or serfs, there is no way in which the slave-owner or feudal overlord can assert his or her claim. Article 2 of the European Convention on Human Rights, which guarantees the right to life, and which states that it 'shall be protected by law' and that '[n]o one shall be deprived of his life intentionally save in the execution of a sentence of a court', must mean that States Parties may not allow individuals and private organizations a licence to commit murder.[57]

The position with regard to some of the other traditional rights is more debatable, however. Advocates of expansive human rights might be astonished if it were found that States which were Parties to the European Convention on Human Rights but did not prohibit private torture were not in violation of the Article 3 guarantee that '[n]o one shall be subject to torture or to inhuman or degrading treatment or punishment'. Yet torture is defined by the United Nations Declaration on the subject as severe pain or suffering intentionally inflicted 'by or at the instigation of a public official' for specified purposes.[58] Article 5 of the European Convention guarantees 'liberty and security of the person'; and it might be thought that this requires States Parties to provide adequate redress against kidnapping, assaults and the like. Yet the traditional view of what personal liberty and security in these contexts means is freedom from restraint by the State; and the structure of Article 5 would indicate that this is its meaning there. Other examples could be given.

(b) *Preambles and General Clauses*

Where it is not clear from the text whether or not an instrument extends to purely private interferences with the protected interests, the preamble to the relevant convention, or some of its more general clauses, may throw some light on the matter. The two central international Covenants (i.e. those on Civil and Political Rights and on Economic, Social and Cultural Rights), the Racial Discrimination Convention and the European and the American Conventions on Human Rights in their preambles refer to the Universal Declaration of Human Rights,[59] in which the UN General Assembly proclaimed that '[e]veryone has duties to the community . . .'.[60] The preambles to the two international Covenants, moreover, speak of

[56] Cf. *Runyon* v. *McCrary* (1976), 427 US 160, and *Van der Mussele* v. *Belgium*, European Court of Human Rights, 23 November 1983, Series A, No. 70, 6 EHRR 163 (1984).

[57] Cf. *Application no. 9348/81* v. *United Kingdom*, European Commission of Human Rights, March 1983, 5 EHRR 504 (1983), and *Paton* v. *United Kingdom*, above, p. 260 n. 43, with Decision of the Austrian Constitutional Court, 11 October 1974 (abortion) reproduced in Cappelletti and Cohen, *Comparative Constitutional Law* (1979), pp. 615–22.

[58] Article 1.

[59] Of 10 December 1948. For text, see Brownlie, op. cit. above (p. 260 n. 40), pp. 21–7.

[60] Article 29 (1).

'the individual, having duties to other individuals [and being] under a responsibility to strive for the promotion and observance of the rights recognized . . .' . These statements seem merely to acknowledge that States are permitted to regulate specific rights enjoyed by individuals, a power which is expressly granted by a number of these instruments' articles.

Some writers contend that the key to the non-governmental action debate lies in the convention in question's effective national remedies clause, which in the European Convention is Article 13:

> Everyone whose rights and freedoms as set forth in this Convention are violated shall have an effective remedy before a national authority notwithstanding that the violation has been committed by persons acting in an official capacity.

The argument is that since this appears to assume that State officials may violate the Convention in their private capacities, it must be concluded that the Convention's guarantees are capable of being infringed by any private person or body as well.[61] But as more than one commentator has noted, the wording of this Article is 'puzzling' and 'strange', and betrays a 'basic confusion of thought as to [its] real purpose and function'.[62] The proviso on which the argument is based is more probably a proscription against the withdrawal of any local remedies on *raisons d'état* grounds.

Many of the rights enumerated in these conventions are prefixed by statements that 'everyone has the right to' or that 'no one shall be deprived of' those rights. This suggests to some that the States Parties must ensure protection against interferences with the rights by private persons. But as the rights in question, for example, to freedom of expression, assembly, association etc., have traditionally been perceived as connoting freedom from governmental interference[63] and as their formulation does not clearly suggest a State obligation in respect of private prima facie violations, the burden of persuasion lies on those who argue for their having a more extensive reach. This is especially the case with the European Convention on Human Rights where this aspect of the guarantees was hardly discussed in the *travaux préparatoires*, and where many of the States Parties must have believed that they were assuming obligations only with reference to direct governmental interferences with the rights contained in it.

(c) *General Principles of State Responsibility*

According to Article 3 of the draft Articles on State Responsibility drawn up by the International Law Commission[64]

[61] See, e.g., Eissen, *Nordisk Tidsskrift for International Ret*, 32 (1962), p. 230.

[62] See Castberg, *The European Convention on Human Rights* (1974), pp. 157–9; Fawcett, *The Application of the European Convention on Human Rights* (1969), pp. 227–32; Jacob, *The European Convention on Human Rights* (1975), pp. 215–16.

[63] See Braud, *La Notion de liberté publique en droit français* (1968), pp. 45–84.

[64] *Yearbook of the International Law Commission*, 1980, vol. 2 (ii), pp. 30–4.

There is an internationally wrongful act of a State when:

(a) conduct consisting of an action or omission is attributable to the State under international law; and

(b) that conduct constitutes a breach of an international obligation of the State.

This draft goes on to provide in Article 11 (1) that States cannot be held responsible for private action:

The conduct of a person or a group of persons not acting on behalf of the State shall not be considered as an act of the State under international law.[65]

Voluminous authority for these propositions is cited in the reports of Mr Ago,[66] the Commission's Special Rapporteur on the subject.

This does not mean that purely private action can never trigger State responsibility. First, the draft Articles provide in Article 7 (2) that

The conduct of an organ of an entity which is not part of the formal structure of the State . . . but which is empowered by the internal law of that State to exercise elements of the governmental authority, shall also be considered as an act of the State under international law, provided that organ was acting in that capacity in the case in question . . .

and in Article 8 that

The conduct of a person or a group of persons shall also be considered as an act of the State under international law if:

(a) it is established that such person or group of persons was in fact acting on behalf of that State . . .

Secondly, as Mr Ago points out,

With regard to the conduct which must be susceptible of being considered as conduct of the State, what can be said in general is that it can be either positive (action) or negative (omission). It can even be said that the cases in which the international responsibility of a State has been invoked on the basis of an omission are perhaps more numerous than those based on action taken by a State. There have been innumerable cases in which States have been held responsible for damage caused by individuals . . . [T]hese alleged cases of State responsibility for the acts of individuals are really cases of responsibility of the State for omissions by its organs: the State is responsible for having failed to take appropriate measures to prevent or punish the individuals' act.

. . .

[M]oreover, there are many cases in which an international delinquency consists in an omission, and whenever international jurisprudence has found a wrongful omission to be a source of international responsibility, it has done so in terms just as unequivocal as those used with reference to active conduct.[67]

[65] Para. 2 of Article 11 adds: 'Paragraph 1 is without prejudice to the attribution to the State of any other conduct which is related to that of persons or groups of persons referred to in that paragraph and which is to be considered as an act of State by virtue of articles 5–10.'

[66] In particular, in his Second Report, in *Yearbook of the International Law Commission*, 1970, vol. 2, pp. 177, 187–90, and his Fourth Report, in ibid., 1972, vol. 2, pp. 71 and 95–126.

[67] In his Second Report, loc. cit. (previous note), at p. 188.

To use terminology which has been roundly condemned for its inaccuracy[68] but which nonetheless highlights the distinction to be made, the extent to which a State is 'directly' responsible for private action should be considered, with particular reference to the questions of implicating the State through litigation and of responsibility for complicity in private prima facie breaches.[69]

1. *Acting for the State*

Private conduct is attributed to the State where it was 'in fact . . . on behalf of that State'.[70] In his Third Report, Mr Ago refers to incidents such as that involving Adolf Eichmann, where the Israeli Government contended that he had been abducted from Argentina by a group of volunteers acting on their own initiative and without the knowledge of the Israeli authorities, but nevertheless expressed its regret for any infringement of Argentine sovereignty and laws.[71] He cites the following less controversial examples:

> A private undertaking may, for instance, be engaged to provide public transport, postal communications or some other public service; non-official associations or groups of private persons may be used as auxiliaries in official health units, the police or armed forces; drivers of private vehicles may be used to carry troops to the front etc.[72]

In its Report to the General Assembly, the International Law Commission stressed that

> in each specific case . . . it must be genuinely proved that the person or group of persons were actually appointed by organs of the State to discharge a particular function or to carry out a particular duty, that they performed a given task at the instigation of those organs.[73]

2. *Entity empowered to exercise governmental authority*

In his Third Report, Mr Ago provides examples of entities which as a matter of municipal law are not part of the formal State apparatus, but whose activities nonetheless are attributed to the State for the purposes of State responsibility. One is the political entity organized outside the machinery of the State, though closely and indissolubly linked to it, such as the Communist Party in the USSR, and, in the past, the Kuomintang in China, the National Socialist or Nazi Party in Germany and the Fascist Party in Italy.[74] Another is the public corporation that has separate legal

[68] Freeman, *The International Responsibility of States for Denial of Justice* (1938), pp. 19–22.

[69] See Mössner, *German Yearbook of International Law*, 24 (1981), p. 63; Starke, this *Year Book*, 19 (1938), pp. 104 and 112–15; and Eagleton, *The Responsibility of States in International Law* (1928, 1970 reprint).

[70] Article 8 (a) of the International Law Commission's draft Articles.

[71] *Yearbook of the International Law Commission*, 1971, vol. 2 (i), p. 265.

[72] Ibid. at p. 263.

[73] Ibid., 1974, vol. 2 (i), p. 285, Cf. *Van der Mussele* v. *Belgium*, European Court of Human Rights, 23 November 1983, Series A, No. 70, 6 EHRR 163 (1984).

[74] Loc. cit. above (n. 71), at p. 254; and see Friedmann, this *Year Book*, 19 (1938), pp. 118, 144, and Friedmann, *American Journal of International Law*, 50 (1956), pp. 475 and 492.

personality and a degree of autonomy but which performs 'functions [of] a distinctly public character' or which 'provides services for the community'.[75] International judicial decisions and State practice, however, provide few examples of actions by such bodies and groups being attributed to States. As the International Law Commission points out in its report to the General Assembly:

> The choice of criteria for designating [such] entities . . . is not easy, for the entities in question vary widely in characteristics, in the matters falling within their field of activity and, sometimes, in the regimes which govern them. The fact that an entity can be classified as public or private according to the criteria of a given legal system, the existence of a greater or lesser State participation in its capital or, more generally, in the ownership of its assets, and the fact that it is subject to such control to a greater or lesser extent, and so on, do not emerge as decisive criteria for the purposes of attribution or non-attribution . . . Hence the Commission has come to the conclusion that the most appropriate solution is to refer to the real common feature which these entities have: namely that they are empowered, if only exceptionally and to a limited extent, to exercise specified functions which are akin to those normally exercised by the organs of a State.[76]

There is an enormous divergence of opinion in the international community as to what the functions 'normally exercised' by the State are. Indeed, has not this very matter been the principal ideological source of international tension since 1945? This tension exists even among the capitalist countries, for example in broadcasting; while broadcasting in France has been a government monopoly,[77] it is in the US entirely in private hands (including the so-called public broadcasting service, Channel 9)[78] and in the UK is shared between the BBC and private companies (though it should be added that the private broadcasters in the UK and the US are subject to a degree of public regulation). The US Supreme Court was prepared to consider the editorial policy, sustained by the Federal Communications Commission, of a private broadcasting network as 'State action' for the purposes of the First Amendment's freedom of expression guarantee;[79] but the same Court ruled in another case that the action of a privately owned (though publicly regulated) electric power company with a monopoly in the supply of electricity in New York, in cutting off the plaintiff's supply without prior notice for alleged non-payment of charges, was not 'state action' for the purposes of the Constitution's due process guarantee.[80] On the international plane, it would indeed be anomalous if action by a State-owned or -controlled

[75] Loc. cit. above (p. 266 n. 71), at pp. 254 and 256.

[76] Ibid. at p. 282.

[77] Cf. Conseil Constitutionnel, 27 July 1978, *Recueil Dalloz Sirey*, 1980, p. 169, and Conseil Constitutionnel, 30 and 31 October 1981, *Recueil Dalloz Sirey*, 1982, p. 557.

[78] Cf. *Yale Law Journal*, 89 (1980), p. 719.

[79] *Columbia Broadcasting System* v. *Democratic National Committee* (1973), 412 US 94; and compare the '*Oswald Moseley Application*', below, p. 272 n. 107.

[80] *Jackson* v. *Metropolitan Edison Co.* (1974), 419 US 345.

broadcasting service, public utility, or professional organisation,[81] is to be judged against standards set down in human rights conventions whereas the virtually identical actions of similar entities in another State, but which are privately controlled and subject to little or no governmental regulation, are not required to abide by the same standards.

3. *Implicating the State through litigation*

Article 6 of the International Law Commission's draft Articles classifies as an act of the State under international law the conduct of State judicial organs. Accordingly, even where the guarantee in question neither renders States 'directly' responsible for private infringements[82] nor requires States to take affirmative steps of one form or another to prevent, punish or compensate for such action, it would appear possible to attribute the private conduct to the State where the courts lend their support to such conduct.

The US racially restrictive covenant cases provide parallels. In *Shelley* v. *Kraemer*,[83] the (white) plaintiffs were awarded an injunction by a state court restraining the (black) defendants from taking possession of property the defendants had bought because it had been subject to a covenant proscribing its sale to non-whites. Chief Justice Vinson, writing for a unanimous Court, stated that when state courts enjoin the taking of possession by purchasers of property which is subject to such covenants, there is 'State action . . . in the full and complete sense of the phrase . . . It is clear that but for the active intervention of the State courts, supported by the full panoply of State power, [the purchasers] would have been free to occupy the properties in question without restraint.'[84] In a later case, *Barrows* v. *Jackson*,[85] similar reasoning was applied in dismissing a damages action for breach of such a covenant; the US Supreme Court could 'not permit or require [a state] to coerce [the seller] to respond in damages for failure to observe a restrictive covenant that this Court would deny [a state] the right to enforce in equity . . .'.[86] The notorious *Veit Harlan* case[87] in Germany provides another parallel: there the interference with the defendant's effort to organize a boycott of the ex-Nazi plaintiff's film was an injunction issued by a lower court.

But US law does not treat as State action every instance where a state court upholds private prima facie human rights violations. Court backing has been thus classified only where it is invoked to compel a person to

[81] Cf. *Van der Mussele* case, loc. cit. above (p. 266 n. 73), and *X* v. *United Kingdom* (*Re Solicitors' Advertising*), European Commission of Human Rights, 16 July 1981, 4 EHRR 350 (1982).

[82] Bearing in mind Freeman's exhortation about use of the term 'directly' in the context of State responsibility: op. cit. above (p. 266 n. 68).

[83] (1948), 334 US 1.

[84] Ibid. at p. 19.

[85] (1953), 346 US 249.

[86] Ibid. at p. 258.

[87] Judgment of 15 January 1958, *Entscheidungen des Bundesverfassungsgerichts*, 1958, p. 198 (No. 28).

engage in conduct—for instance, where the court orders private discrimination (e.g., *Shelley* v. *Kraemer*) or it awards damages against persons who, in violation of contract, chose not so to discriminate (e.g., *Barrows* v. *Jackson*). Court backing does not constitute State action where the victim of private discrimination simply fails to obtain court recognition of his or her claim.[88] Thus in *Black* v. *Cutter Laboratories*[89] the plaintiff was discharged by her employer allegedly for being a member of the Communist Party. She successfully contested her dismissal in private arbitration proceedings, where it was found that the charge of Communism was a pretext to get rid of her for her trade union activities. But when she sought enforcement of the award, the California Supreme Court ruled that Communist Party membership constituted 'just cause' for her dismissal under the collective agreement between her employer and union and, alternatively, that to decree specific performance of the award would contravene state public policy. The US Supreme Court denied certiorari; but in a dissenting judgment Mr Justice Douglas took the position that the Court 'sanction[s] a flagrant violation of the First Amendment [freedom of opinion] guarantee when we allow California acting through her highest court, to sustain [the plaintiff's] discharge because of her belief'.[90] In his view, when the judicial organs of government give legal effect to a contract which requires discrimination on political grounds, then the State itself becomes involved; and 'if the courts lend their support to any such discriminatory [action], *Shelley* v. *Kraemer* . . . teaches that the Government has thrown its weight behind an unconstitutional scheme to discriminate against citizens by reason of their political ideology'.[91] The majority of the Court avoided the issue by ruling that the contested decision involved only California's construction of a local contract under local law, and therefore no substantial federal question was presented.[92]

On the international plane, and assuming that by its very terms the right in question neither makes States 'directly' responsible for private interferences with it nor requires States to adopt measures to prevent such action, the question arises whether court endorsement of a private interference with that right is to be attributed to the State and thus trigger State responsibility. Little guidance on this matter can be obtained from the classic law on the denial of justice because it is based on the overriding premiss that States have affirmative obligations with respect to the treatment of aliens.[93] The answer would appear to be no. For if the State does not have analogous obligations with respect to its own citizens' human rights, the courts act merely as impartial arbiters of private claim and counterclaim. To take the recent English cases involving discriminatory

[88] For a consideration of this distinction, see Lewis, *Columbia Law Review*, 60 (1960), pp. 1083 and 1108–20; Pollak, *University of Pennsylvania Law Review*, 108 (1959), pp. 1 and 6–18.

[89] (1956), 351 US 292.

[90] Ibid. at p. 304.

[91] Ibid. at pp. 302–3.

[92] Ibid. at p. 299.

[93] Freeman, *The International Responsibility of States for Denial of Justice* (1938).

trusts,[94] the courts did not discriminate against the disappointed beneficiaries on account of their choice in relation to religion; the discrimination was by private individuals, the courts merely upholding their wishes. Nor does the general law on the denial of justice warrant making a distinction, as the US law has, between court action which in a sense compels private prima facie violations and court action which simply refuses to recognize the plaintiff's claim that he has been denied his human rights. In his book, *International Law and Human Rights*,[95] Sir Hersch Lauterpacht expressed the view that States would violate a general non-discrimination obligation where their 'courts . . . are called upon to lend the assistance of the State to the enforcement of the private (discriminatory) act in question'.[96] But he nevertheless felt the matter was of sufficient importance—by which, presumably, he meant open to dispute—to warrant special mention in the Bill of Rights he proposed.[97]

4. *State complicity in private action*

According to Borchard, writing in 1922:

> A long line of cases has established certain qualifications upon the non-liability of the government for the wrongful acts of private individuals. These consist in certain manifestations of the actual or implied complicity of the government in the act, before or after it, either by directly ratifying or approving it, or by an implied, tacit or constructive approval in the negligent failure to prevent the injury, or to investigate the case, or to punish the guilty individual, or to enable the victim to pursue his civil remedies against the offender. . . .[98]

If governmental complicity of one form or another in private prima facie human rights violations triggered State responsibility, then many forms of private incursions into various freedoms would be required to conform to international standards. The US cases classifying as State action activities where there is significant State involvement, or 'State nexus', or 'symbiotic relationship', such as *Burton* v. *Wilmington Parking Authority*,[99] provide parallels.

However, the complicity doctrine in the international law of State responsibility is rejected by most writers today, and occupies no place in

[94] *Blathwayt* v. *Baron Cawley*, [1976] AC 397, and *In re Tuck's Settlement Trusts*, [1978] 1 Ch. 49 (CA).

[95] 1950 (1968 reprint).

[96] Ibid. at pp. 340–1; and see ibid. at pp. 154–60.

[97] Article 8: 'No State shall lend the assistance of its judicial and other organs and resources for the purposes of enforcing or practising discrimination . . .'.

[98] Borchard, *The Diplomatic Protection of Citizens Abroad* (1928), p. 217. See *Répertoire de la pratique française en matière de droit international public* (1965), vol. 3, pp. 579–90, where the State practice collected is headed 'L'Etat est responsable des actes de particuliers lorsque ses organes sont complices de ces actes. Par contre, sa responsabilité n'est pas engagée lorsqu'il s'agit d'actes qu'il n'est pas tenu de réprimer et qu'il n'y a aucune collusion de sa part.'

[99] (1961), 365 US 715, and above, p. 256 n. 19.

the International Law Commission's draft Articles. The Commission instead takes the view that although the acts of private entities

> which cause injury to foreign States . . . are often the occasion of an internationally wrongful act of the State . . . this is a wrongful act which is the conduct of State organs. [The private acts] frequently constitute an external event which acts as a catalyst in setting in motion the wrongful conduct of those organs with respect to the actual situation. But the State is internationally responsible only for the action, and more often the omission, of its organs where they are guilty of not having done everything within their power to prevent the injurious act of the private individual or to punish it suitably if it has occurred despite everything.[100]

It is not inconceivable, however, that in relation to human rights obligations, a place will be made for the complicity doctrine. For it should not be overlooked that the principal concern of the writers who contend that it has no place in the general law of State responsibility has been responsibility for injuries to aliens. Since customary and conventional international law requires States to take some positive steps to protect aliens within their jurisdiction, and to take measures against persons who inflict injury on aliens,[101] there is therefore no real need for the concept of complicity in that field of law. But in the human rights field there is no authoritative ruling that States owe an analagous all-pervasive duty to their own citizens, at least with regard to rights such as non-discrimination and freedom of expression, of assembly, of association and the like.

IV. The European Convention on Human Rights

The European Court of Human Rights has yet to pronounce on whether and in what circumstances the European Convention on Human Rights makes States Parties responsible for essentially private or non-governmental action that could be regarded as inconsistent with the Convention's guarantees. Although the issue was put to the Court in a number of cases regarding Article 11 and trade union freedoms, in three of these[102] the action complained of was that of the defendant State itself; and in another,[103] which concerned arrangements made between a State-owned public utility and trade unions, the defendant State conceded that its responsibility had been engaged by virtue of related legislation.

(a) *The Commission of Human Rights*

A case can be brought before the European Court of Human Rights only by a State Party to the Convention or by the European Commission of

[100] *Yearbook of the International Law Commission*, 1975, vol. 2, pp. 25 and 81. Cf. Brierly, this *Year Book*, 9 (1928), p. 42.

[101] Lillich, *Recueil des cours*, 161 (1978–III), p. 330.

[102] *National Union of Belgian Police* case, judgment of 27 October 1975, Series A, No. 9, 1 EHRR 578 (1979–80); *Swedish Engine Drivers' Union* case, judgment of 6 February 1976, Series A, No. 20, 1 EHRR 617 (1979–80); and *Schmidt and Dahlström* case, judgement of 6 February 1976, Series A, No. 21, 1 EHRR 632 (1979–80).

[103] *Young, James and Webster* case, judgment of 26 June 1981, Series A, No. 44, 4 EHRR 38 (1982).

Human Rights.[104] One of the Commission's functions is to decide on the admissibility of applications lodged against the States Parties. Applications are rejected *ratione loci* where they concern what was done in a territory not in fact subject to the Convention; *ratione materiae* where the complaint is against the violation of some right not in fact guaranteed by the Convention; and *ratione personae* where the basic complaint is against action taken by private individuals or institutions, or by some other entity not a party to the Convention itself.[105] The Commission has frequently held inadmissible *ratione personae* allegations concerning the actions of lawyers assigned under public legal aid systems to represent applicants in civil and criminal proceedings.[106] It has rejected on these grounds a complaint by Sir Oswald Moseley against the UK alleging violation of freedom of political expression when the BBC, the State-owned broadcasting service, refused to allow him to broadcast in support of the British Union of Fascists, a political party;[107] against Belgium concerning an applicant's discharge from a State-owned steel company allegedly on account of his non-membership of a trade union;[108] against Austria concerning credits, allegedly given originally to the applicant at the behest of public authorities, and which were later withdrawn by a private savings bank;[109] and against the FRG concerning allegedly defamatory reports about the applicant in the press, radio and television.[110] Yet in a later (though unreported) application, where the Belgian Government was accused of violating Articles 6 and 10 for refusing to prosecute newspapers which allegedly defamed the applicant,[111] the Commission held itself incompetent *ratione personae* because 'the newspapers were independent of the government', and also *ratione materiae* because the applicant still had a right to have criminal proceedings instituted against the papers. The Commission expressly left open the question whether, assuming there were prima facie violations of these Articles, 'the contracting States are obliged to ensure that these rights are respected in relations between private individuals'.[111]

In *X* v. *Ireland*[112] the Commission indicated where, in its view, States

[104] See O'Boyle, *Santa Clara Law Review*, 20 (1980), p. 697.

[105] See Mikaelsen, *European Protection of Human Rights* (1980), chap. 6, esp. pp. 90–3.

[106] e.g. *De Courcey* v. *United Kingdom* (1966–9), *Yearbook of the European Convention on Human Rights*, 10 (1967), pp. 368 and 388, at p. 380.

[107] *X and the Association of Z* v. *United Kingdom* (1971), *Yearbook of the European Convention on Human Rights*, 14 (1971), p. 538; and see too *X* v. *United Kingdom* (1968), *Collection of Decisions of the European Commission of Human Rights*, 28 (1969), p. 89.

[108] *X* v. *Belgium* (1970), *Yearbook of the European Convention on Human Rights*, 13 (1970), p. 708.

[109] *X* v. *Austria* (1966), *Collection of Decisions of the European Commission of Human Rights*, 21 (1967), p. 34.

[110] *X* v. *Federal Republic of Germany* (1966), *Collection of Decisions of the European Commission of Human Rights*, 23 (1967), p. 1.

[111] Decision of 18 December 1963 (unpublished), referred to by Eissen in *René Cassin Amicorum Discipulorumque Liber* (1971), vol. 3, pp. 151 and 158–9.

[112] Decisions of 24 July 1970 (partial) and 1 February 1971 (final), *Yearbook of the European Convention on Human Rights*, 14 (1971), pp. 188 and 198.

Parties may incur responsibility in respect of the anti-trade union activities of non-governmental bodies. There the applicant complained *inter alia* that the Irish Electricity Supply Board (ESB), a public corporation with a practical monopoly in the supply of electricity in Ireland, discriminated against him on account of his trade union activities, in violation of Article 11. The Irish Government contended that it could not be held responsible for the activities of the ESB:

the Board is . . . a body established by a statute which sets out its essential features and functions and is financed, at least in the first instance by public funds . . . and it is clear from the provisions of the statute that the Board is solely responsible for matters relating to exercise of its functions, including the relationship between the Board and its employees . . . accordingly, the applicant's complaint is in respect of alleged actions by or on behalf of a body independent of the Government and such actions cannot involve the *direct* responsibility of the Government under the Convention.[113]

Against this, the applicant emphasized that a Government Minister appoints the board of the ESB, including its Chairman, and reference was made to a letter of that Minister which stated that he exercised general supervision over the Board's policies. The Commission decided that, even assuming that the Government was responsible, in the circumstances the action complained of was not a violation of the substantive rights guaranteed by Article 11. Consequently, there was no need to consider the question of Government liability for the ESB's actions, except to observe that 'the Government exercises, at least, general supervision over the policy of the Board, the day to day administration is solely in the hands of the Board; [but] the acts alleged by the applicant clearly fall within the domain of such day to day administration for which the Government is not *directly* responsible'.[113] However, the Commission suggested that a State might still be 'indirectly' responsible for infringements committed by non-governmental actors if its own laws did not adequately protect against interferences with the guaranteed right:

insofar as the acts alleged have not been committed in circumstances involving the *direct* responsibility of the Government, a breach by the Government in connection with these acts may not be established otherwise than by showing either that the domestic law does not protect a right or freedom guaranteed by the Convention which has been infringed or that there is no adequate remedy for enforcing the law's protection in this respect. . . .[114]

But even this analysis does not resolve the central question: does the Convention require protection against private prima facie violations of particular rights? It is only on the assumption that it does that the question of whether the domestic law adequately secures those rights can arise.

[113] Ibid. at p. 218 (emphasis added).

[114] Ibid. at p. 220 (emphasis added).

(b) *The Court of Human Rights*

The vast majority of instances that are brought before the European Court of Human Rights concern actions by States Parties' legislatures, executives and courts but where there is no suggestion whatsoever of private involvement in the alleged breaches. As for the few instances where private interests were implicated, those interests were very much peripheral. Thus in the *Sunday Times* case,[115] it was the English Attorney-General who instituted proceedings for the gagging injunction, and not the Distillers Co.[116] In the *Le Compte* case, the Belgian *Ordre des médecins* was no private body but was established and given its powers by legislation.[117] In the *Van der Mussele* case,[118] it was contended that the obligation imposed by the Belgian *Ordres des avocats* on the applicant to co-operate in providing legal aid arose from rules adopted by the bar associations themselves and was not imposed by the Belgian State. But this argument was rejected on the grounds that the duty under Article 6 of the Convention to provide legal aid is imposed by legislation on these associations.[119] And in the *Campbell and Cosans* case[120] which concerned corporal punishment in schools, the Court held that the UK Government was responsible for the practices that were complained of because in Scotland 'the State has assumed responsibility for formulating general [educational] policy and the schools attended by the applicants' children were State schools. Discipline is an integral, even indispensable, part of any educational system, with the result that the functions assumed by the State in Scotland must be taken to extend to questions of discipline in general . . .'.[121] The Court there made the interesting observation that when a teacher 'administers corporal punishment he is exercising not a power delegated to him by the State but a power vested in him by the common law by virtue of his status as a teacher',[121] which suggests that corporal punishment in private schools would not fall foul of the Convention's provisions.

The non-governmental action question engendered considerable debate in two of the substantive labour law cases decided by the Court. In the *Swedish Engine Drivers' Union* case,[122] which concerned a claim by a minority trade union to be a party to a collective agreement with the State agency that employed its members, the argument for a US-style State action gloss on Article 11 was put eloquently by Mr Danelius, agent

[115] Judgment of 26 April 1979, Series A, No. 30, 2 EHRR 245 (1979–80).

[116] Cf. the *Veit Harlan* case, loc. cit. above (p. 268 n. 87).

[117] Judgment of 10 February 1983, Series A, No. 58, 5 EHRR 533 (1983).

[118] Judgment of 23 November 1983, Series A, No. 70, 6 EHRR 163 (1984).

[119] Cf. *X* v. *United Kingdom* (*Re Solicitors' Advertising*), European Commission of Human Rights, 16 July 1981, 4 EHRR 350 (1982).

[120] Judgment of 25 February 1982, Series A, No. 48, 4 EHRR 293 (1982).

[121] Ibid., para. 34.

[122] Judgment of 6 February 1976, Series A, No. 20, 1 EHRR 617 (1979–80). See Forde, *American Journal of Comparative Law*, 31 (1983), p. 301.

for the Swedish Government, and an eminent authority on the European Convention:[123]

Clearly this Article prevents the Government . . . from interfering with the activities of a trade union whose policy is not agreeable to the Government . . . [and] prevents the Parliament . . . from adopting a law which prohibits trade union activities [etc.] and it also prohibits interference with trade union activities by way of judicial decisions.

But does Article 11 go further than that? Does it put an obligation on the State to ensure that employers do not improperly take action which is detrimental to trade unions? Does it impose . . . an obligation to enact legislation in the field of labour law, which adequately protects trade unions against certain acts by employers or employers' associations and which protects employers' associations against certain acts by trade unions? Does Article 11 perhaps even cover other aspects of relations between organizations and private individuals in the labour market, for instance the relations between trade unions and their members?[124]

To take an example of particular relevance to the UK: assuming that a State Party is in violation of the article where the government refuses to employ persons on account of their trade union, political or religious affiliations, is the UK then in violation of the article because private employers are allowed thus to discriminate at the point of hiring?[125]

Danelius' answer was that as regards the rights enumerated in Articles 8, 9, 10 and 11 of the Convention,

States may be required to ensure by appropriate means that these freedoms can in fact be exercised without risk of physical harm or violent action of some kind; [but] this does not mean that a State is obliged . . . to regulate various sorts of contractual relations or other private law relations between individuals. [For t]he history of these rights shows that their purpose was to guarantee that the State did not, by means of legislation or otherwise, suppress or restrict the freedom of expression, the freedom of religion and the other freedoms concerned . . .

This was their 'overriding purpose' and 'primar[y] aim'.[126] In support of this view, he contrasts the International Convention on the Elimination of All Forms of Racial Discrimination, which by express terms reaches certain forms of private discrimination,[127] with Article 14 of the European Convention which contains no indication of its application to relations between individuals.[128] He focuses then on the other right referred to in Article 11, freedom of assembly, which is

basically a right to non-interference by the public authorities. It means that no legislation may be enacted to forbid peaceful meetings or to restrict them. It also

[123] See, e.g., Danelius, *Revue des droits de l'homme*, 2 (1969), p. 284.

[124] European Court of Human Rights, Series B, No. 18, at p. 146.

[125] *Allen* v. *Flood*, [1898] AC 1, esp. Lord Davey at p. 172, and *City of Birmingham* v. *Beyer*, [1978] 1 All ER 910. There are now four major statutory exceptions to the power to discriminate at the point of hiring: the Sex Discrimination Act 1975, s. 6(1)(c), the Race Relations Act 1976, s. 4(i)(c), the Fair Employment (Northern Ireland) Act 1976 and the complex rules regarding closed shops (below, p. 278 n. 141).

[126] Loc. cit. above (n. 124), at p. 152.

[127] p. 262 n. 50 above.

[128] p. 261 nn. 46 and 47 above.

means that public authorities such as the police must not break up meetings or interfere with them in any other way. It does not, however, affect any private law relations which may exist, any agreements which may be concluded between landlord and tenant, between employer and employee and which may restrict the right to hold public gatherings in certain private premises, or, for instance, during working hours.[129]

He goes on to reject the conclusions *a contrario* which may be drawn from the references in Articles 8 and 10 to interferences by 'public authority';[130] those references 'may be seen merely as a clarification of the meaning of that Article, a clarification which was natural in the context but which does not justify the conclusion that the other freedom-rights . . . should also be understood as rights vis à vis private individuals.'[131] Having pointed out that reference to the *travaux préparatoires* of the UN Covenants was inconclusive as to the position under the European Convention, he concluded by warning the Court of the undesirable consequences that could ensue if Article 11 was applied to private conduct: this could require that the Court construct a single labour relations code for the diverse industrial relations systems in the States Parties to the Convention.

The Commission on Human Rights' response to these points was based primarily on the principle that treaties must be construed in the light of their objects and purposes, and that the European Convention must be interpreted in a way that makes the protection of the individual effective. Thus, in respect of Article 11,

if unions are to achieve their purpose . . . it would be compatible with the text to provide them with some kind of protection against certain types of interference not only by the State but also by employers in which case protection would have to be ensured by legislation. . . . It is true that the Convention fundamentally guarantees traditional 'liberal' rights in relation to the State as a holder of public power. This does not, however, imply that the State may not be obliged to protect individuals through appropriate measures taken against some forms of interference by other individuals, groups, or organizations. While they themselves cannot, under the Convention, be held responsible for any such acts which are in breach of the Convention, the State may, under certain circumstances, be responsible for them. This consideration should in particular apply to Article 11 which combines the aspects of a traditional liberal right or a civil liberty and an economic right. . . . Social and economic rights . . . may correspond to a duty to enact legislation to govern 'private' relations.[132]

During the oral hearings in the *Swedish Engine Drivers' Union* case, Professor Fawcett, the Commission's principal delegate, cited the example of a trade union denying admission to applicants on the grounds of race. In his view, Article 14, the non-discrimination provision, 'would immediately come into the issue; and if the State allowed this situation to

[129] Loc. cit. above (p. 275 n. 124), at p. 165.
[130] p. 260 nn. 42 and 43 above.
[131] Loc. cit. above (p. 275 n. 124), at p. 166.
[132] Ibid. at pp. 41–2.

continue, there would be a breach of the Convention'.[133] In the event, the Court declined to pronounce authoritatively on the non-governmental action question, given that the complaint concerned policies of the State bargaining agency and that these did not violate Article 11.

This issue was raised again in the *Young, James and Webster*, or 'closed shop' case,[134] which has close parallels with State action controversies under US constitutional law.[135] A closed shop agreement (sometimes called a union security, or union membership, agreement) is an arrangement between an employer and a trade union, or between employers and unions, whereby persons working for an employer are required to join a trade union on pain of losing their jobs. A closed shop agreement concluded in 1970 between British Rail, the State-owned railway, and three railway unions, known for short as the NUR, TSSA and ASLEF, was, following the repeal of the Industrial Relations Act 1971, revived in 1975. At the relevant time the agreement contained an exception for persons who genuinely objected on grounds of religious belief to being members of any trade union. The three applicants' original terms of employment included the provision that their contracts would be subject to such terms and conditions of employment as might be settled from time to time in negotiations with any trade unions or other organizations. There was no closed shop agreement in existence when they were hired. Subsequently, British Rail informed them that, following implementation of the 1970 agreement, it would be a condition of their employment that they join either the NUR or TSSA. Two of the applicants had ideological objections to joining either of those unions, while the third, who previously had had some dispute with NUR officials, simply refused to join it. In consequence, they were dismissed. They claimed in their application to the Commission of Human Rights that their right to freedom of association under Article 11 had been violated, as had their rights to freedom of thought and conscience under Article 9 and to freedom of expression under Article 10. A divided Court held that the applicants' rights under Article 11 had been contravened.

As regards the non-governmental action question, the legal status of closed shop agreements in the UK has been complex. At common law such agreements would not be enforced by a court because they are unreasonable restraints of trade,[136] but industrial action to secure or to enforce a closed shop is not unlawful *per se*.[137] The Trade Disputes Act of 1906

[133] Ibid. at p. 199.

[134] Judgment of 26 June 1981, Series A, No. 44, 4 EHRR 38 (1982). See Forde, *American Journal of Comparative Law*, 31 (1983), p. 301.

[135] Especially with *Buckley* v. *American Federation of Television and Radio Artists* (1974), 496 F 2d 305 (2d Cir.), cert. denied, 419 US 1093, and *Railway Employee's Department, American Federation of Labor* v. *Hanson* (1955), 351 US 225.

[136] *Faramus* v. *Film Artistes' Association*, [1964] AC 925. Cf. *Reynolds* v. *Shipping Federation*, [1924] 1 Ch. 28.

[137] *Crofter Handwoven Harris Tweed Co. Ltd.* v. *Veitch*, [1942] AC 435. Cf. *Rookes* v. *Barnard*, [1964] AC 1129, and *Huntley* v. *Thornton*, [1957] 1 WLR 321.

authorized strikes and peaceful picketing for these purposes.[138] Over the last fifteen years numerous legislative measures have been adopted to deal with the closed shops. The Conservative Government's Industrial Relations Act 1971 virtually proscribed them,[139] but the Act was repealed by the Labour Government's Trade Union and Labour Relations Act 1974 (the TULRA) and the TULRA (Amendment) Act of 1976 abolished some remaining restrictions on closed shop agreements.[140] Since the present Conservative Government first came to power in 1979, extensive restrictions on closed shops have been introduced.[141]

Essentially the same arguments as Mr Danelius and Professor Fawcett made in the *Swedish Engine Drivers' Union* case were repeated before the Commission and the Court in this case. The circumstances indeed provide a text-book example of the 'State complicity' or 'symbiotic relationship' situation referred to above. A significant twist in the case was that by the time it came before the Court the Labour administration had been replaced again by the Conservatives, who came into office with anti-closed shop pledges. The British representatives before the Court conceded that Britain should be held responsible if it was shown that the applicants' dismissal constituted a 'relevant interference' with their Article 11 rights which was a 'direct consequence of' the TULRA. The Court found that there was such a causal relationship, and consequently did not have to examine the broader question. As the majority judgment put it,

> Under Article I of the Convention, each Contracting State shall secure to everyone within [its] jurisdiction the rights and freedoms defined in . . . [the] Convention'; hence, if a violation of one of those rights and freedoms is the result of non-observance of that obligation in the enactment of domestic legislation, the responsibility of the State for that violation is engaged. Although the proximate cause of the events giving rise to this case was the 1975 agreement between British Rail and the railway unions, it was the domestic law in force at the relevant time that made lawful the treatment of which the applicants complained. The responsibility of the respondent State for any resultant breach of the Convention is thus engaged on this basis. Accordingly, there is no call to examine whether . . . the State might also be responsible on the ground that it should be regarded as employer or that British Rail was under its control.[142]

V. Conclusions

Occasionally the text of a human rights guarantee will stipulate that States Parties to the international convention in question incur responsibility for private infringements of particular rights; and the very nature of certain other human rights leads to the conclusion that they are protected

[138] *White* v. *Riley*, [1921] 1 Ch. 1.
[139] *Sarvent* v. *Central Electricity Generating Board*, [1976] IRLR 66.
[140] *Taylor* v. *Co-operative Retail Services Ltd.*, [1982] ICR 600.
[141] See Davies and Freedland, *Labour Law Text and Materials* (2nd edn., 1984), chap. 5.
[142] Loc. cit. above (p. 277 n. 134), para. 49.

against some non-governmental interferences as well as against violations by the very instruments of State. Moreover, there are some exceptional provisions that render private individuals responsible for violations, notably the Genocide Convention and Article 117 of the EEC Treaty, and arguably the Convention on *Apartheid*. As a general rule, however, international human rights guarantees do not impose legal obligations directly on the shoulders of individuals; and usually the texts of and the *travaux préparatoires* relating to many of the guarantees indicate that they do not make governments responsible for merely private interferences with the interests protected.

On the few occasions where the entire question of State responsibility for private infringements of human rights has been debated before an international tribunal, the tribunal (the European Court of Human Rights) did not have to address itself squarely to the main issues in this controversy, the first and foremost of which is the intrinsic nature of human rights. In the past, these were considered as interests that required protection only against governmental action. It was assumed that the State would always act to prevent its citizens from treating each other in unacceptable ways, but it was paramount to protect individual citizens and minorities from abuses of State power. Against this, it could be argued that the very essence of human rights is that they are inalienable rights of individuals and not just restrictions on what the government may do; that the protection of individual rights is the primary, direct and basic content of human rights rather than a consequence of restrictions on public power.[143]

While this latter view obviously appeals to those who champion universal respect for human rights, it could if it gained general acceptance in fact contribute to a decline in the actual protection for human rights—at least at the international level and in the short to medium term.[144] It would, for example, lead to a huge increase in the workload of the European Commission and Court of Human Rights, which in turn could hamper those bodies' efforts to combat the many atrocities committed by the States Parties 'directly'. And as Mr Danelius pointed out in the *Swedish Engine Drivers' Union* case, many States Parties might object if the European Convention were to be translated into virtually a comprehensive code governing numerous aspects of private relations for societies that possess diverse attitudes to many questions. Extensive interpretation of the Convention in this respect, as Judge Sir Gerald Fitzmaurice remarked in a slightly different context in the *National Union of Belgian Police* case, could even induce some of the States Parties not to renew their acceptance of the right of individual petition under

143 See Nelson in Pennock and Chapman (eds.), *Nomos*, vol. 23: *Human Rights* (1981), chap. 14, and Konvitz (ed.), *Law and Social Action, Selected Essays of Alexander H. Pekelis* (1950), pp. 91–127.

144 Cf. Weil, *American Journal of International Law*, 77 (1983), p. 413.

Article 25 of the Convention, thereby demonstrating the truth of the saying that *le meilleur est l'ennemi du bon*.

Where it is not abundantly clear from either the text or the nature of the right in question, or from the *travaux préparatoires*, whether States Parties are to be held responsible under international law for private interferences with that right, the answer will involve a combination of considerations. One is the background and nature of the convention which proclaims the right. Thus, according to its preamble, the European Convention was adopted as one of 'the first steps for the collective enforcements of certain rights'; and it could plausibly be argued from this that the intention was to found the Convention on the then conventional assumption about the most basic human rights, viz. that they are principally entitlements against abuses of public power. Another consideration is that what at the outset may appear to be a private interference with some human right may also be seen as an individual asserting some other human right that is protected by the very same instrument. This is particularly the case with private discrimination on such grounds as race, sex or religion: the private employers, landlords and testators who discriminate on these grounds can claim to be standing on their own rights to private property, privacy and association. An important element in finding the proper solution to the entire dilemma may lie in the law of State responsibility. Already the International Law Commission has decided to devote special attention to one distinct area of human activity—State responsibility on the basis of risk for certain lawful endeavours, such as spacial and nuclear activities.[145] This paper suggests that State responsibility in the context of human rights obligations requires separate examination by that Commission, and furthermore that in drawing up human rights conventions greater attention be given to the question of the circumstances in which essentially private conduct is to be deemed a violation of the substantive guarantees.

145 Cf. Handl, *American Journal of International Law*, 74 (1980), p. 525, and Christenson in Lillich (ed.), *International Law of State Responsibility for Injuries to Aliens* (1983).

REVIEWS OF BOOKS

New Horizons of International Law and Developing Countries. Edited by S. K. AGRAWALA, T. S. RAO and J. N. SAXENA. University Law Teachers' Research Group Series. Bombay: N. M. Tripathi Private Ltd., 1983. xxiii + 427 pp. + Foreword and Preface. Rs. 90.

This volume incorporates papers contributed at seminars of 1977, 1979 and 1981 organized under the auspices of the Indian Regional Branch of the International Law Association which in 1969 set up a University Law Teachers' Research Group (to promote the study of, and research into, international law), and represents the second publication in this series. Responsibility for the publishing enterprise was entrusted to a Board of three senior Indian Professors of International Law.

As the preface states, the articles included cover 'diverse themes' but 'do not aim at exhausting any theme in any sense'. The latter, unfortunately, only too often proves to be an understatement, as many of the contributions consist of little more than very short, descriptive exposition, often superficial, without any real attempt at critique or evaluation. As far as the 'themes' are concerned, these have been divided up into five sections: 'Human Rights', 'International Criminal Law', 'The New Economic Order', 'Law of the Sea', and what is described as 'Other Essays'. As is often the case with symposium papers, several of the topics dealt with tend to overlap with each other—as, for example, the contributions in Chapters 17 and 18 by S. P. Sharma and D. W. Wadegaonkar on delimitation of maritime boundaries in the 'Law of the Sea' section. Another problem arising for the editors in this section is that a good deal of updating has had to be done to cater for the supervening advent of the 1982 Convention on the Law of the Sea. As some papers were given as early as 1979, an emphasis on the earlier texts still remains (as, for example, on p. 299 in regard to the ICNT delimitation principles). Unfortunately, also throughout the book, the English language exposition is of uneven quality which detracts at times from easy comprehension of the text; and misprints abound, so that, for example, the Draft Convention (Informal Text) 1980 becomes the 'Draft Convention (Informed Text) 1980'! (p. 267).

Space forbids an analysis of all the contributions by the twenty-four Indian scholars involved, but certain of them deserve special mention. In Chapter 2 ('Human Rights in Developing Countries') Professor T. S. Rama Rao discusses what he sees as the 'key role' played by the developing nations in the areas of self-determination and apartheid (p. 20). Controversially, he views any armed assistance to movements against colonial or racist regimes as 'forming an exception to the Charter prescription against "the threat or use of force" under Art. 2 (4) of the Charter' (p. 21), on the basis not just of GA Resolutions, but also of the OAU Charter; and additionally, in the case of *apartheid*, he views the use of force against South Africa as 'a form of humanitarian intervention' which, as such, should be 'deemed to be a tacit exception' to Article 2 (4) (ibid.). As for the application of self-determination itself, he notes that developing nations intended it only for 'the traditional western overseas colonies' (p. 25). But he does admit allowance for extension of the principle to 'exceptional cases' like Bangladesh where a 'segment of a State's population' is subjected to 'undemocratic and brutal measures' (p. 25); and he cites paragraph 7 of the 1970 Declaration on Friendly Relations, *inter alia*, as embodying such a notion of 'internal' self-determination (p. 27).

In Chapter 7, Professor S. K. Agrawala ('The Concept of International Criminal Law') finds the purpose of international criminal law not very different from that of municipal law (p. 71), but points out the interesting fact that not all the relevant conventions even declare the offence concerned to be 'international', and that the Convention on the Crime of *Apartheid* (1973) comes 'nearest to universalising the offence' (p. 80). In Chapter 9 ('Some Basic Issues of International Criminal Law'), L. N. Mathur, in repeating the plea for setting up an International Criminal Court (p. 109), emphasizes the practical problems this would entail such as a 'prosecuting agency' and 'efficacious constabulary' (p. 110) having to be set up, rules of evidence to be settled, and a decision made on where and how the sentence is to be carried out (p. 111).

Two of the other most interesting essays for the Western reader are contained in the 'omnibus' section at the end entitled 'Other Essays'. First, Professor U. Baxi in his piece ('Teaching of International Law in India in 2000 AD—Some Utopian Proposals') claims that on an Olympic games analogy, India would merit a medal for its contribution to international law to date (p. 392), even if the teaching thereof in India 'can only be branded conventional, if not mediocre' (ibid.), and if 'dogmatic assertions of the text or treatise' in this area have become unsatisfactory (p. 395). For such failings he prescribes a 'reorientation' of teaching (p. 396) so that, for instance, teachers develop 'inter-disciplinary skills at least to the point of becoming specialists in some aspects of international law', with a radically revised curriculum distributing some traditional contents to other courses (p. 397) (though his denial that this might overload the other courses (p. 398) may be doubted!). Secondly, Professor M. K. Nawaz in Chapter 26 ('On the Ways and Means of Improving Research of International Law in India'), after pointing out that India has not yet produced an 'authoritative' textbook on international law, nor even a digest of State practice, concludes that, *inter alia*, India should have a Research and Development Board (pp. 411, 412) which might prepare a research manual on international law suggesting 'researchable topics' and applicable methods of research.

On the other hand, other contributions contain dubious, if not erroneous, statements. For example, in Chapter 6 ('Jurisprudence of the European Court of Human Rights') C. K. N. Rajah and J. S. Patil describe the European Court of Human Rights receiving 'petitions' from the Commission or States parties; and in Chapter 17 ('Role of Equidistance Principle in the Process of Delimitation of Continental Shelf and EEZ between Opposite and Adjacent States') S. P. Sharma comes to the remarkable conclusion that the authority of the equidistance principle being unquestionable 'is affirmed by its recent elimination in the Draft Convention presumably implying that it is already part of the international law . . .' (p. 253)! One might have hoped, also, that in Chapter 23 ('Unilateralism and the Emerging Law of Seabed Exploitation'), S. Ramo Rao in alleging that any 'mini-treaties' would be 'without any legal effect' (p. 363), 'contrary to public policy' (p. 370) or 'liable to be unlawful' (p. 371) would anchor his argument on more legalistic grounds by, for example, referring to the implicit *jus cogens* argument of the Group of 77 in its 1979 memorandum (mentioned in footnote 9) or to Article 311 of the 1982 Convention on the Law of the Sea.

This volume, then, provides a useful insight into the Indian viewpoint on aspects of international law. But, like the proverbial curate's egg, it is only good in parts.

C. R. Symmons

Development of Judicial Control of the European Communities. By Gerhard Bebr. The Hague: Martinus Nijhoff, 1981. xviii + 822 pp. (including bibliography and index). *f*360; $150.

Dr Bebr's monograph entitled *Judicial Control of the European Communities* was first published in 1962, before the European Court had pronounced its judgments in *Toepfer*, *Costa* v. *ENEL* or *Consten and Grundig*. The development of Community law by the European Court during the subsequent twenty years has been rapid and varied. For example, we now have, as we did not have in 1962, a substantial jurisprudence upon the supremacy of Community law over national law; upon the availability of damages under Article 215 of the EEC Treaty for acts of a legislative nature; upon human rights as a source of European Community law; and upon the direct effectiveness of directives and of agreements between the Community and third States. For these reasons, Dr Bebr's monograph stood in need of substantial revision. In his new work, *Development of Judicial Control of the European Communities*, Dr Bebr presents more than a fresh edition of an earlier work: rather, it is a new study designed to reflect the new dimensions of the subject.

After an introductory chapter, the book falls into two parts, entitled 'Direct Judicial Control' and 'Indirect Judicial Control'. Those titles are less than felicitous. By 'direct' control, Dr Bebr means actions initiated in the European Court, and by 'indirect' control he means actions initiated before national courts which may refer them to the European Court for preliminary ruling. Thus, collateral attacks upon the applicability of Community legislation by means of pleas of illegality are characterized as aspects of direct judicial control, whereas the attribution of direct effects to a treaty provision is considered as an aspect of indirect judicial control. Moreover, by this selection of terminology, Dr Bebr is obliged to avoid one or two expressions which have gained an established meaning among Community lawyers: he does not speak of 'direct actions' under Article 169 but of actions for infringement, directed at member States.

Most of the part entitled 'Direct Judicial Control' is organized conventionally. There is a long chapter on actions for annulment, containing a particularly useful section on admissibility. Four shorter chapters follow. These deal respectively with actions for default or inactivity; the plea of illegality; actions for damages; and actions for infringement. The next chapter appears at first sight to be anomalous. Entitled 'Infringement Procedure against Defaulting Private Parties', it deals with the imposition of sanctions on private parties by Community institutions. Essentially, this is a brief analysis of the Commission's power under Article 87 of the EEC Treaty and under Council Regulations 11 and 17 to impose fines on undertakings for breaches of competition rules and of rules relating to transport. It is both novel and illuminating to examine this issue from the perspective of jurisdiction, rather than from the customary vantage point of competition law. This part of the book ends with a brief chapter entitled 'Preventive Judicial Control', which is concerned with the European Court's power to review draft agreements in advance of their entry into force.

The part entitled 'Indirect Judicial Control' comprises six chapters, roughly equal in length. Two of these deal with general problems of Article 177 of the EEC Treaty. One deals with the purposes, scope, grounds and effects of a review under Article 177 and one with the practice of national courts in cases based on that article. The remaining three chapters are devoted to the doctrine of direct effect, the supremacy of Community law and the practice of national courts in relation to supremacy.

The main strength of this book lies in its thoroughness. It is comprehensive in its coverage of decisions of the European Court (even though the Court's jurisdiction in staff cases and its power to give judgments based on arbitral clauses in contracts receive scant attention). It devotes much attention to the provisions of the ECSC Treaty and the Euratom Treaty and the judicial decisions thereon, whereas other writers tend to reduce these aspects of the Court's jurisdiction by confining them to the footnotes. Dr Bebr's tendency is to offer an objective appraisal of the Court's decisions, together with an analysis or criticism, but to avoid lengthy conjecture. He shows a healthy scepticism for the more speculative propositions advanced by others. For example, he doubts that the European Court has jurisdiction to review decisions of the representatives of the member States meeting in Council (p. 467). His emphasis is constantly upon the established case law and not upon the literature (even though the bibliography and some of the footnotes show that he has not ignored the latter).

For these reasons, Dr Bebr's book is likely to appeal principally to the practitioner of Community law, for whom it will be indispensable. For the student, the style is likely to prove too dense and the references to the ECSC and Euratom Treaties too frequent and detailed. In view of its use to practitioners, the author and publishers would do well to consider the publication of a supplement, or of periodical supplements, designed to keep the work up to date. Two years seem to have elapsed between the completion of Dr Bebr's study and its publication and a further three years between then and the writing of this review. Those five years have proved no less formative for Community law than the periods between 1962 and 1967, or 1973 and 1978, even though the recent tendency has been to arrest, in some respects, the progress made in those earlier periods towards an enlarged jurisdiction for the European Court.

The informed reader nowadays would like to have Dr Bebr's comments on Case 230/81, *Luxembourg* v. *Parliament*, or on Case 8/82, *Wagner*. He may predict, but would like to read, Dr Bebr's views on Case 246/81, *Lord Bethell*, and on Case 60/81, *IBM*. He may know from other sources what Dr Bebr thinks of Joined Cases 100–3/80, *Pioneer*, and on Cases 104/79 and 244/80, *Foglia* v. *Novello*, but is apt to regret that the judgment in *Pioneer* appeared after the publication of Dr Bebr's book, and the first of the decisions in *Foglia* v. *Novello* reached Dr Bebr too late to prevent him from writing (at p. 377): 'Nor may national courts be deprived of the independent exercise of discretion to make a referral to the Court by an agreement of private parties seeking to oblige the courts of the Member States to do so, as the Court has ruled. . . .'

With or without supplements, this is liable to prove an enduring work. It is the product of much scholarship and it cannot but remain a standard work of reference for years to come.

RICHARD PLENDER

Encyclopaedia of Public International Law. Volume 7: *History of International Law, Foundations of International Law, Sources of International Law, Law of Treaties*. Published under the auspices of the Max Planck Institute, under the direction of RUDOLF BERNHARDT. Amsterdam: North Holland Publishing Company, 1984. 555 pp.

This latest volume covers the history of international law, foundations and principles, sources and the law of treaties. With over one hundred separate entries, it becomes invidious to select only a few for comment, but it is nevertheless of interest to sample those entries dealing with 'controversial' topics.

The volume begins with a well-balanced article on abuse of rights by Kiss, followed by a rather brief treatment of acquiescence by Muller and Cottier, but there is a good entry on estoppel by the same two authors. The entry on 'Consensus' by Erik Suy is disappointing, for it describes the origin and forms of the technique of decision-making without really examining the evidential value of such decisions as 'sources' of international law. In contrast, Van Hecke's treatment of contracts between States and foreign private law persons is excellent. He emphasizes the difficulty in assuming that a reference in a choice of law clause to 'general principles of law' does in fact lead to a coherent set of legal principles. His sensible conclusion is that such a choice of law is really the expression of confidence in the discretion of the arbitrator, which parties may choose in preference to being left at the mercy of the State party's legislature.

This same theme of arbitral, or judicial, discretion is taken up in the entry on 'Equity in International Law' by Janis. But here the treatment of the maritime delimitation cases, in which equitable principles figure prominently, is too slight, for it does not attempt to explain why some factors are relevant in producing an equitable result, and others are not. In the other domain in which equity is increasingly appealed to—the new international economic order—Janis rightly treats it as a concept having more to do with political or economic justice than with rules of law.

Bernhardt's six-page entry on 'Customary International Law' is a masterly summary of an increasingly difficult topic. He maintains the traditional requirement of *opinio juris*, but is prepared to accept 'instant' custom. He notes the different values, or importance, of customary rules, and distinguishes that category which forms the *jus cogens*. Perhaps the one question not sufficiently addressed is whether persistent objection by a State to a new customary rule can prevent such a rule from becoming binding on that State.

Mosler's entry on 'General Principles of Law' makes a useful supplement to Bernhardt's, for he relates these general principles to customary international law extremely well and then goes on to identify various general principles dealing with liability, unjust enrichment, expropriation, denial of justice and so on. It is a very comprehensive treatment of the topic.

One sees, with some surprise, an entry on 'International Law' by Judge Sir Robert Jennings. Given that the whole encyclopaedia is concerned with international law, one wonders what the purpose of this entry might be, or how such an entry could possibly be drafted. The result is nevertheless successful, and it might well be just the 'bird's-eye view' that students ought to have as preliminary reading.

Jaenicke's discussion of 'International Public Order' is wider than *jus cogens*, for he tends to identify, as part of this public order, all those rules which are fundamental to the system, and mostly rules which contain obligations *erga omnes*. The article on '*Jus Cogens*' by Frowein to some extent overlaps, but he takes a very broad view of *jus cogens*, including human rights and the right to self-determination within the category of rights which have as their correlative duties obligations forming part of *jus cogens*.

Judge Manfred Lachs contributes an exceedingly interesting entry on '*Pacta sunt servanda*', tracing its history and analysing its relationship to seemingly contradictory principles such as *rebus sic stantibus* and the right to enter reservations.

The volume concludes with a whole series of entries on treaties, providing a most comprehensive treatment. All in all, this volume is a particularly successful one, providing a very high quality of entries on topics of major importance.

D. W. Bowett

Le Régime juridique des îles dans le droit international de la mer. By Hartini Dipla. Geneva: Publications de L'Institut Universitaire de Hautes Études Internationales, 1984. 243 pp. (including bibliography) + index. 125 F.

In the preface (p. 13), Professor Caflisch describes this work as ranking amongst the premier monographs in the French language dedicated to the phenomenon of islands. Certainly this is true, as the only other recent French language monograph on the regime of islands, that of the Turkish lawyer, Pazarci (*La Delimitation du plateau continental et les îles* (1982)), is essentially concerned with islands in the Aegean dispute. However, in the English language, Mme Dipla has been preceded in 1979 by two other monographs on the same issue (Bowett, *The Legal Regime of Islands in International Law*, and the reviewer's own book, *The Maritime Zones of Islands in International Law*). To a large degree, Mme Dipla covers the same ground as both these monographs, but, of course, has the advantage of being able to take into account later developments in the UNCLOS III proceedings and the finalized 1982 text of the Law of the Sea Convention. Thus, for example, she is able to mention the interesting, but unsuccessful, move by the United Kingdom to suppress Article 121 (3) (which purports to deprive 'rocks' without habitation or economic viability of any continental shelf or EEZ) (p. 41). Also she is able to include a full discussion of the Conciliation Commission's finding in the *Jan Mayen* delimitation (pp. 188–95), the ICJ's judgment in the *Libya–Tunisia* case (pp. 202 ff.), and the *Dubai–Abu Dhabi* arbitration 1981 (pp. 128, 195–200), where she points out that the Tribunal's treatment of the islet of Abu Musa (giving it a 12-mile zone of waters) was based not only on equitable principles, but also on elements drawn from regional practice (p. 200), though she disagrees that such a practice can really be said to exist (p. 202).

Unfortunately, the latest ICJ cases which touch on the problems of islands, the

Canada–USA *Gulf of Maine Delimitation* case (*ICJ Reports*, 1984, p. 4) (see, especially, paras. 198, 201, 210, 211, 222) and the *Libya–Malta* case (ibid., 1985, p. 13), came too late for inclusion, and so now make her categorical statement at p. 224 that there are as yet no customary law rules relating to delimitation of the EEZ somewhat dubious, in so far as the Court in the former case attempted to spell out rules that might be suitable to the division of the 'superjacent water column' (para. 194), and stated that it could be foreseen that with the gradual adoption by the majority of maritime States of an EEZ, criteria of a 'neutral character' would inevitably be given greater preference in the future (ibid).

The monograph deals in the first part with the definition of insular formations, in the second part with the maritime zones of islands, and in the third part with the influence of islands on the delimitation of maritime spaces. But there is a curious omission of any detailed discussion of archipelagos and Archipelagic States; and in the introduction (p. 18) no reason is given for this apart from the fact that archipelagic States were subject to the 'particular regime' of Part IV of the Convention. On the other hand, formations that are strictly 'non-insular' such as low-tide elevations are exhaustively discussed, as are 'fringing reefs' and 'atolls'. In the latter case, she points out that there is no definition of 'atolls' in the LOSC (p. 47), and concludes (p. 77) that the novelty of Article 6 of the LOSC (allowing use of the seaward low-tide line of a reef as a territorial sea baseline) is to allow States having such formations to use such low-tide elevations irrespective of their distance from the island proper, so allowing such States to extend their territorial seas considerably, and, on an analogy with Article 7, possibly to treat the interior lagoon waters as internal (p. 78).

Throughout the book State practice in relation to the treatment of islands is broadly and competently discussed, though on occasion the author has fallen into error by over-reliance on secondary sources, sometimes seemingly owing to a lack of familiarity with English-language sources. Thus, for example, she is incorrect in implying that the 1974 UK continental shelf designation around Rockall was justified on the basis of the rock alone having the ability to generate it (p. 80) (the major UK justification was on the basis of prolongation of the Scottish mainland); nor is it correct that in 1976 Ireland extended its *jurisdiction* over the *rock* (p. 81 n. 137): see the corrigendum in *Revue générale de droit international public*, 81 (1977), pp. 1173, 1175. Sometimes, also, her analysis of material is weak. For example, on the vital matter of the tidal datum requirement of 'above-water' manifestation for insular definition in Article 10 of the 1958 Territorial Sea Convention she unfortunately expresses no opinion (p. 37), whereas on the analogous problem relating to low-tide elevations (p. 45), she commits herself to maintaining, without any convincing supporting evidence, that it is enough for such formations to uncover at 'la marée la plus basse' ('lowest tide'). Also, in her analysis of the present-day status of paragraph 3 of Article 121 of LOSC (p. 100), her conclusion (p. 101) that this paragraph has as yet no customary law status (largely because, it appears, State practice in the form of internal legislative acts makes no distinction between the different 'categories of islands') takes no account of the fact that such alleged 'practice' has not gone unchallenged: see, for example, the continuing Danish and Irish protests concerning the 1974 UK 'Rockall designation' and the imposition by the UK of a 200-mile fishery zone around it in 1976.

This monograph is a useful addition to the existing literature on the law of the sea, and its heavy reliance on French language sources in fact makes it particularly valuable to the English international lawyer, like the reviewer, who tends to be relatively ignorant of such continental sources.

C. R. Symmons

The Regulation of Nationality in International Law. By RUTH DONNER. Helsinki: Finnish Society of Science and Letters (Societas Scientarium Fennica), 1983. 287 pp.

The international and municipal law aspects of the concept of nationality cannot be satisfactorily separated. Consequently, despite its title, Donner's work on the regulation of nationality in international law includes a wealth of references to municipal laws.

The book consists of six chapters (I—Nationality in the Context of Public International Law, II—The Principle of Effective Link in Nationality Law, III—The Imposition and Withdrawal of Nationality, IV—Human Rights Conventions and Other Instruments, V—Nationality and State Succession, VI—Nationality and International Organizations).

The first chapter is devoted to the theory of the sovereign State and its role in the creation of nationality law. It examines the period from Macchiavelli to contemporary times and provides an introduction to the remainder of the work. It is disappointing not to find any examination of the fundamental notions concerning the subject. It would have contributed to a better understanding of the book had the author tried to explain at the beginning the differences between the notions of nationality-citizenship and national-citizen, for these do not always bear the same meaning.

The section of the book which deals with effective nationality is of great importance to the whole dissertation. As practice shows, it is a very sensitive sphere of international relations, the more so as the number of people with more than one nationality is today increasing. The author gives a fairly broad picture of how the principle of effective nationality was born and in doing so she employs various cases in which international tribunals faced the question of multinationality, and analogous questions. The *Nottebohm* case is the central one. It is interesting to note that Donner uses the notion of the 'effective link' (p. 44) whereas the ICJ in its judgment in the *Nottebohm* case explicitly referred to the 'genuine connection'. The author may well have been right in employing the notion of 'effective link' in the title of Chapter II for it has a broader meaning than the principle of the genuine link, but this point is not developed by the author. Her research has led her to this conclusion:

> As a standard of international law the meaning of the link differs from that of domicile. It is a mixture of fact and law. Of the various definitions of the link that have been handed down two ingredients are essential. There must be the fact of permanent residence in a State and also it must be evident that in that State lies the centre of the individual's interest. There must be the fact of commitment to a society as a whole. Nationality defines a person's political status and his duty of allegiance so the bond of attachment must be proof of a political commitment to a State. (p. 95)

It may be worth mentioning that practice has made yet another step forward in the direction of the application of the principle of effective nationality. In 1981 the Iran–United States Claims Tribunal was established in order to decide, among others, claims of Iranian nationals against the US and claims of US nationals against Iran. Frequently the Tribunal has been required to decide the question of the nationality of claimants. In *Esphahanian* v. *Bank Tejerat* a Chamber of the Tribunal adopted the principle of dominant and effective nationality and in applying this principle it took into account place of residence, voting records, property ownership, schooling, payment of taxes, family ties, military service, investments (Iran–US Claims Tribunal Reports, vol. 2, p. 157). The full Tribunal subsequently adopted the same principle in Case A/18.

The Iran–US Claims Tribunal is an example of an international tribunal to which individuals have direct access. Donner mentions one exception (the European Commission of Human Rights) to the rule that individuals have no access to international tribunals (p. 74). One may add to these also the International Centre for the Settlement of Investments Disputes of 1965, bearing in mind that in the past there were other such tribunals too, for example the Upper Silesia Arbitral Tribunal.

In Chapter III Donner discusses another complex issue, the imposition and withdrawal of nationality. In examining different systems of municipal law she goes back to the nineteenth century and gives the reader many examples of legal regulations of the issue. Her survey of a number of cases and doctrine on the question leads her to draw certain general conclusions. One is that, under international law, nationality may not be imposed on a person without his consent and laws purporting to do this are not binding on third States. This consent must be given at the time of naturalization or there must be an act constituting express or implied consent after the imposition in order to render it valid under international law (pp. 141–2). This seems to be an important point because of its possible consequences for all those cases in which the persons concerned did not have the capacity to consent owing to their age at the time when the imposition of nationality took place.

Donner expresses the view that an example of implied consent to a forcible naturalization is shown where there is a strong factual tie between the State and the national (p. 142). One may wonder, however, whether the use of the term 'the national' is correct in this context. If we assume that consent is required in order to become a national by a forcible naturalization, then we cannot speak of a person who has not yet passed 'the test of consent' as a national. Therefore Professor Brownlie's conclusion that the objective principle to emerge from the practice concerned is simply that nationality is not to be conferred on those already having a nationality unless the new nationality is based upon adequate links is to be preferred (*Principles of Public International Law* (3rd edn., 1979), p. 405).

Many interesting remarks are contained in that part of Chapter III which concerns the problem of deprivation or withdrawal of nationality. The question is one of contemporary importance, for as a result of such acts the number of stateless persons is increasing. Donner admits that it is not certain that laws depriving citizens of their nationality are equally invalid under international law, but points out that municipal courts have generally recognized foreign denationalization decrees passed by authorities of a State recognized *de jure*. She stresses, none the less, that the denationalization may be disregarded as contrary to public policy if openly discriminatory and unjust.

The question of withdrawal of nationality is also treated in Chapter IV, where it is considered against the background of human rights documents from the Universal Declaration of Human Rights through the International Covenants on Human Rights to the Final Act of the CSCE.

Once more the author returns to the genuine link between a State and its national, this time in relation to nationality problems arising from State succession. After a very thorough analysis of the problem covering not only doctrine but also State practice and judicial decisions of different countries, Donner concludes that 'according to the modern practice . . . those persons domiciled or habitually resident in territory over which the sovereignty, and hence the nationality, has been transferred, to another or to a new State acquire the nationality of the successor State, provided they have a genuine link with the bulk of the population' (p. 215).

The last chapter, although interesting in itself, gives an impression of being slightly detached from the rest of this valuable work; the problems there covered seem to be more connected with international institutions than with nationality.

It has to be admitted that the book is, in a way, unique, for its author has made a real attempt to examine the question of nationality from many angles. It is very concise and yet full of substance. The book is an excellent survey of the problem of nationality.

ZBIGNIEW WLOSOWICZ

Outer Space: New Challenges to Law and Policy. By JAMES E. S. FAWCETT. Oxford: Clarendon Press, 1984. vi + 170 pp. £16.

This is Professor Fawcett's second book on outer space. In 1968, when *International Law and the Use of Outer Space* was published, the Outer Space Treaty had just come into force and the extent and frequency with which space activities are now carried out was hardly envisaged. The rapid development of space science and technology since then has brought about new challenges for policy-makers. For international lawyers space law has been one of the fastest growing legal disciplines. Therefore the new work by Fawcett after sixteen years is to be welcomed.

The task he has set himself looks promising. As the publisher notes, 'this work seeks to give a concise account of the development of the uses of outer space since the conclusion of the Outer Space Treaty (1967), and of the interaction in them of international regulations and national policies'. However, the work itself only partly succeeds in accomplishing this objective.

Fawcett's book is divided into two parts. The first deals with some basic issues of space law which are summarized under the headings 'The Province of Mankind', 'Uses of Outer Space' and 'Space Operators'. In the second part the main fields in which space activities are relevant are reviewed. These include telecommunications, remote sensing, space stations, astronomical observation and strategic uses of outer space. The work is supplemented by two appendices (chronological and documentary).

The narrative style of the writing is supplemented by a vast number of quotations from several legal instruments. The various tables, graphs and definitions, of both scientific and technical issues such as acronyms of spacecraft, satellite transmission or the method of astronomical distance measurement, are very helpful to the non-professional reader. Thus Fawcett succeeds in revealing the complexity and the scope of the developments taking place in outer space. Unfortunately, however, his analysis of the legal and political issues lacks the care and precision he gives to technical matters.

His section on the 'province of mankind' principle (p. 3) may serve as an example of this. After stating that the perception of outer space as 'the province of all mankind', which was codified in the Outer Space Treaty in 1967, was a 'broad political principle' indicating the growing influence of the developing countries, Fawcett surprises with a comparison of this principle with the later 'common heritage of mankind' principle, which is now established with regard to the moon and other celestial bodies as well as the deep sea-bed. He writes that although the two concepts are overlapping, 'they contain two important and distinct ideas: the "province of mankind" has rather a jurisdictional sense, while the "common heritage of mankind" has property overtones' (p. 4). Surely this is a statement which needs more elaboration. Also missing is an appreciation of the progress which has taken place in this area of space law, namely, the ripening of the rather vague, political concept in the Outer Space Treaty into a legal concept of 'common heritage of mankind' in the Moon Treaty. There are many other examples of this tendency towards enigmatic statements which are not further explained and which cause frustration to the interested reader. This frustration is enhanced by the lack of any useful footnoting and by the somewhat poor bibliography, which makes the book of but limited use as a research tool.

The documents in the appendix, which include the Outer Space Treaty, the Agreement on Activities of States on the Moon and Other Celestial Bodies, the Convention on International Liability for Damage caused by Space Objects and the Convention on Registration of Objects launched into Outer Space, are useful. It is not clear, however, why the fifth major UNCUPOUS agreement, the Rescue and Return Agreement of 1968, has been omitted although it is referred to in the text.

However, in spite of these defects, the present book can be recommended for anyone seeking basic technical information on international space activities or looking for an account of actual or potential operations in outer space.

SABINE LOEPER

Las Islas Malvinas y el Derecho Internacional (*The Falkland Islands and International Law*). By ENRIQUE FERRER VIEYRA. Buenos Aires: Ediciones Depalma, 1984. xvi+368 pp.

The title of this book promises more than is actually delivered by it. As is explicitly stated in the introduction, this study of the relationship between the Falkland Islands and international law is not meant to cover the problem of the legality of the recent Argentinian attempt to impose its sovereignty over the islands through the use of armed force. The illegality under international law of the Argentinian operation of 1982 is, for the author, beyond question. For this reason this work finds its place outside the large part of literature about the Falklands conflict and is, to this extent, quite interesting. Its main aim is to examine the basis, in international law, of the claims of both parties over the islands, with the avowed purpose of demonstrating the superiority of the Argentinian title.

The attempt to do so is made through a one-by-one analysis of the legal grounds put forward by Britain to defend its position, mostly with the support of works and statements made by British authors. The first chapter is thus devoted to a general consideration of the legal position of both parties through documents and reports presented on various occasions in the British Parliament. This is followed by a more detailed evaluation of the contents and history of the Convention of Nootka Sound of 1790 (whose alleged violation by the British constitutes, in the author's view, the basis for asserting the illegality of the occupation of the islands by Britain in 1833). An examination of the concept of prescription, of its relevance to the situation of the islands since 1833, and of the value of the protests issued by Argentina since then, follows the chapter just mentioned. The fourth chapter is devoted to the principle of self-determination of peoples and its application to the inhabitants of the islands. Finally, the last chapter deals with the juridical link between the status of the Falkland Islands and the British Antarctic possessions. Since the official position of the Argentinian Government is one of keeping the question of the sovereignty over the islands distinct from that of the aforementioned Antarctic territories, the last chapter contains a criticism of this position from a legal point of view.

Altogether, this work contains more a collection of materials on the subject than the author's direct analysis of the question. Each chapter consists mainly of the texts relevant to the topic of the chapter itself (all translated into Spanish), and the conclusions of the author. Regrettably, the consequential link between the latter and the former is not always clear and the style of the conclusions themselves is more reminiscent of pleadings before a court than of an academic work. The decision to devote the first chapter to a general exposition of the respective claims, with the one-by-one examination of each ground in the subsequent chapters, is the reason for the numerous repetitions in the course of the text. The subject of self-determination of peoples, in the fourth chapter, is rather unsatisfactorily treated: the impression received is that the avowed purpose of demonstrating the superiority of the Argentinian position is achieved at the cost of a rather superficial and partial analysis of the principle, and of the role played by it in the dispute. The legal and factual issues in the previous two sections, on the other hand, are explained in great detail. These sections contain a good deal of useful information about the origins of the dispute, the applicable conventions, and the often complicated succession of events.

As a whole, the book provides very good and interesting materials for anybody interested in studying the Falklands dispute in depth, but its quality is somewhat uneven. Some parts of it, particularly the links between the material published and the conclusion drawn, leave something to be desired. This also applies to the amount of references provided. It is finally regrettable that, since this work expressly chooses not to deal with the armed conflict between Argentina and the United Kingdom, a section on possible alternative solutions of the dispute between the two countries has not been included.

ANTONIO TANCA

Australia's Antarctic Policy Options. Edited by STUART HARRIS. Canberra: Centre for Resource and Environmental Studies, Australian National University, 1984. xxi+412 pp.

The Antarctic Treaty, which entered into force on 23 June 1961, comes up for review in 1991. The general consensus is that the Treaty has been successful, in so far as militarization of Antarctica has not occurred, the environment has been protected and no new assertions of territorial sovereignty have been made. Moreover, scientific exploration has continued at a brisk pace. There is a growing feeling, however, that the present calm may soon be displaced. A number of factors account for this.

The demands of the various groupings within the international community are changing. In particular the petroleum and mineral industries, prominent in the industrial countries, appear to be turning their attention to the region and the less-developed States, often suffering from food and mineral shortages, are pressing their claim that the 'common heritage of mankind' principle, as embodied in the United Nations Convention on the Law of the Sea, be applied to Antarctica. Moreover, a conflict is developing between the growing environmental awareness which is leading to increased activism for the region's protection, and the discovery of large quantities of exploitable living resources, leading to calls for the region's development. As politics and technology change, so the law will follow, and over the next few years the growth of interest in Antarctica, which has already markedly picked up, will continue to attract international legal attention.

This volume contains eleven papers, each followed by a commentary, discussing a variety of factors to be taken into account in assessing Australia's policy options towards the region. The editor of the collection reviews the perceived options, and concludes that four possibilities exist. The first is to 'increase international acceptability of the treaty system' and to pursue change within the framework it provides. The second is to compromise on the sovereignty claim and give higher priority to the establishment of an effective minerals regime, either within the framework of the Treaty or through the development of the common heritage principle or a trustee system. The third is to give high priority to the sovereignty claim and accept the possibility of a breakdown of the minerals regime and of the Treaty system. A fourth option is to compromise on mineral objectives and either continue the moratorium on mining or develop the concept of a world park. Each option concedes a normative role for international law, a theme which runs through the volume, either expressly or implicitly.

The collection successfully achieves its purpose of providing a basis for 'public' understanding of issues involved, and does so in a thorough and accessible manner. Several essays are of particular interest. Triggs and Greig disagree as to the role of the lawyer, the nature of the law and its relationship to the political realities. Prescott, discussing the boundaries in Antarctica, concludes that as a result of the Treaty, boundaries associated with national claims have no practical significance. Spencer describes the competing interests of Treaty members, non-consultative parties and those entirely outside the Treaty. Quilty and Auburn focus on the mineral aspects of the region, an understanding of which provides a key to future developments, and Chittleborough reviews the history of the exploitation of living resources in the region, concern over which has led to the Commission for the Conservation of Antarctic Marine Living Resources. Finally, Mosley and Horsley put the case for an Antarctica world park, the so-called 'wilderness' option.

Whilst the focus is on Australia, the issues and options discussed reflect those of the wider world. As such, the volume will be useful for all those contributing their own resources to the question of what to do with those in the Antarctic.

PHILIPPE SANDS

Toward a New International Marine Order (Proceedings of the NIO Youth Seminar held in Amsterdam, August 1980). Edited by FINN LAURSEN. The Hague: Martinus Nijhoff, 1982. 198 pp.

The title of this collection of papers is an indication of their age, and of the now sadly disappointed idealism about the law of the sea prevalent only a very few years ago. Indeed, this reviewer's initial reaction upon opening the book was to wonder whether, in view of subsequent events, there would be any point at all in either reading or reviewing it. The 'New International Economic Order', referred to so often in the various essays, appears to have vanished, or at least to have gone into hibernation, to await a more propitious hour. A parallel fate has befallen the much hoped for 'New International Marine Order', as the deadline for signature of the Law of the Sea Convention has passed, with the United States and other important industrial powers steadfastly going their own way and refusing to participate. The papers reproduced in the volume under review were originally presented at an NIO Youth Seminar in August 1980, while the Third United Nations Conference on the Law of the Sea was still in session, and the prospect of a successful conclusion was still in sight. At the time of the Seminar, the eventual result of a divisive vote, instead of agreement by consensus, and the continuing refusal of some of the world's maritime States to sign the treaty could not, of course, have been predicted.

And yet the title, to a certain extent, belies the contents of the book. By the time the Proceedings went to press in late 1981, the unfortunate events of the following year were at least beginning to be feared. Most of the papers were rewritten before publication and reflect the fact that, after the Youth Seminar, the Reagan administration had decided to review the American approach to the Law of the Sea Conference. Some of the Seminar participants express in their comments an apprehension as to the results of the Reagan initiative that later proved to be only too justified. This book, therefore, provides a fascinating snapshot of attitudes and expectations of those involved in the law of the sea issues at an important point in time, immediately prior to the 'failure' of the treaty negotiations.

The book is divided into four parts: I. UNCLOS, National Enclosures, and the Common Heritage; II. Resources, Military Uses, and Ecology; III. The European Community and the Law of the Sea; IV. Deep Sea-bed Mining. Parts I and II contain three essays each, while Parts III and IV have two. The whole is framed by a preface from Jesper Grolin, Chairman of NIO Youth, and an introduction and concluding remarks by Finn Laursen, who in 1981 was visiting lecturer at Aarhus University and assistant professor at Odense. The distinguished contributors include Jens Evensen on 'UNCLOS: Origin and Process of Negotiation', Barry Buzan on 'The Coastal State Movement', John J. Logue on the common heritage, Jorge A. Vargas on the Latin American contribution to the law of the sea, Alan Pickaver of Greenpeace on the 'Ecological Impact of Ocean Exploitation', Tullio Treves and Albert Koers on the European Community and the law of the sea, and Jesper Grolin, Jerome D. Davis and Clive Archer on deep sea-bed mining. Editor Finn Laursen also contributes the chapter on the law of the sea and international security.

Possibly the most interesting section of the book, however, is the transcription of the discussion of John Logue's views on the Common Heritage Fund proposal by the various seminar participants. While the CHF proposal has passed into history, the debate illuminates the vivid contrasts between the idealists and the cynics (or, as fate would have it, the realists). The CHF came to naught because Third World countries with extensive coastlines proved to be no more altruistic than their industrialized colleagues.

For all these reasons, the book is an interesting historical document. It is also a potentially useful teaching tool. Individually and as a group, the ten chapters explain in a clear and impartial manner the origins and development of the UN Conference on the Law of the Sea, and explore the complex policy disputes that ultimately became impossible to resolve.

LOUISE DE LA FAYETTE

The Iran–United States Claims Tribunal 1981–1983. Edited by RICHARD B. LILLICH. Charlottesville, Virginia: University Press of Virginia, 1984. viii + 175 pp. $25.

When the participants gathered for the Seventh Sokol Colloquium at the University of Virginia School of Law in April 1983, the Iran–US Claims Tribunal had been sitting for only a year and a half. The papers presented at the colloquium and now published together in this short volume bear the marks of a limited gestation period. In the majority of the essays, the approach tends to the descriptive rather more than the analytical. Moreover, the sources available to the authors were necessarily sparse. Some contributors have undertaken to update their material to September 1983, but Professor Sohn is nevertheless representative when he notes in his paper that the case sample available to him amounted to no more than 1 per cent of the potential total and was 'not necessarily representative' (pp. 92–3). As a consequence, descriptions of the same cases appear and reappear in many of the papers. For example, the admittedly important jurisdictional cases involving forum selection clauses are discussed fully by Professors Sohn (pp. 95–100) and Lowenfeld (pp. 79–87), and to a lesser extent by David Stewart and Laura Sherman (pp. 18–20). The contributors were also forced by the lack of raw data to devote themselves to mere speculation, attempting to divine deliberative techniques and substantive solutions which the Tribunal might ultimately adopt. Professor Carbonneau's lengthy ode to comparative law methodology is typical, but it is a cry in the wilderness when matched against subsequent Tribunal practice.

With but one exception, all of the papers are by Americans. The introductory piece, a general review of Tribunal activity from 1981 to 1983, is the work of the US State Department's Administrator for Iranian Claims and of a 'Paralegal Specialist'. Another US Government Official is responsible for the contribution on domestic American litigation involving claims against Iran. An American lawyer who has appeared before the Tribunal contributes a 'practitioner's perspective'. Three American academics were called upon to discuss substantive aspects of the Tribunal's decisions, Professor Lowenfeld offering an impressionistic 'interim appraisal', Professor Sohn examining briefly the Tribunal's impact upon the development of international case law and Professor Carbonneau investigating the Tribunal's potential for the elaboration of substantive legal norms. The only non-American contributor is David Lloyd Jones, a British academic and barrister, who has appeared before the Tribunal on behalf of Iran. His paper focuses upon the character and status of the Tribunal.

Although recognizing that the perhaps over-eager release of this collection has dictated its predominantly speculative tone, one would have welcomed more broadly based speculation. It would have been instructive, for example, to read the views of scholars from the developing world, especially as one of the Tribunal's greatest tasks will be to elaborate principles governing the awarding of compensation for the expropriation of foreign-owned property, an issue of great importance for less-developed, capital-importing States. The law governing such compensation is unsettled, as illustrated by the controversy surrounding the various drafts of the latest *Restatement on Foreign Relations Law* of the American Law Institute. An argument can be made that the issue of compensation for expropriation will be simplified for the Tribunal by the existence of the 1955 US–Iranian Treaty of Amity, which prescribes the payment of 'just' compensation representing the 'full equivalent of the property taken', but the Tribunal's sometimes idiosyncratic attitude towards governing law should make any observer loath to predict the course that will be adopted. It would have been helpful to see rehearsed the substantive arguments that Iran is likely to present to the Tribunal. Scholars from developing States could also have brought valuable perspectives to bear upon the evaluation of the entire Tribunal process. The Iranian arbitrators have complained bitterly that arbitration is 'an institution which is designed to safeguard the interests of the capitalist world'. One wonders if that statement is merely the product of rhetorical excess or if it reflects sincere and widespread resentment.

A number of papers contain concise and valuable histories of the hostage crisis and the negotiations leading to the creation of the Tribunal. The Tribunal's early case law is also recounted in detail. The contribution of Michael Hertz of the US Department of Justice focuses upon a wider context, providing an exhaustive account of the domestic 'litigation history' of American claims against Iran and its controlled entities. His paper is addressed expressly to 'practitioners, governmental officials, and judges' in an effort to help them devise 'appropriate strategies to handle similar litigation in the future' (p. 136).

From the perspective of 1985, much of the discussion contained in the volume already seems dated. Examples could be drawn from every paper, but it will suffice to note that David Stewart and Laura Sherman, in criticizing the lassitude of Tribunal proceedings, rely upon statistics updated only to September 1983. The pace of Tribunal decision-making has quickened markedly in the last two years, despite serious internal wrangling. Professor Sohn's contribution includes a brief review of the decisions of Chamber Two concerning jurisdiction over claims presented by dual nationals, but the issue has since been resolved authoritatively by the plenary Tribunal in *Case A-18*. Even the documentary sources cited by many of the authors have often been replaced by more easily accessible collections. It is no longer necessary, for example, to write to the Tribunal or to the US State Department to obtain copies of the Final Tribunal Rules of Procedure, for all the basic Tribunal documents, including orders and awards, have now been reprinted in the *Iran–United States Claims Tribunal Reporter*, a publication of the Research Centre for International Law at the University of Cambridge. Materials may also be found in the *Iranian Assets Litigation Reporter*, but its prohibitive cost ensures that only the best endowed institutions (and American law firms) will be able to subscribe.

One contribution does stand out as having passed the test of time. David Lloyd Jones's paper raises difficult theoretical questions concerning the nature of arbitrations involving States and foreign private parties, the resolution of which will have important consequences for the Iran–US Claims Tribunal and for all tribunals of a 'mixed', public law and private law status. It should be noted, however, that this paper was published previously in the *Virginia Journal of International Law* and is already widely available. The contributions of Professor Lowenfeld and of David Stewart and Laura Sherman are also reprinted from periodicals and contain no significant alterations.

In his preface to the volume under review, Professor Lillich suggests that 'the seven chapters constitute the most extensive description, critique and evaluation of the Tribunal's work that has been published to date' (p. viii). That summation remains true for the present, but this collection is by no means definitive and its long-term utility is likely to be restricted to its historical interest as an evaluation of the Iran–US Claims Tribunal at a very early stage in its development.

STEPHEN J. TOOPE

Extraterritorial Jurisdiction: An Annotated Collection of Legal Materials By A. V. LOWE. Cambridge: Grotius Publications Ltd., 1983. xxiii + 273 pp. £25.

This most valuable collection of materials is described in the introduction as being 'concerned with the problems arising from the extraterritorial application of laws regulating economic activities'.

The work is divided into three parts. Part I—The Claims—is 78 pp. long. For the most part it contains examples of United States practice (and that comprising mainly decisions of the federal courts) in claiming extraterritorial jurisdiction for its anti-trust laws by applying them to that behaviour outside its territory which has economic effects within it. The 'odd man out' is the extract from the report of the *Dyestuffs* case, i.e. Cases 48 et seq./69, *ICI et al.* v. *Commission*, [1972] ECR 619, which is a decision of the European Court of Justice on the construction of Article 85 of the EEC Treaty. The Court avoided reliance upon the 'effects' doctrine, and has yet to confirm that it forms part of Community law, though the European Commission acts on the assumption that it does. Since not all member States of the EEC either claim or recognize the extraterritorial reach of other countries' anti-trust laws, this is perhaps a rash assumption, even if the Court could be said to have hinted at recognition of the 'effects' doctrine in Case 22/71, *Béguelin*, [1971] ECR 949. Indeed, in its note to the US State Department protesting at the US 'pipeline' legislation, the EEC itself, in its executive capacity, described the 'effects' doctrine as having found 'less than general acceptance under international law' (Lowe, pp. 204, 205). The extract from *Dyestuffs* is preceded by an excellent note which surveys the status of the 'effects' doctrine in countries other than the US, demonstrating, for example, that jurisdiction may be claimed on this basis—according to national law—by Austria, the Federal Republic of Germany and Greece.

Part II of the book is entitled 'The Responses to the Claims' (pp. 79–225). It contains some thirty or so evidences (mainly legislative texts but including *aides-mémoire* and like statements of practice) of resistance by States to the application of US legislation to activity outside its borders. Many of the examples, unsurprisingly, are of national 'blocking' legislation responding to US attempts to require individuals outside its borders to reveal to the US authorities business records, etc., in connection with alleged violations of US law.

Part III is entitled 'The Resolution of Jurisdictional Conflicts' (pp. 226–67). The materials included therein demonstrate the steps that have latterly been taken to resolve conflicts of jurisdiction through bilateral agreements, and the recommendations of international organizations. A helpful editorial note (pp. 239, 240) makes the point that provisions on the enforcement of competition laws may appear in bilateral treaties of friendship, commerce and navigation, and lists a number of examples.

A very readable survey of the materials contained in the three sections of the book is to be found in the introduction (xv–xxiii), along with an historical outline, which puts the extensive practice to be found in the volume in its chronological context.

Extraterritorial Jurisdiction is obviously the product of considerable research on the part of Mr Lowe. It is an invaluable reference book, and legal practitioners and scholars alike will benefit greatly from it.

DERRICK WYATT

Essays in International Law in Honour of Judge Manfred Lachs (Institute of State and Law of the Polish Academy of Sciences). Edited by JERZY MAKARCZYK. The Hague, Boston, Lancaster: Martinus Nijhoff, 1984. 757 pp. No index.

This substantial celebration of the first seven decades of the life of Judge Manfred Lachs comes with a foreword by Adam Lopatka and an impressive bibliography. The essays very adequately reflect the varied intellectual interests and broad experience of Judge Lachs and the editor is to be congratulated. The collection contains fifty-one pieces whose authors encompass twenty-six nationalities and eleven Judges or former Judges of the International Court. The essays are generally rather brief, but the pleasant result of the discipline of brevity is that they tend to be lively and to the point. With the exception of the thoughtful and original piece from Professor Graveson ('The Contribution of Private International Law and Comparative Law to International Harmony and Understanding'), the subjects treated fall within the spheres of public international law and international organizations.

Given the variety of backgrounds of the contributors, the collection provides a panorama of different styles and approaches to the materials of the law, and yet overall perhaps it is the substantial degree of consistency which is remarkable. The vast majority of the essays are concerned with practical and technical problems of contemporary international law. However, a minority of writers look at the law in a broad perspective and in terms of its general capabilities (Madame Bastid, Judges Jennings and Lacharrière and Professor Tunkin).

Several contributions are concerned with the role of the International Court as perceived by its members. Thus Judge Mosler writes candidly about the issue of justiciability, and Judges Elias and Schwebel study the advisory opinion jurisdiction. The essay on 'the judicial philosophy of Manfred Lachs' from the hand of Lyndel Prott is attractively presented and of very great interest. This and the contribution of Judge Mosler, already noticed, very effectively elucidate those issues central to the role of the Court in dealing with disputes.

The reviewer, in common with other readers of these essays, will have his preferences among the topics which feature, but at least those preferences will provide a sample of the many offerings. Judge Mbaye expounds the law of development, a subject more or less ignored in the anglophonic literature. Professor McWhinney gives a spirited survey of the 'time dimension' in the law, in which he looks at the problem of the intertemporal law but also gives the issues a much wider context. Dr Barbosa and Professor Salmon examine the concept of necessity in the light of the work of the International Law Commission. Professor Zemanek analyses some problems of reservations to treaties in the Vienna Convention. Professor Paul De Visscher writes a carefully nuanced commentary on unilateral declarations with special reference to the *Nuclear Tests* cases. The editor, Professor Makarczyk, makes a frank and useful survey of the implied powers of organizations in the context of the jurisprudence of the International Court.

The two subjects which figure most prominently in this volume are the sources of the law and the law of the sea, areas which have always attracted the interest of Judge Lachs. Studies relating to the former include Professor Wolfke's essay, 'Can codification of international law be harmful?', which is a critique of the position adopted by Richard Baxter in his lectures to the Hague Academy in 1970. There is a particularly impressive series of pieces on the modern law of the sea. Eduardo Jiménez de Aréchaga examines the relation of the 1982 Convention and customary international law. The essay concludes with several candid observations, of which the following is a good example:

> A final word to point out that the generating effect of the Convention is not exhausted by the acceptance of the Exclusive Economic Zone. It may yet cause other significant developments, such as a broader acceptance of the notion of 'common heritage of mankind' as a legal principle rendering illegal the unilateral exploitation by individual States of the mineral resources of the sea-bed and ensuring that such an exploitation is carried out collectively, 'taking into particular consideration the interests and needs of developing States'. (p. 585)

Professor Castañeda provides a most helpful account of the negotiations on the EEZ at UNLOSC III. Judge Oda subjects the dispute settlement clauses of the 1982 Convention to rigorous analysis. The relation of the maritime flag and State responsibility are examined by President Nagendra Singh. Daniel Vignes concludes the series with a lively account of the recent schism resulting from the conclusion of the Third United Nations Conference.

Of the pieces which do not readily fit into the more familiar categories, the study by Professor Verwey of the legal significance of the classification of LDCs stands out particularly. As he says, this is one of the 'grey zones' of international law. In this excellent essay the topic receives a balanced treatment.

It is popular, especially among those ignorant of the world of international affairs, to criticize the Court—and other courts for that matter—on the ground that its members are supposedly 'cut off' from reality; but reality is most often referred to by those with the least experience of affairs. The fact is that the career of Judge Lachs embodies a variety of experience, military, diplomatic, legal and judicial, which is in its way typical of the membership of the Court, at least of his generation, who experienced the Second World War in their adult lives. Yet even by the standards of his peers, the experience of Manfred Lachs has been unusually rich. It is pleasant for his friends and colleagues to see his contribution to international law and the diplomacy of dispute settlement saluted with style.

IAN BROWNLIE

Risoluzione e Sospensione dei Trattati per Inadempimento (*Termination and Suspension of Treaties for Breach*). By RICCARDO PISILLO MAZZESCHI. Milan: Giuffrè Editore, 1984. viii + 352 pp. L. 22.000.

Although in State practice the right of termination and suspension of international treaties as a consequence of their breach is frequently invoked, and it plays a role in more than one area of the literature of public international law, it has seldom constituted the autonomous subject of a research work. This book represents a significant contribution in this sense, both as a clarification of the subject, and as an evaluation of its development in the light of the progressive codification of customary international law which has been taking place in recent years. This work, however, is not confined to ascertaining the existence of the right and its possible limits; it goes further in an attempt to identify the nature of the right itself which finds a place in several areas of international law, namely the law of treaties as such, the law of State responsibility and the legal regulation of peaceful reprisals. The method adopted is that of a systematic inquiry into the scope and the 'position' of the right in question on several planes: general international law, its subsequent codifications *ratione materiae* and the relationship between the two.

The first two sections seem to be by and large the two most important ones. They are devoted to the identification of the scope and limits of the right before the coming into force of the Vienna Convention on the Law of Treaties, and to the changes and clarifications brought about by this convention. In the first section, about bilateral termination, an impressive survey of the literature is provided; the legal principle is systematically analysed from the point of view of its existence, its nature and its procedural and substantive limits. Great importance is then given to the preparatory works of the Vienna Convention, especially to the extent to which the approach to the question adopted in them differs from that which prevailed in the codification of Article 60. To this end the reports of the International Law Commission are analysed in great detail. On the whole, the systematization of the subject achieved with the Vienna Convention is very carefully evaluated in all possible aspects, with remarkable clarity. Great stress is given to the limits of this convention *vis-à-vis* the scope of the right in general international law, and the aspects which are left unimpaired by the former. The subject of the right of termination and suspension with respect to multilateral treaties, which was left rather vague in the section devoted to customary law, is treated here in greater detail.

Particularly interesting is the following section, on the reports of the International Law Commission on the draft Convention on State Responsibility, especially where it points out the existence of a divergence of approach to the problem between the first two parts of the draft. The remaining chapters deal with recent developments of the subject as they emerge from a series of international judicial and arbitral decisions, with the role of the right of termination and suspension for breach in the context of international organizations, and, finally, with the relationship between the aforementioned right and the legal regulation of peaceful reprisals. An attempt to individuate tendencies, rather than reach definitive conclusions, characterizes these last chapters and this aim has been satisfactorily achieved.

As a whole, the subject seems to be covered in this work in every possible aspect, and the limits of the research are certainly more attributable to the grey areas and loopholes of the subject as it is conceived in the literature and applied by States than to the way the work has been carried out. In fact, great restraint can be noticed, on the part of the author, in issuing general statements or drawing absolute conclusions, while no statement is made without substantive support, both in logical terms, and in terms of coherence with the prevailing views in the literature and with State practice.

The positive judgement given to the contents of the book can undoubtedly be extended to the more formal aspects of it. The drafting is extremely clear and readable. Even if the author deals with a rather specific and technical topic in a rigorous way, this does not seem to affect his capability of keeping awake the attention of the reader. The book is well bound (although some reservations could be expressed on the 'polished' cover), the editing is excellent, and so is the amount of references provided. A small addition with an index of the cases cited would have been very useful.

ANTONIO TANCA

La Codification de la succession d'états aux traités. By Z. MÉRIBOUTE. Paris: Presses Universitaires de France, 1984. 272 pp. 135 F.

This book provides an interesting analysis of the *travaux préparatoires* of the Vienna Convention of 1978 on Succession of States in Respect of Treaties, and of the extent to which the Convention codifies customary law. The author's conclusion is that the rules contained in the Convention accurately reflect customary law, with the exception of the rule that a new State created by secession inherits most of the predecessor State's treaties; he argues that this rule is not supported by State practice and was inserted in the Convention as a result of Afro-Asian hostility to secession. He is also critical of illegal annexations of territory by certain Afro-Asian States (West Irian, East Timor, Western Sahara, Eritrea).

The author is Algerian, and it is therefore natural that he bases the 'clean slate' principle (the principle that an ex-colony is not bound by treaties made by the former colonial power) on the principle of self-determination. But, unlike some Afro-Asian writers, he does not restrict his analysis to post-1945 practice; he also makes a comparatively brief examination of pre-1945 practice, and concludes that it does not differ very much from post-1945 practice.

Some of the author's interpretations of State practice are questionable. For instance, he often cites denunciation of treaties by newly independent States as evidence that those States have not inherited the treaties, whereas many writers would interpret such denunciations as evidence that the treaties were binding on the denouncing States from the moment of independence to the moment of denunciation. Another defect is that the author does not examine why so few States have ratified the 1978 Convention. On the whole, however, the book is a useful addition to learning on State succession. All the more pity, then, that it is spoilt by many misprints and by the lack of an index.

MICHAEL AKEHURST

Human Rights in International Law: Legal and Policy Issues. Edited by THEODOR MERON. Oxford: Clarendon Press, 1984. 2 volumes. 566 pp. £20 per volume.

This book is the nearest there is to a comprehensive textbook on the international law of human rights and is as such a very welcome addition to the bibliography on the subject. Arranged in two volumes, the book consists of thirteen chapters on different topics, each one having been written by an eminent authority on the subject. The subjects include an overview of the jurisprudence of human rights, civil, political and economic rights, the United Nations system, the International Labour Organization, regional systems and the work of non-governmental organizations. All the contributions, although inevitably brief, are admirable for their clarity of expression which has the result that the material is readable and interesting. At the end of each chapter, there are teaching suggestions and bibliographies for either a long or short course on the subject. Having already taught the 'International Protection of Human Rights' for several years as a single post-graduate course, this reviewer read the teaching suggestions as well as the contributors' approach to their subjects with interest. This reviewer's personal experience has been one of considerable difficulty in adequately covering the vast amount of factual material necessary for an intelligent discussion of the issues raised in the context of international human rights law. In particular, most of the contributors thought it important to teach the procedural systems developed under the UN and regional organizations, but this takes time and thus the tedium involved seems unavoidable. Of much geater interest is the substantive law and its interpretation, and in this context the European Convention is unique for its enormous case law. Here again, however, the pressures of time are an inhibiting factor. One feels obliged to familiarize the students with the major Court cases on selected rights, yet the lesser known cases on admissibility are often a truer reflection of the jurisprudence of the European organs. A study of selected cases since the coming into force of the Convention provides a truly illuminating picture of the shifts in attitudes which have occurred, particularly in the late 1960s and 1970s, and indicates the extent to which the Convention has been interpreted so as to be in conformity with the prevalent views in Europe at the time. A study of human rights in an historical, philosophical and societal context is certainly the most interesting approach but, if one is to avoid being parochial, it also involves an input of material which is virtually impossible to achieve in the light of the time restraints of a course.

The topic of discrimination, however, should pose less of a problem in this respect as there is greater discussion of the subject in the popular press. Greenberg's chapter on discrimination is disappointing in that it is basically United States orientated and approaches the question of sex discrimination in a particularly superficial way. Given that this is the most deeply rooted and widespread form of discrimination in the world, some sociological consideration, and a study of legal problems arising therefrom, is called for. It would also have been useful to have pointed out that discrimination can take two forms, the denial of fundamental civil rights to a section of the population on the one hand, and on the other a difference in treatment based on custom or prejudice which leads to such gross social and economic inequalities that it affects the very dignity of the individual. It is this latter type that is in practice the most pervasive in modern times and which is not dealt with in the standard human rights documents covering civil rights, including the European Convention. On the subject of economic and social rights, Trubek's chapter on 'social welfare rights', as he conveniently calls them, persuasively argues that successful development depends on their implementation and outlines the work of the ILO and WHO in this respect and their possible contribution to the implementation of the ESC Covenant. In addition to the measures indicated, this reviewer would have additionally stressed the importance of adequate education to *all* sections of the population as essential for both development and the curbing of excessive population growth in the poorest countries.

Another chapter on which this reviewer would like to comment is Lillich's review of civil rights. Of particular interest is the fact that Lillich attempts to assess whether certain rights in the Universal Declaration have attained the status of international customary law or even *jus cogens*. It is refreshing that such an exercise has been undertaken for there have been too many facile generalizations to the effect that the Universal Declaration as a whole is international customary law. Although this reviewer would agree with most of Lillich's conclusions, the method of assessing whether a right represents customary law seems somewhat cavalier. Of particular importance in human rights law is the credibility gap between statements as to principle and actual behaviour within a State. Some discussion as to the difference between *opinio juris* representing State practice and mere lip-service is surely called for. Also to be questioned is the method of comparing human rights instruments and concluding that if they all coincide in one respect, this is custom. Treaty Law cannot, *ipso facto*, indicate the existence of custom. Conversely, it is surely not a negative factor in itself, as Lillich appears to indicate, that a right should be described in general terms or that limitations are permissible for public reasons. Finally, it might be questioned whether there is such a thing as a 'weak right', which is the term used by Lillich when referring to the right of religion.

Dinstein's chapter on human rights in armed conflict is particularly useful in that, apart from usefully summarizing the scope of this vast subject, he pinpoints popular misconceptions relating to the content and application of this field of law and effectively disproves them. Dictates of space prevent a discussion of all the chapters which are, as earlier stated, generally very clear and useful. Finally, it might be mentioned that although this is the most up-to-date work, human rights law moves fast, and apart from the constant stream of new cases being decided under the European Convention, new books appear, amongst which Van Dijk and Van Hoof's volume on the European Convention should be mentioned. This reviewer would also have included Pomerance's excellent book on self-determination amongst Humphrey's literature on that subject in his chapter on political rights.

LOUISE DOSWALD-BECK

Contract Conflicts. Edited by P. M. NORTH. Amsterdam and New York: North Holland Publishing Co., 1982. xviii+404 pp. US $53.50; *f*115.

This collection of papers presented at the 1981 Colloquium of the United Kingdom National Committee on Comparative Law forms a comparative study of the EEC Convention on the Law Applicable to Contractual Obligations of 1980.

Given its origin, the contributions vary greatly in length, particularity and in the degree to which they are 'comparative'. The two main parts which follow the editor's general account of the Convention consist, first, of eight detailed studies of particular topics and, secondly, of six discussions of the Convention in relation to, or comparison with, national laws of both EEC member States and non-member States.

Of the former, Jackson and Philip both discuss the somewhat complex provisions of the Convention concerning the role of mandatory rules and public policy from the points of view of an English and a European lawyer. Particularly interesting are the acute comments of Hartley and Morse on the consumer protection and contracts of employment provisions respectively. The latter's words make one wonder with the writer what advantages could really be derived from the enactment of the Convention rules into domestic law. In the 'comparative' contributions, Collins, a consistent sceptic where the Convention is concerned, shows from an examination of some decided English cases how difficult it may be to apply the Convention with any certainty in very important commercial contexts. Von Hoffman, Giardina and von Overbeck examine the Convention in the light of German, Italian and Swiss law. A devastatingly rumbustious American discussion which compares the Convention with the equivalent rules of the United States *Restatement* (*Second*) comes from Juenger; it comes as a bit of a surprise to find a couple of paragraphs at the end which are complimentary of the Convention.

Some of the contributors, among them those who had something to do with the formulation of the Convention, are for it, others are either critical or hostile. Its two notorious features come in for the greatest and most frequent attack. These are the concept of the place of 'characteristic performance' as a means of selecting the proper law of a contract in the absence of an express choice (Article 4 (2)) and the application of mandatory rules of a legal system other than that of the forum or of the proper law (Article 7 (1)). Of course, the latter was the subject of a reservation by the UK when signing the Convention.

Most of the English contributors seem to feel that the adoption of the Convention into English law would make little appreciable difference from the present dispensation. This may be true, but the Australian, Pryles, strongly believes that it would lead to future divergence between English and Commonwealth conflict of laws in this field.

After reading this book one is left with the feeling one had before picking it up, that this Convention was unnecessary in the first place, and that it resembles a scissors and paste job done from various legal systems. The real trouble is that such a Convention, like most previous choice of law conventions, must tend to freeze the law at a particular stage of its development and thereby hamper its proper evolution. As Juenger says, a convention differs from a restatement which 'merely purports to say what the courts have said already'; unlike a treaty, 'it is not a code directed towards the future'. The lack of legislative activity that the Convention has generated amongst most member States is, perhaps, some comfort.

J. G. COLLIER

Dispute Settlement in Public International Law. Texts and materials compiled by K. OELLERS-FRAHM and N. WUHLER. Publication of the Max Planck Institute for Comparative Public Law and International Law. Berlin, Heidelberg, New York, Tokyo: Springer-Verlag, 1984. xx+913 pp. $87.40 approx.

This is an extremely useful compilation, both for reference and as a teaching tool in any course concerned with settlement of disputes.

Part I contains general agreements, both universal (Hague Convention 1907, ICJ texts, General Acts of 1928 and 1949, ILC Model Rules on Arbitral Procedure, Swiss Model Treaty of 1960, Vienna Convention on Law of Treaties, Article 66 and Annex) and regional (i.e. various texts of Council of Europe, Central America, OAS, OAU, Arab League). It also contains some bilateral treaties of general application (i.e. Jay Treaty, 1794; Bryan Treaties, 1914).

Part II covers instruments dealing with human rights in Europe, the United Nations, America, Africa and the Arab region. Part III contains treaties on economic co-operation, such as GATT, the European Economic Communities, and related instruments like the Yaoundé and Lomé agreements, Benelux, the American organizations (CACM, LAFTA and ALADI), some African organizations (the East African Common Market, CEAU and ECOWAS).

Part IV covers a rather disparate range of subjects of a technical nature such as traffic and communications (ICAO, Intelsat, carriage of goods conventions), disarmament, nuclear energy, law of the sea, international rivers and lakes, investment and export (including ICSID and the Judicial Board of OAPEC) and State immunity.

Part V is devoted to post-war settlement agreements (MATs, Locarno, conciliation commissions, restitution court, external debts, etc.). Part VI includes dispute settlement provisions in various treaties on topics such as diplomatic relations, space liability, telecommunications, pollution, INMARSAT, the UPU, air transport agreements, river basin treaties, investment guarantees, protection of investments. Finally, Part VII includes a range of special agreements or compromis, both those relating to the ICJ and those relating to arbitration.

The one area excluded, perhaps necessarily on grounds of space, is international commercial arbitration agreements between private parties (except for the ICSID Convention, which is included).

The volume is primarily a volume of texts. There are introductory notes to each part, which, though short, are helpful in putting the texts in their context. There is also quite a useful, selected bibliography on each section, and even some reference to cases where these are publicly reported. But the notes do not purport to embody value-judgments, or critiques or even analyses: they are simple factual statements. So the note to the OAU Protocol of 1964 simply reports its non-use, without further comment.

It is hard to think of material which ought to have been included, but which is omitted: the selection is sensible and very comprehensive. Its utility is therefore considerable.

D. W. BOWETT

Extra-Territorial Application of Laws and Responses Thereto. Edited by CECIL J. OLMSTEAD. Oxford: International Law Association in association with ESC Publishing Limited, 1984. xv + 236 pp.

Defining a State's competence under public international law to prescribe and apply its laws beyond its territory causes particular theoretical problems for students and scholars of the subject. With the growing economic interdependence of States, and the developing facility for transborder communications and transactions for private individuals and corporations, the question has assumed increasing importance for the practitioners of domestic and international law. This volume, the product of the International Law Association Conference on Extra-Territorial Application of Laws and Responses Thereto, held in May 1983, presents a collection of essays by a distinguished group of international legal scholars and practitioners attempting to cover wide-ranging aspects in a systematic and comparative manner.

The Conference and the book are divided into six parts. Part I is of the greatest interest to the theoretician, and deals with 'State Jurisdiction and International Law'. Much attention is devoted to the content and effect of the decision in the *Lotus* case (*PCIJ*, Series A, No. 10), the source of much mystery to students of the subject. Both Professor Higgins and Professor Weil provide illuminating papers, the latter being of particular interest for its blunt analysis of whether international law does indeed provide any rule at all in this area, and its preference for the declared existence of a rule under which 'states are permitted by international law to define extra-territorial norms but, at the same time, they are also permitted by international law not to recognize and give effect to, extra-territorial norms adopted by other states' (p. 36). Professor Meessen suggests the existence of an 'international law rule of balancing interest', particular support for which is found by the incorporation of the principle in section 40 of the United States *Second Restatement of the Foreign Relations Law*. He accepts, however, that this is not a widely accepted rule, which is not yet referred to in the general textbooks. The difficulties of definition and application are clear, and are referred to throughout the book.

Part II is concerned with 'Specific Extra-Territorial Applications of Jurisdiction Resulting in Conflicts'. One section discusses export, trade and financial controls, with particular emphasis on US legislation. Professor Richard Portes discusses economic motives for extra-territorial intervention in economic processes, a key factor for understanding why States adopt the positions they do. The second section, on restrictive business practices, consists of papers by national authors on the US, French, German and European Community approaches to the extra-territorial application of laws, and contrasts in varying degrees of detail the meanings of principles such as 'comity', 'reasonableness' and 'effects'.

Part III is concerned with 'Securities Regulation'. Arthur Fleischer Jun. covers a wide-ranging subject-matter thoroughly in his analysis of the position in the US, including the general approach of the courts and some recent developments by the Securities Exchange Commission to address insider trading through foreign banks. Sir Patrick Neill compares the approach of the courts in the United Kingdom, and finds that when they are faced with a foreign bank secrecy law, preventing disclosure of the identity of a purchaser of shares, their freezing of the rights attaching to the shares 'looks a little bit more legitimate' than the approach of the US. The viewpoint of the European Community is described by Donald Holley as being 'a little vague', with no general position of principle discernible as yet.

Part IV deals with the 'Responsibilities of Directors and Officers for Acts of Foreign Subsidiaries and Affiliates'. William Park discusses some of the effects of the determination by the International Court of Justice in the *Barcelona Traction* case that the nationality of a corporation is determined by the place of incorporation, and finds that this principle is 'clear, sensible and capable of application without uncertainty' (p. 153). Furthermore it 'could and should be extended to the actions of directors in relation to the corporation' (ibid.). Dr Mann believes that the attitudes of judicial and administrative authorities in the

US are inconsistent with international law as developed by the practice of the majority of civilized States, but finds that 'perhaps they are not altogether alien to the fundamental approach of the United States itself' (p. 159). The developing position of the European Community is analysed by both Kuper and Gill, and the much criticized and now amended Vredeling Directive receives attention.

Part V deals with the 'Discovery of Documentary and other Evidence in a Foreign Country' and is almost wholly concerned with the procedure within the US, and with the decisions of US courts.

Part VI deals with 'Responses to Extra-Territorial Exercises of Jurisdiction'. Sir Ian Sinclair discusses 'The Diplomatic Response', and Serge April the purpose, legality and effect of blocking statutes.

In so far as it presents traditional analyses and answers to traditional problems this is an excellent collection of essays, which would form an admirable central text for a seminar course. The volume is particularly helpful in that it brings together into a manageable and organized whole a vast array of factual examples and conflicting arguments. The reader's task would be greatly facilitated by a general or case index, both of which are missing. Unfortunately, the participants represent and discuss only the perspectives, actions and reactions of the numerically small but economically powerful and interdependent Western liberal democracies. As such, the practice of these could only develop into customary regional international law, and it would be useful and necessary, in the context of a volume on general international law, to have at least noted the attitudes and responses of economically developing and less-developed and powerful States, particularly those in the Far East and Latin America. Professor Olmstead, the Conference chairman, in drawing together the threads, notes the participants' consensus that 'international law does limit a state's authority to prescribe rules applicable to foreign persons outside the territorial limits of the state, . . . that efforts to enforce such rules extra-territorially may well constitute a violation of international law', and that 'a state should consult with states likely to be affected by such prescriptions prior to any enforcement attempts . . .'. The consensus of writers has not been translated into the practice of States. To a certain extent the volume has been overtaken by events, and the signals conflict as to whether the US has become more or less sensitive to the interests of others. Dr Mann believes that the excesses of jurisdiction committed by the US 'will cease only when an international tribunal has established their illegality'. Given the nature of the economic interests involved, and the attitude displayed by the US to at least one decision of an international tribunal since that was written, such sentiments are perhaps over optimistic.

PHILIPPE SANDS

Third United Nations Conference on the Law of the Sea: Documents. Edited by R. PLATZÖDER. Dobbs Ferry, New York: Oceana Publications, Inc., 1982– . 15 volumes.

The extensive documentation—official and unofficial—of the Third United Nations Conference on the Law of the Sea is now being organized in a fifteen-volume series: *Third United Nations Conference on the Law of the Sea: Documents*, by Dr R. Platzöder. The first seven volumes of the series have been published and the remaining eight volumes will become available throughout 1985 and 1986. The documents are organized according to the system of the 1982 Convention on the Law of the Sea. The first two volumes and part of the third volume contain the five negotiating texts, the draft Convention—both the informal and formal texts—and the 1982 Convention plus the Resolutions adopted on 30 April 1982. The remaining volumes contain documents related to the preamble, the Second Committee, the First Committee, the Third Committee, dispute settlement, and the plenary. The series closes with an index.

The chapter headings reflect the method according to which UNCLOS III worked: informal and formal papers, informal and formal sessions and informal and formal proposals. For example, with respect to the work of the Second Committee the following chapter headings are included: Formulation of Main Trends, Main Trends, Second Committee Blue Papers, Second Committee Informal Meetings, Second Committee Proposals and Second Committee Summary Records. Within each chapter the documents are organized chronologically.

The series presents real improvements over other series compiling UNCLOS III documents: *Third United Nations Conference on the Law of the Sea: Official Records* published by the UN and Dr Platzöder's earlier series *Documenten der Dritten Seerechtskonferenz der Vereinten Nationen* published by the Stiftung Wissenschaft und Politik. A first improvement over the other series is the fact that the documents are organized according to the system of the 1982 Convention—an improvement that could only be attained once UNCLOS III had concluded its work. As the other two series appeared as the Conference progressed, their organization was by definition a chronological one. Another advantage over the other series is that the table of contents, generally, includes the title of a document, its number and date. This gives the user three ways to locate a document by way of the table of contents. Adding to this the fact that an index will be included in the series, one must conclude that the accessibility of the documents of UNCLOS III has been greatly improved. In comparison to the *Official Records* this series also has the significant advantage of containing both the official and unofficial documents of UNCLOS III, the *Official Records* containing only the summary records of the official sessions and the formal proposals and other formal documents presented. Given the fact that virtually all of the negotiations at UNCLOS III took place in informal meetings—many of which were not officially documented—the availability of as much information as possible on these informal negotiations is essential if the background to the provisions of the 1982 Convention is to be understood. A final advantage of this series over both other series is that the volumes are hardbound books of long-lasting quality. This is important for a series that will remain required reference for many over a long period of time.

In short the series *Third United Nations Conference on the Law of the Sea: Documents* should be available for use by anyone concerned with the law of the sea. It is an essential research tool both for the practitioner and the scholar of the law of the sea.

A. W. KOERS

Protection of Officials of Foreign States according to International Law. By FRANCISZEK PRZETACZNIK. The Hague: Martinus Nijhoff, 1983. 390 pp.

The publication of this monograph on the special protection accorded by international law to officials of foreign States is timely in that it appears when kidnappings and murders of State representatives have reached alarming proportions and States are giving fresh and urgent consideration to means of co-ordinating their attempts to counteract international terrorism. Professor Przetacznik argues that the response of lawyers, statesmen and diplomats to recent crises has revealed a lack of knowledge of the exact norms governing the protection of officials of foreign States and has demonstrated the need for a scientific and systematic study of the subject. His extensive analysis is likely to assist in improving understanding of the subject.

The field surveyed by the work is deliberately restricted by the author. Its subject is the personal inviolability of foreign officials within the territory of the receiving State and, concentrating on this, the author excludes from consideration linked questions such as the protection of the premises of diplomatic missions or other aspects of the law of inter-State representation. However, the personal inviolability of visiting officials and the legal consequences of its infringement, including the means by which individuals may be brought to justice and the circumstances in which States may bear responsibility for failure to fulfil their duties in international law, are considered in exhaustive detail. After a consideration of the legal basis and scope of the special protection to which visiting officials are entitled, the author examines the content of the obligations on States not to infringe their personal inviolability, to prevent such infringements by private individuals, to punish those who commit such infringements and to co-operate with other States in the prevention and punishment of such infringements. Within each area there is an examination of customary international law, doctrine and attempts at codification. The lengthy catalogues of attacks on State officials in recent years to which reference is made make chilling reading. The author then examines the character of crimes against officials of foreign States before dealing with the international responsibility of States and the means of settlement of inter-State disputes in this field.

It is a feature of the work that its author intends that it should serve 'as a practical basic handbook' for diplomats and State officials as well as international lawyers. The subject is likely to be made more intelligible to a non-lawyer by the way in which the specific topic is related to more general subjects and concepts. In this way, in the course of considering the character of crimes against visiting officials, the author explains the concept of asylum and the nature of the political offence exception in existing systems of extradition. Similarly, the central section on the international responsibility of States for failure to fulfil duties towards officials of foreign States expounds more general principles of the law of State responsibility such as those governing attribution of acts to States and the relevance of fault. As a result, while one may consider that the author's specific subject might have benefited from examination in conjunction with the other legal aspects of representation of States, the work succeeds in setting the chosen topic in the wider context of the system of public international law.

The book contains an extensive bibliography. The text of the Convention on the Prevention and Punishment of Crimes against Internationally Protected Persons, including Diplomatic Agents, of 1973 is usefully included as an appendix.

DAVID LLOYD JONES

The Vienna Convention on the Law of Treaties. By SIR IAN SINCLAIR. 2nd edition. Manchester: Manchester University Press, 1984. x+270 pp. (including index). £29·50.

This extensively revised and enlarged second edition of what has become the standard companion to the Vienna Convention on the Law of Treaties has been published at a most appropriate time. The original work was published in 1973, only four years after the Vienna Convention was opened for signature on 23 May 1969. In that short span of time there was no widespread opportunity for the Vienna Convention to come into play. The first edition was written, as the author readily acknowledges, when the Vienna Convention 'was still in its infancy'. However, in the ten years since publication of the first edition much has happened to merit this excellent second edition: the Vienna Convention has entered into force (on 27 January 1980, after the deposit of the thirty-fifth instrument of ratification or accession); relevant instances of State practice have occurred; international courts and tribunals have referred to the Vienna Convention in their decisions; and a wealth of scholarly writings on the law of treaties has become available. The second edition cogently reflects those occurrences, while, at the same time, it preserves substantially all of the material from the first edition. The result is that the new edition is nearly double the length of the first edition, but it remains a relatively slim book.

The first edition focused primarily on three areas of discussion. First and foremost it analysed and commented on the most significant provisions of the Vienna Convention. Secondly, it explored the relationship between the Vienna Convention and customary international law. And thirdly, it discussed at length the elusive concept of *jus cogens*. The second edition revises and expands those areas of discussion by adding new comment and additional useful notations and by breaking out as separate chapters the original material on reservations and treaty interpretation which understandably received somewhat cursory treatment in the first edition. The new edition also adds a new chapter on the significance of the Vienna Convention in the light of the past fourteen years since its adoption in 1969.

The chapter on reservations (Chapter 3, pp. 51–82) goes into greater depth than did the first edition on the history and origins of the so-called unanimity rule, under which traditionally all signatories to a multilateral convention had to accept a reservation for it to have any effect. The chapter notes the movement away from the unanimity rule and towards a compatibility standard under which essentially a State may be considered a party to a multilateral convention even if a reservation it has made has been objected to by one or more other signatory States, as long as the reservation is compatible with the objects and purposes of the convention involved. That movement towards a more liberal, compatibility criterion is traced from its judicial origins in the International Court's advisory opinion in 1951 on *Reservations to the Genocide Convention* through the subsequent work of the International Law Commission in attempting to codify the law of treaties (including questions of reservations to multilateral conventions), to the final adoption of the present articles on reservations (Articles 19 to 23) by the Vienna Conference. The author, in the first edition, expressed uncertainty over whether the flexible approach taken by the Vienna Convention with regard to reservations would be 'abused' by States and would 'result in the fractionalisation of treaty regimes'. In the second edition the author feels less uncertain and after ten years concludes, and correctly so, that experience to date shows that the discretion left by the Vienna Convention to individual States to determine, for the most part, their own attitude towards particular reservations has not resulted in 'the fragmentation of treaty regimes' as some adherents to the traditional unanimity rule originally had feared (pp. 77–8).

Of significant note is the author's lucid discussion of two decisions that issued after the first edition was published and which deal, in part, with the topic of reservations (pp. 68–77). The author examines the four dissenting opinions in the International Court's decision in the 1973 *Nuclear Tests* cases (France, Australia and New Zealand) in so far as these opinions deal with the thorny problems associated with the applicability of reservations. In addition, he sets out with particular clarity the complex questions involved in the legal effect of objections to reservations that were addressed in the 1977 decision in the *UK–French Continental Shelf* arbitration.

The chapter on interpretation of treaties (Chapter 5, pp. 114–58) contains new material, absent from the first edition, on the general rules of treaty interpretation reflected in Articles 31 to 33 of the Vienna Convention. The author examines in some detail such elements of treaty interpretation as good faith, ordinary meaning, the objects and purposes of a treaty and the use of *travaux préparatoires*. He reviews prior State practice and relevant international case law on treaty interpretation. Here the exposition and the wealth of citation are particularly rich and constitute a vast improvement to the first edition. The author also offers some insight into the reasons why the Vienna Convention is silent on such interpretation doctrines as *ejusdem generis* and *expressio unius est exclusio alterius*. However, his explanation that they were omitted to achieve an 'economical code of principles' (p. 153) raises as many questions as it answers. The author concludes by stating that Articles 31 to 33 of the Vienna Convention constitute a non-exclusive 'general expression of the principles of customary international law relating to treaty interpretation' (p. 153).

The second edition's final chapter (Chapter 8, pp. 242–60) presents the author's view of the Vienna Convention's significance fourteen years after it was adopted. The author expresses disappointment that only forty-odd States have ratified or acceded to the Vienna Convention, thereby severely restricting the Convention's effect as a treaty in its own right. That disappointment, while understandable, is unduly pessimistic. After all, the real utility of the Vienna Convention, as the author acknowledges, lies not so much in its existence as a treaty but in its role as a written articulation or restatement, if you will, of existing and emergent principles of treaty law. To that extent the Vienna Convention has fulfilled its role splendidly over the past fourteen years and will continue to do so in the future. The Vienna Convention has now entered into force and notwithstanding the paucity of ratifying or acceding States it increasingly will be the primary source to be relied upon by States and international courts on questions of treaty law. And the publication of this second edition assures that this book will continue to be the standard companion to the Vienna Convention.

One minor criticism made of the first edition remains uncorrected in the second edition (see *American Journal of International Law*, 68 (1974), pp. 351–2). The author often paraphrases articles rather than quoting them in full, which really demands having a copy of the Vienna Convention readily at hand. However, the publishers unfortunately did not include the text of the Vienna Convention in an appendix.

JAMES E. HICKEY, JR.

Non-Appearance before the International Court of Justice. By H. W. A. THIRLWAY. Cambridge: Cambridge University Press, 1985. vii + 184 pp. £25. *Non-Appearance before the International Court of Justice: Functional and Comparative Analysis. By* JEROME B. ELKIND. Dordrecht: Martinus Nijhoff, 1984. xv + 223 pp. £27·95.

Both books were stimulated by the Institute of International Law, and their publication testifies to the general concern over the increasing tendency of States to decline to appear before the Court, a tendency of which the statement by the United States that it will not participate in the future proceedings of the Court in the *Nicaragua* case is but the latest example.

Elkind begins with a comparative survey of 'default' in municipal law, a chapter which has no counterpart in Thirlway. Both review the cases in which default or non-appearance has occurred; and both review the drafting history of Article 53 of the Court's Statute. But it is Thirlway who faces most directly the questions whether a State has a 'duty' to appear, and whether, despite non-appearance, the State can be regarded as a 'party'.

On the first question, he rightly concludes that there is no such duty, and the State exercises the privilege of not appearing—and accepts the consequential risks—at its discretion. This has important consequences, for it means that the Court's approach should not take on the character of a sanction for a breach of a supposed 'duty' to appear. On the second, he concludes, very sensibly, that the issue is not of real relevance (despite Judge Gros's view in *Nuclear Tests*) except in those cases where the lack of jurisdiction is clear and admitted.

The problem of applying Article 53 at the early stage of a request for interim measures really arises from a supposed contradiction between the Court's view that, in applying Article 41 (1) on interim measures, it need only require prima facie evidence of jurisdiction; whereas, under Article 53 it must be 'satisfied' that it has jurisdiction. So the question arises, can there be a default at the interim measures stage?

Thirlway's answer, essentially, is to take the particular stage of the proceedings in question, and to pose the question whether the Court is satisfied that it has the jurisdiction necessary *at that stage*. So that if, at the stage of interim measures, a prima facie jurisdiction suffices, that is all the Court has to satisfy itself about. Elkind takes a different view, for his conclusion is that only a manifest absence of jurisdiction can prevent the Court from dealing with a request for interim measures (pp. 111–12). He has a point, of course, in saying that the further the Court goes, at this stage, in affirming its jurisdiction, the more reluctant will a State contesting the jurisdiction be to appear. But it does seem unlikely that the Court will shift away from the prima facie test, when Article 41 is in question.

Elkind then devotes a very substantial Chapter 5 to self-judging reservations. The justification for including this in a discussion of non-appearance is that the essential purpose of such reservations is to justify non-appearance without incurring the risk of default (p. 168). In a sense, this is true. But the issue of self-judging reservations is a much wider one, having no necessary connection with non-appearance, and this rather long treatment is surprising. Moreover, Elkind agrees, basically, with Judge Lauterpacht's approach on such reservations: he finds his reasoning 'inescapable'. But this ignores the rather persuasive argument by Crawford (this *Year Book*, 50 (1979)) that, since no State has ever objected to such reservations, it is difficult to argue that they are incompatible with the object and purpose of the Statute.

Thirlway stays more closely to the problems specific to non-appearance, with two chapters on procedure, followed by a discussion of 'attitudes concomitant with non-appearance' and, finally, an important chapter on 'diagnoses and remedies'. It is this final chapter which is the real test of his analysis.

He doubts whether a new 'special appearance' procedure, based on analogy with some municipal systems, will help, at least in the case of a State which accepts that, ultimately, it is for the Court to determine whether it has jurisdiction. For the existing preliminary objection procedure already safeguards such a State against being deemed to have waived its objection to jurisdiction by appearing. Moreover, if a State is unwilling to accept that the Court's finding on jurisdiction is binding upon it, he finds it unlikely that such a State would use a 'special appearance' procedure. He is lukewarm over the six conclusions, or proposals, offered by Fitzmaurice (this *Year Book*, 51 (1980)): in short, he finds them 'unworkable' (p. 171). But he does agree with Sinclair (*International and Comparative Law Quarterly*, 30 (1981)) that the Court should allow the appearing party to respond fully, if necessary at a reopened hearing, to arguments furnished to the Court by the non-appearing party in an unofficial, and usually tardy, manner. This is the better solution, rather than have the Court decline to receive such communications from the non-appearing party. Thirlway would also favour the abandonment by the Court of separate procedural phases devoted to 'jurisdiction' or 'admissibility', in favour of a reversion to the treatment of irregular challenges to jurisdiction or admissibility as preliminary objections, as in the *Nottebohm* case.

Elkind gives a useful survey of various proposals for reform of the Court (some of them not related specifically to the problem of non-appearance), but he does not himself appear to have particular proposals for change or reform. He is doubtless right in viewing non-appearance as but one facet of a general dislike of independent, third-party settlement.

Thus, both books seem to accept that there are no obvious, easy answers to the problem: it will not be solved by a revision of the Statute or Rules. Both books are useful contributions, although Thirlway's has more elegance and directness.

D. W. Bowett

Consensus and Confrontation: The United States and the Law of the Sea Convention. Edited by Jon M. von Dyke. Honolulu: The Law of the Sea Institute, University of Hawaii, 1985. x+576 pp. (including appendices and index).

This book is an edited record of a workshop held by the Law of the Sea Institute from 9 to 13 January 1984, in Honolulu, Hawaii. The twenty-eight participants in the workshop, whose papers and views appear in the book, were primarily representatives of the Reagan administration, diplomats from the Asia–Pacific region, who had represented their nations at the Law of the Sea Conference, and interested scholars from the United States and the Asia–Pacific region, including the Soviet Union and the People's Republic of China.

The purpose of the workshop, according to the editor of the book, was twofold: first, to 'air' 'nagging doubts' that have 'persisted' concerning the decision of the US Government not to sign the Law of the Sea Convention which opened for signature on 10 December 1982; and secondly, 'to look at the benefits and costs of the Convention as a whole' in the light of the US rejection of the Convention (p. 2). Most of the book, seven of its nine chapters, is devoted to an airing of the participants' views with a final chapter which addresses the costs and benefits of the failure of the US to join the Convention.

The book presents in each chapter competing viewpoints of the Asian–Pacific and US participants on a particular topic, followed by portions of the sometimes lively discussion of the workshop participants on those competing viewpoints. Each chapter contains a brief, non-analytical summary introduction by the editor.

The 'airing' of competing views recorded in the book runs the gamut of current law of the sea issues affected by the US rejection of the Convention: whether the Convention should be accepted or rejected as a whole, and the charge that the US is effectively 'picking and choosing' the parts of the Convention of which it approves while it rejects other parts, in particular the Convention's section on deep sea-bed mining (Chapter 2); the relation between customary international law and the Convention (Chapter 3); the US position that deep sea-bed mining is a protected freedom of the high seas (Chapter 4); the navigational issues of innocent passage, passage through straits and the navigation rights of warships within 200-mile exclusive economic zones (Chapter 5); fishing and living resources issues including the position of the US that coastal States do not have jurisdiction over tuna (Chapter 6); issues involving the environmental protection provisions of the Convention that were strongly insisted upon by the US (Chapter 7); and the Convention's dispute resolution procedures including the question of the ability of non-signatories, such as the US, to make use of them (Chapter 8).

In the final chapter (Chapter 9), the book presents the workshop participants' attempts to weigh the benefits and costs to the US of its decision to stay outside the Convention. Among the perceived costs to the US are the uncertainty created with regard to US navigational rights, the loss to the US of the Convention's dispute resolution mechanisms, and the increased isolation of the US from the world community. Against those perceived costs is weighed the asserted benefit to the US of an opportunity to attempt to construct a viable alternative deep sea-bed mining regime which would provide US companies with greater access to sea-bed mineral resources than those companies would have under the present Convention.

It is a bit difficult to discern the audience for this book. It is not a book that will be understood easily by one who is not familiar, to some extent, with the new Law of the Sea Convention and its negotiating history. To follow much of the discussion it is advisable to have a copy of the text of the Convention readily at hand (the book does not include a copy in an appendix). To those who are familiar with the Convention and the negotiating sessions leading up to its adoption, the book may offer little that is new—or thought-provoking. The book does succeed in drawing into focus within one volume most, if not all, of the issues that eventually will need to be addressed if the US remains a non-signatory to the Convention. To that extent it constitutes a useful contribution to literature on the law of the sea.

JAMES E. HICKEY, JR.

International Law: The Essential Treaties and Other Relevant Documents. Edited by INGO VON MÜNCH and ANDREAS BUSKE. Berlin, New York: de Gruyter, 1985. xix + 702 pp.

There has always been a substantial need for the publication of a collection of international legal materials in a form that would allow 'diplomats, administrative officers, employees of international organizations, lawyers, scientists and students' (p. vi) to make everyday use of them. Even today access to certain international legal materials is sometimes fairly limited for individuals. A collection as such also has drawbacks. Not being an official publication, anyone engaged in research on international law must, as a matter of course, go further—to an official text. Furthermore, any collection that is selective inevitably reflects the priorities of the author. Collections fulfil nevertheless a very important role in revealing the subject to those who are interested in it, and for this reason the present volume is most welcome.

The book covers the post-war period and has seven sections: (A) General International Law; (B) Diplomatic and Consular Law; (C) Law of the Sea; (D) Air and Space Law; (E) International Legal Protection of Human Rights; (F) International Environmental Law; (G) International Law of Peace and Security.

It begins with the Charter of the United Nations and then gives a picture of, in the words of Article 13 of the Charter, 'the progressive development of international law and its codification'. Amongst the fifty documents presented in the collection there is the Montego Bay Convention of 1982, which is the most extensive document of all (188 pp). It may be worth noting that the authors have also included texts of the four Geneva Conventions of 1958 on the law of the sea. These must not be overlooked because they still constitute law binding upon States.

Air and space law and international environmental law are newly developed branches of international law, and it may be said that they are adequately treated by the authors. There are various relevant treaties, for example the Agreement Governing the Activities of States on the Moon and other Celestial Bodies, 1979, the Convention on the Conservation of Antarctic Marine Living Resources, 1980 and the Convention on Long-Range Transboundary Air Pollution, 1979.

As Professor Ingo von Münch has put it: 'the internationalization of human rights protection belongs to the remarkable development of international public law' (p. xvii). Based on this view, the reader is given a survey of 'global and regional, general and specific rules provid[ing] a variety of means for the protection of human rights' (pp. xvii–xviii).

The last section of the book includes documents concerning international peace and security, giving appropriate prominence to the Final Acts of the Helsinki and Madrid Conferences on Security and Co-operation in Europe.

There is no doubt that here we have a very valuable and helpful publication, that should find its way into every university library as well as any institution dealing with international relations. The English language in which the book is published makes it suitable for use in various countries all over the world, although it is to be noted that it does not attempt complete coverage of the whole subject of international law (*inter alia*, humanitarian law and the law relating to international institutions have not been included). In certain cases it would have been interesting to have had information as to the parties to particular instruments, but perhaps the authors were right in stating that they wanted 'to avoid the presentation of information already outdated at the time of publication of this collection' (p. v).

ZBIGNIEW WLOSOWICZ

DECISIONS OF BRITISH COURTS DURING 1985 INVOLVING QUESTIONS OF PUBLIC INTERNATIONAL LAW*

Proposed army firing range in British Sector of Berlin—capacity in which British agencies act in Berlin—amenability to suit in United Kingdom courts—reviewability of certificates under State Immunity Act 1978, section 21

Case No. 1. Trawnik v. *Gordon Lennox*, [1985] 1 WLR 532, [1985] 2 All ER 368, CA, reversing *Trawnik* v. *Ministry of Defence*, [1984] 2 All ER 791, Sir Robert Megarry VC. *Case No. 2. R.* v. *Secretary of State for Foreign and Commonwealth Affairs, ex parte Trawnik*, [1985] TLR 250, Div. Ct. These two cases arose out of an attempt by two residents of the British sector of Berlin to find a court before which they could argue that the proposed use of a firing range by British forces in Berlin would constitute an unlawful nuisance. As will appear, the merits of this argument were never reached. It has been said that the law of nuisance is not an appropriate vehicle to adjust conflicting claims over land use. But it is certainly better than the creation of a series of procedural obstacles in the way of persons seeking to vindicate legal rights.

The plaintiffs occupied houses adjoining Gatow Airfield in the British sector of Berlin. The airfield was occupied by British forces. It was proposed to use part of the airfield as a firing range in circumstances which, the plaintiffs claimed, would constitute a nuisance by noise at common law, and which, presumably, was not justifiable under the law in force in the British sector.[1] The plaintiffs first commenced proceedings in the Administrative Court in Berlin, but the German courts in Berlin can, under Law No. 7 of the Allied Kommandatura, only hear cases to which the allied forces are parties with the permission of the Allied Kommandatura or the appropriate sector kommandant. That permission was refused. Although Ordinance No. 68 of the Berlin Military Government provides for a High Court and other courts to be established in the British sector, no such courts have been established. Accordingly there was no court in Berlin with jurisdiction to hear the case.

The plaintiffs next commenced proceedings in the High Court against the Ministry of Defence. The Ministry is not separately incorporated, and can only be sued in its own name under section 17 of the Crown Proceedings Act 1947. However, that Act does not authorize proceedings to be taken in respect of any alleged liability of the Crown arising otherwise than in respect of Her Majesty's Government in the UK (section 40 (2) (b)), and a certificate of a Secretary of State is, under section 40 (3), conclusive as to whether an alleged liability so arises. A certificate was given, certifying that the alleged liability here arose otherwise than

[1] The fact that the case involved land outside the UK did not deprive the British courts of jurisdiction because no question of title or the right to possession of the land was involved: Civil Jurisdiction and Judgments Act 1982, section 30 (b). See [1985] 1 WLR 532 at pp. 535–6.

in respect of Her Majesty's Government in the UK. Accordingly, the action could not be maintained against the Ministry of Defence.[2]

The plaintiffs then sought to join as defendants the British Commandant in Berlin, Major-General Gordon Lennox, and the Attorney-General. Whether they were entitled to join the Attorney-General depended in part at least on whether the proceedings were, despite section 40, brought under the 1947 Act. As Sir Robert Megarry VC pointed out, counsel for the plaintiffs had

> . . . contended that in reaching my conclusion I should if possible give effect to the opening sentence of article 6 (1) of the European Convention for the Protection of Human Rights and Fundamental Freedoms . . . This states:
>
> > 'In the determination of his civil rights and obligations . . . everyone is entitled to a fair and public hearing within a reasonable time by an independent and impartial tribunal established by law. . . .'
>
> I do not need the European Convention on Human Rights to tell me that it is deplorable that, as [counsel for the Attorney-General] accepts and asserts, there is no court with power to decide whether the plaintiffs are entitled to the remedy that they seek. If heard, their claim might fail, or the court might reach the conclusion that in all the circumstances of the case (including the special position of Berlin) it would not be right to grant the discretionary remedy of declaratory relief; but at least the plaintiffs would have had their day in court. . . . The Convention is not, of course, law, though it is legitimate to consider its provisions in interpreting the law; and naturally I give it full weight for this purpose.[3]

In the result he gave leave to join the two additional defendants, on the basis that:

> I do not feel sufficiently sure of the inevitability of success of [counsel's] argument on behalf of the Attorney-General to say that the claim against him should be struck out. Nor am I at all clear about the status of the commandant or the government of the British sector of Berlin; and it would be lamentable if the claim proceeded against the commandant alone, and then the plaintiffs were to be met by a contention that he was the wrong defendant, and that they ought to have sued some general representative of the Crown instead.[4]

The Court of Appeal, however, rejected this view and struck out the claim so far as it concerned the Attorney-General. Since the actions could not succeed under the 1947 Act (because of the combination of sections 17 (3) and 40) it could only be pursued apart from that Act, and the Crown's common law immunity in tort could not, the Court held, be evaded by bringing proceedings for a declaration, or by relying on the fact that the proceedings were anticipatory or *quia timet* proceedings. Different views were, however, expressed about whether the Attorney-General was in any event the proper defendant. Lawton LJ said:

> The Attorney-General of England, Wales and Northern Ireland can represent the Crown in these parts of Her Majesty's Dominions. He has no functions as Attorney-General outside them and, in particular, he has no functions in the British sector of Berlin. The plaintiffs have been unable to discover from the Treasury Solicitor who in Berlin performs functions similar to those of the Attorney-General of England, Wales and Northern Ireland or who, as a matter of law, can represent the Crown in causes of action arising there. The plaintiffs may be suffering a wrong for which there is no remedy in our courts. This is to be regretted; but sympathy for the plaintiffs is no justification for adding as a defendant an officer of state who, as a matter of law, has no interest in the proceedings.[5]

[2] At pp. 536–7 *per* Sir Robert Megarry VC.
[3] At p. 541.
[4] At p. 544.
[5] At pp. 549–50.

On the other hand, Browne-Wilkinson LJ (with whom Sir David Cairns agreed) refused to express a concluded view to this effect, and indeed it seems that he inclined to the opposite view. He referred to counsel's submission

. . . that the certificate given by the Foreign Secretary shows that the case is not brought against the Crown in right of the Government of the United Kingdom and the Attorney-General of England is not the proper respondent to such proceedings. I express no concluded view on this submission since I am not satisfied that it has been demonstrated that the case is brought against the Crown otherwise than in right of the Government of the United Kingdom. The Foreign Secretary's certificate is conclusive for the purposes of the Act of 1947 since section 40 (3) so provides. But it is not conclusive for other purposes and I am far from clear how liability for the acts of the British Army (as opposed to the forces of any other part of the Commonwealth) can be said not to arise from the acts of the Crown in respect of the Government of the United Kingdom.[6]

The proceedings against the Attorney-General having been struck out, that left only Major-General Gordon Lennox. However, a further certificate was issued under the State Immunity Act 1978 section 21, to the effect that Germany was a State for the purposes of section 21 of that Act, and that the persons to be regarded as the Government of Germany, for the purposes of Part I of the Act, included members of the Allied Kommandatura, including Major-General Gordon Lennox. A further certificate was issued under section 40 (3) (a) of the Crown Proceedings Act 1947 to the effect that any liability of Major-General Gordon Lennox was otherwise than in respect of Her Majesty's Government in the UK. If valid, the effect of those certificates was to preclude the plaintiffs from suing, because Major-General Gordon Lennox would have to be treated as part of the government of a State for the purposes of Part I of the 1978 Act, and none of the exceptions from State immunity in Part I applied in this case. In separate proceedings the plaintiffs then sought judicial review of the Secretary of State's decision to issue the certificates, on the ground that in doing so he had taken into account irrelevant considerations and ignored relevant considerations. Again they failed, although, according to the only available report of the decision,[7] the members of the Divisional Court gave slightly different reasons for this.

Kennedy J pointed out that section 21 of the State Immunity Act 1978 made a certificate 'conclusive evidence on any question' of the kind specified in section 21 (a)–(d). It was not limited to proceedings to which the foreign State was a party, provided that the certificate related to a question of the immunity of a 'State' under the Act (as was the case here). Accordingly, he held:

. . . the content of the certificate, provided that it was a certificate, could not be challenged. The content of the certificate could not be challenged because in many cases the matters certified would be facts of state, involving questions of the recognition of foreign states, and of the rights and privileges to be granted to the representatives of foreign states—matters within the realm of the royal prerogative and outside the scope of any form of judicial review. Accordingly, the applicants in the present case could not use any information from any external source to challenge the information in the section 21 certificate. . . . That did not mean that in a proper case the Divisional Court might not be prepared to consider whether a certificate given under either Act was indeed a certificate, or whether it was a nullity, but once it was clear that the document was what it purported to be, as in the instant case, namely a certificate given by the appropriate person under the relevant Act, dealing

[6] At p. 552. [7] [1985] TLR 250.

with matters which the Act enabled the appropriate person to certify, any possibility of judicial review was at an end. If there was an abuse of power in its issue, the court could not give redress.

This argument is acceptable, in that it relies on the plain language of section 21. On the other hand, Forbes J appeared to treat the reviewability of the certificate as a matter governed by the common law rather than section 21. He is reported to have said:

> The position at common law was that questions concerning the identity and recognition of foreign states were matters of which the courts would take judicial notice and thus were strictly not matters to be proved by evidence at all. Once given, such certificates were conclusive of the facts stated therein and no evidence could be adduced by parties to contradict them. In the case of doubt, insufficiency of information, or ambiguity the court would ask for supplementary information. . . . In order to succeed in an application for judicial review of the section 21 certificate, the applicants would have to establish that the facts were contrary to those stated by the secretary of state. Even assuming that the certificates were only conclusive for the limited purposes stated in section 40 (3) (a) and section 21 and could not be said to be conclusive in judicial review proceedings where there was no civil suit against the Crown and no foreign government involved, neither section was intended to exclude the common law position. How could the applicants establish the necessary facts? The facts were notorious facts which were the subject of judicial notice and in respect of which the court was entitled to ask for information of the secretary of state to refresh its memory. The court was entitled to regard a certificate as equivalent to such requested information. Since, at common law, the section 21 certificate was conclusive evidence of the facts stated in it, no evidence could be called to rebut or contradict the facts. It had to be remembered that the only arbiter of the truth of a notorious fact lying within the sphere of foreign relations was the secretary of state when he gave the certificate. Thus at common law the statements contained in the section 21 certificate could not be contradicted by evidence. The certificate was unequivocal in its terms and there was no ambiguity or lacuna requiring further recourse to the secretary of state. . . . Thus, even if the certificates were reviewable, the necessary factual basis on which review could proceed could not be laid by the applicants because the facts were concluded by the statements in the certificates.

This is, with respect, as doubtful as it was unnecessary. One does not need to postulate a common law rule excluding evidence about the existence of a foreign State or government in order to explain the conclusiveness of an executive certificate as to the recognition of the State or government. In cases where a certificate is not given, or is deliberately left incomplete or equivocal, the courts have always had power to determine the matter on the evidence and in accordance with law.[8] They have, it is true, sometimes taken judicial notice of notorious facts lying within the sphere of foreign relations, but judicial notice is not a substitute for evidence or argument in cases of uncertainty. The idea that the executive is the 'only arbiter of the truth of a notorious fact lying within the sphere of foreign relations' is an absurd and outdated fiction—the more so in view of the changed policy of the UK Government with respect to recognition of governments.[9] The independence manifested, admittedly *obiter*, by Browne-Wilkinson LJ is much to be preferred.

None the less, it followed from all of this that there was no body in the UK or Berlin whom the plaintiffs could sue in respect of the alleged nuisance. And not merely were the merits of their claim not reached, but neither were the interesting

[8] e.g. *The Jupiter* (*No. 3*), [1927] P 122.

[9] See this *Year Book*, 51 (1980), pp. 367–8.

questions that arise relating to the capacity or capacities in which the British army is present in Berlin, or as to whether acts performed by UK officials or personnel in Berlin can ever be attributed to Her Majesty's Government in right of the UK as distinct from the Allied Kommandatura.[10]

Jurisdiction—extra-territorial application of Companies Act 1981 sections 74, 77—distinction between inquiry provisions and criminal penalties

Case No. 3. In re F. M. Loyd Holdings plc, [1985] TLR 236, Nourse J. This interesting case raised a short point concerning the application of certain provisions of the Companies Act 1981 to foreign companies. Section 74 of the Act enables a public company which knows or reasonably suspects 'any person' to have been interested in shares in the company within the past three years to require the person to disclose that interest, and that of any other person interested (e.g. as beneficiary or nominee) in the shares. Section 77 (1) enables the court, on application by the company, to restrict transfer in the shares or the exercise of voting rights under section 174 of the Companies Act 1948 if the notice under section 74 is not complied with. In addition it is an offence under section 77 (5) for 'any person' to fail to comply with a notice under section 74.

The applicant company in this case was concerned that persons interested in acquiring substantial shareholdings in it were doing so through the use of overseas nominees, thereby avoiding disclosure provisions in the Companies Act and associated takeover rules. It issued a notice to a foreign corporation, TDB, incorporated in Liechtenstein, which had no presence and conducted no business in the UK. TDB held shares in the applicant company 'for account client', but claimed to be prohibited by Liechtenstein law from disclosing the client's identity. The applicant sought a restriction order in respect of the shares under section 77 (1). In the words of Nourse J:

> The primary contention on behalf of TDB was that 'any person' in sections 74 (1) and 77 (1) of the 1981 Act did not include a foreign corporation which could not and did not carry on business in the United Kingdom and had no presence here of any kind. It was convenient to refer to such an entity or an individual having an equivalent status, as 'a true foreigner'. . . . To what state of affairs was it sought to apply section 74 (1) and 77 (1)? The company was an English company whose articles constituted a contract, the proper law of which was English, between the company and its members. . . . TDB's beneficial interest was also situated in England. [Counsel for TDB] submitted that in construing the words 'any person' in the sections, unless the contrary was expressly enacted or so plainly implied that the courts must give effect to it, United Kingdom legislation was only applicable to British subjects or to foreigners who by coming to this country, whether for a short or a long time, had made themselves subject to British jurisdiction. . . . Superficially that had the appearance of a powerful argument founded on a fundamental principle of statutory interpretation, but closer scrutiny had convinced his Lordship that it failed. It would be difficult to think of words more often used in imposing criminal penalties, and, as such, less fitted to be words of art, than 'any person'; his Lordship saw nothing heretical in imputing to Parliament the twofold intention to include a true foreigner in sections 74 (1) and 77 (1), but to exclude him from section 77 (5) which imposed a criminal penalty.[11]

Thus the same words ('any person') in the same section were given a more

[10] On the status of Berlin and of quadripartite control over it, see Crawford, *The Creation of States in International Law* (1979), pp. 277–81, and works there cited.

[11] [1985] TLR 236.

restricted interpretation in the case of the criminal as distinct from the civil sanction, on the basis of a differential presumption of territoriality. This had the further advantage of refuting TDB's argument from double jeopardy, since the restriction on transfer and voting rights under section 77 (1) affected the client, not itself, and there was no question of a direct conflict of criminal laws of the two countries concerned.[12]

Foreign law expropriating shares in foreign company—whether consequential controlling interest of foreign State in British company should be recognized—effect on pre-existing causes of action under English law—foreign expropriatory laws and English public policy

Case No. 4. Williams & Humbert Ltd. v. *W. & H. Trade Marks (Jersey) Ltd., Rumasa SA* v. *Multinvest (UK) Ltd.*, [1986] 1 All ER 129, HL, affirming [1985] 2 All ER 619, CA, affirming [1985] 3 WLR 501, [1985] 1 All ER 208, Nourse J. The relevance of international law in determining the content of the English rules of law or public policy concerning the recognition of foreign penal or expropriatory laws has long been a matter for debate. Positions vary greatly, from the assertion that English courts will apply international law in refusing to recognize or enforce

[12] A number of other cases in 1985 concerned the territoriality principle or its application in particular cases. In *R* v. *Berry*, [1985] AC 246, the respondents manufactured electronic timers in England for use (presumably in time bombs) in the Middle East. They were convicted of making explosive devices in circumstances which gave rise to reasonable suspicion that they were not being made for a lawful object, contrary to the Explosive Substances Act 1883, section 4. The Court of Appeal ([1984] 1 WLR 824) held that the 'lawful object' within section 4 had to be an object within the jurisdiction, relying in part on the difficulty of proving foreign law, and quashed the conviction. The House of Lords, relying in part on 'considerations of comity', allowed the Crown's appeal, on the basis that, once the circumstances disclosed a reasonable suspicion that the eventual use of the article would not be lawful by the law of the place where it was used, the onus was on the defendant to show that this was not so ([1985] AC 246, 254). As Lord Roskill pointed out, the case did not strictly concern the territoriality principle but rather the interpretation of section 4. See the note at *Criminal Law Review*, 1985, p. 103. In *R* v. *Beck*, [1985] 1 WLR 22, the defendant used stolen travellers cheques and a credit card in France. The cheques and credit card vouchers were honoured by the issuing English bank, for commercial reasons and in the knowledge that they had been used fraudulently. The Court of Appeal upheld the defendant's conviction for procuring the execution of a valuable security under section 20 (2) of the Theft Act 1968, on the basis that the security was executed when it was honoured by the English bank in England. On the other hand, in *R* v. *Tomsett*, *Criminal Law Review*, 1985, p. 369, the appellants' conviction for conspiring to steal was quashed. They had sent telexes from the London branch of a Swiss bank to New York aimed at diverting the credit balance in a New York account to another account for the credit of a Swiss account opened by the appellants. Following *Board of Trade* v. *Owen*, [1957] AC 602, the Court of Appeal held that the conspiracy was committed where the crime itself would have occurred (namely, in New York). The defendants were, however, rightly convicted of forgery and false accounting in respect of the telexes. In *Inland Revenue Commissioners* v. *Stype Trustees (Jersey) Ltd.*, [1985] 1 WLR 1290, the foreign trustees of a settlement governed by the law of Jersey, the settlor of which died domiciled in England, were held liable to render accounts under the Finance Act 1975 in respect of their tax liability as trustees of the settlement. Walton J held that once the substantive liability to tax was established, the machinery provisions for an account needed no further territorial limitation to be implied, and accordingly applied to trustees outside the UK: ibid., 1299. See also *South India Shipping Corporation Ltd.* v. *Export–Import Bank of Korea*, [1985] 2 All ER 219 (CA), pet. all. [1985] 1 All ER 740 (HL) (held: unregistered foreign bank had, on the facts, a place of business in Great Britain for the purposes of service of process, although no local banking business was done there and although the proceeding bore no relation to the business actually carried on within the jurisdiction); *Spiliada Maritime Corporation* v. *Consulex Ltd.*, [1985] 2 Lloyd's Rep. 1167 (CA) (extent of onus to justify leave to serve outside the jurisdiction based on 'exorbitant' ground that contract governed by local law).

foreign expropriatory laws contrary to international law[13] to the assertion that international law is irrelevant, and that the matter is regulated only by English conflicts rules based on the established categories of penal, revenue and, perhaps, public laws, and the established distinction between recognition and enforcement.[14] Neither view gained much support in this case: rather, the courts, and especially the House of Lords, emphasized the international law underpinnings of the distinction between recognition and enforcement, as well as the point that this will usually if not invariably lead to the recognition of expropriatory laws applying to property located within the State in question.

Admittedly the facts of the two actions involved did not raise these issues in any very central or obvious way. An English company, W. & H. Ltd., the plaintiff in the first action, marketed Spanish sherry and was the proprietor of the trade mark 'Dry Sack'. Control of W. & H. Ltd. was held by a Spanish company, Rumasa, which was effectively controlled by the second defendant in the action, M, and his family. In 1976, in the uncertainty following the death of General Franco, M had a company set up in Jersey, the first defendant, to which the trade marks were transferred and granted back to W. & H. Ltd. on licence terminable without notice if the shares in Rumasa or any intermediate holding company were expropriated. In 1983 under a special law, all the shares in, and control of, the Spanish company and its subsidiaries were vested in the Spanish State, with a 'fair price' to be negotiated or determined by local legal proceedings (which had not yet been concluded). Accordingly Spain as owner and controller of Rumasa under the law of 1983 was in a position to control W. & H. Ltd. The licence to use the trade mark was revoked, and W. & H. Ltd. commenced proceedings claiming that the 1976 arrangements were void as *ultra vires* or as an unauthorized reduction in the capital of W. & H. Ltd. In the second action, Rumasa and two Spanish banks (the shares in which were also compulsorily acquired by Spain in 1983) claimed various orders and damages in respect of M's alleged breach of fidiciary duties to the plaintiffs relating to the diversion of $46 million in loans from one of the banks, breaches in which three defendants in the action were said to be involved. The details of the various claims are of limited relevance. The point is that they arose independently of, and in most cases before, the 1983 law. The effect of that law was not legal but practical: it replaced M and his affiliates with managers, appointed by Spain, in the control of the various companies involved, who were prepared to take action against M for the alleged breaches of duty.

Moreover, it was very difficult to see how the compulsory acquisition of the shares in the Spanish companies violated international law. Compensation was provided for, through an apparently appropriate procedure. The companies and their shareholders were Spanish. The acquisition was apparently for a public purpose, and did not appear to be invidiously discriminatory.[15] There was no international law obstacle to holding that the shares, and therefore control in the companies, vested in Spain.

None the less, it was argued by the defendants that to allow the actions to

[13] Cf. *Anglo-Iranian Oil Co. Ltd.* v. *Jaffrate* (*The Rose Mary*), [1953] 1 WLR 246, as to which see the comments of Nourse J, [1985] 2 All ER 208 at p. 214.

[14] Cf. *Oppenheimer* v. *Cattermole*, [1976] AC 249, 265–6 (Lord Pearson, dissenting).

[15] Nourse J rejected the view that a specific or *ad hoc* confiscation (not based on invidious grounds such as race or religion) would not be recognized in any way: 'if it does not operate by reference to unacceptable criteria there is nothing so inherently abhorrent in selective confiscation in peacetime as to warrant the fiction that the foreign law does not exist': [1985] 2 All ER 208 at pp. 214–15.

proceed would involve recognizing and enforcing the penal or expropriatory decree of 1983. Nourse J, the Court of Appeal (by majority) and the House of Lords (unanimously) struck out the defence in each case on the ground that it disclosed no reasonable cause of defence. For present purposes the most interesting aspect of the case was the discussion by Lord Templeman in the House of Lords of the argument that it would be contrary to public policy to grant the plaintiffs relief in the two cases. He said:

> This [argument] could be justified if English law abhorred the compulsory acquisition legislation of every other country, or if international law abhorred the compulsory acquisition legislation of all countries. But in fact compulsory acquisition is universally recognised and practised. As early as 1789 the Declaration of the Rights of Man, more recently repeated in the French Constitutions of 1946 and 1958, provided that no one should be deprived of property 'except in case of evident public necessity legally ascertained and on condition of just indemnity'. In the United States the Fifth Amendment to the Constitution of 1791 provided that private property should not 'be taken for public use, without just compensation'. In modern times written constitutions recognise compulsory acquisition in the public interest subject to the payment of compensation: see, for example, the 1949 Basic Law of the German Federal Republic, the 1949 Constitution of India, the 1969 South American Convention on Human Rights, and the written constitutions of the African states which achieved independence from colonial rule. The United Nations and European conventions recognise compulsory acquisition in the public interest and in accordance with domestic law and international law. In the United Kingdom, the courts are bound to accept and enforce any compulsory acquisition authorised by the United Kingdom Parliament and to recognise compulsory acquisitions by other governments subject only to limitations for the safeguarding of human rights.
>
> There is undoubtedly a domestic and international rule which prevents one sovereign state from changing title to property so long as that property is situated in another state. In the present case, the Spanish government acquired all the shares in Rumasa and Jerez. Ownership of the shares in Williams & Humbert was and remained vested in Rumasa. Ownership of any right of action to recover the Dry Sack trade mark and to recover damages was and remained vested in Williams & Humbert. Ownership of any right of action to recover $46m was and remained vested in Jerez.
>
> There is another international rule whereby one state will not enforce the revenue and penal laws of another state. This rule with regard to revenue laws may in the future be modified by international convention or by the laws of the European Economic Community in order to prevent fraudulent practices which damage all states and benefit no state. But at present the international rule with regard to the non-enforcement of revenue and penal laws is absolute.
>
> It is, in my view, doubtful whether the Spanish law dated 20 June 1983 can properly be described as a penal law for present purposes, but in any event the respondents are not seeking to enforce the Spanish law. In the trade marks action the respondents, Williams & Humbert, and in the banks' action Rumasa, Jerez and Norte, are seeking to enforce English private law which can be invoked, subject to exceptions not here relevant, by a plaintiff of any nationality against any defendant within the jurisdiction and against any property within the jurisdiction. Nourse J succinctly observed that the object of the Spanish law of 20 June 1983 . . .
>
>> 'was to acquire ownership and control of Rumasa and the two banks and indirect ownership and control of Williams & Humbert. The object has been clearly achieved by perfection of the state's title in Spain. Accordingly, on a simple but compelling view of the matter there is nothing left to enforce'.
>
> . . . If the principles of English domestic law and international law are applied and if the respondents succeed in establishing liability against any of the appellants in tort,

misfeasance or breach of fiduciary duty then an English court will grant the appropriate relief. If the Mateos family had remained in charge of the Rumasa group perhaps no action would have been brought by any of the companies comprised in the Rumasa group against the appellants. But that consideration is irrelevant to the actions which have now been brought.[16]

The interesting feature of this passage is not merely its reference to international law as relevant in determining the scope of public policy in the field of non-recognition of foreign laws: *Oppenheimer* v. *Cattermole*[17] established that proposition. It is rather the emphasis on international law (by which Lord Templeman evidently meant public international law and not, or not only, English conflict of laws) as providing a basic justification for recognizing a foreign expropriatory law affecting property within the jurisdiction of the foreign State. But because of the indirect way in which the issue was raised in the case (the foreign law being irrelevant to the local cause of action relied on), and because of the apparently inoffensive character, so far as international law is concerned, of the Spanish law, the limits of the rule of recognition of foreign expropriations did not need to be discussed.

The only judicial disagreement in the case occurred in the Court of Appeal, where Lloyd LJ was persuaded in particular by the arguments of Dr F. A. Mann ('happily not yet authoritative in the strict sense'),[18] in a series of articles dealing with recognition of foreign expropriations affecting corporate assets, to hold that the defence was not unarguable, and therefore should not be struck out at a preliminary stage.[19] Of course, the articles were not concerned specifically with the situation before the court; but the tenor of the speeches in the House of Lords appears to be that if appeal is to be made to international law in underwriting or helping to constitute the rules for recognition of foreign public laws, regard should also be had to the content of international law in determining the scope of those rules.

A subsidiary point was the procedural problem of dealing with the company affected if the foreign law is not recognized. Counsel for the defendants relied on Dr Mann's suggestion of local receivership in the interests of company creditors, with the residue held on trust for those previously entitled to the assets in question (in this case, the shares), but this suggestion was firmly rejected by Lord Templeman.[20] This was probably a reflection of the view his lordship took of the merits of the case. There may perhaps be situations where receivership is the only solution, although, given the insistence in this case on the distinction between legal control of the company and the ownership of its shares, such situations will undoubtedly be rare.[21]

[16] [1986] 1 All ER at pp. 133–5, citing Nourse J, [1985] 2 All ER 208 at pp. 217–18. Lords Scarman, Bridge and Brandon agreed. Lord Mackay delivered a separate speech agreeing in the result, for substantially the same reasons.

[17] [1976] AC 249.

[18] [1985] 2 All ER 619, 632. The articles referred to were 'The Confiscation of Corporations, Corporate Rights and Corporate Assets and the Conflict of Laws', *International and Comparative Law Quarterly*, 11 (1962), p. 471, and 'Conflicts of Laws and Public Law', *Recueil des cours*, 132 (1971–I), p. 107 at pp. 176–80. The latter article was not cited by counsel, and Lloyd LJ cited it at length but 'with diffidence' (at p. 634).

[19] At p. 640.

[20] [1986] 1 All ER 129 at p. 135.

[21] The problems of substance and form in this area give rise to equivalent difficulties of evidence and proof, as *Settebello Ltd.* v. *Banco Totta & Acores*, [1985] 1 WLR 1050, reveals. Liberian shipowners

Judicial review—unimplemented treaty—UK–Philippines Air Services Agreement—whether relevant in exercise of powers under Air Navigation Order 1980

Case No. 5. R v. *Secretary of State for Transport, ex parte Philippine Airways Ltd.*, [1984] TLR 273, McNeill J; [1984] TLR 570, CA. Philippine Airways, which had for three years held an operating permit for flights between London and Manila, sought judicial review of a decision of the Secretary of State for Transport provisionally suspending the permit. The provisional suspension purported to be an exercise of the general power under Article 59 of the Air Navigation Order 1980,[22] which allows provisional suspension or variation of a permit, pending inquiry into or consideration of the case. Article 59 makes no

had a contract with a Portuguese State-owned shipbuilding company, under which the shipbuilding company had an obligation to return advance payments (some $25 million) if the contract was cancelled on grounds of delay. The obligation was guaranteed by a Portuguese State-owned bank. The contract was apparently governed by Portuguese law. There was a delay of four years in delivery. The shipowners sought to cancel the contract. In defence to the claim for repayment the bank relied on a Portuguese decree law giving certain companies (including the shipbuilders) the right to extra time to perform their contracts. The shipowners argued that the decree law should not be recognized because

> 'under the cloak of legislating for public purposes, the decree law was promulgated in order to serve the particular commercial interests of the shipbuilders and the defendants, both of whom were wholly owned by the Portuguese state'

(at p. 1028 *per* Sir John Donaldson MR). The shipowners applied for letters of request to be issued to obtain evidence in Portugal and West Germany relevant to this question. The Court of Appeal, without going into the merits of the recognition question, refused to grant the letters of request. In the words of Sir John Donaldson MR:

> 'effect should be given to [the decree law] unless there has been some degree of failure to comply with the standards accepted amongst civilised nations or unless the law can be characterised as abhorrent in its nature or there has been some degree of "iniquity" on the part of the government or ministers of the Portuguese state. Any letters of request issued in these circumstances involve inviting the Portuguese courts to assist the English courts to investigate such an allegation.
>
> Such a request would, in my judgment, be deeply embarrassing and indeed offensive to the Portuguese courts and would be likely to be embarrassing to the courts of West Germany. Counsel for the plaintiffs replies that he is only asking for a request to be made of these courts and that it will be open to them to refuse. This is literally true, but judicial comity or good neighbourliness between the judges of different friendly foreign states requires that they refrain from making such requests of each other. It would be quite otherwise if the issue to which the evidence was directed had been whether some constitutional formality had been observed and whether, as a consequence, the law was invalid or ineffective as a matter of Portuguese law' (at p. 1030).

In two other cases involving letters of discovery under the Evidence (Proceedings in Other Jurisdictions) Act 1975 the courts exercised their powers so as to limit as far as possible the scope of discovery and to avoid 'fishing expeditions'. In *Re Asbestos Insurance Coverage Cases*, [1985] 1 WLR 331, the House of Lords construed strictly the words 'particular documents specified in the order' in section 2 (4) (b) of the Act so as to require documents sought in relation to US proceedings to be clearly described or indicated. The second case involved almost the converse situation. In *South Carolina Insurance Co.* v. *Assurantie Maatschappij 'De Zeven Provincien' NV*, [1985] 3 WLR 739, the Court of Appeal upheld an injunction preventing the appellants from seeking pre-trial discovery in the US in respect of proceedings in England. The *Laker Airways* case, [1985] AC 58, this *Year Book*, 55 (1984), p. 331, was distinguished on the ground that the US proceedings in this case were not based on a separate cause of action but were ancillary to proceedings properly commenced in the UK. It was inconsistent with acceptance of the procedural law of the forum to rely on different and much wider US discovery rules. Griffiths LJ cited the UK declaration under Article 23 of the Hague Convention on the Taking of Evidence Abroad in Civil or Commercial Matters of 18 March 1970 as evidence of the 'deeply entrenched . . . attitude towards pre-trial discovery' in the UK: [1985] 3 WLR 739 at p. 745. Leave to appeal to the House of Lords has been given: [1985] 1 WLR 1336.

[22] SI 1980, no. 1965.

reference to the matters to be considered by the Secretary of State in the subsequent inquiry into the 'case'. Philippine Airways' permit was issued pursuant to a bilateral Air Services Agreement.[23] Article 4 (6) of the Agreement provides that each contracting party may suspend an airline's privileges under Article 3 (2)

> . . . in any case where the airline fails to comply with the laws or regulations of the Contracting Party granting those privileges or otherwise fails to operate in accordance with the conditions prescribed in the present Agreement; provided that, unless immediate suspension or imposition of conditions is essential to prevent further infringements of laws or regulations, this right shall be exercised only after consultation with the other Contracting Party.

Article 6 (3) provides that passenger capacity on approved routes should be related to:

(*a*) traffic requirements to and from the territory of the contracting party which had designated the airline;
(*b*) traffic requirements of the areas through which the airline passed, after taking account of other transport services established by airlines of the States comprising the area; and
(*c*) the requirements of through airline operations.

The Secretary of State wished to prevent the airline operating more than two flights a week, on the basis of sampling in London of traffic on the routes which, it was thought, revealed that Philippine Airlines was encroaching improperly on the UK–Australia route. The UK view, expressed in consultations with the Government of the Philippines which were held under Article 11 (1) of the Agreement and which were attended by the airline's representatives as observers, was that this traffic pattern revealed a breach of Article 6 (3) of the Agreement. It was conceded that there was no breach by the airline of the Air Navigation Order itself. The airline denied that it was in breach of the Agreement (by which, it said, it was not bound), and also denied that traffic sampling in London only could reveal traffic patterns accurately enough to determine the 'case'.

The crux of the airline's application for judicial review concerned the relationship between the Agreement (which was not part of UK law) and the exercise of the Secretary of State's power under the Air Navigation Order. As McNeill J said:

> The position of a designated airline in circumstances such as these has its unusual features, not perhaps unusual in aviation law, but unusual in the normal business of this court. Its operations are subject both to inter-state agreement and to state regulation. What then is the obligation of the state carrying out a regulatory function?[24]

Of course, it was not possible for the airline to rely directly on the Agreement, as McNeill J pointed out, citing *Pan-American World Airways* v. *Department of Trade*.[25] But the relationship between the international disagreement and the exercise of domestic powers under the Order was in fact a close one and the Agreement itself, in Article 4 (6), subjected airlines to disabilities under domestic law if they operated contrary to the Agreement. Not only were international and domestic powers linked, they were entangled.

[23] *United Kingdom Treaty Series*, no. 68 (1955).
[24] Reasons for Judgment, 13 April 1984, p. 29.
[25] [1976] 1 Lloyds Rep. 257; this *Year Book*, 48 (1976–7), pp. 345–8. See Reasons for Judgment, 13 April 1984, pp. 23, 30.

McNeill J's treatment of the entanglement was somewhat equivocal. He discounted Article 4 (6) of the Agreement on the ground that:

> The only powers which the Secretary of State has sought to exercise are those conferred upon him by the Air Navigation Order, 1980. . . . [T]he Secretary of State has not sought or purported to act under any powers which he may have under Article 4 (6) for 'failure to operate in accordance with the conditions prescribed in' the ASA. This, I accept, would be justiciable only under public international law.[26]

So far as the exercise of domestic law powers was concerned, however, counsel did rely on the Agreement indirectly. According to McNeill J:

> [Counsel for the airline] put the point in this way. Where the Secretary of State, in taking the action complained of, has misdirected himself as to the meaning of the agreement and/or as to the question of whether the agreement was broken or not, that misdirection can be challenged in the courts, even if the agreement forms no part of the domestic law. Where, as here, the agreement creates neither rights in nor obligations upon the applicants under domestic law, the decision, he said, can be challenged if the Secretary of State, intending to comply with the agreement, gets it wrong. Here, the Secretary of State has consistently misinterpreted and misdirected himself upon Article 6 (3) of the ASA. . . . I have already canvassed the factual material on traffic statistics. If this point stood alone, I should not have found it possible to say that the Secretary of State was not entitled to reach the conclusion which he did upon the material before him . . . [Counsel for the Secretary of State] put his case in this way. It being conceded that the Secretary of State can have regard to rights under the ASA, he can have regard also to contraventions by either government or airline, notwithstanding that the airline is not a party to the ASA and that the ASA is not justiciable under municipal law, provided the Secretary of State acts *bona fide* and has what could reasonably be regarded as a sound basis for asserting the contravention. In those circumstances, he said, the municipal court will not inquire further into the correctness of his view, either as to the proper legal construction of the ASA or as to the factual substratum upon which his view is formed. Indeed, he said, the court would be obliged to find perversity before it could interfere. [Counsel for the airline], in reply, rejected the submission that only perversity, or the lack of honest decision making on the part of the Secretary of State, or the absence of *bona fides* in him would justify review. Here, he said, the Secretary of State purported to deprive the applicants of well-established rights and so the *Wednesbury* principle applies, particularly if, as here, the Secretary of State has misconstrued the agreement. If he chooses to take the agreement into account, 'he must get it right'.
>
> So far as this narrow point is concerned, I agree with [counsel for the airline]. . . . My firm impression, at the end of this hearing, is that the Secretary of State never considered the propriety of the course which he proposed to take; still less considered whether it was reasonable to invoke regulation 59. On the contrary, he was directing his mind entirely to the statistical traffic material. Having decided that matter in his own mind provisionally, in a manner adverse to the applicants, he was concerned only to inquire into or consider further additional material on traffic figures and the like. There is nothing to indicate that the problem of the airline's liability to the domestic law, in respect of the alleged non-conformity with the ASA, was ever recognised as a problem. The Secretary of State treated as fundamental and indeed as the only question the statistical material which it had gathered or was prepared further to consider only material bearing on that question. It failed to recognise as fundamental the question whether or not the ASA imposed any obligations on PAL under the domestic law relevant for the purposes of the [Order] and, in failing to recognise the question, failed to consider it.[27]

Accordingly McNeill J granted judicial review by way of *certiorari* quashing the provisional suspension of the permit.

[26] At pp. 25–6.

[27] At pp. 32, 33–4, 35–6, 37, 38, 39.

However, the short answer to this rather formalistic point—although perhaps a prospective answer—was that the general power conferred by Article 59 of the Order did enable the provisions of international aviation agreements to be taken into account, and that Article 4 (6) of the Agreement in question did contemplate the exercise of domestic powers in case of operations inconsistent with its provisions. It was accordingly open to the Secretary of State, if he maintained his view about the airline's operations, to act again under Article 59 of the Order. This he did. The airline applied again to McNeill J for judicial review of the subsequent decision, which was refused, and then appealed to the Court of Appeal which, by a majority (Dillon LJ dissenting), and in somewhat curious circumstances, quashed the subsequent decision. Lawton LJ (with whom Griffiths LJ agreed) commented that the earlier provisional variation quashed by McNeill J

> . . . could have been quashed on another ground, namely, that in relying on imperfect figures which were inaccurate and unreliable the secretary of state had taken into account facts which ought not to have been taken into account.[28]

The subsequent decisions provisionally and then permanently varying the permit also took the 'imperfect figures' into account. It was, Lawton LJ pointed out, only during argument in the Court of Appeal that counsel for the airline

> . . . learned that in the course of the discussions referred to in the decision letter PAL had produced what seemed to be full and accurate traffic figures together with figures showing the kind of fares paid by passengers passing through Manila from or to Australia. Those new figures showed that all the time PAL had been running the Manila–London service, more than half the traffic had originated from or had been destined for the Philippines and a substantial proportion, between one fifth and one third, had been taken up by passengers from the areas through which PAL's services had passed but without reaching London. About three-quarters of PAL's traffic was clearly in conformity with what was envisaged in article 6 (3). The revised and detailed figures produced by PAL showed for the first time what was the proportion of transit traffic as a whole, where it had originated and how much of it was made up by passengers paying promotional fares and to whom PAL had unrestricted access. The Secretary of State thought it was too large a proportion. Maybe he was justified in being of that opinion; but in basing his decision on that ground, he was looking at the issue from a different standpoint from that which he had taken up when making his provisional variations. He did not tell PAL what he had in mind and gave them no oppportunity of commenting on the traffic pattern which the revised figures revealed.[29]

Accordingly the final decision was not based on 'due inquiry' as required by Article 59 (1) of the Order and was void.

Clearly the decisions depend very much on their own facts, but they are none the less revealing as to the way in which administrative law principles inescapably interact with considerations of international law and treaty provisions in areas such as this. No doubt a strong case is needed before the courts will interfere,[30] but the distinction between unimplemented and implemented treaties is no justification for arbitrary decision-making, in a case where the decision-maker is mistaken as to the meaning or effect of treaty provisions, or completely fails to take them

[28] [1984] TLR 570.

[29] Ibid.

[30] In the *Laker* case Lord Diplock commented that, where a decision 'concerns international relations between the United Kingdom and a foreign sovereign state a very strong case needs to be made out to justify a court of law in holding the decision to be ultra vires under the *Wednesbury* principle' (i.e. the principle that a decision is *ultra vires* if the court is satisfied that no reasonable person in the circumstances could have reached it): [1985] AC 58 at p. 92.

into account where they are relevant. For this reason the alternative ground, referred to by Lawton LJ,[31] for McNeill J's decision is to be preferred to the one actually adopted.

Acquisition of land in New Territories of Hong Kong—whether valid notwithstanding provisions of Peking Convention of 1898 ceding Territories—whether provisions of Convention justiciable in courts of Hong Kong

Case No. 6. Winfat Enterprise (HK) Co. Ltd. v. *Attorney-General for Hong Kong*, [1985] AC 733, [1985] 2 WLR 786 (PC). This case concerned land in the New Territories of Hong Kong, ceded by China to Britain for ninety-nine years by the Peking Convention for Extension of Hong Kong of 9 June 1898.[32] The Convention provided in part that:

> It is further understood that there will be no expropriation or expulsion of the inhabitants of the district included within the extension [sc. the New Territories], and that if land is required for public offices, fortifications, or the like official purposes, it shall be bought at a fair price.

The appellants were land developers who were successors in title to Chinese inhabitants of the New Territories in 1898. When British administration was extended to the New Territories, the New Territories Land Ordinance 1900, section 3, provided that all land in the Territories was the property of the Crown for the period of the cessions under the Convention, and made provision for land grants to be made by the Governor. The New Territories Order in Council 1898 gave the Governor, with the advice and consent of the Legislative Council, power to make laws for the peace, order and good government of the Territories as part of the Colony of Hong Kong. Occupiers of land in the Territories were subsequently issued with Block Crown Leases over their land, subject to a restriction on building other than as incidental to the existing use of the land for agriculture or gardens.

The appellants acquired various parcels of the land between 1974 and 1976 and applied for permission to use the land for low-density housing development, but permission was refused. Subsequently part of the land was compulsorily acquired for temporary housing. They sought declarations that they held the land on the same basis as the original inhabitants did in 1898, free from restrictions on building, and that its compulsory acquisition was a violation of the 'fair price' guarantee in the Convention. In counsel's words:

> Since there was a non-expropriation provision in the Convention the British Crown could only exercise its prerogative power to legislate in relation to the New Territories in a manner which was consistent with the Convention. The New Territories Order in Council 1898 did not give the Governor power to make laws inconsistent with the Convention. The Order in Council must be read as a whole including the preamble, which refers to the Convention, and it is apparent that it was intended to implement the Convention. The Crown therefore only had power to legislate in accordance with the Convention and the Order in Council must be interpreted accordingly. Paragraph 2 of the Order in Council is limited in that the Governor could not make laws contrary to the non-expropriation provisions in the Convention. . . . The power to make laws for the 'peace, order and good government' of the New Territories should be construed consistently with international law, which regards treaties as binding, and those words should be interpreted in accordance

[31] See p. 323 n. 28, above.

[32] *Hertslet's Commercial Treaties*, vol. 21, p. 293.

with the Convention, especially the non-expropriation provisions. When subordinate legislatures are created it is not intended that they should have power to legislate contrary to international law.[33]

Counsel for the Attorney-General argued that any limitations on plenary legislative power over Hong Kong embodied in the Convention were non-justiciable and unenforceable in the courts, although it was also argued that the Convention had been complied with. Speaking for the Privy Council, Lord Diplock confined himself to the former argument. He said:

The elementary fallacy of British constitutional law which vitiates the land developers' claim is the contention that this vaguely expressed understanding, stated in the Peking Convention, that there shall not be expropriation or expulsion, is capable of giving rise to rights enforceable in the municipal courts of Hong Kong or by this Board acting in its judicial capacity. Although there are certain obiter dicta to be found in cases which suggest the propriety of the British Government giving effect as an act of state to promises of continued recognition of existing private titles of inhabitants of territory obtained by cession, there is clear long-standing authority by decision of this Board that no municipal court has authority to enforce such an obligation. . . . The only reference to the Peking Convention in the New Territories Order in Council 1898 is for the purpose of identifying the area of land and the period of time to which the Order in Council relates. The relevant Ordinances are unambiguous and their Lordships agree with the courts below that there is no ground for recourse to the principle of *Salomon* v. *Commissioners of Customs and Excise* [1967] 2 Q.B. 116 in an attempt to construe their unambiguous words so as to give effect to some guess, for it can be no more, as to what was intended by the respective sovereigns to be meant by the paragraph in the Convention which their Lordships have already cited.[34]

[33] [1985] 1 AC 735, 739.

[34] At pp. 747–8. A number of other cases in 1985 involved more or less indirect reliance on treaties or international arrangements not given the force of UK law. The most important was *R* v. *Secretary of State for the Home Department, ex parte Musisi*, briefly reported only in [1985] TLR. 354. A Ugandan citizen claimed to be a political refugee. His claim was rejected by the Home Secretary, but he claimed the right to remain in the UK, notwithstanding an order for his removal to Kenya, to conduct an appeal against the refusal of refugee status to an immigration adjudicator under the Immigration Act 1971 section 14. He relied in particular on Article 32 (2) of the Convention relating to the Status of Refugees of 1951 as amended by the 1967 Protocol. His claim was rejected by the Court of Appeal, on the gound that

'the right of appeal under article 32 (2) applied only where a decision was taken that a refugee should be expelled on the grounds therein specified. It did not have any application to a decision whether or not a person was a refugee' (*per* Watkins LJ).

In *Wheeler* v. *Leicester City Council*, [1985] 2 All ER 1106, a local council banned a rugby club from use of its ground for twelve months because the club had not taken action against club members participating in a tour of South Africa. The House of Lords quashed the council's decision on grounds of unreasonableness and abuse of power. Their Lordships agreed that the council was entitled to take local race relations into account, but that its action against the club went beyond persuasion and amounted to illegitimate pressure or coercion in respect of an area Parliament had deliberately left free for individual decision. Lord Roskill commented (at pp. 1109–10):

'It is important to emphasise that there was nothing illegal in the action of the three members in joining the tour. The government policy recorded in the well-known Gleneagles agreement made in 1977 between the Commonwealth heads of government, has never been given the force of law at the instance of any government, whatever its political complexion, and a person who acts otherwise than in accordance with the principles of that agreement commits no offence even though he may by his action earn the moral disapprobation of large numbers of his fellow citizens.'

In *Council of Civil Service Unions* v. *Minister for the Civil Service*, [1985] AC 374, the House of Lords

International convention—relation to statute—Brussels Convention on the Arrest of Sea-Going Ships 1952—Administration of Justice Act 1956 section 47 (2) (d) (e)—relevance of travaux préparatoires—*whether claim for insurance premiums within Admiralty jurisdiction*

Case No. 7. Gatoil International Inc. v. *Arkwright-Boston Manufacturers Mutual Insurance Co.*, [1985] AC 255, [1985] 2 WLR 74, [1985] 1 All ER 129, [1985] 1 Lloyd's Rep 181, HL.

The appellants were a Panamanian company alleged to be the owners of a ship, the *Sandrina*. The respondents, six insurance companies and an insurance broker, claimed almost $4 million in respect of unpaid insurance premiums under a war risk open cover on cargo. They procured the arrest of the *Sandrina* in Scotland on the dependence of their action against the appellants, under section 47 (2) (e) of the Administration of Justice Act 1956. That provision, unlike its English counterpart section 1 (now enacted as Supreme Court Act 1981 section 20), does not require a nexus between the claim and the ship in question (or a sister-ship), but it does limit the previously broad power under Scots law to arrest ships *ad fundandam jurisdictionem*. It thus brings Scots law more closely into conformity with the 1952 Brussels Convention on the Arrest of Sea-Going Ships.[35] Thus for the arrest to be valid the claim had to come within one of the heads enumerated in section 47 (2): in fact the respondents relied on section 47 (2) (e), on the basis that the insurance contract was an 'agreement relating to the carriage of goods in any ship whether by charterparty or otherwise'.

The House of Lords held unanimously that an insurance contract did not fall within section 47 (2) (e), for two distinct reasons. Lord Keith came to that conclusion after a lengthy analysis of earlier cases[36] and of the language of section 47 (2) (e) in its context. Lord Wilberforce also relied on the *travaux préparatoires* of the Brussels Convention, which revealed that the identical words of Article 1 (e)

declined to follow the Court of Appeal in discussing the meaning of certain ILO Conventions (especially ILO Convention No. 87 concerning Freedom of Association and Protection of the Right to Organize of 1948) on the ground that their meaning was unclear and that in any event they were not part of UK law: at p. 403 *per* Lord Fraser. Counsel for the union also referred to Article 11 (2) of the European Convention on Human Rights (at p. 379) but this was not referred to by their Lordships. In *X* v. *Commissioner of Police of the Metropolis*, [1985] 1 All ER 890, a police officer had given information about the plaintiff's criminal record to the Paris Office of the International Criminal Police Commission (Interpol) in response to a request arising from investigations into suspected offences to be committed in Andorra. The criminal offences disclosed were 'spent offences' and the plaintiff was a 'rehabilitated person' under the Rehabilitation of Offenders Act 1974. He sought a declaration that the disclosure of the offences occurred 'otherwise than in the course of [official] duties' within section 9 (2) of the 1974 Act and therefore constituted an offence. Whitford J commented that under Interpol's constitution and in accordance with its practice:

> 'for a good many years this country as a member of Interpol has accepted obligations relating to the transmission of information following requests received, with this safeguard, that information is just not broadcast on request without reason being given. As matters stand today, international crime has assumed a significance which, so far as this country is concerned, makes its suppression as important to the inhabitants of this country, and perhaps in some cases more important, as the suppression of domestic crime' (at p. 895).

He accordingly held that the information was disclosed in the course of official duties under the 1974 Act.

[35] *United Nations Treaty Series*, vol. 439, p. 195.

[36] Especially, *The Zeus* (1888), 13 PD 188; *The Aifanourios*, [1980] SC 346. See [1985] AC 255 at pp. 267–70.

of the Convention were not intended to include claims for unpaid insurance premiums. He said:

My Lords, there is here, no doubt, no more than a degree of doubt as to the meaning of statutory words not significantly greater than often arises, particularly in such cases as reach this House. They can be, and are, solved by a judicial process of interpretation. My noble and learned friend, Lord Keith of Kinkel, has followed this path, and if there were no other material to help us, I would be content to follow him. However, I believe that contentment can be converted to conviction by legitimate reinforcement ab extra, namely, by resort to the travaux préparatoires of the International Convention relating to the Arrest of Seagoing Ships, signed at Brussels on 10 May 1952. The case for a cautious use of travaux préparatoires in aid of the interpretation of conventions or treaties of private law received some acceptance in this House in *Fothergill* v. *Monarch Airlines Ltd.* I there suggested that two conditions must be fulfilled before they can be used: first, that the material is public and accessible; secondly, that it clearly and indisputably points to a definite legislative intention. The case for resort to them here is, in my opinion, a strong one. The Administration of Justice Act 1956, Part V (which included section 47) was enacted to give effect to the obligations of the United Kingdom consequent on its accession to the Brussels Convention of 1952 . . . and in particular to displace, in Scotland, the wide common law powers of arrestment in favour of statutory provisions which were narrower and precisely defined. . . . The proceedings of the conference which led to the Brussels Convention are public and accessible: they have been published by the International Maritime Committee as regards the preparatory conference at Naples held in 1951, and as regards the Diplomatic Conference of 1952 by the Foreign Ministry of Belgium (Conference Internationale de Droit Maritime). . . . The conference decided not to include premia on policies of insurance among the maritime claims justifying arrest. It did so, moreover, not because it thought that these premia were already covered (so that explicit reference was unnecessary) but because it considered it unnecessary as a matter of policy to provide for their protection by means of arrestment. The legislative intention is manifest: not by any provision in article 1 to provide for the inclusion of premia among arrestable maritime claims. In the face of this legislative intention the adoption of the provisions of article 1 of the Convention in the Act of 1956 must be treated as carrying the same meaning as that evidently placed upon them in the Convention and as not extending to premia on insurance policies.[37]

Although Lord Keith referred to the Convention he did not find it necessary to discuss the argument from its *travaux préparatoires*.[38] However, the other three Law Lords, Lords Fraser, Scarman and Roskill, expressly agreed with both Lord Keith and Lord Wilberforce.[39]

As was pointed out in an earlier volume of this *Year Book*,[40] and as Lord Wilberforce implied, the discussion of the relevance of *travaux préparatoires* in the leading case, *Fothergill* v. *Monarch Airlines Ltd.*,[41] though authoritative, did not constitute part of the ratio of that case. It is equally clear that the point was part of the ratio of the present case, as well as a good illustration of the application of the principle.[42]

[37] At pp. 263–4, 265. See also at pp. 264–5 for Lord Wilberforce's summary of the relevant proceedings at the two conferences.

[38] At p. 270.

[39] At p. 262 (Lord Fraser), p. 271 (Lord Roskill). Lord Scarman (at p. 262) expressly affirmed Lord Wilberforce's reasoning based on the *travaux préparatoires*.

[40] This *Year Book*, 51 (1980), p. 321.

[41] [1981] AC 251.

[42] On the point of substance, the tendency in more recent Admiralty legislation has been to include claims for unpaid insurance premiums expressly within Admiralty jurisdiction. See, e.g., Admiralty

Diplomatic immunity—appointment not yet notified to receiving State—whether diplomat entitled to immunity

Case No. 8. R v. *Lambeth Justices, ex parte Yusufu*, [1985] TLR 114, Div. Ct. This important case, involving the vexed question of when the diplomatic immunities of an ordinary diplomatic agent commence, is surprisingly reported only in *The Times* 'Law Reports'. Major Yusufu was committed for trial on a charge of kidnapping a former Nigerian minister resident in London, Mr Umaru Dikko.[43] He claimed diplomatic immunity. He had entered the UK on a diplomatic passport on 'official business' for one month, and had joined the staff of the Nigerian High Commission in London. However, his appointment had not been notified by the Nigerian Government to the UK Government, nor had his credentials been presented to the Queen.

Jurisdiction Regulation Act 1983 (South Africa) section 1 (1) (r); Comité Maritime International, *Draft Revision of the International Convention for the Unification of Certain Rules relating to the Arrest of Sea-Going Ships* (Lisbon, May 1985) (LIS I ARREST—30), Article 1 (1) (q); Australian Law Reform Commission, *Civil Admiralty Jurisdiction* (1986), para. 173. Other cases during the period under review involving the interpretation of statutes implementing treaties included *The Antonis P. Lemos*, [1985] AC 771 (also involving the 1952 Brussels Convention), *Centrocoop Export-Import SA* v. *Brit European Transport Ltd.*, [1984] 2 Lloyd's Rep. 618 (Carriage of Goods by Road Act 1965). A number of cases concerned the question whether the classic Islamic *talaq* divorce was to be recognized as 'other proceedings' within section 2 (a) of the Recognition of Divorces and Legal Separations Act 1971. That Act was passed in part so as to implement the Hague Convention on Recognition of Divorces and Legal Separations of 1970 (*United Kingdom Treaty Series*, no. 123 (1975)). As pointed out in this *Year Book*, 50 (1979), p. 232, it is clear from the *travaux* of that Convention that it was not intended to cover the unilateral *talaq*, or similar forms of divorce where no official intervention of any kind is necessary. The 1971 Act might still be held to cover such *talaqs* (it is no violation of the Convention to recognize divorces not covered by it), but some indication of an intention to go beyond the scope of the Convention might fairly be required. The point was left open by the House of Lords in *Quazi* v. *Quazi*, [1980] AC 744. In *R* v. *Secretary of State for the Home Department, ex parte Fatima*, [1984] 2 All ER 458, the Court of Appeal held that the pronouncement of *talaq* was itself part, at least, of the proceedings: a *talaq* pronounced in the UK which was followed by various administrative steps in Pakistan was not obtained by 'proceedings in any country outside the British Isles' within section 2 of the Act, since that phrase requires the proceedings to occur entirely abroad. In *Chaudhary* v. *Chaudhary*, [1985] 2 WLR 350, the Court of Appeal held that a bare *talaq* was not 'other proceedings' within the meaning of the 1971 Act. The Court relied on the presumed intention of the draftsmen of the Convention, without expressly referring to the *travaux préparatoires*: see especially at p. 365 *per* Cumming-Bruce LJ. In any event recognition would have been refused on grounds of public policy under section 8 (2) (b) of the Act (Article 10 of the Convention) since the parties were domiciled in the UK and the husband's visit to Kashmir to pronounce *talaq* was principally if not solely for the purpose of evading the matrimonial jurisdiction of the UK's courts. The House of Lords refused leave to appeal: [1985] 2 WLR 375. Also on the 1971 Act, see *Lawrence* v. *Lawrence*, [1985] 3 WLR 125 (CA). Finally, *R* v. *Her Majesty's Treasury, ex parte Smedley*, [1985] QB 657 involved the question whether an agreement by EEC member States to contribute to a supplementary community budget (the UK share was over £120 million) constituted 'a treaty ancilliary to any of the [Community] Treaties' within the meaning of section 1 (2) of the European Communities Act 1972. If it did, an Order in Council, supported by an affirmative resolution of both Houses of Parliament, was a sufficient authority for the payment of the contribution (section 1 (3)). However, it was argued that the agreement could not be 'ancillary' because it conflicted with the decision, embodied in Article 127 of the Treaty of Accession, that the Community's budget would be funded from its own resources, without additional contributions. The Court of Appeal emphasized the need for flexibility and the vagueness of the term 'ancillary'. While accepting that not all treaties would qualify as 'ancillary', it held that an agreement containing partial variations or inconsistencies with the Community Treaties could none the less be 'ancillary': see especially at p. 669 *per* Sir John Donaldson MR, at pp. 673–4 *per* Slade LJ.

[43] See Akinsanya, 'The Dikko Affair and Anglo-Nigerian Relations', *International and Comparative Law Quarterly*, 34 (1985), p. 602, for an account.

The Diplomatic Privileges Act 1964 gives the force of law to certain articles of the Vienna Convention on Diplomatic Relations of 1961.[44] Yusufu relied on two distinct grounds to establish his immunity. A subsidiary argument involved Article 40 of the Convention. While in London Yusufu had been granted a multiple entry diplomatic visa for the United States. He argued that as a result he was 'in the territory of a third State . . . while proceeding to take up or return to his post . . .'. The argument was, rightly, summarily rejected. Watkins LJ said that 'article 40 could not begin to apply unless the person in question was at the relevant time in a country which was neither the sending nor the receiving state, in transit from one to the other'.[45] On Yusufu's other argument, the UK was the receiving State, and in any event he was not in transit. Moreover (though this point was apparently not taken), Article 40 only accords 'inviolability and such other immunities as may be required to ensure his transit or return'. Yusufu's activities had nothing to do with any 'post' in the US.

A much more substantial argument involved Articles 7 and 39 of the Convention, both given the force of law by the 1964 Act, and Article 10, which is not. Article 7 provides that, subject to certain exceptions, the sending State 'may freely appoint the members of the staff of the mission'. Article 39 provides that diplomatic privileges and immunities apply 'from the moment [the person entitled to them] enters the territory of the receiving State on proceeding to take up his post'. Article 10 provides that the Ministry for Foreign Affairs of the receiving State shall be notified of the appointment of members of the mission and of their arrival in that State. On the basis of Articles 7 and 39, Yusufu argued that his entitlement to immunity did not depend upon the prior consent or acceptance of the UK Government. The Divisional Court rejected this argument. Watkins LJ is reported as having said:

> The applicant had contended that since article 10 of the Vienna Convention, which required the sending state to give such notification, was not part of English law as it had not been included in Schedule 1 to the Diplomatic Privileges Act 1964, failure to comply with it could not of itself deprive a person of diplomatic immunity. Although his Lordship accepted that the provisions of article 10 were only of evidentiary value, it was clear that it was incumbent upon the sending state under international law to comply with it; if it did not, then no question of diplomatic status or immunity could arise. . . . It had then been contended that article 39, also in Schedule 1, which provided that a person entitled to diplomatic immunity should enjoy it from the moment that he entered the receiving state, conferred diplomatic immunity on the applicant from the time of his entry to the United Kingdom, rendering the lack of notification to, or of acceptance by the Foreign and Commonwealth Office immaterial in determining whether he was a diplomat. That submission was surprising in the light of the decision in *R* v. *Governor of Pentonville Prison, ex parte Teja* ([1971] 2 QB 274) that diplomatic immunity could not be conferred by the unilateral action of the sending state. The court was bound by the decision, with which it in any event agreed. His Lordship agreed with what had been said in argument in *Teja*'s case: that article 39 was procedural in effect, and could not confer immunity on someone who was not otherwise entitled to immunity; it merely extended the scope of the immunity to which a person was already entitled.

Accordingly the applications for judicial review of the decision to commit Yusufu

[44] *United Nations Treaty Series*, vol. 500, p. 95.
[45] [1985] TLR 114. Nolan J agreed.

for trial failed. Yusufu was subsequently convicted and sentenced to twelve years' imprisonment.

The case illustrates the strains that flagrant abuses of diplomatic immunity are placing on the law as stated in the Vienna Convention. Since a codified text such as the Convention allows little flexibility, change has to occur, in the absence of some formal revision of the text, through judicial interpretations which may appear strained and even contrary to the intentions of the draftsmen. *Yusufu* was such a case. The Convention is quite clear in requiring prior agreement to the appointment of certain categories of diplomatic personnel (in particular, heads of mission (Article 4) and military, naval and air attachés where the receiving State so requires (Article 7)) and in not requiring it in other cases. Article 7 is stated to be subject to certain other provisions where local agreement for an appointment is required (namely, Article 5 (multiple accreditation) and Article 8 (local nationals)), and it is also subject to the *persona non grata* rule (Article 9) and to limits imposed on the size of mission (Article 11). But it is not subject to Article 10. It was presumably for this reason that the UK Government which, unlike some other States, made no reservation to Article 7 to preserve the receiving State's right to agree to all appointments, did not include Article 10 in the Schedule to the Diplomatic Privileges Bill 1964.

Watkins LJ's view of the Convention is contradicted also by the *travaux préparatoires*. A proposal (made by Verdross) in the International Law Commission to require agreement to the appointment of all diplomatic agents was lost by one vote.[46] A proposal to similar effect failed at the Vienna Conference.[47] The International Law Commission's Commentary on the text clearly implies that prior agreement is not necessary.[48] That is also the view of most authors.[49] It is probably the case as a matter of general international law (apart from the Convention) that prior agreement, express or implied, is necessary.[50] The general international law position may well have represented a better balance between receiving and sending State interests. But a different view was taken at the Conference.

So far as UK law is concerned, there are further difficulties with the decision. There can be no objection to interpreting the scheduled articles of the Convention by reference to the Convention as a whole. But it is curious to treat a non-scheduled article as in effect overriding a scheduled one, or to reintroduce general international law rules in the context of a Convention which appears to have been intended to reverse the international law rule in question. To rely on *Teja*'s case[51] was also questionable. That case concerned an *ad hoc* mission, a situation where it is clear that express consent is required. Moreover, there was in that case a certificate of the Secretary of State under section 3 (4) of the 1964 Act denying that Teja was a diplomatic agent. Lord Parker's statement in *Teja*'s case that prior agreement is required[52] was thus plainly *obiter*, as well as distinguishable.

[46] *Yearbook of the International Law Commission*, 1975, vol. 1, p. 29. See Hardy, *Modern Diplomatic Law* (1968), pp. 27–8.

[47] Ibid. (although Hardy notes that certain minority views were expressed at the Conference as to the meaning of the relevant provisions).

[48] *Yearbook of the International Law Commission*, 1958, vol. 2, p. 91.

[49] For example, Hardy, op. cit. above (n. 46), p. 81; Brownlie, this *Year Book*, 45 (1971), p. 399.

[50] *Oppenheim's International Law*, vol. 1 (8th edn., by Lauterpacht, 1955), p. 784; *In re Solvan Vitianu* (1949), 16 *Annual Digest* 281 (Swiss Federal Tribunal); H. Lauterpacht, *International Law. Collected Papers* (ed. E. Lauterpacht), vol. 3 (1977), p. 433.

[51] [1971] 2 QB 274.

[52] Ibid., p. 282. See the criticism by Brownlie, loc. cit. above (n. 49), p. 388.

If the view of Article 7 taken in this case is maintained, either some procedure will need to be adopted to ensure advance agreement, or at least prompt agreement, by the receiving State to appointments of diplomatic agents, or the status and immunities of diplomatic agents permitted to enter the receiving State will remain obscure and uncertain, perhaps for considerable periods of time. The latter alternative is inconvenient, but the former is perhaps not to be expected. The Vienna Convention's failure to stipulate an *agrément* procedure in all cases provides strong support for the view that such a procedure was not intended to apply.[53]

Extradition—relation to deportation—'disguised extradition'—whether relevant in examining legality of subsequent decision to try deportee in England

Case No. 9. R v. *Plymouth Magistrates' Court, ex parte Driver*, [1985] 2 All ER 611, [1985] 3 WLR 689, Div. Ct. The difficulties increasingly encountered with transnational crime, and toughening attitudes towards 'organized crime', seem to be leading to a sharp reduction in the guarantees available in the courts against extradition. That is to say, a number of guarantees long thought to exist, by implication at least, in extradition law and treaties have been held to be either non-existent or illusory. Thus the so-called principle of 'double criminality' does not exist as a general principle, apart from stipulations in particular treaties.[54] And the rule about 'disguised extradition', applied or assumed by the courts to exist in cases such as *R* v. *Bow Street Magistrates, ex parte Mackeson*,[55] and *R* v. *Guildford Magistrates' Court, ex parte Healy*,[56] has now also been held to be non-existent.

Driver, an English-born Australian citizen, was suspected of a murder committed in Plymouth. He left England, intending to travel overland to Australia, and was found in Turkey, with which the UK has no extradition treaty. He was held by the Turkish police (in circumstances which, under Turkish law, were of doubtful legality) but was then told that the British police were no longer interested in him and was 'released' by being placed on a direct flight to London. On arrival he was arrested and charged with murder. He sought orders of *certiorari* to quash the charge and prohibition to prevent the hearing of committal proceedings against him, on the grounds that his deportation was a disguised extradition without treaty and was accordingly unlawful. The Divisional Court

[53] Another case in the year under review reveals the difficult position a foreign State may find itself under in resisting claims that it is obliged to arbitrate a dispute. In *Republic of Liberia* v. *Gulf Oceanic Inc.*, [1985] 1 Lloyd's Rep. 539, the respondent initiated an arbitration against the appellant State, alleging it to be an undisclosed party to the contract in question. The appellant commenced proceedings seeking a declaration that it was not a party to the contract, and the respondent then counterclaimed against it for damages for breach of contract and in tort. The counterclaim could not have been commenced as a separate proceeding against the Republic of Liberia because it was not a case where service outside the jurisdiction was available. The counterclaim was held to be properly brought, although the question whether the appellant was none the less immune from the jurisdiction under the State Immunity Act 1978 (UK) section 2 (6) or otherwise was reserved to a later stage in the proceedings: [1985] 1 Lloyd's Rep. 539, 542, 545 (Oliver LJ). That question is not a straightforward one, since in a sense the counterclaim arose out of 'the same . . . facts as the claim' (section 2 (6)) even though it did not (on the assumption that Liberia was not a party to the contract) arise out of the 'same relationship'. But it is an open question how strict an identity the courts will require for the 'same facts' to be held to underlie the claim and counter-claim.

[54] *Government of Denmark* v. *Nielsen*, [1984] AC 606; this *Year Book*, 55 (1984), p. 343.

[55] (1981) 75 Cr. App. R. 24; this *Year Book*, 54 (1983), p. 295.

[56] [1983] 1 WLR 108; this *Year Book*, 54 (1983), p. 295.

declined to follow the 'disguised extradition' cases such as *Mackeson* and *Healy*, and refused the relief sought.

It was not, and could not have been, argued that the courts lacked jurisdiction to try Driver: it is well established that the criminal jurisdiction of the English courts over crimes against English law depends on and requires only the accused's presence within the jurisdiction.[57] But it was argued that the court had inherent power to stay proceedings where the accused's presence was obtained irregularly, by collusion between the police forces of the two States concerned and in violation of the law of the deporting State. Stephen Brown LJ, delivering the judgment of the court, held that there had been no irregularity or impropriety on the part of the English police, who 'did not at any time seek his detention or continued detention in Turkey'.

> It is true that they notified the Turkish authorities that the applicant was wanted in the United Kingdom on suspicion of having committed the murder . . . and said that if it was within the power to deport him to the United Kingdom it would assist the police to interview him. I stress that both the affidavits make it clear that this request was subject to the important condition that any action taken should be within their power. There was no request by the British police to encourage the Turkish authorities to act illegally in any way, although they agreed to pay his fare. In these circumstances, it is not established that the authorities in this country were guilty of any improper dealing. The fact that a request was made in the terms indicated in the affidavits to which I have referred cannot in my judgment amount to improper dealing which would justify a court in taking the step sought by the application of refusing to try him, always assuming that the court has the discretionary power so to do.[58]

But he went on to hold that such a discretionary power did not exist. *Soblen*'s case,[59] which was relied on, concerned the review of an executive decision to deport a suspect to another country in circumstances where extradition may not have been available. It was irrelevant in the converse situation, that is, where the UK was the receiving State. After a review of British and US authorities, the Court held that it had 'no power to inquire into the circumstances in which a person is found in the jurisdiction for the purpose of refusing to try him'.[60] The decisions in *Mackeson* and *Healy* were *per incuriam* and did not have to be followed.

However the notion of 'irregularity' is to be applied in particular situations, it is regrettable that the courts have denied themselves all power to deal with these kinds of cases. A suspect's return might result from patently illegal action by the authorities of the forum State (e.g. kidnapping):[61] apparently this too would be irrelevant. A suspect returned by informal means is in a worse position than one extradited: for example, the principle of speciality does not apply and there is no preliminary opportunity to test the evidence against him. Moreover, in this case, unlike *Soblen*, *Mackeson* or *Healy*, the suspect was not a British citizen, but was returned to a 'third' country.[62] A premium is thus placed on manipulation of local law, deception or coercion of suspects, and evasion of extradition arrangements.

[57] See, e.g., *R* v *O/C Depot Battalion RASC, Colchester, ex parte Elliott*, [1949] 1 All ER 373.

[58] [1985] 2 All ER 681 at p. 691.

[59] [1963] 2 QB 243; this *Year Book*, 38 (1962), p. 479.

[60] [1985] 2 All ER 681 at p. 697.

[61] Cf. *United States* v. *Sobell*, 142 F Supp. 515 (1956).

[62] There was evidence that Australian embassy authorities colluded in Driver's return to the UK.

Indeed, it may be wondered on what basis extradition would ever be sought from countries with direct air links to the UK, co-operative local authorities and an effective absence of remedies against illegal or improper detention.[63]

JAMES CRAWFORD

[63] Two other, unreported, extradition decisions in the period under review concerned the relationship between the extradition treaty and the evidentiary provision, section 14, of the 1870 Act. In *R* v. *Governor of Pentonville Prison, ex parte Rodriguez*, *The Times*, 29 November 1984, it was held that Article 14 of the Anglo-Portuguese extradition treaty, which requires the Government of Portugal to produce evidence in support of an extradition requisition to the Home Secretary within two months, should be liberally construed in accordance with its intent, so that there was no requirement that within the time limit the evidence should be in a form admissible before justices. In *R* v. *Secretary of State for the Home Office, ex parte Rees*, [1985] TLR 190, it was held that Article 11 of the extradition treaty with West Germany, which requires the court to receive in evidence any sworn and authenticated statements taken in Germany, did not impair the discretion under section 14 to admit statements taken in third countries. As Watkins LJ pointed out:

> 'Since article 10 of the treaty envisaged that extradition would take place "according to the laws of the state applied to" there was no reason why such laws should not include the full width of the section 14 discretion.'

DECISIONS ON THE EUROPEAN CONVENTION ON HUMAN RIGHTS DURING 1985*

The applicability of Articles 6 (1) and 8 to paternity proceedings—discrimination on grounds of sex (Article 14)

Case No. 1. Rasmussen case.[1] In this case the Court held unanimously that the fact that under Danish law a man's right of access to the courts to challenge paternity was subject to time-limits, whereas a woman's was not, did not constitute a violation of Article 14 taken in conjunction with either Article 6 or Article 8 of the Convention.

The applicant, Mr Rasmussen, married in 1966 and in 1971 his wife gave birth to a girl, Pernille. Doubts arose as to the child's paternity, but in an attempt to save the marriage the applicant refrained from contesting the issue. The applicant and his wife divorced in 1975 and in an agreement he undertook not to contest paternity in return for his wife's abandonment of any claim for maintenance of the child. In 1976 the wife indicated that she did not regard herself as bound by the agreement. Mr Rasmussen therefore sought leave from the Danish courts to institute proceedings to contest paternity. However, this was refused on the grounds that his application was out of time and that there were no special circumstances warranting an exception.

In his application to the Commission in 1979 Mr Rasmussen claimed that he had been the victim of discrimination based on sex since under the relevant Danish legislation his right of access to the courts to challenge paternity was subject to time-limits, whereas his former wife could have applied at any time.[2] In its report in 1983 the Commission, by a narrow majority, expressed the opinion that there had been a breach of Article 14 taken in conjunction with Articles 6 and 8. It then referred the case to the Court.

Article 14 of the Convention provides:

> The enjoyment of the rights and freedoms set forth in this Convention shall be secured without discrimination on any ground such as sex, race, colour, language, religion, political or other opinion, national or social origin, association with a national minority, property, birth or other status.

As the wording indicates, Article 14 is complementary to the other substantive provisions in the sense that it can be applied only where the facts fall within the ambit of one or more of the other articles. The first question in the present case was therefore whether the facts were such as to raise an issue under Articles 6 and 8.

 I should like to express my gratitude to the Registrar of the Court and to my colleagues V. T. Bevan and K. W. Lidstone for their co-operation in the preparation of these notes.

[1] European Court of Human Rights (ECHR), judgment of 28 November 1984, Series A, No. 87. The Court consisted of the following Chamber of Judges: Wiarda (President); Ganshof van der Meersch; Bindschedler-Robert; Matscher; Macdonald; Russo; Gersing (Judges).

[2] The Danish legislation provided that paternity proceedings must be instituted by the husband within twelve months of his becoming aware of the circumstances which might give grounds for his renunciation of paternity, and not later than five years after the birth of the child.

Article 6 concerns *inter alia* the determination of 'civil rights and obligations'. The Government pointed out that paternity proceedings are not a purely private matter, but involve a strong element of public interest. The Court, however, decided that this element was not enough to exclude Article 6 where litigation by its very nature was civil in character and an action contesting paternity had that character because it was a matter of family law. Article 8 includes the right to respect for 'private and family life'. Although the Government again disputed the applicability of the provision, here the Court held that whilst 'the paternity proceedings which the applicant wished to institute were aimed at the dissolution in law of existing family ties, the determination of his legal relations with Pernille undoubtedly concerned his private life'.[3] The facts accordingly fell also within Article 8.

The main question in the case was whether the difference of treatment which the Court found to exist in Danish law had an 'objective and reasonable justification', i.e. pursued a 'legitimate aim' and exhibited a 'reasonable relationship of proportionality between the means employed and the aim sought to be realised'.[4] The Government pleaded that the difference of treatment was justified by the interests of the child and that regard should be had to the margin of appreciation enjoyed by the national authorities in matters of this kind. The Court agreed. Pointing out that in its previous jurisprudence it had often held the latter to be highly relevant in cases involving Article 14, the Court explained that an important factor in determining the scope of the margin of appreciation can be the extent to which the legislation of the Contracting States adopts a uniform approach. The fact that there was no such common ground in the treatment of paternity proceedings supported the Government's argument. This was reinforced by the background of the legislation and the purpose of time-limits which was to ensure legal certainty and to protect the interests of the child, whilst: 'The difference of treatment established on this point between husbands and wives was based on the notion that such time-limits were less necessary for wives than for husbands since the mother's interests usually coincided with those of the child, she being awarded custody in most cases of divorce or separation.'[5]

There had also been no transgression of the principle of proportionality. For although the desired end could have been achieved without legislation,[6] having regard again to the margin of appreciation, the authorities were entitled to regard a statutory time bar as the best solution. Accordingly, the difference in treatment complained of was not discriminatory within the meaning of Article 14 and there had been no violation of that article taken in conjunction with Article 6 or Article 8.

While the present case was pending before the Commission, the Danish Government introduced legislation establishing uniform time-limits for men and women in paternity proceedings. This legislation, which came into force in 1982, did not, of course, relieve the Court of the need to consider Mr Rasmussen's application, nor was it regarded by the Court as an admission that the previous state of the law was incompatible with the Convention. Such caution is commendable. Family law is a matter on which the Court should tread warily and

[3] Judgment, para. 33.

[4] Ibid., para. 38. Article 14 also only protects individuals who are 'placed in analogous situations' against discriminatory treatment. The Court, however, considered that it was unnecessary to deal with this issue.

[5] Ibid., para. 41.

[6] It was this fact, which arose from the 'doctrine of acknowledgement' in Danish law, that led the Commission to conclude that the Convention had been violated.

where the sensitivity of the subject-matter, changing social mores and the cultural diversity of the Contracting States mean that the margin of appreciation can be given considerable play.[7]

Less satisfactory is the treatment of Article 8 which seems to indicate that any legal problem with a bearing on private life falls within the Convention. This certainly goes beyond the broad and somewhat controversial interpretations already to be found in the Court's jurisprudence on this provision.[8] As Judge Gersing pointed out in his separate opinion, the Court's reading is particularly difficult to reconcile with the treatment of spouses' relations with their children in Article 5 of Protocol No. 7,[9] which might be thought to indicate that the Contracting States regard this matter as outside the scope of Article 8.

Just satisfaction (Article 50)—compensation for loss of opportunities—costs and expenses

Case No. 2. Sporrong and Lönnroth case (Application of Article 50).[10] The Court held by a majority of 12 votes to 5 that Sweden should pay 800,000 Swedish crowns (SEK) to the Sporrong Estate and 200,000 SEK to Mrs Lönnroth, as compensation for damage, and by a majority of 13 votes to 4 that Sweden should pay 723,865.75 SEK, less 24,103 French francs, to the applicants jointly, in respect of their costs and expenses.

In its judgment on the merits in 1982 the Court held that the right of property of the Sporrong Estate and of Mrs Lönnroth had been violated by long-term expropriation permits relating to their land, accompanied by prohibitions on construction, and their case could not have been taken before a tribunal competent to determine all aspects of the matter. Accordingly, there had been breaches of Article 1 of Protocol No. 1 and of Article 6 (1) of the Convention.[11] The question of just satisfaction under Article 50 was reserved for later consideration.

Article 50 of the Convention provides:

If the Court finds that a decision or a measure taken by a legal authority or any other authority of a High Contracting Party is completely or partially in conflict with the obligations arising from the present Convention, and if the internal law of the said Party allows only partial reparation to be made for the consequences of this decision or measure, the decision of the Court shall, if necessary, afford just satisfaction to the injured party.

In the present proceedings the applicants sought over 24 million SEK as compensation for alleged financial loss, an unspecified sum for non-pecuniary

[7] The *Marckx* case, Series A, No. 31, which concerned the law relating to illegitimacy in Belgium, is an interesting comparison. The dissenting judgment of Sir Gerald Fitzmaurice contains a particularly forceful statement of the case for recognizing a margin of appreciation. See Merrills, this *Year Book*, 53 (1982), pp. 139–43.

[8] For a comprehensive review of the Court's jurisprudence on Article 8 see Duffy, *Yearbook of European Law*, 2 (1982), p. 191.

[9] Protocol No. 7 was opened for signature in 1984. Article 5 provides:

'Spouses shall enjoy equality of rights and responsibilities of a private law character between them, and in their relations with their children, as to marriage, during marriage and in the event of its dissolution. This Article shall not prevent States from taking such measures as are necessary in the interests of the children.'

[10] ECHR, judgment of 18 December 1984, Series A, No. 88. French text authentic. The case was decided by the plenary Court.

[11] ECHR, judgment of 23 September 1982, Series A, No. 52, and see this *Year Book*, 53 (1982), p. 319.

damage and almost 1 million SEK in respect of costs and expenses. The scale and legitimacy of most of these claims was disputed by the Government.

The Court first determined the periods over which any loss to the applicants could be taken into account. The expropriation permits were in force for twenty-three years in respect of one property and eight years in respect of the other. However, the Court decided that it was reasonable for a municipality to require some time to undertake and complete the planning needed to prepare a final decision on a contemplated expropriation. In the present case four years should have been sufficient for the Stockholm City Council to make its decisions. The relevant 'periods of damage' were therefore nineteen and four years respectively.

The constituent elements of the damage were a more complex issue. At the end of the periods concerned, the applicants had not been prejudiced financially because the market value of the properties had not fallen and they had been let continuously with no loss of income. On the other hand, the applicants' utilization of their properties had been limited in respect of construction; loans secured by way of mortgage had proved difficult to obtain; the properties had fallen in value while the expropriation permits were in force and any scheme for redevelopment during that period was impracticable. There was therefore a loss of opportunities. A final factor was the prolonged uncertainty and the non-pecuniary damage occasioned by the breach of Article 6 (1).

The most problematical issue was the actual assessment of compensation, particularly what the Court termed 'the virtual impossibility of quantifying, even approximately, the loss of opportunities'.[12] The applicants' argument that compensation should be assessed on the assumption of a maximum hypothetical development of the properties was found by the Court to be unsupported by the facts. The Government's argument that since the properties had maintained their value, the loss of opportunities should be ignored altogether was also rejected. Making an overall assessment of the factors found to be relevant and without detailing its calculations, the Court awarded the applicants 'on an equitable basis' just satisfaction amounting to about 4 per cent of their initial claim.

Costs and expenses were also awarded on a reduced basis, though here the reductions were less drastic and related only to particular items. Although the amount claimed for costs and fees was high, the Court found that it could be explained by the length of the proceedings and the complexity of the case, which made the employment of experts reasonable. However, certain expenses were rejected because the Court decided that they had not been 'necessarily' incurred.

This was one of the most difficult cases the Court has had to decide under Article 50. The assessment of compensation in this type of situation is a problem that is bound to arise again and it is a pity that the Court was unable to be more explicit in its calculations. Four of the five judges who considered the decision on compensation over generous would also have reduced the sum awarded for costs and expenses. The discrepancy between the claim under Article 50 and the sum eventually awarded led them to conclude that as regards costs 'a significant part of those incurred in relation to the claim for material damages must be regarded as unnecessary and out of proportion'.[13] This seems a very harsh view. If the Court

[12] Judgment, para. 27.

[13] Joint dissenting opinion of Judges Thór Vilhjálmsson, Lagergren, Sir Vincent Evans and Gersing. The question of compensation was dealt with in a second joint dissenting opinion with Judge Walsh.

is prepared to say no more than that its assessment is made on equitable grounds, it is difficult to see the basis on which applicants are expected to moderate their claims.

Right to a fair hearing (Article 6 (1))—just satisfaction (Article 50)—striking off—the meaning of 'fact of a kind to provide a solution of the matter' in Rule 48 (2)

Cases Nos. 3 and 4. Colozza case;[14] *Rubinat* case.[15] In the first of these cases the Court held unanimously that Italy had contravened Article 6 (1) of the Convention by instituting criminal proceedings against the applicant without his knowledge. The applicant was awarded 6 million lire by way of just satisfaction. In the second case the Court held that having regard to the subsequent action of the Italian authorities and other circumstances, the case should be struck off its list.

These cases originated in applications lodged with the European Commission in May 1980 by Mr Colozza, an Italian, and in July 1978 by Mr Rubinat, a Spaniard. Both had been tried in Italy—Mr Colozza *in absentia* for fraud and Mr Rubinat by default for murder—and convicted without being informed of the proceedings against them. In their applications they relied on Article 6 (1) of the Convention and in its report of May 1983 the Commission expressed the unanimous opinion that there had been a violation in both cases. Mr Colozza subsequently died in prison, but his widow expressed the wish to see the proceedings continued. The Commission referred the cases to the Court.

The relevant portion of Article 6 (1) of the Convention provides:

> In the determination of . . . any criminal charge against him, everyone is entitled to a fair . . . hearing . . . by [a] . . . tribunal . . .

The question in the first case was whether the Italian authorities' recourse to the procedure for notifying individuals who are untraceable, and to the procedure for holding a trial by default, together had the effect of depriving Mr Colozza of his right to a fair hearing.

The right to take part in criminal proceedings is not expressly mentioned in Article 6 (1), but the Court had no hesitation in finding it implicit in both the object and purpose of the article and the various rights of defence set out in sub-paragraphs (c), (d) and (e) of Article 6 (3). Two points therefore called for decision: whether on the facts the applicant could be said to have waived his right to appear, and if not, whether the circumstances disclosed a violation by the authorities.

On the issue of waiver the Court decided that it was unnecessary to establish the precise scope of the doctrine since previous case law demonstrated that the waiver of the exercise of a right guaranteed by the Convention, if it is possible at all, must be established in an unequivocal manner, which was not the case here. The applicant had not absconded, but simply moved house. The authorities sought him at his old address and having failed to find him, treated him as a fugitive. The Rome police, however, had succeeded in tracing him for the purpose of other

[14] ECHR, judgment of 12 February 1985, Series A, No. 89. The Court consisted of the following Chamber of Judges: Wiarda (President); Cremona; Thór Vilhjálmsson; García de Enterría; Pettiti; Russo; Gersing (Judges).

[15] Ibid. This case was decided by the Chamber constituted to hear the *Colozza* case (Case No. 3, above).

criminal proceedings. He could therefore hardly be said to have disappeared, or to have waived his right to defend himself.

What then was the scope of the right? The Government argued that trial by default was an essential part of the criminal justice system and that without it a great many practical problems would arise. The Court agreed, but distinguished between the procedure and its consequences. In the key passage of its judgment the Court held that:

> When domestic law permits a trial to be held notwithstanding the absence of a person 'charged with a criminal offence' who is in Mr Colozza's position, that person should, once he becomes aware of the proceedings, be able to obtain, from a court which has heard him, a fresh determination of the merits of the charge.[16]

The Court further explained that it is for the Contracting States to decide exactly how this is to be done, but the relevant domestic law must be shown to be effective and an individual in the applicant's position must not have 'the burden of proving that he was not seeking to evade justice or that his absence was due to *force majeure*'.[17]

Judged by the above criteria, Italian law was, the Court found, defective. The applicant had lodged a 'late appeal' on becoming aware of the proceedings against him, but the case could be reopened only if it could be shown that the authorities had failed to comply with the proper domestic procedure. In addition, it was for the individual to prove that he was not seeking to evade justice. Thus the applicant's case was never heard in his presence by a 'tribunal' competent to determine all aspects of the matter. This was not something which could be regarded as the applicant's responsibility.[18] There had therefore been a breach of Article 6 (1).

There remained the question of just satisfaction under Article 50. As already noted, Mr Colozza had died and the claimant was his widow, who maintained that her husband's time in prison had caused both of them physical and mental suffering and financial loss. The Court was not prepared to speculate as to whether the outcome of the applicant's trial would have been different had he been present, but confined itself to the observation that it was 'not . . . unreasonable to regard Mr Colozza as having suffered a loss of real opportunities'.[19] Bearing in mind also the non-pecuniary damage suffered by the applicant and his widow, the Court calculated that on an equitable basis an indemnity of 6 million lire would constitute just satisfaction.

Mr Rubinat's case can be dealt with more briefly. The applicant had been tried and convicted while abroad, extradited to Italy, imprisoned following an unsuccessful attempt to challenge his conviction, then pardoned. He was currently abroad again and all efforts to contact him had failed. In these circumstances the Government requested that the case be struck off the list, relying on Rule 48 (2) of the Rules of the Court, which provides:

> When the Chamber is informed of a friendly settlement, arrangement or other fact of

[16] *Colozza* judgment, para. 29.

[17] Ibid., para. 30.

[18] The Government's argument that the applicant was himself responsible for the situation because he failed to notify the authorities of his change of address (thereby committing a regulatory offence) was rejected with the observation that 'the consequences which the Italian judicial authorities attributed to it are manifestly disproportionate, having regard to the prominent place which the right to a fair trial holds in a democratic society within the meaning of the Convention': ibid., para 32.

[19] Ibid., para. 38.

a kind to provide a solution of the matter, it may, after consulting, if necessary . . . the Delegates of the Commission and the applicant, strike the case out of the list.

In the present case there was no 'friendly settlement' or 'arrangement' because the pardon was granted to the applicant as a unilateral measure. The Court considered, however, that the pardon could be regarded as a 'fact of a kind to provide a solution of the matter', since Mr Rubinat had been released well before the expiry of his sentence and appeared to have no further interest in the proceedings. Although the case raised issues of principle which transcended the applicant's interests and could therefore be retained if desired, the Court saw no reason to adopt this course. Having just examined analogous legal issues in the *Colozza* case, the Court decided that it would be appropriate to strike the case from its list, subject only to its right to restore it in the event of fresh circumstances justifying such a course.

The treatment of trial *in absentia* in the first of these two cases breaks new ground,[20] but the Court's insistence on the fundamental importance of the rights of the accused in that situation is exactly what might have been expected. Mr Colozza's success does not, of course, mean that absentee defendants are entitled to a fresh hearing in all cases; rather that, here, as in other areas of the criminal process, it is not enough for the authorities merely to go through the motions; an *effective* regard for the individual's rights is required. Although it is not unknown for applicants to lose interest in proceedings at Strasbourg, few are as elusive as Mr Rubinat. *Vallon* (Case No. 11) and *Can* (Case No. 12) show a more familiar side of Rule 48 (2).

Freedom of expression (Article 10)—application to the prohibition of activities entailing publicity for members of a profession—the meaning of 'prescribed by law' and 'necessary in a democratic society' in Article 10 (2).

Case No. 5. Barthold case.[21] In this case, which concerned the Federal Republic of Germany, the Court held that an injunction issued against a veterinary surgeon by virtue of unfair competition legislation and rules of professional conduct was not consistent with freedom of expression and violated Article 10 of the Convention.

The applicant was a veterinary surgeon who ran a clinic in Hamburg. In August 1978 a local newspaper published an article describing how his clinic had provided treatment for a cat at night and outside the normal working hours of veterinary clinics. The article included Dr Barthold's name and photograph, described his position and quoted his view that there was a need for a regular night veterinary service in the city. Publication of the article prompted the Frankfurt am Main Central Agency for Combatting Unfair Competition, a private association, to bring an action against the applicant in the civil courts in Hamburg, alleging that the article contained advertising matter contrary to the rules of professional conduct of veterinary surgeons and to relevant legislation. In January 1980 the Hanseatic Court of Appeal upheld the association's claims and granted

[20] For a previous case involving appellate proceedings and Article 6 (3) (c) see the *Goddi* case, Series A, No. 76, and this *Year Book*, 55 (1984), p. 376.

[21] ECHR, judgment of 25 March 1985, Series A, No. 90. The Court consisted of the following Chamber of Judges: Wiarda (President); Thór Vilhjálmsson; Bindschedler-Robert; Pettiti; Russo; Bernhardt; Gersing (Judges).

an injunction against Dr Barthold, restraining him, on pain of fine or imprisonment, from repeating statements of the kind published in the article in the general press. A constitutional complaint against this judgment was unsuccessful.

Dr Barthold's application to the Commission invoked various articles of the Convention. In its report in July 1983 the Commission expressed the unanimous opinion that there had been a violation of Article 10 and subsequently referred the case to the Court.

Article 10 of the Convention provides:

> 1. Everyone has the right to freedom of expression. This right shall include freedom to hold opinions and to receive and impart information and ideas without interference by public authority and regardless of frontiers . . .
>
> 2. The exercise of these freedoms, since it carries with it duties and responsibilities, may be subject to such formalities, conditions, restrictions or penalties as are prescribed by law and are necessary in a democratic society . . . for the protection of health or morals, for the protection of the reputation or rights of others . . .

The main issue in the case was whether the judgment of the Hanseatic Court of Appeal, which clearly constituted an 'interference by public authority' with the applicant's freedom of expression, could be justified under Article 10 (2).[22]

The first question was whether the interference was 'prescribed by law'. In the *Sunday Times* case[23] and a number of subsequent decisions the Court has explained that to satisfy this requirement 'the interference must have some basis in domestic law, which itself must be adequately accessible and be formulated with sufficient precision to enable the individual to regulate his conduct, if need be with appropriate advice'.[24] Applying these criteria to the relevant provisions of German law, including the veterinary surgeons' Rules of Professional Conduct, which qualified as 'law' for the present purpose, the Court noted that the accessibility of these texts was not disputed, and that absolute precision cannot be expected in an area like competition law 'where the relevant factors are in constant evolution in line with developments in the market and in means of communication'.[25] Since there was no evidence that domestic law had been misapplied, something which was in any case primarily a matter for the German courts, the Court was satisfied that in all the circumstances the measures complained of were 'prescribed by law'.

The second question was whether the interference had an aim that was legitimate under Article 10 (2). Here the Court pointed out that the Hanseatic Court of Appeal issued the injunction to prevent the applicant from acquiring a commercial advantage over colleagues who were prepared to refrain from advertising in accordance with their professional code. The decision was thus grounded on the protection of the 'rights of others'. As such, the interference fell within Article 10 (2) and there was no need for the Court to consider whether, as the Government argued, it might also be justified as a protection of 'health' or 'morals'.

The third, and crucial, question was whether the interference was 'necessary in a democratic society' for the attainment of the above aim. The Government argued that the restraint imposed on Dr Barthold was a legitimate restriction on advertising and that since it was narrowly circumscribed and did not bar him

[22] The applicant's allegation of a breach of Article 11 (freedom of association), which was declared inadmissible by the Commission, was held to fall outside the ambit of the case referred to the Court.

[23] ECHR, judgment of 26 April 1979, Series A, No. 30. See this *Year Book*, 50 (1979), p. 257.

[24] Judgment, para. 45.

[25] Ibid., para. 47.

from expressing an opinion on the issue of a night veterinary service in Hamburg, it was consistent with the principle of proportionality.

The Court's evaluation of this argument took as the point of departure its previously expressed ruling that 'whilst the adjective "necessary", within the meaning of Article 10 para. 2 of the Convention is not synonymous with "indispensable", neither does it have the flexibility of such expressions as "admissible", "ordinary", "useful", "reasonable" or "desirable"; rather, it implies a "pressing social need". The Contracting States enjoy a power of appreciation in this respect, but that power of appreciation goes hand in hand with a European supervision which is more or less extensive depending upon the circumstances.'[26]

The circumstances of the present case were, the Court found, that the newspaper article was intended to inform the public about a genuine problem of current interest. The object of the injunction was not to prevent Dr Barthold from participating in the controversy, but to stop him obtaining publicity by recounting his personal professional experiences. Nevertheless, in view of the importance of freedom of expression in a democratic society, the interference went further than the aim justified. Any publicity which Dr Barthold might obtain was altogether secondary, having regard to the content of the article and the nature of the issue. The German Court failed to achieve a fair balance between the interests at stake when it decided that there was an intent to act for the purposes of commercial competition unless that intent was entirely overriden by other motives. For in the opinion of European Court:

> A criterion as strict as this in approaching the matter of advertising and publicity in the liberal professions is not consonant with freedom of expression. Its application risks discouraging members of the liberal professions from contributing to public debate on topics affecting the life of the community if ever there is the slightest likelihood of their utterances being treated as entailing, to some degree, an advertising effect. By the same token, application of a criterion such as this is liable to hamper the press in the performance of its task of purveyor of information and public watchdog.[27]

The measures complained of were therefore not proportionate to the legitimate aim pursued and accordingly were not 'necessary in a democratic society' for the protection of the rights of others. There had therefore been a violation of Article 10.

The Court arrived at its decision by a majority of 5 votes to 2[28] and reserved the question of just satisfaction under Article 50 for later consideration.

On a preliminary point concerning the applicability of Article 10 the Government argued that the subject-matter of the injunction complained of was not the applicant's opinion as to the veterinary service in Hamburg, but the unflattering comparisons he made between his own practice and the activities of his professional colleagues. According to the Government, these statements amounted to commercial advertising and as such were altogether outside the scope of Article 10. Before examining the question of compliance, the Court considered this

[26] Ibid., para. 55

[27] Ibid., para. 58.

[28] In a short dissenting opinion Judges Thór Vilhjálmsson and Bindschedler-Robert held that in view of the national authorities' margin of appreciation, there was no transgression of the principle of proportionality.

submission,[29] but ruled against the Government. Its grounds for doing so were that the various components of the prohibited statements overlapped to make a whole, the gist of which was the expression of 'opinions' and the imparting of 'information' on a topic of general interest. In the Court's view it was 'not possible to dissociate from this whole those elements which go more to manner of presentation than to substance and which, so the German courts held, have a publicity-like effect. This is especially so since the publication prompting the restriction was an article written by a journalist and not a commercial advertisement.'[30]

Accordingly, the Court was able to find that Article 10 was applicable on the facts, while leaving open the general issue of whether advertising falls within the scope of this part of the Convention.[31]

Right to respect for private life (Article 8)—obligation of the State to take positive measures including use of the criminal law—the margin of appreciation—just satisfaction (Article 50)

Case No. 6. X and Y v. *Netherlands*.[32] In this case the Court held unanimously that the victim of a sexual assault had not had the protection of the criminal law which, in the circumstances, was required to secure respect for her private life in accordance with Article 8 of the Convention. The applicant was awarded 3,000 Dutch guilders by way of just satisfaction under Article 50.

Miss Y was a mentally handicapped person, living in a special home in the Netherlands. In December 1977, when she was 16 years old, she was sexually assaulted by Mr B, the son-in-law of the institution's governor. The next day her father, Mr X, lodged a complaint with the local police. However, the authorities decided not to prosecute because the complaint had not been lodged by the victim herself. In the law of the Netherlands Miss Y was incapable of acting because of her mental handicap. The Arnhem Court of Appeal nevertheless dismissed Mr X's appeal against the decision not to prosecute, holding that the relevant article of the Criminal Code could only be invoked by the victim. Since Miss Y was incapable of acting and a complaint by the father was not a substitute, there was a gap in the law through which Mr B escaped prosecution.

In an application to the Commission on his own behalf and on behalf of his daughter Mr X claimed that Miss Y had been subjected to 'inhuman and degrading treatment' contrary to Article 3 of the Convention, that he and his daughter had both been victims of a breach of their right to 'respect for private life' guaranteed by Article 8 and that there had also been breaches of Article 13 (right to an effective remedy) and Article 14 (discriminatory treatment). In its report of July 1983 the Commission expressed the opinion that as regards Miss Y, there had been a breach of Article 8, but not of Article 3, and that it was unnecessary to examine the other complaints. The case was then referred to the Court.

[29] An argument that the Government was estopped from raising this issue because they had conceded it before the Commission was rejected. In accordance with earlier case law the Court held that, 'For the purposes of procedure before the Court, the applicability of one of the substantive clauses of the Convention constitutes, by its very nature, an issue going to the merits of the case, to be examined independently of the attitude of the respondent State': judgment, para. 41.

[30] Ibid., para. 42.

[31] In a concurring opinion, however, Judge Pettiti explained why he considered that 'commercial speech' is included within the sphere of freedom of expression.

[32] ECHR, judgment of 26 March 1985, Series A, No. 91. The Court consisted of the following Chamber of Judges: Ryssdal (President); Wiarda; Walsh; Sir Vincent Evans; Russo; Bernhardt; Gersing (Judges).

Article 8 of the Convention provides everyone with 'the right to respect for his private and family life, his home and his correspondence'. To perform this obligation, as the Court has previously indicated, the Contracting States must refrain from acts of arbitrary interference and, furthermore, take whatever positive steps are needed to ensure that the right is effectively respected.[33] In the present case the question was whether the requisite degree of protection to individuals in the position of Miss Y calls for use of the criminal law, or whether, as the Government maintained, the Convention leaves it to each State to decide upon the means to be used, so permitting reliance on the civil law.

The Court acknowledged that in principle issues of this type are a matter for the Contracting States:

> . . . the choice of the means calculated to secure compliance with Article 8 in the sphere of the relations of individuals between themselves is in principle a matter that falls within the Contracting States' margin of appreciation. In this connection, there are different ways of ensuring 'respect for private life', and the nature of the State's obligation will depend on the particular aspect of private life that is at issue. Recourse to the criminal law is not necessarily the only answer.[34]

In the particular circumstances, however, the various civil remedies which the Government claimed were available could not be regarded as adequate. 'This', said the Court, 'is a case where fundamental values and essential aspects of private life are at stake. Effective deterrence is indispensable in this area and it can be achieved only by criminal-law provisions; indeed, it is by such provisions that the matter is normally regulated.'[35] Since it was evident that, according to the decision of the Arnhem Court of Appeal, the present case was not covered by the criminal law,[36] Miss Y was the victim of a violation of Article 8.

The other claims on behalf of Miss Y were quickly dealt with. The Court held that it was unnecessary to examine the case under Article 14 in conjunction with Article 8 in view of its finding in relation to Article 8 taken alone. It was similarly unnecessary to examine the case under Articles 3 or 13. The complaints which Mr X had put to the Commission on his own behalf had not been pursued before the Court. Accordingly, these too were not examined.

The final issue was the matter of compensation under Article 50. Evidence indicated that seven years after the assault Miss Y was still suffering its effects. Dismissing the Government's submission that these consequences should be attributed to her assailant, rather than to the breach of the Convention, the Court held that the Netherlands authorities had 'a degree of responsibility'[37] for her situation and awarded a sum of 3,000 Dutch guilders as just satisfaction.

Cases involving Article 8 fall into two groups: those in which the applicability of the article is a contested issue and those in which everything turns on its application. The present case was of the second type. The decision neatly illustrates both the positive obligations entailed by the notion of respect for private life and the limits of the margin of appreciation. The Court's finding that the

[33] See the *Airey* case, Series A, No. 32, and this *Year Book*, 50 (1979), p. 264.

[34] Judgment, para. 24.

[35] Ibid., para. 27.

[36] In its examination of the law of the Netherlands the Court observed that 'It is in no way the task of the European Court of Human Rights to take the place of the competent national courts in the interpretation of domestic law': ibid., para. 29. An argument by the Government that proceedings might have been instituted on the basis of another provision of the Criminal Code was rejected as implausible.

[37] Ibid., para. 40.

Convention had been violated was almost inevitable given that the absence of a criminal sanction was a lacuna in the law rather than a matter of deliberate policy. Further consideration of the margin of appreciation in the context of Article 8 will be found in *Abdulaziz, Cabales and Balkandali* (Case No. 10).

Just satisfaction (Article 50)—friendly settlement

Case No. 7. Malone case (Application of Article 50).[38] In view of the settlement agreed between Mr Malone and the United Kingdom Government in respect of the former's claims to just satisfaction under Article 50 of the Convention, the Court unanimously decided to strike this case out of its list.

In its judgment on the merits in 1984 the plenary Court held that the applicant had been the victim of a breach of Article 8 of the Convention (right to respect for private life) by reason of the existence in England and Wales of laws and practices permitting the interception of postal and telephone communications and the 'metering' of telephones by or on behalf of the police in the course of criminal investigations.[39] The question of just satisfaction to the applicant was reserved and referred back to the Chamber originally constituted to hear the case.

In his original memorial the applicant claimed just satisfaction under four heads:

(*a*) legal costs, assessed at £9,011, which he had been ordered to pay to the Metropolitan Commissioner of Police in his unsuccessful action in the High Court,
(*b*) costs which he had paid to his own lawyers in connection with the same action, assessed at £5,443.20,
(*c*) legal costs incurred in the proceedings at Strasbourg, which at that stage were unquantified, and
(*d*) 'compensation of a moderate amount' for interception of his telephone conversations.

In February 1985 after several months of negotiations the Court was notified of a friendly settlement between Mr Malone and the Government. Under its terms the Government agreed to reimburse the domestic costs, i.e. claims (*a*) and (*b*), and to pay £3,774.10, less the sums received under the Commission's and Court's legal aid schemes, in respect of claim (*c*). Nothing was said about claim (*d*).

In cases of this kind the Court's function is defined by Rule 53 (4) of the Rules of the Court, which provides:

> If the Court is informed that an agreement has been reached between the injured party and the Party liable, it shall verify the equitable nature of such agreement and, where it finds the agreement to be equitable, strike the case out of the list by means of a judgment . . .

Having regard to the terms agreed between Mr Malone and the Government, and to the absence of any objection on the part of the Commission's Delegate, the Court had no difficulty in deciding that the settlement here was equitable and that the case should be removed from its list.

Cases in which the parties succeed in agreeing upon appropriate satisfaction are

[38] ECHR, judgment of 26 April 1985, Series A, No. 92. The Court consisted of the following Chamber of Judges: Wiarda (President); Bindschedler-Robert; Lagergren; Gölcüklü; Walsh; Sir Vincent Evans; Gersing (Judges).

[39] ECHR, judgment of 2 August 1984, Series A, No. 82, and see this *Year Book*, 55 (1984), p. 387.

relatively rare. Here, unlike *Sporrong and Lönnroth* (Case No. 2), compensation was obviously not the applicant's main concern, a point which was underlined when during the period under review Parliament passed the Interception of Communications Act 1985 with the object of implementing the Court's earlier ruling on the merits.[40]

Right to a fair hearing (Article 6 (1))—right to examine witnesses (Article 6 (3) (d))—application to court-appointed expert

Case No. 8. Bönisch case.[41] In this case, which concerned certain provisions in Austrian law relating to the use of expert evidence in criminal proceedings, the Court held unanimously that there had been a violation of the applicant's right to a fair hearing as guaranteed by Article 6 (1) of the Convention.

The applicant was a German who ran a meat smoking firm in Vienna. In 1976 and the two years following samples of the firm's products were analysed by the Federal Food Control Institute, which decided they were adulterated and dangerous to health and reported him to the authorities. In 1977 and 1979 criminal proceedings were brought against Mr Bönisch in the Vienna Regional Court, which in accordance with the relevant legislation appointed the Director of the Institute as its expert. In the 1977 proceedings the applicant was allowed to challenge the Director's evidence by calling a witness, though in the 1979 proceedings he was not. On the basis of the Director's expert opinion the Regional Court found the charges proved and sentenced Mr Bönisch to short terms of imprisonment, which were later commuted to substantial fines.

In 1979 Mr Bönisch applied to the Commission alleging that the handling of the evidence in his case had violated Articles 6 (1) and 6 (3) (d) of the Convention. In its report in March 1984 the Commission expressed the unanimous opinion that these allegations had been substantiated. The Commission and the Government then referred the case to the Court.

Article 6 (3) of the Convention provides:

> Everyone charged with a criminal offence has the following minimum rights:
>
> . . .
>
> (d) to examine or have examined witnesses against him and to obtain the attendance and examination of witnesses on his behalf under the same conditions as witnesses against him.

The rights set out here are one aspect of the right of defence which forms the subject-matter of Article 6 (3) and which has been examined by the Court on a number of occasions.[42] Read literally, however, paragraph (d) relates to witnesses, not experts, and in the Government's submission had no relevance to the position of the Director. On the other hand, the Court has consistently made the point that the various guarantees of Article 6 (3) are themselves constituent elements of a larger whole, namely the concept of a fair trial, contained in Article 6 (1).[43] In view

[40] An outline of the Act and an explanation of its significance are to be found in Leigh, *Police Powers in England and Wales* (2nd edn., 1985), ch. 12.

[41] ECHR, judgment of 6 May 1985, Series A, No. 92. The Court consisted of the following Chamber of Judges: Wiarda (President); Cremona; Bindschedler-Robert; Gölcüklü; Matscher; Walsh; Bernhardt (Judges).

[42] See, e.g., *Artico*, Series A, No. 37, and this *Year Book*, 51 (1980), p. 332, and, more recently, *Goddi*, Series A, No. 76, and ibid. 55 (1984), p. 376.

[43] For the most recent example, see *Colozza* (Case No. 3, above).

of this the Court decided that it should avoid resolving the issue of classification and review the proceedings in the Regional Court for conformity with the more general obligation.

To assess the role played by the Director of the Institute in the particular circumstances the Court examined his procedural position and the manner in which he performed his function. It noted that he drafted the reports which set the criminal proceedings against Mr Bönisch in motion and then, as expert, had the duty of explaining and supplementing these findings. Pointing out that 'it is easily understandable that doubts should arise, especially in the mind of an accused, as to the neutrality of an expert when it was his report that in fact prompted the bringing of a prosecution',[44] the Court concluded that in appearance the Director was more like a witness against the accused. From this it followed that in accordance with the principle of equality of arms, there must be equal treatment as between the hearing of the Director and the hearing of persons called by the defence.

On the facts the Court found that equal treatment had not been afforded. Because of his appointment as expert the Director's statements must have carried greater weight than those of the witness which Mr Bönisch was allowed to call in the 1977 proceedings. Yet, as already noted, his independence and impartiality were capable of appearing open to doubt. The Director's dominant role was shown by the fact that he could attend throughout, put questions to the accused and to witnesses with the leave of the Regional Court and comment on their evidence. In contrast, the applicant's expert witness could appear only when called upon to give evidence, was examined by the judge and the Director and was then relegated to the public gallery. Finally, there was little opportunity for the defence to obtain the appointment of a counter-expert. The Court therefore concluded that there had been a violation of the applicant's right to a fair trial, as guaranteed by Article 6 (1), and that it was unnecessary to give a separate ruling on Article 6 (3) (d).

In his memorial the applicant also complained of a violation of Article 6 (2), which concerns the presumption of innocence. The Court held that it had jurisdiction to entertain this complaint, despite the fact that it had not been raised before the Commission,[45] but in view of its conclusion with respect to Article 6 (1), decided that it was unnecessary to consider it further. The question of just satisfaction under Article 50 was reserved for later decision.

This was the Court's one hundredth decision, and it was fitting that it should involve Article 6, the most frequently invoked provision of the Convention, and in particular the right to a fair hearing in criminal proceedings, one of the cornerstones of any system of human rights protection.

Right to liberty (Article 5 (1))—application to conditions of detention of person of unsound mind—right to have the 'lawfulness' of detention decided (Article 5 (4))—right of access to the courts (Article 6 (1))

Case No. 9. Ashingdane case.[46] In this case, which concerned the United Kingdom, the Court held that the continued compulsory confinement of a mental

[44] Judgment, para. 32. [45] Ibid., para. 37.

[46] ECHR, judgment of 28 May 1985, Series A, No. 93. The Court consisted of the following Chamber of Judges: Wiarda (President); Thór Vilhjálmsson; Bindschedler-Robert; Lagergren; Pettiti; Walsh; Sir Vincent Evans (Judges).

patient in a special secure psychiatric hospital after he had been declared fit for transfer to an ordinary psychiatric hospital had not contravened Article 5 (1) of the Convention. It also held that there was no breach of either Article 5 (4) or Article 6 (1) when the patient was unable to take domestic proceedings to rectify the situation.

In 1970 the applicant, a British citizen, was convicted of dangerous driving and four offences of unlawful possession of firearms. Medical evidence indicated that he was suffering from paranoid schizophrenia and so the court made a hospital order under section 60 of the Mental Health Act 1959. After a short period in the local psychiatric hospital, Oakwood, he was transferred to Broadmoor, a special hospital for those requiring treatment under conditions of special security on account of their dangerous, violent or criminal propensities. In October 1978 the psychiatrist in charge of Mr Ashingdane's case reported that he might properly be treated in an open hospital and recommended his transfer back to Oakwood. However, the local branches of the nursing staff's trade union (COHSE) were operating a ban on the admission of offender patients subject to restriction orders, on account of a lack of resources. The hospital authorities therefore refused to transfer Mr Ashingdane until October 1980, when an agreement was finally reached with the nursing staff. On arrival at Oakwood he was first placed in a closed ward, then, some ten months later, moved to an open ward.

In his application to the Commission Mr Ashingdane invoked the right to liberty guaranteed by Article 5 (1) of the Convention and also claimed that his inability to have his case heard by the English courts constituted a violation of Article 5 (4) and Article 6 (1). In its report of May 1983 the Commission by various majorities expressed the opinion that there had been no breaches of the Convention and then referred the case to the Court.

Article 5 (1) of the Convention provides:

> Everyone has the right to liberty and security of person. No one shall be deprived of his liberty save in the following cases and in accordance with a procedure prescribed by law;
>
> . . .
>
> (e) the lawful detention . . . of persons of unsound mind . . .

Despite the applicant's personal view that at no time had his mental disorder been such as to warrant his confinement, there was no doubt that his detention throughout the relevant period was based on objective and reliable medical evidence of the sort that the Court has held is necessary in this type of case.[47] The crucial question was therefore not whether Mr Ashingdane had been properly classified as a mental patient, but whether his continued detention in Broadmoor when he was regarded as fit to be transferred to Oakwood meant that his right to liberty had been infringed.

The applicant's first argument was that the two institutions were so different that the choice between them was in effect a choice between detention and liberty. In its judgment in the *Guzzardi* case[48] the Court decided that the distinction between deprivation and mere restriction of liberty is one of degree or intensity and not one of nature or substance. In the present case the question was whether if Mr Ashingdane had been transferred, the regime at Oakwood would merely have restricted his liberty, or whether, as the Government maintained, at either

[47] See, e.g., *Luberti*, Series A, No. 75, and this *Year Book*, 55 (1984), p. 374.

[48] ECHR, judgment of 6 November 1980, Series A, No. 39. See this *Year Book*, 51 (1980), p. 335.

establishment he would have been deprived of his liberty within the meaning of Article (5) (1) (e). The Court decided that on the facts the Government's view of the situation was correct. Despite the differences between the two hospitals, when the applicant was eventually transferred, his move was from one regime of hospital confinement to another. Accordingly, the delay in carrying out the transfer did not result in Mr Ashingdane's continued detention at a time when he had been declared fit to return to liberty.

The applicant's second argument was that even if his detention at Oakwood might have been justifiable, his continued detention at Broadmoor was not, because in the circumstances it could not be regarded as 'lawful'. This raised an important issue of principle, namely whether the expression 'lawful detention of a person of unsound mind' in Article (5) (1) (e) concerns not only actual deprivation of liberty, but also matters relating to the execution of the detention, such as the place, environment and conditions of confinement. The question is not a simple one and the Court's answer was as follows:

> Certainly, the 'lawfulness' of any detention is required in respect of both the ordering and the execution of the measure depriving the individual of his liberty. Such 'lawfulness' presupposes conformity with domestic law in the first place and also, as confirmed by Article 18, conformity with the purposes of the restrictions permitted by Article 5 para. 1. More generally, it follows from the very aim of Article 5 para. 1 that no detention that is arbitrary can ever be regarded as 'lawful' . . . The Court would further accept that there must be some relationship between the ground of permitted deprivation of liberty relied on and the place and conditions of detention. In principle, the 'detention' of a person as a mental health patient will only be 'lawful' for the purposes of sub-paragraph (e) of paragraph 1 if effected in a hospital, clinic or other appropriate institution authorised for that purpose. However, subject to the foregoing, Article 5 para. 1 (e) is not in principle concerned with suitable treatment or conditions . . .[49]

On the particular facts the Court found that the applicant's detention had not been shown to be contrary to domestic law. Furthermore, although the regimes at Oakwood and Broadmoor were different, both were psychiatric hospitals where 'qualified staff displayed a constant preoccupation with the applicant's treatment and health'.[50] Oakwood was a more liberal institution and in view of the applicant's improvement, more appropriate to his needs. In the circumstances, however, the place and conditions of Mr Ashingdane's deprivation of liberty did not cease to be those capable of accompanying 'the lawful detention of a person of unsound mind'. Since the Court was also satisfied that the applicant's continued detention at Broadmoor was not arbitrary, or effected for an ulterior purpose, there had been no violation of Article 5 (1).

The applicant's other claims concerned his unsuccessful attempts to challenge his continued detention at Broadmoor in the English courts. In August 1979 he had instituted proceedings against the Department of Health and Social Security and the Kent Regional Health Authority, alleging that they were in breach of their statutory duty to provide appropriate hospital accommodation. In February 1980, however, the Court of Appeal held that these claims were barred by section 141 of the Mental Health Act 1959, which provided immunity from suit in respect of acts done in pursuance of the Act, unless there was bad faith or lack of reasonable care. In the applicant's submission, the lack of a domestic remedy for his grievance amounted to a breach of Articles 5 (4) and 6 (1).

[49] Judgment, para. 44. [50] Ibid., para. 47.

Article 5 (4) of the Convention provides:

> Everyone who is deprived of his liberty by arrest or detention shall be entitled to take proceedings by which the lawfulness of his detention shall be decided speedily by a court and his release ordered if the detention is not lawful.

In an earlier case involving the detention of a mental patient the Court held that this article does not guarantee a right to the judicial control of the legality of all aspects of detention. Rather, 'the domestic remedy available under paragraph 4 should enable review of the conditions, which, according to paragraph 1 (e), are essential for the "lawful detention" of a person on the ground of unsoundness of mind'.[51] The applicant, however, did not challenge the legal basis for his detention or seek his release. Instead, his claims concerned his accommodation and treatment, which, as already noted, the Court regarded as matters not covered by Article 5 (1) (e). Thus the Court concluded that the claims which the applicant was prevented from pursuing before the English courts did not fall within the scope of the judicial determination of 'lawfulness' which Article 5 (4) guarantees. Accordingly, there was no breach of this provision.

In its celebrated judgment in the *Golder* case the Court held that 'Article 6 para. 1 secures to everyone the right to have any claim relating to his civil rights and obligations brought before a court or tribunal'.[52] Although there was no breach of Article 5 (4) in Mr Ashingdane's case, could it be said that the immunity from suit which the authorities enjoyed under English law meant that his 'right to a court' had been denied? The right of access to the courts is not absolute, but may be subject to limitations. Moreover, in deciding its scope the Contracting States enjoy a certain margin of appreciation. On the other hand, as the Court recalled:

> . . . the limitations applied must not restrict or reduce the access left to the individual in such a way or to such an extent that the very essence of the right is impaired . . . Furthermore, a limitation will not be compatible with Article 6 para. 1 if it does not pursue a legitimate aim and if there is not a reasonable relationship of proportionality between the means employed and the aim sought to be achieved.[53]

Applying these principles to the facts, the Court found that the objective pursued by section 141 of the Mental Health Act was to protect those responsible for the care of mental patients from the risk of being unfairly harassed by litigation. This objective was clearly legitimate in relation to individual members of a hospital's staff, but the immunity of the DHSS and the local Health Authority called for closer scrutiny. The claims which the applicant wished to assert in the English courts were based on the duty to provide hospital accommodation. This, since it was couched in rather general terms, left a wide discretion to the authorities. Thus, the matter would not be amenable to full judicial control even without the immunity provided by section 141. In addition, the section did not preclude action entirely, since a claim alleging bad faith or negligence in respect of a refusal to transfer a patient would have been allowed to proceed. In the light of all these circumstances, the Court concluded that the restriction imposed in the present case did not impair the very essence of the applicant's 'right to a court', nor transgress the principle of proportionality.

[51] Ibid., para. 52, and see *X* v. *United Kingdom*, Series A, No. 46, and this *Year Book*, 52 (1981), p. 347.

[52] ECHR, judgment of 21 February 1975, Series A, No. 18, para. 36.

[53] Judgment, para. 57.

In view of its conclusion that the 'right to a court' had not been violated, the Court decided that it was unnecessary to consider whether the claims asserted before the English courts lay outside the ambit of Article 6 (1) because no 'civil right' of the applicant was involved. However, this issue was discussed by Judge Lagergren, who emphasized the autonomy of the concept, and by Judge Pettiti, who held that Article 6 (1) was applicable and had been violated. The latter also dissented on the issue of Article 5 (1), explaining that the authorities superintending Mr Ashingdane could have done more and that as the body with ultimate responsibility, the Government ought not to be allowed to 'shelter behind the mere threat of a strike or industrial dispute'.

Section 139 of the Mental Health Act 1983 has removed the protection from suit which the DHSS and local Health Authorities enjoyed under the 1959 Act, but the implications of this case for mental patients and others detained in inappropriate institutions are clearly of considerable significance. The meaning of 'civil rights and obligations', which the Court declined to address here, is examined in some detail in Case No. 13.

Right to respect for family life (Article 8)—application to immigration control—discrimination on grounds of sex, race and birth (Article 14)—degrading treatment (Article 3)—right to an effective remedy before a national authority (Article 13)—just satisfaction (Article 50)

Case No. 10. Abdulaziz, Cabales and Balkandali case.[54] The Court held unanimously that since wives could be accepted for settlement in the United Kingdom more easily than husbands, the applicants had been victims of discrimination on grounds of sex in violation of Article 14 taken in conjunction with Article 8 of the Convention. Since they had no effective remedy on this point there had also been a violation of Article 13. The UK was ordered to pay the applicants a specified sum in respect of their costs and expenses. Various other claims under Articles 3, 8 and 14 of the Convention were dismissed.

The applicants were women of foreign birth who were lawfully settled in the UK. Each had a foreign husband and sought permission from the authorities for him to remain in or enter the UK. Under the immigration rules then in force a foreign husband wishing to join or remain with his wife lawfully living in the UK would not be granted leave to enter or to stay if she was not a citizen of the UK and Colonies who was herself born, or one of whose parents was born, in the UK. Permission was consequently refused. No such restriction existed for a foreign wife wishing to join or remain with her husband lawfully living in the UK, whether or not he was a citizen of the UK and Colonies with a territorial birth link.

Before the Commission the applicants claimed that they had been victims of a practice of discrimination on the grounds of sex, race and, in the case of Mrs Balkandali, birth. They also alleged violations of Article 8, taken alone and in conjunction with Article 14, Article 3 and Article 13. In its report of May 1983 the Commission upheld several of these claims and then referred the case to the Court.

The foundation of the applicants' case was Article 8 of the Convention, which provides:

> 1. Everyone has the right to respect for his private and family life, his home and his correspondence.

[54] ECHR, judgment of 28 May 1985, Series A, No. 94. The case was decided by the plenary Court.

2. There shall be no interference by a public authority with the exercise of this right except such as is in accordance with the law and is necessary in a democratic society in the interests of national security, public safety or the economic well-being of the country, for the prevention of disorder or crime, for the protection of health or morals, or for the protection of the rights and freedoms of others.

This is the first case in which immigration control has been considered by the Court and the Government's principal submission was that neither Article 8 nor any other article of the Convention covers this matter, for which Protocol No. 4 is the only appropriate text.[55] Like the Commission, the Court had no hesitation in rejecting this argument. Repeating its view that the Convention and its Protocols must be read as a whole and that a matter dealt with mainly by one provision may in some respects be subject to other provisions, it concluded that while some aspects of the right to enter a country may be regulated by Protocol No. 4, measures of immigration control may also affect the right to respect for family life and so engage Article 8.

Two further points concerning the scope of Article 8 were also examined. The Government argued that the Convention is concerned only with respect for existing family life, whereas at the relevant time none of the couples concerned in the present case had established a family life with a legitimate expectation that it would be enjoyed in the UK. This argument the Court rejected on the ground that while this aspect of Article 8 presupposes the existence of a family, 'this does not mean that all intended family life falls entirely outside its ambit. Whatever else the word "family" may mean, it must at any rate include the relationship that arises from a lawful and genuine marriage, such as that contracted by Mr and Mrs Abdulaziz and Mr and Mrs Balkandali, even if a family life of the kind referred to by the Government has not yet been fully established.'[56] Mrs Cabales was slightly different because the validity of her marriage, which was contracted in the Philippines, had been questioned. However, since it was clear that she had gone through a ceremony of marriage and that she and her husband believed themselves to be married, wished to cohabit and subsequently did so, the Court held that in the circumstances 'the committed relationship thus established'[57] was enough to fall within Article 8.

The question of compliance with Article 8 turned on precisely what the right to respect for family life can be said to demand of the Contracting States in the present context. According to the applicants it entailed an acknowledgement of the right to establish a home with one's spouse in the State of one's nationality or lawful residence. The Court was not prepared to go so far. There are certainly positive obligations inherent in an effective respect for family life. However, as already noted in *Rasmussen* (Case No. 1) and *X and Y* v. *Netherlands* (Case No. 6), the Court has consistently emphasized the significance of the margin of appreciation in this area. This the Court regarded as a point of particular significance in the present case. Holding that 'the extent of a State's obligation to admit to its territory relatives of settled immigrants will vary according to the particular circumstances of the persons involved', it explained that 'the Court cannot ignore that the present case is concerned not only with family life but also with immigration and that, as a matter of well-established international law and subject to its

[55] Protocol No. 4 includes provisions dealing with a number of aspects of freedom of movement, but not the subject-matter of the present case. The UK is not yet a party.

[56] Judgment, para. 62.

[57] Ibid., para. 63.

treaty obligations, a State has the right to control the entry of non-nationals into its territory'.[58]

In the light of the above the Court held that 'the duty imposed by Article 8 cannot be considered as extending to a general obligation on the part of a Contracting State to respect the choice by married couples of the country of their matrimonial residence and to accept the non-national spouses for settlement in that country'.[59] On the particular facts the applicants, who at the time of their marriage could or should have known the effect of the immigration rules, had not shown that there were obstacles to establishing family life in their own or their husbands' home countries, or that there were special reasons why this could not be expected. There had therefore been no lack of respect for their family life and no breach of Article 8 taken alone.

The applicants' other main argument concerned Article 14. As noted earlier,[60] this article complements the other substantive provisions and has effect solely in relation to 'the enjoyment of the rights and freedoms' safeguarded by those provisions, which, according to Article 14, must be secured without discrimination. Although Article 8 had not been violated, the facts of the case fell within its ambit. As a result Article 14 was applicable and the Court had to decide whether, as the applicants alleged, their right to respect for family life had been secured in a way that was discriminatory and contrary to the Convention.

It was not disputed that under the relevant immigration rules it was easier for a man settled in the UK to obtain permission for his non-national spouse to enter for settlement than for a woman to do so. Unless this difference of treatment had an objective and reasonable justification, it would amount to discrimination on grounds of sex. The Government argued that the aim of the immigration rules was to protect the domestic labour market at a time of high unemployment. The Court accepted this and that such an aim was legitimate. It pointed out, however, that whether the Government could justify treating male and female immigrants differently was a quite separate question. Although the margin of appreciation was again relevant, its scope must vary with the circumstances, subject-matter and background. Specifically, 'it can be said that the advancement of the equality of the sexes is today a major goal in the member States of the Council of Europe. This means that very weighty reasons would have to be advanced before a difference of treatment on the ground of sex could be regarded as compatible with the Convention.'[61]

On the evidence before it the Court held that no such reasons had been shown. The statistics supplied by the Government failed to convince the Court that any difference there might be between the impact of men and women on the labour market was sufficiently important to justify treating them differently. Neither was it persuaded that the additional aim of advancing public tranquillity by regulating immigration was served by distinguishing between men and women. The Court thus concluded that the three applicants had been victims of discrimination on grounds of sex, contrary to Article 14, in conjunction with Article 8, in securing their right to respect for family life.

In the opinion of a minority of the Commission the applicants had also been victims of discrimination on grounds of race. The Court, however, endorsed the view of the majority and rejected this part of the claim. Noting that the

[58] Judgment, para. 67.
[59] Ibid., para. 68.
[60] See Case No. 1, above.
[61] Judgment, para. 79.

immigration rules made no distinction on grounds of race, but were applicable 'across the board' to all intending immigrants, the Court found their basis to be the need to reduce immigration in order to protect the domestic labour market, and not objections relating to prospective immigrants' origins. It was true that the main effect of the rules was to prevent immigration from the New Commonwealth and Pakistan, but this fact, which had impressed the minority in the Commission, according to the Court, was 'not a sufficient reason to consider them as racist in character: it is an effect which derives not from the content of the 1980 Rules but from the fact that, among those wishing to immigrate, some ethnic groups outnumbered others'.[62]

The final argument on Article 14 concerned discrimination on grounds of birth. Mrs Balkandali complained that as between women citizens of the UK and Colonies settled in the UK, only those born there, or having a parent so born, could have their non-national husbands accepted for settlement. The Commission took the view that this difference of treatment was indeed contrary to Article 14. The Court disagreed. Finding that the Government's concern was to avoid the hardship which women having close ties to the UK stemming from birth would encounter if, on marriage, they were obliged to move abroad in order to remain with their husbands, the Court found the difference in treatment here to have an objective and reasonable justification. Consequently, Mrs Balkandali had not been the victim of discrimination on grounds of birth.

A number of points under other provisions of the Convention should also be mentioned. A somewhat far-fetched claim under Article 3 was rejected on the ground that the discrimination complained of did not amount to 'degrading' treatment. On the other hand, since the Convention has not been incorporated into domestic law in the UK and the violation in this case related not to a misapplication of the immigration rules, but to the rules themselves, recourse to the available channels of complaint could not have been effective. Accordingly, there had been a violation of Article 13 which provides:

> Everyone whose rights and freedoms as set forth in this Convention are violated shall have an effective remedy before a national authority notwithstanding that the violation has been committed by persons acting in an official capacity.[63]

Finally, on the issue of just satisfaction under Article 50 the Court rejected a claim for 'substantial', but unquantified, compensation for non-pecuniary loss. Although it was prepared to accept that the applicants had suffered distress and anxiety, the Court held that its findings on the merits were enough to constitute just satisfaction. It noted in particular that the couples concerned could have lived in Portugal, the Philippines or Turkey, respectively; that they knew when they were married that they were not entitled to live together in the UK and that thanks to the subsequent action of the authorities, they had not in fact been prevented from doing so. In these circumstances the Court, perhaps not surprisingly, held that its award under Article 50 was limited to the costs and expenses claimed by the applicants in respect of the Strasbourg proceedings.

[62] Ibid., para. 85.

[63] Although the judgment on this point is consistent with the Court's recent decisions in *Silver and Others*, Series A, No. 61, and *Campbell and Fell*, Series A, No. 80, Judges Bernhardt, Pettiti and Gersing indicated that they preferred a narrower reading of Article 13.

In terms of both domestic reaction[64] and the law of the Convention this was the most important case involving the UK in the period under review. Although the decision was unanimous, two members of the Court indicated that their conclusion that there was no violation of the right to respect for family life derived not from the restricted scope of Article 8 (1), but from the qualifications to be found in Article 8 (2).[65] It should also be noted that the Court was careful to indicate that its decision relates only to immigrants who contract marriage after settling in the UK. Where therefore an immigrant already has a family when he settles here, different considerations may apply. The Court's handling of the various issues under Article 14 demonstrates once again the difficulty of deciding whether a difference of treatment, especially in a politically sensitive area, has an objective and reasonable justification. With respect to the question of discrimination on grounds of sex, the Government sought to argue that it should not be condemned merely because in respect of the admission of non-national wives and fiancées it had acted more generously than the Convention requires. The argument was rejected as irrelevant to Article 14, but is a reminder that in circumstances like those of the present case a decision that discrimination contrary to the Convention has occurred may turn out to be something of a Pyrrhic victory.[66]

Pre-trial detention in criminal proceedings (Article 5 (3))—trial within a reasonable time (Article 6 (1))—friendly settlement (Rule 48 (2))

Case No. 11. Vallon case.[67] In this case, which concerned Italy, the Court held unanimously that, having regard to the friendly settlement arrived at between the Government and the applicant, the case should be struck off its list.

Mr Vallon, who was wanted in France for murder and attempted murder, fled to Italy, where he was arrested in December 1976. The French authorities requested his extradition, but this was refused on the ground that the death penalty, to which Vallon would be liable in France, is a punishment prohibited by the Italian Constitution. Instead, the Italian authorities themselves prosecuted him on the same charges. Mr Vallon was held in custody from his arrest until March 1982, when he was sentenced to fourteen years' imprisonment. This sentence was upheld by the Genoa Court of Appeal in January 1983, when the judgment became final.

In his application to the Commission Mr Vallon complained of both the length of his detention on remand (Article 5 (3)) and the length of the proceedings against him (Article 6 (1)). In its report of May 1984 the Commission expressed the unanimous opinion that there had been a violation of both articles. In April 1985 the Court was informed that a friendly settlement had been reached between the Government and the applicant: the Government acknowledged its violation of

[64] *The Times* stated that the case demonstrated the 'defectively broad, declamatory and imprecise' law the Court was called upon to apply, while reaction to the decision in Parliament was predictably mixed.

[65] Judge Thór Vilhjálmsson and Judge Bernhardt made this point briefly in their separate opinions.

[66] Having changed the immigration rules before the case reached the Court, the Government's response to the decision was to make further changes with the object of removing the advantages enjoyed by foreign wives and fiancées. See *Statement of Changes in Immigration Rules*, Parliamentary Papers, 1985, HC, Paper 503.

[67] ECHR, judgment of 3 June 1985, Series A, No. 95. The Court consisted of the following Chamber of Judges: Wiarda (President); Evrigenis; Lagergren; Pettiti; Walsh; Sir Vincent Evans; Russo (Judges).

the Convention and undertook to pay the applicant 6 million lire, an offer which he accepted.

In view of the settlement the Government requested the Court to strike the case off its list in accordance with Rule 48 (2), which has been quoted earlier.[68] Taking formal note of the friendly settlement, the Court held that as far as the general interest was concerned there were no reasons of public policy to justify a continuation of the proceedings. In particular, the Court recalled that in several previous cases it had determined issues under Articles 5 (3) and 6 (1) analogous to those arising in the present case.[69] With the obligations of the Contracting States thus clarified by its earlier jurisprudence, the Court decided that it was appropriate to accede to the Government's request.

Right of defence in criminal cases (Article 6 (3) (c))—pre-trial detention (Article 5 (3))—friendly settlement (Rule 48 (2))

Case No. 12. Can case.[70] Having regard to the friendly settlement concluded between the Austrian Government and the applicant, the Court unanimously decided to strike this case out of the list.

The applicant was a Turkish citizen resident in Austria. In August 1980 he was arrested on suspicion of having been involved in arson at a restaurant of which he was manager. The applicant's brother and the owner of the restaurant were also arrested. Two days after the arrest an investigating judge ordered the applicant to be detained on remand. Over the next year Mr Can made several unsuccessful applications for release; finally, in November 1981 he was released subject to depositing 20,000 schillings as security. At the outset of his detention the applicant was permitted to consult with his lawyer only under the supervision of a court officer. This was because the Austrian Code of Criminal Procedure provided that until the indictment had been served such supervision was obligatory if a suspect's detention was grounded either wholly or in part on the danger of suppression of evidence. In January 1983 the applicant was convicted and sentenced to fourteen months' imprisonment. At the time of the present proceedings he had returned to Turkey.

In his application to the Commission in 1981 Mr Can complained that the duration of his detention on remand—almost fifteen months—violated Article 5 (3) of the Convention, and that the supervision of his consultations with his lawyer violated Article 6 (3), which reads:

> Everyone charged with a criminal offence has the following minimum rights:
> . . .
> (c) to defend himself in person or through legal assistance of his own choosing or, if he has not sufficient means to pay for legal assistance, to be given it free when the interests of justice so require.

In its report in July 1984 the Commission expressed the opinion that there had been a violation of both articles. In June 1985 the Court was informed that a

[68] See *Rubinat* (Case No. 4, above).

[69] See, e.g., *Ringeisen*, Series A, No. 13, this *Year Book*, 46 (1971–2), p. 470; *Eckle*, Series A, No. 51, ibid. 53 (1982), p. 317; and *Foti and Others*, Series A, No. 56, ibid. 54 (1983), p. 314. On the Court's earlier jurisprudence, see Harris, ibid. 44 (1970), p. 87.

[70] ECHR, judgment of 30 September 1985, Series A, No. 96. The Court consisted of the following Chamber of Judges: Wiarda (President); Gölcüklü; Matscher; Pinheiro Farinha; Pettiti; Walsh; Russo (Judges).

friendly settlement had been negotiated. Within the framework of the comprehensive reform of the Code of Criminal Procedure which was in preparation the Government would propose new rules on the supervision of consultations between a suspect in detention on remand and his lawyer and these would take into account the Commission's observations on this matter. The Government also undertook to pay the applicant 100,000 schillings by way of compensation, together with a reimbursement of his costs and expenses.

In the light of the settlement the Government requested the Court to strike the case off its list in accordance with Rule 48 (2). The Commission had no objection and the applicant clearly regarded the settlement as in his interests. Therefore the only question was whether considerations of public policy necessitated a continuation of the proceedings. The Court ruled that they did not. Explaining that in several previous cases it had decided issues analogous to those arising in the present case under Article 5 (3),[71] it noted that the same could not be said of the question concerning Article 6 (3) (c). However, there were, the Court found, 'certain indications' in its case law as to the relevance of this part of the Convention at the stage of preliminary investigations.[72] In view of this, and the Government's undertaking to put forward proposals for reform taking into account the unanimous report of the Commission on the point, the Court considered that in all the circumstances it was appropriate to strike the case from its list.

Two members of the Court expressed only qualified support for this approach. In their view when a settlement satisfies the individual interest in the case the Court needs merely to satisfy itself that the cause of the problem will be eliminated. Thus:

> . . . there is no room in a judgment striking a case out of the list for the inclusion of any observations on what the Court's opinion might have been if it had had to determine the merits of the case, or on the opinion it had expressed in similar cases, the existence of any established case-law of the Court on the issue in question being a matter that is totally irrelevant for a decision to strike out.[73]

This is not the first case in which the Court's handling of a friendly settlement has produced disagreement.[74] However, *Rubinat* (Case No. 4) and *Vallon* (Case No. 11) indicate that at least as regards treating earlier jurisprudence as relevant, the Court on this occasion was not breaking new ground, but following its consistent practice.

Meaning of 'contestation' *and of 'civil rights and obligations' in Article 6 (1)—right to a hearing by a 'tribunal' (Article 6 (1))—just satisfaction (Article 50)*

Case No. 13. Benthem case.[75] The Court held by 11 votes to 6 that there had been a violation of Article 6 (1) of the Convention when the authorities in the

[71] For references to the Court's previous jurisprudence on Article 5 (3), see *Vallon* (Case No. 11, above).

[72] The cases mentioned by the Court in this connection were: *Engel and Others*, Series A, No. 22, this *Year Book*, 48 (1976–7), p. 386; *Luedicke, Belkacem and Koç*, Series A, No. 29, ibid. 49 (1978), p. 315; and *Campbell and Fell*, Series A, No. 80, ibid. 55 (1984), p. 381. From these decisions and *Bönisch* (Case No. 8, above), it may be inferred that when the Court addresses this aspect of Article 6 (3), it may do so in terms of the general right to a fair trial guaranteed by Article 6 (1).

[73] Separate opinion of Judges Matscher and Pinheiro Farinha.

[74] In *Skoogström*, Series A, No. 83, the disagreement concerned the Court's decision rather than its reasoning. See this *Year Book*, 55 (1984), p. 391.

[75] ECHR, judgment of 23 October 1985, Series A, No. 97. The case was decided by the plenary Court.

Netherlands refused to grant the applicant a licence for an installation needed for his business without a hearing before an independent and impartial tribunal. The Court also decided unanimously that this finding constituted sufficient just satisfaction for the purposes of Article 50.

The applicant was a garage proprietor who wanted a licence to operate an installation for the delivery of liquid petroleum gas. In August 1976 the authorities in his municipality granted the licence, but the Regional Health Inspector, who had opposed the application on grounds of safety, lodged an appeal with the Crown. In accordance with the normal procedure the matter was referred to the Administrative Litigation Division of the Council of State which advised that the municipal authorities' decision should be quashed. In June 1979 a Royal Decree conforming to this advice was issued and Mr Benthem, who had been operating the installation, was eventually forced to close it down.

In his application to the Commission in December 1979 Mr Benthem maintained that he was the victim of a violation of Article 6 (1) of the Convention, the relevant portion of which provides:

> In the determination of his civil rights and obligations . . . everyone is entitled to a fair and public hearing within a reasonable time by an independent and impartial tribunal established by law . . .

The first question was whether Article 6 (1) was applicable to the type of proceedings here in issue. This depended on whether Mr Benthem's application for a licence gave rise to a dispute ('*contestation*') over his 'civil rights and obligations'. As regards the existence of a dispute the principles to emerge from the case law, said the Court, included the following:

(*a*) conformity with the spirit of the Convention requires that the word 'dispute' should not be construed technically, but be given a substantive rather than a formal meaning;
(*b*) the dispute may relate not only to the actual existence of a right, but also to its scope or the manner in which it may be exercised, and may concern both questions of fact and questions of law;
(*c*) the dispute must be genuine and of a serious nature;
(*d*) Article 6 requires that there be a direct link between the dispute and the right in question.[76]

In the light of the facts the Court concluded that a genuine and serious dispute had arisen between the applicant and the Netherlands authorities and that the result of the proceedings complained of was directly decisive for the right which he claimed.

Was what was at stake a 'civil' right within the meaning of the Convention? As the Court pointed out, this could not be decided solely by reference to domestic law. Moreover, Article 6 is not confined to private law disputes in the traditional sense. Accordingly, the character of the legislation and of the authority with jurisdiction are of little consequence. Only the character of the right at issue is relevant.[77] Applying these principles to the situation in the present case the Court

[76] Judgment, para. 32. Principles (*a*) and (*b*) were put forward in the case of *Le Compte, Van Leuven and De Meyere*, Series A, No. 43; principle (*c*) in the *Sporrong and Lönnroth* case, Series A, No. 52; and principle (*d*) in the *Ringeisen* case, Series A, No. 13.

[77] See the *König* case, Series A, No. 27, and this *Year Book*, 49 (1978), p. 317.

emphasized that the licence which the applicant sought was 'one of the conditions for the exercise of part of his activities as a businessman'.[78] It was closely associated with his right to use his possessions in accordance with the law. It also had a proprietary character, indicated by, among other things, the fact that it could be assigned. The Court was not persuaded by the Government's argument that Mr Benthem could have sought a licence for a different locality, since a change of that kind might have adversely affected the value of the business and his contractual relations. The Court's conclusion was therefore that Article 6 (1) was applicable to the proceedings in the appeal to the Crown.

The second question was whether the proceedings complained of were in conformity with Article 6 (1). For this purpose the Administrative Litigation Division of the Council of State and the Crown were the two institutions to be considered. The problem with the former was that although it reviewed all aspects of the case and acted very much like a court, it had no power to decide disputes, but simply tendered advice to the competent Ministry. True, as the Government pointed out, its advice was followed in the majority of cases, but this, the Court held, was not enough. Explaining that 'a power of decision is inherent in the very notion of "tribunal" within the meaning of the Convention',[79] the Court concluded that the proceeding before the Administrative Litigation Division did not provide the 'determination by a tribunal of the matters in dispute' which is required by Article 6 (1).

The Crown was empowered to determine the dispute and was therefore in a different position. However, the difficulty here was that the term 'tribunal' connotes independence and impartiality and is intended to provide a guarantee of judicial procedure. In the present case the Royal Decree by which the Crown had rendered its decision constituted an administrative act by a Minister responsible to Parliament. Moreover, the Minister was the hierarchical superior of both the Regional Health Inspector, who was appellant, and of the experts who had been consulted. Finally, the Royal Decree was not susceptible to review by a judicial body. In the circumstances, therefore, since neither the Crown nor the Administrative Litigation Division satisfied the Convention's requirements, there had been a violation of Article 6 (1).

The third and final question was the matter of just satisfaction under Article 50. The applicant alleged that his bankruptcy and divorce were directly attributable to the cancellation of his licence to operate the controversial installation and sought substantial sums as compensation. These claims were rejected. Pointing out that the applicant had not in fact closed down the installation until February 1984, the Court held that there was nothing to prove that the Royal Decree was the cause of his misfortunes. Since no claim had been made in respect of costs and expenses, the Court held that its finding of a breach of Article 6 (1) was sufficient to constitute just satisfaction.

This was the last case decided in the period under review and may turn out to be the most important. The bearing of Article 6 (1) on non-criminal proceedings has been the subject of examination on numerous occasions and, as the present decision indicates, the relevant principles are now well established. The application of those principles to different types of proceedings is another question,

[78] Judgment, para. 36.

[79] Ibid., para. 40. For a recent application of this principle in another context, see *de Jong, Baljet and van den Brink*, Series A, No. 77, and this *Year Book*, 55 (1984), p. 377.

however. In *Albert and Le Compte*[80] and earlier cases the Court came close to holding that Article 6 (1) protects the right to practise a profession. The present judgment appears to go further and to suggest that decisions with a bearing on any business or commercial activity may fall within the Convention. The six judges who dissented held that to extend Article 6 (1) to cover decisions concerning the interests of the community, which they described as 'a typical function of administrative law', was too radical a step.[81] Since a majority of the Commission also favoured a narrower reading of the Convention, it is likely that the relevance of Article 6 (1) to cases of this type will be a matter of controversy for some time to come.[82]

J. G. Merrills

[80] ECHR, judgment of 10 February 1983, Series A, No. 58. See this *Year Book*, 54 (1983), p. 319.

[81] See the joint dissenting opinion of Judges Bindschedler-Robert, Gölcüklü, Matscher, Pinheiro Farinha, Sir Vincent Evans and Dubbink.

[82] For discussion of the bearing of the Convention on administrative law, see Harris, this *Year Book*, 47 (1974–5), p. 157, and, more recently, Bradley, *Osgoode Hall Law Journal*, 21 (1983), p. 609.

UNITED KINGDOM MATERIALS ON INTERNATIONAL LAW 1985*

Edited by GEOFFREY MARSTON[1]

[*Editorial note*: Attention is drawn to the editorial note in UKMIL 1983, p. 361. The publication schedule of the present edition of UKMIL has permitted the citation of column references in the bound, definitive, volumes of the Parliamentary Debates]

INDEX[2]

[1] LLM, Ph.D. (Lond.): Lecturer in Law, University of Cambridge; Fellow of Sidney Sussex College. The assistance of Mr A. D. Watts, CMG, Deputy Legal Adviser, and Mr C. A. Whomersley and Ms J. S. Foakes, Assistant Legal Advisers, Foreign and Commonwealth Office, is gratefully acknowledged.

[2] Based on the *Model Plan for the Classification of Documents concerning State Practice in the field of Public International Law* adopted by the Committee of Ministers of the Council of Europe in Resolution (68) 17 of 28 June 1968.

Part Nine: Seas, Waterways, Ships

Abbreviations

HC Debs.	*Hansard*, House of Commons Debates (6th series)
HL Debs.	*Hansard*, House of Lords Debates
Cmnd.	Command Paper (5th series)
UKMIL	*United Kingdom Materials on International Law*
UKTS	*United Kingdom Treaty Series*

Part One: II. A. *International law in general—relationship between international law and municipal law—in general*

(See Part Ten: II. A. 2., below)

Part One: II. D. *International law in general—relationship between international law and municipal law—implementation of international law in municipal law*

(See also Part Three: II. A. 1. (c) (item of 25 February 1985) and Part Three: II. B. 3., below)

The Foreign and Commonwealth Office presented a memorandum, dated 8 November 1984, on the subject of the external competence of the European Community to the House of Lords Select Committee on the European Communities which was examining that topic. The memorandum contained the following passages:

A. *Parliamentary Procedure and Practice on Treaties of the United Kingdom*

2.1 The power to make treaties which are binding on the United Kingdom and the power to carry out the international procedures relating to it, such as signature, ratification and accession, fall within the prerogatives of the Crown, exercised on the advice of Her Majesty's Ministers.

2.2 However, where the implementation of the treaty requires legislation by Parliament, the practice is that ratification takes place only when the approval of Parliament, normally given by enacting the necessary legislation, has taken place. Such legislation may be necessary for example for accession of territory, for authorising use of public funds requiring the statutory authorisation of Parliament, or for changes in the law by enactment of original or amending Acts of Parliament, so that the law of the United Kingdom gives effect to the treaty.

2.3 In addition, since 1929, the practice known as 'the Ponsonby Rule' has been applied. Under this practice, every treaty which is subject to ratification is laid before Parliament for a period of twenty one sitting days before it is ratified. The practice is also applied to procedures where signature is followed by acceptance or approval and to accession. This gives the Houses of Parliament an opportunity to debate such an agreement, if they so desire.

Exceptions have sometimes to be made where considerations of urgency demand earlier ratification and where there is insufficient Parliamentary time; and there have been a number of cases where the practice has been wholly or in part waived. Where the treaty in question has in fact come before Parliament, because legislation or a resolution approving a draft Order is required or otherwise, the practice under the Ponsonby rule ceases to be relevant.

(*Parliamentary Papers*, 1984–5, HL, Paper 236, Evidence, pp. 1–2)

D. *Implementation in United Kingdom Law of Obligations resulting from International Treaties of the Community. The position under the EEC Treaty*

5.1 Under Article 228(2) agreements concluded under the conditions envisaged in that Article are binding on the institutions and on Member States. Their binding force on the United Kingdom would not of itself without the aid of statute incorporate them into the corpus of United Kingdom law.

The 'Community Treaties' as defined in United Kingdom law

5.2 The European Communities Act 1972, however, provides in Section 1 (2) that certain treaties are 'Community Treaties'. The Act deals with all three communities together.

5.3 The treaties which are 'Community Treaties' for the purpose of the Act are not only the three main Treaties establishing the Communities and a number of other pre-1972 treaties indicated in Schedule 1 to the Act but also any treaty entered into by any of the Communities, with or without the Member States, or entered into, as a treaty ancillary to any Community treaty, by the United Kingdom subject to Section 1(3) (see paragraph 5.5 below).

5.4 If the Community concludes a treaty at any time without the United Kingdom being a party, it automatically becomes a Community treaty.

5.5 But, because of the second sentence of Section 1(3), if, after 22 January 1972, the United Kingdom is a party to a treaty ancillary to the existing Community Treaties or is a party together with the Community to a treaty, then the treaty in question can only become a 'Community treaty' if it is specified by an Order in Council approved in draft by both Houses of Parliament.

5.6 As an illustration, the following are examples of 'Community treaties' *without* any need for a Section 1(3) Order.

(i) The original three Community Treaties establishing the EEC, ECSC and EURATOM.

(ii) The agreements listed in Schedule 1 to the Act, for example the Merger Treaty of 1965 establishing a single Council and a single Commission.

(iii) An agreement between the Community and other States (without the Member States as parties) of any date, such as a trade agreement concluded under Article 114, for example the Agreements with the States of the European Free Trade Association of 1972 and agreements concluded under Article 228 which permit third countries to be associated with the Community in joint research and development programmes.

5.7 The following are examples of treaties which become 'Community Treaties' when specified by a Section 1(3) Order.

(i) An internal agreement (that is not involving outside States) between the United Kingdom and the other Member States since 1972 supplementing in some way the existing Community arrangements.

(ii) An external Agreement since 1972 to which the Community and the United Kingdom is a party.

The European Communities (Definition of Treaties) (Second ACP/EEC Convention of Lomé) Order 1980 S.I.1077/80 gives examples of each of these. In the Schedule to that Order the main Convention is external and falls within (ii) above while the Internal Agreement is limited to the Member States and falls within (i).

The consequences of status as a 'Community Treaty' under the Act

5.8 If an agreement is a 'Community Treaty' (where necessary as a result of a section 1(3) Order), it falls within the scope of Section 2(1). In brief summary, this Section provides that all such rights and obligations under the Community Treaties in accordance with the Community Treaties are without further enactment to be given legal effect in the United Kingdom, shall be recognised and available in law and be enforced, allowed and followed accordingly. Governmental authorities are entitled under United Kingdom law to take the actions envisaged for them in the treaty in question.

5.9 A number of provisions of the Treaty establishing the EEC have been held by the European Court of Justice to have direct effect under the Treaty as part of the national law of Member States, so as not only to bind governmental authorities but also to operate for the benefit of individuals. Some provisions of external agreements, even in fields where Community competence is established and the Community has been active, have been held not to have direct effect for example in Cases 21 to 24/72, *the International Fruit Co.*, GATT. But the provisions of a few agreements, even with outside states, have been held by the European Court under Community law to have direct effect as part of the law of the Member States for example in Case 87/75 *Bresciani*, the Yaoundé Convention which preceded the Lomé Convention, and Case 104/81, *Kupferberg*, the Agreement of 1972 between the EEC and Portugal.

5.10 Status as a Community Treaty is not only relevant to possible direct effect under United Kingdom law but has other consequences for the application of subsequent sections of the Act. A Community Treaty gives rise to Community obligations and rights for the purpose of the Act; Section 2(2) allows these to be implemented by Orders in Council or regulations. Section 2(3) gives statutory authority for recourse to public funds to meet Community obligations to the Communities and to other Member States.

The part played by Section 1(3) Orders

5.11 Section 1(3) Orders ensure that Community treaties for the purposes of the Act include post 1972 treaties where the United Kingdom is a party to a treaty ancillary to existing Community treaties or is a party together with the Community, when such a treaty is specified by the Order.

5.12 Community treaties are thus brought into the system of Community law for the United Kingdom as established by the Act. The Orders authorise the necessary actions by Governmental authorities, including subordinate legislation under Section 2(2) and financial payments under Section 2(3). In addition, if the provisions of the Community treaty have under Community law direct effect to and for the benefit of individuals, effect is given to these provisions in United Kingdom law.

The part played by Section 2(2) Orders and Regulations

5.13 Section 2(2) Orders and Regulations are most familiar as a means of implementing directives of the Community, which under Article 189 are binding on the Member States but which normally have no direct effect in United Kingdom law. They require further legislative action. Similarly, though Council Regulations are directly applicable, they may require implementing action on matters not regulated by them. In each of these cases there is a clear Community obligation to take legislative steps.

5.14 In relation to Community Treaties, there may also be need for implementing action. In some cases this is done by EEC Council Regulations, which, being directly applicable, may leave no requirement for national action for implementation. But in many cases, there will be a need for national legislation.

5.15 Where national legislation is to give effect to obligations under a Community treaty either falling within the definition in Section one, or, where necessary, specified by a Section 1(3) Order, Section 2(2) is available as a basis for making implementing Orders in Council or regulations.

(*Parliamentary Papers*, 1984–5, HL, Paper 236, Evidence, pp. 3–5)

The Cabinet Office presented a memorandum to the same Committee in which the following passages appeared:

THE LEGAL DOCTRINES OR PROCEDURES FOR MAKING TREATY OBLIGATIONS EFFECTIVE IN THE LAW OF THE UNITED KINGDOM

16. Community proposals for international agreements come before Parliament through the scrutiny procedures. Because of the confidential nature of the

negotiating mandates, these are not normally deposited in the Houses of Parliament. But where negotiations are complete and the results are embodied in draft decisions or other instruments to be adopted by the Council, the documents containing these draft decisions or instruments are deposited together with appropriate explanatory memoranda. Once a document has been deposited, it is subject to the general arrangements for scrutiny.

17. Once the Council has adopted a decision to conclude an international agreement, the procedure to be adopted to give effect to the agreement in United Kingdom law depends on two things: first, whether the Council has adopted under the EEC Treaty measures to implement the agreement within the Community and secondly, whether the United Kingdom is a party to the agreement along with the Community. When the Council adopts measures under the EEC Treaty to give effect to the agreement within the Community, for example, by adopting a Regulation, section 2 of the European Communities Act 1972 will apply to such a measure in the same way as it applies to other Acts adopted under the Treaty. The European Court has held, however, that provisions of international agreements concluded by the Community can have direct application (*Bresciani*—Case 87/75 [1976] ECR 129). If the Community alone is party to the agreement, no legislative steps in the United Kingdom are necessary, as the agreement will fall within the definition of 'Community Treaties' in section 1(2) of the 1972 Act, thereby attracting the provisions of section 2. If, however, the United Kingdom is also a party to the agreement an Order in Council specifying the Treaty as one of the Community Treaties under section 1(3) of the 1972 Act will be required before any directly applicable provisions of the agreement can have effect by virtue of section 2(1) of the Act. A specification under section 1(3) would also permit any necessary consequential United Kingdom regulations to be made under section 2(2).

18. Draft Orders in Council to specify agreements as Community Treaties are introduced by the Departmental Minister responsible for the subject matter of the agreement, and, under section 1(3) of the 1972 Act, have to be approved by resolution of each House of Parliament. Normally only one agreement is specified in any one Order. It is also the practice of Her Majesty's Government to ensure that, before draft Orders are laid, the agreement concerned has been published either as a Command Paper or in the Official Journal of the European Communities. Whenever possible, the Command Paper number is quoted in the Schedule to the draft Order, in preference to a reference to the Official Journal. Departments will also arrange publication of a notice in the London, Belfast and Edinburgh Gazettes, giving the date of entry into force of the agreement, if this cannot be specified in the Order itself.

(*Parliamentary Papers*, 1984–5, HL, Paper 236, Evidence, pp. 163–4)

In moving the Second Reading in the House of Commons of the Education (Corporal Punishment) Bill, the Secretary of State for Education and Science, Sir Keith Joseph, stated:

The objective of the Bill is to secure compliance with the judgment of the European Court of Human Rights in February 1982. Under article 2 of the first protocol to the European Convention on Human Rights, states are obliged to respect the philosophical convictions of their citizens. The court's judgment means that a parental conviction against corporal punishment in schools comes within the terms of that article.

The United Kingdom Government ratified the convention in March 1951 and undertook to abide by the decision of the court in any case to which they were a party. There is no provision for appeal, and the court's judgment in February 1982 is therefore binding.

The question for the Government, therefore, was to decide on the means of compliance. One way of complying would be to legislate to abolish corporal punishment in state schools. That is not required by the judgment, which was concerned with respect for a philosophical conviction, and the Government reject that option. The Government are opposed in principle to forcing abolition.

(HC Debs., vol. 72, col. 38: 28 January 1985)

Later in the debate, the Parliamentary Under-Secretary of State for Education and Science, Mr R. Dunn, observed:

The Bill is before the House because of a judgment of the European Court of Human Rights in the case of Campbell and Cosans. We cannot accept some judgments and discard others, picking and choosing between those that we like and those that we do not like. The case was vigorously defended by the United Kingdom, but the judgment went against us. We have an obligation to abide by the judgment of the court, and that obligation will be fulfilled by the scheme that the Bill introduces. Failure to act would place us in breach of a treaty obligation and expose us to the possibility of a succession of cases under the European Convention on Human Rights and the further possibility of compensation awards.

(Ibid., col. 108; see also HL Debs., vol. 463, col. 479: 3 May 1985)

In moving the Second Reading in the House of Lords of the Child Abduction and Custody Bill, the Lord Chancellor, Lord Hailsham, stated:

The object of the Bill is to enable the United Kingdom to ratify the Hague Convention on the civil aspects of child abduction and the European Convention on the recognition and enforcement of custody decisions.

. . .

Obviously the main provisions of the Bill cannot immediately confer benefits on a parent in this country seeking to recover a child taken from this country abroad. But enactment of this Bill is essential to permit ratification of the two conventions by the United Kingdom, and by virtue of those conventions parents here will enjoy reciprocal arrangements in contracting states by being able to invoke the jurisdictions of local courts elsewhere to enforce orders of British courts.

I will now, if I may, turn to the contents of the Bill and the two conventions which are reproduced in part in Schedules 1 and 2. Part I and Schedule 1 deal with proceedings under the Hague Convention on the Civil Aspects of International Child Abduction of 1980. Credit for the first move in this goes to Canada, which first put forward proposals for a convention in January 1976, and these were included in the programme for the 14th Session of the Hague Conference on Private International Law. A draft convention was prepared and circulated to Governments in 1979, and the convention was opened for signature in October 1980. It was signed by us on 19th November last, and has been ratified by France,

Portugal, Switzerland and Canada. It will probably, I am told, be ratified by Australia, West Germany, the Netherlands and the United States of America—and, if this Bill goes through, the United Kingdom—within the next year or so.

. . .

Part II relates to the European Convention which is about the reciprocal recognition and enforcement of child custody decisions. It has a number of points in common with Part I, so I shall be able to deal with it rather shortly.

The European Convention has its origins in a recommendation accepted by the Seventh Conference of European Ministers of Justice held at Basle in May 1972. Following this recommendation, a committee of experts drew up the convention, which was finally agreed in February 1979 and opened for signature on 20th May 1980. The European Convention requires decisions on custody made in one contracting state to be recognised and enforced in any other contracting state. Up to the present time the European Convention has been ratified by France, Luxembourg, Portugal, Spain and Switzerland, and I am told is likely to be ratified by another 10 members of the Council of Europe.

The first three clauses (Clauses 12, 13 and 14 of the Bill) do much the same for the European Convention as Clauses 1, 2 and 3 do for the Hague Convention. They deal respectively with giving effect to the relevant parts of the European Convention in United Kingdom law, designating contracting states by Order in Council and creating a central authority in each part of the United Kingdom. Of course, the central authorities will be the same as those for the Hague Convention. They will have similar functions of co-operation and assistance, and will operate in much the same way through solicitors instructed upon the grant of legal aid.

(HL Debs., vol. 460, cols. 1248–52, *passim*: 5 March 1985)

In its document *Invitation to promoters for the development, financing, construction and operation of a Channel Fixed Link between France and the United Kingdom*, dated April 1985, the Department of Transport wrote:

25 *International railway conventions*

25.1 The promoters should be aware that the Government would expect to designate any Link involving a railway line for the purposes of the Convention concerning International Carriage by Rail (COTIF) (Berne, 1980). This Convention is implemented in the law of the United Kingdom through the International Transport Conventions Act 1983. In France, it has been implemented by a Decree of 3 September 1982.

(Text provided by the Foreign and Commonwealth Office)

[*Editorial note*: The following item in explanation of the above may be read as part of UKMIL 1982:

In moving the second reading in the House of Lords of the International Transport Conventions Bill, the Government spokesman, the Earl of Avon, stated:

I should like to begin by explaining briefly the background to this Bill. The first international convention dealing with rail transport dates from 1890 when the organisation which continues to administer the current conventions—known from their administrative headquarters as the 'Berne Union' Conventions—was set up. The 1890 convention covered the international carriage of goods by rail within Central Europe and was followed in 1924 by a further convention covering the carriage of passengers and their luggage. The United Kingdom acceded to the conventions in 1952 and is currently one of 33 member states now covering Western and Eastern Europe (except for the USSR), North Africa and the Middle East.

The conventions currently in force are the International Convention concerning the Carriage of Goods by Rail; the International Convention concerning the Carriage of Passengers and Luggage by Rail; and the Additional Convention relating to the liability of the Railway for Death of, and Personal Injury to, Passengers. These conventions have been the subject of regular revisions at approximately ten-year intervals.

The rules contained in these three conventions and their four annexes specify the rights and duties of the railway, of passengers and of consignors and consignees of goods. They cover, for instance, the contract of carriage and the liability of the railway for delay and for death and injury in the case of passengers; and they deal with compensation for loss or damage in the case of goods. The conventions also deal with the relationship with national law and the administration of the international provisions. They will cease to be valid when the new convention concerning international carriage by rail comes into force. This is the *Convention Relative aux Transports Internationaux Ferroviaires*, otherwise known as COTIF.

The new COTIF Convention, which the United Kingdom signed at a joint Revision and Diplomatic Conference in 1980, revises and consolidates these rules by bringing together the three existing conventions and their annexes, together with new institutional provisions, into a single basic convention. It also involves the establishment of a permanent treaty between member states to provide continuity of relations, with a new revision procedure. The convention also sets up a new inter-governmental organisation with legal personality—*Organisation Inter Gouvernementale pour les Transports Internationaux Ferroviaires*—otherwise known as OTIF to administer the convention. All present member states will be party to this organisation and the administration will continue to be carried out by the existing Central Office for International Rail Transport in Berne; there is no question either of increased bureaucracy or of any financial contribution beyond that which all members are already paying towards the administration of the organisation in Berne.

As noble Lords can see, therefore, the COTIF Convention itself contains no new principles; it is basically a consolidation and updating measure for a long-standing set of conventions on the contractual duties and rights of the railways in respect of international journeys. It does not touch upon any critical financial issues affecting the railways, either nationally or internationally; nor does it institute any new administrative system.

The main purpose of this Bill is simply to give the force of law in the United Kingdom to the convention and thus allow us to ratify it. Its provisions cover the United Kingdom as a whole and will bind both British Rail and also the Northern Ireland Railway. The Bill also makes provisions for the necessary consequential action for dealing with revisions to the convention; and it sets out the relationship with national law on key points such as damages in the event of a fatal accident.

Additionally the Bill makes minor changes to four other existing United Kingdom Acts of Parliament—the Carriage by Air Act 1961, the Carriage of Goods by Road Act 1965, the Carriage of Passengers by Road Act 1974 and the

International Carriage of Perishable Foodstuffs Act 1976. These Acts, like the present Bill, give force of law in the United Kingdom to a series of international conventions and provide for a procedure of amendment by Order in Council to take account of revisions to the conventions agreed to by the United Kingdom.

(HL Debs., vol. 436, cols. 978–9: 25 November 1982)]

In moving the second reading in the House of Lords of the Interception of Communications Bill, the Lord President of the Council, Viscount Whitelaw, stated in part:

. . . the Bill, in the Government's view, fully meets the United Kingdom's obligations under the European Convention on Human Rights. It clearly establishes in law the circumstances in which interception can be undertaken and thereby meets the judgment of the European Court last year. Noble Lords will wish to bear in mind that in that judgment the court did not criticise the purpose for which interception was authorised or the manner in which it was undertaken, but simply the absence of a clear statutory framework. The criteria in the Bill on which interception may be authorised are all set out in the convention. The Bill itself narrows the application of certain of these criteria. A number of other grounds set out in the convention, such as public safety, have not been included because in the Government's view they cover areas where interception would be entirely inappropriate.

(Ibid., vol. 463, col. 1256: 16 May 1985)

In opening the debate in committee on the Education (Corporal Punishment) Bill, the Government spokesman in the House of Lords, Baroness Cox, stated:

I begin by emphasising the point that the reason for the Bill is to secure compliance with the ruling of the European Court of Human Rights which obliges us to change our law in order to respect the rights of parents—parents who have a philosophical conviction against corporal punishment.

(Ibid., vol. 464, col. 625: 4 June 1985)

In reply to the question whether Her Majesty's Government 'will introduce legislation to restrict the powers of the European Court of Human Rights as regards United Kingdom law such that it has no status with regard to political as distinct from purely legal issues', the Prime Minister wrote:

The United Kingdom has signed and ratified the European Convention for the Protection of Human Rights and Fundamental Freedoms. It would not be practicable or possible to distinguish between judgments of the European Court which the United Kingdom has, under the convention, an obligation to abide by. Amendments to the convention, including any affecting the role of the European Court, need to be agreed by the contracting parties and could not be imposed by domestic legislation.

(HC Debs., vol. 80, Written Answers, col. *435*: 12 June 1985)

In the course of a debate on the subject of the decision of the European Court of Human Rights in the cases of *Abdulaziz, Cabales and Balkandali*, the Parliamentary Under-Secretary of State, Home Office, Lord Glenarthur, stated:

The judgment is binding and we shall of course abide by it.

(HL Debs., vol. 464, col. 1545: 14 June 1985; see also Written Answer of 10 July 1985, below)

Later in the debate, the same Minister observed:

Before I turn to the options, perhaps I may take up the particular question asked . . . concerning incorporation of the European Court of Human Rights into domestic law. The possibility of incorporating the ECHR as part of the domestic law of this country has been canvassed for a number of years, as the noble Lord will be aware. The issues are complex, raising matters of basic constitutional importance, and they cannot quickly be resolved. I have to tell the noble Lord that the Government have no plans at present for legislation in this direction.

(Ibid., col. 1548)

In reply to a question on the same subject, the Secretary of State for the Home Department wrote:

In order to comply with the judgment it will be necessary to change the immigration rules so that the provisions for the admission of husbands and wives for settlement are brought into line with each other. The Government therefore propose to allow husbands to join women who, though not British citizens, have permanent residence here, and to apply to wives seeking admission for settlement (other than wives to whom the provisions of section 1(5) of the Immigration Act 1971 apply) the requirements, including the requirement to satisfy the entry clearance officer that the marriage was not entered into primarily for immigration purposes, which at present apply only to husbands. The opportunity will be taken to clarify and strengthen the provisions of the existing rules relating to maintenance and accommodation and the entry clearance officer will need to be satisfied that adequate accommodation will be available for the partners to a marriage, and for any children, and that they will be able to maintain themselves without recourse to public funds.

Similar changes, including the introduction of an entry certificate requirement for fiancées, will be made to bring the provisions for the admission of fiancés and fiancées into line with each other.

I am satisfied that these changes, taken together, will enable us to comply with the judgment in a way that preserves the firm and fair immigration control to which the Government remain fully committed.

(HC Debs., vol. 82, Written Answers, cols. *427–8*: 10 July 1985; see also HL Debs., vol. 466, cols. 308–9: 10 July 1985 and HC Debs., vol. 83, cols. 893–900, *passim*: 23 July 1985)

In the course of a later debate on the same subject, the Minister of State, Home Office, Mr David Waddington, stated:

Several hon. Members have mentioned incorporation. That question raises complex constitutional issues. . . . Many think that it could lead to considerable difficulties in the relationship between Parliament and our courts. Certainly the Government have no plans for incorporation.

(HC Debs., vol. 83, col. 954: 23 July 1985)

The Minister then made reference to Article 13 of the European Convention on Human Rights, which provides: 'Everyone whose rights and freedoms as set forth in this Convention are violated shall have an effective remedy before a national authority notwithstanding that the violation has been committed by persons acting in an official capacity.' He continued:

We do not accept that lack of incorporation puts us in automatic and continuing breach of the convention. The decision in the present case means no more than that, as there was a breach of substantive provision, there was also a breach of article 13 because we had not incorporated. If there had not been a breach of a substantive provision, there would not have been a breach of article 13. When we remedy the breach of the substantive article, we shall no longer be in breach of article 13.

(Ibid.)

In moving the approval of the draft European Communities (Definition of Treaties) (Third ACP–EEC Convention of Lomé) Order 1985, the Minister of State for Overseas Development, Mr Timothy Raison, stated:

. . . the Lomé convention is the treaty which governs economic relations between the European Community and the African, Caribbean and Pacific group of developing countries. The third ACP–EEC convention, or Lomé III as it is commonly known, was signed on 8 December last year and covers the period 1985 to 1990.

The draft Order in Council, to which the motion refers, allows effect to be given to the provisions of the convention in United Kingdom law. This in turn opens the way for ratification of the convention by the United Kingdom. The convention will come into force when it has been ratified by all the member states, the European Community and two thirds of the ACP states. This will probably be early next year.

(Ibid., vol. 81, col. 725: 24 June 1985)

In the course of a debate on the subject of the Human Rights and Fundamental Freedoms Bill, the Government spokesman, Lord Glenarthur, stated:

The reason for the Government's opposition to incorporation is not because of any desire to inhibit the pursuit of human rights. Indeed, it has nothing to do with human rights as such. Our concern is that incorporation could cause a shift in the balance of our democratic system. Our machinery of government does not depend on a written constitution. Our statutes are specific in nature and set out measures that the Government of the day decide are necessary for our democratic society. If society does not approve of the Government's actions, the Government will not be re-elected.

My noble friend Lord Broxbourne suggested that if this Bill became law the provisions of the convention would be integrated and applied by British judges in British courts instead of by the members of the European commission and court. The only comment I should make on that is that people who did not succeed before our courts could go on to Strasbourg afterwards and, if the Strasbourg organs disagreed with our courts, they would have the last word and the United Kingdom Government would be obliged under the convention to give effect to their decision even if it conflicted with that of our courts.

Were we to incorporate the provision of the European Convention in accordance with the provisions of this Bill, we should have taken a major step towards a written constitution and we should have on the statute book a series of non-specific provisions with no precise definition. For example, Article 8 requires that everyone has the right to respect for his private and family life, his home and his correspondence. Who then will have to decide what is necessary for our democratic society within that article? Not the elected Government, not Parliament, but the judiciary. With all respect to the learned members of the judiciary, and with all due deference to the noble and learned Lord, Lord Scarman, who foreshadowed a little of what I have to say, I must ask whether it is right that they should be required to take such decisions, many of which, as the noble and learned Lord, Lord Elwyn-Jones, the noble Lord, Lord Lloyd of Hampstead, and the noble Lord, Lord Allen of Abbeydale, suggested, will be politically charged, and that they should take those decisions with no requirement to answer to Parliament or to society itself.

One has to ask whether this is a role that would be welcome to the judiciary. Judging by the remarks of the noble and learned Lord, Lord Denning, he at least did not seem to think that they would welcome it.

Both the noble Lord, Lord Banks, and the noble and learned Lord, Lord Scarman, referred to the delays that occur before a case reaches the European Court. The fact is that few cases reach the court because the commission acts as a screen, as the noble and learned Lord, Lord Denning, suggests, particularly in rejecting cases that it considers not to be admissible. There appears to be no provision for such a screen in this Bill and there would be access to our courts for all those who could relate their cases, spuriously or otherwise, to one of the general articles of the convention. The only reservation that I can find refers to frivolous or vexatious proceedings, but this would cover only a tiny minority of cases.

Not only would there be this shift away from the determination of society's needs by its elected representatives to the determination of society's needs by a non-elected judiciary, but we should have the problems associated with the uncertain interpretation of the non-specific articles of the convention. If we were to enact the provisions of this Bill, could we be certain that the present statute book would not be open to challenge? If not, 'so be it' is a not unreasonable answer. But can we be sure that the present statute book and the laws we pass after incorporation will not be struck down a few years later as the interpretation of the articles of the convention evolves either in this country or at Strasbourg—and evolve it no doubt will. Who would have thought when the convention was drafted that our laws bearing upon homosexuality, corporal punishment in schools and marriage in prison would be found to be defective?

Of course, the Bill makes provision in Clause 4, which has been referred to by many including my noble friend Lord Campbell, for Acts to contain a provision expressly excluding the application of the incorporated provisions. Presumably Parliament will be hesitant to apply this because it will, as now, frame legislation to conform with the current interpretation of the convention. But will Parliament be able to be confident about the future? I do not think it will be. An express provision would, of course, insure the Bill. But it seems to me that to do this would be to negate the effect of the Bill before us.

The Government's view is that we cannot readily predict what effect the enactment of this Bill would have on our constitutional heritage and what consequences would arise from the inevitable uncertainties which it would create. Were the Bill necessary to confer basic human rights on the individuals of our society, we should regard it differently. However, it is not necessary for this purpose and we consider the risks I have mentioned such that we should be taking a completely unjustifiable gamble were we to support the Bill. For those reasons, I have to tell your Lordships and my noble friend that the Government cannot support this measure.

(HL Debs., vol. 469, cols. 193–4: 10 December 1985)

In moving the approval of the draft Merchant Shipping (Prevention of Oil Pollution) (Amendment) Order 1985, the Government spokesman in the House of Lords, the Earl of Caithness, stated:

Protection of the marine environment from pollution by oil from ships is considered by the Marine Environment Protection Committee (MEPC) of the International Maritime Organisation. At its 20th session held on 7th September 1985 amendments were adopted by Resolution MEPC 14(20) to annex 1 of the protocol of 1978, relating to the International Convention for the Prevention of Pollution from Ships 1973 (known as Marpol 73/78). The amendments come into force on 7th January 1986 and the order will enable changes to be made to the Merchant Shipping (Prevention of Oil Pollution) Regulations 1983, which gave effect to annex 1 of Marpol 73/78.

It is the desire of parties to the Marpol 73/78 Convention to aim for the complete elimination of intentional pollution of the marine environment by oil and the minimisation of accidental discharge. These amendments are yet a further step in realising those objectives. In general, the amendments make provision for improvements in ship construction, pollution prevention equipment and operational procedures. The United Kingdom, which is particularly active in IMO proceedings, were responsible for initiating certain of these amendments.

The powers for making the order are contained in Section 20 of the Merchant Shipping Act 1979. In particular, Section 20(1)(*d*) empowers the Secretary of State for Transport to give effect to any international agreement ratified by the United Kingdom so far as the agreement relates to the prevention, reduction or control of pollution of the sea or other waters by matter from ships. Under Section 20(6) of that Act the order is required to be laid under affirmative procedure.

The making of this instrument, which supplements existing legislation, is yet another important step toward reducing oil pollution of the marine environment and is in keeping with the United Kingdom's international obligations.

(Ibid., col. 409: 12 December 1985)

Part Two: II. *Sources of international law—custom*

(See also Part Nine: XIV. (Written Answer of 27 February 1985), below)

In reply to the question which articles of the United Nations Convention on the Law of the Sea are considered by Her Majesty's Government to have achieved the status of customary international law, the Minister of State, Foreign and Commonwealth Office, stated:

Customary international law is based on state practice. In order to prepare the list requested, it would be necessary to examine each point in detail to assess how far the specific provisions in the text of the convention reflected state practice. That would not be practicable.

(HC Debs., vol. 73, Written Answers, col. *359*: 18 February 1985)

Part Two: XI. *Sources of international law*—jus cogens

On 8 November 1985 in the Sixth Committee of the General Assembly of the UN, discussing the International Law Commission's latest work on State responsibility, the United Kingdom representative, Sir John Freeland, observed of draft Article 12, sub-paragraph (b):

The concept of *jus cogens* may have a role to play in the context of the law of treaties, but we are not satisfied that it has in the law of state responsibility. We see no need, as a matter of law, for the inclusion of a reference to *jus cogens* in Part 2 of the present draft articles. Indeed, the inclusion of such a reference would in our view serve to add elements of confusion to an already difficult text. Our preference would therefore be for the deletion of sub-paragraph (b)—if not, since sub-paragraph (a) seems to us probably otiose, of draft article 12 as a whole.

(Text provided by the Foreign and Commonwealth Office; see also A/C. 6/40/SR. 32, p. 7)

Part Three: I. A. 1. *Subjects of international law—States—international status—sovereignty and independence*

In moving the second reading in the House of Commons of the Brunei and Maldives Bill, the Parliamentary Under-Secretary of State, Foreign and Commonwealth Office, Mr Timothy Renton, stated in part:

The purpose of the Bill, which has been approved in another place, is to make minor amendments to certain United Kingdom enactments to take account of the recently acquired status of Brunei and the Maldives as members of the Commonwealth. It will have no effect on the laws of Brunei and the Maldives.

Britain's historical connections with those two countries are particularly interesting. The sultanate of Brunei first entered special treaty relations with the United Kingdom in 1846 and subsequently enjoyed the status of a protected state until 1971. Subsequently, the United Kingdom continued to exercise direct responsibility for Brunei's external relations until 31 December 1983. On that date, Brunei resumed her status as a sovereign and independent state and was admitted to the Commonwealth with effect from 1 January 1984.

Britain's connections with the Maldives date back to the 18th century when, on taking possession of Ceylon, we extended our protection to the Maldives. In 1948 the Maldives were granted self-government, but the United Kingdom continued to maintain control of their external relations. In 1965, the Maldives became a fully independent sovereign state outside the Commonwealth, but were admitted to the Commonwealth, at their own request, as a special member in July 1982.

. . .

The amendments which the Bill makes to United Kingdom enactments follow the precedents of the Papua New Guinea, Western Samoa and Nauru (Miscellaneous Provisions) Act 1980 and the New Hebrides Act 1980. These precedents relate to countries which, like Brunei and the Maldives, required only such legislative provision as was consequent on their accession to membership of the Commonwealth.

In the case of former British colonies, the relevant independence Act passed on the achievement of independence, and almost simultaneous accession to the Commonwealth, includes these necessary amendments to other United Kingdom legislation which place the state on the same footing as other Commonwealth countries. However, both Brunei and the Maldives have achieved full sovereignty and membership of the Commonwealth without the need for such an independence Act.

Clause 1 and the schedule provide for the necessary modification of United Kingdom enactments. Paragraphs 1 and 2 of the schedule provide for amendments to section 427(2) of the Merchant Shipping Act 1894 and to the Whaling Industry (Regulation) Act 1934. Because nationals of Brunei and the Maldives will be brought within the definition of 'British subjects' in enactments passed before the coming into force of the 1981 Act, it is necessary to amend the Merchant Shipping Act 1894 and the Whaling Industry (Regulation) Act 1934 in such a way as to exclude Brunei and the Maldives from their application.

Paragraph 3 of the schedule provides for an amendment to the Imperial Institute Act, as amended by the Commonwealth Institute Act 1958. Brunei and the Maldives will thereby be included as countries which may be represented on the board of governors who are consulted when arrangements for the Commonwealth Institute are changed.

Paragraphs 4, 5, 6 and 7 of the schedule provide for amendments to Acts relating to Commonwealth forces and their discipline while on visits to the United Kingdom. These amendments make provisions for forces raised in Brunei and the Maldives similar to those which apply to forces raised in other Commonwealth countries.

Paragraph 8 provides for an amendment to the British Nationality Act 1981. The Maldives will be added to the list of Commonwealth countries under schedule 3 of that Act. Paragraph 8 applies to the Maldives only. The similar consequential change with regard to Brunei has already been effected by Order in Council.

(HC Debs., vol. 72, Written Answers, cols. *118–20*: 28 January 1985)

In the course of a speech in the Security Council on 7 March 1985, the UK representative, Mr Maxey, stated:

The sovereignty, unity, independence and territorial integrity of Lebanon within its internationally recognized boundaries must be strictly respected.

(S/PV. 2570, p. 39)

On 12 March 1985, in the Security Council, Mr Maxey stated:

We strongly support the Security Council's calls for the complete withdrawal of all Israeli forces from Lebanon and for strict respect for the sovereignty, independence, unity and territorial integrity of Lebanon within its internationally recognized boundaries.

(S/PV. 2573, pp. 84–5)

In the course of the case *Matsushita Electric Industrial Co. Ltd.* v. *Zenith Radio Corporation and National Union Electric Corporation*, the Governments of Australia, Canada, France and the UK sought leave, and were permitted, to file an *amici curiae* Brief before the Supreme Court of the United States. The Brief, stated to be the first *amicus curiae* brief presented to the Supreme Court by more than one foreign government, was dated 15 June 1985 and contained *inter alia* the following passages:

The related doctrines of foreign sovereign compulsion and act of state are judicial acknowledgements of the fundamental principle of international law that a sovereign's exercise of its authority within its territory is not reviewable by the courts of another nation.[10]

. . .

. . . since 1978 the U.S. Government has encouraged foreign governments to address U.S. courts directly. If this Court now holds that such filings properly may be disregarded by U.S. courts, the Executive Branch will have the very difficult task of convincing foreign sovereigns that there is any acceptable mechanism in the U.S. legal system for friendly foreign sovereigns to express the nature and effect of their regulatory actions within their territory. It clearly would not be acceptable to such sovereigns that they be required to submit the determination of such questions of fact to the courts of another sovereign.

. . .

In analyzing the act of state doctrine in a recent antitrust case, the Ninth Circuit made the following perceptive comments in illuminating the underpinnings of that doctrine:

> 'The doctrine recognizes the institutional limitations of the courts and the peculiar requirements of successful foreign relations. To participate adeptly in the global community, the United States must speak with one voice and pursue a careful and deliberate foreign policy. The political branches of our government are able to consider the competing economic and political considerations and respond to the public will in order to carry on foreign relations in accordance with the best interests of the country as a whole. The courts, in contrast, focus on single disputes and make decisions on the basis of legal principles. The timing of our decisions is largely a result of our case-load and of the random tactical considerations which motivate parties to bring lawsuits and to seek delay or expedition. When the courts engage in piecemeal adjudication of the legality of the sovereign acts of states, they risk disruption of our country's international diplomacy. The executive may utilize protocol, economic sanction, compromise, delay, and persuasion to achieve international objectives. Ill-timed judicial decisions challenging the acts of foreign states could nullify these tools and embarrass the United States in the eyes of the world.'

International Association of Machinists v. Organization of Petroleum Exporting Countries, 649 F.2d 1354, 1358 (9th Cir. 1981), *cert. denied*, 454 U.S. 1163 (1982).

Amici submit that the preceding explanation of the bases of the act of state doctrine, as well as *United States v. Pink*, 315 U.S. 203, 218–21 (1942), and its progeny, explain why U.S. courts may not adjudicate the veracity of an official statement by a friendly foreign government that it mandated private conduct. Such an adjudication of a friendly foreign sovereign's official statement would be an unacceptable intrusion into the sovereignty of that friendly foreign government. It could, as a practical matter, render the act of state and foreign sovereign compulsion doctrines meaningless and would, at minimum, create uncertainty in international economic relations. Amici believe that the U.S. Government would have the same reaction to such adjudications of its statements by foreign courts.

[10] 'The sovereignty and equality of states represent the basic constitutional doctrine of the law of nations. . . . The principal corollaries of the sovereignty and equality of states are: (1) a jurisdiction, *prima facie* exclusive, over a territory . . .; (2) a duty of non-intervention in the area of exclusive jurisdiction of other states. . . .' I. Brownlie, *Principles of Public International Law* 287 (3d ed. 1979).

(*International Legal Materials*, 24 (1985), pp. 1293–1301, *passim*)

In the course of a debate on the subject of the European Community, the Minister of State, Foreign and Commonwealth Office, Baroness Young, stated:

. . . there has been a committee, known as the Dooge Committee, which has been sitting and looking at the institutions of the Community. In *Europe: the Future* it was stated that the objective should be the progressive attainment of a common external policy—that is, of the Community. The United Kingdom is firmly committed to a strengthened foreign policy co-operation among the Ten for the reasons that have been given and reasons which have frequently been advanced in your Lordships' House. But I can confirm that sovereignty for foreign policy matters rests firmly with member governments.

(HL Debs., vol. 466, col. 131: 9 July 1985)

In reply to a question on the subject of the visit to London of two representatives of the Palestine Liberation Organization, the Minister of State, Foreign and Commonwealth Office, set out the following text of a statement prepared by the representatives:

The members of the joint delegation reiterated their personal support for a peaceful settlement between Israel and its Arab neighbours on the basis of the relevant United Nations resolutions, including Resolutions 242 and 338 of the Security Council, under the appropriate auspices. They stated that in accordance with these resolutions a settlement should recognise the inalienable rights of the Palestinian people, including the right to self-determination within the context of a Jordanian/Palestinian confederation, as well as the right of all states in the area to exist within the secure recognised boundaries. They confirmed their opposition to all forms of terrorism and violence from whatever source.

He then wrote:

We made clear our view that the statement would only be acceptable if it contained an explicit reference to the right of Israel to exist within secure and recognised borders.

(HC Debs., vol. 84, Written Answers, col. *358*: 28 October 1985)

Part Three: I. A. 2. *Subjects of international law—States—international status—non-intervention and non-use of force*

(See also Part Three: I. A. 1. (*amici curiae* Brief of 15 June 1985), above)

In reply to a question, the Secretary of State for Foreign and Commonwealth Affairs, Sir Geoffrey Howe, stated in part:

. . . it was clearly understood at the Lancaster House conference that the operation of the Zimbabwean constitution would be a matter for the Zimbabwean Government and courts. That constitution established Zimbabwe as an independent country and gave us no right to interfere in its internal affairs.

(Ibid., vol. 83, Written Answers, col. *592*: 24 July 1985)

Part Three: I. A. 3. *Subjects of international law—States—international status—domestic jurisdiction*

(See also Part Three: I. A. 2., above)

In reply to the question what action will be taken within the Commonwealth to inhibit civil conflict in Zimbabwe, the Minister of State, Foreign and Commonwealth Office, wrote:

The domestic affairs of a member are not discussed within the Commonwealth without the express approval of the Government concerned.

(Ibid., vol. 75, Written Answers, col. *525*: 20 March 1985)

Part Three: I. B. 1. *Subjects of international law—States—recognition—recognition of States*

(See Part Three: I. B. 5. (Written Answers of 1 and 20 March 1985), below)

Part Three: I. B. 2. *Subjects of international law—States—recognition—recognition of governments*

(See also Part Three: I. B. 5. (items of 24 January 1985 and 16 May 1985), below)

In reply to a question, the Parliamentary Under-Secretary of State, Foreign and Commonwealth Office, wrote:

We do not have normal Government to Government dealings with the regime in Kabul which depends on an occupying army of over 115,000 Soviet troops.

(Ibid., vol. 83, Written Answers, col. *294*: 19 July 1985; see also ibid., cols. *580–1*: 24 July 1985)

In reply to a later question on the same subject, the Parliamentary Under-Secretary of State, Foreign and Commonwealth Office, wrote:

We have no substantive relations with Afghanistan. Following the Soviet invasion in December 1979, we withdrew Her Majesty's ambassador in Kabul and suspended our aid programme to Afghanistan.

(HC Debs., vol. 87, Written Answers, col. *143*: 19 November 1985)

Part Three: I. B. 5. *Subjects of international law—States—recognition—non-recognition*

(See also Part Three: I. B. 2., above and Part Three: III. D. (item of 6 December 1985), below)

In reply to a question, the Minister of State, Foreign and Commonwealth Office, wrote in part:

Since 1950 Her Majesty's Government have dealt with the Government of the People's Republic of China as the sole legal Government of China. Accordingly there can be no question of entering into diplomatic or other official relations with the authorities in Taiwan.

(Ibid., vol. 71, Written Answers, col. *549*: 24 January 1985)

In reply to the question whether 'the Government still hold firm to their decisions not to recognize the so-called Turkish State in northern Cyprus', the Minister of State, Foreign and Commonwealth Office, Mr Richard Luce, stated:

Our position remains precisely the same.

(Ibid., vol. 73, col. 1018: 20 February 1985)

In reply to the question 'in what respect Bophuthatswana fails to satisfy the accepted Foreign and Commonwealth Office criteria for the recognition of a sovereign State', the Minister of State, Foreign and Commonwealth Office, wrote:

We do not recognise Bophuthatswana as an independent State on the grounds that it does not enjoy genuine independence.

(Ibid., vol. 74, Written Answers, col. *305*: 1 March 1985)

In reply to further questions asking him to elaborate on this answer, the Minister of State wrote:

Amongst the criteria for recognition is that the country in question shall have an independent position, in the sense that it has full internal autonomy as well as full freedom of action in respect of external relations. We are not satisfied that Bophuthatswana, which came into existence as a result of South Africa's apartheid policies, possesses these attributes.

(Ibid., vol. 75, Written Answers, col. *532*: 20 March 1985)

The receipt of external economic, military or other assistance, does not necessarily detract from the attributes of a defined territory, an effective

Government, and independence in its internal autonomy and external relations which are the criteria for recognition.

(Ibid.)

In reply to a later question on the same subject, the Minister of State wrote:

It is our judgment, after taking all factors into account, including the circumstances of Bophuthatswana's creation, the agreements then concluded, its fractured territory and its relationship with South Africa, that Bophuthatswana does not meet our criteria for recognition as an independent state.

(Ibid., vol. 76, Written Answers, col. *447*: 1 April 1985)

In reply to oral questions, the Prime Minister, Mrs Margaret Thatcher, stated:

. . . We recognise the state of Cambodia but in common with the overwhelming majority of the international community will not countenance having relations with the present regime in Phnom Penh which depends on the Vietnamese occupation forces for its existence.

. . .

The Government withdrew formal recognition from the Pol Pot regime in December 1979. In accordance with the recommendation of the United Nations General Assembly credentials committee, we continue to accept the representatives of the democratic parts of Kampuchea as representing the Cambodia seat.

(Ibid., vol. 79, col. 486: 16 May 1985; see also ibid., vol. 80, Written Answers, col. *488*: 12 June 1985)

In reply to a question on the subject of the 'Turkish Republic of Northern Cyprus', the Minister of State, Foreign and Commonwealth Office, wrote in part:

We do not recognise the 'TRNC' and do not therefore recognise any so-called constitutional developments in Northern Cyprus.

(HL Debs., vol. 465, col. 359: 19 June 1985)

In reply to a question, the Parliamentary Under-Secretary of State, Foreign and Commonwealth Office, wrote in part:

The following, among others, are sometimes referred to as independent sovereign states but are not recognised as such by Her Majesty's Government:

North Korea
Taiwan
Turkish Republic of Northern Cyprus
Transkei or any of the other Black Homelands established in South Africa

(HC Debs., vol. 81, Written Answers, col. *149*: 19 June 1985)

In reply to the question what action is currently taken by Her Majesty's ambassador in Moscow in acknowledgement of the fact that Her Majesty's Government do not recognize the incorporation of the Baltic States into the Soviet Union *de jure*, the Minister of State, Foreign and Commonwealth Office, wrote:

Her Majesty's ambassador in Moscow avoids any contact with the authorities in the Baltic states which could be taken to imply de jure recognition. The Soviet Government has been made aware of our position on a number of occasions.

(HC Debs., vol. 82, Written Answers, col. *273*: 5 July 1985)

In reply to the further question what contacts Her Majesty's Government has with any of the Baltic States which do not imply *de jure* recognition, the Minister of State, Foreign and Commonwealth Office, wrote:

There have on occasions been limited contacts between members of Her Majesty's embassy and officials of the Baltic Republics related to specific events when these were in our interests. A case in point was over the organisation of the British element in a trade exhibition in Riga in 1974.

(Ibid., vol. 83, Written Answers, col. *908*: 26 July 1985)

In reply to a question, the Minister of State, Foreign and Commonwealth Office, wrote:

We do not recognise North Korea as a state and have no diplomatic relations with the authorities there.

(Ibid., col. *384*: 22 July 1985)

In reply to a question, the Minister of State, Foreign and Commonwealth Office, wrote in part:

We do not recognise the Democratic Republic of the Western Sahara.

(Ibid., vol. 89, Written Answers, col. *134*: 17 December 1985)

In the course of answering oral questions on the subject of the Middle East, the Minister of State, Foreign and Commonwealth Office, Mr Timothy Renton, stated:

. . . we agreed to the inclusion of two Palestinians in the recent Jordanian–Palestinian delegation that came to London. Unfortunately, in the end, they were not willing to sign the resolution that had been agreed in advance. The question of the recognition of the PLO does not arise, because we recognise states only.

(Ibid., col. 287: 18 December 1985)

Part Three: I. C. 1. *Subjects of international law—States—types of States—unitary States, federal States and confederations*

On 6 December 1984, the Government of the UK concluded an Agreement on Certain Commercial Debts with the Government of Yugoslavia. The latter was described in the instrument as 'The Federal Executive Council of the Assembly of the Socialist Federal Republic of Yugoslavia'.

(Cmnd. 9431)

Part Three: I. C. 4. *Subjects of international law—States—types of States—dependent States and territories*

The following Joint Communiqué was agreed by the Foreign Ministers of the UK and Spain in Brussels on 27 November 1984:

1. The Foreign and Commonwealth Secretary, the Right Hon. Sir Geoffrey Howe, and the Spanish Foreign Minister, His Excellency Sr. Don Fernando Morán López, held a meeting in Brussels on 27 November during which they agreed on the way in which the Spanish and British Governments will apply by not later than 15 February 1985 the Lisbon Declaration of 10 April 1980 in all its parts. This will involve simultaneously:

(a) The provision of equality and reciprocity of rights for Spaniards in Gibraltar and Gibraltarians in Spain. This will be implemented through the mutual concession of the rights which citizens of EC countries enjoy, taking into account the transitional periods and derogations agreed between Spain and the E.E.C. The necessary legislative proposals to achieve this will be introduced in Spain and Gibraltar. As concerns paid employment, and recalling the general principle of Community preference, this carries the implication that during the transitional period each side will be favourably disposed to each other's citizens when granting work permits.

(b) The establishment of the free movement of persons, vehicles and goods between Gibraltar and the neighbouring territory.

(c) The establishment of a negotiating process aimed at overcoming all the differences between them over Gibraltar and at promoting co-operation on a mutually beneficial basis on economic, cultural, touristic, aviation, military and environmental matters. Both sides accept that the issues of sovereignty will be discussed in that process. The British Government will fully maintain its commitment to honour the wishes of the people of Gibraltar as set out in the preamble of the 1969 Constitution.

2. Insofar as the airspace in the region of Gibraltar is concerned, the Spanish Government undertakes to take the early actions necessary to allow safe and effective air communications.

3. There will be meetings of working groups, which will be reviewed periodically in meetings for this purpose between the Spanish and British Foreign Ministers.

(Text provided by the Foreign and Commonwealth Office)

In the course of a letter dated 24 January 1985 from the UK Permanent Representative to the UN, Sir John Thomson, addressed to the Secretary-General, it was stated:

As administering Power of the Falkland Islands, the Government of the United Kingdom will continue to be guided by its obligations under Article 73 of the United Nations Charter (notably, in the present context, to promote to the utmost the well-being of the inhabitants of the Falkland Islands, to ensure their economic and social advancement and to promote constructive measures of development) and under the two international covenants. In the view of the Government of the

United Kingdom measures such as these, undertaken to promote the economic development of the Falkland Islands, are in no way relevant to the question of the normalization of relations between the United Kingdom and Argentina.

(A/40/97, p. 2)

In the course of a debate on the subject of the Foreign Affairs Committee's report on the Falkland Islands, the Secretary of State for Foreign and Commonwealth Affairs, Sir Geoffrey Howe, mentioned the proposal to create separate constitutions for the Falkland Islands and for their dependencies. He went on:

Even so, there is good reason to make separate constitutional provision for the two territories. Although the dependencies have for convenience been administered from Port Stanley, they are a separate dependent territory with their own requirements. Unlike the Falkland Islands, they have no permanent population and, therefore, no need for representative government.

. . .

I come now to the close relationship between the two constitutions about which I was speaking. The close relationship that has long existed between the two territories will be reflected in the new arrangements that we propose. The Governor of the Falkland Islands will also be commissioner for South Georgia and the South Sandwich Islands. In this capacity, he will consult the Executive Council of the Falkland Islands on matters relating to the dependencies which might affect the Falkland Islands.

. . .

The constitutions are being promulgated in accordance with the normal procedures. They were approved by the islands' Legislative Council on 16 January. They are embodied in Orders in Council which will be made under the provisions of the British Settlement Acts 1887 and 1945. Drafts of the two orders were placed in the Library of the House on 24 January. A revised text, taking account of further consultations with the islands' councillors, was placed in the Library on 11 March.

There is one new point in the revised text that I should mention to the House. We have accepted the wish of the islanders to revert to the title of Governor rather than Civil Commissioner. The latter title was introduced, at the same time as that of Military Commissioner, immediately after the liberation of the islands in June 1982. We have taken the view that the introduction of the new constitution is the right time to return to the more familiar titles of Governor and Commander British Forces. The title of Governor is, of course, the customary one for a dependent territory of this kind.

(HC Debs., vol. 75, cols. 493–4: 14 March 1985)

Speaking on 9 August 1985 to the UN Special Committee on the Situation with regard to the Implementation of the Declaration on the Granting of Independence to Colonial Countries and Peoples, the Acting Permanent Representative of the UK to the UN, Mr P. Maxey, stated:

The Falkland Islands Constitution

Article 73b of the Charter enjoins us to 'develop self-government, to take due account of the political aspirations of the peoples, and to assist them in the progressive development of their free political institutions, according to the particular circumstances of each territory and its peoples and their varying stages of advancement'.

The present constitution of the Falkland Islands dates from 1948. Before the events of 1982, Falkland Islands Councillors had taken the first steps towards a review of the constitutional arrangements then existing. After the invasion, a Select Committee of the Legislative Council resumed its work, and submitted a report in July 1983, having consulted the electorate fully. Drafts of new constitutions for the Falkland Islands and for South Georgia and the South Sandwich Islands were approved on 16 January 1985 by the Falkland Islands Legislative Council, and embodied in Orders in Council laid before Parliament on 28 March. Both constitutions will enter into force at the time of the general election to be held in the Falkland Islands on 3 October.

The new Falkland Islands constitution is designed, in accordance with Article 73 of the Charter, to develop the political institutions of the Falkland Islanders. Among its new features, the revised constitution provides for the abolition of nominated members in the Executive Council; for an increase in the number of elected members in both the Legislative and the Executive Councils; and for removal of the right to vote from the two ex officio members of each Council. It also includes for the first time a chapter on human rights, the preamble to which reflects the provisions regarding self-determination in Article 1 of the International Covenant on Civil and Political Rights.

(Text provided by the Foreign and Commonwealth Office)

S. 3 of the South Georgia and South Sandwich Islands Order 1985, which entered into force on 3 October 1985, reads:

As from the date of commencement of this Order all islands and territories whatsoever between the 20th degree of west longitude and the 50th degree of west longitude which are situated between the 50th parallel of south latitude and the 60th parallel of south latitude shall cease to be governed as Dependencies of the Falkland Islands and shall be known as South Georgia and the South Sandwich Islands.

(Statutory Instrument 1985 No. 449)

Speaking in explanation of vote in the Fourth Committee of the General Assembly on 8 November 1985, the UK representative, Mr H. Mortimer, stated:

The resolution underlines the responsibilities placed on administering powers to submit information to the Secretary General on the non-self-governing territories for which they are responsible, under Article 73(e) of the Charter. We have no objection to the resolution on that score. But we part company over the assumption in paragraph 2 of the resolution which leaves it to the General Assembly to determine at which point in the constitutional advance of a non-self-governing territory the administering power is no longer obliged to submit information to the Secretary General. We do not accept this assertion since we believe that such a decision is best left to those most directly concerned, namely the administering power and the local government.

(Text provided by the Foreign and Commonwealth Office; see also HC Debs., vol. 87, Written Answers, col. *421*: 25 November 1985)

Part Three: I. E. *Subjects of international law—States—self-determination*

(See also Part Three: III. D. (item of 2 December 1985), below)

In the course of a debate on the subject of Anglo-Argentine relations, the Minister of State, Foreign and Commonwealth Office, Baroness Young, stated:

. . . I think it might be helpful to confirm that the Government have agreed that the human rights chapter of the new constitution for the Falkland Islands should have in its preamble a reaffirmation of the islanders' right to self-determination. The wording repeats the provisions regarding self-determination in Article I of the International Covenant on Civil and Political Rights.

(HL Debs., vol. 458, col. 1073: 17 January 1985)

In the course of a letter dated 24 January 1985 from the UK Permanent Representative to the UN, Sir John Thomson, addressed to the Secretary-General, it was stated:

On 19 July 1984 the Falkland Islands Government granted to a British company, Firstland Oil and Gas PLC, a licence to prospect for oil and gas in an area known as Douglas Station on West Falkland. This fact was reported in the British and Argentine press last July and was confirmed shortly thereafter in the British Parliament. The licence was granted under the Falkland Islands Mining Ordinance. Its grant was an example of the exercise by the people of the Falkland Islands of the right freely to dispose of their natural resources. This right is recognized by article 1 of the International Covenant on Economic, Social and Cultural Rights and article 1 of the International Covenant on Civil and Political Rights, both of which have been ratified by the United Kingdom. Under the licence, rent and royalties are payable to the Falkland Islands Government.

(A/40/97)

In reply to an oral question, the Prime Minister, Mrs Margaret Thatcher, stated in part:

Let me make it clear, that the statement of 27 November 1984 underlined Her Majesty's Government's intention fully to maintain their commitment to honour the freely and democratically expressed wishes of the people of Gibraltar, as set out in the preamble of the Gibraltar constitution of 1969. As my hon. Friend says, Her Majesty's Government have given assurances to the people of Gibraltar that Gibraltar will remain part of Her Majesty's dominions unless and until an Act of Parliament provides otherwise, and, furthermore, that Her Majesty's Government will never enter into arrangements under which the people of Gibraltar would pass under the sovereignty of another state against their freely and democratically expressed wishes.

(HC Debs., vol. 72, col. 744: 5 February 1985)

In the course of a debate on the subject of Gibraltar, the Secretary of State for Foreign and Commonwealth Affairs, Sir Geoffrey Howe, remarked:

I repeat that our commitment as set out in the 1969 constitution stands unqualified.

(Ibid., col. 940; see also HL Debs., vol. 459, cols. 1077–9: 6 February 1985; HC Debs., vol. 75, Written Answers, col. *533*: 20 March 1985; and ibid., vol. 77, col. 861: 24 April 1985. For the text of the preamble to the 1969 Constitution, see UKMIL 1982, p. 373)

In reply to a question about action taken to implement the objectives of the Venice declaration, the Minister of State, Foreign and Commonwealth Office, stated in part:

The Heads of State and Government of the European Community reaffirmed in Dublin in December 1984 their desire to see urgent efforts made to establish peace and stability in the Middle East, and their willingness to assist efforts to that end. With our partners we shall continue to do all we can to encourage a negotiated solution on the basis of a balanced approach which safeguards Israel's right to exist within secure and recognised borders and the right of the Palestinian people to self-determination.

(Ibid., vol. 73, Written Answers, col. *473*: 20 February 1985; see also ibid., vol. 75, Written Answers, col. *523*: 20 March 1985)

Following the publication in December 1984 of the Fifth Report from the Foreign Affairs Committee of the House of Commons, which dealt with the Falkland Islands (*Parliamentary Papers*, 1983–4, HC, Paper 268-i), Her Majesty's Government made certain observations on it in February 1985. In particular, it stated:

5. The Argentines claim that the Falkland Islanders should be denied the right of self-determination. The people of the Falkland Islands are small in number. But this in no way detracts from the rights which international law, including provisions of the United Nations Charter and of the International Covenants on human rights, accords to them and requires States to respect. They are a peaceful and homogeneous community which has developed democratic institutions over a period of a century and more. Many Falkland Islands families have been established there far longer than many Argentines in Argentina. The Government have consistently defended the Islanders' right of self-determination and will continue to do so.

6. The Report refers (paragraphs 74–83) to proceedings at the United Nations General Assembly since 1982. The Resolutions adopted by the Assembly in 1982, 1983 and 1984 all reflected the unacceptable Argentine approach calling for negotiations which would pre-judge the outcome: they must, in the Argentine

view, lead only to the transfer of sovereignty irrespective of the wishes of the people of the Falkland Islands. These Resolutions also deliberately failed to take account of the principle of self-determination. The outcome of the debate in the Assembly in 1984 (89 votes in favour of the Argentine resolution, nine against, and 54 abstentions) showed that the margin between those supporting Argentina and those not prepared to do so was exactly the same as in 1982 and differed by only two votes from that in 1983.

7. In this context, the Government have noted the suggestion in the Report (paragraph 104) that it should consider inviting the United Nations De-colonisation Committee to visit the Falklands. We would need to be persuaded, however, that such a visit would permit an impartial consideration of the situation in the Islands, especially the central question of self-determination. Since the conflict, the majority of the Committee of 24 have proved to be strong supporters of the Argentine position.

(Cmnd. 9447, pp. 4–5)

In the course of a debate on the subject of the Foreign Affairs Committee's above report on the Falkland Islands, the Secretary of State for Foreign and Commonwealth Affairs, Sir Geoffrey Howe, stated:

The new constitution for the Falkland Islands contains one important new element. The island councillors expressed the view that the constitution should include a reference to their right of self-determination. We agree with them. Accordingly, the preamble to the human rights chapter of the constitution now recalls the provisions on self-determination from article 1 of the International Covenant on Civil and Political Rights. This was adopted by the United Nations General Assembly in 1966. The United Kingdom ratified it in 1976.

Argentina has not subscribed to that covenant. On the contrary, the Argentine Government seek to deny the Falkland Islanders the right of self-determination. In our view, the Falkland Islanders, like any other people, have that right. They make up a peaceful and homogeneous community which has developed democratic institutions over more than a century. Their right to self-determination will now be reflected in their constitution, and we shall uphold it.

(HC Debs., vol. 75, col. 493: 14 March 1985; see also Cmnd. 9447, p. 14)

The preamble to the new Constitution, which entered into force on 3 October 1985, reads in part as follows:

Whereas all peoples have the right of self-determination and by virtue of that right they freely determine their political status and freely pursue their economic, social and cultural development and may, for their own ends, freely dispose of their natural wealth and resources without prejudice to any obligations arising out of international economic co-operation, based upon the principle of mutual benefit and international law;

And whereas the realization of the right of self-determination must be promoted and respected in conformity with the provisions of the Charter of the United Nations;

. . .

(Statutory Instrument 1985 No. 444, Schedule 1)

By a letter addressed to the Secretary-General of the UN, dated 13 March 1985, the Permanent Representative of the UK to the UN in New York, Sir John Thomson, replied to a letter (A/40/132) from the Government of Argentina. He stated in part:

Article 73 of the Charter of the United Nations obliges the United Kingdom, as the Administering Power for the Non-Self-Governing Territory of the Falkland Islands, to promote to the utmost the well-being of the inhabitants of that Territory and, *inter alia*, to ensure their political, economic, social and educational advancement. The United Kingdom is also bound by its obligations under the International Covenant on Civil and Political Rights, adopted by the United Nations General Assembly in 1966 and ratified by the United Kingdom in 1976, to promote the realization of the right of self-determination and to respect that right in conformity with the provisions of the Charter. The intention of the Government of the United Kingdom to promulgate a new constitution for the Falkland Islands is thus entirely consistent with the United Kingdom's international obligations. It is a matter of regret that the International Covenant on Civil and Political Rights has not yet been ratified by Argentina, but this is not relevant to the international obligations of the United Kingdom.

Falkland Islands Councillors had taken the first steps towards a review of the present constitutional arrangements in the Falkland Islands before the Argentine invasion took place in 1982. A Select Committee of the Islands' Legislative Council resumed its work after the invasion and submitted a report in July 1983 after a full consultation of the electorate. Drafts of new constitutions for the Falkland Islands and for South Georgia and the South Sandwich Islands were approved on 16 January 1985 by the Falkland Islands Legislative Council, subject to further consideration of a few detailed points. The British Government intends that the new constitutions should be promulgated in the spring and enter into force at the time of the general election to be held in the Falkland Islands this autumn.

The new Falkland Islands constitution will replace the existing constitution which dates from 1948. It is designed, in accordance with Article 73 of the United Nations Charter, to develop the Islanders' political institutions. For example, it will provide for the abolition of nominated members in the Executive Council, an increase in the number of elected members in both Legislative and Executive Councils, and removal of the right to vote from the two *ex officio* members of each Council.

The new constitution includes for the first time a chapter on human rights, the preamble to which reflects the provisions regarding self-determination in article 1 of the International Covenant on Civil and Political Rights.

The Argentine Government seeks to deny to the Falkland Islanders the right of self-determination. But the Islanders are a peaceful and homogeneous community which has developed democratic institutions over more than 150 years of continuous settlement. There was no indigenous population of the Falkland Islands when the British Captain, John Strong, made the first recorded landing on the islands in 1690. A British settlement was established in 1776, before Argentina had come into existence. Nor was there a settled Argentine population on the islands in 1833. Many Falkland Island families have been established there far longer than many Argentines in Argentina. That the Islanders enjoy British citizenship cannot deprive them of their right to self-determination or of their right to live in peace and security under a government of their own choosing. The British Government has consistently defended the Islanders' right of self-determination and will continue to do so.

The Argentine Government claims that introduction of the new constitution disregards General Assembly resolution 31/49, in which the Assembly called upon the United Kingdom and Argentina to refrain from taking decisions that would unilaterally modify the then existing situation. The United Kingdom voted against that resolution. What the Argentine Government's claim ignores entirely however are the events of 1982, when Argentina invaded the Falkland Islands in breach of the fundamental principles of the United Nations. The Argentine Government must recognize that it was that brutal attempt to modify the situation unilaterally which caused a profound change in the situation in the south Atlantic.

The Argentine statement seeks to argue that, under the new constitution, the people of the islands 'could exercise the right to veto potential decisions of the United Kingdom Parliament.' The provisions in the constitution do not confer any such veto, nor do they derogate from the sovereignty of the British Parliament. These provisions recall the Islanders' right of self-determination, but any significant proposal regarding the future of the islands would be a matter for Parliament to decide.

(A/40/177)

Speaking in respect of the vote taken to adopt Security Council Resolution 562 (1985) on 10 May 1985, the Permanent Representative of the UK to the UN, Sir John Thomson, stated:

I should like to explain why, in the paragraph voting, my delegation abstained on what were originally the sixth preambular paragraph and operative paragraph 3. The original operative paragraph 3, of course, became the operative paragraph 1 in the resolution as adopted.

That paragraph refers to the inalienable right freely to decide on political, economic and social systems. My delegation is second to none in upholding this right, but we must insist that it is a right which belongs to people, not to States. That is what the United Nations Charter says; that is what both international Covenants on Human Rights say; that is what the Declaration of Principles of International Law Concerning Friendly Relations and Co-operation among States says. And indeed that is what the fourth preambular paragraph of the resolution before us says.

The Charter refers to 'the principle of equal rights and self-determination of peoples'. Both of the International Covenants in their first articles state that:

> 'All peoples have the right of self-determination. By virtue of that right they freely determine their political status and freely pursue their economic, social and cultural development.'

The Declaration on Principles of International Law concerning Friendly Relations and Co-operation among States similarly holds that:

> '. . . all peoples have the right freely to determine, without external interference, their political status and to pursue their economic, social and cultural development . . .'. (*General Assembly resolution 2625 (XXV), annex*)

According to that Declaration, all States have the duty 'to respect this right' and 'to promote realization of the principle of equal rights and self-determination of peoples'.

These basic instruments, as well as General Assembly resolution 38/10, on the situation in Central America, which is quoted in the fourth preambular paragraph of the resolution, make it crystal-clear that the right to self-determination is one that belongs to peoples and not to States. It is for States to respect and promote this right, but it is peoples which enjoy it. This is a fundamental distinction.

We deplore the distortion of this principle in operative paragraph 1 of the resolution as adopted.

(S/PV. 2580, pp. 2579–80)

[The fourth preambular paragraph as adopted reads:

Recalling also General Assembly resolution 38/10 which reaffirms the inalienable right of all the peoples to decide on their own form of government and to choose their own economic, political and social system free from all foreign intervention, coercion, or limitation.

Operative paragraph 1 as adopted reads:

1. *Reaffirms* the sovereignty and inalienable right of Nicaragua and the rest of the States to freely decide on their own political, economic and social systems, to develop their international relations according to their people's interests free from outside interference, subversion, direct or indirect coercion or threats of any kind.]

Speaking on 9 August 1985 to the UN Special Committee on the Situation with regard to the Implementation of the Declaration on the Granting of Independence to Colonial Countries and Peoples, the Acting Permanent Representative of the UK to the UN, Mr P. Maxey, stated:

The principle of self-determination—as vital to the Falkland Islanders as to the peoples of the other territories before this Committee—will be undermined if the resolution fails to take account of the views and wishes of the people of the Falkland Islands. There can be no justification for discriminating in this respect against those people. The Falkland Islanders are a peaceful and homogeneous community, and have developed democratic institutions over a century and a half. The 1980 census showed a population of 1,813 of whom 1,360 were born in the Islands: most of them can trace their origins in the territory to the nineteenth century. Many Falkland Islands' families have been established in the islands far longer than, for example, many Argentines in Argentina. Their number is small but this in no way detracts from the rights which international law, including provisions of the UN Charter and of the International Covenants on Human Rights, accords to them and requires States to respect. In this Committee last year, the distinguished Permanent Representative of Argentina acknowledged that the islanders enjoyed rights under the International Covenant on Civil and Political Rights, which the United Kingdom ratified in 1976. Article 1.3 of the Covenant obliges States parties to 'promote the realisation of the right of self-determination'. More recently, we note that a consultative document commissioned by the Argentine Government and leaked to an Argentine newspaper, which published it on the 3rd of July, acknowledged the existence of native Falkland Islanders, to whom political rights should be accorded, and implicitly recognises that the islanders are a culturally distinct people. Sadly, the consultative paper then contradicted itself by refusing to accept the Islanders' right to self-determination and, specifically, by rejecting the notion of a plebiscite in the Falklands concerning a proposed Pact of Incorporation, if it should seem certain that the islanders would vote against it. It can surely not be acceptable to this Committee that self-determination should be exercised only to the extent that the people concerned are prepared to subject themselves to the preconceived wishes of an alien power.

(Text provided by the Foreign and Commonwealth Office)

In the course of a statement to the Third Committee of the General Assembly on 11 October 1985, the UK representative, Ms Edna Young, stated:

Item 93: Importance of the Universal Realisation of the Right of Peoples to Self-Determination etc

It is clearly right that we should link our discussion of the related issues of racism and self-determination. The system of apartheid in South Africa is particularly obnoxious because its institutionalised racism serves to deny to the majority of the people of South Africa any role in determining how the society in which they live should be organised. In other words, they are denied the right of self-determination.

It is no accident that the first article of each of the International Covenants proclaims the right of self-determination. We should always remember that under the Covenants self-determination is a right of peoples and not of governments. Moreover, it is not only peoples suffering occupation by a foreign power which are deprived of their right of self-determination. We are all aware of appalling violations of the right of self-determination, accompanied by equally appalling violations of many other fundamental rights, perpetrated against peoples by their own countrymen. Amin's atrocities in Uganda and Pol Pot's in Cambodia are perhaps the most glaring contemporary examples. But they are by no means the only ones.

Self-determination is not a single event, but a continuous process. It cannot simply be achieved and then ignored. If peoples are to be able, in the words of the Covenants, to 'freely determine their political status and freely pursue their economic, social and cultural development', they must have regular opportunities to choose their governments and their social systems, and to change them when they so wish. This in turn means that they must be able to exercise other rights set out in the Covenants, such as the rights to freedom of thought and expression; the rights of peaceful assembly and freedom of association; the right to take part in the conduct of public affairs, either directly or through freely chosen representatives; and the right to vote and be elected at genuine periodic elections.

To enumerate these basic rights is to realise that all too many peoples in our world are deprived of them and thus of the right of self-determination, not by foreign occupation but by groups of their own fellow citizens who have contrived to monopolise power for themselves. They maintain that power by refusing to allow free expression to political views different from their own; by refusing to seek a genuine popular mandate from their people; and by denying their people the opportunity to practise beliefs different from their own. These systems are by definition based on oppression and inequality; and not infrequently by more violent abuses of the rights of their peoples such as torture, summary executions and disappearances.

My delegation considers that all peoples are entitled to expect the United Nations to protect their right of self-determination, not only from abuse by their own countrymen but also by outsiders. Foreign invasion and occupation are equally appalling violations of the right of self-determination, as well as of the UN Charter itself.

Turning to the situation in Afghanistan, the speaker continued:

The occupation of Afghanistan by an ever-growing foreign garrison continues to deprive the people of Afghanistan of their right of self-determination.

After mentioning the situation in Cambodia, she went on:

Regrettably these are not the only parts of the world where the right of self-determination is being denied. That right applies with equal force to the peoples of Namibia and of the Middle East. Those peoples have been denied that right for too long. In Namibia, the unlawful South African presence should be ended by implementing the UN settlement plan which provides a timetable for elections to a constituent assembly. The implementation of this plan will thereby provide the people of Namibia with the opportunity for self-determination so long denied to them.

Respect for the right of self-determination is also fundamental to resolving the problems of the Middle East. There has been over many years a fundamental failure to achieve a reconciliation of the right of all states in the region, including Israel, to a secure existence, with justice for all peoples, including the recognition of the right of the Palestinian people to self-determination, with all this implies. A balanced peace settlement must embrace both these rights: Israel's right to existence and security and the Palestinian right of self-determination.

. . .

The right of self-determination applies with equal force to the peoples of Namibia, of the Middle East, of Afghanistan and Cambodia. It applies to the smallest peoples among us just as much as to the largest. It applies, as the United Nations has consistently recognised, to the 569 people in the Cocos Keeling Islands who have opted, significantly, for integration with the former administering power, Australia, rather than independence; as well as to the 5,000 on St Helena, and the tiny populations of the British dependencies in the Caribbean. It applies to all peoples, without discrimination, including the 1,800 Falkland Islanders. On this last issue, the United Kingdom delegation will have more to say in Plenary under Item 23 of the Assembly's agenda. Suffice it to say here that the right of self-determination is both inalienable and indivisible. It is an inherent right that clearly cannot be taken away by the General Assembly. The United Kingdom will continue to uphold it wherever it is threatened or violated. It is a right which is fundamental to international peace and security, and to the protection of national integrity. As nation states, every one of us has a vital interest in it. It is not simply that we have the duty not to be selective about its implementation, we cannot afford to be selective, because none of us can be sure that no threat will be posed to our own right of self-determination.

(Text provided by the Foreign and Commonwealth Office; see also A/C. 3/40/SR. 7, pp. 2–4)

In the General Assembly of the UN on 27 November 1985, the Permanent Representative of the UK, Sir John Thomson, spoke in the debate on the subject of the Falkland Islands, and in particular on draft resolution A/40/L. 19, sponsored by Argentina. He stated:

I was talking about the phrase in paragraph 1 of draft resolution A/40/L.19: 'including all aspects on the future of the Falkland Islands (Malvinas)'. It is perhaps typical of Argentine drafters that they should constantly refer to the future of the Falkland Islands and never—perhaps because of some psychological blockage—to the future of the Falkland Islanders. The reason, of course, is that they find the existence of the inhabitants inconvenient. That leads them into the strange doctrine of claiming that self-determination does not apply to the Islanders. There is no question about that Argentine attitude. We heard it repeated this morning. If anyone was doubtful about the meaning of what he heard this morning, let me refer him to what the Permanent Representative of Argentina said on 16 November 1983:

> 'My country respects the self-determination of peoples, but it has the support of the countries of the Latin American region and the Non-Aligned Movement, which consists mainly of States which have come to independence recently, in maintaining that the right to self-determination does not apply to the specific case of the Malvinas . . .' (*A/38/PV. 57, p. 96*)

Thus, when the Argentine-drafted draft resolution talks about resolving problems 'in accordance with the Charter of the United Nations', we have been put on notice, sadly, that the principle of self-determination cannot be applied to the Falkland Islanders, that the phrase 'in accordance with the Charter of the United Nations' does not, for the Argentines, include the principle of self-determination —at any rate, not in this instance.

That is a sad conclusion. The people of the Falkland Islands have the right to self-determination, like other people, and my Government is committed to it. It would therefore be another monumental fudge for us to pretend that we did not know what the Argentines mean when they speak of the Charter of the United Nations not applying in this instance to the Falkland Islanders.

. . .

Let us consider what our amendments are. The first—the insertion of a new second preambular paragraph—is based textually on the common article 1 of the two International Covenants, that on civil and political rights and that on economic and social rights. I quote from the first paragraph of that article, as follows:

> 'All peoples have the right to self-determination. By virtue of that right they freely determine their political status and freely pursue their economic, social and cultural development.' (*General Assembly resolution 2200 A (XXI), Annex, art. 1*)

Already 81 members of the United Nations have signed those Covenants, and I have no doubt that others will do so.

Our second amendment—a short addition to the end of paragraph 1—is equally based on United Nations texts. After the words 'in accordance with the United Nations Charter', which, as I have just shown does not, for the Argentines, mean self-determination in this case, we propose to add 'and the right thereunder of peoples to self-determination'. That is Charter language. Is there anyone who will deny that under the United Nations Charter there is a right of peoples to self-determination? Of course not, and that is what our amendment says.

The Argentine text is intended to include sovereignty and to exclude self-determination. We object to it on both those grounds. The Argentines object to our amendment, because they claim that the principle of self-determination cannot apply to the Falklands. There is a clear opposition here, and it will not profit us to fudge it. I regret this clash—I expect the Argentines do, too—but let us consider what it is that we are weighing in the opposite scales.

I do not think it is unreasonable to say that there is a certain disproportion between the Argentine demand for sovereignty and the British reaffirmation of the principle of self-determination. There are a great many territorial disputes around the world, though fortunately not all of them lead to fighting. No one wishes to sweep under the rug such dangerous and emotional things as territorial disputes. But all the same they have to be taken separately and *ad hoc* with due consideration to all the circumstances.

Self-determination on the other hand is a general principle which is enshrined in the Charter and in innumerable United Nations documents. It is frequently described as an inalienable right. It is the basis on which the great decolonization movement took place and it is to the application of the principle of self-determination that most of the countries in this Chamber owe their existence. Self-determination is therefore of a different order of importance and generality to the rights and wrongs of particular territorial disputes. Self-determination is not a matter for negotiation.

If you do not have self-determination, how are you going to have sovereignty? How have the Argentines come to have sovereignty in Argentina? I do not know what to make of the phrase in the speech by the Foreign Minister of Argentina where he spoke of the 'limited rights of a foreign people to legitimize' (A/40/PV. 92, pp. 9–10) the occupation of territories by force. But, whatever that means, I accept that the present democratic Government of Argentina—which we very much welcome and which came to power as a result of the failure of the previous military régime to conquer the Falklands—is a fully legitimate Government and that it draws its legitimacy from the freely expressed will of the electorate of Argentina. In the same way the people of the Falklands have recently had an election—on 3 October, as a matter of fact. They, too, have elected by free and fair elections their representatives to speak for them. Two of those elected representatives will be speaking tomorrow morning in the Fourth Committee.

I want to be very clear and fair about this crucial matter of self-determination. I listened with care to the Ambassador of Brazil. He is a man who is universally respected in this Assembly, and with justice. He said that the draft resolution was 'a neutral document' (*p. 13*), and I believe that he means it. Nevertheless, as I have explained, it is not a neutral document. It could hardly be, when it is 100 per cent crafted in Buenos Aires without a single British contribution. But, leaving that aside, I am not quite sure that the Ambassador of Brazil has quite seen to the bottom of the Argentine text. Unless the Argentines have changed their position—

and they say they have not—they are asking us to change our position and go into talks on sovereignty. They are also not saying that they will accept the principle of self-determination. And I am afraid that my suspicions are aroused by two sentences in the speech by the Ambassador of Brazil. He says:

> 'In saying "in accordance with the Charter", the draft intends to include in that expression all the pertinent principles and provisions of the Charter and the rights thereunder; in other words, it does not exclude the possible invoking . . . of any provision of the Charter that may be applicable to questions being negotiated.' (*p. 16*)

'The pertinent principles' of the Charter, provisions 'that may be applicable'—those words might sound fine if we did not know that the Argentines in fact say that self-determination is not pertinent and that it is not applicable. So those words do not seem to me to be balanced. They do not seem to me to be neutral. I would prefer to omit the adjectives.

My suspicions are increased when the Ambassador of Brazil says that he is distressed by the United Kingdom amendments—and I must say I take it a bit hard when the Foreign Minister of Argentina describes them as ludicrous. Self-determination ludicrous? What are those amendments except the principle of self-determination? If the principle of self-determination is pertinent and applicable, why can it not be included? I am glad that the Permanent Representative of Brazil says that the principle or right of self-determination is beyond question; but if it is a right, it is a right. As I have said, it is a right for the Falkland Islanders and not a matter for negotiation.

Once again I say that we must not fudge the issues. It distresses me that the Foreign Minister of Argentina says that Argentina has always been and will always be a staunch defender of the principle of self-determination of peoples, while at the same time he says: 'the reference to the principle of self-determination can cast doubt on Argentina's attitude towards the population of the islands.' (*p. 11*)

Well, yes, indeed his unwillingness to apply self-determination does cast doubt on the Argentine attitude regarding the population of the islands. He accepts the principle but when it comes to the point he will not apply it. That is fudge and more fudge.

At one point in his speech the Foreign Minister of Argentina said: 'Does the United Kingdom truly want self-determination to be applied . . .?' (*A/40/PV. 92, p. 12*). I answer yes, and I would be glad if he would join me in that answer.

I hope that I have dealt with the reasons for our amendment and why we cannot accept the Argentine-crafted resolution.

(A/40/PV. 93, pp. 11–18, *passim*)

Later in his speech, Sir John Thomson stated:

Namibia was also mentioned—very strangely, since my Government was one of that small group that put together the agreement to be implemented by Security Council resolution 435 (1978), and that provides, as we all know, precisely for self-determination. I challenge the Foreign Minister of Argentina to find anything on the record in which the British deny the right of self-determination of Namibia. We have constantly held the opposite.

(Ibid., pp. 19–20)

In concluding his speech, Sir John Thomson remarked:

Let us have balance and clarity. That is what our amendment is intended to achieve. With their reference to 'all aspects' the Argentines already have their version of sovereignty in the draft resolution. Whether they want to say it in plain terms or in disguised terms is for them, but the sovereignty is there. We must assert the relevance of the principle of self-determination, and I trust the General Assembly will support us.

The Foreign Minister of Argentina quoted from Article 1 of the United Nations Charter, but he quoted somewhat selectively. He did not quote paragraph 2 of Article 1, which speaks of: 'respect for the principle of equal rights and self-determination of peoples'. We base our position on the language of the Charter. Surely the world's press is not going to report that the General Assembly, when it came to the point, refused to act on a fundamental principle of the Charter, which has also been called an inalienable right.

(Ibid., pp. 24–6)

Introducing two amendments to the draft resolution, Sir John Thomson stated:

The first amendment reads as follows:

> 'Reaffirming that in accordance with the Charter of the United Nations all peoples have the right to self-determination and by virtue of that right they freely determine their political status and freely pursue their economic, social and cultural development'.

That is intended as a new second preambular paragraph. It is based textually on the common article 1 of the two International Covenants, one on civil and political rights and the other on economic and social rights. I quote from the first paragraph of that common article:

> 'All peoples have the right of self-determination. By virtue of that right they freely determine their political status and freely pursue their economic, social and cultural development.' (*resolution 2200 (XXI) (1966), Annex*)

It can be seen how closely the amendment is based on the Covenants. These Covenants have been signed by 81 members of the United Nations.

Our second amendment, a short addition to the end of operative paragraph 1, is equally based on United Nations texts. After the words 'in accordance with the Charter of the United Nations', we propose to add the words 'and the right thereunder of peoples to self-determination'. That is Charter language. Is there anyone who will deny that under the United Nations Charter there is a right of peoples to self-determination? Of course not, but that is exactly what our amendment says, and there are some people who deny our amendment. There is a grave inconsistency there.

These two amendments are so evidently at the root of the doctrine and practice of the United Nations, they are so much in accord with what has been done in other colonies, that it is hard to believe that we are being asked to vote on them. They should be passed by consensus.

However, since Argentina insists on a vote, we should be clear about what is at stake. First and foremost, it is the future of the Falkland Islanders. It is elementary justice that they should have a say in their own fate.

. . .

We are faced with a vote we do not want, because we think this is something that should be adopted by consensus. We must now see what the parliament of nations here at the United Nations makes of it. In this Assembly there is sovereign equality. Each country has one vote. This is a moment when the small countries come into their own. However small or lacking in power, they have an equal position with the big and powerful nations. The small countries, including the small island countries, must now say whether it is right or wrong that a small island community of peaceful people with no army of their own should be able, as our amendments say, to exercise their right of self-determination and by virtue of that right freely to determine their political status and freely to pursue their economic, social and cultural development.

This is the question which each country must answer for itself. The answer seems obvious to us, especially given the wording of the Charter and of resolution 1514 (XV).

(A/40/PV. 95, pp. 2–6)

Speaking in the General Assembly on 2 December 1985, Sir John Thomson stated:

With the exception of Namibia the process of decolonisation is virtually at an end. Nevertheless insofar as it still has a future, my Government reaffirms that our policy towards our remaining dependent territories will continue to be guided by the principle of self-determination. We regret that the overriding importance of that principle which was so lightly treated in last week's vote on the future of the Falkland Islanders does not appear to be shared by others including notably members of the Committee of 24. However, Mr President, we will stick by our principles. We respect the wishes of the peoples of our dependent territories as we take seriously the obligations placed on us by the Charter of the United Nations as an administering power; and we shall do nothing to stand in their way if independence is what they want. Meanwhile those who attack the small peoples who wish to exercise their right of self-determination in favour of retaining their links with the United Kingdom should re-read the Charter and re-dedicate themselves to the principle of self-determination. That would be appropriate to a 25th commemoration.

(Text provided by the Foreign and Commonwealth Office; see also A/40/PV. 99, pp. 104–5)

In the course of answering oral questions on the subject of the Middle East, the Minister of State, Foreign and Commonwealth Office, Mr Timothy Renton, stated:

We have always maintained the right of the Palestinians to self-determination . . .

(HC Debs., vol. 89, col. 289: 18 December 1985)

Part Three: II. A. 1. (b). *Subjects of international law—international organizations—in general—legal status—powers, including treaty-making power*

In September 1984, the Cabinet Office presented a memorandum on the subject of the external competence of the European Community to the

House of Lords Select Committee on the European Communities which was examining that topic. The memorandum contained the following passages:

THE LEGAL BASIS FOR COMMUNITY PARTICIPATION IN INTERNATIONAL AGREEMENTS

3. Generally speaking, the Community participates in international agreements wherever such agreements concern matters within the competence of the Community. Matters are within Community competence where the EEC Treaty gives the Community such competence, whether expressly or by implication. All other matters are within the competence of Member States.

4. The EEC Treaty confers *express treaty making powers* on the Community in two areas: the common commercial policy (Articles 113 and 114), and association between the Community and a third state or states or an international organisation (Article 238). In addition, Article 28 lays down a procedure for conclusion of agreements for which the EEC Treaty provides.

5. However, treaty making powers may be *implied* from the existence of internal competence, as was established in European Court of Justice (ECJ) Case 22/70 (*Commission v Council* on the European Road Transport Agreement (AETR)) [1971] ECR 263, in which the Court upheld the view that the treaty making powers of the Community were not confined to matters covered by Articles 113 and 238, but embraced in addition an implied power to conclude treaties with third countries, 'which may flow from other provisions of the Treaty and from measures adopted, within the framework of these provisions, by the Community institutions'. The Court held that this implied power became vested in the Community automatically whenever the Community had laid down common rules to give effect to common policies, and it was necessary to conclude international agreements with third countries relating to the subject matter of those rules. The Court further held that, when such common rules were laid down, the Member States ceased to have the right, either individually, or collectively, to conclude treaties with non Member States affecting those rules. The underlying thesis of the AETR judgement was that it cannot be right for the Member States to agree on common rules to give effect to an internal 'common policy' and then to undermine that policy by subscribing to international obligations which are inconsistent or in conflict with the agreed rules.

(*Parliamentary Papers*, 1984–5, HL, Paper 236, p. 161)

In reply to a question, the Minister of State, Foreign and Commonwealth Office, wrote:

We have not supported any resolutions passed by the United Nations General Assembly (which are not in any event obligatory) which prohibit the use or threatened use of nuclear weapons; and the United Nations Security Council has not passed any resolutions in this sense.

(HL Debs., vol. 467, col. 462: 14 October 1985)

Speaking in explanation of vote on a draft resolution on trust and non-self-governing territories in the Third Committee of the General Assembly on 19 November 1985, the UK representative, Ms Young, said:

In regard to the reference in operative paragraph 3 to co-operation on the part of administering powers, I can state categorically that the United Kingdom is absolutely scrupulous in the fulfilment of all its obligations in this connection whether under the Charter or the Convention.

My delegation has taken careful note of the advice of the Legal Counsel, in particular on the question of reporting obligations of States Parties under the Convention. We were consequently obliged to vote against operative paragraph 4 of the draft since it fails to take proper account of all the reporting obligations of States Parties which are also administering powers.

(Text provided by the Foreign and Commonwealth Office; see also A/C. 3/40/SR. 46, p. 14)

[Operative paragraphs 2 and 3 of the draft resolution read:

The General Assembly

. . .

2. *Takes note also* of the part of the report relating to Trust and Non-Self-Governing Territories and other Territories to which General Assembly resolution 1514 (XV) of 14 December 1960 applies;

3. *Draws the attention* of the relevant United Nations bodies to the opinion and recommendations of the Committee relating to the Territories mentioned in paragraph 2 above, calls upon those bodies to ensure that the Committee is supplied with all relevant information on those Territories and urges all administering Powers to co-operate with the relevant United Nations bodies by providing all the necessary information in order to enable the Committee to discharge fully its responsibilities under article 15 of the International Convention on the Elimination of All Forms of Racial Discrimination; . . .

Operative paragraph 4 read:

4. *Considers* that the Committee should not take into consideration information on Territories to which General Assembly resolution 1514 (XV) applies unless such information is communicated by the competent United Nations bodies in conformity with article 15 of the Convention; . . .

During the debate, Mr Scott, Office of Legal Affairs, UN Secretariat, had made the following remarks:

. . . the Committee on the Elimination of Racial Discrimination (CERD) was not a subsidiary organ of the General Assembly but an autonomous treaty body established pursuant to the International Convention on the Elimination of All Forms of Racial Discrimination, to which not all States Members of the United Nations were parties. Therefore, paragraph 4 of draft resolution A/C. 3/40/L. 14/Rev. 1, if adopted, would constitute a recommendation to the Committee and not a binding instruction. Furthermore, the right to give authoritative interpretations of the Convention, and the powers of the Committee thereunder, rested not with the General Assembly but, in the first instance, with CERD itself, as the body responsible for monitoring compliance with the Convention, and ultimately with the States parties. Hence, were paragraph 4 to be adopted, it would be the responsibility of CERD to determine the extent to which it could be given effect, consistent with the Committee's understanding of its obligations and those of the

States parties to the Convention, including, of course, the obligations set forth in articles 3 and 9.

(A/C. 3/40/SR. 46, p. 8)]

Part Three: II. A. 1. (c). *Subjects of international law—international organizations—in general—legal status—privileges and immunities*

In moving the approval by the House of Lords of the draft Specialized Agencies of the UN (Immunities and Privileges) (Amendment) Order 1985 and the draft International Union for the Protection of New Varieties of Plants (Legal Capacities) Order 1985, the Minister of State, Foreign and Commonwealth Office, Baroness Young, stated:

This order would add the World Intellectual Property Organisation (WIPO) to the list of United Nations specialised agencies on which we confer a range of privileges and immunities. . . . I should like, at the same time, to speak to the draft International Union for the Protection of New Varieties of Plants (Legal Capacities) Order 1985.

The United Kingdom was among the founders of the World Intellectual Property Organisation (WIPO), which came into being in 1970. It was formed by uniting two existing organisations, the International Union for the Protection of Literary and Artistic Work, and the International Union for the Protection of Industrial Property. The General Assembly of the United Nations adopted a recommendation making WIPO the 14th specialised agency, with its headquarters in Geneva. It aims to promote internationally the protection of inventions, trade marks, industrial designs and copyright.

It is proposed that the United Kingdom should undertake to apply the Convention on the Privileges and Immunities of the Specialised Agencies of the United Nations in respect of WIPO; and the order before your Lordships will enable this to be done. The order amends the Specialised Agencies of the United Nations (Immunities and Privileges) Order 1974 by adding WIPO to the list of Specialised Agencies on which the order confers privileges and immunities. The order will place WIPO on the same footing as the eight other specialised agencies in relation to which we have accepted the Specialised Agencies Convention.

The WIPO has no current plans to establish an office in the United Kingdom; but its staff, including the director-general, visit London in their official capacity. Expert level meetings are held in London from time to time, and the organisation's officials attend. This order will assist the WIPO to perform its functions in this country.

The order before your Lordships will confer the full range of privileges and immunities normally accorded to such UN organisations in accordance with the Specialised Agencies Convention. This includes immunity from legal process for the organisation with a range of fiscal privileges, and full diplomatic immunities and privileges on the four high officers. Other staff members of the organisation, and representatives attending meetings, will enjoy limited privileges and immunities; in particular they will enjoy immunity from legal process only in respect of official functions.

I turn now . . . to the draft order relating to the International Union for the Protection of New Varieties of Plants. This order would accord only legal capacities to the union.

The union promotes international co-operation in the introduction of plant variety legislation. Its member states are required to acknowledge the achievements of breeders of new plant varieties by making a law which confers an exclusive property right in the form of a special title or patent. The United Kingdom was the first country to ratify the original convention in 1965. In 1978 a revised convention was adopted, and the order before your Lordships is required to give effect to Article 24(1) of that revised convention. The order would confer upon the union the legal capacities of a body corporate. In other words, the order will enable the union to contract, sue and be sued, and to hold property. It accords no immunity from jurisdiction either to the organisation or to staff members.

The United Kingdom ratified the convention in 1983, and this order, which is necessary to ensure that the United Kingdom is in a position to implement its obligations under Article 24 of the convention, clearly should have been made before ratification. I regret this oversight. Steps are being taken to underline once more to departments the need to draw the attention of the Foreign and Commonwealth Office to any treaty provisions relating to legal capacities or privileges and immunities as early as possible, and certainly before ratification.

(HL Debs., vol. 460, cols. 817–18: 25 February 1985)

In moving the approval in the House of Lords of the draft Specialized Agencies of the UN (Privileges and Immunities) (Amendment) (No. 2) Order 1985, the Minister of State, Foreign and Commonwealth Office, Baroness Young, stated:

The first draft order before your Lordships relates to the World Health Organisation. The order is very specific, conferring only exemptions in respect of social security contributions on officers of WHO who are neither United Kingdom [nationals] nor permanently resident in the United Kingdom. This order would enable effect to be given to an Exchange of Notes between Her Majesty's Government and WHO.

This draft order will have no effect on the Exchequer. WHO currently employs only one staff member in the United Kingdom and he is permanently resident here, and is therefore unaffected by this order. If in future there are in the United Kingdom officers of WHO not contributing to the national insurance scheme, they will, by the same token, be unable to claim from it; so again there will be no effect on the Exchequer. WHO currently enjoys other immunities and privileges under the Specialised Agencies of the United Nations Order 1974.

(Ibid., vol. 463, col. 76: 29 April 1985)

The Minister of State then moved the approval of the draft EUMETSAT (Legal Capacities) Order 1985. She said:

I now turn to the draft order concerning the European Organisation for the Exploitation of Meteorological Satellites (EUMETSAT). Under an international convention of 1983 its objective is to co-ordinate and develop European satellite systems for weather forecasting. The signatories to the convention include most Western European countries, including the United Kingdom.

Article 1 of the EUMETSAT Convention provides that the organisation shall have legal personality, and that it shall in particular have the capacity to acquire and dispose of movable and immovable property and to be a party to legal proceedings. That is the sole purpose of the draft order before your Lordships. It would confer no immunity from jurisdiction on the organisation or its staff.

(Ibid.)

In reply to a question, the Parliamentary Under-Secretary of State, Foreign and Commonwealth Office, wrote:

We have just concluded a review of the Vienna Convention on Diplomatic Relations and reported to Parliament (Cmnd. 9497). Our policy towards international organisations is based on the principle that they should receive only such privileges and immunities as are necessary to enable them to carry out their functions. This principle is elaborated in Resolution (69)29 of the Committee of Ministers of the Council of Europe, a copy of which is available in the Library of the House (in an appendix to Council of Europe Assembly Document No. 2623).

(HC Debs., vol. 81, Written Answers, col. *36*: 17 June 1985)

On 21 October 1985, the Foreign and Commonwealth Office issued the following certificate in respect of the case of *Peter Hannan* v. *Fawcett*. (A certificate in substantially similar terms had been issued on 5 January 1984 in respect of the case of *Tajendrasingh* v. *Fawcett*.)

Under the authority of Her Majesty's Principal Secretary of State for Foreign and Commonwealth Affairs conferred on me in accordance with the provisions of Section 8 of the International Organisations Act 1968, I, Peter Marcus Newton, Head of the Protocol Department of the Foreign and Commonwealth Office, hereby certify that James Edmund Sandford Fawcett was elected as a member of the European Commission of Human Rights on 30 January 1962; he was re-elected as a member in 1966, 1972 and 1978, and he continued to hold that office until 17 May 1984.

(Text provided by the Foreign and Commonwealth Office)

[*Editorial note*: S. 8 of the International Organizations Act 1968 reads:

If in any proceedings a question arises whether a person is or is not entitled to any privilege or immunity by virtue of this Act or any Order in Council made thereunder, a certificate issued by or under the authority of the Secretary of State stating any fact relating to that question shall be conclusive evidence of that fact.]

In moving in the House of Commons the draft European Communities (Definition of Treaties) (North Atlantic Salmon Conservation Organization) Order 1985 and the draft European Communities (Immunities and Privileges of the North Atlantic Salmon Conservation Organization) Order 1985, the Minister of State, Foreign and Commonwealth Office, Mr Malcolm Rifkind, stated in part:

The North Atlantic Salmon Conservation Organisation—known as NASCO—was established by the convention for the conservation of salmon in the north Atlantic ocean. This convention was opened for signature at Reykjavik on 2 March 1982. NASCO's principal objective is to contribute to the conservation, restoration and rational management of salmon stocks in the north Atlantic, with the aid of the best available scientific information.

The establishment of the organisation was welcomed by the Government as a significant development in the management of salmon stocks in the high seas, thus having a beneficial effect on salmon stocks in our rivers. We have a strong interest in restricting as far as possible catches of salmon originating from our rivers, but caught in the waters of the Faroe Islands and Greenland where they feed—the intercepting fisheries. We hope, therefore, that the convention, through NASCO, will enable these fisheries to be carefully managed and preserved.

. . .

The convention entered into force on 1 October 1983. The European Economic Community is a party to the convention and a member of the organisation, together with Canada, Denmark—in respect of Greenland and the Faroe Islands—Finland, Iceland, Norway, Sweden and the United States. The headquarters agreement with the organisation, which implements article 3 of the convention, was signed on 26 April at its new offices in Rutland Square, Edinburgh. It will enter into force when the necessary legislation is in place—in other words, once the two draft orders now under consideration have been made.

As the EC is a party to the convention, it is a Community treaty for the purposes of the European Communities Act 1972. It is proposed that the first draft order before the House—that relating to definition of treaties—should be made under section 1(3) of the 1972 Act specifying the headquarters agreement as a Community treaty. This order provides the basis for the second order—that relating to the immunities and privileges of NASCO provided by the headquarters agreement, which will be made under section 2(2) of the European Communities Act. The headquarters agreement implements article 3 of the convention by specifying the privileges and immunities that NASCO is to enjoy in the United Kingdom. This agreement is similar to other headquarters agreements entered into by the United Kingdom with international organisations having their headquarters here—for example, the International Tin Council, the international lead and zinc study group and the Commonwealth Foundation.

Certain principal privileges and immunities will be conferred. NASCO will be provided with legal capacity, inviolability of archives, exemptions from taxes on income and capital gains, the same rating relief as is accorded to a diplomatic mission, relief from car tax and VAT and exemption from import duties.

The representatives of parties will be provided with immunity from suit and legal process in respect of their official acts and inviolability for official papers and documents.

Staff members of NASCO will be provided with immunity from suit and legal process in respect of their official acts, exemption from income tax, 'first arrival' customs privileges and exemption from social security legislation.

Those privileges and immunities are conferred on a strict basis of functional necessity. The House will note that nobody is given the full immunity from jurisdiction of a diplomatic agent.

The House will wish to know that NASCO currently employs only two staff members and both are permanently resident in the United Kingdom.

(HC Debs., vol. 84, cols. 743–4: 28 October 1985; see also HL Debs., vol. 467, cols. 1571–81 *passim*: 30 October 1985)

Later in the debate, the same Minister observed:

The hon. Member . . . asked a crucial question about whether the two employees of NASCO would be immune from parking fines as a result of the immunities and privileges provided under the order. Although I suppose that the two gentlemen in question will be less happy to hear it, I am happy to assure him that they will not be so immune. As I said in my opening remarks, they are receiving not the privileges available to diplomatic agents but simply those which are essential to the carrying out of their proper responsibilities.

(HC Debs., vol. 84, col. 776: 28 October 1985)

In reply to a question on the subject of the possible liability of the International Tin Council for default in its obligations, the Government spokesman in the House of Lords, Lord Brabazon of Tara, stated in part:

Regarding the International Organisations Act, our view is that the tin council is liable on any arbitration award made against it under the arbitration clause which is found in the council's London Metal Exchange tin contracts, and there is no immunity in such a case. This is provided for in a headquarters agreement between Her Majesty's Government and the council which is implemented by an order under the 1968 Act. It is a complicated legal position and we are studying it most carefully.

(HL Debs., vol. 468, col. 140: 12 November 1985)

Part Three: II. A. 2. (b). *Subjects of international law—international organizations—in general—participation of States in international organizations—suspension, withdrawal and expulsion*

In a letter dated 5 December 1984 addressed to the Director-General of UNESCO, the Secretary of State for Foreign and Commonwealth Affairs, Sir Geoffrey Howe, referred to various reforms which the UK Government wished to see implemented by the organization. He continued:

Following our assessment, we concluded that it would be right to safeguard our position should our hopes for reform be disappointed at the 23rd Session of the General Conference. I am accordingly writing to inform you that the British Government has decided to submit notice of withdrawal from UNESCO. Unless rescinded, this notice will become effective on 31 December 1985. This letter constitutes formal notification thereof in accordance with Article 11.6 of the Constitution.

In submitting this formal notice of withdrawal I wish to emphasise that we shall continue to work positively and vigorously with other Member States and within the Governing Bodies for the programme of essential reforms I have indicated above. A further review of British policy will be held after the 23rd Session of the General Conference. The views of the UK National Commission for UNESCO will be sought at that stage. If we were satisfied that substantial progress had by then been made in carrying through the reform programme we have set out, we would be willing to reconsider our decision to withdraw by the end of 1985.

(Text provided by the Foreign and Commonwealth Office)

In a statement in Parliament, the Minister for Overseas Development, Foreign and Commonwealth Office, Mr Timothy Raison, stated in respect of the UK's relationship with UNESCO:

The Government have . . . decided that the notice to leave given by . . . the Foreign and Commonwealth Secretary in his letter of 5 December 1984 to the Director-General will not be withdrawn. The UK will cease to be a member from 31 December 1985.

(HC Debs., vol. 88, col. 448: 5 December 1985)

Part Three: II. A. 3. *Subjects of international law—international organizations—in general—legal effect of acts of international organizations*

In reply to a question, the Minister of State, Foreign and Commonwealth Office, wrote:

The United Kingdom does not obtain its arms and military equipment of the type covered by Security Council resolution 558 from South Africa. We supported the adoption of SCR 558 and expect other UN member states to consider carefully its provisions, but it is a non-mandatory resolution.

(Ibid., vol. 71, Written Answers, col. *87*: 15 January 1985)

Part Three: II. B. 1. *Subjects of international law—international organizations—particular types of organizations—universal organizations*

On 22 July 1985, the Foreign Affairs Committee of the House of Commons, in examining witnesses on the subject of the UK's intention to withdraw from UNESCO at the end of December 1985, put the following question to Mr H. J. Arbuthnott, Under-Secretary, International Organizations Division, Overseas Development Administration, Foreign and Commonwealth Office:

What priority does the Foreign and Commonwealth Office give to the principle of universality of the United Nations family, particularly as we are founder members of the whole concept of the United Nations?

In reply, Mr Arbuthnott stated:

We give considerable importance to the principle of universality, but our interpretation of it [is] different to that of some. Our interpretation of universality . . . is that everybody has the *right*, not the obligation, to join the United Nations and its bodies. Universality, in other words, applies to the right to join, and we uphold that right absolutely.

(*Parliamentary Papers*, 1984–5, HC, Paper 461, p. 123)

In reply to a question, the Parliamentary Under-Secretary of State, Foreign and Commonwealth Office, wrote:

The United Kingdom is currently a member of the following United Nations intergovernmental agencies.

FAO, Food and Agriculture Organisation
GATT, General Agreement on Tariffs and Trade

ITC, International Trade Centre
IAEA, International Atomic Energy Agency
ICAO, International Civil Aviation Organisation
IFAD, International Fund for Agricultural Development
ILO, International Labour Organisation
IMO, International Maritime Organisation
IMF, International Monetary Fund
ITU, International Telecommunication Union
UNESCO, United Nations Educational Scientific and Cultural Organisation
UNIDO, United Nations Industrial Development Organisation
UPOV, International Union for the Protection of New Varieties of Plants
UPU, Universal Postal Union
WHO, World Health Organisation
WIPO, World Intellectual Property Organisation
WMO, World Meteorological Organisation

We participate actively in the policy making of all United Nations agencies and seek, where necessary, to improve the management of their programmes. Our continued membership is dependent on a conviction that the programmes are soundly based and offer good value for money. In the case of UNESCO this is no longer so and the United Kingdom's membership will cease from 31 December 1985.

(HC Debs., vol. 89, Written Answers, col. *813*: 13 December 1985)

Part Three: II. B. 3. *Subjects of international law—international organizations—particular types of organizations—organizations constituting integrated communities*

(See also Part One: II. D. (House of Lords Select Committee on the European Communities), above)

Opening the debate in the House of Lords on the second reading of the European Communities (Spanish and Portuguese Accession) Bill, the Minister of State, Foreign and Commonwealth Office, Baroness Young, stated:

It gives me particular pleasure to introduce a Bill giving legal force in the United Kingdom to the instruments of accession of Spain and Portugal to the European Communities. The strict legal purpose of the Bill is to ensure that, once Spain and Portugal accede to the Community on 1st January 1986, the United Kingdom is able to honour in full the obligations undertaken in the Treaty of Accession between the applicant countries and the Communities. The Bill achieves this by amending the European Communities Act 1972 to provide that the Spanish and Portuguese treaties of accession to the EC, Euratom and the European Coal and Steel Community are included among the basic Community treaties referred to in Section 1 of the European Communities Act 1972.

(HL Debs., vol. 468, col. 497: 19 November 1985)

Part Three: III. D. *Subjects of international law—subjects of international law other than States and organizations—mandated and trust territories, Namibia*

(See also Part III: I. E. (speeches of 11 October and 27 November 1985), above)

In reply to the question whether the UN Institute for Namibia is recognized by the Government as a legal agency of the UN, the Minister of State, Foreign and Commonwealth Office, wrote:

The United Nations Institute for Namibia (UNIN) was established by the United Nations Council for Namibia with the agreement of the United Nations General Assembly. Although we do not recognise the Council's claim to be the administering authority of Namibia we accept that in other respects it is a subsidiary organ of the United Nations General Assembly. We regard its establishment of UNIN as proper. We have supported UNIN's work as benefiting a future independent Namibia.

(HC Debs., vol. 71, Written Answers, col. *41*: 14 January 1985)

In reply to the question why Her Majesty's Government refuse to grant development aid to Namibia until after the implementation of Security Council Resolution 435, the Minister of State, Foreign and Commonwealth Office, wrote:

Because to do so would imply recognition of South Africa's occupation of the territory which we regard as unlawful . . .

(Ibid., vol. 76, Written Answers, col. *281*: 28 March 1985)

In reply to the question whether Her Majesty's Government will review its policy of not accepting the advisory opinion of the International Court of Justice on the subject of Namibia, the Minister of State, Foreign and Commonwealth Office, wrote:

No. There are legal difficulties—which have been acknowledged by successive Governments—in accepting the International Court of Justice's advisory opinion of 1971. I do not believe that further examination would resolve these.

(Ibid., vol. 79, Written Answers, col. *459*: 22 May 1985)

In reply to a question, the Minister of State, Foreign and Commonwealth Office, wrote:

The South African Government announced on 18th April their decision to establish an interim internal administration in Namibia. As we made clear to the South African Government at the time, we shall not recognise the new administration. We remain committed to the United Nations plan, which is the only internationally acceptable basis for Namibian independence.

(HL Debs., vol. 464, col. 1122: 10 June 1985; see also ibid., cols. 1356–8: 13 June 1985, HC Debs., vol. 80, Written Answers, col. *555*: 14 June 1985, and ibid., vol. 81, cols. 906–8: 26 June 1985)

In the course of a speech to the Security Council on 14 June 1985, the UK representative, Mr P. Maxey, stated:

Security Council resolution 435 (1978) is central to the process of achieving self-determination for Namibia, and to this debate. It is our responsibility to ensure that nothing is done by the Council to undermine its own achievement in adopting resolution 435 (1978).

It was above all for this reason that my Government, like other contact-group Governments which first sponsored the United Nations settlement proposal, expressed deep concern in April when the South African Government was considering the proposal made by some of the Namibian internal parties for a transitional government. We told the South African Government that we would regard any unilateral measures taken by South Africa in relation to the establishment of constitutional bodies and to the transfer of power in Namibia as null and void. We said that any arrangements that could be established as a result of such measures would have no status whatsoever under the United Nations settlement plan. We made clear that the South African Government's responsibility to bring about the implementation of the United Nations plan could not be delegated to any Namibian party.

For the same reason, the United Kingdom gave its full support to the statement made by the President of the Security Council on 3 May in which he reiterated that the members of the Council rejected any unilateral action leading towards an internal settlement as unacceptable.

(S/PV. 2590, pp. 41–2)

In the course of a debate in the House of Lords on the UN (Namibia) Bill, the Minister of State, Foreign and Commonwealth Office, Baroness Young, referred to the administration in Namibia and continued:

Let me say here that our attitude to the current interim administration is that we do not recognise it. We will not hold discussions with the new administration in its official capacity. This does not affect the negotiations towards Security Council Resolution 435. Indeed, the previous internal arrangements in 1978 and 1981 did not last and already there are signs of disagreement within the MPC on key constitutional issues. In our view, the establishment of the multi-party conference interim administration in Windhoek by the South African Government earlier this year in no way alters their responsibility to implement the United Nations plan and to bring Namibia into internationally recognised independence. We shall continue to press home this inescapable fact.

(HL Debs., vol. 467, col. 1056: 22 October 1985)

Later in her speech, the Minister stated:

The Bill does not restrict itself purely to the question of economic measures. Paragraph 4 permits the enactment of, 'such provisions as appear . . . necessary or expedient for enabling the United Nations Council for Namibia Decree No. 1 for the protection of the natural resources of Namibia to be effectively applied'. These provisions would have the effect of recognising that the United Nations Council for Namibia has exclusive rights over the management and exploitation of Namibia's natural resources.

In establishing a body with the powers that it purported to confer on the Council for Namibia, we consider that the General Assembly acted beyond its competence under the United Nations charter. Consequently, the United Kingdom does not recognise the claim of the council to administer the territory. Successive United Kingdom Governments have therefore taken the view that pronouncements of the council, such as Decree No. 1, do not impose any obligations upon us. Indeed, there are no mandatory United Nations measures at all which prohibit trade with Namibia. In no way therefore does the Government's position conflict with our international obligations. Thus, the Government see no reason to interfere with trade or investment in Namibia.

(HL Debs., vol. 467, col. 1058: 22 October 1985)

In the course of a statement in explanation of vote in the General Assembly on 2 December 1985, the Permanent Representative of the UK to the UN, Sir John Thomson, stated:

The Resolution does indeed have a good deal to say about the situation in Namibia. It is right that it should do so since with the exception of Namibia, the process of decolonisation is close to an end. No-one is more concerned than we to see the peaceful transition of Namibia to independence. We are staunch upholders of the principle of self-determination in Namibia as elsewhere. Nevertheless Namibia is sui generis. It is in effect a ward of the United Nations and is in a different legal position from all other territories. Accordingly the special provisions that apply to Namibia should be taken for what they are, namely special arrangements to apply to a unique and particular set of circumstances; they do not apply elsewhere.

(Text provided by the Foreign and Commonwealth Office; see also A/40/PV. 99, p. 103)

In reply to a question, the Minister of State, Foreign and Commonwealth Office, wrote in part:

We do not recognise the so-called 'Transitional Government of National Unity' in Namibia.

(HC Debs., vol. 88, Written Answers, col. *384*: 6 December 1985)

Part Four: I. *The individual (including the corporation) in international law—nationality*

In a speech to the American Bar Association in Atlanta in 1983, the Attorney-General, Sir Michael Havers, made the following statement:

Nationality is of course a basis long recognized in academic writings for the assertion of jurisdiction, at least to the extent that this does not conflict with territorial jurisdiction. But the extent to which it is justifiable to rely on a formal link of nationality is also now controversial.

. . .

The assertion that a state is entitled to prescribe rules of conduct for its own nationals wherever they are resident, and to seek to apply them so long as there is no conflict with a directly opposite mandatory command in the law of the territorial state, goes too far. What I mean by this is perhaps best shown by two illustrations. The first arises from the Foreign Boycott Regulations. The second concerns recent problems over supplying equipment for the Siberian pipeline.

The Foreign Boycott Regulations were made in pursuance of the policy of the United States to oppose restrictions or boycotts aimed at U.S. persons or friendly countries. I would not in any way challenge the right of the USA to seek that objective, even though Britain's dependence on world trade leads us not to pursue such a positive policy. It is the reach of the U.S. measures into Britain and their denial of a place for British policy in certain cases in Britain itself which we cannot accept and which I strongly suspect in a hypothetical reciprocal case no United States administration would accept.

The reason for this strong reaction lies in the purported application of the foreign Boycott Regulations to a wide range of persons outside the USA who are not United States nationals. These extend from foreign subsidiaries, affiliates and so on of U.S. companies to any permanent foreign establishment which is, in the terms of the Regulations, 'controlled in fact' by a U.S. domestic concern. The test of such control, put in general terms, is 25% beneficial ownership where no one else controls a larger share. The Foreign Boycott Regulations are in this regard an example of what is found in other U.S. regulatory measures.

We find this objectionable for a reason of principle, which I shall amplify in a moment—that the nationality of a company is that of its place of incorporation.

. . .

The objection on principle to the extent claimed by the USA for the reach of nationality jurisdiction in the case of subsidiaries follows from the particular nationality of the companies concerned.

We would regard companies incorporated in the United Kingdom as having British nationality even if they are entirely foreign owned. A company is a legal entity that owes its personality to a particular system of law and its nationality is that of the state which has established that system of law. We believe that it is generally accepted internationally, and supported in effect by the International Court of Justice, that the general test of the nationality of a corporation is not the 'control' test, but that which follows the traditional rule attributing the right of diplomatic protection to the state under the laws of which the company is incorporated and in whose territory it has its registered office. There are indications in the *Sumitomo* case that the Supreme Court also favors the test of place of incorporation.

My second illustration of the problems in this area is the difficulty last year over the Siberian pipeline. Under the U.S. regulations promulgated by the President, foreign subsidiaries of U.S. companies were forbidden to execute existing contracts for the Siberian pipeline project. This would mean that such a company incorporated or registered in the United Kingdom and doing business there, employing a British workforce and manufacturing equipment of British design and using British materials would have been prohibited by United States regulations from carrying out existing contracts. Even without taking account of the background of high unemployment in the United Kingdom and any policy factors arising from British membership of the European Community, there were clear grounds here for questioning whether the U.S. claim to jurisdiction could be properly founded on the basis of nationality.

(The full text of the speech is reproduced in *International Lawyer*, 17 (1983), pp. 784–95. The above extract is taken from pp. 790–2)

In reply to the question why the new category of British nationality (overseas) is proposed for Hong Kong instead of the existing category of British overseas citizenship, the Minister of State, Foreign and Commonwealth Office, wrote:

We believe that the circumstances of Hong Kong are unique and should be reflected in a unique status. There are also reasons why British overseas citizenship would not be an 'appropriate status' within the terms of the United Kingdom memorandum. For example, British overseas citizenship may be acquired at any time by registration, but the United Kingdom memorandum imposes time limits on the acquisition of the new status.

The benefits to be accorded to holders of the proposed new status of 'British National (Overseas)' are still under detailed consideration and will be subject to parliamentary approval. The Government intend, however, that they should be broadly the same as those enjoyed by British dependent territories citizens, except for transmissibility. This means that there are unlikely to be major differences under United Kingdom law in the benefits enjoyed by holders of the proposed British national (overseas) status and the existing British overseas citizenship.

(HC Debs., vol. 71, Written Answers, cols. *550–1*: 25 January 1985)

In the course of a debate on the Third Reading of the Hong Kong Bill, the Minister of State, Foreign and Commonwealth Office, Mr Richard Luce, stated:

The purpose of amendment No. 2 is to incorporate in the Bill the title of the proposed new form of nationality. As my right hon. and learned Friend the Foreign Secretary announced on Second Reading, this will be, as we all now know, 'British National (Overseas)'.

. . .

It was not easy to devise a title that meets all the necessary requirements. On the one hand, it needs to make clear that we are dealing with a form of British nationality. That was the strongest desire of the people of Hong Kong. On the other hand, it is essential that the title can be used after 1997, and, therefore, that it carries no implication of a continuing constitutional relationship between Britain and Hong Kong after 1997. The title 'British National (Overseas)' meets both those criteria.

The benefits of the new status will be set out in the Order in Council and will be subject to parliamentary approval, but the Government's intention is that the new form of nationality will carry broadly the same benefits as British dependent territory citizen except that it will not be transmissible by descent. Holders of the new status will be able to use British passports. They will be eligible for British consular protection in third countries. They will have a right to registration as British citizens under section 4 of the British Nationality Act 1981 on the same terms as the British dependent territory citizen.

(Ibid., vol. 72, cols. 1065–6: 6 February 1985; see also HL Debs., vol. 460, cols. 481–6 and 505–6: 19 February 1985)

In reply to the question what advice Her Majesty's Government is giving British citizens affected by the Citizenship of Zimbabwe Act 1984, the Minister of State, Foreign and Commonwealth Office, wrote in part:

They are being advised that the Zimbabwean legislation abolishes dual citizenship with effect from 1st December 1985. Similar restrictions on the possession of another nationality are contained in the laws of many countries, including a number in the Commonwealth. It is for each individual who holds both British and Zimbabwean citizenship to decide what course to adopt.

I understand that, under Zimbabwean law and regulations, dual citizens who wish to opt for mono-Zimbabwean citizenship must sign a declaration to that effect in the Zimbabwean Registrar General's Department. If they have a British passport, they are obliged to submit it to the Zimbabwean authorities, who will subsequently return it to the British High Commission. Dual British-Zimbabwean citizens who do not take this action will, in Zimbabwean law, become mono-British citizens on 1st December 1985.

Under the British Nationality Act 1981, British citizenship can be lost only by those who voluntarily renounce it and whose declaration of renunciation is registered at the Home Office in accordance with the British Nationality Act 1981. A person who renounces British citizenship in order to retain or acquire some other citizenship or nationality is entitled to reacquire it by registration, but this provision may be taken advantage of only once.

(HL Debs., vol. 464, col. 740: 4 June 1985)

Part Four: V. *The individual (including the corporation) in international law—statelessness, refugees*

In reply to a question, the Parliamentary Under-Secretary of State, Foreign and Commonwealth Office, wrote:

Our policy on Vietnamese refugees in Hong Kong is kept under constant review. In the case of Vietnamese refugees the relevant legislation is the Hong Kong Immigration Ordinance, which contains a special provision under which Vietnamese refugees may be allowed to remain in Hong Kong pending their resettlement elsewhere. Under the terms of the agreement on the future of Hong Kong the ordinance, unless amended, or unless it conflicts with the basic law, will remain in force after 30 June 1997. The Agreement also provides that the International Covenant on Civil and Political Rights and the International Covenant on Economic, Social and Cultural Rights as applied to Hong Kong shall remain in force.

(HC Debs., vol. 71, Written Answers, cols. *211–12*: 17 January 1985)

In the course of the debate on the Third Reading in the House of Commons of the Hong Kong Bill, the Minister of State, Foreign and Commonwealth Office, Mr Richard Luce, stated:

It is our intention that no former Hong Kong BDTC [British Dependent Territories Citizen], nor any child born on or after 1 July 1997 to such a person, should be made stateless as a result of the arrangements envisaged in the Bill. All former Hong Kong BDTCs will be able to acquire BN(O) [British National (Overseas)] status if they wish before 1 July 1997. If they do this, they will retain that status for the rest of their lives. Any BDTCs who do not acquire BN(O) status and would otherwise be stateless—for example, if they are not Chinese nationals and hold no other nationality—will become British overseas citizens on 1 July

1997. The children born on or after 1 July 1997 to former Hong Kong BDTCs who are Chinese nationals will, of course, have Chinese nationality. Children born to non-Chinese former BDTCs will acquire British overseas citizen status at birth if they would otherwise be stateless.

. . .

The proposal that children born after 30 June 1997 to non-Chinese former BDTCs should acquire BOC [British Overseas Citizen] status automatically at birth if they would otherwise be stateless is intended to apply to the first post-1997 generation. However, we appreciate that there may be concern about potential statelessness arising among subsequent generations of non-Chinese Hong Kongers. It would not be appropriate as a general principle to grant British nationality indefinitely and without restrictions to the descendants of British nationals. However, problems of further generations and potential statelessness—and we are looking here into the next century—are being urgently examined in response to representations made by the non-Chinese community in Hong Kong. In this category we include some 5,000 Indian citizens.

(HC Debs., vol. 72, col. 1069: 6 February 1985; see also HL Debs., vol. 460, cols. 485 and 505–6: 19 February 1985)

In the course of a debate on the subject of refugees in the Third World, the Parliamentary Under-Secretary of State for the Armed Forces, Lord Trefgarne, stated:

The noble Viscount, Lord Buckmaster, asked whether the Government could adopt a more flexible approach on the granting of political asylum to refugees from the third world. The 1951 Convention on Refugees defines a refugee as a person outside his home country who is unable or unwilling to return there because of a well-founded fear of persecution for reasons of race, religion, nationality, membership of a particular social group or political opinion. We not only comply scrupulously with the obligations under the convention and protocol, but already in fact go beyond the obligations under it. A person who is not considered to be a refugee under the convention may still be allowed to remain here exceptionally because of the particular circumstances of his case or in the light of the situation prevailing in his home country.

Indeed, the situation in some countries has caused us to establish several exceptional policies for certain nationals. In recent years the countries concerned have included Afghanistan, Iran, Lebanon, Poland and Uganda. Under these policies less stringent tests than the criteria for refugees are applied in deciding whether a person should be allowed to remain here exceptionally, normally for 12 months in the first instance. Extensions are normally granted if there have been no material changes of circumstances.

He later remarked:

The noble Lord, Lord Chitnis, asked me too about the application of the 1951 convention to Hong Kong. I can tell the noble Lord that it was decided not to extend the convention to Hong Kong because of the territory's small size and geographical vulnerability to mass, illegal immigration. The 1967 protocol was applied only to those territories to which the 1951 convention was extended. The Hong Kong Government nevertheless co-operates fully with the office of the

UNHCR, and Hong Kong has, as I am sure he will agree, made a major contribution to the international effort to assist Indo-Chinese refugees.

(HL Debs., vol. 460, cols. 966 and 968: 27 February 1985)

In reply to a question on the subject of Tamils leaving Sri Lanka to come to the UK, the Government spokesman in the House of Lords, Lord Glenarthur, stated:

. . . as I understand it they are not refugees within the terms of the [1951 Convention relating to the Status of Refugees]. Furthermore, the United Nations High Commissioner for Refugees accepts that. So the notification requirements of the convention do not apparently apply in this case.

(Ibid., vol. 464, col. 535: 3 June 1985; see also ibid., vol. 465, cols. 540–1: 21 June 1985)

Part Four: VI. *The individual (including the corporation) in international law—immigration and emigration, extradition, expulsion and asylum*

In the course of a debate on the subject of international fraud, the Parliamentary Under-Secretary of State, Home Office, Mr David Mellor, stated in part:

It is true that our older extradition treaties are framed in terms that implicitly acknowledge only offences that are committed within the territorial boundaries of countries that are party to the agreements. Our more recent treaties, however, are framed in terms of the respective jurisdiction of the judicial authorities of the parties. As I have endeavoured to explain, the concept of extraterritorial jurisdiction causes difficulties in our law, but our general lack of such jurisdiction does not inevitably make for an enforcement loophole, because in this country we have no objection to extraditing our own nationals, provided that the normal extradition arrangements are met. For the most part, our extradition arrangements are based on bilateral treaties that set out in detail the conditions governing surrender to and from the United Kingdom. At present, there are 43 bilateral treaties in force.

(HC Debs., vol. 73, col. 318: 12 February 1985)

In February 1985, the Secretary of State for the Home Department presented to Parliament a consultative paper on the subject of possible future proposals to change the law relating to extradition. Attached to the paper was the following Annex A:

THE EXISTING LAW

THE EXTRADITION ACT 1870

1. The principal domestic legislation which governs United Kingdom extradition arrangements is the Extradition Act 1870. The Act provides the only basis on which fugitive criminals may lawfully be detained and surrendered to foreign countries. It sets out the conditions on which, and the crimes for which, extradition from the United Kingdom may be granted; and it lays down the procedure

for dealing with applications for extradition made by foreign countries. The Act is applied by Order in Council to each foreign state with which an extradition arrangement has been made, and the text of the arrangement must be incorporated in the Order in Council. The terms of the arrangement must be consistent with the requirements of the Act, but within these limits there may be minor variations in individual arrangements. The Act provides that an arrangement may include safeguards for the fugitive which go beyond those contained in the Act, but it must not derogate from the safeguards laid down in the Act.

2. The Act contains a number of general restrictions and safeguards. First, it stipulates that a fugitive may be surrendered only for an extradition crime; that is, conduct which amounts to one of the crimes listed in the schedule to the Act and which would be an offence against English law if committed in this country. In addition, a fugitive may not be surrendered for a political offence, or if he proves to the satisfaction of the courts or of the Secretary of State that his return has in fact been requested in order to try or punish him for an offence of a political character. In the case of an accused person the application must be supported by evidence which would justify committal for trial if the crime had been committed in this country (the *prima facie* case requirement). In addition, under the speciality rule, a person who has been extradited may not be detained or tried in the country to which he is returned for any offence other than the crime for which he has been returned.

3. Since extradition is concerned with the removal of a fugitive criminal from one Sovereign territory to another, it involves in substance a transaction between governments. Hence there is a role for the Executive as well as for the Judiciary. In the United Kingdom, extradition hearings take place in London at Bow Street Magistrates' Court. The Metropolitan Stipendiary Magistrate (who will generally hear the case) may proceed to hear the case only if the Home Secretary issues an order requiring him to do so. If the magistrate, having heard the case, commits the fugitive to await his surrender, then subject to his right to apply to the High Court for habeas corpus, it falls to the Home Secretary to decide whether to issue the warrant for surrender. In addition the Home Secretary may at any time order the fugitive to be discharged if he is of the opinion that the alleged offence is political, or that extradition has been sought with a view to trying or punishing the fugitive for an offence of a political character. In this respect the functions of the Home Secretary and the courts overlap; both are required to consider the question whether the offence is political.

4. The Act also forms the basis for extradition arrangements between United Kingdom dependent territories and foreign countries.

The Basis of our Extradition Arrangements

(i) *Bilateral treaties*

5. For the most part, our extradition arrangements with foreign states are based on bilateral treaties which set out in detail the conditions governing surrender to and from the United Kingdom. Reliance on bilateral treaties has enabled the United Kingdom to ensure that extradition arrangements are concluded only with those states whose standards of justice and penal administration we find acceptable. Treaties also afford a degree of flexibility, since they permit the incorporation of additional safeguards for the fugitive without the need for amending legislation.

6. There are at present 43 bilateral treaties in force between the United Kingdom and foreign countries.* But we have regular extradition traffic with only about a dozen of these.

(ii) *European Convention on Extradition*

7. The United Kingdom has not signed the European Convention on Extradition, which was concluded in 1957, although we played an active part in its negotiation and in the elaboration of the two additional protocols. The main obstacle to accession has been the difficulty of reconciling our own criminal law procedures with those of Continental countries.

(iii) *International conventions as bases for extradition*

8. Over the past 14 years the United Kingdom has ratified or is now in a position to ratify a number of international conventions which deal with various types of serious crime.† In order to give effect to these conventions the Extradition Act has been applied, in suitably amended form, not only to foreign contracting states which have bilateral extradition arrangements with the United Kingdom but also those which do not. In the legislation which applies the Extradition Act to these arrangements in relation to such states, it has been the practice to incorporate certain safeguards which go beyond those contained in our bilateral treaties. These additional safeguards include a requirement along the lines of section 4(1) of the Fugitive Offenders Act 1967 that a person shall not be returned if his extradition is sought for the purpose of punishing him on account of his political opinions or if he might be prejudiced at his trial or punished, detained or restricted in his personal liberty by reason of his political opinions.

Arrangements within the Commonwealth

9. Extradition from the United Kingdom to other Commonwealth countries and United Kingdom dependencies is governed by the Fugitive Offenders Act 1967. This Act is based on the 1966 Scheme for the Rendition of Fugitive Offenders within the Commonwealth. The Commonwealth Scheme was reviewed in 1982 and some minor changes were agreed by Commonwealth Law Ministers meeting at Colombo in February 1983. If legislation is introduced to amend the Extradition Act, the opportunity could be taken to implement the changes recently agreed to the Commonwealth Scheme.

Arrangements with the Republic of Ireland

10. There is a simplified procedure for the return of offenders between the United Kingdom and the Republic of Ireland based on endorsed warrants of arrest. Return from the United Kingdom is governed by the Backing of Warrants (Republic of Ireland) Act 1965, and from the Republic by the largely reciprocal provisions of its own Extradition Act 1965. These Acts provide for the return of

* Albania, Argentina, Austria, Belgium, Bolivia, Chile, Colombia, Cuba, Czechoslovakia, Denmark, Ecuador, Finland, France, Federal Republic of Germany, Greece, Guatemala, Haiti, Hungary, Iceland, Iraq, Israel, Italy, Liberia, Luxembourg, Mexico, Monaco, Netherlands, Nicaragua, Norway, Panama, Paraguay, Peru, Poland, Portugal, Romania, El Salvador, San Marino, Sweden, Switzerland, Thailand, USA, Uruguay and Yugoslavia.

† These include the Convention for the Suppression of the Unlawful Seizure of Aircraft (1970), the Convention for the Suppression of Unlawful Acts against the Safety of Civil Aviation (1971), the Convention on the Prevention and Punishment of Crimes against Internationally Protected Persons, including Diplomatic Agents (1973), the International Convention against the Taking of Hostages (1979) and the Convention on the Physical Protection of Nuclear Material (1980).

persons accused or convicted of indictable offences, or of offences punishable on summary conviction with 6 months' imprisonment, for which there is a corresponding offence under the law of the requested country. There is a safeguard against the return of political offenders, but the simplified procedure omits certain important features of the Extradition Act 1870 and the Fugitive Offenders Act 1967, for example the need to establish a *prima facie* case against an accused person. This comparatively simple and expeditious procedure is justified by the special circumstances of the two countries, in particular the similarity of our systems of law, geographical proximity, ease of communication and lack of immigration controls.

(Cmnd. 9421, pp. 18–20)

In reply to a question, the Secretary of State for the Home Department wrote:

Agreement has been reached with the United States Government on a supplementary treaty to the United Kingdom/United States extradition treaty for which, in due course, the United States Senate's advice and consent to ratification will be sought and an order under the Suppression of Terrorism Act laid before Parliament for approval. The effect of the supplementary treaty would be to deny fugitives accused or convicted of certain serious offences of violence the ability to avoid extradition on the grounds that their offences were political. Both Governments believe that the present political offence exception to extradition, as it applies to violent offences, is not suitable to extradition arrangements between two democratic countries sharing the same high regard for the fundamental principles of justice and operating similar independent judicial systems. The supplementary treaty would represent a most significant contribution to the efforts now being made by Western democracies to counter the threat posed by international terrorism. It is also intended to make some further, minor amendments to the present treaty.

(HC Debs., vol. 81, Written Answers, cols. *285–6*: 24 June 1985)

Part Four: VII. *The individual (including the corporation) in international law—protection of human rights and fundamental freedoms*

(See also Part One: II. D., above)

In the course of a debate in the House of Lords on the subject of the Helsinki Agreement, the Minister of State, Baroness Young, stated:

. . . the fact is that we all agreed at Helsinki that, however different our systems of government, we would respect the human rights and fundamental freedoms set out in Principle VII. That is the commitment we all made.

(HL Debs., vol. 462, col. 215: 2 April 1985)

During the committee stage of the debate in the House of Commons on the subject of the Interception of Communications Bill, the Minister of State, Home Department, Mr David Waddington, observed:

. . . there is nothing in the Bill that restricts the right to go to the Strasbourg Commission and Court in connection with breaches of the European Convention.

(HC Debs., vol. 76, col. 1267: 3 April 1985)

In reply to a question, the Parliamentary Under-Secretary of State, Foreign and Commonwealth Office, wrote:

A member state is not officially notified when an individual application is made against it to the European Commission of Human Rights. Such information becomes available only when the Commission communicates the case to the Government. At the end of 1984 a total of 132 cases against the United Kingdom were before the Commission. The subject matter of these was:

	Number
Prisoners' complaints on conditions	18
Prisoners' access to correspondence	4
Prisoners' letters censorship	27
Nationalisation compensation	2
Deportation orders	6
Refused entry to United Kingdom	11
Leasehold reform	2
Mental health detainees	6
Wardship cases	5
Corporal punishment	8
Freedom of expression	2
Unlawful detention	3
Immigrants rule	25
Video piracy	1
Trade union disputes	3
Sex change	3
Injury compensation	1
Criminal injury in Northern Ireland	1
Contempt of Court	1
Compulsory purchase order	1
Aircraft noise	1
Legal aid	1
Total	132

(Ibid., vol. 78, Written Answers, cols. *226–7*: 2 May 1985)

In reply to a question, the Parliamentary Under-Secretary of State, Foreign and Commonwealth Office, wrote:

For the period since 1966, when the United Kingdom recognised the competence of the Commission to receive individual petition and the compulsory jurisdiction of the court, up to the end of June 1985 there have been 20 cases referred to the European Court of Human Rights against the United Kingdom. There were 12 findings of violation, two findings of non-violation and six cases are pending. The figures for other member states of the Council of Europe are as follows:

	Accepted right of individual petition since:	Accepted right of individual petition and compulsory jurisdiction of Court since:	Accepted compulsory jurisdiction of Court since:	No. of cases referred:	Violations	Non-Violations	Pending	Terminated in some other way
United Kingdom	—	14 January 1966	—	20	12	2	6	0
Austria	—	3 September 1958	—	10	5	2	3	0
Belgium	—	5 July 1955	—	14	9	3	0	2
Denmark	—	13 April 1953	—	2	0	2	0	0
France	2 October 1981	—	3 May 1974	1	0	0	1	0
Federal Republic of Germany	—	5 July 1955	—	13	6	4	3	0
Ireland	—	25 November 1953	—	3	1	1	1	0
Italy	—	1 August 1973	—	9	7	1	0	1
Netherlands	28 June 1960	—	31 August 1954	9	6	0	3	0
Portugal	—	9 November 1978	—	1	1	0	0	0
Sweden	4 November 1952	—	15 June 1966	5	2	2	0	1
Switzerland	—	28 November 1974	—	5	2	2	1	0

(HC Debs., vol. 82, Written Answers, cols. *395–8*: 9 July 1985)

In reply to a question, the Parliamentary Under-Secretary of State, Foreign and Commonwealth Office, wrote in part:

We take every opportunity to make clear our grave concern over the gross violations of human rights in Afghanistan, a situation clearly documented by the United Nations Special Rapporteur. That situation continues to deteriorate, with the evident Soviet determination to deploy massive forces without thought for the suffering of the local population.

(Ibid., vol. 83, Written Answers, col. *582*: 24 July 1985)

In reply to a question asking for details of the judgments of the European Court of Human Rights, the Parliamentary Under-Secretary of State, Foreign and Commonwealth Office, set out an answer in tabular form, from which the following is an extract:

	Country and Date of Judgment	Articles in Question	Brief Details of the Subject Matter	Name of Case
	United Kingdom			
1.	21 February 1975	6, 8	Prisoner's access to Court	Golder
2.	18 January 1978	3	Interrogation techniques (N. Ireland)	Government of Ireland
3.	25 April 1978	3	Judicial birching (Isle of Man)	Tyrer
4.	26 April 1979	10	Freedom of expression: contempt of court	Sunday Times
5.	13 August 1981	11	Closed Shop	Young, James and Webster
6.	22 October 1981	8	Homosexuality (N. Ireland)	Dudgeon
7.	25 February 1982	Protocol I Article 2	Corporal punishment in schools (respect for parents' philosophical convictions)	Campbell and Cosans
8.	5 November 1981	5	Mental patient: right to have detention reviewed	X

	Country and Date of Judgment	Articles in Question	Brief Details of the Subject Matter	Name of Case
9.	25 March 1983	6, 8, 13	Prisoners' correspondence	Silver and Others
10.	28 June 1984	6, 8, 13	Boards of Prison visitors: conduct of disciplinary proceedings	Campbell and Fell
11.	2 August 1984	8	Telephone tapping	Malone
12.	28 May 1985	8 with 14, 13	Immigration—discrimination on grounds of sex	Abdulaziz, Cabales and Balkandali

(Ibid., cols. *911–12*: 26 July 1985)

In reply to a question, the Secretary of State for the Home Department wrote:

The Government have decided to renew, for a period of five years from January 1986, their acceptance of the right of individual petition to the European Commission of Human Rights and the jurisdiction of the European Court of Human Rights.

(Ibid., vol. 84, Written Answers, col. *211*: 24 October 1985; see to the same effect HL Debs., vol. 467, col. 1373: 24 October 1985)

In the course of a debate on the subject of the activities of UNESCO, in particular its programme XIII on peace, disarmament and human rights, the Minister of State, Foreign and Commonwealth Office, Mr Timothy Raison, stated:

Overall, the outcome on major programme XIII was mixed. The resolution that was adopted did not go as far as we had hoped in limiting UNESCO's role in relation to disarmament issues, but we were successful in preventing UNESCO, in its proposed activities for 1986–87, from endangering the supremacy of individual human rights as defined in the three universally recognised instruments. It was made clear that the in some ways questionable concept of people's rights had a different status from human rights and required further clarification.

. . . The questionable element in the concept of people's rights is the point at which they are held to override individual rights. As I have said, there are international conventions which give a supremacy to individual human rights which we have always regarded as being of very great importance. People's rights, if they are abused, can be a way of determining that the collective power of the Government should override the rights of individuals. That is the area which concerns us.

(HC Debs., vol. 87, col. 521: 22 November 1985)

Speaking on 2 December 1985 in explanation of vote on a draft resolution of the Third Committee of the General Assembly with the title 'Indivisibility and interdependence of economic, social, cultural, civil and political rights', the UK delegate, Ms Young, stated in part:

My delegation abstained on the draft resolution contained in document L. 55, despite the importance we attach to the implementation of both Covenants, since we have a number of serious reservations about the preamble to the text.

Firstly my delegation cannot accept the assertion made in preambular paragraph 8, operative paragraph 8, and indeed in the title of the draft, that all human rights are 'interdependent' for the reasons expressed by the distinguished representative of the FRG. While we agree that certain rights are interrelated, and the enjoyment of some may contribute to the enjoyment of others, we cannot accept any implication that the enjoyment of economic, social and cultural rights can be a precondition for the enjoyment of civil and political rights. Nor can my delegation accept the implicit claim in preambular paragraph 10 that the principal obstacles to the full realisation of human rights are those listed in the paragraph. If they were to be a complete list, totalitarian ideologies would certainly have to appear in it.

Moreover my delegation does not accept that the fact that certain territories are not self-governing means that this status is in itself an obstacle to the full realisation of the human rights of the peoples of those territories, provided those peoples are free to 'exercise their right to self-determination'.

My delegation voted against preambular paragraph 11 since the language of that paragraph does not correspond to the language of the International Covenant on Economic, Social and Cultural Rights.

(Text provided by the Foreign and Commonwealth Office; see also A/C. 3/40/SR. 60, pp. 19–20)

[Preambular paragraph 8 of the above draft resolution read:

The General Assembly

. . .

Convinced that the full realization of civil and political rights is inseparably linked with the enjoyment of economic, social and cultural rights

Preambular paragraph 11 read:

Recognizing the fundamental rights of every people to exercise full sovereignty over its natural wealth and resources

Operative paragraph 8 read:

1. *Recognizes* that equal attention should be given to the implementation, promotion and protection of both economic, social, cultural and civil and political rights]

In reply to a question, the Minister of State, Foreign and Commonwealth Office, wrote:

We continue to take all suitable opportunities to raise human rights matters with the Government of Iran. We co-sponsored the resolution on violations of human rights in Iran adopted by the United Nations General Assembly on 13 December, which called for the Government of Iran to respect and ensure to all individuals within its territory the rights enshrined in the international covenant on civil and political rights, to which Iran is a party.

(HC Debs., vol. 89, Written Answers, col. *363*: 20 December 1985)

In the course of a debate on the subject of the Soviet incursion into Afghanistan, the Parliamentary Under-Secretary of State, Foreign and Commonwealth Office, Mr Eggar, stated:

The tragedy is that none of that should be necessary. The presence of Soviet troops in Afghanistan has been consistently condemned by the international community, most recently on 13 November this year at the United Nations, when a record 122 voted for the motion calling for the withdrawal of Soviet troops, with only 19 countries against. There can be no doubt that both the Kabul regime and the Soviet Union are, in Afghanistan, in breach of the Geneva convention and of the International covenants on Human Rights, of which both are signatories.

(Ibid., cols. 689–90: 20 December 1985)

Part Five: IV. *Organs of the State—diplomatic agents and missions*

(See also Part Five: VIII. A. and B., below)

On 7 February 1985, Mrs E. M. Denza, Legal Counsellor, Foreign and Commonwealth Office, made the following affidavit in respect of habeas corpus proceedings in the Divisional Court of the Queen's Bench Division in *Re Mohammed Ahmadu Jarma Yusufu*:

. . .

2. The Applicant applied to the British High Commission in Lagos Nigeria for a United Kingdom entry certificate. A copy of his application form is annexed hereto and exhibited as 'EMD 1'. On that form in reply to questions 15 and 17, he describes himself as going on 17 May 1984 to London on official duty for a stay of one month.

3. The application for a United Kingdom entry certificate was supported by a Note from the Ministry of External Affairs of the Federal Republic of Nigeria a copy of which is annexed hereto as exhibit 'EMD 2'. This form could be used either for notification of a prospective diplomatic posting or for notification of an official duty visit, as can be seen from the words 'posting/official duty' which appear half-way down the form.

4. Both the United Kingdom application form and the Note from the Nigerian Ministry of External Affairs are inconsistent with the Applicant's assertions in his Affidavit of February 1985 that he was posted as a diplomat to the Nigerian High Commission. If that had been the case I would have expected the reply to question 15 on the United Kingdom application form to have been to the effect that he was travelling to the United Kingdom on a diplomatic posting. Further, I would have expected the Note from the Nigerian Ministry of External Affairs to have deleted the reference to 'official duty', leaving the reference to 'posting' as the reason for his proceeding to London.

5. The Applicant states in paragraphs 2, 4 and 7 of his Affidavit of February 1985 that he was issued with a diplomatic passport. This fact does not show that he was appointed to the United Kingdom as a diplomatic agent.

6. In paragraphs 4 and 7 of his Affidavit of February 1985 the Applicant states that he was admitted to the United Kingdom as a Diplomat by one of HM Immigration Officers at Heathrow Airport. This is incorrect. The diplomatic entry certificate on the Applicant's passport was issued by the British High Commission in Nigeria as can be seen from the round stamp showing the words 'High Commission' which is placed over the diplomatic entry certificate (see exhibit 'MAJY 2' of the applicant's Affidavit of February 1985). The United

Kingdom Immigration Authorities merely issued date stamps on 17 May 1984 and 1 June 1984, without any reference to the status of the Applicant.

7. As a matter of Foreign and Commonwealth Office practice members of the diplomatic service of Foreign or Commonwealth States proceeding to or returning from their posts as diplomatic agents and those members of the diplomatic service who are travelling to or through United Kingdom territory on official business are given the same form of visa or prior entry clearance in either case. Whether or not a member of the diplomatic service is a diplomatic agent depends on his being validly appointed by his own Government and accepted by the Host State. There was no acceptance of the Applicant as a diplomatic agent by Her Majesty's Government as is explained in paragraph 8 below; insofar as it is suggested that the Applicant was appointed by his own Government, none of the normal procedures has been followed or invoked.

8. It is normal practice for notification of arrival of a diplomat in London to be lodged with the Protocol Department of the Foreign and Commonwealth Office on form TX9, a copy of which is annexed hereto at exhibit 'EMD 3'. Such a notification is required by Article 10.1 of the Vienna Convention on Diplomatic Relations signed in 1961. The fact that no such notification was received in respect of the Applicant is shown by the copy of the certificate issued under the authority of the Secretary of State for Foreign and Commonwealth Affairs annexed hereto as exhibit 'EMD 4'.

(Text provided by the Foreign and Commonwealth Office. Exhibits not reproduced)

In reply to questions on the subject of diplomatic relations with Albania, the Parliamentary Under-Secretary of State for the Armed Forces, Lord Trefgarne, stated:

. . . it is a matter of regret that we have been unable to establish diplomatic relations with Albania. But, as I have explained, the objections come from the Albanian side and not from Her Majesty's Government. The Albanian Government have made it clear that they are not prepared to enter into relations with the United Kingdom until the quantity of gold (currently in the control of the Tripartite Commission for the Restitution of Monetary Gold) to which they have laid claim, is delivered to them.

. . . As for the gold being negotiable, I should make it clear that the United Kingdom is not a totally free agent in this matter because we are of course only one member of the tripartite commission which controls the gold. The other members are the French and the United States. Before anything can happen to it, we have to have the agreement of all three of those parties.

. . . there are, I believe, meetings of the commission from time to time, but there are a number of difficult problems to be resolved.

. . . I am not aware that the other governments have disclaimed any ownership of the gold or any claim to it. But then, of course, I cannot speak for either the French Government or the United States Government.

(HL Debs., vol. 462, cols. 1119–20: 24 April 1985)

The Report of the Secretary-General of the UN, dated 23 August 1985, on the topic of the consideration of effective measures to enhance the protection, security and safety of diplomatic and consular missions and representatives, set out the text of a note verbale from the Permanent Mission of the UK to the UN in New York, dated 30 May 1985, which began as follows:

The Permanent Mission [of the United Kingdom] deeply regrets to have to inform the Secretariat of the kidnapping and subsequent murder of a senior official of the Indian High Commission in the United Kingdom and of the subsequent prosecution and conviction of six persons against whom criminal charges were brought in that connection.

(A/40/453, p. 17)

In response to a letter dated 8 November 1985 from the Soviet Permanent Mission to the UN in New York addressed to the Secretary-General of the UN, in which reference was made to certain alleged infringements of the inviolability of its diplomatic premises in London, in particular that such premises had been fired upon, the Permanent Mission of the UK wrote to the Secretary-General on 16 December 1985 in part as follows:

The Government of the United Kingdom regrets all such incidents, and has taken, and will continue to take, all appropriate steps to prevent their occurrence. In the event of such incidents, appropriate steps are taken to investigate the circumstances and to apprehend those responsible. In taking such steps the co-operation of the foreign mission concerned is, of course, necessary.

The Government of the United Kingdom rejects the allegations contained in document A/40/453/Add. 5 concerning the security of foreign missions and representatives in London. In relation to the protection of all such missions and representatives the Government observes strictly its international legal obligations in the field of consular and diplomatic relations, including those under the two applicable conventions: the Vienna Convention on Diplomatic Relations of 1961 and the Vienna Convention on Consular Relations of 1963.

(Ibid., Add. 10)

In a press statement on 17 December 1985, the Foreign and Commonwealth Office referred to a break-in at the premises of the press section of the Soviet Embassy and a Soviet protest asking for a thorough investigation. The statement continued:

In reply, the Foreign and Commonwealth Office had said that it had already been in touch with the police and had been assured that urgent investigation was indeed in train. Her Majesty's Government took its responsibilities under the Vienna Convention seriously.

(Text provided by the Foreign and Commonwealth Office)

Part Five: VIII. A. *Organs of the State—immunity of organs of the State—diplomatic and consular immunity*

On 17 April 1984 the Governments of the UK and the People's Republic of China signed an agreement, which entered into force on

14 January 1985, for the establishment of a British Consulate-General at Shanghai and a Chinese Consulate-General at Manchester. The agreement contains the following Articles:

ARTICLE 3

(1) The consular premises shall be inviolable. The authorities of the receiving State may not enter the consular premises without the consent of the head of the consular post or the head of the diplomatic mission of the sending State, or a person designated by one of those persons.

(2) The receiving State is under a special duty to take all appropriate steps to protect the consular premises against any intrusion or damage and to prevent any disturbance of the peace of the consular post or impairment of its dignity.

. . .

ARTICLE 6

The receiving State shall treat consular officers with due respect, and shall take all appropriate steps to prevent any attack on their person, freedom or dignity.

ARTICLE 7

(1) Members of the consular post and members of their families shall be immune from the criminal jurisdiction of the receiving State and shall not be liable to arrest or detention pending trial.

(2) Members of the consular post shall be immune from the civil and administrative jurisdiction of the receiving State in respect of acts performed by them in the exercise of consular functions.

(3) The provisions of paragraph (2) of this Article shall not apply in respect of a civil action:

(*a*) relating to private immovable property situated in the receiving State, unless the member of the consular post holds it on behalf of the sending State for the purposes of the consular post;
(*b*) relating to succession in which the member of the consular post is involved as executor, administrator, heir or legatee as a private person and not on behalf of the sending State;
(*c*) relating to any professional or commercial activity exercised by the member of the consular post in the receiving State outside his official functions;
(*d*) arising out of a contract concluded by the member of the consular post in which he did not contract, expressly or impliedly, on behalf of the sending State;
(*e*) by a third party for damage arising from an accident in the receiving State caused by a vehicle, vessel or aircraft.

(4) No measures of execution shall be taken against any of the persons mentioned in this Article, except in the cases coming under subparagraphs (*a*), (*b*) and (*c*) of paragraph (3) of this Article and provided also that the measures concerned can be taken without infringing the inviolability of the person concerned or of his residence.

(5) Members of the consular post and members of their families may be called upon to attend as witnesses in the course of judicial or administrative proceedings. If a consular officer or a member of his family should decline to give

evidence, no coercive measure or penalty shall be applied to that person. Consular employees and members of their families, as well as members of the service staff and members of their families, may not decline to give evidence except as provided in paragraph (6) of this Article.

(6) Members of the consular post are under no obligation to give evidence concerning matters relating to the exercise of their official functions or to produce official correspondence or documents. They are also entitled to decline to give evidence as expert witnesses with regard to the law of the sending State.

(7) In taking evidence from members of the consular post, the authorities of the receiving State shall take all appropriate measures to avoid interference with the performance of their consular functions. At the request of the head of the consular post, such evidence may, when possible, be given orally or in writing at the consular premises or at the residence of the person concerned.

(8) Members of the consular post who are nationals or permanent residents of the receiving State and members of their families, as well as those members of the families of the members of the consular post who are themselves nationals or permanent residents of the receiving State, shall not enjoy the rights, facilities and immunities provided for in this Article, except the immunity provided for in paragraph (6) of this Article.

(Cmnd. 9472)

In the course of a debate on the subject of the Immobilization of Vehicles Illegally Parked (London Boroughs of Westminster, and Kensington and Chelsea) (Continuation) Order 1985, the Government spokesman in the House of Lords, Lord Brabazon of Tara, stated:

As regards diplomats, it was very disappointing when we had to suspend clamping diplomatic vehicles because of legal advice that this was in fact contrary to the Vienna Convention on diplomatic relations. The Government therefore urgently reviewed the problem of the number of diplomatic vehicles in London and my noble friend Lord Elton announced changes in the system of special 'D' and 'X' registration plates designed to reduce the number exempted from parking regulations. Immunity from clamping is now restricted to vehicles with 'D' registration plates and these are limited to those diplomats with full immunity; the number of 'D' plates issued has also been curtailed both for cars used officially and for diplomats' private vehicles. Those not entitled to full diplomatic immunity, but only to immunity when on official duty, now receive 'X' registration plates and are liable for clamping. Forty such vehicles were clamped in the last quarter of 1984.

(HL Debs., vol. 461, col. 330: 18 March 1985)

In reply to a question on the subject of diplomatic immunity in respect of British diplomats abroad, the Parliamentary Under-Secretary of State, Foreign and Commonwealth Office, wrote in part:

Our policy is that we would not expect diplomatic immunity to be unreasonably maintained in cases where waiver would be without prejudice to the work of the mission.

(HC Debs., vol. 76, Written Answers, col. *74*: 25 March 1985)

In reply to a question, the Minister of State, Foreign and Commonwealth Office, wrote:

Since 1980 we have only once, in 1985, requested a waiver of the immunity of a diplomat alleged to have committed a drug-related offence. The waiver was promptly granted by the Zambian Government, to whom we expressed our satisfaction with their helpful response.

In the same period there were only two other cases of alleged drug offences by persons entitled to immunity, both involving cannabis. In the first case, in 1980, where the alleged offender was the son of a diplomat, we made strong representations. In the second case, in 1981, the diplomat was withdrawn before representations could be made.

(Ibid., vol. 75, Written Answers, col. *52*: 11 March 1985)

In a circular dated 19 April 1985 to the Heads of Diplomatic Missions in London on the subject of illegal parking, the Vice Marshal of the Diplomatic Corps, Mr Eustace Gibbs, wrote in part:

I must once again draw your attention to the problem of the parking of diplomatic vehicles in London. The number of unpaid fixed penalty notices for parking offences by diplomatic vehicles is now running at the enormous figure of over 100,000 a year. This is double the figure of only 5 years ago and represents a much higher proportion of the total number of such offences.

. . .

In my circular of 1 June 1983 I noted that 'several Heads of Mission have told me that their staff (like those of UK Missions abroad) are under instructions to pay their parking penalties except where they have been unavoidably incurred on essential official duty—not simply on daily travel to and from work'. It is clear however from the statistics either that many Missions do not have such instructions or alternatively that compliance with them is far from being fully effective.

As you will be aware, diplomats are obliged under Article 41 of the Vienna Convention to respect the laws and regulations of the receiving state. Deliberate and persistent disregard of this obligation cannot be ignored or regarded as acceptable behaviour by those concerned. In his letter of 15 August 1984 the Permanent Under-Secretary at the Foreign and Commonwealth Office drew attention to the Secretary of State's statement to the Foreign Affairs Committee of the House of Commons on 18 July that we would henceforth expect and apply more stringent standards.

. . .

In my letter of 12 December 1983 I informed you that cars bearing diplomatic registration plates would be exempted from wheel-clamping. This remains the position but the exemption of the diplomatic corps has, as you will be aware, continued to arouse criticism from the press and Londoners generally. This is all the more reason for impressing upon your staff the importance of scrupulous adherence to parking regulations. In cases where diplomatic vehicles cause obstruction or danger, they will continue to be towed away. We expect the towing charge to be paid on the basis that it is a legal obligation in respect of a service performed.

As from 1 May 1985 detailed records will be kept of unpaid parking tickets by all cars with diplomatic registration plates. Persistent and deliberate failure by individual diplomats in their *private cars* to respect parking regulations and to pay fixed penalty notices will henceforth call into question their continued acceptability as members of diplomatic Missions in London. Where necessary particular cases will be drawn to your personal attention with a warning about the possible consequences. Due account will be taken if the parking tickets are subsequently paid or appropriate contributions made to the Central Ticket Office. Further unpaid parking tickets incurred by individuals will lead to a request for the withdrawal of the offender. An alternative in certain cases could be to grant a waiver of immunity so that the person concerned can be prosecuted.

Note will also be made of the total number of fixed penalty notices incurred by individual *official cars* of diplomatic Missions and left unpaid. In particular cases these will be drawn to your personal attention with a request, in the first instance, for appropriate action. If this has no effect, we shall be obliged to take further measures. This could include exercising the right under Article 9 of the Vienna Convention to declare a chauffeur unacceptable.

(Text provided by the Foreign and Commonwealth Office)

In an appendix to the circular giving the number of fixed penalty notices cancelled on grounds of diplomatic immunity in the Metropolitan Police District by country or organization, it was stated that the totals were as follows:

1981	1982	1983	1984
68,940	76,223	102,179	108,932

(For the detailed breakdown for the years 1981–3 inclusive, see HC Debs., vol. 73, Written Answers, cols. *193–5*: 13 February 1985)

In a statement to the House of Commons on 1 May 1984, the Secretary of State for Foreign and Commonwealth Affairs, Sir Geoffrey Howe, stated that he had 'instituted a full Review of the Vienna Convention, its operation and enforceability' and that he would report the outcome of this Review to the House. He also stated that he would welcome the views of the Foreign Affairs Committee of the House of Commons. The Committee's Report on 'The Abuse of Diplomatic Immunities and Privileges' was published on 23 January 1985 (*Parliamentary Papers*, 1984–5, HC, Paper 127), including records of evidence provided by the Foreign and Commonwealth Office, the relevant parts of which were set out in UKMIL 1984, Part Five: IV. and VIII. A. In April 1985, the Secretary of State for Foreign and Commonwealth Affairs presented to Parliament a document entitled 'Government Report on Review of the Vienna Convention on Diplomatic Relations and Reply to "The Abuse of Diplomatic Immunities and Privileges"'. Extracts from this Government Report (Cmnd. 9497) are set out below.

General Scope of the Review

4. The commitment to undertake the Review was given in the aftermath of the

events outside the Libyan People's Bureau in St. James's Square on 17 April 1984. It received added impetus from the events relating to the attempted abduction of Mr. Umaru Dikko on 5 July 1984. Wider questions concerning immunities and privileges arose out of evidence considered by the Foreign Affairs Committee. The abuse of diplomatic immunity has caused serious and legitimate public concern, and particularly when it leads to acts of terrorism.

5. Given this context the Government set itself the following specific objectives:

(*a*) to examine the Articles of the Vienna Convention, and in particular those relating to immunity and inviolability; and to consider whether it would be (i) desirable and, if so, (ii) practicable *either* to propose amendments of the Convention *or* to apply more stringently any of its existing provisions in ways which would help to prevent abuse and at the same time be consistent with Her Majesty's Government's overall interests;

(*b*) to seek international support for any measures that may be desirable and practicable to improve the operation and enforceability of the Vienna Convention.

6. The Government accept the Committee's observation that the events involving the Libyan People's Bureau and the attempted abduction of Mr. Umaru Dikko have not been the only source of concern about diplomatic immunities and privileges in the UK, merely the most serious (para 5 of their Report). Thus, while taking full account of the lessons learnt from these events, we have decided to take a wider and forward-looking approach.

7. The Government have studied the provisions of the Vienna Convention in relation to two broad categories of abuse;

(*a*) deliberate abuse of the diplomatic bag, diplomatic premises or diplomatic status for activities of a terrorist or political nature;

(*b*) incidental abuse covering matters of a more personal nature, in particular breaches of the criminal law.

8. The main areas of difficulty, some of which have only arisen in acute form since the Vienna Convention was drawn up in 1961, include:

(*a*) the opportunity for members of diplomatic missions to take advantage of their immunity to carry out, or escape prosecution for, serious criminal activities extending even to terrorism;

(*b*) the freedom of sending states to appoint members of diplomatic missions and thus to provide diplomatic cover for persons not carrying out legitimate diplomatic functions;

(*c*) reliance on diplomatic immunity for relatively petty offences often unrelated to any perceived function of a diplomatic mission;

(*d*) more cars and more traffic congestion which has led to a proliferation of driving and parking offences for which immunity is claimed;

(*e*) the constraints on receiving states in applying the main sanctions that exist in the Vienna Convention in dealing with or preventing abuse.

AMENDMENT OF THE VIENNA CONVENTION

9. The Government have studied the views of the Committee on the desirability and practicability of seeking to amend the Vienna Convention in specific cases of

abuse (paras 53–57). This would alter the balance between immunities and obligations. Existing obligations include the duty of all persons enjoying privileges and immunities to 'respect the laws and regulations' of the receiving state (Article 41.1). Any change that strengthened this provision and enabled receiving states to enforce their own laws in respect of foreign diplomats could be valuable in dealing both with state-sponsored terrorism and more petty abuses. It could also however mean a corresponding reduction in the protection given to the personnel and facilities of sending states. This could bear hardly on states that generally abide by the existing rules and lead in some cases to unjustified harassment. It could also restrict the ability of Governments, acting on behalf of their country and its citizens, to carry out legitimate business overseas.

10. Moreover the Vienna Convention is a codification of international law and practice going back many hundred years which was re-examined carefully by the international community before it was agreed in 1961. As such it is almost universally respected. 145 states have become parties. The 1964 Diplomatic Privileges Act gave effect to it in the UK. Those very few states which are not parties give general effect to its terms. In practice it has become the modern customary law so that termination of our acceptance of the Convention (even if legally possible) would leave us in substantially the same position. It has provided a framework which is explicit and clear in many respects but nevertheless leaves room for common sense in its detailed interpretation and application.

11. We have made extensive international soundings on the feasibility of amending the Vienna Convention through renegotiation. There is a widespread consensus that attempts to do so would not succeed. They could in fact create more problems than they would solve by opening up issues on which disagreements could surface and thrive. Given the ambiguities and grey areas, the process would be complex and time consuming and would lead to a very confused position until the great majority of states accepted any amendments by ratification. We have therefore agreed with the Committee's conclusion that:

> 'Given the difficulties in the way of achieving any restrictive amendment to the Convention, and the doubtful net benefit to the UK of so doing, it would be wrong to regard amendment of the Vienna Convention as the solution to the problem of abuse of diplomatic immunities. Accordingly, the Government are right not to concentrate on amendment of the Convention as a major element in new policies to restrict abuse of immunities'.

(Cmnd. 9497, pp. 5–7)

The Government then examined various areas of action.

General Interpretation and Application of the Vienna Convention

14. The Committee have stated that a firmer policy towards application of the Vienna Convention is the only effective weapon that the Government possess and should be strongly pursued (para 123). After a full review of the subject including the legal and practical possibilities, the Government have reached the same conclusion.

15. In pursuing a firmer policy, there are a number of important principles that will need to be respected:

(*a*) adherence to agreed international rules to which we subscribe. Therefore any administrative action to apply the Vienna Convention restrictively must have a sound legal basis;

(*b*) preservation of a balance between a general level of immunities for our functions overseas and an adequate means to enforce obligations on others in the UK. Therefore any administrative action we apply to others we must be prepared in principle to accept for ourselves. Our ability to protect British interests overseas could be affected by any limitations we impose as a receiving state. As the Committee recognise (para 56) the concept of reciprocity is crucial;

(*c*) application of the Vienna Convention consistently and on an equal basis. Section 3 of the Diplomatic Privileges Act 1964 gives power to withdraw privileges and immunities where it appears that those accorded to a British mission in a particular country or to persons connected with it are less than those conferred by the Act on the mission of that country or persons connected with it. Use of this power can be effective in some cases but it is best used selectively.

(Cmnd. 9497, p. 9)

The Government turned to ways in which a stricter application of the Vienna Convention has already been implemented, the first one of which was in respect of notification of staff.

19. Problems of abuse or attempted abuse arise mainly out of the interpretation of Article 7 of the Convention which states that 'the sending state may freely appoint the members of the staff of the Mission', though this is partly circumscribed by the *persona non grata* provision in Article 9 and the provision in Article 11 that enables the receiving state to limit the size of a Mission. Particular problems include:

(*a*) notification as diplomatic staff of persons who should more properly be regarded as administrative and technical staff; and apparent disproportion in certain cases between diplomatic staff and administrative and technical staff;

(*b*) notification of staff (such as students and teachers) whose functions do not appear properly or fully to fall within those of a diplomatic Mission;

(*c*) imprecise definition of 'members of the family forming part of the household';

(*d*) notification as administrative and technical staff, entitled to immunities and privileges, of persons originally appointed as locally engaged staff (whom we would treat as permanently resident and therefore not so entitled);

(*e*) failure by missions to reclassify members of diplomatic or administrative and technical staff (or their dependants) who have become UK nationals or permanently resident, e.g. following marriage to British citizens.

We have also been concerned about the employment as locally engaged mission staff of persons who would not otherwise be permitted to stay and work in the UK. These include members of the service staff, e.g. chauffeurs and cleaners, who are thereby able to evade the enforcement of immigration rules.

20. Article 10.1 requires notification to the receiving state of new appointments and of the termination of the functions or status of persons entitled to immunities

and privileges. *Agrément* is required in advance for Heads of Mission (except those from Commonwealth countries of which the Queen is also the Head of State). Other new appointments are notified to the FCO on arrival on a prescribed form. Each form has to be signed by the Head of Mission or, in certain cases, his designated nominee. These notification forms are scrutinised carefully by the FCO. Further information is sought or queries are raised with the mission concerned in about one in five cases.

21. Since the Vienna Convention contains no objective definition of staff categories, checks carried out after notification usually relate to questions of nationality, designation, residence or family status. Doubts about official status or duties are rarely apparent from the notification form and it is virtually impossible in most cases for the FCO to tell whether a person should more properly be described as a diplomat or as a member of the administrative and technical staff or indeed as a member of the mission at all. In certain cases we refuse to accept notifications and they are withdrawn by the mission concerned. The *persona non grata* sanction is exercised where there is good reason to do so. Where appropriate we make use of our exchanges of information with European Community and other countries which have recently been increased.

22. There is a visa requirement for certain countries which enables prior checking to be carried out on those expecting to take up appointments in diplomatic and consular missions in the UK. If we had good reason to believe that any such person was likely to engage in unlawful activities he would normally be made *persona non grata* under Article 9 before arrival. This procedure has been followed in certain cases. A wider system of requiring prior notification would not be enforceable under the Vienna Convention (Article 10.2 provides for it only 'where possible') and would be administratively cumbersome without necessarily providing useful information on which effective action could be taken. The visa requirement effectively provides advance notice in cases where it is most likely to be needed.

(Ibid., pp. 10–11)

25. Any notification of a person whose relationship to the new official is other than that of spouse or minor child is queried. The Vienna Conference tried, but failed, to reach agreement on a definition of 'members of the family forming part of the household'. Our practice is to accept children aged 18 or over provided they are clearly resident with the member of the mission (including students) and not engaged in employment on a permanent basis. In exceptional circumstances other relatives, e.g. dependent parents living with the member of the mission, are accepted. Our acceptance or rejection of a notification is not itself conclusive of status. In doubtful cases it is for a court to rule on the status of a dependant should he for instance be accused of a criminal offence.

26. The Government have generally regarded all locally engaged staff as 'permanent residents' of the UK and treated them accordingly for the administrative purposes of the Diplomatic Privileges Act 1964. Attempts made to classify as non-permanent residents those appointed or previously employed on a locally engaged basis are normally queried and often refused unless convincing evidence is provided that they should properly be regarded as overseas based. The status of locally engaged staff that come to our attention in connection with the immigration rules is also queried.

(Ibid., p. 12)

The Government then turned to another way in which the Vienna Convention has been more strictly applied.

SIZE OF DIPLOMATIC MISSIONS

28. The Government have reviewed the practical and legal options available to limit the size of diplomatic missions under Article 11.1 of the Vienna Convention. This reads:

> 'In the absence of specific agreement as to the size of the mission, the receiving state may require that the size of a mission be kept within limits considered by it to be reasonable and normal, having regard to circumstances and conditions in the receiving state and to the needs of the particular mission.'

Two different approaches have been considered:

(*a*) the development of a policy of applying ceilings across the board on all missions;

(*b*) the limiting of the size of individual missions to levels we regard as appropriate to our relations.

29. We have over the past 15 years imposed ceilings on a number of diplomatic missions in London. But we have concluded that a general policy of restrictions cannot be justified. There has been no overall increase in the size of diplomatic missions in the UK in the past 10 years. The majority of them do not abuse their immunity and the level of unacceptable activities would not necessarily be reduced by imposing overall limits. Such a policy could make us vulnerable to reciprocal action, and retaliation against British missions overseas would almost certainly follow.

30. The Government accept the Committee's view of the need to be 'significantly readier than in the past to use the power to limit the size of a mission in cases where there is cause for significant concern about the overall nature of the mission's activities' (para 59). We have concluded that a case by case approach remains the most appropriate means of dealing with existing problems of abuse or potential abuse. The discretion to limit the size of individual missions has been extended in the past year in certain cases and will continue to be applied in the future where there are grounds for doing so and British interests will not be at undue risk. Account has to be taken of the general state of, and likely impact on, bilateral relations with the country concerned and the likelihood of retaliation in some form. Where formal ceilings are already in force they will be rigorously applied.

31. There are no objective criteria for considering what might be regarded as a 'reasonable and normal' size for a particular mission and for considering whether a limit should be imposed. We apply one or more of the following criteria:

(*a*) active involvement in espionage or terrorism, the two major categories of offence which clearly require exemplary action. In these cases those directly involved are expelled. Specific ceilings may also be imposed since the mission has no need for those 'diplomats' whose activities are not properly diplomatic. A ceiling was placed on the Soviet Union in 1971 following the expulsion of 105 Soviet officials for 'inadmissible activities';

(*b*) the pattern of behaviour of certain missions, or Governments, which suggest possible future involvement in unacceptable activities. In effect this means imposing, or possibly agreeing, ceilings *before* any offence or incident;

(*c*) a numerical comparison between the size of a mission in London and that of a UK mission in the country concerned. This yardstick is not normally in itself sufficient to justify action without taking into account the reasons for any significant discrepancy. Diplomatic missions in London are in many cases larger than the corresponding British missions overseas. This reflects the particular importance of London as an economic, financial and political centre, including the Headquarters of various international commodity organisations. Moreover some missions use London as a base from which to cover other countries in addition to the UK.

In the light of these criteria and the wording of Article 11, we have reviewed the sizes of individual missions in London and are querying staff levels in certain cases with a view to obtaining a reduction in a number of cases. We will continue to pursue this approach.

(Cmnd. 9497, pp. 13–14)

Moving on to the next manifestation of a stricter approach, the Government continued:

DIPLOMATIC PREMISES

33. The Government have considered whether it would be possible, legally and practically, to exercise greater control over the premises of diplomatic Missions in London; whether limitations can be placed on their number, location or management; and whether specific measures can be taken to prevent or limit abuse.

34. Under Article 22 of the Vienna Convention on Diplomatic Relations not only are the premises of diplomatic Missions inviolable, but the receiving State has a special duty to take all appropriate steps to protect them. Similar provisions apply to the private residences of diplomatic staff (Article 30), and of administrative and technical staff unless they are nationals of or permanently resident in the receiving state (Article 37). Moreover, the receiving state should facilitate the acquisition of premises or otherwise assist the sending state in obtaining accommodation (Article 21). If diplomatic relations are broken, and even in the case of armed conflict, the receiving state is still required to respect and protect the premises of a Mission, though the sending state may entrust the custody of the premises to a third state acceptable to the receiving state (Article 45).

35. A further relevant factor is that under Article 23 'the sending state and the Head of Mission shall be exempt from all municipal dues and taxes in respect of the premises of the Mission, whether owned or leased, other than such as represent payment for specific services rendered'. Article 1(i) of the Vienna Convention defines the premises of a diplomatic Mission as the buildings or parts of buildings and the land ancillary thereto, irrespective of ownership, used for the purposes of the Mission including the Head of Mission's residence. Under Articles 30, 34 and 37, the residences (in connection with their work for the Mission) of all diplomats and members of the administrative and technical staff and their families are given inviolability and rating relief.

36. Claims for rating relief are made to the FCO with full details of the premises and a statement on the purpose for which they are to be used. Buildings or properties that we accept as constituting premises of the mission qualify for rating

relief and are also regarded as having diplomatic status. They are therefore entitled to inviolability and protection. Some buildings or properties constitute diplomatic residences even if rating relief has not been sought, e.g. because it is the residence of a diplomat where rates have been included in the rent. Some, but not all, the addresses of these properties are made known to the FCO on the form notifying a diplomat's arrival.

37. The main concern relates to incidents of an unacceptable nature such as terrorist attacks or demonstrations that take place in or near diplomatic premises. Because of the immunity of the premises the police are unable to enter and search them for evidence of criminal offences including public order offences and illegal possession of firearms or explosives except with the permission of the Head of Mission or the diplomatic occupant. Apart from the risk of demonstrations or violent attacks the existence of diplomatic premises can also give rise to a number of lesser inconveniences, such as disregard of planning or public health legislation, general obstruction or parking offences in the immediate neighbourhood.

38. Problems concerning diplomatic premises are often caused by the behaviour of the occupants but some can be related specifically to their number, location, general management or use. These are considered below:

(*a*) *Number*. Of the 147 Governments in diplomatic relations with the UK, 132 have diplomatic missions resident in London. (In addition 18 of the 28 international organisations established in the UK have inviolable premises.) Many missions have several separate office premises; the reasons for this include convenience for specific functions, cost and availability. Inviolability also applies to the individual residences of all diplomatic and administrative and technical staff;

(*b*) *Location*. There is no power under British law to control the location of diplomatic premises and therefore no legal means of preventing missions from establishing premises in areas which might pose risks for security, public order or traffic and crowd control arising from demonstrations or other incidents. Existing planning permission procedures, which are administered by Local Authorities and subject to public enquiry and appeal, can only be used on planning grounds, i.e. land use and public amenity;

(*c*) *Management*. Diplomatic Missions are expected to comply with UK laws and regulations concerning planning permission, listed buildings' consent and building regulations, and in practice most do so. However the management of empty premises, for instance after relations have been broken, can cause problems;

(*d*) *Use*. Premises of the mission are defined by the Vienna Convention as premises 'used for the purposes of the mission' (Article 1(i)). The functions of a mission as described in Article 3 include 'promoting friendly relations between the sending state and the receiving state, and developing their economic, cultural and scientific relations'. A mission's functions can therefore cover wide and sometimes ill-defined areas of activity.

39. We are taking the following measures to tackle these problems:

(*a*) we will take appropriate administrative action in the event of abuse or suspected abuse, including withdrawal of diplomatic status from existing premises where they are not being used for purposes compatible with the legitimate functions of a mission. As a general rule we regard the following types of activity as being incompatible with the functions of a mission: trading or other activities conducted for financial gain (e.g. selling tickets for airlines or holidays, or charging fees for language classes or public lectures) and educational activities (e.g. schools or students' hostels);

(*b*) we have tightened the procedures on notification of the addresses and occupiers of all diplomatic premises, including residential properties. Normally we are notified of these addresses as part of a claim to rating relief and in that context they have always been carefully scrutinised. In the absence of legislation we cannot however stipulate that any premises or properties not so notified are not inviolable. Under the Vienna Convention the status of premises depends on use for mission or residence purposes. A court would therefore recognise diplomatic status even without notification if it should be in issue in legal proceedings;

(*c*) we have considered whether any existing diplomatic premises are being used for purposes which, although in themselves legitimate and even Governmental in character, are not properly diplomatic as the term is understood in the Vienna Convention and international practice. In the case of separate Tourist Offices our application of the phrase 'premises of a mission' may have been more generous than is strictly required by international law. Most other countries do not accord them diplomatic status. We therefore believe it is right in principle no longer to accord diplomatic status to separate Tourist Offices. With these considerations in mind we intend to withdraw diplomatic status from the small number of Tourist Offices in London that currently hold it;

(*d*) The Government has under active consideration proposals for legislation to control in exceptional circumstances the acquisition and disposal of diplomatic premises in London. The proposals now under consideration would enable the Secretary of State for Foreign and Commonwealth Affairs:

(i) to require diplomatic missions to obtain his express consent before office premises acquired by them, or following a change of use, could be regarded as premises 'used for the purposes of the mission', and therefore entitled under the Diplomatic Privileges Act to inviolability and rating relief;

(ii) to provide that such consent could be withdrawn in respect of existing premises in certain circumstances and that the premises would then cease after a specified period to be premises of the mission (with consequent loss of inviolability and rating relief);

(iii) to acquire the title, after a further specified period, of premises formerly used for the purposes of a diplomatic mission which the Government concerned refused to dispose of (with a view to selling the premises and remitting the proceeds to the foreign Government in question).

The Government regard these proposals as fully consistent with all their obligations under the Vienna Convention. We have made careful comparisons with laws and practice of other countries and in particular the United States Foreign Missions Act 1982;

(*e*) we have also considered whether new measures are required to prevent demonstrations disrupting the peace of diplomatic missions or impairment of their dignity (as required under Article 22), or becoming so provocative as to lead to violent incidents. The Government fully share the Committee's view (paras 45–52) that the UK's duty to protect the peace of diplomatic missions cannot be interpreted so widely that no demonstrations are allowed outside them. The Government also agree with the Committee that the essential requirements are that the work of the mission should not be disrupted, that mission staff are not put in fear, and that there is free access for both staff and visitors. How each demonstration is policed in order to ensure that these requirements are met without undue infringement of freedom of speech is primarily a matter for the police. There are some 350 demonstrations a year outside embassies in London. In most cases the police keep demonstrators on the opposite side of the road from a mission so the question of Article 22 being breached seldom arises. But the practice varies depending on the geography and may be varied in special circumstances (such as the holding of a function at the embassy). The police are the best judges in each case of the controls required: how to preserve the peace and dignity of a mission is essentially a matter of sensible policing practice rather than a question of law. Only rarely will consultation with the Home Office and the FCO be required, e.g. at time of increased tension. The police already have powers to deal with demonstrations and marches outside mission premises. These include their statutory powers under the Public Order Act 1936 to control marches which may result in serious public disorder and to prevent obstruction of the highway; and their common law powers to control numbers or to disperse an unlawful assembly when a breach of the peace has occurred or is reasonably apprehended. The general law of demonstrations is, however, being considered in the context of the public order review, whose conclusions the Government expect to announce shortly.

(Cmnd. 9497, pp. 14–18)

The Government turned to the subject of the diplomatic bag.

DIPLOMATIC BAGS

41. The Government share the concern expressed by the Committee on abuse of the diplomatic bag (paras 25–38). We have carefully considered measures that might be taken to prevent such abuse. In particular we have examined whether it would be desirable and if so practical to seek international agreement for restrictions on the use of the bag and to introduce scanning.

42. Article 27.4 of the Vienna Convention states that a diplomatic bag 'may contain only diplomatic documents or articles intended for official use'. This phraseology is clearly open to wide interpretation. A restrictive revision or modification of the rules in the Vienna Convention on Diplomatic Relations would significantly improve our ability to reduce abuse of foreign diplomatic bags entering and leaving the UK. The parallel Convention on Consular Relations contains provision to enable a state suspecting that a bag contains illicit material to request that it be opened in the presence of an authorised representative of the sending state. If this request is refused the bag must be returned to its place of

origin. This possibility of challenge and supervised search also existed for diplomatic bags in customary law before the Vienna Convention on Diplomatic Relations.

43. In the Government's view it is unacceptable that bags should be used to transmit items prohibited in UK law whether or not it is claimed that they may be 'for official use'. We do not accept for instance that weapons may be imported by bag since the use of firearms for personal protection of diplomats is not permitted in the UK. It could nevertheless be desirable in principle to seek a restriction that would in specific terms exclude from the bag a limited number of items whose unauthorised import or export does not conform to local laws and regulations, regardless of any claim that they may be intended for official use. In the UK guns and explosives as well as narcotics would fall into this category. Under such a restriction, if a state had serious reason to suspect a bag contained any of these prohibited items, it could demand that it be opened or returned to the place of origin.

44. To be effective any agreed limitation on the use of the bag would have to carry with it the possibility of challenge. Even if no challenge were carried out, the very existence of a possible threat to do so could in itself be a deterrent against serious abuse. In practice any actual challenge could normally be expected to lead to the return to the sending authority of a suspect bag rather than agreement to submit to search.

45. The major difficulty would be the certainty of reciprocal action against British diplomatic bags with consequent prejudice to the security of our confidential correspondence and system of communications. Our bags could be put at indiscriminate risk of harassment and disruption while traffic by others in arms or drugs or other prohibited items would not necessarily be prevented. Even if it were reduced, there are other doubts about the practicality and effectiveness of a challenge and search provision. Diplomatic missions would not be deprived of their ability to acquire illicit items from other sources. Furthermore the limits of any action against suspect bags would be difficult to define. The simple opening of a bag, whether it be a hand held pouch or larger container, would be unlikely in itself to reveal the object of suspicion. Little practical purpose would be served if it could not apply to packages within a bag at least to the point where the nature of its contents became clear. There would be risk of breaching other provisions in the Vienna Convention, e.g. Article 24 on the inviolability of archives and documents and Article 27.1 on permitting and protecting free communication.

46. Thus any formal restriction on the content or use of bags would have both advantages and disadvantages for the UK. Even if it were desirable to proceed in this way, we would not find easy or universal acceptance. There is widespread concern internationally to prevent improper use of the bag and a number of states are anxious about threats to their own security arising from it. But there is a marked reluctance to take any action that could endanger the security of communications. A particular difficulty is that many states see no objection in principle to the carriage of arms in diplomatic bags for personal defence. As the Committee have clearly recognised, the practical and procedural difficulties involved in securing a restrictive amendment are formidable.

47. This has not inhibited the Government from making plain its concern about abuse of the bag in a variety of international meetings and bilateral exchanges over the past year. The question has been, and remains, under scrutiny within the

European Community. The International Law Commission (ILC), which was responsible for the preparatory work leading to the Vienna Convention, is currently considering new draft Articles on the status of the courier and the diplomatic bag. It is the best forum for pursuing detailed work on limiting the use of the bag. The need to prevent abuse of the bag for the illicit importation of firearms, explosives and drugs was expressed by the UK representative in the Sixth Committee of the UN General Assembly in November 1984 with a view to further study by the ILC.

48. Whatever measures it may prove possible to achieve internationally to curb abuse of the bag, the Government remain ready to deal promptly and firmly with any exceptional cases. For instance, where the evidence is good that the contents of a bag might endanger national security or the personal safety of the public or of individuals the Government will not hesitate to take the necessary action on the basis of the overriding right of self defence or the duty to protect human life. This latter consideration applied in the case of the attempted abduction of Mr. Umaru Dikko and would have done so even if the crate in which he was found had in fact constituted a diplomatic bag. We note that the Committee welcomed this.

49. The Government have meanwhile taken administrative measures to tighten up safeguards within the Vienna Convention against abuse. Article 27.4 states that 'the packages constituting the diplomatic bag must bear visible external marks of their character'. In October 1984 diplomatic missions in London as well as HM Customs & Excise were given revised clarification of our rules on the identification (including labels and seals) and the handling of foreign diplomatic bags. These rules, which reflect international law and practice, are being rigorously applied in the UK and ensure that we are able to check the official origin and endorsement of all items purporting to be diplomatic bags.

50. *Scanning of Bags*. The Government have given detailed and careful study to the arguments in favour of scanning and to the Committee's recommendation that we should be prepared to scan bags on specific occasions if in our judgment the need arises (paras 29–33). There is no reference to scanning in the Vienna Convention. In our view this does not rule it out, though it is arguable that any method for finding out the contents of a bag is tantamount to opening it, which is illegal. Since however we do not regard scanning as unlawful we have considered whether it would provide an effective and practical solution to the problem of abuse of diplomatic bags. We have also taken into account the risk of retaliation against our own bags.

51. Scanning could in theory deter some abuse, especially if a threat to scan were made explicit. When carried out it might also detect the outlines of certain articles that could provide grounds for suspicion. Those grounds would however need to be extremely strong to justify moving to the further step of requesting a search. Moreover a determined sending state could in particular instances take steps to disguise suspect contents. Thus scanning in itself would only be of limited practical value. It might reveal a problem but it could not solve it. These limitations are widely recognised internationally.

52. A major disadvantage of scanning is that it would make our own bags vulnerable to generalised and indiscriminate challenge. For security reasons we could not allow the protection of our bags to be impaired. These reservations are shared by many other Governments and international opposition to the introduction of scanning would be considerable. The element of uncertainty and the

potential disruption that could be caused, either by retaliatory action or by a widespread introduction of such a practice, could seriously undermine our freedom of communication.

53. Because scanning would not be a wholly effective procedure and because of the consequences for our own bags the Government have decided against the introduction of scanning as a matter of routine. We accept however the Committee's view that there may be circumstances in which it may be helpful. We will therefore be ready to scan any bag on specific occasions where the grounds for suspicion are sufficiently strong.

Individual cases would require specific authorisation from the FCO and would be treated strictly on their merits. A representative of the sending state would be notified of an intention to scan a particular bag and be invited to be present. Should the sending state not wish the bag to be scanned it would be required to return the bag to the originator.

(Cmnd. 9497, pp. 18–21)

The Government next examined the problem of diplomatic immunity in the UK.

57. The Government have reviewed carefully the application in the UK of the provisions of the Vienna Convention relating to immunity from criminal and civil jurisdiction. In particular the statistics on alleged serious offences by diplomats and the criteria for handling individual cases have been closely examined. We have also noted the Committee's views (paras 39–44).

58. The Vienna Convention on Diplomatic Relations substantially limited the immunities formerly enjoyed within the UK by staff of diplomatic missions. (Under previous English law, the Diplomatic Privileges Act 1708, complete immunity from all criminal and civil jurisdiction was given to all members of missions, including domestic service staff and to private servants.) The tone is set in the Preamble to the Convention which states that: 'the purpose of such privileges and immunities is not to benefit individuals but to ensure the efficient performance of the functions of diplomatic missions as representing states'. Article 29 provides that 'the person of a diplomatic agent shall be inviolable'. The concept of inviolability covers *inter alia* immunity from 'any form of arrest or detention'. A diplomatic agent is also immune from 'the criminal jurisdiction of the receiving state' and, with exceptions in regard to certain private matters, from its 'civil and administrative jurisdiction' (Article 31.1). Moreover similar immunities are enjoyed by 'the members of the family of a diplomatic agent forming part of his household' provided they are not nationals or permanent residents of the receiving state. These immunities persist when the appointment ends until the diplomat leaves the country or has had a 'reasonable period' in which to do so, even in the case of armed conflict.

59. Members of the administrative and technical staff and their families also enjoy personal inviolability and the same immunities except that their immunity from civil jurisdiction does not apply to 'acts performed outside the course of their duties'. Members of the service staff have immunity only 'in respect of acts performed in the course of their duties'.

(Ibid., pp. 21–2)

Having analysed the statistics of criminal offences by persons entitled to diplomatic immunity, the Government continued:

62. Of course, criminal offences by those entitled to immunity and serving in a representative capacity cannot be condoned. The main abuse lies, not so much in the comparative number of alleged offences (which is small) or in their relative gravity, but in the reliance on immunity to protect individuals for offences without any obvious connection to the efficient performance of the functions of a diplomatic mission. This applies to most cases involving dependants as well as to many particular types of case, especially theft from shops. However claims to immunity in doubtful cases are seldom tested in court, e.g. where dependants are involved or where the person concerned might be found to have permanent resident status (and therefore no entitlement to immunity).

63. Guidelines for practice in the UK were set out in the following terms in the report on Diplomatic Immunity presented by the then Secretary of State for Foreign and Commonwealth Affairs to Parliament in 1952:

> '. . . If a person possessing diplomatic immunity is alleged to have committed a criminal offence and there is a *prima facie* case which, in the ordinary way, would lead to the institution of a prosecution, the Foreign Office approaches the foreign mission concerned and, unless the offence is such that it is considered that an admonition by the Head of the Mission is sufficient, the Foreign Office requests a waiver of immunity in order that the case may be tried, on the footing that, if the immunity is not waived, it may be impossible for the Foreign Secretary to continue to accept the individual concerned as a person possessing diplomatic status in this country'.

The practice of seeking a waiver or, in appropriate cases, the withdrawal of the official concerned has been consistently followed in subsequent years. All missions have been treated on a similar basis.

64. In each case the normal procedure is to take into account the strength of available evidence (usually from detailed police reports), the degree of gravity of the alleged offence, whether it was a first or subsequent one, aggravated for example by violence or injury or committed by a dependant, the likely penalty which an offence would have received in the absence of immunity, the recommendation of the Home Office, legal advice (where appropriate) and any other relevant considerations.

65. A diplomat is not able to waive his own immunity. Waivers can be granted only by the sending state, which means that even a Head of Mission will normally consult his home Government. In drink/driving cases a waiver, even if granted, will come too late to allow the necessary medical evidence for conviction to be obtained. A person entitled to diplomatic immunity cannot because of his inviolability under Article 29 be required to undergo a breath test or other medical examination.

66. In view of the nature and extent of abuse, we have examined whether it would be feasible (or even desirable) to obtain agreement either internationally or bilaterally to restrict diplomatic immunity to cover only actions performed in the course of official duties (on the lines of the Vienna Convention on Consular Relations), or alternatively to exclude certain types of offence. We have however found no support within the European Community or elsewhere for the idea of bilateral or limited mutual agreements to waive immunity either generally or in

specific cases. There would in any case be a risk that a restriction on immunity could in certain countries be exploited for political or retaliatory purposes against British diplomats and communities overseas.

67. We have therefore implemented the only realistic alternative. That is to introduce an improved and more detailed code of practice based on a strict application of the measures available under the existing provisions of the Vienna Convention. The main objective is to achieve a better standard of behaviour and a reduction in the number of offences for which immunity can be claimed. In practice this has meant a tightening of the criteria and their application in the handling of individual cases, and specific warnings to missions and individual diplomats about the consequences.

68. Heads of Mission were informed in August 1984 of the statement by the Secretary of State for Foreign and Commonwealth Affairs to the Foreign Affairs Committee of 18 July that 'it would be right in future to expect and to apply more stringent standards'. They were in particular asked for co-operation in waiving immunity or arranging for the withdrawal of any members of staff who may be responsible for serious offences. In accordance with the Committee's recommendation (para 44), specific guidance is now being issued to all diplomats newly appointed to London on the attitude likely to be taken in the event of any breach of UK laws and regulations, including driving and shoplifting offences. They are asked to ensure that dependant members of their families are aware of this guidance. It has also been brought to the attention of existing staff of diplomatic missions.

69. As a general rule espionage and incitement to or advocacy of violence require an immediate declaration of *persona non grata*. Those involved in violent crime or drug trafficking are also declared *persona non grata* unless a waiver of immunity is granted. In addition the following categories of offence normally lead to a request for withdrawal in the absence of a waiver:

(*a*) firearms offences;
(*b*) rape, incest, serious cases of indecent assault and other serious sexual offences;
(*c*) fraud;
(*d*) second drink/driving offence (or first if aggravated by violence or injury to a third party);
(*e*) other traffic offences involving death or serious injury;
(*f*) driving without third party insurance;
(*g*) theft including large scale shoplifting (first case);
(*h*) lesser scale shoplifting (second case);
(*i*) any other offence normally carrying a prison sentence of more than 12 months.

The criteria for dealing with alleged offences are applied with both firmness and discretion, but not automatically. Full account is taken of the nature and seriousness of the offence and any inadequacies in the evidence.

70. Reminders have regularly been sent to missions in recent years on regulations relating to the import, acquisition, possession and use of firearms and the grave view that is taken of any deliberate breach. In June 1984 missions were warned that a breach would normally result in a request for withdrawal of the offender. They were also told that firearms certificates would not be issued for

weapons for use by security staff of missions or personal protection of individuals. They are well aware of the rôle of the Diplomatic Protection Group and the care taken by the Government to fulfil their responsibility to provide appropriate security protection.

71. The application of more stringent standards together with the clarification of guidelines and criteria should lead to a reduction in the number of serious offences involving diplomats and members of their families. The onus is on missions and individuals to respect the basic ground rules or face the consequences. Where a diplomat is transferred because of involvement in a particularly serious criminal offence, the Government will also consider the possibility of reducing a mission's size with regard to the criteria already set out in para 31.

72. A serious view is also taken of any reliance on diplomatic immunity from civil jurisdiction to evade a legal obligation, or to impose on another party to a dispute the person's own view as to liability. Many difficulties over civil claims however arise because of a dispute as to liability or a failure to secure remission of necessary funds from overseas. Again each case has to be treated individually, but the FCO remain ready to make representations calling for a waiver of immunity or for private arbitration where immunity from civil jurisdiction has prevented settlement of an apparently valid claim and where a direct approach to the Head of Mission has yielded no result.

73. UK staff serving overseas are expected to respect the laws and regulations of the receiving state in accordance with Article 41 of the Convention. The Government would not maintain diplomatic immunity from criminal jurisdiction in cases where a waiver would be without prejudice to the work of the mission and the fair treatment of the individual.

(Cmnd. 9497, pp. 22–5)

Turning to the subject of parking offences, the Government stated:

77. In May 1983 wheel-clamps were introduced on an experimental basis in certain parts of Central London. Our initial view was that the wheel-clamping of a car which could be identified by its number plate as belonging to a diplomatic mission or a diplomat was not ruled out by the wording of Article 22.3 of the Vienna Convention, which states that '. . . the means of transport of the mission shall be immune from search, requisition, attachment or execution'. It became clear however that clamping (unlike towing away) is a measure which must be regarded as penal in intent and effect, and thus contravenes Article 31.1 of the Vienna Convention, which provides that a diplomatic agent shall enjoy immunity from criminal jurisdiction of the receiving state. The Minister of State for the Home Department, Lord Elton, therefore announced in the House of Lords on 12 December 1983 that the clamping of cars belonging to diplomats would be discontinued.

79. In addition at least 200 cars belonging to diplomats have been towed away every year over the past few years before wheel-clamping was introduced in 1983. Since then the figures have been somewhat lower. Where the purpose is to relieve obstruction or danger towing away is entirely justified under the Vienna Convention. In so far as resources permit this policy will be vigorously pursued.

(Ibid., pp. 26–7)

The Government next dealt with matters relating to the Libyan People's Bureau in London. Having set out the conclusions of the Foreign Affairs Committee in this respect, the Government stated:

82. . . .

It was not legally possible to cease to recognise the Bureau buildings as premises of the Mission while we remained in diplomatic relations with Libya and the buildings were being used for the purposes of the mission.

83. On matters relating to the FCO's handling of events after 17 April 1984 the Committee concluded (para 127(7)):

(i) whatever answer is given to the question of whether self defence is a concept applicable to the circumstances of St. James's Square, it could not have acted as a lawful basis for the forcible entry of the Bureau premises;
(ii) despite the outrage that had occurred, the bags in principle remained inviolable;
(iii) the decision not to search the Libyan bags was not directed by the requirements of the Vienna Convention (as was commonly supposed), but by the requirements of political judgment; we do not dissent from the judgment that was made;
(iv) the searching of those leaving the Bureau was justified;
(v) we agree with the Government's assessment of their obligations in respect of 5 St. James's Square following its evacuation on 27 April 1984'.

The Government accept the Committee's conclusions.

(Ibid., p. 29)

In the course of a debate on the subject of foreign affairs, the Secretary of State for Foreign and Commonwealth Affairs, Sir Geoffrey Howe, stated:

We are applying the Vienna convention more firmly. Stricter standards are being enforced—in particular, on the size of diplomatic missions, notification of new staff, use of diplomatic premises, handling of diplomatic bags, breaches of criminal law and illegal parking. Heads of diplomatic missions in London have been left in no doubt about the Government's resolve to deal with abuse of diplomatic immunity. We have made it clear that the small minority of diplomats who seriously abuse their immunity—especially for purposes connected with terrorism—are not acceptable in this country.

(HC Debs., vol. 77, col. 1020: 25 April 1985)

In reply to a question which asked on what basis 'certain diplomatic courtesies' were accorded to Mr Vincas Balickas, the Minister of State, Foreign and Commonwealth Office, wrote:

Mr. Balickas enjoys certain personal diplomatic courtesies because he is an individual who held diplomatic rank in the Lithuanian mission in London at the time of the Soviet annexation in 1940.

(Ibid., vol. 79, Written Answers, col. *583*: 24 May 1985)

In reply to a question on the subject of Mr Ahmed Walid Rajab, Counsellor at the Syrian Embassy in London, the Parliamentary Under-Secretary of State, Foreign and Commonwealth Office, wrote:

This case first came to our notice in August 1983 when the Syrian ambassador told officials that the landlord, Mr. Chaffey, had forced an entry into the flat at 21 Stonor Road where Mr. Rajab was living. Our policy in civil disputes of this kind is that the parties should exhaust all legal remedies open to them before the Government can consider intervening. In response to questions from both parties, we gave advice on this basis. We also gave factual information on the status of Mr. Rajab.

The Foreign and Commonwealth Office became directly involved in February 1985 when we were told by Mr. Chaffey's solicitors that Mr. Rajab was not ready to observe a court order to vacate Mr. Chaffey's flat.

The head of protocol department in the Foreign and Commonwealth Office wrote to the Syrian ambassador on 16 April and on 14 May, and summoned him to the Foreign and Commonwealth Office on 31 May to protest strongly about Mr. Rajab's unacceptable behaviour in ignoring a court order.

The ambassador was warned at that stage that we would request the removal of Mr. Rajab from this country if he did not vacate the flat by 14 June.

In view of the stringent standards which we now expect from the Diplomatic Corps in accordance with the criteria laid down in the recent White Paper on diplomatic immunities and privileges, we have today told the Syrian ambassador that, in view of Mr. Rajab's unacceptable behaviour, it would be best to transfer him from this country soon.

(HC Debs., vol. 80, Written Answers, cols. *488–9*: 12 June 1985; see also Written Answer of 26 June 1985)

In reply to a question, the Parliamentary Under-Secretary of State, Foreign and Commonwealth Office, wrote:

Requests by landlords to tenants to vacate premises may lead to a dispute about the legal rights of each side. As was stated in the recent White Paper on Diplomatic Immunities and Privileges (Cmnd. 9497), we take a serious view of any reliance on diplomatic immunity from civil jurisdiction to evade a legal obligation, or to impose on another party to a dispute the person's own view as to liability. In such cases we try to bring the parties together to ensure a satisfactory outcome. But if it is thought appropriate we are prepared to consider the removal of a diplomat who abuses his immunity in this way.

(Ibid., vol. 81, Written Answers, col. *36*: 17 June 1985)

In a letter to the press, the Acting Head of the News Department, Foreign and Commonwealth Office, Mr I. A. Roberts, stated the following on the subject of the above dispute:

. . .

Until February of this year the dispute between Mr Rajab and Mr Chaffey revolved around Mr Rajab's use of British legal procedures—the Rent Act etc.—to protect his position as tenant of Mr Chaffey's flat.

A court gave judgement in favour of Mr Rajab, but ordered him to vacate the premises by the end of February 1985. It was only when Mr Rajab failed to carry out this order that the Foreign and Commonwealth Office became directly involved because the order could not be enforced.

We immediately contacted the Syrian Embassy and when there was inadequate progress we promptly called in the Syrian Ambassador to inform him that Mr Rajab must leave the property within a fortnight. This he did.

Complex legal issues are involved in cases like this. The Foreign Office is not there to settle British legal disputes. But it is our job to ensure that when the court gave judgement, that judgement was not frustrated by misuse of diplomatic immunity. This we did.

(*The London Standard*, 24 June 1985)

In reply to the question whether Her Majesty's Government 'will consider establishing a method of compensation to individuals for any losses they may incur which they are unable to recover through legal action in cases when the defendants have diplomatic immunity', the Minister of State, Foreign and Commonwealth Office, Baroness Young, stated:

No, my Lords. Arrangements already exist with authorised motor insurers to ensure that claims against diplomats in respect of traffic accidents are settled in the usual way. These cause few problems in practice. In other cases where diplomats rely on their immunity from civil jurisdiction to evade a legal obligation, we take action with their head of mission where appropriate. Our intervention is usually successful.

(HL Debs., vol. 465, col. 543: 24 June 1985)

In reply to later questions on the same subject, Baroness Young stated:

. . . the Government's view is that compensation out of public funds for the wrongful acts of diplomats would be inappropriate. The loss that is suffered does not flow directly from the Government's obligation under international law, and even if it did that would be no reason to provide compensation out of public funds.

(Ibid.)

. . . the position so far as diplomats are concerned is that under Article 14 of the Vienna Convention all persons enjoying the privileges and immunities are asked to respect the laws and regulations of the receiving state. In the case of diplomats who have offended against the law in some respect, we draw the attention of the head of mission to all serious offences alleged to have been committed by diplomats. In some cases we request either a waiver of immunity or the removal of the offender. Of course, to be sent home in disgrace can be a severe punishment.

(Ibid., col. 544)

In reply to a further question on the subject of Mr Rajab (Written Answer of 13 June 1985), the Parliamentary Under-Secretary of State, Foreign and Commonwealth Office, wrote:

Before taking any action against diplomats alleged to have used their immunity to default on a civil obligation we need to be satisfied that there has been such an abuse; that legal remedies have been exhausted; and that the diplomat has had time to state his side of the case and to rectify the default.

The Foreign and Commonwealth Office became directly involved in this case in February 1985 when we were told by Mr. Chaffey's solicitors that Mr. Rajab was not ready to observe a court order to vacate Mr. Chaffey's flat. Mr. Rajab eventually vacated the flat before expiry of the deadline for doing so given him by the Foreign and Commonwealth Office. In the circumstances, however, we consider that the early transfer of Mr. Rajab from this country would be in the best interests of relations between the United Kingdom and Syria. We have made this clear to the Syrian authorities, from whom we expect an early response.

(HC Debs., vol. 81, Written Answers, col. *406*: 26 June 1985)

Her Majesty's Government was asked the following question:

... whether they will study as a method of compensating individuals for any losses they may incur which they are unable to recover through legal action in cases where the defendants have diplomatic immunity, the method used in the United States of America of requiring embassies to carry insurance policies for this purpose.

In reply, the Minister of State, Foreign and Commonwealth Office, Baroness Young, made the following remarks:

No, my Lords. I understand that the United States Foreign Missions Amendment Act 1983 ... covers only vehicle insurance. In the United Kingdom the position is as described in the Answer I gave ... on 24th June. We would normally request the transfer of any diplomat found to be driving without third-party insurance.

...

... There are many cases where diplomatic immunity is waived. Indeed, it may in effect be waived by the diplomat himself, who may go before the court and not indicate that he is a diplomat with immunity to waive. It is perfectly possible that such might be done.

(HL Debs., vol. 466, cols. 858–9: 18 July 1985)

The following question was then put to the Minister:

... supposing that in a civil case diplomatic immunity is not waived, could not consideration be given to compensating the person concerned out of public funds, provided he can satisfy the appropriate tribunal that but for the diplomatic immunity he would have a valid claim?

In reply, Baroness Young stated:

... We believe that it would be impossible for officials or a special tribunal to determine the facts of any case without compulsory powers to obtain documentary or written evidence.

Where the facts are clear there is no difficulty in applying political pressure, such as the threat of withdrawal of a diplomat who is found to have committed an offence. The difficult cases are those where the facts or law are in dispute. We could not award compensation simply on the basis of the claimant's version of the case. Furthermore, the existence of the right to compensation could encourage diplomats to flout their obligations, and claimants to inflate or invent claims against diplomats.

(Ibid., col. 860)

In reply to a question, the Minister of State, Foreign and Commonwealth Office, gave the following written statement:

In April this year my department prepared a memorandum for all new diplomats in London drawing attention to various matters of public concern and giving guidance about their behaviour. It is now being issued to all members of diplomatic missions on arrival. In addition, the Permanent Under-Secretary of State for Foreign and Commonwealth Affairs circulated it to all heads of diplomatic missions on 22nd April, asking them to ensure that it was seen by all members of their staff and their dependants who were entitled to diplomatic immunity.

The text of the memorandum is as follows:

Memorandum For All New Diplomats In London
Diplomatic Immunity

This memorandum is intended to be of assistance to all persons entitled to diplomatic privileges and immunities and particularly to those newly appointed to London. It draws attention to a number of matters of public concern.

It would be helpful if you could make sure that members of your family who are with you in London are aware of its contents, since they also apply to all those in a position to claim immunity. Your co-operation and that of your family in maintaining the high standards of conduct expected of the Diplomatic Corps, and in ensuring friendly relations between the corps and the residents of London, will be greatly appreciated.

Diplomats and their families are expected to respect the laws and regulations of the United Kingdom, in accordance with Article 41 of the Vienna Convention on Diplomatic Relations. Diplomatic immunity in no way absolves diplomats from their duty to obey the law. All allegations of breach of the law which come to the attention of the police are thoroughly investigated and the results reported to the Foreign and Commonwealth Office. The Foreign and Commonwealth Office draw these to the attention of the head of mission (or sometimes a senior official) in the expectation of disciplinary action.

In serious cases additional action will be taken. Where a waiver of immunity is not granted to permit trial in this country, violent crime, incitement to or advocacy of violence, espionage and drug trafficking will, as a general rule, result in the offender being declared *persona non grata*. In addition the following categories of offence normally lead to a request for the transfer from post of the offender in the absence of a waiver:

(*a*) *Firearms offences*. A firearm or shotgun certificate from the police is required for all firearms, whether acquired in the UK or imported. In no circumstances will certificates be granted for firearms or shotguns used for personal protection. Any breach of firearms regulations will result in a request for withdrawal of the offender. This is almost always an automatic consequence of an offence of this kind. It should be noted that the possession of other types of weapon, including gas canisters, is also illegal in this country;

(*b*) *Drink-driving offences.* Driving while under the influence of alcohol (or drugs) is a very serious offence. Even a first offence of this kind could lead to a request for withdrawal, particularly if aggravated by violence or injury to a third party. For a second offence this would be automatic;

(*c*) *Other serious traffic offences.* These include incidents involving death or serious injury or driving without third party insurance. Drivers must not only hold a valid driving licence but also be covered by third party insurance. A failure by a diplomat to hold third party insurance for himself or any member of his family who drives a car is likely to lead to a request for his transfer from the UK. Cars must be kept in roadworthy condition; if they are more than three years old, they have to have an annual MOT test of their roadworthiness. Drivers are required to stop if they are involved in an accident and to report the accident to the police within 24 hours unless no personal injury was caused and they provide details of driving licence and insurance to the other driver at the scene of the accident. Exceeding the speed limit can also be regarded as a serious offence;

(*d*) *Theft, including shoplifting.* Customers found outside shop premises with goods which they have taken and intentionally not paid for are normally prosecuted for theft. If a diplomat or a member of his family should be found in this position with no satisfactory explanation, the police will be called and the facts reported to the Foreign and Commonwealth Office. This type of offence may lead to a request for the transfer of the diplomat from the UK and will certainly do so if repeated;

(*e*) *Other serious breaches of criminal law.* These include fraud and serious sexual offences as well as any other offence normally carrying a prison sentence of more than 12 months;

(*f*) *Civil claims.* A serious view is taken of any reliance on diplomatic immunity from civil jurisdiction to evade a legal obligation. Such conduct could call into question a diplomat's continued acceptability in the UK.

The criteria for dealing with alleged offences are applied with both firmness and discretion, but not automatically. Full account is taken of the nature and seriousness of the offence and any inadequacies in the evidence.

Parking. Diplomats are required to comply with local parking regulations and to pay any charges for parking meters and residents' parking spaces. Illegal parking is a matter of considerable public concern in London. It can cause traffic congestion as well as great inconvenience to local residents and traders. The very large number of cases involving cars with diplomatic number plates brings the Diplomatic Corps into disrepute. Cars are liable to be towed away if they cause obstruction or danger. Detailed records are kept of unpaid parking tickets by both individual diplomats and official cars. Persistent failure by individual diplomats to respect parking regulations and pay fixed penalty notices will call into question their continued acceptability as members of diplomatic missions in London.

Finally, diplomats are expected to show consideration towards their neighbours. Inconsiderate behaviour, such as the holding of noisy parties late at night, can bring the name of the mission of the sending state and of the Diplomatic Corps as a whole into disrepute. It can in some cases also constitute a breach of the law.

Whatever action the British Government may decide to take following an incident involving a diplomat or a member of his family will of course depend on a most careful consideration of the nature of that incident. The purpose of this memorandum is to explain informally the possible consequences of breaches of British law. It cannot be taken as determining any particular course of action in any particular case.

More detailed guidance and information on many of these subjects has been communicated in separate notices to diplomatic missions. Protocol Department will be glad to provide further information or answer specific queries.

(HL Debs., vol. 466, cols. 1191–3: 23 July 1985; see also HC Debs., vol. 83, Written Answers, cols. *519–21*: 23 July 1985)

On 8 November 1985, in the Sixth Committee of the General Assembly of the UN, discussing the work of the International Law Commission on the subject of the status of the diplomatic courier and the diplomatic bag not accompanied by diplomatic courier, the UK representative, Sir John Freeland, stated:

The Committee will be well aware from the remarks made on this topic in successive years by United Kingdom representatives that we have always seen the need to control abuse of the diplomatic bag as the real justification of the International Law Commission's work. This remains our central concern; and on reading the Commission's Report we are gratified by the evidence we find that this concern is shared by so many members of the Commission. We welcome the rigorous analysis by the Commission of the difficult issues and the conflicting interests involved. We have also been impressed by the constructive way in which the Special Rapporteur has responded to criticism of his earlier draft and has sought to reconcile the conflicting views expressed in the Commission.

A year ago I informed this Committee that the Select Committee on Foreign Affairs of our House of Commons and our Secretary of State for Foreign and Commonwealth Affairs were separately reviewing the Vienna Convention on Diplomatic Relations, with the particular objective of seeking to curtail abuse of diplomatic immunities and privileges. Both these Reviews have been concluded and their results published. But in spite of the considerable effort that all those concerned with these two investigations have made, in particular in examining the possibilities for international action to control abuse of the diplomatic bag, I am bound to admit that I do not come today with clear and easy solutions to the problems. As was pointed out by my Government in its Review of the Vienna Convention on Diplomatic Relations:

> 'There is widespread concern internationally to prevent improper use of the bag and a number of states are anxious about threats to their own security arising from it. But there is a marked reluctance to take any action that could endanger the security of communications.'

Although our own deliberations have led us to adopt a cautious approach to radical changes in the rules—an approach which, I may say, is shared by many of the other countries with whom we have discussed the matter—we remain highly receptive to new ideas which may be developed by the Commission. We have ourselves found that the rules of the Vienna Convention, supplemented by more general rules of customary international law relating in particular to self-defence and the duty to protect human life, offered greater flexibility of response than was perhaps thought at first. In examining any changes to these familiar rules as supplemented by general international practice, we will wish to ensure that they do not endanger the necessary fundamental balance between, on the one hand, security of communications and, on the other, restraints on possible abuse; and, secondly, that they do not inhibit some of the international practices which have become very widespread in recent years and which do act as a safeguard. I would refer in particular to the very general practice whereby diplomatic agents and couriers, notwithstanding their entitlement to personal inviolability, voluntarily pass through a screening arch before boarding an aircraft and on occasion agree to personal search in the interests of aviation security. Although the Commission has endorsed this practice in regard to screening, we remain concerned that the prohibitions on personal examination of the diplomatic courier in Article 19 and the requirement that waiver from any immunities—not only immunity from legal proceedings—must be express and communicated in writing could cast doubt on existing practices and procedures which are generally thought to be essential in the interests of the safety of air transport and are accepted on that basis.

The overall regime envisaged for diplomatic couriers is now apparent from those articles provisionally adopted by the Commission. We welcome the moves made to reduce the level of new privileges and immunities proposed and to eliminate provisions which would be impracticable to administer or would have no real effect. But we continue to take the view that inviolability for a courier's temporary accommodation would impose an unrealistic and unnecessary burden on the authorities of the receiving state. And although the immunity from jurisdiction now proposed is substantially reduced we continue to be opposed to the grant of any immunity from jurisdiction whatsoever. Our own couriers have travelled for many years in almost every country in the world without immunity from jurisdiction and have never found this gave rise to difficulties. I suspect that the experience of virtually all, if not all, other States is similar. Many of the matters on which a courier is likely to be sued will relate in some way to his functions—an obvious example is the renting of hotel accommodation or transport. Although the commentary makes clear that immunity is not intended to apply to such a case, the question cannot be regarded as beyond argument. Immunity from civil jurisdiction might be thought to be a less sensitive matter than the kind of abuse which so greatly concerned my Government last year. But there is increasing concern in my own country and in a number of others at certain highly publicised incidents of reliance by diplomats on immunity to avoid their civil obligations. There would be no disposition on our part to extend the categories of persons who might be tempted to abuse their immunity.

Article 24 on the identification of the diplomatic bag deals with a matter to which my Government have given careful attention. As our Review of the Vienna Convention makes clear, we have recently issued revised clarification of our rules on the identification and handling of foreign diplomatic bags. Our new rules carefully reflected our own understanding of international law and practice and enable us to check the official origin and endorsement of all items purporting to be diplomatic bags. We strongly agree with the Commission's view set out in the commentary to Article 24 that the rigorous application of the rules on the external marks of the bag operates not only in the interest of the sending State but also in the interest of the receiving State by enabling it to ascertain the *bona fide* character and authenticity of any diplomatic bag. I would however suggest that the

Commission might consider modifying the text of Article 24 so as to incorporate into the concept of 'visible external marks' the indication of destination and consignee. Our own requirements on markings include 'a tag or stick-on label, addressed to the Head of Mission, to the Head of a consular post or to the Minister of Foreign Affairs, and carrying the official stamp of the sending State or the sending diplomatic mission'. We have doubts whether a bag or label simply saying 'Diplomatic Bag' would be a sufficient guarantee of authenticity if the consignment were addressed to some private or commercial enterprise having no connection with the Government.

On Article 25 we have found the commentary helpful in its list of items which may properly be consigned by the diplomatic bag. We have made it very clear in London that no items may be sent by the diplomatic bag where the import or export violates United Kingdom law, as with arms or explosives. This is so regardless of any claim that weapons, for example, might be needed for official use. We find in the Commission's commentary helpful support for this position. We have studied with great interest the account of the conclusion of the Commission's first reading of Articles 36 to 43. Many of the draft articles there we find acceptable and helpful, in particular Articles 37, 39 and 40. But the key provision of the entire draft is obviously Article 36. We have studied with particular interest the Commission's deliberations on scanning—an issue which our own Parliamentary Select Committee and my Government have also considered in some depth. We agree with those members of the Commission who expressed the view 'that although electronic scanning should not be practised as a matter of routine, it should be allowed under specific circumstances when the grounds for suspicion were sufficiently strong to justify scanning'. This view is in line with the conclusions reached by the United Kingdom Government in its Review. We concluded that scanning would not be a wholly effective procedure and that its introduction could make our own bags vulnerable to generalised and indiscriminate challenge, thus seriously undermining our freedom of communication. We have also studied with interest the discussion of the possibility of setting up an optional regime under which States making a written declaration might as among themselves agree to treat diplomatic bags in the way in which consular bags are treated under the Vienna Convention on Consular Relations. This would enable like-minded States to agree that where a State had serious reason to suspect that a bag contained prohibited items it could demand that it be opened or returned to its place of origin. There are undoubted attractions in this idea. I do however have certain misgivings, particularly when reading Article 36 together with the drafts of Articles 42 and 43, as to whether the separate regimes might not in practice become too complex. A uniform regime for bags is of great benefit to all States maintaining diplomatic relations and can be guaranteed only if the rules on treatment are standard in each capital and can be easily applied by Customs Officers. A great variety of possibilities could arise if some States were to agree to treat diplomatic bags like consular bags and others agree to treat consular bags like diplomatic bags, while a third group of States in addition made special agreements modifying as between themselves a regime which already has certain options built into it. This would, I fear, mean that the clearance of diplomatic bags through the airports of major capitals would require the permanent attendance of a qualified international lawyer. It is our hope that in their further deliberations on this the Commission will not lose sight of the ideal of a uniform, and properly balanced, regime. Such a regime cannot match exactly the wishes of all States on the matters of principle at stake but it would undoubtedly prove a great practical benefit to the freedom of all diplomatic communications.

(Text provided by the Foreign and Commonwealth Office: see also A/C. 6/40/SR. 32, pp. 7–8)

Part Five: VIII. B. *Organs of the State—immunity of organs of the State—immunity other than diplomatic and consular*

(See also Part Five: IV., above)

On 6 or 7 June 1983 (the precise date is not clear from the documents below), a Sea Harrier military aircraft of the British Royal Navy made a forced landing on containers stowed on the deck of the Spanish merchant ship *Alraigo* when that ship was about 120 miles west of Oporto in Portugal. The ship, with the aircraft on board, sailed to the Spanish port of Santa Cruz de Tenerife. The following documents, which have been made available to the Editor by the Foreign and Commonwealth Office, take up the story.

The British Embassy in Madrid handed the following Note Verbale to the Spanish Ministry of Foreign Affairs on 9 June 1983:

Her Britannic Majesty's Embassy present their compliments to the Ministry of Foreign Affairs and wish, on instructions from Her Majesty's Government, to refer to the forced landing of a British Sea Harrier aircraft on board the Spanish container ship Alraigo on 6 June 1983. The Alraigo arrived in Tenerife on 9 June with the aircraft on board. Preparations began for the removal of the aircraft from the Alraigo on 9 June but were stopped in the afternoon by the owner.

The Embassy wish to state that this aircraft is a state aircraft, is immune from seizure under international law and should accordingly be handed over to Her Britannic Majesty's Government. At the same time Her Britannic Majesty's Government wish to give the assurance that they will negotiate fairly in respect of any claims with the owners of the Alraigo and will submit to arbitration if necessary. However Her Britannic Majesty's Government cannot submit to the jurisdiction of a Spanish court on this matter. They are ready to agree to submit to a British court matters arising out of this forced landing.

In view of the foregoing Her Britannic Majesty's Government would be most grateful if the Spanish Government would make the necessary arrangements to secure the immediate release of the aircraft from the Alraigo and its transfer to Her Britannic Majesty's Government. Representatives of Her Britannic Majesty's Government in Tenerife will, in cooperation with the appropriate Spanish authorities, make all the necessary arrangements for the return of the aircraft back to the United Kingdom.

On 10 June 1983, the British Consul in the Canary Islands filed a statement before the Permanent Maritime Court in Tenerife. The statement was written in the Spanish language. The following translation has been provided by the Foreign and Commonwealth Office and modified slightly by the Editor:

TO THE PERMANENT MARITIME COURT

Mr. DAVID G. ALEXANDER, British Consul in the Canary Islands, resident in Las Palmas de Gran Canaria, carrier of identity card number 6 issued in 1980 by the Spanish Ministry of Foreign Affairs appears before Your Honour and, representing the British Government, STATES:

First.—That on 9 June 1983 the Spanish vessel 'ALRAIGO', which had on its deck a 'SEA HARRIER' type military aircraft belonging to the British Royal Navy, berthed in the Port of Santa Cruz de Tenerife.

Second.—That the said military aircraft, piloted by Royal Navy Sub-Lieutenant Ian Watson, took off from the ship H.M.S. ILLUSTRIOUS at approximately 1600 hours G.M.T. on Tuesday 7 June 1983 at about one hundred and fifty nautical miles N.E. of the said ship.

Three.—That as a result of a failure in the aircraft's navigating equipment, the pilot tried to make contact with H.M.S. ILLUSTRIOUS by radio, which he was unable to do because of a breakdown in the latter, and he also tried to locate the ship by sight without success. Finding himself in this situation, the pilot Sub-Lieutenant Ian Watson located a ship by radar and flew directly over it, then he found that he only had fuel in his tanks for a further ten minutes of flying.

Four.—That on flying over the said ship, Sub-Lieutenant Watson established that the vessel was wide enough for him to make a vertical landing, and he proceeded to do so on the deck of the said ship which at that moment was in international waters about one hundred and twenty miles off the coast of Portugal, level with the town of Oporto.

Five.—That the ship on which he made the landing turned out to be the 'ALRAIGO', of Spanish nationality, which proceeded to transport the aircraft and pilot to Santa Cruz de Tenerife, in which port it berthed on 9 June 1983 at about 13.20 hours.

Six.—That the appearer, in the capacity of representation which he has, declares that the said military aircraft is the property of the United Kingdom and in the service of its Royal Navy.

Seven.—That as a result of the landing made by the aircraft in operation, according to the shipowners some damage was apparently caused to the cargo, the extent of which the appearer has no evidence of.

Eight.—That in order to reach an agreement with the shipowner and crew of the vessel 'ALRAIGO' in respect of fixing and paying for however much might be due to them as a result of the aircraft's landing and transportation of the aircraft to this port of Santa Cruz de Tenerife, the appearer wishes to state that he offered them a guarantee consisting of the signing of a 'Lloyd's Standard Form of Salvage Agreement' which they did not accept.

Nine.—That the appearer, in the capacity of representation which he has, states that the 'SEA HARRIER' type military aircraft referred to above is public property belonging to the United Kingdom and as such, in accordance with the principle in International Public Law of 'Sovereign Immunity', it cannot be the object of any kind of insurance or preventive measure for guaranteeing payment of any compensation and/or payment which might be in order, and he furthermore believes that, with regard to the said principle of 'Sovereign Immunity', Spanish courts are not competent to try the present case.

On the basis of the legal principles pleaded in this statement, he puts forward the following

LEGAL CONSIDERATIONS

First.—The 1969 Vienna Convention on Diplomatic Relations, signed and ratified by Spain and Great Britain, confirms the principle in International Public Law of 'Sovereign Immunity', which has been adopted in numerous legal cases.

Thus, in the 'Arantzazu Mendi' case and many others, the 'de facto' possession of property by a foreign State has been sufficient to prevent the Courts from admitting any claim by the owners for recovering possession thereof, if not asserting their right. In this legal case, which took place during the Spanish Civil War, the Republican Government claimed before the British Government for the possession of a vessel which the said Republican Government intended to requisition but which had been placed by its Captain at the order of General Franco. The British Court was informed by the Foreign Office that Great Britain recognized Franco's government as the one which had 'de facto' administrative control of the greater part of Spain, including Bilbao, the port at which the ship was registered, and that it was not subordinate to any other government. This declaration was interpreted by the Court to the effect that it implied recognition that General Franco's government was the 'de facto government', and the petition was rejected.

Likewise, I cite the case 'Baccus Srl v. Servicio Nacional del Trigo' [1957] 1 Q.B. 438, in which the principle of 'Sovereign Immunity' was applied in favour of a Spanish State Body, namely the Ministry of Agriculture.

International legal thinking considers that the principle of 'Sovereign Immunity' consists of the following: 'As a consequence of the absolute independence of every sovereign authority, and of the international obligation which induces every Sovereign State to respect the independence and dignity of any other Sovereign State, each and every one of them decline to exercise through their courts any territorial jurisdiction over the person of any Sovereign or Ambassador of any other State, or over the public property of any State, which is intended for public use, or over the property of any Ambassador. In principle it is a provision of customary law and means that a foreign Sovereign State, its public property and its official agents are generally immune from local jurisdiction, except where the foreign State itself chooses to renounce its privilege. If any dispute arises between the territorial sovereign and the foreign State, it may only be dealt with through the diplomatic channel or in any international court of justice, except when the foreign State renounces its immunity in favour of local jurisdiction.

International legal thinking also considers that war ships and war planes, and other vessels of a public nature, raise the special problem of being more than property, forming a closely linked unit, with their crews, and constitute in the military sphere a part of the State which is not very different from an Embassy, or a Delegation in the diplomatic sphere. At any rate, not only can no proceedings be brought against the vessel or aircraft, but also the latter are inviolable, and the local authorities may not enter them, on any pretext, without the consent of the officers; under the command of the latter.

Second.—Article 44 of the General Budgetary Law (Law 11/1977), and Article 18 of the Law on State Proprietorship (Law 1,022/1964), which confirms the principle of non-attachability of Spanish State property, as goods which come under public law; which takes the form in our international law of a principle of international public law sanctioned by Spanish law, with the old precedent of the Law on Administration and Accounting of the Public Treasury, of 1 July 1911, and in Great Britain by the [State Immunity Act of 1978].

Third.—Article 7 of our Civil Code on the abuse of process.

By virtue of which he proceeds and,

REQUESTS

that the COURT, taking cognizance of the fact that this writ has been presented before it, should deign to accept it, consider the aforementioned statements to have been made and, following the appropriate steps in the proceedings, should order: (a) the immediate return of the military aircraft which is on board the vessel ALRAIGO which is anchored in this port and that the said aircraft be placed at the disposal of the hearer as representative of the British Government; (b) that the appropriate orders and/or authorisations be given for transfer of the aircraft in question to the vessel designated by the appearer so that it may be conveyed to the United Kingdom; (c) that the said transfer be carried out by technical personnel, designated by the appearer, following the instructions which this personnel gives in order to carry out the said operation; (d) that whilst the said aircraft is in the port of Santa Cruz de Tenerife, it is given the necessary protection for its safekeeping; (e) that whilst the aircraft in question is on board the vessel ALRAIGO, anchored in this port, the said vessel should be prevented from putting to sea, and should therefore remain in this capital city; (f) that, on the basis of the 'sovereign immunity' principle, the Court to which I am making this application should declare itself without competence, consequently disqualifying itself from hearing the present case, once the necessary measures in this plea have been taken.

On 13 June 1983, the Permanent Maritime Court issued a decision in the following terms:

. . . this Court has not made an order withholding the Royal Navy 'Sea Harrier' aircraft in port, since in the view of this Court it is free property at the disposal of its legitimate owners.

In a Note Verbale of the same day, the British Embassy in Madrid informed the Ministry of Foreign Affairs in part as follows:

The Embassy wish to assure the owners, Captain and crew of MV Alraigo of the Ministry of Defence's recognition that this incident will be treated as a matter of maritime salvage, and of the Ministry of Defence's firm and irrevocable commitment to pay any reasonable salvage claim made in respect of the aircraft. The Embassy acknowledges, on behalf of the Ministry of Defence, that the physical return of the aircraft does not prejudice any claim which may arise as a result of this incident.

On 15 June 1983, the following 'Letter of Guarantee' was issued from the British Embassy 'on behalf of Her Majesty's Government' addressed to Naviera García Miñaur SA, the owners of the *Alraigo*:

1. We wish to inform you of our acknowledgement of the assistance given to the Sea Harrier and pilot some 120 miles off the Portuguese coast on the 6th June by the vessel named Alraigo owned by Naviera García Miñaur SA and by its Captain and crew.

2. We wish to assure you of our recognition that this incident will be treated as a matter of maritime salvage, and of the vital part taken in the recovery of the aircraft by the presence of MV Alraigo and the timely efforts of the Master and crew of the Alraigo.

3. We also wish to assure you of our firm and irrevocable commitment to pay any reasonable salvage claim made in respect of this incident. The amount of the claim should take into account any damage to the ship and all reasonable costs that may have fallen to the Owners of the ship heretofore as a result of delay in delivering their cargo.

4. The matter of payment for damage caused to the containers, their contents and any other cargo, in particular the vehicle, will be dealt with separately between ourselves and the Owners of such cargo. If, however, the cargo owners bring a successful action against the shipowners in respect of such damage, we will indemnify the shipowners provided notice of proceedings is given to us.

5. We formally agree, on behalf of Her Britannic Majesty's Government, to pay on demand any total amount that may be determined by negotiation and amicable agreement between our representatives and the representatives of the Owners and the Captain and crew of the Alraigo.

6. We regret that, because the aircraft and its contents are the property of Her Britannic Majesty's Government, it is not possible to submit the case to arbitration before courts other than those of Her Britannic Majesty.

7. We nevertheless formally agree that if it is not possible to agree a total amount of salvage by negotiations and amicable agreement, the Ministry of Defence are prepared to submit to an agreement that the assessment of the total amount shall be submitted to independent arbitration in London, namely by the applicable Lloyds arbitration proceedings.

An appeal to the Central Maritime Court from the decision of 13 June 1983 above was made by two seamen from the *Alraigo*. In the 'Grounds for Appeal' it was stated *inter alia*:

There does not exist in our Positive Law, whether of domestic or international origin, any provision which exempts an aircraft salvaged at sea from being withheld owing to the fact that it is foreign military aircraft.

The provision that warships and war aircraft are not attachable is limited to a privilege of Spanish State property before our own Courts and cannot be extended by analogy, it being an exceptional rule limiting individual rights.

Furthermore, it should be stressed that Spain did not ratify the 1926 Brussels Convention on the Immunity of State Vessels, nor the 1967 Brussels Protocol amending the 1910 Convention on Assistance at Sea, on account of which these conventions cannot be put forward or taken into account, since it is not possible to suppose that our legislator, who ratified so many Maritime Conventions, omitted these through error or oversight. The fact that they were not ratified shows a clear wish on the part of the Spanish legislator not to uphold the provision of non-attachability in cases such as the present one.

The Spanish–British Consular Agreement of 1961 and the 1963 Vienna Convention on Consular Relations are obviously not applicable to the case which concerns us, since they refer exclusively to 'vehicles or aircraft of the Consulate', which in no way is the case in this instance.

On 27 June 1983, this appeal was abandoned.

The issue was submitted to arbitration in London. On 12 July 1984, the arbitrator, Mr Gerald Darling QC, delivered an award under which the owner, master and crew of the *Alraigo* were awarded a total of £412,000.

On 12 October 1984, the Governments of the UK and Kenya concluded an agreement concerning the status of UK forces in Kenya. The Agreement contains the following Article:

EXEMPTION FOR VESSELS, VEHICLES AND AIRCRAFT

13. (*a*) Vessels, vehicles and aircraft which are the property of the British Forces in Kenya or on charter to them and are for the time being exclusively in their service shall be exempt from any form of compulsory insurance, registration, licensing or compulsory testing.

(*b*) The movement of vessels, vehicles or aircraft belonging to the British Forces in Kenya, in and over Kenya and territorial waters of Kenya under this agreement shall be free from compulsory pilotage, harbour charges and all dues or tolls, except landing fees, air navigation, service charges and charges for specific services rendered at the request of the United Kingdom service authorities. Landing fees at Kenyan military airfields will continue to be waived in favour of aircraft in the service of the United Kingdom Government.

(*c*) The clearance for entry into or exit out of Kenya of all vessels and aircraft connected with the official use thereof by the British Forces shall be directed through normal diplomatic channels. British military vehicles entering Kenya by road on official duties shall be cleared through other official channels.

(Cmnd. 9446).

On 8 November 1985, in the Sixth Committee of the General Assembly of the UN, discussing the recent work of the International Law Commission on the subject of jurisdictional immunities of States and their property, the UK representative, Sir John Freeland, stated:

. . . it continues to be our view that State-owned ships employed in commercial service should not enjoy immunity. We accordingly do not favour the inclusion of the double criterion of 'commercial non-government service', which we consider would pose difficulties of interpretation and involve a narrowing of the exception to an unacceptable extent. We therefore consider that the expression 'non-governmental', wherever it appears in square brackets in the draft article [19], should be omitted.

(Text provided by the Foreign and Commonwealth Office; see also A/C. 6/40/SR. 32, p. 9).

Part Six: I. A. *Treaties—conclusion and entry into force—conclusion, signature*

In reply to the questions in what respects the wording of the Dublin version of the Anglo-Irish agreement differs from the London version, and which text is authoritative, the Parliamentary Under-Secretary of State, Foreign and Commonwealth Office, wrote:

In accordance with standard international practice, precedence is given to the United Kingdom in the original retained in London and to the Republic of Ireland in the original retained in Dublin. In addition, and in line with long established precedent in bilateral treaties with the Republic, each country's original of the agreement uses its own nomenclature in reference to itself and to the other country. There are no substantive differences between the texts, both originals of which are authoritative.

(HC Debs., vol. 89, Written Answers, col. *132*: 17 December 1985)

Part Six: I. B. *Treaties—conclusion and entry into force—reservations and declarations to multilateral treaties*

(See also Part Eight: II. C. (item of 25 January 1985), below)

In reply to a question, the Parliamentary Under-Secretary of State, Foreign and Commonwealth Office, wrote:

The following statement was made on signature of the United Nations Convention Against Torture and Other Forms of Cruel, Inhuman or Degrading Treatment or Punishment.

'The United Kingdom reserves the right to formulate, upon ratifying the Convention, any reservations or interpretative declarations which it might consider necessary.'

This was to reserve our position should we consider any such reservations or declarations necessary for technical or legal reasons on ratification.

Of the countries which have signed thus far, none has made similar statements.

(Ibid., vol. 77, Written Answers, col. *35*: 15 April 1985)

In reply to a question in respect of the UN Convention on the Elimination of All Forms of Discrimination against Women, the Minister of State, Foreign and Commonwealth Office, Baroness Young, stated:

. . . if we decided to ratify the convention we would enter a number of reservations. They are still of course under discussion so I cannot go into all the details. But they would cover such areas as succession to the throne and hereditary titles, the right of education authorities to determine curricula and text books, as they do at present, and the affairs of religious ministries. In fact, a number of other countries, including some of our European Community partners, have entered reservations upon ratification.

(HL Debs., vol. 464, col. 1124: 11 June 1985; see also ibid., vol. 465, col. 360: 19 June 1985)

Part Six: I. C. *Treaties—conclusion and entry into force—entry into force, ratification and accession*

(See also Part One: II. D. (item of 8 November 1984), above)

The Department of Transport presented a memorandum to the House of Lords Select Committee on the European Communities which was examining the subject of the external competence of the European Community. The memorandum, which was discussed in December 1984, contained the following passage:

There is in principle no reason why the Community should not legislate by reference to an international instrument but there is an obvious difficulty in doing so by requiring Member States to ratify or accede to an international agreement . . . Ratification or accession to, an international agreement, is an exercise by the Member State of its national sovereignty and it is not therefore open to the Community to require ratification or accession by the Member States who have not already done so.

(*Parliamentary Papers*, 1984–5, HL, Paper 236, Evidence, p. 44)

In reply to a question, the Paymaster General set out in tabular form the titles of the 161 conventions adopted by the International Labour Organization, indicating that the UK had ratified and was currently bound by seventy-one of them.

(HC Debs., vol. 84, Written Answers, cols. *236–8*: 24 October 1985)

Part Six: II. A. *Treaties—observance, application and interpretation—observance*

(See Part Ten: II. A. 2., below)

In the course of a statement on 29 November 1985 to the First Committee of the UN General Assembly on the subject of Antarctica, the UK representative, Dr J. A. Heap, remarked:

I believe it important that we should all be clear as to what is happening here in this Committee. In the view of my Government, it is that a Treaty which has been concluded by sovereign States outside the United Nations is under attack within this Committee of the United Nations.

The representative of New Zealand has already drawn our attention to that part of the United Nations Charter which such an attack calls into question. He quoted the third preambular paragraph, which if I may remind members, says:

> 'We the peoples of the United Nations determined to establish conditions under which justice and respect for the obligations arising from treaties and other sources of international law can be maintained'.

Now, my Government sees here an issue of principle which is important to the United Nations as a whole, namely, the principle of *pacta sunt servanda* to which I referred in my statement to the Committee last year. It is a serious thing to my Government that as this debate unfolds it becomes progressively more difficult to see the purposes of the instigators as being conducive to the establishment of conditions for the maintenance of 'respect for the obligations arising from treaties'.

That is the nature of the attack, and it is one which my Government sees as being important to oppose as a matter of principle. We will not be parties to a precedent which calls into question one of the basic tenets upon which international law and order are based.

(A/C. 1/40/PV. 53, pp. 2–5)

Part Six: II. C. *Treaties—observance, application and interpretation—interpretation*

In the course of a written answer, the Parliamentary Under-Secretary of State, Department of Trade and Industry, stated:

. . . the Soviet Union notification to the Universal Postal Union of prohibited articles is so widely drawn as to allow the Soviet authorities, in theory, to refuse entry or to confiscate items that we should consider quite innocuous. In our view, the Soviet Union's interpretation of the UPU Convention in this respect is unsatisfactory and we will continue to take every suitable opportunity to press the Soviet authorities to adopt a more reasonable attitude.

(HL Debs., vol. 467, col. 331: 31 July 1985)

Part Six: II. D. *Treaties—observance, application and interpretation—treaties and third States*

(See Part Eight: IV. (item of 29 November 1985), below)

Part Six: IV. C. *Treaties—invalidity, termination and suspension of operation—termination, suspension of operation, denunciation*

In reply to a question on the subject of International Labour Organization Convention No. 26, the Parliamentary Under-Secretary of State, Department of Employment, wrote:

Her Majesty's Government intends to communicate the instrument of denunciation to the Director General of the International Labour Office for registration on 25 July 1985. The denunciation will become effective one year after it is registered.

(HC Debs., vol. 83, Written Answers, col. *366*: 22 July 1985)

Part Six: V. *Treaties—depositaries, notification, corrections and registration*

In reply to a question on the subject of Her Majesty's Government's execution of its obligations as a depositary power under the nuclear non-proliferation treaty, the Parliamentary Under-Secretary of State, Foreign and Commonwealth Office, wrote:

As required by article IX(5) of the treaty, we have promptly informed all signatory and acceding states of the date of each signature, the date of deposit of each instrument of ratification or accession, and the date of the treaty's entry into force. As required by article IX(6), we registered the treaty pursuant to article 102 of the United Nations Charter. We have also played a full part in setting up the third non-proliferation treaty review conference to be held in Geneva in September 1985.

(Ibid., vol. 78, Written Answers, col. *260*: 3 May 1985)

The Foreign and Commonwealth Office issued the following press statement on 13 June 1985:

In accordance with our obligation under Article 102 of the UN Charter, the United Kingdom Mission to the United Nations registered, on 12 June, with the UN Secretariat in New York, the Joint Declaration of the Government of the United Kingdom of Great Britain and Northern Ireland and the Government of the People's Republic of China on the question of Hong Kong. The Chinese Mission to the United Nations registered the Joint Declaration simultaneously. We welcome this. The registration ceremony was attended by the British and Chinese Permanent Representatives to the United Nations. This early action to register the Joint Declaration underlines once again the serious commitment of the two sides to its full implementation.

(Text provided by the Foreign and Commonwealth Office)

Part Seven: I. *Personal jurisdiction—general concept*

(See Part Four: I. (speech of the Attorney General in 1983), above)

Part Eight: II. A. *State territory and territorial jurisdiction—territorial jurisdiction—territorial sovereignty*

In reply to a question on the subject of the transfer to Chile of the Adelaide base in Antarctica, the Parliamentary Under-Secretary of State, Foreign and Commonwealth Office, wrote:

Article IV of the Antarctica Treaty states, inter alia, that 'no acts or activities taking place while the present Treaty is in force shall constitute a basis for asserting, supporting or denying a claim to territorial sovereignty in Antarctica.' The arrangements made with Chile over the use of the Adelaide base thus have no legal effect on the sovereignty positions of either the United Kingdom or Chile in Antarctica and would have no direct bearing on any future review of the treaty.

(HC Debs., vol. 71, Written Answers, col. *138*: 16 January 1985)

In the course of a debate in the House of Lords on the subject of Anglo-Argentine relations, the Minister of State, Foreign and Commonwealth Office, Baroness Young, stated:

. . . we have no doubt as to our sovereignty over the Falkland Islands.

(HL Debs., vol. 458, col. 1073: 17 January 1985)

In the course of a letter dated 24 January 1985 from the Permanent Representative of the UK to the UN, Sir John Thomson, to the Secretary-General, it was stated:

The Government of the United Kingdom rejects the assertion that the Falkland Islands are an integral part of Argentine national territory. The Falkland Islands are British territory. It is worth repeating here that the United Kingdom's title to the Falkland Islands is derived from early settlement, reinforced by formal claims in the name of the Crown and completed by open, continuous, effective and peaceful possession, occupation and administration of the islands since 1833 (with the exception of an involuntary hiatus in 1982). The exercise of sovereignty by the United Kingdom over the islands has, furthermore, consistently been shown to accord with the wishes, expressed through their democratically elected representatives, of the islanders themselves.

(A/40/97)

In reply to the question whether 'Her Majesty's Government have sought outside legal advice as to the comparative validity of the United Kingdom's constitutional and territorial claims to the Falkland Islands and South Georgia, respectively', the Prime Minister wrote:

Communications between the Government and legal advisers are confidential and it would not be in accordance with the practice in matters such as this to disclose the source of the advice which the Government have received.

The Government have stated on numerous occasions that they have no doubt about British sovereignty over the Falkland Islands or the Falkland Islands Dependencies.

(HC Debs., vol. 72, Written Answers, col. *387*: 4 February 1985)

In the course of a debate on the subject of Gibraltar, the Secretary of State for Foreign and Commonwealth Affairs, Sir Geoffrey Howe, stated:

There is no parallel between the case of Gibraltar and that of the Falkland Islands. They are historically, legally and constitutionally quite different. Perhaps the most important difference is that Spain recognises the validity of our title under the treaty of Utrecht whereas Argentina refuses to acknowledge our sovereignty over the Falkland Islands. Spain's attitude to the rights of the inhabitants of Gibraltar is also markedly different. Spain is an ally in NATO and a prospective partner in the European Community and has publicly stated that it intends to pursue its claim by peaceful means. The right hon. Gentleman will appreciate that that is in total contrast with the historical, geographical and constitutional position of the Falkland Islands. Our position in relation to the Falkland Islands remains unchanged.

(Ibid., col. 938: 6 February 1985)

Later in the debate, the Secretary of State observed:

. . . British sovereignty over Gibraltar is plainly founded upon the treaty of Utrecht without any limit to its term. That is in total contrast to Hong Kong where 92 per cent. is held on a lease that is due to expire in 1997.

(Ibid., col. 944)

In reply to the question whether (*a*) NATO and (*b*) the European Economic Community consider Ceuta and Melilla 'European Territory', the Minister of State, Foreign and Commonwealth Office, wrote:

Ceuta and Melilla do not form part of the North Atlantic Area as defined in the North Atlantic Treaty. It is common ground that the terms of Spain's accession to the European Community will apply to all parts of the Kingdom of Spain, of which, under Spanish law, Ceuta and Melilla form a part.

(HL Debs., vol. 460, col. 668: 20 February 1985)

In reply to an oral question on the subject of the sovereign base areas in Cyprus, the Minister of State for the Armed Forces, Mr John Stanley, remarked:

. . . The base is sovereign British territory as laid down in the 1960 treaty. It has the full rights of sovereignty that we associate with the use of that word.

(HC Debs., vol. 74, col. 161: 26 February 1985)

Following the publication of the Fifth Report from the Foreign Affairs Committee of the House of Commons, which dealt with the Falkland Islands (*Parliamentary Papers*, 1983–4, HC, Paper 268-i), Her Majesty's Government made certain observations on it in February 1985. In particular, it stated:

INTRODUCTION

1. Prior to the invasion of the Falkland Islands by Argentina on 2 April 1982, successive British Governments had been engaged in an effort to find a negotiated solution to the long-standing differences between Britain and Argentina over the status of the Falkland Islands and their people. The British aim had been to try to reconcile our own position on sovereignty, and the wishes and interests of the Falkland Islanders, with Argentina's deeply held belief in its own claim to the Islands. The attempts to reach a negotiated solution have been thoroughly documented in the Report of the Committee of Privy Councillors under the Chairmanship of Lord Franks published in 1983 (Cmnd. 8787).

2. Argentina broke off this search for a negotiated solution by its resort to force in 1982, in breach of the fundamental principles of the United Nations Charter. That action created a new situation. Its impact on opinion in Britain and in the Islands will be long-lasting. The restoration of confidence will require realism and patience on both sides. The British Government took the initiative in seeking to improve our relations with the democratically elected Government of Argentina and will continue to pursue this objective. But we are not prepared to resume discussion of the future of the Islands with Argentina. The question of sovereignty must be set aside, and efforts made to restore the traditionally good relations which existed between the United Kingdom and Argentina without prejudice to our differing positions over the Islands.

SOVEREIGNTY AND SELF-DETERMINATION

3. The Government regret the Committee's reluctance to reach a categorical conclusion on the legal validity of Britain's title to the Islands (paragraph 22). The

Government's position on sovereignty over the Falkland Islands has been made clear on numerous occasions. The Islands are British territory. Britain's title is derived from early settlement, reinforced by formal claims in the name of the Crown and completed by open, continuous, effective and peaceful possession, occupation and administration of the Islands since 1833 (save for the 10 weeks of forcible Argentine occupation in 1982). The exercise of sovereignty by the United Kingdom over the Falkland Islands has, furthermore, consistently been shown to accord with the wishes of the Islanders, expressed through their democratically elected representatives.

4. The Government also find it surprising that the Report seeks to argue (paragraph 42) that our assertions of confidence in the strength of British title are belied by the fact of the negotiations with Argentina between 1967 and 1982, and by doubts expressed by officials during the first half of this century. That successive British Governments were prepared to seek a negotiated resolution of our differences with the Government of Argentina over the Islands should not be taken as a reflection of any doubts about British title. And it is hardly surprising that, with a subject as complicated as the history of the Falkland Islands, differing and in some cases conflicting views on the question of sovereignty should in the past have been expressed from time to time by officials. These comments were made when concepts of international law, such as prescription and self-determination, were less clearly established than they are today. Successive British Governments have made it clear that they have no doubts about our sovereignty over the Falkland Islands.

(Cmnd. 9447, pp. 3–4)

In the course of a debate on the subject of the above report of the Foreign Affairs Committee, the Secretary of State for Foreign and Commonwealth Affairs, Sir Geoffrey Howe, stated:

Some concerns were expressed in the islands about the Government's decision to promulgate separate constitutions for the Falkland Islands and for the dependencies on the ground that this might imply an intention to relinquish sovereignty over the Falkland Islands while retaining the dependencies. I can assure the House that there are absolutely no grounds for that anxiety. We have no such intention. Our position on sovereignty is firm.

That is one of the few points on which we take a different view from the Committee. I have to say that we were disappointed that its report did not reach a categorical conclusion on the legal validity of Britain's title to the Falkland Islands. Successive British Governments have had no such doubts. In their view—and in our view—the islands are British territory.

(HC Debs., vol. 75, cols. 492–3: 14 March 1985)

In reply to a question on the subject of discussions between the UK and Irish Governments on the sovereignty of Rockall, the Parliamentary Under-Secretary of State, Foreign and Commonwealth Office, wrote:

Discussions have taken place in the past about the delimitation of the continental shelf in the area of the Hatton Rockall plateau, but there have been no discussions about our sovereignty over the island of Rockall.

(Ibid., vol. 84, Written Answers, col. *176*: 23 October 1985)

Speaking on a motion to approve the Anglo-Irish Agreement of 15 November 1985, the Prime Minister, Mrs Margaret Thatcher, stated:

Article 1 of the agreement makes it abundantly clear that there is no threat whatsoever to Unionists' heartfelt desire to remain part of the United Kingdom. It provides, in a formally binding international accord, a recognition by the Irish Government that the status of Northern Ireland will remain unchanged as long as that is the wish of a majority of the people of Northern Ireland.

(Ibid., vol. 87, col. 748: 26 November 1985)

Later in her speech, the Prime Minister said:

. . . I want to make it clear that the agreement does not detract from British sovereignty in Northern Ireland—or, for that matter, from Irish sovereignty in the republic.

(Ibid., col. 750)

Speaking in the debate on the subject of the Falkland Islands in the General Assembly on 27 November 1985, the Permanent Representative of the UK, Sir John Thomson, stated:

My Government, I repeat, takes the clear position that our sovereignty, on which we have no doubts, is not for negotiation.

(A/40/PV. 93, p. 11)

Later in the same debate, Sir John Thomson remarked:

South Georgia and South Sandwich islands were mentioned. They are a quite separate matter from the Falkland Islands. They were claimed by the Argentines many, many years after they began their claim to the Falkland Islands. They have a totally different history. I must say that my Government has no doubt about our sovereignty over those islands, as we have no doubt in the case of the Falklands.

(Ibid., p. 17)

Part Eight: II. C. *State territory and territorial jurisdiction—territorial jurisdiction—concurrent territorial jurisdiction*

On 12 October 1984, the Governments of the UK and Kenya concluded an agreement concerning the status of UK forces in Kenya. The agreement contains the following Article:

JURISDICTION

3. (*a*) Subject to the provisions of this paragraph:

(i) the United Kingdom service authorities may exercise, within Kenya or on board any ship or aircraft of Kenya all criminal and disciplinary jurisdiction conferred on them by the law of the United Kingdom over members of the British Forces in Kenya and civilian component and dependants;

(ii) the courts of Kenya may exercise jurisdiction over members of the British Forces in Kenya and civilian component and dependants with respect to offences committed in Kenya and punishable by the law of Kenya.

(*b*) In cases where the right to exercise jurisdiction is concurrent the United Kingdom service authorities shall have the primary right to exercise jurisdiction if:

(i) the offence is an offence against the property or security of the United Kingdom, or against the property or person of another member of the British Forces in Kenya or civilian component or dependants, or Loan Service Personnel or their dependants; or
(ii) the offence arises out of an act or omission done in the course of official duty.

In any other case the courts of Kenya shall have the primary right to exercise jurisdiction with respect to offences committed in Kenya and punishable by the Laws of Kenya. If the State having the primary right decides not to exercise jurisdiction, it shall notify the authorities of the other State as soon as practicable. The authorities of the State having the primary right shall give sympathetic consideration to a request from the authorities of the other State for a waiver of its right in cases where the other State considers such waiver to be of particular importance and in cases of minor offences where the courts of Kenya have the primary right and where the United Kingdom service authorities can impose a suitable punishment by disciplinary action without recourse to a court.

. . .

(Cmnd. 9446)

The following three items are representative of many along similar lines made during the period.

In a letter dated 14 December 1984, the Soviet delegation to the Eighth Session of the Steering Body to the Co-operative Programme for Monitoring and Evaluation of the Long-Range Transmission of Air Pollutants in Europe (EMEP) protested against the inclusion in the delegation of the Federal Republic of Germany of an employee of the Federal Environment Agency located in the Western sectors of Berlin. In its reply dated the same day, the Ambassador of France to the UN in Geneva, on behalf also of the delegations of the United States of America and the UK, stated:

L'établissement de l'Agence fédérale de l'Environnement dans les secteurs occidentaux de Berlin a été approuvé par les autorités américaines, britanniques et françaises, agissant dans l'exercice de leur autorité suprême. Ces autorités se sont assurées que l'Agence fédérale n'accomplit pas dans les secteurs occidentaux de Berlin d'actes dans l'exercice d'une autorité étatique directe sur les secteurs occidentaux de Berlin. Par conséquent l'établissement et les activités de cette Agence dans les secteurs occidentaux de Berlin ne sont contraires à aucune des dispositions de l'Accord quadripartite du 3 septembre 1971.

En outre, aucune disposition de l'Accord quadripartite ne peut être utilisée à l'appui de l'affirmation selon laquelle des résidents des secteurs occidentaux de Berlin ne peuvent pas être inclus dans les délégations de la RFA dans les Conférences internationales. L'annexe IV de l'Accord quadripartite stipule que, à condition que les questions de sécurité et de statut ne soient pas affectées, la RFA peut représenter les intérêts des secteurs occidentaux de Berlin dans les Organisations et Conférences internationales et que les résidents permanents des secteurs occidentaux de Berlin peuvent participer, ensemble avec les représentants de la RFA, aux échanges et expositions internationaux.

(Text provided by the Foreign and Commonwealth Office)

In a letter dated 10 May 1985, the Soviet delegate to the Thirty-Eighth World Health Assembly advised its President:

The delegation of the USSR at the Thirty-eighth World Health Assembly, referring to the list of participants in the Assembly (document WHA38/DIV/3 Rev. 1 of 9 May 1985), deems it necessary to state in connection with the inclusion of Dr Ruth Mattheis, Director of the Public Health Department of West Berlin, in the delegation of the Federal Republic of Germany, that this inclusion may be recognized only with due regard for the political status of West Berlin and for the fact that the participation of permanent residents of West Berlin in international meetings jointly with representatives of the Federal Republic of Germany is possible only on the basis of the provisions of the four-power agreement of 3 September 1971, according to which West Berlin is not a component part of the Federal Republic of Germany and cannot be administered by it.

In reply, the delegate of the United States of America wrote to the President on 14 May 1985 as follows:

On behalf of the delegations of France, the United Kingdom of Great Britain and Northern Ireland and the United States of America I wish to state that the statement by the Soviet delegate contains an incomplete and consequently misleading reference to the Quadripartite Agreement of 3 September 1971. The relevant passage of that Agreement to which the Soviet representative referred provides that the ties between the Western Sectors of Berlin and the Federal Republic of Germany will be maintained and developed, taking into account that the sectors continue not to be a constituent part of the Federal Republic of Germany and not to be governed by it.

Furthermore, there is nothing in the Quadripartite Agreement which supports the contention that residents of the Western Sectors of Berlin may not be included in the delegation of the Federal Republic of Germany to international conferences.

In fact, Annex 4 of the Quadripartite Agreement stipulates that, provided matters of security and status are not affected, the Federal Republic of Germany may represent the interests of the Western Sectors of Berlin in international conferences and that permanent residents of the Western Sectors of Berlin may participate jointly with participants from the Federal Republic of Germany in international exchanges. Furthermore, as a matter of principle, it is for the Federal Republic of Germany alone to decide on the composition of its delegations.

Regarding other communications on this subject, we would like to take this opportunity to bring to your attention that States which are not parties to the Quadripartite Agreement are not competent to comment authoritatively on its provisions.

(WHO A38/INF.DOC./14)

On 12 November 1985, the Soviet delegate to the UN conference to review all aspects of the set of multilaterally agreed equitable principles and rules for the control of restrictive business practices sent a letter to its chairman protesting against the inclusion in the delegation of the Federal Republic of Germany of an employee of the Federal Cartel Office located in the Western sectors of Berlin. In a reply dated 13 November 1985, the representative of the United States of America, on behalf also of the Governments of the UK and France, wrote:

The establishment of the Federal Cartel Office in the western sectors of Berlin was approved by the French, American and British authorities acting on the basis of their supreme authority. These authorities are satisfied that the Federal Cartel Office does not perform in the western sectors of Berlin acts in exercise of direct State authority over the western sectors of Berlin. Neither the location nor the activities of that office, in the western sectors of Berlin, therefore, contravene any of the provisions of the Quadripartite Agreement.

Furthermore, there is nothing in the Quadripartite Agreement which supports the contentions that residents in the western sectors of Berlin may not be included in delegations of the Federal Republic of Germany to international conferences; in fact Annex IV of the Quadripartite Agreement stipulates that, provided matters of security and status are not affected, the Federal Republic of Germany may represent the interests of the western sectors of Berlin in international conferences and that western sectors of Berlin residents may participate jointly with participants from the Federal Republic of Germany in international exchanges. Furthermore, as a matter of principle, it is for the Federal Republic of Germany alone to decide on the composition of its delegation.

Regarding other communications on this subject, I would like to state that States which are not parties to the Quadripartite Agreement are not competent to comment authoritatively on its provisions.

(TD/RBP/CONF. 2/L.1)

On its ratification of the International Cocoa Agreement in 1984, the Government of the German Democratic Republic made the following declaration:

With regard to the application of the Agreement to Berlin (West) it is the position of the German Democratic Republic that the provisions of the Agreement will be applied to Berlin (West) in compliance with the Quadripartite Agreement of 3 September 1971 according to which Berlin (West) is not a constituent part of the Federal Republic of Germany and is not to be governed by it.

In response to this, the following statement dated 25 January 1985 was communicated to the Secretary-General of the UN by the Mission of the United States of America:

With regard to the note of the German Democratic Republic referred to above, the delegation of the United States reaffirm on behalf of the Governments of France, the United Kingdom of Great Britain and Northern Ireland, and the United States of America that states which are not parties to the Quadripartite Agreement of September 3, 1971, are not competent to comment authoritatively on its provisions. The Governments of France, the United Kingdom and the United States do not consider it necessary, nor do they intend, to respond to any further communications on this subject from states which are not parties to the Quadripartite Agreement. This should not be taken to imply any change in the position of the three governments in this matter.

(CN 225. 1984. TREATIES—8; see also CN 292. 1985. TREATIES—2 (Three-Power Note of 27 November 1985 responding to Polish declaration on ratification of the Convention on Long-Range Transboundary Air Pollution, 1979))

In reply to a question, the Minister of State, Home Office, Lord Elton, stated:

. . . United States servicemen in this country have to obey the law of the United Kingdom. Jurisdiction is determined by the terms of the Visiting Forces Act 1952. It lies with the courts of the United Kingdom in all circumstances except where an act which is an offence under United States law is not an offence under United Kingdom law or where the act is an offence under the laws of both countries and either arises out of and in the course of duty or is committed solely against persons or property associated with the visiting force. In those cases jurisdiction lies with the authorities of the United States forces unless they choose not to exercise it.

(HL Debs., vol. 459, cols. 935–6: 5 February 1985)

In a subsequent debate on the subject of the Administration of Justice Bill, the same Minister observed:

. . . visiting forces in this country are no more exempt from the rule of law and the doctrine of minimum force than are our forces in, for instance, Germany, who are deployed under the same international agreement.

(Ibid., col. 937)

Part Eight: II. D. *State territory and territorial jurisdiction—territorial jurisdiction—extra-territoriality*

(See also Part Four: I (speech of the Attorney-General in 1983), above)

In the course of proceedings in the US District Court for the District of Columbia in the case of *Laker Airways Ltd.* v. *Pan American World Airways Inc* et al., Pan American requested the consent of the UK Government to produce documents located in England, production of such documents being currently prohibited by a General Direction issued by the Secretary of State under s. 2 of the Protection of Trading Interests Act 1980 (for the text of the General Direction, see UKMIL 1983, pp. 486–7). In reply, the following letter, dated 19 December 1984, was sent by the Solicitor's Office of the Department of Trade and Industry to Pan American's London solicitors:

LAKER AIRWAYS LIMITED *v.* PAN AMERICAN WORLD AIRWAYS INC *ET AL.*

I refer to your letter to me of 10 December and to your earlier application on behalf of Pan American World Airways for consent to permit Pan American World Airways to produce documents located in the United Kingdom to the United States District Court which I understand would be in response to certain discovery requests.

The Secretary of State has been advised by US Counsel that under the US Federal Rules of Civil Procedure such requests must be answered unless objected to and moreover that they have been made in circumstances in which a requirement to the same effect could be or could have been imposed. The Secretary of State has considered your applications in the light of this advice.

As you are aware there is a dispute between Her Majesty's Government and the United States Government concerning the application of US antitrust laws to competition matters regulated by or under the Bermuda 2 Air Services Agreement (under which Pan American World Airways is designated by the US Government) and that this dispute remains unresolved. Her Majesty's Government contends that it is incompatible with Bermuda 2 for the United States to apply or permit the application of its domestic law in relation to tariffs charged pursuant to the Agreement.

Her Majesty's Government objected in particular to the Grand Jury investigation into the activities of British airlines in relation to North Atlantic air fares, which has recently been closed by President Reagan, as well as to the private antitrust proceedings for penal damages to which your application relates. In the view of the Government these proceedings undermine the rights granted to the United Kingdom under the Bermuda 2 Agreement. It is against this background that your applications for consents have been considered and dealt with.

The effect of the decision of the House of Lords, discharging the injunctions against Laker Airways, emphasises the need for the underlying dispute between the two Governments to be resolved as soon as possible. Her Majesty's Government is at present renewing its efforts to this end and is currently discussing the matter with the United States Government.

The Secretary of State has considered your applications in the light of all these circumstances. As matters stand at present he has decided not to grant them.

(Text provided by the Foreign and Commonwealth Office)

In a letter to a member of the public who had requested information on the subject of the operation of the US Export Administration Act 1985, the British Overseas Trade Board replied on 23 October 1985:

The new Act, like the 1979 Act, is extraterritorial in nature; the definitions which determine the scope of the Act still permit controls to be imposed on re-exports from the UK of goods of US origin or which incorporate materials, components or technology of US origin and on exports from the UK by UK subsidiaries of US parent firms. The UK Government has formally registered its disappointment and concern that the extraterritorial provisions, which are in our view inconsistent with international law, have been retained and has noted that the inclusion of powers to impose import sanctions for violation of national security controls introduces another potential source of dispute. We have welcomed the fact that the introduction of new export controls for foreign policy purposes have been subjected to additional constraints, for example the 'contract sanctity' provisions, and the reductions in the licensing requirements with regard to export to other COCOM countries. But these improvements of course only address the margins of the problem. We have reminded the US Administration that the new Act remains a threat to good relations between the US and its allies and urged that the US Government show moderation in its implementation.

(Text provided by Dr A. V. Lowe)

The following statement was made by Her Majesty's Government on 8 November 1985 on the subject of unitary taxation in the United States of America:

The Government welcome the statement by the President that the Administration will support federal legislation to limit state use of the unitary method to the water's edge. They trust that such legislation will be brought forward as soon as possible and that it will take fully into account the criticisms expressed of the water's edge concept as presented in the Regan Working Group Report last year. The Government also welcome the US Administration's intention to pursue enactment of the domestic spread sheet legislation and to ensure that the representation of the United States' interests in current law suits is consistent with the approach now taken on the unitary tax issue.

In the light of the President's statement, the Government will enter into negotiations with the Administration to amend the UK/US double taxation convention so as to prevent the application of the unitary method of taxation to UK companies.

In recognition of what they regard as a major step forward, the Government are prepared to defer initiating action under Section 54 of this year's Finance Act for the present, on the understanding that legislation to resolve the unitary tax issue will be introduced before the end of this year, that it will fully take account of the criticisms expressed of the water's edge concept, and that it will be passed into law and take effect by 31 December 1986. If action were to be taken under Section 54, it would not apply to dividends paid on or before that date.

The Treasury issued the following background note to the above statement:

The internationally accepted principle is that tax authorities charge tax on foreign owned companies only on the profits arising in the country or state for which they are responsible. However, a number of US states tax foreign-owned companies in a conventional share of the worldwide income of the Group. This means, for example, that a UK group operating in California may have to pay tax on income arising outside the state, possibly giving rise to double taxation. It may also face heavy compliance costs in furnishing details of its worldwide operations.

2. The UK Government has consistently opposed the application of unitary taxation to international business. So has the CBI. So have many other countries. It is contrary to internationally accepted principles and results in unreasonable tax and compliance burdens.

3. In 1979 the US Senate rejected the provision (Article 9(4)) included in the US/UK double taxation agreement, as signed, which would have prevented US states from applying the unitary method to UK companies with US subsidiaries.

4. In July 1984 a Working Group under the Chairmanship of (then) US Treasury Secretary Regan agreed on the principle that unitary taxation should be limited to the United States water's edge, but failed to resolve a number of issues. Secretary Regan said in his Chairman's Report (July 1984) that if there were not 'sufficient signs of appreciable progress' at states level by 31 July 1985 he would recommend to the President that the Administration should propose federal legislation.

5. Since July 1984 there has been action to reform unitary tax in six states—Oregon, Florida, Massachusetts, Indiana, Utah and Colorado—though in some cases the application of unitary tax to foreign-owned corporations is limited and not eliminated. Legislation in California failed in September. Legislative initiatives have not succeeded in the remaining five states which apply unitary tax to foreign-owned business (Alaska, North Dakota, Montana, New Hampshire and Idaho).

6. In July 1985 Parliament passed a provision (Section 54 Finance Act 1985) under which the UK could withdraw from US parent companies situated in unitary states the entitlement to tax credits relating to dividends paid by UK subsidiaries. This provision would take effect by statutory instrument, subject to affirmative resolution of the House of Commons.

(Texts reproduced from Treasury Press Release 158/85)

In reply to a question on the subject of the disturbance at the Heysel football stadium in Brussels, the Solicitor-General wrote in part:

Any offence of murder or manslaughter committed by a British subject abroad is triable in this country under English law. The English courts would not have jurisdiction to try any other criminal offences arising out of the events at the Heysel stadium on 29 May 1985.

(HC Debs., vol. 86, Written Answers, col. *291*: 15 November 1985)

In reply to a question, the Minister of State, Department of Trade and Industry, wrote:

My right hon. and learned Friend the Secretary of State and I continue to emphasise to the United States Administration the Government's objections to the claims to extraterritorial control over exports maintained in the new Export Administration Act and to warn of the damaging consequences to our mutual interests of attempts to enforce such claims in the United Kingdom. Efforts to prevent or resolve problems arising from such controls will continue to be made under the consultation arrangements agreed by the United Kingdom and United States Governments in November 1984.

(Ibid., vol. 87, Written Answers, cols. *17–18*: 18 November 1985)

In reply to a question on the subject of US anti-trust laws applied to civil aviation, the Secretary of State for Trade and Industry wrote:

The Government have consistently maintained the view that in so far as the activities of airlines are authorised and regulated in accordance with an air services agreement, the domestic laws of a contracting party may not be used to constrain or regulate those activities, unless that is provided for expressly, or is necessary in order to implement the agreement, or the laws can be applied in a manner which is compatible with the agreement. Regulation under the agreement by the contracting parties jointly of matters such as market access, capacity and tariffs necessarily displaces the unilateral application of the domestic competition laws of each party which implements the national economic philosophy of each country and are not designed to deal with the special characteristics and needs of international civil aviation.

In particular, the Government's view is that the unilateral application of United States anti-trust law to air services operated under the United Kingdom–United States air services agreement (Bermuda 2) is not only incompatible with the United Kingdom's rights under the agreement, but is damaging to the trading interests of the United Kingdom. In 1983 the then Secretary of State for Trade and Industry exercised his powers under the Protection of Trading Interests Act 1980 to prohibit compliance by persons carrying on business in the United Kingdom with requirements for the enforcement of United States anti-trust laws in relation to activities of United Kingdom airlines and concerning the operation of air services under Bermuda 2.

Our policy is unchanged, and I therefore intend to exercise powers under that Act to whatever extent is necessary if proceedings under the anti-trust laws were to be begun in the future in United States courts against any United Kingdom airline in relation to air services operated by it under Bermuda 2, and would not envisage consenting to requests to comply with discovery orders made by United States courts in such cases.

While maintaining this position, the Government's longer-term objective is to reach mutually acceptable arrangements as appropriate with foreign Governments to deal with anti competitive behaviour by airlines. As a first step we have indicated to the United States Government that we are ready to discuss these issues with them.

(Ibid., vol. 88, Written Answers, col. *624*: 11 December 1985)

Part Eight: III. B. *State territory and territorial jurisdiction—acquisition and transfer of territory—transfer*

In the course of moving the Second Reading in the House of Lords of the Hong Kong Bill, the Minister of State, Foreign and Commonwealth Office, Baroness Young, stated:

. . . I have it in command from Her Majesty the Queen to acquaint the House that Her Majesty, having been informed of the purport of the Hong Kong Bill, has consented to place her prerogative and interests, so far as they are affected by the Bill, at the disposal of Parliament for the purposes of the Bill. . . .

The Bill before the House today is short and, I hope, relatively straightforward;

but it is one of great significance. It provides for the termination on 1st July 1997 of British sovereignty and jurisdiction over Hong Kong and on that date will sever the links of government between the United Kingdom and Hong Kong which were first established some 150 years ago.

. . .

Following the signature of the agreement, the Governments of both China and the United Kingdom have to satisfy their constitutional requirements in order to ratify the agreement. The purpose of the Bill before us today is to enable Her Majesty's Government for their part to ratify the agreement.

The central provision of the Bill is Clause 1. This provides for the termination of British sovereignty over the ceded parts of Hong Kong and the termination of British Jurisdiction over the whole territory with effect from 1st July 1997. The clause will enable the Government to meet their obligation under paragraph 2 of the Joint Declaration in which the Government of the United Kingdom declare that they will restore Hong Kong to the People's Republic of China with effect from 1st July 1997. The clause will enter into force on the exchange of instruments of ratification.

In recent years, the Government have, when divesting the United Kingdom of sovereignty over a dependent territory, done so upon the authority of an Act of Parliament. Hong Kong's case is, of course, somewhat different from that of other dependent territories, but the Government still need the authority of an Act of Parliament before they ratify the agreement and thus create an international obligation to terminate sovereignty.

Paragraph 3 of the schedule deals with the modification of United Kingdom Acts and subordinate legislation. It gives the necessary powers to make changes in British law in consequence of, or in connection with, the ending of sovereignty. This paragraph enables Orders in Council to be made to repeal or amend United Kingdom legislation insofar as it is a part of the law of Hong Kong; to enable the legislature of Hong Kong to repeal or amend United Kingdom legislation insofar as it is a part of the law of Hong Kong, and to legislate with extra-territorial effect; and to repeal or amend British legislation which relates to Hong Kong.

Such provisions are normal when this country ceases to have sovereignty over a territory. They are written into independence Acts, and although this Bill is of course different from an independence Bill, a similar provision is necessary. It would of course be inappropriate to continue after 1997 to have references in the laws either of Hong Kong or of the United Kingdom implying the continuation of a constitutional relationship with the United Kingdom.

(HL Debs., vol. 460, cols. 481–5: 19 February 1985)

In reply to the question whether the return of sovereignty to Spain of Gibraltar in return for a long lease has been, or is still being, considered, the Minister of State, Foreign and Commonwealth Office, Baroness Young, stated orally:

No, my Lords, it is not.

(Ibid., col. 816: 25 February 1985)

The Hong Kong Act 1985, which received the Royal Assent on 4 April 1985, reads in part as follows:

1.—(1) As from 1st July 1997 Her Majesty shall no longer have sovereignty or jurisdiction over any part of Hong Kong.

(2) This section shall come into force on the exchange of instruments of ratification of the Joint Declaration of the Government of the United Kingdom and the Government of the People's Republic of China on the Question of Hong Kong which was signed in Peking on 19th December 1984; and notice of the date on which those instruments are exchanged shall be given in the London Gazette.

Part Eight: IV. *State territory and territorial jurisdiction—regime under the Antarctic Treaty*

(See also Part Eight: II. A. (Written Answer of 16 January 1985), above and Part Nine: XVI. (item of 2 April 1985), below)

In reply to a question, the Parliamentary Under-Secretary of State, Foreign and Commonwealth Office, wrote:

As a founder member, we greatly value the Antarctic treaty. It has successfully demilitarised Antarctica, maintained the peace there and helped promote important international scientific cooperation. We shall continue to defend and strengthen the treaty system. We welcome the continuing accession of new member states.

(HC Debs., vol. 71, Written Answers, col. *443*: 23 January 1985)

The Permanent Representative of the UK to the UN in New York, Sir John Thomson, addressed a letter, dated 30 May 1985, to the Secretary-General of the UN in response to a letter from the Government of Argentina (A/40317—S/17196) on the subject of the new airport at Mount Pleasant, Falkland Islands. Sir John Thomson's letter read in part as follows:

The United Kingdom Government regrets the Argentine Foreign Minister's gratuitous references to Antarctica, in relation to which the two Governments maintain working relations within the framework of the Antarctic Treaty system. The Falkland Islands do not lie within the area of application of the Treaty. There is, moreover, no foundation whatsoever for the assertion that the aims of the United Kingdom in the Falkland Islands or in Antarctica are incompatible with British obligations under the Antarctic Treaty. British stations in the Antarctic, like Argentine stations, have recently been inspected under the terms of Article VII of the Antarctic Treaty by the Government of the United States. No activity has been found at any of these stations that is inconsistent with the purposes and principles of the Antarctic Treaty.

(A/40345—S/17229)

In the course of a statement on 29 November 1985 to the First Committee of the General Assembly, the UK representative, Dr J. A. Heap, remarked:

Let us now turn to the third of the grounds upon which the Antarctic Treaty system is attacked, namely, that it denies access to the Antarctic to non-parties.

This is simply not so. As I said in the first of my statements to this Committee and repeated in my second, the obligations assumed by Consultative Parties are denying no one's freedom in the Antarctic other than their own. If a country which had not acceded to the Antarctic Treaty were to send an expedition to the Antarctic, the Consultative Parties would be bound by the Treaty to take steps in accordance with the Charter of the United Nations to ensure that the country in question did nothing contrary to the principles and purposes of the Treaty—that is to say, in effect, that they would take steps to ensure continued non-militarization of the Antarctic, the protection of the Antarctic environment, the conservation of wildlife and avoidance of disturbance to scientific investigations. Action towards such ends by the Consultative Parties acting as a group is the limit of their capability. It does not include denial of access. This ground for attack has no basis in fact.

(A/C. 1/40/PV. 53, p. 13)

Part Nine: I. A. *Seas, waterways, ships—territorial sea—delimitation*

In reply to the question whether Her Majesty's Government will extend the 'territorial limits' of the Falkland Islands to 200 miles, the Parliamentary Under-Secretary of State, Foreign and Commonwealth Office, wrote:

We do not recognise the legality of claims to territorial sea of a breadth of 200 miles.

(HC Debs., vol. 73, Written Answers, col. *475*: 20 February 1985)

In reply to a question, the Minister of State, Foreign and Commonwealth Office, wrote in part:

Her Majesty's Government have been considering the extension of the territorial sea to 12 miles first in the context of a possible signature of the UN Law of the Sea Convention and later in the light of their decision not to sign. The possible timing and circumstances of any such move are among the matters under consideration.

(HL Debs., vol. 463, col. 519: 3 May 1985)

Part Nine: I. B. *Seas, waterways, ships—territorial sea—legal status*

(See Part Nine: XVI., below)

Part Nine: I. B. 1. *Seas, waterways, ships—territorial sea—legal status—right of innocent passage*

(See also Part Nine: VII. A. 1. (item of 1 June 1984), below)

In reply to a question, the Minister of State, Foreign and Commonwealth Office, wrote:

. . . the United Kingdom has, in our view, the right under customary international law to authorise the undertaking of works such as those connected with a Channel Fixed Link provided that due account is taken of the interests of navigation. United Kingdom jurisdiction within the territorial sea reflects the 1958 Geneva Convention on the Territorial Sea and subsequent developments in international law and practice.

(Ibid.)

Part Nine: I. B. 6. *Seas, waterways, ships—territorial sea—legal status—fishery*

In a memorandum, dated 5 July 1985, submitted to the Scottish Affairs Committee of the House of Commons for its deliberations on the subject of fishery protection, the Department of Agriculture and Fisheries for Scotland observed:

Title to Salmon Fishings

1. In both inland waters and the territorial sea (*i.e.* within the 3-mile limit) the rights of salmon fishing are private property. They were originally part of the private estate of the Crown which, over the centuries, made grants of rights to others. . . . Beyond the 3-mile limit there is theoretically a public right of fishing for salmon but all practicable methods of exploiting it are prohibited.

(*Parliamentary Papers*, 1984–5, HC, Paper 433-iv, p. 49)

Part Nine: III. *Seas, waterways, ships—internal waters, including ports*

(See Part Nine: I. B. 6, above and Part Nine: VII. A. 1 (item of 1 June 1984) and VII. H. (item of 26 November 1985), below)

Part Nine: IV. *Seas, waterways, ships—straits*

In an Invitation to Promoters for the development, financing, construction and operation of a Channel Fixed Link between France and the UK, issued by the Department of Transport in April 1985, the following passage appeared:

24.1 Any project which involves construction work or the building of permanent structures in the Straits of Dover must not hamper the freedom and safety of navigation.

24.2 A routeing system operates in the Dover Straits which has been adopted by the International Maritime Organisation (IMO). It consists of two traffic lanes, for north-east and south-west bound vessels; a separation zone between those lanes; and inshore traffic zones between the outer edges of the lanes and the coasts of the UK and France. The traffic lanes and the separation zone together constitute a traffic separation scheme, and (as a consequence of having been adopted by IMO) are subject to Rule 10 of the International Regulations for Preventing Collisions at Sea 1972, as amended in 1981. Under the law of the United Kingdom the International Regulations are given effect through the Merchant Shipping (Distress Signals and Prevention of Collision) Regulations 1983 (SI 1983/708) and apply to UK vessels wherever they may be and to other vessels while they are in UK territorial waters. The latest versions of the system for organising navigation in the Straits of Dover were made applicable in France by Decree No. 83.448 on 27 May 1983 published in the Official Journal on 5 June 1983.

24.3 Promoters should be aware that any structure (such as ventilation shafts, bridge piers, artificial islands and embankments) that in any respect involved a permanent modification of the traffic separation scheme would require acceptance by the IMO and any modification of the traffic system would have to be adopted by the IMO. It is difficult to estimate how long such a process would take but it would be time consuming (probably more than 12 months) and of uncertain result. The timetable might be shortened if there were additional meetings of the relevant IMO Committees, but a part of the cost might have to be borne by the promoters. It should be noted that any structure, whether temporary or permanent, that did not entail modification of the traffic separation scheme, e.g. a structure in the separation zone, would not require IMO's approval. However, all information relating to any such structure would be made available to the IMO, which would, of course, be consulted on navigational warnings and notification.

24.4 Permanent modifications to the arrangements in the Inshore Traffic Zones of the system could be made without the approval of IMO. Notification to the IMO would however be necessary and, in the interests of securing the cooperation of the other member states, prior consultations would also be desirable.

(Text provided by the Foreign and Commonwealth Office)

In reply to the question whether it would be within the terms of the Montreux Convention for the Soviet Union to send the aircraft carrier now under construction in the Black Sea through the straits into the Mediterranean, the Minister of State, Foreign and Commonwealth Office, wrote:

We have taken the view that the passage of aircraft carriers through the straits is not compatible with the Montreux Convention. As the noble Lord will be aware, this view is not shared by all parties to the convention.

(HL Debs., vol. 469, col. 882: 8 December 1985)

Part Nine: VII. A. 1. *Seas, waterways, ships—the high seas—freedom of the high seas—navigation*

In a speech to the Security Council on 4 April 1984 on the subject of events in Central America, the UK Permanent Representative, Sir John Thomson, referred to the laying of mines by a foreign power in Nicaraguan waters. He added:

Our position is well known and consistent: as a maritime nation, we are committed to freedom of navigation, including innocent passage through the territorial sea and access to foreign ports for peaceful trade. We deplore any threats to navigation whenever and wherever they occur. I reaffirm our adherence to that principle.

(S/PV. 2529, pp. 77–8)

In a speech in the Security Council on 1 June 1984, Sir John Thomson referred to attacks by Iran upon merchant shipping *en route* to and from Saudi Arabian and Kuwaiti ports. He then remarked:

The attacks which have taken place in international waters and in the territorial sea of the States concerned are in clear breach of international law. They are both reprehensible and unjustified.

(S/PV. 2546, pp. 31–2)

Later in his speech, Sir John Thomson stated:

As a maritime nation of long standing the United Kingdom considers the principle of freedom of navigation as of paramount importance. As we said in a recent debate here on another matter:

'we are committed to freedom of navigation, including innocent passage through the territorial sea and access to foreign ports for peaceful trade.

'We deplore any threats to navigation, whenever and wherever they occur.' (*S/PV. 2529, pp. 77, 78*)

For the United Kingdom, this is a fundamental principle.

It must therefore apply equally to the Gulf. The draft resolution concentrates for understandable reasons on one particular act of escalation, but clearly this does not mean that it condones other attacks on merchant shipping in the Gulf. We are therefore particularly pleased that the draft resolution in its revised form contains a clear and general reaffirmation of the right of free navigation. This right is laid down in international law, and we look to all States of the region to respect it. In our view neither side has the right to attack neutral shipping indiscriminately, whatever its destination. The breach of international law is flagrant if the shipping attacked is in transit to the ports of third countries and compounded if the attacks take place in the territorial waters of the third countries. Such attacks violate the sovereignty of the coastal States as well as the rights of the flag State.

(Ibid., p. 33)

In reply to a question on the subject of attacks on ships in the Gulf by Iran and Iraq, the Minister of State, Foreign and Commonwealth Office, wrote in part:

We remain in close contact with interested parties, both at the United Nations in New York and elsewhere, concerning all aspects of the tragic and wasteful conflict between Iran and Iraq, including attacks on shipping in the gulf. We deplore such attacks and fully supported Security Council Resolution 552 which stressed the importance of freedom of navigation in international waters.

(HC Debs., vol. 83, Written Answers, col. *591*: 24 July 1985)

Part Nine: VII. F. *Seas, waterways, ships—the high seas—conservation of living resources*

In reply to the question whether Her Majesty's Government will seek to extend the Convention on the Conservation of Antarctic Marine Living

Resources, 1980, to the Falklands waters, the Parliamentary Under-Secretary of State, Foreign and Commonwealth Office, wrote:

The Convention on the Conservation of Antarctic Marine Living Resources (CCAMLR) was specifically designed to deal with conservation in the Antarctic marine ecosystem which is quite different from that of Falkland waters. Extension of CCAMLR would require the unanimous consent of the parties.

(HC Debs., vol. 83, Written Answers, col. *49*: 15 July 1985)

Part Nine: VII. G. *Seas, waterways, ships—the high seas—pollution*

(See Part One: II. D. (item of 12 December 1985), above)

Part Nine: VII. H. *Seas, waterways, ships—the high seas—jurisdiction over ships*

In a speech in Atlanta to the American Bar Association in 1983, the Attorney-General, Sir Michael Havers, stated:

. . . in the case of oil pollution at sea, no state which has a coast wants that coast polluted by oil. States which have merchant fleets do not want their ships to be subject to uncontrolled interference on the high seas. Successive negotiations on this subject have prohibited discharge of oil within a certain distance from the coast but have respected the primary jurisdiction of the flag state to prosecute for offenses on the high seas. However, in order to protect, where possible, coastal states from potential damage to their coasts, the flag state undertakes to prosecute if the coastal state can provide the proper evidence in respect of a particular ship.

On a bilateral basis an example of a good compromise on questions of jurisdiction is to be found in the Exchange of Notes between the United Kingdom and the United States of November 13, 1981 on Co-operation in the Suppression of the Unlawful Importation of Narcotic Drugs into the USA. Obviously our two countries have a common view on suppression of drug traffic; but for the UK to allow the USA to stop and search British commercial vessels on the high seas and then exercise US enforcement jurisdiction, applying US law does involve quite a compromise of important principles. In this case negotiation achieved a result enabling the USA to extend its defenses against drug smuggling as it wished within a defined area beyond its territorial sea but with certain safeguards for the UK against unwarranted interference with shipping on the high seas and against forfeiture of British vessels and prosecution of British nationals without consent.

(The full text of the speech is reproduced in *International Lawyer*, 17 (1983), pp. 784–95. The above extract is taken from p. 791)

In reply to a question on measures to be taken to eliminate extra-territorial pirate radio broadcasting, the Parliamentary Under-Secretary of State, Department of Trade and Industry, wrote:

The unauthorised broadcasting stations currently operating outside United Kingdom territorial waters in the North Sea are based on Panamanian register vessels. Their operation contravenes International Radio Regulation 2665 which prohibits the establishment of broadcasting stations outside national territories and Recommendation No. 9 of the World Administrative Radio Conference 1979 which calls on Administrations to prevent their operations.

My Department has written to the International Telecommunication Union (ITU) about the stations' unauthorised operations. We and the ITU have been in contact with the Panamanian Administration. Since the stations' offices are reportedly based in the United States of America, my officials have also written to and had discussions with members of the United States Administration, drawing their attention to obligations of ITU members and seeking their assistance to remove the stations. At a recent Commission of the European Post and Telecommunications (CEPT) meeting in Italy, we sought the co-operation of all other European Administrations to remove the stations. We shall continue to pursue the matter at the next CEPT meeting to be held in France in June.

The Marine &c. Broadcasting (Offences) Act 1967 makes it an offence for anyone in the United Kingdom to supply or promote the stations and for a British national to engage in the stations' operations. When my Department receives information of possible offences it is immediately passed to the Office of the Director of Public Prosecutions, who usually asks for a police investigation before deciding whether to institute proceedings under the Act.

These unauthorised stations interfere with the radio communications of the North Sea oil and gas industry and jam frequencies which should be allocated to legitimate radio stations. I am determined, within the resources available and the constraints of our jurisdiction, to take all possible action to prevent their continued operation.

(HC Debs., vol. 80, Written Answers, cols. *11–12*: 3 June 1985)

In reply to a question on the subject of Laser 558, a Panamanian-registered vessel, the Government spokesman in the House of Lords, Lord Brabazon of Tara, stated:

The Government have no power to detain the vessel in Harwich because of its illegal broadcasting as it was in international waters when broadcasting illegally.

(HL Debs., vol. 468, col. 790: 26 November 1985)

Part Nine: VIII. *Seas, waterways, ships—continental shelf*

(See also Part Nine: XVI., below)

On 7 May 1985, the Danish Government published a communication concerning the designation of the continental shelf area around the Faroe Islands. In a press statement issued with the communication, the Ministry of Foreign Affairs of Denmark stated in part:

What is the Faroe–Rockall micro-continent?

The Faroe-Rockall plateau is an elevated plain which with its summit in the Faroe Islands forms what is known as a micro-continent under the sea. Parts of the area have already been designated by the British and Irish authorities which consider the plateau an extension of their respective national territories. Iceland does not contest the Danish right to exercise jurisdiction over the plateau, but claims that Iceland also has such right. The present Danish designation is being made on the assumption that the Faroe Islands are part of the micro-continent formed by the plateau.

The relatively narrow center corridor of the designated area is due to the fact that the designation—without prejudice to the legal positions of the countries concerned—allows for a 200 mile zone of the United Kingdom and Iceland. Towards the United Kingdom and Ireland the micro-continent is delimited by a steep drop of the seafloor to a depth of approx. 2.5 km and up to a width of 250 km, the so-called Rockall Trough. Towards Iceland the micro-continent is delimited by a similar drop of the seafloor.

The United Kingdom and Ireland have previously designated parts of the plateau without taking the Rockall Trough and other factors into consideration.

Referring to present knowledge about the local geological conditions Denmark for its part contests claims made by the United Kingdom, Ireland and Iceland to parts of the micro-continent.

As designated by Denmark the aggregate area of the Faroe-Rockall plateau is approx. 300,000 sq. km. The part of the plateau designated by the United Kingdom is approx. 50,000 sq. km while Ireland has designated approx. 180,000 sq. km.

What are the implications of the designation?

The term 'designation' connotes a national legal act which indicates an area within which Denmark will until further notice exercise its right to jurisdiction over the seabed. The delimitation of this area must be determined by agreements between Denmark and any other affected countries.

The importance of who has the right to the seabed in these wind-swept areas of the North Atlantic may seem a question of academic rather than practical interest.

It is a fact, nevertheless, that as early as the mid-1970s the United Kingdom and Ireland put on record their claims to parts of the area which in the Danish opinion is part of the Faroese continental shelf.

If and when exploration and exploitation of potential resources in the area should come up for consideration it will be important for Denmark to have announced that we consider the right to exercise jurisdiction over the seabed belongs to Denmark.

The present situation regarding the Faroe–Rockall plateau is one of diplomatic contacts between the countries involved. Today no one can predict what developments lie ahead, but Denmark has stressed its will to negotiate at any time on the delimitation of the continental shelf between the Faroes and the other countries.

What is the importance of the Rockall skerry?

The famous rock, Rockall, which is seen above the water's surface barely 200 nautical miles west of Scotland *is of no importance in the context referred to here.*

Denmark does not contest the sovereignty claimed by the United Kingdom over the Rockall skerry. The argument concerns the implications of the sovereignty. The British authorities maintain that Rockall is entitled to a 200-mile fisheries zone. Denmark and others plead that the uninhabited skerry cannot be granted status as an island in the sense of international law, and that under international law the United Kingdom can make no claim to maritime zones beyond a 12-mile territorial sea around Rockall. The new UN Convention on the Law of the Sea clearly confirms this view.

However, this last problem is *not* affected by the Danish designation of the continental shelf around the Faroe Islands.

(Text provided by the Royal Danish Embassy, London)

In response to the above, the British Embassy, Copenhagen, issued the following press statement dated 13 May 1985:

Designation of Faroes Continental Shelf

1. On 7 May the Danish Government published a communication claiming in respect of the Faroes Islands an extensive area of continental shelf to the north and west of Scotland. The Danish claim covers areas already designated by the United Kingdom in 1974 as well as other areas which the British Government consider form integral parts of the continental shelf appertaining to the United Kingdom in accordance with international law.

2. Acting on instructions, the British Ambassador has today delivered a note protesting at the action of the Danish Government, and reserving fully all the rights of the United Kingdom in accordance with international law. The note also expressed regret that Denmark chose to proceed with this measure at a time when a request from the British side for a further round of informal talks about this issue had not been met.

(Text provided by the Foreign and Commonwealth Office)

In reply to the question 'whether the "deep water frontier areas of the Rockall and Faroes troughs", concerning which conditional awards of petroleum production licences have recently been announced, are fully recognised by all neighbouring states as being subject to exclusive British sovereign rights for the purposes of exploration and exploitation', the Minister of State, Scottish Office, wrote:

No neighbouring states have challenged the United Kingdom's sovereign rights in those areas of the Rockall and Faroes troughs where petroleum production licences have been issued. The United Kingdom designated this area in 1974 by Order in Council under the Continental Shelf Act 1964.

(HL Debs., vol. 464, cols. 1475–6: 13 June 1985)

By an instrument dated 9 May 1985, the Ministry for Foreign Affairs of Iceland issued regulations concerning the delimitation of the Icelandic continental shelf to the west, south and east. The regulations state that Article 76 of the UN Convention on the Law of the Sea is used, where applicable, to define the boundary. The boundary is stated to be in part a median line, in part a 200-nautical mile distance line from the Faroes, Greenland, the UK and Ireland, in part a 350-nautical mile distance line from Iceland, and in part, extending beyond 350 nautical miles from Iceland, a line sixty nautical miles beyond the foot of the continental slope.

On 19 June 1985, the British Embassy in Reykjavik, Iceland, issued the following press statement:

The British Embassy have today delivered a Note protesting at the action of the Icelandic Government in claiming an extensive area of Continental Shelf to the west of the British Isles. The Note reserved all the rights of the UK in accordance with International Law. The British Government note that the Regulations were issued when a response from Iceland was still awaited to an offer to continue bilateral talks between legal experts.

The following background note was also provided by the Embassy:

The Icelandic Regulations have no basis in International Law. The Icelandic claim encroaches on the Continental Shelf appertaining to the UK and in other places goes beyond the outer limit of the Continental Shelf prescribed by International Law.

There is no link of any kind between Iceland and the Hatton/Rockall plateau.

First, Iceland is of recent volcanic origin: the plateau is composed of old rocks similar to those in Scotland. There is no geological link between Iceland and the plateau.

Secondly, Iceland stands on a separate volcanic platform. There is a sharp edge to the south of Iceland, beyond which the seabed has the characteristic of deep ocean floor. There is a fundamental error in the Icelandic regulations, which overlook the fact that there is a clear line for the foot of the Continental Slope close to the south coast. Accordingly, there is no geomorphological link between Iceland and the plateau.

Thirdly, Iceland lies further away from the plateau than the UK. Thus, there is no geographical link between Iceland and the plateau.

The absence of geological, geomorphological and geographical links between Iceland and the plateau means that there is no legal basis for a claim by Iceland to the plateau.

(Texts provided by the Foreign and Commonwealth Office)

In an interview given on BBC Radio on 25 July 1985, the Minister of State, Foreign and Commonwealth Office, Mr Timothy Renton, stated in part:

No one knows precisely yet just how important Rockall is going to be to Britain, or more particularly the Hatton–Rockall Plateau. But there obviously is potential there and that is the reason why we are going to stand very firmly on our rights to the area.

. . . Our rights stem from what are known as the three geos: geography, because we are the largest and most populous country nearby; geology, because the rocks on the plateau are the same as in the United Kingdom (whereas they are quite different in Iceland and the Faroes); and finally geomorphology, the last of the three geos, because the sea-bed of the Hatton–Rockall Plateau is an extension of the United Kingdom mainland. So on all these three technical points, we are totally confident of our sovereign rights.

. . . we dispute very definitely both the Danish claim, which is the reverse of ours, and the Icelandic. The Icelandic, for example, we think is actually based on a misinterpretation of the United Nations Convention on the Law of the Sea, and of existing international law.

(Extracted from BBC tape No. TLN30646R673 with slight punctuation and grammatical amendments made by the Editor)

Part Nine: IX. *Seas, waterways, ships—exclusive fishery zone*

(See also Part Nine: I. B. 6, above)

In the course of a debate on the subject of the Select Committee on Foreign Affairs' report on the Falkland Islands, the Secretary of State for Foreign and Commonwealth Affairs, Sir Geoffrey Howe, stated:

Another of Lord Shackleton's recommendations was the proposed declaration of a 200-mile exclusive fisheries limit around the Falklands. The Government are of course well aware of the activity of foreign fishing fleets in Falklands waters and the consequent danger of over-exploitation of fish stocks. Under normal conditions, the unilateral declaration of a 200-mile limit could well have been an appropriate response because it would offer a means of ensuring conservation and management of this valuable resource. In considering that possibility in the circumstances of the Falklands, however, the Government have had to give full weight to the serious difficulties that could arise in that context. The Select Committee, quite rightly, drew attention to the political and practical problems of enforcing and policing a unilaterally imposed fisheries zone in an area where British sovereignty was in dispute. For that reason, the Committee was not convinced that the establishment of such a zone could be justified.

The Government take the same view. For the same reason, we have decided instead to explore possible ways in which to establish a multilaterally based conservation and management regime. We are therefore taking steps to develop that approach.

(HC Debs., vol. 75, col. 495: 14 March 1985)

Part Nine: X. *Seas, waterways, ships—exclusive economic zone*

(See Part Nine: XVI., below)

Part Nine: XII. *Seas, waterways, ships—bed of the sea beyond national jurisdiction*

(See also Part Nine: XIV., below)

Her Majesty's Government was asked

Whether they recognise as having the force of law the licences issued by the United States Department of Commerce to various consortia for prospecting on the seabed of the Pacific Ocean, beyond zones of national jurisdiction as generally defined and accepted in international law, and whether any British firms are involved, and if so which.

In reply, the Minister of State, Foreign and Commonwealth Office, wrote:

We regard licences for exploration of the deep seabed issued by the United States as lawful and respect them in accordance with agreements between the two countries. One of the United States licences has been issued in favour of the Kennecott Consortium, in which British Petroleum, Consolidated Goldfields and Rio Tinto Zinc have an interest through subsidiaries.

(HL Debs., vol. 465, col. 947: 28 June 1985)

In the course of a debate on the subject of the fortieth anniversary of the UN, the Minister of State, Foreign and Commonwealth Office, Baroness Young, stated:

I should like to confirm that the Government decided that this country should not sign the UN Law of the Sea Convention. However, we decided not to stand in the way of the signature of the convention by the European Community whose competence as regards the convention is limited to fisheries, pollution, Customs matters between land-locked states, and commercial policy to a limited extent. Although much of the convention was recognised as valuable, the proposed regime for deep sea-bed mining was unacceptable. Potential United Kingdom mining operators made it clear that they would not wish to commence operations under the mining regime as presently proposed in the convention. We hope that as the drawbacks of the convention as presently envisaged become clear, it may yet be possible to establish a regime for marine matters which would be built on consensus among the whole international community.

(HL Debs., vol. 467, col. 1523: 29 October 1985)

Speaking in the General Assembly on 10 December 1985, the UK representative, Mr D. M. Edwards, stated in part:

. . . we do not accept that activities relating to the seabed that take place outside the Convention are illegal. It will be recalled that UN General Assembly Resolution 2749 (XXV) states, in paragraph 9, that an international regime applying to the area and its resources, including appropriate international machinery, is to be established by an international treaty of a universal character 'generally agreed upon'. Given the objections raised during the Conference to certain aspects of the Convention, and the continuing objections of a number of States interested in deep sea mining, this has yet to be achieved. Despite the outcome of the Conference and the Convention, in the absence of a regime which is generally accepted and is thus likely to be effective, a State retains its rights and freedom of action in relation to the seabed. It remains the wish of my Government that a universally acceptable regime should be established, and we shall continue to work towards this goal.

(Text provided by the Foreign and Commonwealth Office; see also A/40/PV. 111, pp. 8–10)

Part Nine: XIV. *Seas, waterways, ships—international regime of the sea in general*

(See also Part Nine: XII. (item of 29 October 1985), above)

In reply to a question, the Minister of State, Foreign and Commonwealth Office, wrote in respect of the UN Convention on the Law of the Sea, 1982:

The convention will enter into force one year after sixty ratifications and accessions in respect of states ratifying or acceding to it. So far, there have been 14 ratifications. In respect of states ratifying or acceding subsequently, it enters into force 30 days after the deposit of the instrument of accession by the state in question. The United Kingdom, as a state which has not acceded to the convention, would become bound by the rules envisaged in the convention only in so far as they were generally accepted and regarded as rules of customary international law. How far they are or may come to be so regarded depends on the past and future state practice of countries generally. As for deep sea mining, British operators have made it clear they would not wish to operate under the convention's present mining regime.

(HC Debs., vol. 74, Written Answers, col. *211*: 27 February 1985)

Part Nine: XV. A. 2. *Seas, waterways, ships—ships—legal status—public ships other than warships*

(See Part Five: VIII. B. (item of 8 November 1985), above)

Part Nine: XV. B. *Seas, waterways, ships—ships—nationality*

In May 1983, the Government of the UK, on behalf of itself and other States in Group B of UNCTAD (industrialized market economy countries), commented on a document entitled 'A set of basic principles concerning the conditions upon which vessels should be accepted on national registers', proposed in November 1982 by an Intergovernmental Preparatory Group set up in advance of a meeting of the Preparatory Committee of the UN Conference on Conditions for Registration of Ships. The comments read in part as follows:

1. The 1958 Geneva High Sea Convention, as well as the newly agreed United Nations Convention on the Law of the Sea, cover matters regarding the registration of ships and duties of flag States which are regarded as highly important by Group B Member countries. Group B Governments fully subscribe to the concept of a genuine link between the State and the ships flying its flag, as elaborated in Article 5 of the 1958 Convention on the High Seas, which states that 'Each State shall fix the conditions for the granting of its nationality to ships, for the registration of ships in its territory, and for the right to fly its flag. Ships have the nationality of the State whose flag they are entitled to fly. There must exist a genuine link between the State and the ship; in particular, the State must effectively exercise its jurisdiction and control in administrative, technical and social matters over ships flying its flag.' These principles were also taken up in the recently signed Convention on the Law of the Sea. In particular Article 91 of the Convention states:

'*Nationality of ships*

1. Every State shall fix the conditions for the granting of its nationality to ships, for the registration of ships in its territory, and for the right to fly its flag. Ships have the nationality of the State whose flag they are entitled to fly. There must exist a genuine link between the State and the ship.

2. Every State shall issue to ships to which it has granted the right to fly its flag documents to that effect.'

Group B countries strongly support the principles set out in Article 91 and also Article 92 which spells out the duties of the flag State and believe that they should guide all future deliberations in the Preparatory Committee, as well as the forthcoming Diplomatic Conference.

2. Article 91, as well as all the others dealt with in Part VII of the new United Nations Convention, do not make any reference to any kind of economic requirements for ship registration. This is why Group B countries firmly believe that any future registration convention should base itself on accepted principles of international law and respect the 'national sovereignty concept' as regards economic policies and legislations covering fields such as investment and nationality of ownership, crews and management of ships. It was shown by a survey carried out by the UNCTAD secretariat in document TD/B/AC. 34/2 that, while many member countries of UNCTAD have certain economic requirements for ship registration, they nevertheless differ very considerably.

3. However, the international community has an interest in eliminating any abuses of ship registration that may become possible through the failure of flag States to meet their international obligations that they have accepted of effectively exercising their jurisdiction and control over ships flying their flag. Any set of basic principles concerning registration conditions has, therefore, in Group B's view to try to strengthen the genuine link and to ensure that a flag State is in a position to exercise its jurisdiction and control. This has necessitated the Intergovernmental Preparatory Group considering many areas which are subject to a variety of international instruments, national laws and regulations, questions of maritime safety, labour conditions, environmental protection, the insurance of ships and company law, all matters that a flag State must consider in registering ships and exercising effective control.

4. On the other hand, Group B has considerable doubts whether the introduction of economic requirements formulated at international level would in fact promote the development of merchant fleets in the developing countries and is of the view that this would result in increased over-all costs to world shipping.

(TD/RS/CONF/PC/3, pp. 13–14)

The comments concluded:

The core of Group B's position was, and still is, that it opposes the imposition of economic requirements in the field of ship registration on sovereign States.

(Ibid., p. 17)

At the meeting of the Preparatory Committee in November 1983, the UK representative, Mr Fielder, on behalf of the UK and the other Group B States, made the following observations:

He stated that the policy of Group B countries as regards ship registration rested upon the principles enshrined in the 1958 Convention on the High Seas and the United Nations Convention on the Law of the Sea of 1982. He stressed that all States must ensure the existence of a genuine link between the State and the ship, and effectively enforce their jurisdiction over their vessels, particularly with regard to the safety of ships, the qualification and protection of their crews, and protection of the marine environment and of the welfare and working conditions of seafarers in order to ensure compliance with internationally agreed standards.

Referring to the position of Group B countries on the set of principles, as stated in document TD/RS/CONF/PC/3, he reaffirmed that his Group was unable to accept the imposition of principles proposed by other groups directed towards limiting registration to vessels which met specific requirements on the nationality of ownership, crew and management. He emphasized that it should be left to each State to determine the conditions upon which it would grant its nationality to merchant vessels. The fact that certain States already laid down nationality requirements was within their sovereign right but did not invest those requirements with a compelling character or make them a rule of international law, as they merely reflected economic and social decisions taken by those States.

(TD/RS/CONF/PC/4, p. 6)

In reply to a question, the Parliamentary Under-Secretary of State, Department of Transport, wrote in part:

In order to be registered in the British Isles (i.e. the United Kingdom, the Isle of Man and the Channel Islands) a fishing vessel must be wholly owned by either British subjects or by companies incorporated and having their principal place of business in the British Isles. For this reason there are no fishing boats on the British Isles register that are owned by non-British individuals. But some vessels may be owned by companies that are controlled by non-British parties. The department has no information on the number of such vessels or the nationality of the non-British parties (if any). Nor does the department have any information about the chartering of fishing vessels. In addition, there are fishing vessels under the British flag that are registered in British Dependent Territories. There are 13 such territories and the regulations governing their registries are different both from those in the British Isles and from one territory to another.

(HL Debs., vol. 468, col. 892: 26 November 1985)

Part Nine: XV. C. *Seas, waterways, ships—ships—diplomatic and consular protection*

At a press conference held on 24 September 1985, a spokesman for the Foreign and Commonwealth Office drew attention to the sinking of the Greenpeace vessel *Rainbow Warrior* in Auckland Harbour, New Zealand, by French secret service agents. The report continued:

Spokesman said that the British Ambassador in Paris, Sir John Fretwell, had this morning called on a senior official at the French Ministry of External Relations to deliver a note drawing the French authorities' attention to the British Government's standing in the matter of the Rainbow Warrior (in that it was a British ship) and urging them to make swift compensation to those who had suffered losses. Spokesman added that the Permanent Under Secretary at the Foreign and Commonwealth Office, Sir Antony Acland, would be taking the opportunity of a call by the French Ambassador, which had already been arranged for tomorrow afternoon, to deliver a similar note.

(Text provided by the Foreign and Commonwealth Office; see also HC Debs., vol. 84, Written Answers, col. *292*: 25 October 1985, and ibid., vol. 87, Written Answers, cols. *270–1*: 21 November 1985)

Part Nine: XV. D. *Seas, waterways, ships—ships—jurisdiction*

(See also Part Nine: XV. B. (material of 1983), above)

In a speech on 19 July 1985 at the end of the Third Session of the UN

Conference on Conditions for the Registration of Ships, the UK delegate, Mr Fielder, summed up the agreement to date in part as follows:

139. First, the Conference had agreed to a text on the role of the maritime administration. It had agreed that the flag State should have an adequate and competent maritime administration which would enforce the international rules and standards which had been developed by the international community in order to make shipping as safe as possible. This text touched on an essential obligation of the flag State to the international community: a flag State must do its utmost to secure that its vessels were not a risk to the ships and seafarers of other countries and that they would not pollute the marine environment to the detriment of all States.

140. Secondly, the Conference had agreed to address the draft agreement exclusively to the flag State. Various Groups including Group B had proposed texts which touched upon the possible role of the port State in the context of this agreement. These were interesting texts, but the Conference had concluded that they had no place in the agreement, which addressed the responsibilities of the flag State: it was for the flag State alone to set the conditions on which it would accept ships on its register and to ensure that those responsible for its vessels were readily identifiable and accountable.

(TD/RS/CONF/19, p. 22)

Part Nine: XVI. *Seas, waterways, ships—marine scientific research*

The Foreign Office provided a memorandum, *The State of Marine Science and Technology in the United Kingdom: International Aspects*, to the House of Lords Select Committee on Science and Technology (Sub-Committee II). The memorandum, dated 2 April 1985, read in part as follows:

Diplomatic Clearances

3. The FCO attaches considerable importance to United Kingdom marine research work, which it recognises is expensive, is planned years in advance and may involve international groups of scientists who will probably have built continuing research projects around the information they expect to gather. We are fully aware that delay, curtailment or cancellation carries a heavy cost to public funds and the risk of embarrassment in the United Kingdom's bilateral relations with the states concerned. The FCO and overseas Posts will continue to make every effort to meet the needs of British marine scientists. Unfortunately the atmosphere for marine scientific research is deteriorating generally. Most developing countries are suspicious of marine scientific work, especially on their continental shelf. Elsewhere, domestic political issues, for example the disposal at sea of radio-active waste, influence decisions. The advice of the FCO to British research organisation is that the best way to keep the door open and to ensure that British vessels are welcome is to respect the wishes of coastal states, particularly with regard to the period of notification, requests for additional information and early provision of cruise reports. Changes in timing and routes are also best avoided; at best these are irritants in relations with the Foreign Ministries of other states, at worst, causes for further suspicion about the purposes of the cruise.

4. The procedure for obaining clearance from a foreign government for British research vessels should normally be routine and involve little more than passing details of the cruise programme to the Ministry of Foreign Affairs which then obtains clearance from those Government departments which have an interest. Procedures in the FCO for handling applications for clearances were tightened last year to avoid problems which had occurred previously when a request went astray or was not dealt with promptly. Embassies now have a Glossary of Terms used in oceanographic research for use in explaining in layman's language details of the research work proposed.

INTERNATIONAL LAW

5. International law on this topic is based on state practice and several international conventions. The principal international agreements which have implications for United Kingdom marine scientific research are:

(i) Convention on the Territorial Sea and the Contiguous Zone of 1958;
(ii) Convention on the High Seas of 1958;
(iii) the Convention on the Continental Shelf, 1958, and
(iv) the UN Convention on the Law of the Sea, 1982.

The United Kingdom is a party to (i) to (iii) which are in force, but has not signed (iv) which is not in force.

6. *The Convention on the Territorial Sea* recognises the sovereignty of the coastal state over its territorial sea subject to rights of passage. It follows that the consent of the coastal state has to be obtained for research work in its territorial sea. *The Convention on the High Seas* recognises and regulates several freedoms, including that of scientific research. *The Convention on Continental Shelf* requires that the consent of the coastal state be obtained 'in respect of any research concerning the continental shelf and undertaken there' (Article 5(8)). The coastal state is normally expected to give its consent if the request is in connection with purely scientific research and submitted by a qualified institution. The coastal state has the right to participate or be represented in the research. The results must be published.

7. The United Kingdom has not signed the *UN Law of the Sea Convention of 1982* because of our objection to its provisions for deep sea mining (Part XI). It will not enter into force until a year after 60 ratifications or accessions have been received. (So far there have been 15 ratifications). The Convention sets out general principles for the conduct of marine scientific research (Part XIII). Among these are that it should be conducted exclusively for peaceful purposes and shall not unjustifiably interfere with other legitimate uses of the sea, nor prejudice the protection and preservation of the marine environment. The Convention also defines more specific conditions which vary according to the area concerned.

8. In the *territorial sea* the coastal state is entirely free to refuse consent or impose any restrictions or conditions it wishes on the conduct of research and use of results. There is no appeal if consent is refused or unreasonable conditions are imposed. For all research in the *Exclusive Economic Zone* (200 nautical miles) and for seabed research on the *continental shelf*, the Convention lays down certain conditions, both on countries seeking consent for research and on the coastal state. In normal circumstances there is a duty on a coastal state to grant consent. However, it may withhold consent if the project:

'(a) is direct significance for the exploration or exploitation of natural resources, whether living or non-living;
'(b) involves drilling into the continental shelf, the use of explosives, or the introduction of harmful substances into the marine environment;
'(c) involves the construction, operation or use of artificial islands, installations and structures . . .;
'(d) contains information . . . (provided about the project) . . . which is inaccurate or if the researching State . . . has outstanding obligations to the Coastal State from a prior research project.' (Article 246(5)).

A detailed request for consent has to be submitted not less than six months in advance of the expected starting date of the work. Consent may be implied and research proceeded with on expiry of six months from the date of submission of the request unless the Coastal State has within four months withheld its consent, sought additional information or pointed out that there are outstanding obligations in respect of previous projects. On the *high seas* beyond the limits of national jurisdiction, the Convention recognises the freedom of scientific research.

9. To sum up, the UN Convention has taken the principles contained in the three Conventions of 1958 and has elaborated them by specific provisions, especially as far as the Exclusive Economic Zone and the Continental Shelf are concerned. A number of states which are signatories have anticipated the entry into force of the UN Convention in promulgating national legislation, often imposing further restrictions on marine research.

INTERNATIONAL COOPERATIVE RESEARCH PROGRAMMES

10. The main international agreements for cooperation in research are:
(i) the Antarctic Treaty, 1959;
(ii) the Convention for the International Council for the Exploration of the Sea (ICES), 1964;
(iii) the Convention for the Conservation of Antarctic Seals, 1972; and
(iv) the Convention for the Conservation of Antarctic Marine Living Resources, 1980.

11. *The Antarctic Treaty, 1959* provides that the freedom of scientific investigation in Antarctica and cooperation established during the International Geophysical Year should continue, subject to the Treaty's provisions. The contracting parties agreed that
(a) information regarding plans for scientific programmes in Antarctica should be exchanged to permit maximum economy and efficiency of operations;
(b) scientific personnel shall be exchanged in Antarctica between expeditions and stations;
(c) scientific observations and results from Antarctica shall be exchanged and made freely available.

All these obligations relate to research and are taken by the parties to relate to the marine as well as terrestrial environments.

12. *The Convention for the International Council for the Exploration of the Sea, 1964* provides for a new constitution for the International Council for the Exploration of the Sea established at Copenhagen in 1902. The Council's duties, primarily concerned with the North Atlantic, are:

(i) to promote and encourage research and investigation for the study of the sea, particularly those related to living resources;
(ii) to draw up programmes and to organise such research in agreement with the Contracting Parties;
(iii) to publish or otherwise disseminate the results of research and investigations carried out under its auspices.

13. *The Convention for the Conservation of Antarctic Seals, 1972* recognises that in order to improve scientific knowledge and so place exploitation on a rational basis, every effort should be made to encourage biological and other research on Antarctic seal populations. To that end, contracting parties furnish relevant information to the Scientific Committee on Antarctic Research (SCAR) of the International Council of Scientific Unions. The United Kingdom is the depositary government for the Convention.

14. *The Convention for the Conservation of Antarctic Marine Living Resources, 1980*, established machinery for recommending, promoting, deciding upon and coordinating the measures needed to ensure the conservation of Antarctic marine living organisms. The BAS programme provides information relevant to such deciding.

(Text provided by the Foreign and Commonwealth Office)

The UK Government notified the Government of the Soviet Union of a proposal to carry out marine scientific research in the Soviet exclusive economic zone, namely in ICES Fishing Area Barents Sea 1, beyond twelve nautical miles from the coast. It was in respect of this notification and the Soviet response that the following question was asked in the House of Lords:

Whether the Soviet Union's rejection of British requests to carry out marine research in the water column in the Soviet exclusive economic zone in the course of tracing the route of caesium escaped from Sellafield is based on its rights under the United Nations Convention on the Law of the Sea, whether Her Majesty's Government accept that other states should exercise rights under this convention, and what further steps they propose to take.

In reply, the Minister of State, Foreign and Commonwealth Office, wrote:

The Soviet authorities based their rejection of the British notification on Article 8 of the Charter of the Supreme Soviet of the USSR on the 'Economic Zone of the USSR' of 28th February 1984 and Article 5 of the Charter of the Praesidium of the Supreme Soviet on the 'Continental Shelf of the USSR' of 6th February 1968. There is no indication of a link with the United Nations Convention on the Law of the Sea, which is not in force for any country.

(HL Debs., vol. 466, cols. 120–1: 8 July 1985)

In answer to a later question on the same subject, the Minister of State wrote:

We intend to take the matter up within the International Council for the

Exploration of the Sea, which is a more appropriate channel than the International Atomic Energy Agency. Her Majesty's Embassy at Moscow is also being asked to raise the matter with the Soviet authorities when a suitable opportunity arises.

(HL Debs., vol. 467, col. 262: 30 July 1985)

Part Ten: II. A. 2. *Air space, outer space—air navigation—civil aviation—treaty regime*

Speaking on 21 October 1985 at the Third International Civil Aviation Authority Conference in Montreal, the UK representative, Mr A. I. Aust, addressed the subject of unilateral measures which affect international air transport:

The first point I wish to make is that, by persistently resorting to unilateral measures, states call into question the very foundation of scheduled international air services—the bilateral air services agreement. Some unilateral measures may fall outside the ambit of air services agreements, but the vast majority are directly contrary to them and amount to breaches of them. Measures such as the government direction of traffic to the national airline threaten that cornerstone of the air services agreement, the provision that each designated airline shall have fair and equal opportunity to compete. That is just one example; there are a host of others.

By adopting such measures a party to an air services agreement shows disregard for the sanctity of treaties. This is especially disturbing when one considers the extent to which treaties govern so many aspects of international civil aviation.

If one party is unhappy with the deal embodied in an air services agreement—perhaps because it believes circumstances have changed—then it is open to it to seek to renegotiate the agreement or, as a last resort, to terminate it. These are the proper courses of action. Only where the application of domestic law is clearly consistent with the terms of the bilateral agreement can such laws be applied without provoking arguments, uncertainty and—what is perhaps more disturbing—a loss of confidence, not only between the airlines and aeronautical authorities, but between governments. Without confidence and good-will the delicate structure of international air services will suffer.

I spoke just now of the air services agreement as being the foundation of scheduled international air services. Article 6 of the Chicago Convention has spawned many hundreds, if not thousands, of agreements. Together with the Convention they form the structure within which scheduled services are operated. Unilateral measures threaten that structure. It is a structure which states—and mine is no exception—would be loath to see dismantled.

But here I must strike a note of warning. Because we have become so accustomed to operating within a network of air services agreements we tend to forget that, unlike the Chicago Convention, they are not *essential* for the operation of air services. Even today there are many instances where scheduled air services are operated without, or outside, an air services agreement. If a party to an air services agreement, or its designated airline, is persistently in breach of it, and is unwilling to mend its ways, it should not be surprised if the other party terminates the agreement. Nor should it be surprised if the other party has no wish to negotiate a replacement agreement, but it is content for the airlines to operate on the basis of an exchange of operating permits. Once an air services agreement no longer brings with it an assurance of certainty and fair dealing, there may be little point in having one at all.

One unilateral measure which has caused particular concern to the UK has been the application of domestic competition laws to scheduled international air services. The most celebrated cases have of course involved the United States, and certain aspects of US anti-trust law have been picked out for particular criticism—such as the draconian sanctions inherent in the treble damage remedy available to private litigants, the contingency fee system, or the extraterritorial reach of such laws in certain instances—but the main concern must centre on the fundamental incompatibility of domestic competition laws with the bilaterally agreed regulatory regimes established by air services agreements. That is why we have had occasion to make representations not only to the United States Government in relation to its anti-trust laws, but also to the Government of Australia in relation to developments flowing from the Trade Practices Act and the Government of New Zealand in relation to the Commerce Bill which is currently under consideration. Domestic competition laws are designed to deal with the particular circumstances of the State concerned, or its economic policies; and it is presumptuous for any State to believe that what is good for its people or its economy is necessarily good for others.

It is of course true that when a particular foreign company goes to another country to do business it must normally expect to be subject to that country's laws, including its competition laws. But when that business is being carried out simultaneously in two States and concerns the traffic between them, and particularly when it is done under the terms of a treaty which provides an agreed framework of regulation for that business, there can be no place for the unilateral application by either of the two States concerned of domestic competition laws.

International air transport is unique. Only scheduled international air services are governed to such an extent by bilaterally agreed regulatory regimes. An air services agreement is one in which, as in all treaties, the parties relinquish certain sovereign rights in return for mutual benefits. The right of a State, as confirmed by the Chicago Convention, to decide unilaterally which airlines of other States may fly to and from its territory, the routes they may operate and the traffic rights they may exercise, are replaced by provisions empowering each party to designate those of its airlines who will have the right to operate services on the routes (and with such traffic rights) laid down in the agreement. The capacity which airlines may mount, and the tariffs they may charge are regulated by principles and procedures set out in the agreement. In short, the regulation of air services between the territories of the parties is removed from an area largely governed by the unilateral exercise of sovereign powers and placed in a bilateral framework regulated by international law. As a consequence the area in which national law may still be used to regulate the conduct of the designated airlines is reduced to the extent that the activities are governed by provisions of the agreement. This is particularly so in the case of tariff regulation. The normal tariff article will contain a full, self-contained and exclusive scheme for the regulation of tariffs including agreed principles and criteria which the parties must observe when considering whether a proposed tariff should be approved. These agreed bilateral standards necessarily displace the domestic law of the parties.

Where the field is already occupied by an air services agreement domestic competition rules may not be substituted for the bilaterally agreed rules. To enforce such domestic rules (especially where they are designed to promote national economic philosophy) seriously derogates from the provisions of the agreement. And this problem is compounded and the potential conflict made many times worse where, as in the case of anti-trust law, provision is made for private treble damage suits. In a recent celebrated case British airlines (and others) found themselves involved in hugely expensive private law suits as the result of charging tariffs which had been properly approved by *both* governments and, having been approved under the air services agreement, were required to be charged by the airlines. It creates an impossible situation where decisions of governmental regulatory authorities in such matters as tariffs are challengeable in the courts of one of the States concerned under quite different criteria than those which had been laid down in a bilateral agreement. Such a unilateral assertion of the economic interests and policy of one State disregards the legitimate interests of other States. What one State may regard as an undesirable, or even illegal, anti-competitive practice (such as discussions between airlines on matters of mutual interest) may not be considered at all in the same light by other States, and certainly not internationally recognised as meriting sanctions. What is punishable in one State may be permissible or even encouraged in others, and where such matters are regulated by bilateral agreements it should be the function of that agreement to reconcile the differing views of the two States so that the airlines concerned are not caught in uncertainty and legal peril between the conflicting policies and laws of the two States between which they are providing services.

A solution to these problems must be found, and the starting point must be that each side must recognise and respect the legitimate interests of the other. Equally they must re-examine their own laws and policies. Traditionally air services have been subject to very detailed regulation by governments, and governments have therefore exercised almost total control over the limited competition which has been allowed. In many areas of the world where market entry, capacity and tariffs are still tightly controlled by governments this is still the case.

Of course regulation by government is an instrument of policy which may be more or less favourable to competition. That is a matter for each State to decide for itself. In the United Kingdom the Civil Aviation Authority which has a statutory obligation to 'further the reasonable interests of users of our transport services', as well as the economic well being of the airline industry, has followed an increasingly pro-competitive policy in recent years. We now have two or more airlines competing on most of our domestic trunk routes and three British airlines operating services between London and Hong Kong. British carriers also compete with one another on many international routes, and the Authority encourages the filing of innovative tariffs with or without the agreement of other airlines.

It is with the encouragement of more normal competitive conditions in aviation that the potential role for competition law, as distinct from the direct regulation of competition by government, becomes greater. This is recognised in the United Kingdom where we have recently brought domestic air services and international charter services more fully within the scope of our competition laws. Our attachment to the application of the competition provisions of the Treaty of Rome to international services between the Member States expresses the same philosophy in relation to the air services within the European Community. But we have refrained from applying our domestic laws unilaterally to scheduled international air services, because we believe that to do so would bring us into conflict with our international obligations under our bilateral air services agreements.

There is no doubt in my mind that increasing attention must now be paid to arrangements for ensuring fair competition between airlines as the regulatory restraints on competition are relaxed. But it is no solution to apply domestic laws which may not be appropriate to the particular conditions of the aviation industry, and which are liable to be in conflict with one another if they are applied to the same services by the domestic competition authorities at both ends of a route. We have seen what the consequences of that approach are: confusion among airlines, conflict between the courts of two countries, and a serious dispute between Governments. What is needed are arrangements to deal with anti-competitive activities which can be applied bilaterally or multilaterally between States to ensure fair competition in circumstances where it is no longer considered practical or appropriate to achieve such an outcome by the traditional means of detailed and constant regulatory control. We are ready to engage in such discussions about such arrangements bilaterally wherever the need arises, but it would be in the traditions of ICAO to develop such arrangements for Member States to apply bilaterally in their relations with one another if they wished to do so. States must not seek to apply their domestic competition laws unilaterally to international air services, but my Government will be ready to take part in any endeavour designed to ensure that airlines are not free to engage in anti-competitive behaviour. That is the only way forward.

Meanwhile we ask this conference to reaffirm the vital principle that all Member States must ensure that their laws—not just in relation to competition but in all relevant fields—are applied in such a way that there is no conflict with their obligations under air services agreements.

(Text provided by the Foreign and Commonwealth Office)

Part Ten: III. *Air space, outer space—outer space*

In reply to a request to list those treaties to which the UK is party which prohibit the development of directed energy weapons in space, the Minister of State, Foreign and Commonwealth Office, wrote:

United Kingdom is party to the 1963 treaty banning nuclear weapon tests in the atmosphere, in outer space and under water, and the 1967 treaty on principles governing the activities of states in the exploration and use of outer space, including the moon and other celestial bodies. Neither of these treaties prohibits the development of directed energy weapons in space.

(HC Debs., vol. 89, Written Answers, col. *208*: 18 December 1985)

Part Ten: IV. *Air space, outer space—telecommunications including broadcasting*

(See also Part Nine: VII. H., above)

In reply to a question, the Parliamentary Under-Secretary of State, Foreign and Commonwealth Office, wrote:

The Soviet authorities are well aware of our strong feelings about the continued jamming of BBC services in the Soviet Union and elsewhere, which contravenes the spirit and letter of the Helsinki final act as well as article 35 of the Convention of the International Telecommunication Union of which the Soviet Union is a signatory. We continue to take suitable opportunities to remind them of their commitments under these agreements, most recently at the Anglo-Soviet cultural talks in March.

(HC Debs., vol. 79, Written Answers, col. *463*: 22 May 1985; see also ibid., vol. 83, Written Answers, col. *581*: 24 July 1985)

In reply to a question on the subject of radio stations in international waters, the Parliamentary Under-Secretary of State, Department of Trade and Industry, wrote in part:

The Government also have international obligations, as International Radio Regulation 2665 prohibits broadcasting from ships outside national territories. The United Kingdom is a signatory to a 1965 European convention in which signatories undertook to take steps to prevent broadcasts through legislative means.

(Ibid., vol. 87, Written Answers, col. *129*: 19 November 1985)

Part Eleven: II. A. 6. *Responsibility—responsible entities—States—reparation*

(See also Part Nine: XV. C., above)

In reply to a question on the subject of compensation for the sequestration in 1956 by the Egyptian Government of a villa belonging to Mr D. T. W. Forsyth and his late father, the Parliamentary Under-Secretary of State, Foreign and Commonwealth Office, Mr Renton, stated:

The Forsyth family were not alone in the losses which they suffered in 1956. Most of the British community in Egypt suffered similar misfortune following the conflict of that year. Many British people were expelled from Egypt and had their property sequestrated. It was against that background that the Government reached an agreement with the Egyptian authorities in 1959, which provided for the payment of compensation and the return of British property to its former owners.

The villa owned by Mr. Douglas Forsyth's father was, as my hon. Friend said, sequestrated in 1956. It was then let by the Egyptian Sequestrator General on 1 May 1957 at a low rate on an agreement which provided for 15 days' notice of termination on either side. The villa was desequestrated by the Egyptian authorities on 1 March 1960, under the terms of the 1959 agreement, but the Sequestrator General did not give the tenant notice to quit at that time. As a result, the tenant remains in occupation to this day. As my hon. Friend is aware, tenants have considerable legal protection in Egypt, and it is extremely difficult to secure their eviction.

As to the effects of the form of renunciation, I assure my hon. Friend that we do not rely on that form in deciding what representations to make. We have made many representations irrespective of the effect of the form of renunciation that was signed by Mr. Forsyth's father.

I must place it on record that the Forsyth family has not been ungenerously treated in the matter of compensation. Mr. Forsyth submitted several claims to the Foreign Compensation Commission under the provisions of the Orders in Council relating to the distribution of the compensation that had been received from the Egyptian Government. A total of £79,914 was awarded to him as a result and accepted by him in full settlement of his claims. . . .

Included in the total was a payment of more than £3,000 in settlement of a claim for loss in value of his villa resulting from the fact that it had been returned to him with a sitting tenant. The total of nearly £80,000 compensation was a considerable sum 20 years ago, and I should mention that Mr. Forsyth's late father also received a grant of £30,000 from the Egyptian Grants Committee for the comparative hardship he suffered as a refugee from Egypt.

The correspondence that the Foreign and Commonwealth Office has received from my hon. Friend's constituent shows that there has been some misunderstanding of the position of the Foreign Compensation Commission. I take this opportunity to clarify this. The FCC was established under the Foreign Compensation Act 1950 with two principal functions. The first is the administrative function of registering claims. The second is the judicial and administrative functions involved in awarding and distributing payments of lump sum compensation received by Her Majesty's Government from other Governments.

In exercising the latter function, the Commission has the task of inviting claims to participate in such compensation, judicially determining these claims, deciding which are admissible and which are to be rejected, and finally distributing the moneys among the successful claimants. Although the Secretary of State for Foreign and Commonwealth Affairs retains some responsibility for its work and funding, the commission is wholly independent of the Government when it acts in its judicial capacity in determining claims.

The members of the commission and its staff have always tackled the difficult tasks assigned to them with dedication and conscientiousness. In connection with these Egyptian affairs, they received no fewer than 9,000 claims, made 15,000 adjudications and determinations and distributed to claimants sums in excess of £31 million.

(Ibid., vol. 71, cols. 1108–9: 23 January 1985)

On 18 March 1985, the Governments of the UK and Haiti signed an Agreement for the Promotion and Protection of Investments. Instruments of ratification have not yet been exchanged. Articles 4, 5 and 6 of the Agreement read as follows:

ARTICLE 4

Compensation for Losses

(1) Nationals or companies of one Contracting Party whose investments in the territory of the other Contracting Party suffer losses owing to war or other armed conflict, revolution, a state of national emergency, revolt, insurrection or riot in the territory of the latter Contracting Party shall be accorded by the latter Contracting Party treatment, as regards restitution, indemnification, compensation or other settlement, no less favourable than that which the latter Contracting Party accords to its own nationals or companies or to nationals or companies of any third State.

(2) Without prejudice to paragraph (1) of this Article, nationals and companies of one Contracting Party who in any of the situations referred to in that paragraph suffer losses in the territory of the other Contracting Party resulting from:

(*a*) requisitioning of their property by its forces or authorities, or

(*b*) destruction of their property by its forces or authorities which was not caused in combat action or was not required by the necessity of the situation,

shall be accorded restitution or adequate compensation. Resulting payments shall be freely transferable.

ARTICLE 5

Expropriation

(1) Investments of nationals or companies of either Contracting Party shall not be nationalised, expropriated or subjected to measures having effect equivalent to nationalisation or expropriation (hereinafter referred to as 'expropriation') in the territory of the other Contracting Party except for a public purpose related to the internal needs of that Party and against prompt, adequate and effective compensation. Such compensation shall amount to the market value of the investment expropriated immediately before the expropriation or impending expropriation became public knowledge, shall include interest at a normal commercial rate until the date of payment, shall be made without delay, be effectively realisable and be freely transferable. The national or company affected shall have a right, under the law of the Contracting Party making the expropriation, to prompt review, by a judicial or other independent authority of that Party, of his or its case and of the valuation of his or its investment in accordance with the principles set out in this paragraph.

(2) Where a Contracting Party expropriates the assets of a company which is incorporated or constituted under the law in force in any part of its own territory, and in which nationals or companies of the other Contracting Party own shares, it shall ensure that the provisions of paragraph (1) of this Article are applied to the extent necessary to guarantee prompt, adequate and effective compensation in respect of their investment to such nationals or companies of the other Contracting Party who are owners of those shares.

ARTICLE 6

Repatriation of Investment and Returns

Each Contracting Party shall in respect of investments guarantee to nationals or companies of the other Contracting Party the unrestricted transfer to the country where they reside of their investments and returns, subject to the right of each Contracting Party in exceptional balance of payments difficulties and for a limited period to exercise equitably and in good faith powers conferred by its laws. Such powers shall not however be used to impede the transfer of profit, interest, dividends, royalties or fees; as regards investments and any other form of return transfer of a minimum of 20% a year is guaranteed. Transfers of currency shall be effected without delay in the convertible currency in which the capital was originally invested or in any other convertible currency agreed by the investor and the Contracting Party concerned. Unless otherwise agreed by the investor transfers shall be made at the rate of exchange applicable on the date of transfer pursuant to the exchange regulations in force.

(Cmnd. 9731)

In reply to the question whether Her Majesty's Government has claimed compensation from the Soviet Union for the British lives lost when the Soviet military authorities shot down Korean Air Lines flight 007 on 1 September 1983, the Parliamentary Under-Secretary of State, Foreign and Commonwealth Office, wrote:

Yes. Fourteen persons entitled to our protection were killed then and a national claim for compensation of £2 million was handed to the Soviet Embassy on 3 July.

(HC Debs., vol. 82, Written Answers, col. *273*: 5 July 1985)

In the course of a debate on the subject of the operation of the Foreign Compensation (Czechoslovakia) Order 1982, the Parliamentary Under-Secretary of State, Foreign and Commonwealth Office, Mr Timothy Eggar, stated:

I recognise that a significant number of people who suffered losses in Czechoslovakia a long time ago are interested in these questions and hope to receive compensation for their losses; I very much sympathise with them.

The House will be aware that the negotiations with Czechoslovakia which led to the signature of an agreement on 29 January 1982 were extremely complicated and lengthy. They began in 1949 and had many ups and downs. Their successful conclusion was not wholly within our gift nor that of the Czechoslovaks. The French and United States Governments were holding their own bilateral negotiations with the Czechoslovaks at the same time and there was a higher degree of interdependence between the three sets of negotiations.

Although the Order is long and complicated, its principal purpose is straightforward enough. It entrusts to the Foreign Compensation Commission the task of receiving applications to share in the distribution of the compensation received from Czechoslovakia. It reviews and values those claims and deals with the distribution of compensation to claimants in proportion to the valuation assigned by the commission to their claims.

As my hon. Friend has said, the total sum of money handed to the Foreign Compensation Commission for private claimants in October 1982, was almost £4 million. I am pleased to tell the House that with interest that sum now stands at almost £4·75 million. The 1982 Order gave applicants 12 months in which to make their claims to share in the compensation. A large number did so. Whereas our negotiations with the Czechoslovaks had been concerned with only 1,254 private claims with a face value of some £6 million, no fewer than 2,204 persons applied to take part in the distribution. My hon. Friend might like to know that the nominal value of the applications filed up to the closing date, 31 August 1983, had risen to some £21 million rather than the £6 million which we were previously talking about.

I understand that my hon. Friend the Member for Kettering . . . spoke of his concern about the pace at which the Foreign Compensation Commission is reaching decisions. Indeed, he has asked me to review the whole order, with a view both to altering the burden of proof placed upon the applicants and also to setting a target date for the clearance of all the claims. While I share my hon. Friend's concern that matters should be speeded up, I am sorry to have to say that there is no possibility of altering the burden of proof. That must still rest upon the applicants. It seems to me proper that in the case of this order, as with all similar orders, it should be the responsibility of the claimant to establish his own claim. No one else can shoulder that responsibility.

(HC Debs., vol. 86, cols. 665–6: 13 November 1985)

In reply to questions on the subject of claims for compensation for assets seized in Russia at the time of the Bolshevik revolution in 1917, the Parliamentary Under-Secretary of State, Foreign and Commonwealth Office, wrote:

We have no new initiative in mind at present. We believe we should persist with the discussions with the Soviet Union about these claims.

. . .

Some 50,000 private claims were registered between 1918 and the early 1950s. The total value of those claims was earlier set at £400 million.

. . .

. . . We have continued to hold meetings with the Soviet Union at irregular intervals which have been directed towards a settlement both of United Kingdom claims against the Soviet Union and of Soviet claims against us.

(Ibid., vol. 88, Written Answers, cols. *718–20*: 12 December 1985)

Part Eleven: II. A. 7 (a). *Responsibility—responsible entities—States—procedure—diplomatic and consular protection*

In the course of a debate on the subject of persons detained in Zimbabwe, the Minister of State, Foreign and Commonwealth Office, Mr Malcolm Rifkind, stated:

. . . the Government recognise their full responsibility to provide what consular protection they can to any British citizen who is incarcerated in a foreign country. Where a British citizen is detained, we always make representations to the Government of that country that they should either bring charges and allow the person to be tried in open court, or he should be released if no charges are brought.

(Ibid., vol. 76, cols. 1398–400: 4 April 1985)

Part Eleven: II. A. 7. (a). (i). *Responsibility—responsible entities—States—procedure—diplomatic and consular protection—nationality of claims*

In reply to a question on the subject of Mr Robert Astles, imprisoned in Uganda, the Minister of State, Foreign and Commonwealth Office, wrote:

Since Mr. Robert Astles renounced his British citizenship to become a mono-Ugandan citizen we have no right to intervene on his behalf and it is for the Ugandan authorities to decide when to release him.

(HL Debs., vol. 460, col. 179: 12 February 1985)

On 18 March 1985, the Governments of the UK and Haiti signed an Agreement for the Promotion and Protection of Investments. Instruments of ratification have not yet been exchanged. Article 1, paragraphs (c) and (d) of the Agreement reads:

(*c*) 'nationals' means:

(i) in respect of the United Kingdom: physical persons deriving their status as United Kingdom nationals from the law in force in the United Kingdom;

(ii) in respect of the Republic of Haiti: Haitians as defined in the law establishing the rules concerning Haitian Nationality.

(*d*) 'companies' means:

(i) in respect of the United Kingdom: corporations, firms or associations incorporated or constituted under the law in force in any part of the United Kingdom or in any territory to which this Agreement is extended in accordance with the provisions of Article 11;

(ii) in respect of the Republic of Haiti: legal persons, commercial companies or other associations having legal personality whose headquarters are in Haiti: and which are constituted within the framework of the relevant laws.

(Cmnd. 9731)

In reply to a question about the arrest of trade unionists in Zimbabwe, the Minister of State, Foreign and Commonwealth Office, wrote in part:

We have no standing to make formal representations on behalf of non-British citizens.

(HC Debs., vol. 75, Written Answers, col. *525*: 20 March 1985)

In reply to a question on the subject of the treatment of Sr Fernandez Lembach, detained in Chile, the Parliamentary Under-Secretary of State, Foreign and Commonwealth Office, wrote in part:

As Sr Fernandez Lembach is a Chilean national we have no formal standing to intervene with the Chilean authorities on his behalf nor any right of access to him.

(Ibid., vol. 80, Written Answers, col. *76*: 3 June 1985; see also ibid., vol. 83, Written Answers, col. *383*: 22 July 1985)

In reply to a question on the effects of the Citizenship of Zimbabwe Act 1984, the Minister of State, Foreign and Commonwealth Office, wrote in part:

International practice precludes British consular protection being afforded to dual British-Zimbabwean citizens in Zimbabwe, and this will of course continue to be the case for those who opt for Zimbabwean citizenship. Persons who renounce their British citizenship will be ineligible for British consular protection in any country.

(HL Debs., vol. 464, col. 740: 4 June 1985)

In the course of a debate on the subject of the operation of the Foreign Compensation (Czechoslovakia) Order 1982, the Parliamentary Under-Secretary of State, Foreign and Commonwealth Office, Mr Timothy Eggar, stated:

I realise that some claimants were members of the allied armed forces during the second world war and gave distinguished and gallant service then. They have since come to Britain and made their homes here, but they were not British nationals at the relevant time when they lost their pension rights in Czechoslovakia and so, sadly, do not qualify under the provisions of the Czechoslovakia order. I must tell my hon. Friend that we reviewed this matter very carefully last year . . . and concluded that it would be wrong to amend article 21 of the order, which bears upon pension claims. I will explain briefly the reasons behind our decision.

In preparing the 1982 order, the Government thought it right to make provision for some of the compensation received under the 1982 agreement with Czechoslovakia to be used for the benefit of the very limited category of pension claimants described in article 21. Since we had been negotiating with the Czechoslovak Government about compensation for the loss of British property, it was inevitable that the text of this article should be drawn in such a way as to benefit only those who met a strict British nationality requirement.

We also had a duty to consider the position of all the other claimants under this order. We could not act to their detriment without having a sound legal justification for this. In the present case, we concluded that such a legal justification did not exist and that it would not be proper for us to attempt to relax the nationality requirement. All other claims under this order are subject to a strict nationality test based on international law. That has been our consistent practice in all orders in Council providing for the distribution of compensation moneys received from other Governments.

(HC Debs., vol. 86, col. 667: 13 November 1985)

[The Foreign Compensation (Czechoslovakia) Order 1982 provides as follows:

'United Kingdom national' means:—

(a) any individual who was at the material time, or who as regards any material time prior to 1st January 1949 would have been had the British Nationality Act 1948 (*a*) and the British Protectorates, Protected States and Protected Persons Order in Council 1949(*b*) been in force at that time, a citizen of the United Kingdom and Colonies, a British subject by virtue of section 2, 13 or 16 of that Act or the British Nationality Act 1965(*c*), or a British protected person within the meaning of the said Act of 1948: provided that:-

(i) as regards any material time prior to 16th May 1948, the expression 'British protected person' shall be deemed to include a person who was at that time a Palestinian citizen under the Palestinian Citizenship Orders 1925 to 1942 (*d*); and

(ii) any individual who was a British subject at any time before the date of the commencement of the said Act of 1948 only by virtue of the provisions of the Act of 1705(*e*), intituled 'An Act for the Naturalization of the Most Excellent Princess Sophia Electress and Duchess Dowager of Hanover and the Issue of Her Body', shall be deemed not to be a United Kingdom national;

(b) any corporation, firm or association incorporated or constituted under the laws in force in the United Kingdom or in any territory for whose international relations Her Majesty's Government in the United Kingdom were, at the material time, responsible;

(c) any individual who as regards any material time after 31st December 1949 and prior to 18th April 1980 was a citizen of Southern Rhodesia or a citizen of Rhodesia and Nyasaland, and any individual who as regards any material time after 31st October 1957 and prior to 17th September 1963 was a citizen of Singapore;

(d) Her Majesty's Government in the United Kingdom and the Government of any territory for the international relations of which Her Majesty's Government in the United Kingdom were, at the material time, responsible.

(*a*) 1948 c. 56.
(*b*) S.I. 1949/140.
(*c*) 1965 c. 34.
(*d*) S.R. & O. 1925/777, 1931/671, 1939/863, 1941/1121, 1942/1177.
(*e*) 1705 c. 14.

(Statutory Instrument 1982 No. 1073)]

Part Eleven: II. A. 7. (a). (ii). *Responsibility—responsible entities—States—procedure—diplomatic and consular protection—exhaustion of local remedies*

In reply to the question what action Her Majesty's Government were taking about the seizure by the Government of Djibouti of the British-owned company CMAO, the Minister of State, Foreign and Commonwealth Office, wrote:

We have been informed of action which the Djibouti port authority proposes to take against the interests of Compagnie Maritime Auxiliaire d'Outre-Mer (CMAO) in Djibouti. It is our understanding that such action does not involve the seizure of the company but concerns the amount of rent to be paid in the future by CMAO under its lease with the port authority.

It is the responsibility of CMAO to take such action to protect its interests as it deems appropriate having regard to the remedies available under local law. But Her Majesty's ambassador has raised the matter with the Government of Djibouti and the relevant authorities; Foreign and Commonwealth officials have also had discussions with officers of CMAO. We are monitoring developments closely.

(HC Debs., vol. 89, Written Answers, col. *365*: 20 December 1985)

Part Eleven: II. D. 2. *Responsibility—responsible entities—individuals including corporations—responsibility of individuals*

On 8 November 1985 in the Sixth Committee of the General Assembly of the UN, discussing a Draft Code of Offences against the Peace and Security of Mankind, the UK representative, Sir John Freeland, stated:

We believe . . . that once the Commission tackles the issue of general principles it will become all the clearer how great is the need for precision in the definition of those acts of individuals which are to be criminalised. (I add in parenthesis that it continues to be our conviction that the Commission's efforts should be devoted exclusively to the international criminal responsibility of *individuals*; and that, to be a reality, the international criminal responsibility of individuals entails the establishment of an international criminal jurisdiction.) This requirement of precision cannot be satisfied by the inclusion in any list of offences of what an earlier speaker in this debate has, with some justice, referred to as political slogans. I do not propose to add substantially at this stage to what my delegation has said earlier about the categories suggested by the Special Rapporteur for possible inclusion. I will make just two points. First, the category of terrorist acts is one whose inclusion seems to us amply justified in contemporary circumstances and one which is susceptible of the necessary precision of definition. We would not accept, however, that the category should be restricted to State-sponsored terrorism. We believe that all forms of terrorism are vicious and reprehensible and that therefore terrorism in all its forms, and by whomsoever committed, calls for condemnation as an offence against the peace and security of mankind. Secondly . . . we are not impressed by the arguments which have been advanced for the inclusion of a category revolving round the notion of 'colonial domination'. Like some of the other categories suggested, this category is undefined and in all likelihood impossible to define with enough precision to constitute a criminal offence. In any event, if there were to be a category of this kind it should more usefully be approached from the point of view of seeking to criminalise *every* form of subjection of peoples against their will to alien subjugation or domination, in violation of the right of self-determination.

(Text provided by the Foreign and Commonwealth Office; see also A/C. 6/40/SR. 32, p. 6)

Part Twelve: II. A. *Pacific settlement of disputes—modes of settlement—negotiation*

(See also Part Eight: II. A. (item of 27 November 1985), above and Part Twelve: II. G. (UK–Haiti Agreement of 18 March 1985), below)

By a letter dated 13 March 1985, addressed to the Secretary-General of the UN, the Permanent Representative of the UK to the UN in New York, Sir John Thomson, replied to a letter (A/40/132) from the Government of Argentina. He wrote in part:

The Argentine statement refers to British refusal to enter into negotiations on the question of sovereignty. But it is implicit in this statement, and has regularly been made explicit in other statements by the Argentine Government, that such negotiations could, in the Argentine view, have only one pre-determined outcome—the transfer of sovereignty over the Falkland Islands to Argentina irrespective of the wishes of the Falkland Islanders. The British Government regrets that the Argentine Government makes it a pre-condition of progress on any aspect of our bilateral relations that the British Government must first commit itself to negotiations which have the aim of securing the absorption of the Falkland Islands by Argentina. Such a course is unacceptable to the British Government. It looks to the Government of Argentina to respond positively to the British initiatives which have been put forward with the aim of gradually rebuilding confidence in relations between Argentina and the United Kingdom. It hopes that the Argentine Government will come to recognize that the way ahead lies through patient efforts to rebuild the traditionally good relations between the two countries by discussion of practical measures of mutual benefit on which agreement should be feasible in the short term.

(A/40/177)

By a letter dated 30 May 1985, addressed to the Secretary-General, Sir John Thomson replied to a further letter (A/40/345—S/17229) from the Government of Argentina. He wrote in part:

The Argentine Foreign Minister concludes his letter by repeating that the United Kingdom should agree to negotiate on the sovereignty of the Falkland Islands, South Georgia and the South Sandwich Islands, and attempts to argue that there is an obligation in this sense under the United Nations Charter. The United Kingdom Government's attitude is wholly consistent with the provisions of the Charter of the United Nations. It is a misrepresentation of the Charter to suggest that the obligation to seek solutions by peaceful means requires that, irrespective of the circumstances, recourse must be had, solely or even primarily, to negotiations. The United Kingdom is committed to the peaceful settlement of international disputes. We were negotiating on the very subject of sovereignty when Argentina launched its brutal invasion of the Islands in 1982. The United Kingdom cannot ignore those tragic events, nor can the present Government of Argentina escape their consequences.

(A/40/345—S/17229)

Part Twelve: II. G. 1. *Pacific settlement of disputes—modes of settlement—arbitration—arbitral tribunals and commissions*

(See also Part Five: VIII. B. (1983 material on *Alraigo* incident), above)

On 18 March 1985, the Governments of the UK and Haiti signed an Agreement for the Promotion and Protection of Investments. Instruments of ratification have not yet been exchanged. Articles 8 and 9 of the Agreement read as follows:

ARTICLE 8

Settlement of Disputes between an Investor and a Host State

(1) Disputes between a national or company of one Contracting Party and the other Contracting Party concerning an obligation under this Agreement which have not been amicably settled shall after a period of three months from written notification of a claim be submitted to international arbitration if either party to the dispute so wishes.

ARTICLE 9

Disputes between the Contracting Parties

(1) Disputes between the Contracting Parties concerning the interpretation or application of this Agreement should, if possible, be settled through the diplomatic channel.

(2) If a dispute between the Contracting Parties cannot thus be settled, it shall upon the request of either Contracting Party be submitted to an arbitral tribunal.

(3) Such an arbitral tribunal shall be constituted for each individual case in the following way. Within two months of the receipt of the request for arbitration,

each Contracting Party shall appoint one member of the tribunal. Those two members shall then select a national of a third State who on approval by the two Contracting Parties shall be appointed Chairman of the tribunal. The Chairman shall be appointed within two months from the date of appointment of the other two members.

(4) If within the periods specified in paragraph (3) of this Article the necessary appointments have not been made, either Contracting Party may, in the absence of any other agreement, invite the President of the International Court of Justice to make any necessary appointments. If the President is a national of either Contracting Party or if he is otherwise prevented from discharging the said function, the Vice-President shall be invited to make the necessary appointments. If the Vice-President is a national of either Contracting Party or if he too is prevented from discharging the said function, the Member of the International Court of Justice next in seniority who is not a national of either Contracting Party shall be invited to make the necessary appointments.

(5) The arbitral tribunal shall reach its decision by a majority of votes. Such decision shall be binding on both Contracting Parties. Each Contracting Party shall bear the cost of its own member of the tribunal and of its representation in the arbitral proceedings; the cost of the Chairman and the remaining costs shall be borne in equal parts by the Contracting Parties. The tribunal may, however, in its decision direct that a higher proportion of costs shall be borne by one of the two Contracting Parties, and this award shall be binding on both Contracting Parties. The tribunal shall determine its own procedure.

(Cmnd. 9731)

Part Twelve: II. H. 1. *Pacific settlement of disputes—modes of settlement—judicial settlement—the International Court of Justice*

(See Part Three: III. D. (item of 22 May 1985), above)

Part Twelve: II. I. 1. *Pacific settlement of disputes—modes of settlement—settlement within international organizations—the UN*

In the course of a debate in the House of Lords on the subject of the fortieth anniversary of the UN, the Minister of State, Foreign and Commonwealth Office, Baroness Young, stated:

We have had to accept that a body composed of sovereign states cannot, in the modern world, act as an agent of enforcement against recalcitrant members. But the United Nations has nevertheless made an important contribution to international peace.

The Security Council has prime responsibility in this area. Action in the council has at crucial moments been able to defuse regional crises. The Middle East war of 1973, which threatened to escalate into a wider conflict, is a case in point. Negotiations in the Security Council eased tension, and the disputing states were able to agree to the swift deployment of a UN peacekeeping force.

Peacekeeping indeed is perhaps the prime example of the way in which the Security Council has been able to adapt its practices to changing realities. It was not an activity envisaged in the UN Charter. It has developed pragmatically. Peacekeeping operations rely on consent and co-operation to operate effectively.

But where the parties to a dispute commit themselves to its deployment, a peacekeeping force can play a vital role in maintaining an otherwise fragile peace. And it can, as for example in Cyprus, help create the conditions in which negotiations on the underlying problems can begin. Successive British Governments have devoted military and financial resources to UN peacekeeping operations. We can take pride in the important role played by a British citizen—and I was pleased that the most reverend Primate referred to Mr. Brian Urquhart, Under-Secretary General—in the development of UN peacekeeping. This Government will continue fully to support this crucial UN activity.

The Security Council has been able to perform another important role. It has from time to time outlined a possible basis for a comprehensive settlement of some of the major problems facing the international community. Security Council Resolutions 242 and 338 addressed the Middle East conflict; Resolution 435 established the basis for Namibian independence. Such resolutions have not of themselves solved such deep and difficult international problems. But they set out the parameters of the sort of settlement which might be widely acceptable to the international community.

Successive Secretary Generals have worked closely with the Security Council in efforts to preserve peace and resolve disputes. Indeed the Secretary General has on occasion been able to act when the Security Council itself has been paralysed by superpower dissension, as during the Cuba missile crisis in 1962. At other times the independence of his position has enabled the Secretary General to assist governments in conflict. The current Secretary General has, for example, worked tirelessly to bring the Greek and Turkish Cypriots together. The Government fully support those efforts.

(HL Debs., vol. 467, cols. 1460–1: 29 October 1985)

Part Thirteen: I. D. *Coercion and use of force short of war—unilateral acts—intervention*

(See also Part Three: III. D. (item of 28 March 1985), above)

In the course of a speech to the Security Council on 7 March 1985, the representative of the UK, Mr Maxey, stated:

My Government's views on the question of southern Lebanon are clear. We condemned Israel's invasion of Lebanon in June 1982. We have called for the early, complete and orderly withdrawal of all Israeli forces to the south of Lebanon's international border. We have called for the early withdrawal of all foreign forces from Lebanon, except those present at the request of the Government of Lebanon.

(S/PV. 2570, p. 39)

By a letter addressed to the Secretary-General of the UN, dated 13 March 1985, the Permanent Representative of the UK to the UN in New York, Sir John Thomson, replied to a letter (A/40/132) from the Government of Argentina. He stated in part:

What the Argentine Government's claim ignores entirely . . . are the events of

1982, when Argentina invaded the Falkland Islands in breach of the fundamental principles of the United Nations.

(A/40/177)

In the course of a speech to the Security Council on 14 June 1985, the UK representative, Mr Maxey, stated:

In London, early today, the Foreign and Commonwealth Secretary made clear to the South African Ambassador the very serious view which the British Government takes of South Africa's attack on Botswana in the early hours of this morning. He strongly condemned the violation of the sovereignty of a fellow Commonwealth country and deplored this further use of violence which has resulted in much loss of life and injury. Sir Geoffrey Howe told Dr. Worrall that the British Government regarded the attack as indefensible, the more so given the earlier diplomatic exchanges between the Governments of Botswana and South Africa on security matters.

In the course of his speech Mr Maxey referred to an incursion by South African agents into the Angolan territory of Cabinda. He stated:

We unequivocally condemn such violations of sovereignty. We have expressed our strong views to the South African Government.

(S/PV. 2590, p. 40; see also S/PV. 2597, p. 72)

Speaking in the Security Council on 20 June 1985 after a vote to adopt resolution 567 (1985), the UK representative, Mr Maxey, stated:

. . . my delegation considered that the Security Council should express strong condemnation of South Africa's illegal and totally unjustifiable act of force in Cabinda. We have accordingly voted in favour of the resolution. In so doing, we do not endorse every formulation in the present text. We do not consider that the third preambular paragraph, and the first and third operative paragraphs, fall within the provisions of Chapter VII of the United Nations Charter or constitute a finding or decision which has specific consequences under the Charter.

(Ibid.)

[The third preambular paragraph of the resolution reads:

Gravely concerned at the renewed escalation of unprovoked and persistent acts of aggression, committed by the racist régime of South Africa in violation of the sovereignty, airspace and territorial integrity of Angola, as evidenced by the recent military attack in the Province of Cabinda

The first and third operative paragraphs of the resolution read:

1. *Strongly condemns* South Africa for its recent act of aggression against the territory of Angola in the Province of Cabinda as well as for its renewed intensified, premeditated and unprovoked acts of aggression which constitute a flagrant violation of the sovereignty and territorial integrity of that country and endanger seriously international peace and security

3. *Demands* that South Africa should unconditionally withdraw forthwith all its occupation forces from the territory of Angola, cease all acts of aggression against that State and scrupulously respect the sovereignty and territorial integrity of the People's Republic of Angola]

Speaking on 21 June 1985 in respect of the vote on Security Council Resolution 568 (1985), Mr Maxey stated:

As with resolution 567 (1985), adopted yesterday, the United Kingdom does not interpret the term 'act of aggression' in the text of this resolution as falling within the provisions of Chapter VII of the Charter or as constituting a finding or decision which has specific consequences under the Charter. But although we may not endorse every formulation in it, our support for the purpose of this resolution is wholehearted.

(S/PV. 2599, p. 78; see also S/PV. 2631, p. 33 (vote on Resolution 577 (1985)))

[The first and second operative paragraphs of the resolution as adopted read:

The Security Council

. . .

1. *Strongly condemns* the recent unprovoked and unwarranted military attack on the capital of Botswana by South Africa as an act of aggression against that country and a gross violation of its territorial integrity and national sovereignty;

2. *Further condemns* all acts of aggression, provocation and harassment, including murder, blackmail, kidnapping and destruction of property committed by the racist régime of South Africa against Botswana]

In reply to a question on the subject of a raid by South African forces against a target in Botswana, the Minister of State, Foreign and Commonwealth Office, Baroness Young, stated in part:

. . . [The Secretary of State for Foreign and Commonwealth Affairs] summoned the South African ambassador immediately on 14th June and made clear the very serious view we took on this indefensible attack. We strongly condemned this blatant violation of Botswana's sovereignty, and we joined our Community partners in the statement by the Ten on 17th June strongly condemning the South African action.

(HL Debs., vol. 465, col. 640: 25 June 1985; see also HC Debs., vol. 81, col. 906: 26 June 1985, ibid., vol. 83, Written Answers, col. *583*: 24 July 1985, and United Nations Security Council debates S/PV. 2590, p. 38 (14 June 1985) and S/PV. 2598, pp. 23–6 (21 June 1985))

In reply to a question on the subject of the Soviet intervention in Afghanistan, the Parliamentary Under-Secretary of State, Foreign and Commonwealth Office, wrote in part:

We and our Community partners have repeatedly condemned that occupation . . .

(HC Debs., vol. 83, Written Answers, cols. *581–2*: 24 July 1985)

Following a further raid by South African forces into Angola, on 16 September 1985, a spokesman for the Foreign and Commonwealth Office issued the following statement on 19 September 1985:

We strongly condemn this incursion into Angolan sovereign territory by South African Defence Forces. Such acts can only undermine the stability of the region and damage efforts to achieve Namibian independence. We urge South Africa to withdraw her forces at once.

(Text provided by the Foreign and Commonwealth Office)

At a press conference held on 2 October 1985, a spokesman of the Foreign and Commonwealth Office drew attention to the following statement by the Secretary of State for Foreign and Commonwealth Affairs, Sir Geoffrey Howe:

We continue to view with deep concern the persistent violations of Thailand's sovereignty and territorial integrity by the Vietnamese forces which illegally occupy Cambodia. The latest such violations were a subject of a Note sent by the Thai Permanent Representative to the United Nations to the UN Secretary General on 26 September. The United Kingdom calls upon Vietnam to put a stop to these acts which are in defiance of the UN Charter and world opinion, and reiterates its call for Vietnam to withdraw its forces immediately from Cambodia in compliance with successive United Nations resolutions.

(Ibid.)

In a speech in the Security Council on 2 October 1985, the Permanent Representative of the UK, Sir John Thomson, stated:

It was with deep concern that my delegation heard the news of the attack carried out by the Israeli Air Force in Tunisian territory on 1 October. We have listened with attention and sympathy to the characteristically restrained statement made by the Foreign Minister of Tunisia. We have also taken careful note of the public statements made by the Israeli Government in explanation of their action, including the eloquent statement just made by the Ambassador of Israel. We have studied the facts of the case as they have become widely known. Our conclusion is that there can be no question but that the raid constitutes a serious violation of Tunisian sovereignty and that it has been the cause of the indiscriminate killing and wounding of many innocent civilians.

. . . my delegation cannot accept as valid the reasons put forward by the Government of Israel for its action. Member States of the United Nations, in accordance with Article 2 of the Charter, commit themselves to settle their international disputes by peaceful means. Arbitrary and disproportionate violence of this sort, even in retaliation, is in clear breach of this obligation.

(S/PV. 2611, pp. 39–40)

In an explanation of vote on 7 October 1985 on Security Council Resolution 574 (1985) concerning South Africa's military operations in Angola, the UK representative, Mr Maxey, stated:

The United Kingdom does not interpret operative paragraph 6 as endorsing the intervention of foreign combat troops. We would like to see all foreign forces withdrawn from Angola as soon as possible.

(S/PV. 2617, p. 52; see also S/PV. 2631, p. 33 (vote on Resolution 577 (1985)))

[Operative paragraph 6 of the Resolution reads:

6. *Renews* its request to Member States to extend all necessary assistance to the People's Republic of Angola in order to strengthen its defence capability in the face of South Africa's escalating acts of aggression and the occupation of parts of its territory by the South African military forces.]

Speaking on 23 October 1985 in explanation of vote on Resolution A/C. 3/40/L. 7 in the Third Committee of the General Assembly, the UK representative stated:

. . . my delegation has reservations with regard to operative paragraph one. It is the duty of the United Nations under the Charter to work for peaceful solutions to disputes in all circumstances. In our view, therefore, the phrase 'by all available means' in operative paragraph one is to be interpreted in accordance with the relevant provisions of the Charter, and cannot include armed struggle.

(Text provided by the Foreign and Commonwealth Office)

[Operative paragraph 1 of the draft resolution read:

The General Assembly

. . .

1. *Resolves once again* that all forms of racism and racial discrimination, particularly in their institutionalized form, such as *apartheid*, or resulting from official doctrines of racial superiority or exclusivity, are among the most serious violations of human rights in the contemporary world and must be combated by all available means.]

In reply to a question asking for Her Majesty's Government's policy towards the acquisition of territory by force, the Parliamentary Under-Secretary of State, Foreign and Commonwealth Office, wrote:

The United Nations Charter commits member states to refrain in their international relations from the threat or use of force against the territorial integrity or political independence of any state (article 2.4). We believe all states should abide by that commitment.

(HC Debs., vol. 84, Written Answers, col. *248*: 24 October 1985)

Part Thirteen: I. E. *Coercion and use of force short of war—unilateral acts—other unilateral acts, including self-defence*

On 8 November 1985, in the Sixth Committee of the General Assembly of the UN, discussing the latest work of the International Law Commission on State responsibility, the UK representative, Sir John Freeland, stated:

I should record the doubts of my delegation about the inclusion of paragraph 2 of draft article 11. The provisions of that paragraph in our view go too far, in the present state of international organisation, in fettering the right of an injured state to have recourse to counter-measures in response to an internationally wrongful act.

(Text provided by the Foreign and Commonwealth Office; see also A/C. 6/40 SR. 32)

[Draft Article 11 read as follows:

1. The injured State is not entitled to suspend the performance of its obligations towards the State which has committed the internationally wrongful act to the extent that such obligations are stipulated in a multilateral treaty to which both States are parties and it is established that:

(*a*) the failure to perform such obligations by one State party necessarily affects the exercise of the rights or the performance of obligations of all other States parties to the treaty; or

(*b*) such obligations are stipulated for the protection of collective interests of the States parties to the multilateral treaty; or

(*c*) such obligations are stipulated for the protection of individual persons irrespective of their nationality.

2. The injured State is not entitled to suspend the performance of its obligations towards the State which has committed the internationally wrongful act if the multilateral treaty imposing the obligations provides for a procedure of collective decisions for the purpose of enforcement of the obligations imposed by it, unless and until such collective decision, including the suspension of obligations towards the State which has committed the internationally wrongful act, has been taken; in such case, paragraph 1 (*a*) and (*b*) do not apply to the extent that such decision so determines.]

Part Thirteen: II. A. *Coercion and use of force short of war—collective measures—regime of the United Nations*

In reply to a question, the Parliamentary Under-Secretary of State, Department of Trade and Industry, Lord Lucas of Chilworth, stated:

. . . the Security Council Resolution 418 of 4th November 1977 forbids the provision of arms and related material to South Africa and also the provision of equipment and technical knowledge for their manufacture. The resolution is mandatory, and the Government's policy is to comply fully.

(HL Debs., vol. 460, col. 1444: 7 March 1985; see also ibid., vol. 467, cols. 1522–3: 29 October 1985)

In reply to a question on the same subject, the Minister of State, Foreign and Commonwealth Office, wrote:

The United Nations arms embargo is implemented in the United Kingdom by means of the Exports of Goods (Control) Order 1985 (as amended). Her Majesty's Customs and Excise is responsible for implementing the control. Any alleged breaches are fully investigated and, where appropriate, prosecutions follow.

(HC Debs., vol. 88, Written Answers, col. *636*: 11 December 1985)

Part Thirteen: II. B. *Coercion and use of force short of war—collective measures—collective measures outside the United Nations*

At a press conference held by the Foreign and Commonwealth Office on 25 September 1985, details were given of the restrictive measures imposed in respect of South Africa by the ten Member States of the European Economic Community, including the UK. These were:

1. A rigorously controlled embargo on exports of arms and paramilitary equipment to South Africa. Spokesman commented that the UK had already fully implemented this embargo in compliance with UN Security Council Resolution 418.

2. A rigorously controlled embargo on imports of arms and paramilitary equipment *from* South Africa. Spokesman said that the UK supported UN Security Council Resolution 558 calling on states to refrain from importing arms, ammunition and military vehicles from South Africa. In practice the UK did not import arms supplies from South Africa.

3. Refusal to cooperate in the military sphere. Spokesman pointed out that the UK already had a policy of no military cooperation with South Africa.

4. Recall of military attachés accredited to South Africa and refusal to grant accreditation to military attachés from South Africa. On this point Spokesman said that HMG would shortly be taking steps to arrange for the recall of its Defence attachés from South Africa.

5. Discouraging cultural and scientific agreements except where these contribute towards the ending of apartheid or have no possible role in supporting it: and freezing of official contacts and international agreements in the sporting and security spheres. Spokesman commented that HMG's criteria for cultural events already conformed closely to these guidelines.

6. Cessation of oil exports to South Africa. Spokesman referred to guidelines from HMG to companies exporting oil from the UK continental shelf, which require that this oil should be exported only to countries which were either members of the European Community or the International Energy Agency.

7. Cessation of exports of sensitive equipment destined for the police and armed forces of South Africa. Spokesman said that such equipment was already covered for the UK by the terms of the Export of Goods Control Order, and as such was already subject to licence.

(Text provided by the Foreign and Commonwealth Office)

In reply to the questions:

(1) what specific actions have been taken by the United Kingdom in pursuit of its obligations under article VI of the non-proliferation treaty.

(2) what action Her Majesty's Government have taken since 1980 to reduce their stocks of nuclear weapons in accordance with the provisions of the non-proliferation treaty,

the Minister of State for the Armed Forces wrote:

There is no obligation placed on nuclear weapon states in the non-proliferation treaty to reduce their stocks of nuclear weapons unilaterally. Article VI of the treaty commits all parties to negotiations in good faith on measures to halt the nuclear arms race and relating to nuclear disarmament. The first priority must be for reductions in the arsenals of the US and USSR, which hold the vast majority of such weapons. The UK has strongly supported US efforts to achieve agreements aimed at doing this and fully shares the objectives of working out effective agreements aimed at preventing an arms race in space and terminating it on earth, at limiting and reducing nuclear arms and at strengthening strategic stability.

(HC Debs., vol. 74, Written Answers, cols. *301–2*: 1 March 1985)

The Permanent Representative of the UK to the UN in New York, Sir John Thomson, addressed a letter dated 30 May 1985 to the Secretary-General of the UN in response to a letter from the Government of Argentina (A/40/317—S/17196) on the subject of the new airport at Mount Pleasant, Falkland Islands. Sir John Thomson's letter read in part as follows:

The Argentine Foreign Minister accuses the United Kingdom of violating commitments it has undertaken within the inter-American framework and of introducing nuclear weapons into the South Atlantic. We assume this to be a reference to the obligations the United Kingdom has undertaken under the additional protocols to the Treaty of Tlatelolco, which Argentina has not ratified. It is the long-standing practice of nuclear-weapon States for reasons of security and safety, neither to confirm nor deny the presence or absence of nuclear weapons in any location at any particular time. However, the United Kingdom Government has at all times complied, and will continue to comply, with its obligations under the additional protocols:

First, in not deploying nuclear weapons in territories for which the United Kingdom is internationally responsible within the Treaty's zone of application, which include the Falkland Islands;

Second, in not deploying such weapons in the territories for which the Treaty is in force.

(A/40/345—S/17229)

Part Fourteen: I. A. 1. *Armed conflicts—international war—resort to war—definition of war*

(See also Part Fourteen: III., below)

In answer to the oral question whether Her Majesty's Government went to war with the Argentine Republic over the Falkland Islands, and if not why not, the Minister of State, Foreign and Commonwealth Office, Baroness Young, stated:

. . . neither side recognised the existence of a state of war. Our inherent right of self-defence, as recognised by Article 51 of the Charter of the United Nations, was a sufficient basis for our actions.

(HL Debs., vol. 459, col. 646: 30 January 1985)

Part Fourteen: I. A. 3. *Armed conflicts—international war—resort to war—limitation and reduction of armaments*

In reply to a question, the Minister of State, Foreign and Commonwealth Office, wrote:

We are a signatory to the following arms control agreements and treaties:

The protocol for the prohibition of the use in war of asphyxiating, poisonous or other gases, and of bacteriological methods of warfare of 1925 (the Geneva protocol);

the Antarctic Treaty of 1959;

the treaty banning nuclear weapon tests in the atmosphere, in outer space and under water of 1963 (the partial test ban treaty);

the treaty on principles governing the activities of states in the exploration and use of outer space including the moon and other celestial bodies of 1967 (the outer space treaty);

the additional protocols of the treaty for the prohibition of nuclear weapons in Latin America of 1967 (the treaty of Tlatelolco);

the agreement concerning the establishment of a direct communication link between the residence of the Prime Minister of the United Kingdom in London and the Kremlin of 1967 (the Soviet Union–United Kingdom hotline agreement);

the treaty on the non-proliferation of nuclear weapons of 1968;

the treaty on the prohibition of the emplacement of nuclear weapons and other weapons of mass destruction on the seabed and the ocean floor and in the subsoil thereof of 1971 (the seabed treaty);

the convention on the prohibition of the development, production and stockpiling of bacteriological (biological) and toxin weapons and on their destruction of 1972 (the biological weapons convention);

the convention on the prohibition of military or any other hostile use of environmental modification techniques of 1977 (the ENMOD convention);

the (Soviet–United Kingdom) agreement on the prevention of accidental nuclear war of 1977;

the convention on prohibition or restrictions on the use of certain conventional weapons which may be deemed to be excessively injurious or to have indiscriminate effects of 1981 (the UN weaponry convention).

(HC Debs., vol. 87, Written Answers, cols. *417–18*: 25 November 1985)

Part Fourteen: I. B. 7. *Armed conflicts—international war—the laws of war—humanitarian law*

In the course of a speech on the subject of Israeli action in southern Lebanon in the Security Council on 7 March 1985, the representative of the UK, Mr Maxey, stated:

. . . it is imperative that the Israeli occupying forces scrupulously respect the international conventions on humanitarian law applicable to armed conflicts. In particular, they must respect all the provisions of the Fourth Geneva Convention of 1949 relative to the Protection of Civilian Persons in Time of War. Such security measures as Israel may find it necessary to institute must be designed to have the minimum effect on the lives of local inhabitants and must be strictly within the framework of the Fourth Geneva Convention.

(S/PV. 2570, p. 39; see also S/PV. 2573, pp. 84–5)

Part Fourteen: I. B. 8. *Armed conflicts—international war—the laws of war—belligerent occupation*

(See also Part Thirteen: I. D. (press conference of 2 October 1985), above)

In reply to a question, the Minister of State, Foreign and Commonwealth Office, wrote:

We and our European partners have consistently made clear our view that Israel's policy of building settlements in occupied territory is illegal and an obstacle to peace. My right hon. and learned Friend made this point personally to Israeli Ministers during his visit to Israel in October 1984.

The announcement by Israel on 10 January of six new settlements is a negative step which undermines confidence in Israel's intentions.

(HC Debs., vol. 71, Written Answers, col. *512*: 24 January 1985)

Part Fourteen: I. B. 10. *Armed conflicts—international war—the laws of war—nuclear, bacteriological and chemical weapons*

(See also Part Ten: III., above)

In reply to a question, the Minister of State for the Armed Forces wrote in part:

Underground nuclear weapons testing is conducted by the United Kingdom in conjunction with the United States of America and in accordance with treaty commitments.

(Ibid., col. *529*: 24 January 1985)

In reply to a question, the Minister of State, Foreign and Commonwealth Office, wrote:

We believe that the establishment of nuclear weapon-free zones in certain parts of the world could contribute to regional security, to non-proliferation and to disarmament in general, provided that nuclear weapons do not already feature in the security of the region involved and all states concerned are prepared to participate on the basis of agreements freely entered into and in keeping with internationally recognised principles. The zone created by the Treaty for the Prohibition of Nuclear Weapons in Latin America of 1967 is a good example. We give that Treaty our full support, as is evidenced by our ratification in 1969 of Additional Protocols I and II. We would like to see all the states which are entitled to do so become parties and to see the treaty enter into force in the entire region.

(Ibid., vol. 72, Written Answers, col. *747*: 8 February 1985)

In reply to a question, the Minister of State, Foreign and Commonwealth Office, wrote:

We are satisfied that the acquisition of the Trident missile system is consistent with article 1 of the non-proliferation treaty. As the then Minister of State, Foreign and Commonwealth Office . . . told the House on 8 July 1968, at column 37, article 1 does 'Not deal with the transfer of nuclear delivery vehicles, provided that there was no transfer of nuclear weapons or control over them'.

(Ibid., vol. 73, Written Answers, col. *478*: 20 February 1985; see also ibid., vol. 75, Written Answers, col. *437*: 19 March 1985)

In the course of a debate on the subject of the nuclear non-proliferation treaty, the Minister of State, Foreign and Commonwealth Office, Mr Richard Luce, stated in part:

The spread of nuclear weapons to countries that do not now possess them would have the gravest consequences for mankind, . . . The chief barrier against such proliferation is the non-proliferation treaty, which bans the transfer by nuclear weapon states of nuclear weapons to any other recipient, and their acquisition or manufacture by non-nuclear weapon states. The treaty therefore increases the security of the world and the Government are strongly committed to supporting and strengthening it.

Negotiating the treaty in the 1960s was a major diplomatic achievement and Britain can be proud of having helped to draft it and of having been among the earliest to sign it. . . . [T]he third review conference of the treaty will take place this August. We attach considerable importance to this meeting and have played our part as a depositary Government in convening it.

I differ from my hon. Friend [Mr Sayeed, MP] in his judgment about the success or failure of the treaty. I believe that it has been successful. In the 1960s it was predicted that there would be up to 20 additional nuclear weapon states by 1985. In fact, only one further state—India, which is not a party to the treaty in 1974—demonstrated the capacity to detonate a nuclear explosive device. That may be partly because nuclear proliferation is not so straightforward technically as my hon. Friend suggests, but much of the credit must go to the existence of the treaty. The treaty is the most widely supported arms control agreement in existence, with nearly 130 parties or four fifths of the United Nations membership, and no state has exercised its right to withdraw from the treaty.

I do not entirely share my hon. Friend's view that the treaty is failing simply because there are significant non-parties, although the non-participation of those states is clearly a weakness. The vast majority of the world community has adhered to the treaty and that fact alone is of the greatest importance to the security of all states whether or not they are parties to the treaty.

Clearly the treaty would be even more effective if membership were universal. In collaboration with other states party to the treaty we have been lobbying most of the 40 or so non-parties to accede to the treaty. In the past year, eight have done so, four of them in London, thus demonstrating the treaty's continued vitality.

Two states which possess nuclear weapons—France and China—are not parties to the treaty, but France has said that she will act as though she were a party and China has stated that she does not advocate or encourage proliferation.

Among the non-parties which do not possess nuclear weapons several have significant nuclear facilities not open to international inspection. . . . They are Argentina, India, Israel, Pakistan and South Africa. We attach particular importance to membership of the treaty by those countries and will continue to co-operate in international efforts to urge them to accede to the treaty. Pending their accession or their acceptance of internationally supervised safeguards on all their nuclear facilities, our policy is not to export nuclear materials, equipment or technology to them except for unambiguously peaceful purposes and then only on a very carefully controlled basis.

Article 3 of the treaty refers to safeguards, on which my hon. Friend has expressed some interesting and important views. He suggests that the treaty should be amended so that fuel would be leased to recipient countries and returned to the supplier for reprocessing, that the recipient should agree not to build nuclear weapons and that an internationally agreed inspectorate should examine all civil plants as part of what my hon. Friend described as nuclear fuel leasing services.

I sympathise very much with my hon. Friend's motives in putting forward those ideas, and I certainly appreciate his concern for adequate safeguards, which is at the heart of the agreement. Nevertheless, I believe that we should be very cautious about any proposals to amend the treaty itself. Any amendments must be approved by a majority of the nearly 130 parties to the treaty. Even if it were possible to win sufficient support, any proposed change would give rise to floods of other amendments that we might not be able to support. I believe, therefore, that it is much better to leave the text of the treaty unaltered so as not to endanger the whole treaty which has served us well.

I remind my hon. Friend of the vital role already played by the International Atomic Energy Agency safeguards in verifying the binding international legal obligations which the treaty imposes on non-nuclear weapon state parties not to manufacture or acquire nuclear weapons or other nuclear explosive devices. Article III requires such safeguards to be applied to all source or special fissionable material anywhere in the territory of the state concerned or under its jurisdiction or control. Safeguards are designed to detect the diversion of such material away from peaceful uses. All our exports of fissionable material or equipment designed for its processing or use to any non-nuclear weapon state have been subject to safeguards under the existing terms of the treaty. I pay tribute to the valuable role of the IAEA in administering the safeguards system. The United Kingdom will continue to co-operate fully with IAEA safeguards and will assist the agency's efforts further to improve the system . . .

My hon. Friend may also wish to be reminded that we are one of 22 countries which apply the Nuclear Suppliers' Group guidelines to our exports of nuclear materials, equipment and technology to any non-nuclear weapon state for peaceful purposes. The guidelines reinforce the treaty. In addition to requiring IAEA safeguards on the items transferred, the guidelines require formal governmental assurances to be obtained from the recipient that the exported item will not be used to manufacture nuclear explosive devices, that it will be protected against theft or sabotage, and that if it is re-exported the new purchaser will be required to give the same assurances as the original customer. In the case of enriched uranium or plutonium, the prior consent of the original supplier must be obtained before re-transfer can take place. The guidelines also urge restraint on the transfer of sensitive technology such as reprocessing or enrichment facilities. I believe that the existing requirements go far to meet my hon. Friend's concerns.

As to the specific proposal for fuel leasing, the suggestion is not entirely new and certainly has some attractions. However, the system could not now be watertight because the treaty member states are not the exclusive suppliers of nuclear fuel. As for the establishment of an international inspectorate, that already exists in the form of the IAEA. We should continue to support efforts to extend IAEA safeguards to cover all nuclear facilities in all non-nuclear weapon states that are not parties to the treaty. We are doing all that we can to promote universal adherence to the treaty.

Article IV is an important part of the treaty, which deals with the peaceful use of nuclear energy. When the treaty was negotiated, many non-nuclear weapon states believed that if they were to forgo the option to manufacture or acquire nuclear weapons, this should not be at the expense of their right to use nuclear energy for peaceful purposes. For that reason, article IV of the treaty both reaffirms that right and enjoins all parties to facilitate the fullest possible exchange of equipment, materials and technology for peaceful purposes.

In association with the safeguards required for article III, article IV seeks to promote the safe expansion of peaceful nuclear trade, but minimises the risk of nuclear proliferation. That can help the economic development of many of the member states. We have fully complied with our obligations under this article. As one of the first countries to use nuclear energy for peaceful purposes, we have considerable experience in the area and will continue to share our expertise with other countries, within the limits imposed by our overall non-proliferation policy.

The other important article in the treaty—article VI—deals with disarmament negotiations. It embodies the common determination of the parties to work for nuclear disarmament. The Government are strongly committed to the goals of this article. Therefore, we warmly welcome the arms control negotiations in Geneva between the United States and the Soviet Union. We fully support the agreed objective of preventing an arms race in outer space, and terminating it on earth. Negotiations between the superpowers, which possess 95 per cent. of the world's nuclear weapons, are the first priority in pursuing the effective nuclear disarmament measures prescribed by the treaty.

Some critics maintain that the first step towards fulfilment of article VI is the negotiation of a comprehensive test ban. . . . All I say at this stage is that, in my view, it would serve no one's interest for progress towards a comprehensive test ban—which is of great importance—to be artificially linked to the continued adherence to the non-proliferation treaty and its future. The non-proliferation treaty is important in its own right. We must not jeopardise it by holding it hostage to progress in other areas, however important they may be.

(Ibid., vol. 80, cols. 540–3: 6 June 1985)

In reply to the question asking Her Majesty's Government

What arrangements they are making to recover 41 tonnes of depleted uranium exported from the United Kingdom to Luxembourg and from there to Israel and whether they will be providing the Review Conference on the Non-Proliferation Treaty to be held in September with guarantees against future breaches of the Treaty, the Minister of State, Foreign and Commonwealth Office, wrote:

The export to Luxembourg from the United Kingdom was made in full compliance with all our international commitments. The Israeli authorities have told the International Atomic Energy Agency that they imported the material for non-nuclear, non-explosive purposes and that part has already been consumed. They have permitted the Agency to carry out an inspection. The safeguards system was successful in detecting the re-export. We shall not, therefore, raise the matter at the Non-Proliferation Treaty Review Conference, nor have any arrangements been made to recover the material.

Discussions are proceeding in EURATOM to ensure a common interpretation of the safeguards regulations with regard to material transferred for non-nuclear use. We are playing an active part.

(HL Debs., vol. 467, col. 333: 31 July 1985; see also HC Debs., vol. 83, Written Answers, col. *683*: 25 July 1985)

In reply to the question asking Her Majesty's Government

Whether they are aware of the view that the American strategic initiative contains within it collaborative projects which are in breach of the Nuclear Proliferation Treaty, and whether they agree with it,

the same Minister wrote:

The United States Administration has repeatedly stressed that Strategic Defence Initiative research will be conducted in full conformity with treaty obligations. Our firm support for this research is fully consistent with our own obligations, including those under the Non-Proliferation Treaty.

(HL Debs., vol. 467, cols. 333–4; see also HC Debs., vol. 83, Written Answers, col. *685*: 25 July 1985; ibid., vol. 84, Written Answers, col. *26*: 21 October 1985)

In the course of a speech in the First Committee of the General Assembly, the UK representative, Mr Cromartie, stated on 22 October 1985:

The conclusion of the Non-Proliferation Treaty represented a notable joint achievement of this Assembly and of the single multilateral forum in Geneva which is now the Conference on Disarmament. The idea of such a Treaty to put a stop to the wider dissemination of nuclear weapons was born here in this Committee of the General Assembly with the resolution initiated by the Irish delegation in 1961. It took further shape with another General Assembly resolution, resolution 2028 (XIX) of 1965. Flesh was put on these bones by detailed negotiation in the 18-nation Committee on Disarmament in Geneva and the product was commended for signature by this Assembly by a large majority in its resolution 2373 (XXII) of 1968. Since then it has attracted the widest adherence of any multilateral arms control treaty and now has a total of 130 parties, 17 of whom have acceded to the Treaty in the last five years.

(A/C. 1/40/PV. 11, p. 23)

In reply to a question, the Minister of State, Foreign and Commonwealth Office, stated that in the view of Her Majesty's Government, nuclear weapons do not contravene the Hague and Geneva Conventions.

(HL Debs., vol. 467, col. 1369: 24 October 1985)

Part Fourteen: III. *Armed conflicts—self-defence*

(See also Part Fourteen: I. A. 1., above)

The Ministry of Defence presented the following memorandum, dated 16 July 1984, to the Foreign Affairs Committee of the House of Commons examining the Falklands conflict of 1982:

CHANGES IN THE SOUTH ATLANTIC RULES OF ENGAGEMENT DURING OPERATION CORPORATE APRIL–JUNE 1982 . . .

MEMORANDUM BY THE MINISTRY OF DEFENCE

Rules of Engagement (ROE)—the detailed guidance given to Commanding Officers prescribing the circumstances in which they may engage the enemy—were changed very frequently during operation CORPORATE between 2 April and 15 June 1982. The ROE were updated continually, reflecting changes in the Task Force's position and its composition; the allocation of new missions to the Task Force by the War Cabinet; and the nature of the Argentine response. The ROE and their evolution in response to these factors was kept under close political control by the War Cabinet.

2. Examples of this process of evolution include the changes to the ROE for submarines which allowed them discretion to attack certain targets within the zone, following the declaration of the Maritime Exclusion Zone (MEZ) on 12 April. There were special ROE devised on 15/16 April 1982 for the operation to recapture South Georgia, because the ROE under which the task force was making its transit from Ascension were not appropriate for a direct operation against Argentine held territory. Similarly the rules were of necessity changed again when the MEZ was translated into the Total Exclusion Zone on 30 April. Separate ROE existed for the Terminal Control Area established round Ascension. Examples reflecting Argentine response to our operations are the provision of ROE to deal with the Argentine Boeing 707 aircraft which began to shadow the fleet south of Ascension Island, and the change in the ROE by which we allowed our warships to attack the *General Belgrano* outside the Total Exclusion Zone. In connection with the latter change it is, however, important to remember that the legal basis for it was our right to take measures in exercise of our inherent right of self-defence, as recognised in Article 51 of the UN Charter; and, in particular, the warning conveyed to the Argentine Government on 23 April that in exercise of that right 'any approach on the part of Argentine warships, including submarines, naval auxiliaries, or military aircraft which could amount to a threat to interfere with the mission of the British forces in the South Atlantic, will encounter the appropriate response'.

(*Parliamentary Papers*, 1983–4, HC, Paper 268-i, p. 154)

In answer to the oral question whether Her Majesty's Government went to war with the Argentine Republic over the Falkland Islands, and if not why not, the Minister of State, Foreign and Commonwealth Office, stated:

. . . neither side recognised the existence of a state of war. Our inherent right of self-defence, as recognised by Article 51 of the Charter of the United Nations, was a sufficient basis for our actions.

(HL Debs., vol. 459, col. 646: 30 January 1985)

In the course of a debate on the subject of the Falkland Islands, the Parliamentary Under-Secretary of State for the Armed Forces, Lord Trefgarne, stated:

It is worth recalling that on 22nd July 1982 when we announced the lifting of the 200-mile total exclusion zone, we established and replaced it with a protection zone of 150 miles radius. Through the protecting powers we asked the Argentine authorities to ensure that their warships and military aircraft did not enter the zone, but Argentine civil aircraft and shipping were also requested not to enter the zone unless they had the prior agreement of the British Government. It is interesting to note that not one of them has applied for that permission since that time.

(Ibid., vol. 462, col. 949: 22 April 1985)

Part Fifteen: I. *Neutrality, non-belligerency—legal nature of neutrality*

In reply to a question, the Secretary of State for Foreign and Commonwealth Affairs wrote:

The United Kingdom has been strictly impartial in the conflict between Iran and Iraq and has refused to allow the supply of lethal defence equipment to either side. In order to reinforce our policy of doing everything possible to see this tragic conflict brought to the earliest possible end, we decided in December 1984 to apply thereafter, the following set of guidelines to all deliveries of defence equipment to Iran and Iraq:

(i) We should maintain our consistent refusal to supply any lethal equipment to either side;
(ii) Subject to that overriding consideration, we should attempt to fulfil existing contracts and obligations;
(iii) We should not, in future, approve orders for any defence equipment which, in our view, would significantly enhance the capability of either side to prolong or exacerbate the conflict;
(iv) In line with this policy, we should continue to scrutinise rigorously all applications for export licences for the supply of defence equipment to Iran and Iraq.

(HC Debs., vol. 84, Written Answers, col. *450*: 29 October 1985)

In reply to a question, the Minister of State, Foreign and Commonwealth Office, stated in part:

There [have] been occasional informal contacts between Polisario representatives and Foreign and Commonwealth Office officials. These do not denote any change in our neutral policy towards the Western Sahara dispute.

(Ibid., vol. 89, Written Answers, cols. *133–4*: 17 December 1985)

APPENDICES

I. Multilateral Agreements Signed by the United Kingdom in 1985[1]

Title	*Place and Date*	*UK Signature*	*Text*[2]
Convention on a Code of Conduct for Liner Conferences	Geneva, 6.4.1974	28.6.1985 (accession)	Not yet published
Amendment to Article XXI of the Convention on International Trade in Endangered Species of Wild Fauna and Flora signed at Washington on 3.3.1973	Gabarone, 30.4.1983	13.12.1985	Misc. No. 2 (1984) (Cmnd. 9129)
International Convention on the Harmonized Commodity Description and Coding System	Brussels, 14.6.1983	10.6.1985	Misc. No. 17 (1985) (Cmnd. 9666)
Protocol of 1984 to amend the International Convention on Civil Liability for Oil Pollution Damage of 29.11.1969	London, 25.5.1984	4.12.1984	Not yet published
Protocol of 1984 to amend the International Convention on the Establishment of an International Fund for Compensation for Oil Pollution Damage of 18.12.1971	London, 25.5.1984	4.12.1984	Not yet published
Third Additional Protocol to the Constitution of the Universal Postal Union of 10.7.1964	Hamburg, 27.7.1984	27.7.1984	Cmnd. 9624
General Regulations of the UPU	Hamburg, 27.7.1984	27.7.1984	Cmnd. 9624
Universal Postal Convention	Hamburg, 27.7.1984	27.7.1984	Cmnd. 9629
Postal Parcels Agreement	Hamburg, 27.7.1984	27.7.1984	Cmnd. 9631
Giro Agreement	Hamburg, 27.7.1984	27.7.1984	Cmnd. 9630
Cash-on-Delivery Agreement	Hamburg, 27.7.1984	27.7.1984	Cmnd. 9625
Amendment of Article VI.A.1 of the Statute of the International Atomic Energy Agency of 26.10.1956	Vienna, 27.9.1984	10.12.1984	Not yet published
Convention against Torture and Other Cruel, Inhuman or Degrading Treatment or Punishment	New York, 10.12.1984	15.3.1985	Misc. No. 12 (1985) (Cmnd. 9593)
Protocol No. 8 to the Convention for the Protection of Human Rights and Fundamental Freedoms of 4.11.1950	Vienna, 19.3.1985	19.3.1985	Misc. No. 9 (1985) (Cmnd. 9556)
Vienna Convention for the Protection of the Ozone Layer	Vienna, 22.3.1985	20.5.1985	Misc. No. 13 (1985) (Cmnd. 9652)

[1] Information supplied by the Foreign and Commonwealth Office. The table includes some agreements signed by the United Kingdom before 1985, where information was not previously available. The information is correct as at January 1986, although in some cases information available since that date has been included.

[2] Publication is in various series of UK Command Papers, namely: EC = European Communities Series; Misc. = Miscellaneous Series; TS = Treaty Series; Cmnd. = Command Paper number.

Title	Place and Date	UK Signature	Text
Revised Text of the Protocol to the European Agreement on the Exchange of Tissue-Typing Reagents of 17.9.1974 and Annex to the said Protocol	Strasbourg, 28.3.1985	28.3.1985	TS No. 41 (1985) (Cmnd. 9597)
Treaty between the Member States of the European Economic Community and the Kingdom of Spain and the Portuguese Republic concerning the Accession of the Kingdom of Spain and the Portuguese Republic to the European Economic Community and the European Atomic Energy Community	Madrid/Lisbon, 12.6.1985	12.6.1985	EC No. 27 (1985) (Cmnd. 9634)
Agreement establishing an International Foot and Mouth Disease Vaccine Bank	London, 26.6.1985	26.6.1985	TS No. 43 (1985) (Cmnd. 9602)
European Convention on Spectator Violence and Misbehaviour at Sports Events and in particular at Football Matches	Strasbourg, 19.8.1985	19.8.1985	TS No. 57 (1985) (Cmnd. 9649)
Convention for the Protection of the Architectural Heritage of Europe	Granada, 3.10.1985	3.10.1985	Misc. No. 14 (1985) (Cmnd. 9660)

II. Bilateral Agreements signed by the United Kingdom in 1985[1]

Country and Title	Place and Date	Text[2]
ANTIGUA AND BARBUDA		
Agreement between the Government of the UK and the Government of Antigua and Barbuda for Air Services between and beyond their respective Territories	London, 25.3.1985	TS No. 29 (1985) (Cmnd. 9558)
AUSTRALIA		
Exchange of Notes replacing the Schedule to the Agreement between the Government of the UK and the Government of Australia for Air Services between and beyond their respective Territories signed at London on 7.2.1958	Canberra, 29.5.1985	TS No. 49 (1985) (Cmnd. 9612)
AUSTRIA		
Supplementary Convention on Social Security	London, 9.12.1985	Austria No. 1 (1986) (Cmnd. 9746)
BELGIUM		
Exchange of Notes amending Articles IV and XIII of the Treaty for the Mutual Surrender of Fugitive Criminals signed at Brussels on 29.10.1901 as amended	London, 10.9.1985	TS No. 59 (1985) (Cmnd. 9659)

[1] Information supplied by the Foreign and Commonwealth Office. The table includes some agreements signed by the United Kingdom before 1985, where information was not previously available. The information is correct as at January 1986, although in some cases information available since that time has been included.

[2] Publication is in various series of UK Command Papers, including Treaty Series (TS) and Miscellaneous Series (Misc.). Cmnd. = Command Paper number.

Country and Title	*Place and Date*	*Text*
BRAZIL		
Agreement on certain Commercial Debts	Brasilia, 13.12.1984	TS No. 11 (1985) (Cmnd. 9455)
Agreement amending the UK/Brazil Loan Agreement 1973	Brasilia, 31.12.1984	TS No. 17 (1985) (Cmnd. 9484)
CANADA		
Exchange of Letters extending the Films Co-production Agreement signed at London on 12.9.1975	London, 9.7.1985	Canada No. 1 (1985) (Cmnd. 9605)
Protocol further amending the Convention for the Avoidance of Double Taxation and the Prevention of Fiscal Evasion with respect to Taxes on Income and Capital Gains, signed at London on 8.9.1978 and amended by a Protocol signed at Ottawa on 15.4.1980	London, 16.10.1985	TS No. 7 (1986) (Cmnd. 9718)
CHINA, PEOPLE'S REPUBLIC OF		
Agreement for Co-operation in the Peaceful Uses of Nuclear Energy	London, 3.6.1985	TS No. 60 (1985) (Cmnd. 9664)
Agreement on Economic Co-operation	London, 3.6.1985	TS No. 22 (1986) (Cmnd. 9766)
Agreement for the 'Exhibition of Terracotta Figures of Warriors and Horses of the Qin Dynasty, China'	Peking, 2.8.1985	TS No. 2 (1986) (Cmnd. 9698)
CUBA		
Agreement on certain Commercial Debts	London, 3.10.1985	TS No. 4 (1986) (Cmnd. 9704)
EGYPT		
Exchange of Notes regarding the use of British Capital Untransferable Accounts in Egypt	Cairo, 21.1.1985	TS No. 16 (1985) (Cmnd. 9479)
Consular Convention and Exchanges of Notes concerning application to Hong Kong, the Channel Islands and the Isle of Man	London, 23.4.1985	Egypt No. 1 (1985) (Cmnd. 9603)
ETHIOPIA		
Exchange of Notes amending the UK/Ethiopia Aid Grant and Loan 1973	Addis Ababa, 10/28.12.1984	TS No. 21 (1985) (Cmnd. 9509)
FINLAND		
Protocol to amend the Convention for the Avoidance of Double Taxation and the Prevention of Fiscal Evasion with respect to Taxes on Income and Capital signed at London on 17.7.1969, as amended by the Protocols signed at London on 17.5.1973 and 16.11.1979	London, 1.10.1985	Not yet published
GABON		
Agreement on the Development of Economic, Industrial, Technological and Technical Co-operation	Libreville, 26.11.1984	TS No. 38 (1985) (Cmnd. 9591)

Country and Title	*Place and Date*	*Text*
GREECE		
Agreement on Applied Scientific and Technological Co-operation	Athens, 8.2.1985	Greece No. 1 (1985) (Cmnd. 9594)
HAITI		
Agreement for the Promotion and Protection of Investments	Port au Prince, 18.3.1985	Haiti No. 1 (1986) (Cmnd. 9731)
INDONESIA		
Agreement on Scientific and Technological Co-operation	London, 10.7.1985	TS No. 19 (1986) (Cmnd. 9754)
IRELAND, REPUBLIC OF		
Exchange of Notes prolonging the Agreement on the International Carriage of Goods by Road signed at Dublin on 9.4.1980	Dublin, 4.7/15.8.1985	TS No. 54 (1985) (Cmnd. 9651)
Agreement [concerning Northern Ireland]	Hillsborough, 15.11.1985	TS No. 62 (1985) (Cmnd. 9690)
IVORY COAST		
Agreement on certain Commercial Debts	Abidjan, 10.1.1985	TS No. 20 (1985) (Cmnd. 9503)
Convention for the Avoidance of Double Taxation and the Prevention of Fiscal Evasion with respect to Taxes on Income and Capital Gains	Abidjan, 26.6.1985	Not yet published
JAMAICA		
Agreement on certain Commercial Debts	London, 13.5.1985	TS No. 42 (1985) (Cmnd. 9598)
KOREA, REPUBLIC OF		
Agreement on Scientific and Technological Co-operation	Seoul, 14.6.1985	TS No. 5 (1986) (Cmnd. 9709)
MADAGASCAR		
Agreement on certain Commercial Debts	Antananarivo, 7.1.1985	TS No. 15 (1985) (Cmnd. 9473)
MALAWI		
Exchange of Notes further amending the British Expatriates Supplementation (Malawi) Agreement 1971 (The British Expatriates Supplementation (Malawi) Agreement 1971–85)	Lilongwe, 22/31.7.1985	TS No. 55 (1985) (Cmnd. 9646)
MEXICO		
Agreement on certain Commercial Debts	Mexico City, 31.1.1985	TS No. 37 (1985) (Cmnd. 9588)
NIGER		
Agreement on certain Commercial Debts	London, 7.3.1985	TS No. 22 (1985) (Cmnd. 9534)

Country and Title	*Place and Date*	*Text*
NORWAY		
Exchange of Notes replacing Article XIII of the Treaty of 26.6.1873 for the Mutual Surrender of Fugitive Criminals, as continued in force by the Agreement of 18.2.1907	Oslo, 5.8.1985	TS No. 6 (1986) (Cmnd. 9707)
Convention for the Avoidance of Double Taxation and the Prevention of Fiscal Evasion with respect to Taxes on Income and Capital	Oslo, 3.10.1985	TS No. 13 (1986) (Cmnd. 9730)
Agreement relating to the Transmission by Pipeline of Heimdal Liquids to the United Kingdom	Oslo, 21.11.1985	Not yet published
PHILIPPINES		
Convention on Social Security	London, 27.2.1985	Philippines No. 1 (1985) (Cmnd. 9560)
Exchange of Notes extending the Notice of Termination of the Air Services Agreement signed at Manila on 31.1.1955	Manila, 23/24.10.1985	Not yet published
POLAND		
Exchange of Notes concerning the Agreement on certain Commercial Debts signed at Warsaw on 2.7.1981	Warsaw, 15.10/15.11.1985	Not yet published
Agreement on certain Commercial Debts	Warsaw, 30.11.1985	Not yet published
SENEGAL		
Agreement on certain Commercial Debts (resulting from the Paris Conference regarding Consolidation of Senegal's Debts, 21.12.1983)	London, 12.11.1985	TS No. 15 (1986) (Cmnd. 9738)
Agreement on certain Commercial Debts (resulting from the Paris Conference regarding Consolidation of Senegal's Debts, 17/18.1.1985)	London, 12.11.1985	TS No. 16 (1986) (Cmnd. 9739)
SIERRA LEONE		
Agreement on certain Commercial Debts	London, 17.10.1985	TS No. 58 (1985) (Cmnd. 9673)
SOUTH AFRICA		
Exchange of Notes amending the Air Services Agreement of 26.10.1945	Pretoria, 2.11.1985/28.2.1985	TS No. 35 (1985) (Cmnd. 9582)
SPAIN		
Extradition Treaty	London, 22.7.1985	Spain No. 1 (1985) (Cmnd. 9615)
TOGO		
Agreement on certain Commercial Debts	London, 5.2.1985	TS No. 18 (1985) (Cmnd. 9486)
USSR		
Agreement on Relations in the Scientific, Educational and Cultural Fields for 1985 to 1987	Moscow, 25.3.1985	TS No. 61 (1985) (Cmnd. 9663)

Country and Title	*Place and Date*	*Text*
USSR (*cont.*)		
Convention for the Avoidance of Double Taxation with respect to Taxes on Income and Capital Gains	London, 31.7.1985	Not yet published
UNITED STATES OF AMERICA		
Exchange of Notes amending the Defence Areas Agreement of 12.12.1979	Washington, 18.12.1984	Not yet published
Exchange of Notes further amending the Agreement concerning Air Services signed at Bermuda on 23.7.1977, as amended	Washington, 20.2.1985	TS No. 9 (1986) (Cmnd. 9720)
Exchange of Notes further amending and supplementing the Agreement of 27.3.1941, as amended, regarding Leased Naval and Air Bases on Bermuda	Washington, 7.3.1985	TS No. 46 (1985) (Cmnd. 9607)
Exchange of Notes regarding Arrangements for the use by UK Forces of Military Facilities on Ascension Island	London, 25.3.1985	TS No. 39 (1985) (Cmnd. 9590)
Supplementary Treaty concerning the Extradition Treaty of 8.6.1972	Washington, 25.6.1985	US No. 2 (1985) (Cmnd. 9565)
ZAMBIA		
Agreement on certain Commercial Debts	Lusaka, 15.2.1985	TS No. 23 (1985) (Cmnd. 9535)
Exchange of Notes modifying the Public Officers' Pensions (Zambia) Agreement 1978, signed at Lusaka on 8.8.1978	Lusaka, 5.9.1985	Not yet published

III. United Kingdom Legislation During 1985 Concerning Matters of International Law[1]

The Brunei and Maldives Act (1985 c. 3) makes provision in connection with the admission of Brunei and Maldives to membership of the Commonwealth by amending certain enactments. (See Part Three: I. A. 1. (item of 28 January 1985), above.)

The Child Abduction and Custody Act (1985 c. 60) implements the Hague Convention on the Civil Aspects of International Child Abduction of 25 October 1980 and the Council of Europe Convention on Recognition and Enforcement of Decisions concerning Custody of Children and on Restoration of Custody of Children of 20 May 1980. (See Part One: II. D. (item of 5 March 1985), above.)

The European Communities (Spanish and Portuguese Accession) Act (1985, c. 75) extends the meaning in Acts, Measures and subordinate legislation of 'the Treaties' and 'the Community Treaties' in connection with the accession of the Kingdom of Spain and the Portuguese Republic to the European Communities. (See Part Three: II. B. 3., above.)

The Hong Kong Act (1985 c. 15) makes provision for and in connection with the ending of British sovereignty and jurisdiction over Hong Kong as from 1 July 1997. It implements the Joint Declaration of the Government of the United Kingdom and the Government of the People's Republic of China on the Question of Hong Kong of 19 December 1984. (See Part Eight: III. B. (items of 19 February and 4 April 1985), above.)

[1] Compiled by C. A. Hopkins.

TABLE OF CASES[1]

[1] The figures in heavier type indicate the pages on which cases are reviewed.

INDEX